PLEASURE BOATING

GUNTHER;
"HAPPY SAILING"
RICH
'77

PLEASURE BOATING

sail and power

BARRON'S Woodbury, New York

First U.S. Edition
Barron's Educational Series, Inc.

International Standard Book Number
0-8120-5131-9
Library of Congress Catalog Card Number
77-80184.

Printed in Spain.

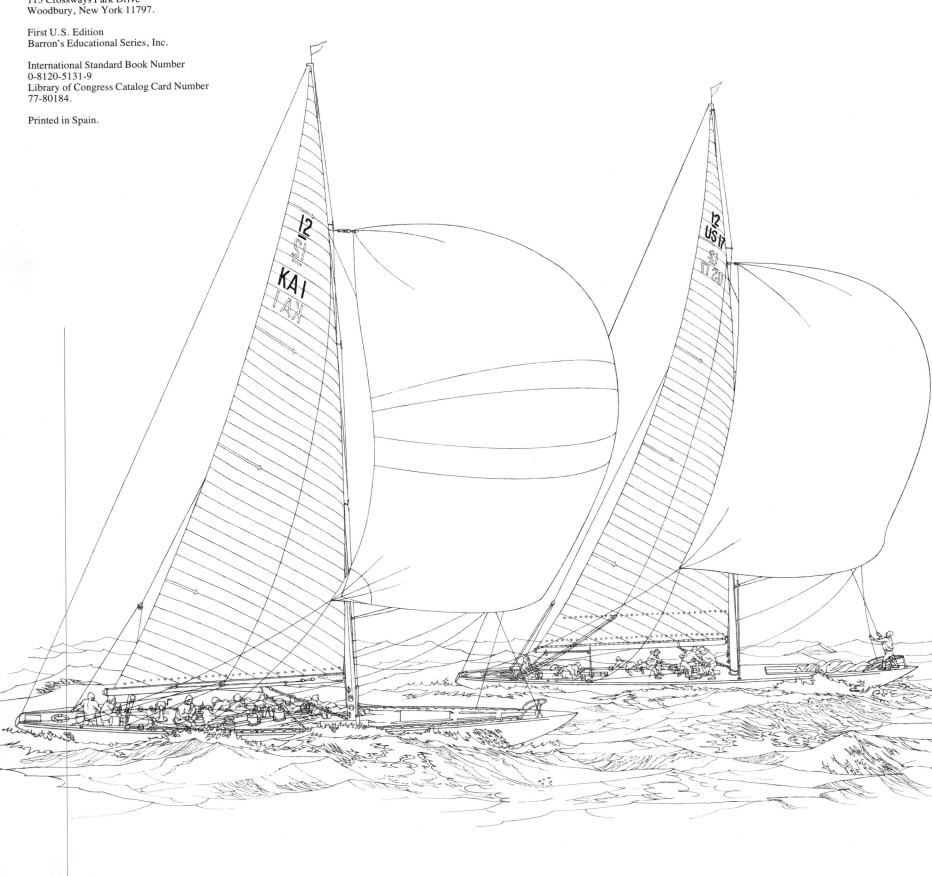

PLEASURE BOATING has been originated, designed, and produced by AB Nordbok, Gothenburg, Sweden.

An international group of authors and experts has worked on the project in close co-operation with the Nordbok art and editorial departments, under the supervision of Einar Engelbrektson and Turlough Johnston.

Colour and graphical design: Roland Thorbjörnsson (principally) and Tommy Berglund.

Artwork: Syed Mumtaz Ahmad, Svend Ahnstrøm, Tommy Berglund, Marie Falksten, Per Fischel, Nils Hermansson, Annette Johansson, Hans Linder, Lennart Molin, Yusuke Nagano, David Penney, Holger Rosenblad, Ulf Söderqvist, Roland Thorbjörnsson.

The water-colour action scenes have been painted by Erland Holmström.

Editors: Turlough Johnston, Kerstin M. Stålbrand.

Nordbok would like to express its sincere gratitude to Göran Petersson, who has advised and assisted on the project since its initiation, and to Göran Nilrud, who has helped with the illustrations.

THE AUTHORS

KEITH BEST, who has written Chapter Eight, ''Meteorology'', is a professional meteorologist. He regularly presents the weather forecast on BBC radio and television. An enthusiastic yachtsman, he is co-author of a training manual written for the Royal Yachting Association.

DOUGLAS PHILLIPS-BIRT is author of the first part of Chapter One, ''History of Sailing''. He is a recognized authority on the subject, and has written over twenty books on design, maritime history, and yachting. He is a committee member of the Royal Southern and Royal Albert Yacht Clubs.

CURT BORGENSTAM has contributed the second part of Chapter One, ''History of Powerboating''. A captain in the Swedish Navy, he is a naval architect and has written several books on powerboats and powerboating. He is the secretary of the Association of Swedish Boat Designers.

PER BROHÄLL, author of Chapter Four, ''Maintenance'', has, during his lifetime, sailed everything from dinghies to four-masters. He is a professional yacht designer, and the 20,000 boats which have been built to his designs are to be found all over the world.

JOHN CHAMIER, contributor of Chapter Ten, ''Safety on Board'', was a yacht-builder for fifteen years. Now an author and journalist, he has a regular yachting column in leading boating journals in several countries, and has written a number of books on practical sailing.

ALAIN GLIKSMAN, author of Chapter Twelve, ''Ocean Racing'', has several books to his credit, besides being a sailor of international repute. He has taken part in most of the famous ocean races, among them the 1968 and 1972 Singlehanded Transatlantic races, and he was RORC champion in 1967.

JACK KNIGHTS has contributed Chapter Six, ''Sail-boat Handling'', and Chapter Eleven, ''Inshore Racing''. He is an active sailor, both of dinghies and ocean racers, as well as being a well-known yachting journalist and author.

JAAP A.M. KRAMER is the author of Chapter Five, ''Theory of Sailing'', and Chapter Thirteen, ''Cruising''. A much-read writer of yachting articles and books, he is a prominent yacht designer, whose designs are internationally known.

COLIN MUDIE has written Chapter Three, ''Design and Construction''. A naval architect, he has designed a wide range of craft, from patrol boats to yachts. Among his designs is REHU MOANA, the first multihull to circumnavigate the world. He has also written several books on powerboats and is a yachting journalist.

GÖRAN PETERSSON, Nordbok's sailing adviser, has written Chapter Two, ''Boat Types and Equipment'', and the glossary. Swedish Keelboat Champion in 1974, he has sailed 505s at world-championship level and was legal adviser and rule tactician to the Swedish America's Cup challenge in 1977.

JOHN TEALE, who has contributed Chapter Seven, ''Powerboat Handling'', and Chapter Fourteen, ''Powerboat Racing'', is a well-known boat designer. He has written several books on powerboats and yachting, and is a regular columnist in boating magazines.

KENNETH WILKES is the author of Chapter Eight, ''Navigation''. He is a certificated ocean yachtmaster and a member of the Royal Institute of Navigation. He has published several books on practical coastal and ocean navigation.

AB Nordbok would like to thank the following persons and organizations for their kind assistance in providing advice, information, and material:
Jan Calvert
Chalmers College of Technology Library
Dantec Marine
Rutger Friberg
Gori Marine
Bengt O. Hult
Bengt Hällqvist
Jofa-företagen
AB Järnförädling
Sture Olsson
Pelle Petterson AB
Seldéns AB
Olin Stephens
Tommy Strömberg
Swedish International Boat Show

Further, AB Nordbok would like to thank the following for their kindness in allowing their artwork to be used as illustration reference material: Airex A.G. for 78–79; Beken of Cowes for 240B; Per Brohäll for 246D and E, and 247G and H; Bruce Banks Sails for 83C; Lars Harry Jenneborg for 89A; Jenniker Sales for 252–253A; Mariner Company Inc. for 248A; Mercury Marine Inc. for 96A; Mirror Group for 67–69; *Motor Boat and Yachting* for 30H, 261C, and 262–263C; Nautor AB for 58A and 59B; *Neptune Nautisme* for 237J and 239D; Royal North of Ireland Yacht Club for 13C; Royal Yachting Association for 182–183; Rydgeway Marine for 247F; *Yachting Monthly* for 80–81; *Yachting World* for 18A.

CONTENTS

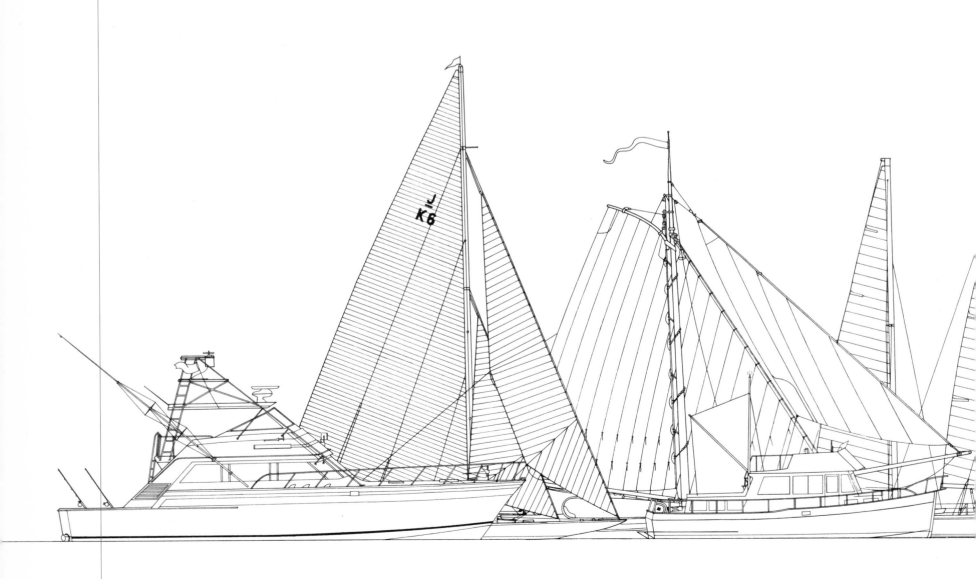

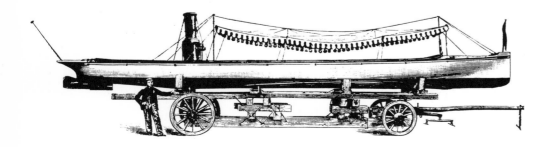

HISTORY OF SAILING

Douglas Phillips-Birt

Very little is known about the earliest days of sailing for pleasure. Kings and high State officials had vessels reserved for their purposes, which sometimes might have been relaxation. This still happens with royal and presidential yachts. Records of any considerable proportion of a nation's ordinary citizens using yachts appear first in Holland. In the sixteenth century, and how much earlier we cannot tell, people in this land, where water is always near, were using private craft for everyday transport and, we may presume, for recreation also.

But everyday things often fail to penetrate the opaque lens of history. By the seventeenth century, we find some accounts of the grander Dutch yachts. But only the diligent social historian is able to dig out facts about the many people who held the noiseless tenor of their way, and kept very small craft by canal-side and river-bank, using them for recreation as well as essential transport. And as it was in Holland, so it must have been all round the coasts of Europe. In areas other than Holland, proportionately fewer people were intimately connected with water, either fresh or salt. But the coastlines and river courses were long; beside them many people lived, some of them using boats for a living, others bound to go afloat for transport, but all of them familiar with small craft. And boats have this in common with horses, that those who have to use them for business will also do so for pleasure.

Pleasure boating, in fact, must be very much older than the records of it in even specialized histories. The difference between then and now, however, is that in the past it was only the coastal-dwelling few who put afloat for pleasure, while today it might appear that nearly everyone does so.

It is with the formation of yacht clubs that recreational sailing comes a little more clearly under the light of history, not that the light is very strong. The first known yacht club—for we believe that such institutions were unknown to the Dutch—was founded in 1720, on an island in Cork Harbour, Ireland. It celebrated its 250th anniversary in 1970, when yachts sailed from America and from all round the European coastlines, from the Baltic to Biscay, to pay convivial and nautical respects to the oldest yacht club, now known as the Royal Cork Yacht Club. The next to be founded was situated by the Thames, in the heart of London. It was originally known as the Cumberland Fleet, now as the Royal Thames Yacht Club. It celebrated its 200th anniversary in 1975 with a splendid programme, involving fleet reviews, banquets, balls, and a transatlantic race. The Prince of Wales is now its Commodore, a post held by two previous Princes of Wales.

In these oldest clubs, something of what we may describe as "Grand Yachting"—which was unknown when the clubs were established, and did not appear until one of them was in its second century and the other approaching it—comes back to life in the egalitarian days of the twentieth century's latter half. An important fact to appreciate is that the clubs were at first concerned with small craft, ones not large even by the diminished standards of today, and that the members who sailed them were, as a rule, amateur seamen of a breed now common enough but rare in the eighteenth and early nineteenth centuries.

The Royal Thames was initially a river sailing club, and some of its best-known yachts, including a series owned by its first Commodore, were clinker-built cutters, 20–25 ft (6.1–7.6 m) in length, beamy, deep-bodied, with heavy displacement, but nevertheless small and steered by the owning member. The boats of the Water Club of Cork, as the Royal Cork was first called, appear to have been somewhat larger, but they were cutters of no great size.

Yacht clubs were being established in quick succession round the coasts of the civilized world during the period 1850–80. They appeared most thickly round the coasts of Britain, with Europe and North America following; but the scatter was wide: Australia, New Zealand, Canada, South Africa, Gibraltar, Malta, the Channel Islands. It was the first rising of the tide which was to surge over the beaches of the world a century later. There was a period, approximately 1860–1914, of "Grand Yachting", when the activity gained its exclusive and gilded reputation, while yachts were certainly at their loveliest and most noble. These were the days of the great racing schooners, with clouds of canvas handled by crowds of paid hands. Then, for racing, the big cutter proved its superiority, and while the schooners remained to grace the yachting scene, first-class racing was conducted in cutters of a size now long unknown, carrying more canvas on a single mast than had ever been set before in the history of sail. It is impossible not to regret their passing.

Racing and sailing in the largest yachts were confined to a very few coastal waters of the western world. Until the latter part of the nineteenth century—perhaps later, for statistics are not available—Britain was the country with the biggest population of recreational sailing-craft of any size, though soon the United States was to take the lead and vastly out-distance her. The Solent was widely regarded as sacred to the finest yachts, and the Camelot of the smartest yachting people. But in Long Island Sound, a fleet that was soon to become much greater was sailing on that larger, bluer stretch of water. Great yachts found their way to the French and Italian coasts of the Medi-

terranean. The third, and last, German emperor, Kaiser Wilhelm II, introduced yachting to Germany and attempted to raise a second Cowes at Kiel.

The sophistication of racing under sail today and the immense experience that has been gained during the last century make it difficult for us to appreciate the problems encountered and, for many years, imperfectly solved by racing yachtsmen. Particularly, there was the question of how yachts should be classified and measured for racing.

Initially, there was a tendency for a fine free-for-all over the racing courses, with craft of all sizes and rigs competing on equal terms, the winner the one that was first over the finishing line. It may be recalled—or be surprising to many—that when AMERICA won that most famous of sailing duels round the Isle of Wight in 1851, the race was conducted in this fashion. The fact that, all else being equal, a good big yacht must inevitably, by the laws of hydrodynamics, be faster than one smaller, was not fully appreciated. When it *was* realized, all the problems of how to assess the size of a yacht on scientific lines leapt into prominence, and they have been with us ever since, never perfectly solved. The latest efforts in this direction have been the several versions of the International Offshore Rule, of such mathematical complexity that computers are demanded to solve the many equations that become involved.

Such matters were beyond the understanding, and far outside the interests, of the salty, unacademic gentlemen of the mid- and later nineteenth century, who revelled in their days out racing on the water, enjoying the skills of handling lovely craft under sail, and who, without knowing how to achieve it, wanted only to assure that the contests were fair. A few among their number, however, with a mathematical and scientific turn of mind, applied themselves to the problem. They began to receive assistance from the members of a new profession, the yacht designers, who were trained in the science of marine architecture and applied themselves particularly to the yachts which were becoming more and more fashionable.

The intricacies of yacht measurement have lain at the heart of yacht development for well over a century. George Watson, the English pioneer in the profession of yacht design, once said, "Throughout the modern story of yachting, the tonnage question has been the all-absorbing one." His contemporary, Lord Dunraven, who owned the America's Cup challengers of 1893 and 1895, expressed the more usual attitude of yachtsmen towards the technicalities of measuring yachts for fair racing, "With shame I confess that the problems and calculations, the combinations of straight and crooked lines, with large and small numerals and Latin and Greek letters, the mathematical contortions and algebraic hieroglyphics ... are meaningless to my uncultured eyes. They are fascinating; I admire their beauty, and can well understand that inventing rules for rating must be a most charming pursuit for intellectual yachtsmen..."

The invention of measurement rules became, indeed, the active pursuit of some racing yachtsmen and their professional technical advisers. These rules may have been uninspiring to the majority, but they became the iron laws that, down the racing years, forced yachts into various shapes, sometimes lovely, sometimes freakish. For it soon became evident that, once yachts began to be measured for racing purposes, so that only those of approximately equal measurement should race together, clever designers—who at the end of each summer became a little cleverer—would learn how to evade the rules without actually breaking them, a practice exactly analogous to that of accountants working through loop-holes in the income-tax laws.

Since it would not always be convenient in regattas to have yachts of exactly equal measurement competing in each race, systems of compensating for variations began to be evolved—methods of handicapping or time allowance—and these, too, are still with us today, the problems involved incompletely solved. For technical reasons, it has proved impossible to evolve a system of time allowance which, in all weathers, is fair to all sizes and types of boat. Time allowance introduces into sail racing an element of chance unconnected with wind, sea, tactical ability, and helmsmanship. For this reason, many dedicated racing people prefer racing in open classes, where no time allowance is involved. But, today, most offshore racing as well as most inshore racing in the larger types of boat are conducted under time allowance, and the International Offshore Rule with various associated time scales is generally used. It is amusing to recall that, in the earliest days of handicapping, there were those who objected strongly to the principle. How unjust, they declared, that the owner of a fine large yacht should be deprived of his winning flag by some much smaller, cheaper craft able to win by time allowance! Was this the way to encourage the best yachts? Let the best boat win and to hell with handicapping, was the undemocratic cry.

The exuberant colours and splendour of the back-cloth of "Grand Yachting" have blinded the eye of history to the amount of recreational sailing and racing that was taking place in smaller craft all round the coasts of the civilized world. A number of clubs organized their own classes of small craft, some of them one-design, built locally to suit the home waters. The Solent itself, for all its exotic reputation, had become, by the 1890s, the busy centre of small-craft racing between amateur helmsmen. The best-known of the boats were those of the several classes known as *Rater*s, ranging in size between one-half and five rating. A very few *Rater*s of similar types are still sailing on the upper Thames today.

The one-design principle took a firm hold, which has grown ever stronger. Today, most dinghy classes are one-design types, as are the great majority of bigger day-racing classes on every coast. The one-design principle was welcomed as a measure of economy. Building yachts to individual designs under a given measurement rule was,

and is, expensive and, in hotly contested racing, leads to the rapid outclassing of even new boats. The United States led the world in the development of one-design classes, applying the principle to big craft as well as small. A well-known American class was composed of yachts 40 ft (12.2 m) on the water-line and 59 ft (18 m) overall; also American was the biggest type of yacht ever to fall into the one-design category, yachts of 70 ft (21.3 m) on the water-line and more than 90 ft (27.4 m) overall.

But it was in the smallest classes that the one-design principle was applied in a way that has led in a smooth, direct line to the sailing world of today. During 1909, an epoch-making event occurred in a quiet way, giving no indication that in it the future was imminent, like song in the egg of a nightingale. On Manhasset Bay, Long Island, a few 17-ft (5.2 m) half-decked, chine-hull racing boats appeared. They had a bug on their sails, and so they were named. In 1911, a slightly enlarged *Bug,* with the more aspiring name of *Star,* appeared in small numbers.

The *Star* was the first successful application, on a world-wide scale, of the one-design principle. By the mid-1970s, there were over 6,000 *Star*s, split into more than two hundred fleets scattered round the coasts of the world. In such mass classes, internationally distributed, was to lie the future of dinghy racing; but not for another half-century or so after the *Star*s had first put in their modest appearance.

Racing and cruising used to be two distinct and even opposed activities. Today, the contrast between them has become less marked, owing to the popularity of handicap and coastal racing. Cruising in large yachts, such as the magnificent schooners, resembled country-house parties afloat, and even the biggest yachts may have spent much of their time in their own home waters. Lacking, however, were many of the comforts expected in the smallest cruisers today. There was inadequate plumbing, lack of refrigeration, poor ventilation, and for some years no motor launches. Throughout even the finest yachts there was liable to be a certain pervasive smell coming from the bilges. To compensate for these discomforts, there were well-trained domestic servants. Cooks and stewards, who were harder-worked than the seamen members of the crew, produced fine meals and a general *douceur de vie.* Yacht-owners and their guests expected to take to sea with them the amenities of civilized life ashore, and a majority of yachtsmen took care that the sea itself should not disturb such comforts.

Very different was a sport that quietly, behind the more showy yachting scene, began to gather devotees; that of cruising in small yachts, in which the owner was skipper and the crew perhaps largely amateur. This was an activity growing in strength during the latter half of the nineteenth century, particularly during the last quarter. It should be made clear that a yacht, described then as "small", would not usually be less than 30 ft (9.1 m) in length and more probably between 35 and 50 ft (10.7 and 15.2 m), and that one or two paid hands would normally be carried. One paid hand was considered a minimum for the general maintenance of the yacht and the less beguiling chores involved in sailing. The crucial feature of this kind of yachting was that the owner was his own master and navigator, and it produced a breed of true amateur seamen. For many years, even until after the Second

World War, there was a great divide between the dedicated racing and cruising people. The difference between them was partly temperamental. The cruising man had a thoughtful love of sea and coast, and a deep interest in the techniques of basic seamanship, an interest particularly strong in the days when auxiliary engines were of low power, unreliable, or altogether absent. He was likely to be a better seaman than his racing contemporary, though the latter may have known far more about how to get the best speed out of a boat racing over a short course. There used to be something like repressed antagonism between the two breeds of yachtsmen. A well-known English writer, who was also a cruising man, once said, "If you let in racing you let in the devil." This was an extreme expression of a prevailing attitude.

Cruising had a great appeal to those of the more erudite professions. A surprisingly high proportion of its devotees belonged to the higher echelons of the legal and medical fraternities; even authors were well-represented. And it was mainly from among cruising yachtsmen that there came books on deep-sea navigation, particularly pilotage, seamanship, ships' husbandry, and all the maritime lore that for many became the enthusiasm of a lifetime.

Yacht cruising of this kind had little public appeal. Newspapers could find nothing in it. Yacht clubs themselves were largely racing organizations, though many purely cruising people joined. However, the waterfront pub, where they could go without changing, having hauled their dinghy through the mud, and have a good salty talk with the locals, was liable to appeal more to cruising men than listening to the events of the day's racing being thrashed through from the depths of club chairs, a process once known to cruising people as "jib-booming and gin-swinging". Until 1880, there was no organization devoted wholly to the interests of cruising people. In this year, the Cruising Club was founded in London, the guiding spirit being, significantly enough, a barrister, later Sir Arthur Underhill. Today, this body is the famous Royal Cruising Club and has behind it almost a century of stimulating the art and science of handling small boats under sail on long voyages.

The boats of the original members were very small indeed by the standards of the 1880s, and in general they have remained small by the measures of their respective periods. For a long time, cruising yachtsmen operated under one serious handicap. There was less money in the cruising world than in the racing, and also less reputation to be made by professional designers, who depended upon producing racing successes. Thus, few good small cruising yachts were produced. During later years, especially in the inter-war period, the professional architects' lack of interest was offset by a small number of amateur yacht-designers, usually experienced seamen themselves, some of whom showed great talent and produced the best small cruising boats yet to have appeared.

One professional was a notable exception. Colin Archer, of Tolderodden, Norway, with his own small yard and a drawing office in his house, made his name celebrated by improving the design and construction of the pilot, fishing, and life-saving boats of his country. He remains the only marine architect whose portrait has ever appeared on a postage stamp. Archer designed and built

FRAM for Nansen's polar expedition in 1892. Some twenty years earlier, he had designed and built what is believed to be the first Norwegian yacht; though, as we have indicated above, sailing for relaxation was no doubt common enough long before this. His name became well-known throughout Europe for the production of what was then regarded as the most ocean-worthy type of small yacht. Many of these craft made famous voyages, and a kind of cruising yacht, widely known as the *Colin Archer* type, though not necessarily designed by him or built at his yard, indicated the respect felt for his work. A number of such yachts are still in service. Archer produced no racing yachts.

In the absence of good professional design, cruising yachtsmen turned to converting suitable types of working boat, the hulls of which might be picked up more cheaply than the products of the yacht yards, and the best of which were commonly believed to be more seaworthy than the generality of yachts influenced by racing fashions. Some conversions were bad, usually owing to excessive economy, and the denigrating term of "tore-out" was reasonably applied to them. Others, well converted, were transformed into fine and able cruisers; some of these, but ever fewer, are still in service.

Today, the situation is transformed. Ocean, offshore, and coastal-passage racing have changed the attitudes of cruising and racing people alike. Two activities have tended to merge, two attitudes to blend. Nowadays, the demand for small cruising yachts, never intended for racing, has become so immense that the best professional architects give these craft their attention. Indeed, in the present day of so few new large yachts, the many small cruisers have become the architects' chief concern.

The racing season of 1912 was memorable for the witnessing of the start of a great technical revolution in sailing. The *International 6-Metres,* small three-quarter-decked craft, formed a class that was often in the forefront of sail developments, and in the above year, one boat of the class in British waters appeared with the Bermudan rig. It was, in fact, an adaptation of the centuries-old leg-of-mutton triangular sail, which had subsequently taken root in Bermuda and which, in 1912, was receiving renewed interest, thanks to the superior aerodynamic qualities it was believed to possess. The advantages of high-aspect ratio were being learned. At that time, the rig carrying the adaptation of the leg-of-mutton sail received the name Marconi, due to its tall mast and elaborate staying, suggesting one of the then new wireless masts.

By the end of the last pre-war season in European waters, the Marconi rig was making a perceptible mark, though confined to the smallest racing craft. It was left to the United States to continue the development while Europe fought. In 1916, a *Class P* sloop was given a moderately tall Marconi rig, and in the following year, a *Larchmont O*-class boat, 38 ft (11.6 m) on the water-line, came out under one. The size of boat carrying the rig was increasing. In the first years of peace, a giant's stride was taken when NYRIA, one of the biggest racing cutters in British waters, adopted Marconi. The rig, soon to become more usually known as Bermudan, made a quick conquest of the racing fleets.

Mechanical defects and fragile staying in the early Bermudan racing rigs made them suspect for serious cruising, and cruising people, not having the same encouragement to achieve the finest edge of windward performance, but having a keen sense of reliability, were slow to adopt them. This was an attitude still prevailing, though growing steadily weaker, until the outbreak of the Second World War.

Of all the developments between the wars, the most important for the future of sail racing outside the dinghy classes was the rise of offshore, or ocean, racing. Between 1920 and 1939, it evolved from a fringe activity of tough amateur seamen, who could be regarded as amiably eccentric, into a form of sport practised by some of the most active and experienced sailing people. Following the Second World War, it became the principal form of yacht racing, again excepting the dinghy classes, and the offshore racing boats also became the principal competitors in regatta sailing.

Ocean racing in craft handled by amateurs began in the United States, and in a very small way indeed. It was mainly associated with the Bermuda race, five of which had been sailed by 1910, drawing little handfuls of rugged devotees—only two boats took part in the 1910 race. But a further series of Bermuda races, starting in 1923, led the way, not only to the races of today drawing hundreds of entries, but also directly to the Fastnet race and the seasonal programmes of the Cruising Club of America (CCA) and the Royal Ocean Racing Club (RORC).

Ocean racing in small, mainly amateur-manned craft was unknown in Europe until the first Fastnet was organized in 1925. One purely English race of a similar kind had been held in 1887, when the Royal Thames Yacht Club held a race round the British Isles, including Ireland, for a large money prize. A fleet of big yachts took part, cutters, schooners, yawls, and ketches, in the fashion of the day mainly professionally manned. The same club, with a series of races over a 53-mile course from the Nore to Dover, sailed every year from 1866 until 1900, originated the practice of port-to-port, round-the-coast racing, which was to become so striking a feature of European yacht racing after the Second World War. But neither the round-Britain race of 1887 nor the series of Nore-to-Dover coastal matches were to have an influence that spread widely. The first Fastnet race was what was needed to send up the star shell that still hangs overhead today.

That star shell, however, went up very slowly and nearly burnt out prematurely. The Fastnet races were for some time no brilliant success. There were signs that the ninth Fastnet race, in 1933, might be the last, while in America the Bermuda race was waxing in strength. It seemed that a sport that was beginning to appeal widely on the western side of the Atlantic had little to attract Europe. There were entries from the United States for the Fastnet; American boats had won the race in 1928 and 1931; and in 1933, when three of the six entries were American, they won again and also took second and fourth places. From Europe, French yachts appeared in 1928, 1929, and 1931, but this was all. There was no widespread interest. After only nine Fastnets had been sailed (the event became biennial after 1931), it was being said by an eminent yachting authority that the world was about to witness "the passing of a great race over a great course".

Between 1925 and 1933, however, and as a direct result of the Fastnet races, other events had occurred which laid the course to the future. The RORC had organized races to Santander in 1929 and 1930 and a transatlantic race in 1931, and each year from 1928 to 1933, the race regarded as the smaller yachts' Fastnet, the now-famous Channel race over a tough course about 225 miles in length, had been held in the English Channel. In addition, there were a few races over shorter coastal courses. After becoming a near-fatality in 1933, European ocean racing began a confident growth.

The Americans had taught Europeans how to design ocean-racing yachts and how to handle them. Perhaps the London-based RORC did something to teach the Americans how to organize ocean racing. The compact British coastline made the task of organization easier in that country than in the United States. The club became an international body, a high proportion of its members European and American. Between 1933 and 1939, events organized by the RORC became an increasingly important element in European yachting. In the course of this trend, an important change of character had occurred. It may reasonably be claimed that anything describing itself as an "ocean race" should be sailed, for at least part of the distance, over an ocean course, or off soundings. But European—and American—events, as they grew in numbers, were offshore rather than oceanic, and during these years ocean racing to a great extent became offshore racing, differing from regatta racing by involving day and night sailing and distances usually in excess of two hundred miles.

By thus extending the range, it proved possible to gain a greater following than could have been won for racing only over long ocean courses. In 1937, the RORC organized six offshore races apart from the Fastnet and Channel events. In 1938, there were ten races. But the augury of the future could have been seen in the Fastnet of 1937. Twenty-eight yachts from five nations entered: eighteen British, seven German, one French, one Dutch, and one American. It was the finest ocean-racing fleet in quality and size yet to have been started outside American waters, and more internationally representative than any. But the future, of which this was the promise, lay on the further side of a war.

During the inter-war years, the top flight of racing was conducted in four International Yacht Racing Union (IYRU) classes, which were sailed round regatta courses only. Here, it was believed, racing was honed to its sharpest edge; indeed, ocean and offshore racers were considered dull performers in comparison—as in fact many of them then were. The significant fact about these peers of the inter-war racing scene, the *J-Class, 12-Metres, 8-Metres,* and *6-Metres,* is that, apart from the *Twelves,* now used for America's Cup racing, their like was to disappear for ever. The first of these classes, used for America's Cup racing until 1937, comprised the biggest kind of racing cutter. The *12-Metres,* very much smaller, was still of handsome size at some 72 ft (21.9 m) overall, while the *8-Metres,* not less than 60 ft (18.3 m) overall, would fall into the biggest of the offshore-racing classes today. Although these three classes of boat had accommodation, enforced by rule, and in the case of the two largest could have provided quite lavish living quarters, they were used purely for day racing round short courses. It would have been regarded as inconceivable to impair their racing performance by equipping them with adequate amenities for living on board. This is an attitude towards yachts of considerable size that must appear remarkably extravagant today.

The new age of yachting and pleasure sailing followed in the trail of six war years. In the most unpromising circumstances of poverty and a partially ruined western world, it burst almost immediately into bold and enthusiastic activity. That age has now run through some thirty years, with enthusiasm soaring on an exponential curve which is not without its embarrassments—it is becoming ever harder to find suitable waters in which to float all the boats.

Today, the period we have described above as "Grand Yachting", whose latter days were passing barely more than half a century ago, appears as remote as maritime activities on the Nile in the days of the pyramid builders. In today's America's Cup contests, yachting still assumes a rich garb, when a few square miles of sea become dense with lavish craft, whose total value is shockingly immense by the egalitarian standards of today. A faint whiff of "Grand Yachting" still rises from the marinas of the Mediterranean. But the world of yachting, in the older sense, has so far receded that the word itself is now regarded as too archaic for respectable use; so we talk of pleasure boating.

When peace returned, it was widely foreseen that yachting, in that old sense, could not be revived. Steps were quickly taken for the international organization of racing. The *12-Metres, 8-Metres,* and *6-Metres* were dismissed as too costly and specialized for the brave new world. Those devoted to such superb racing machines kept the two latter classes, particularly the *Sixes,* alive in a semi-official way, and when the America's Cup contests were revived in 1958, the *12-Metres,* which had become virtually defunct as a racing class on both sides of the Atlantic, were revived. Since then, they have become the most expensive type of racing yacht ever.

But the dominant theme of post-war sailing was the necessity for the dual-purpose yacht, able to race, sail offshore, and provide adequate living accommodation for a wholly amateur crew. The day of the cruiser-racer, foreshadowed during the inter-war years, opened over the yachting waters of the world. The IYRU introduced cruiser-racer classes to replace the *12-Metres* and the *8-Metres,* but it was not these that caught the new fashion, but boats designed for racing with time allowance under

the rules of the RORC in Europe and the CCA in America. The RORC, though a private body, gained an influence in some ways rivalling that of the IYRU as offshore racing became dominant in competitive yachting. The yachts involved also became the principal ones, of a size above day-boats, in regatta sailing. Design developments originated mainly in the offshore fleets, as this kind of racing advanced in technique.

One result of this has been making its appearance during the last few years. It is recognized that, once the racing bug bites, it does not let go. Handicap racing in its several forms—ocean, coastal, and round regatta courses—became an increasingly dedicated affair among the top flight of boats in the various classes. Boats were designed specially to suit the measurement formulae of the RORC and the CCA, and under the pressure of racing competition, the cruiser element in the cruiser-racer compromise lost weight. Once the boats were built mainly or wholly for racing, inshore or offshore, and expensively fitted out for the purpose, the uncertainty unrelated to performance introduced by time allowance—as mentioned above—became irksome. The trend towards pure racing was hurried by the success of the Admiral's Cup series of international races, involving both inshore and offshore events, which was introduced in 1957 and held in alternate years. Two nations, Britain and the United States, entered teams for the first contest; nowadays, about twenty nations enter teams.

Admiral's Cup racing is conducted under time allowance, but with the years, the range of yacht sizes has been reduced, minimizing the effect of handicapping. The further step was inevitable: level racing, without time allowance, between boats of equal rating. In 1965, the famous old racing trophy, the One Ton Cup, was put back into circulation for competition between boats rating 22 ft (6.7 m) under the RORC rule. The success of this was followed by similar events for larger and smaller craft, styled *Two Ton* and *Half Ton.* The term "ton" in this connection is of purely historical derivation, unrelated to tonnage in any sense. It is a pleasing memorial to the fact that the One Ton Cup was originally raced for by yachts measuring one ton under a nineteenth-century French measurement rule.

The wheel has now revolved full circle. International level racing, in boats such as the inter-war *6-Metre* and *8-Metre* classes, was discarded in favour of racing under time allowance in more economical, dual-purpose boats of the cruiser-racer type during the lean years of the 1940s and 1950s. The intense bite of the racing bug assured the return of level racing by the 1960s. There is one difference,

however. The new level-rating boats race offshore as well as inshore, they have some accommodation, and they are tough enough in rig to take the sea as it comes, which was not possible in the pre-war *8-Metres.*

Meanwhile, there emerged the International Offshore Rule, formulated by a committee whose members all belonged to the RORC, the CCA, or both. A single rule was introduced to govern the design of all the major types of racing yachts throughout the world.

In the years since 1945, the racing of dinghies has undergone an explosive growth that makes it rank as a social phenomenon, which will have to be noticed by general historians in the future. Many aspects of dinghies are considered in later pages. I have written elsewhere:

The dinghy world of the 1970s is the yet most extreme manifestation of trends just faintly perceptible in the 1930s. It is the furthest limit to which the "one-design" principle has yet been carried. It has made that principle acceptable in racing as it has never been in the past. The story of one-design racing is rich in class rules, drawn up with painstaking care and then earnestly evaded through an enthusiasm for improvement. Hulls moulded in plastics have precluded such enthusiasm and produced a uniformity hitherto unattainable. Yet still, in mass-produced dinghy classes of seemingly identical boats, individuality is able to persist in sails and rigging arrangements, and wide differences in performance achieved.

One cannot fail to mention, finally, the plastics revolution. It is the most traumatic event in the history of yachting. Yet, so quickly is change accepted, that those whose sailing has been confined to the last decade or so cannot realize how the world of yachting has been transformed by the use of glass-reinforced plastics and manmade fibres. From 1955 onwards, it became clearer with each year that an ever-higher proportion of yachts and sailing-craft would be of the pedigree laboratory out of factory. Until quite recently, our sailing-craft, large and small, owed their being mainly to natural substances—to the trees of the forest, to vegetable fibres, to the products of the glowing cotton fields. All have almost totally disappeared in the course of less than a generation, to be replaced by products from the laboratories where the chemistry of the long molecule is studied. While materials have been thus transformed, so also have methods of construction. The economics of producing hulls of reinforced plastics enforce repetitive moulding processes, the antithesis of building hulls of individually-laid planks.

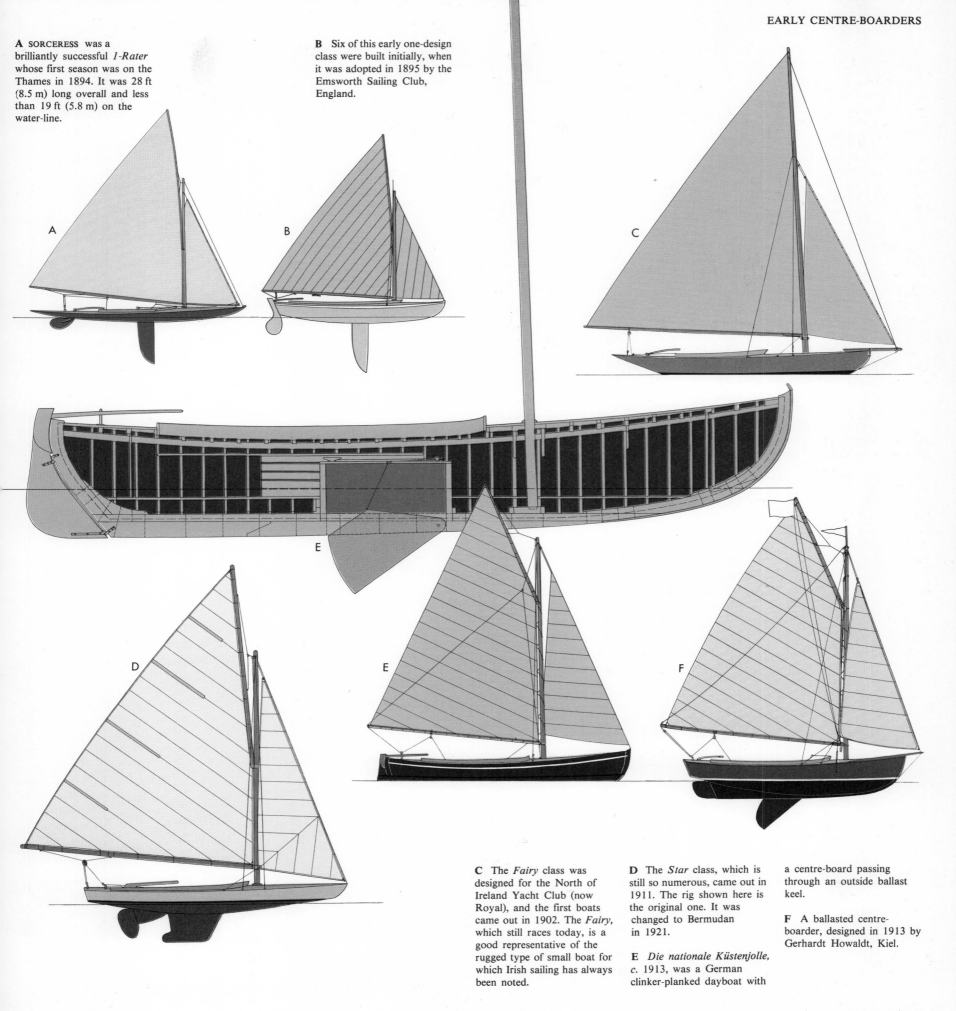

A SORCERESS was a brilliantly successful *1-Rater* whose first season was on the Thames in 1894. It was 28 ft (8.5 m) long overall and less than 19 ft (5.8 m) on the water-line.

B Six of this early one-design class were built initially, when it was adopted in 1895 by the Emsworth Sailing Club, England.

C The *Fairy* class was designed for the North of Ireland Yacht Club (now Royal), and the first boats came out in 1902. The *Fairy*, which still races today, is a good representative of the rugged type of small boat for which Irish sailing has always been noted.

D The *Star* class, which is still so numerous, came out in 1911. The rig shown here is the original one. It was changed to Bermudan in 1921.

E *Die nationale Küstenjolle, c.* 1913, was a German clinker-planked dayboat with a centre-board passing through an outside ballast keel.

F A ballasted centre-boarder, designed in 1913 by Gerhardt Howaldt, Kiel.

13

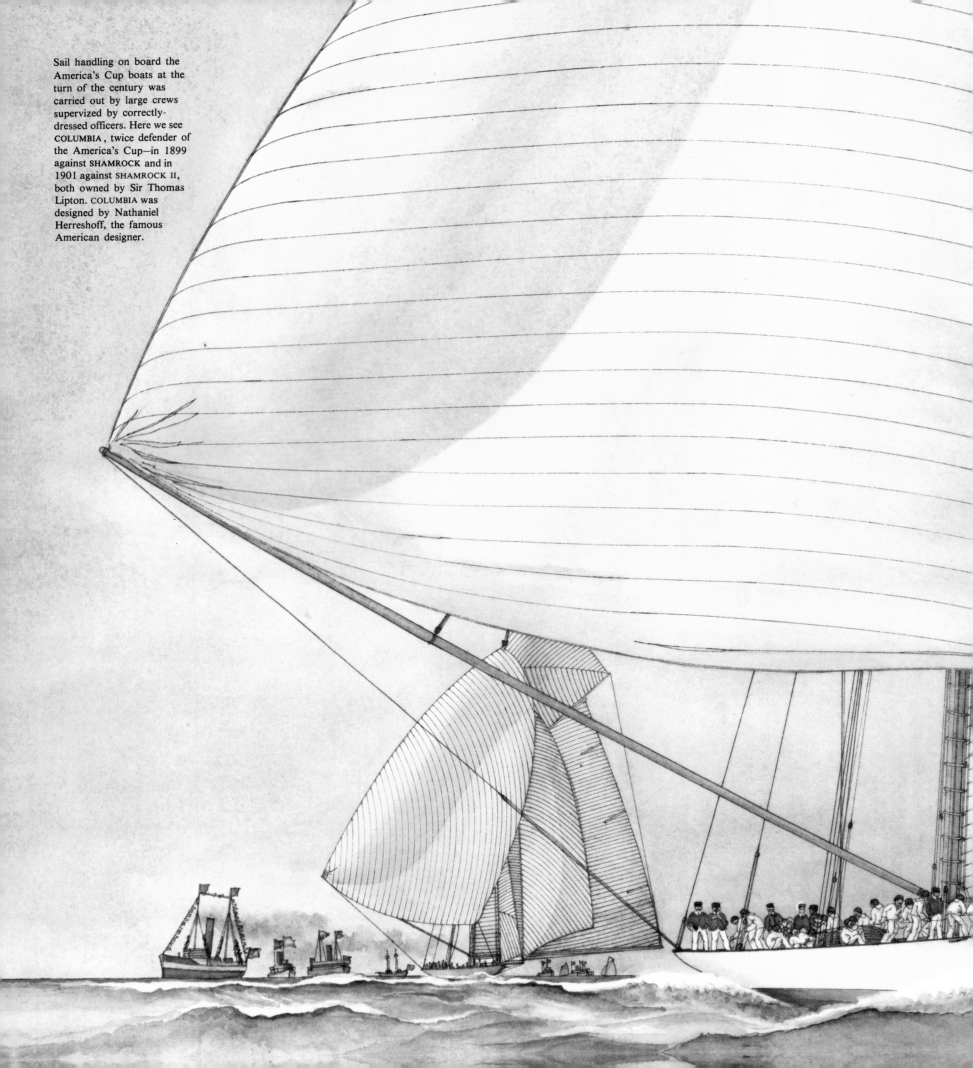

Sail handling on board the America's Cup boats at the turn of the century was carried out by large crews supervized by correctly-dressed officers. Here we see COLUMBIA, twice defender of the America's Cup—in 1899 against SHAMROCK and in 1901 against SHAMROCK II, both owned by Sir Thomas Lipton. COLUMBIA was designed by Nathaniel Herreshoff, the famous American designer.

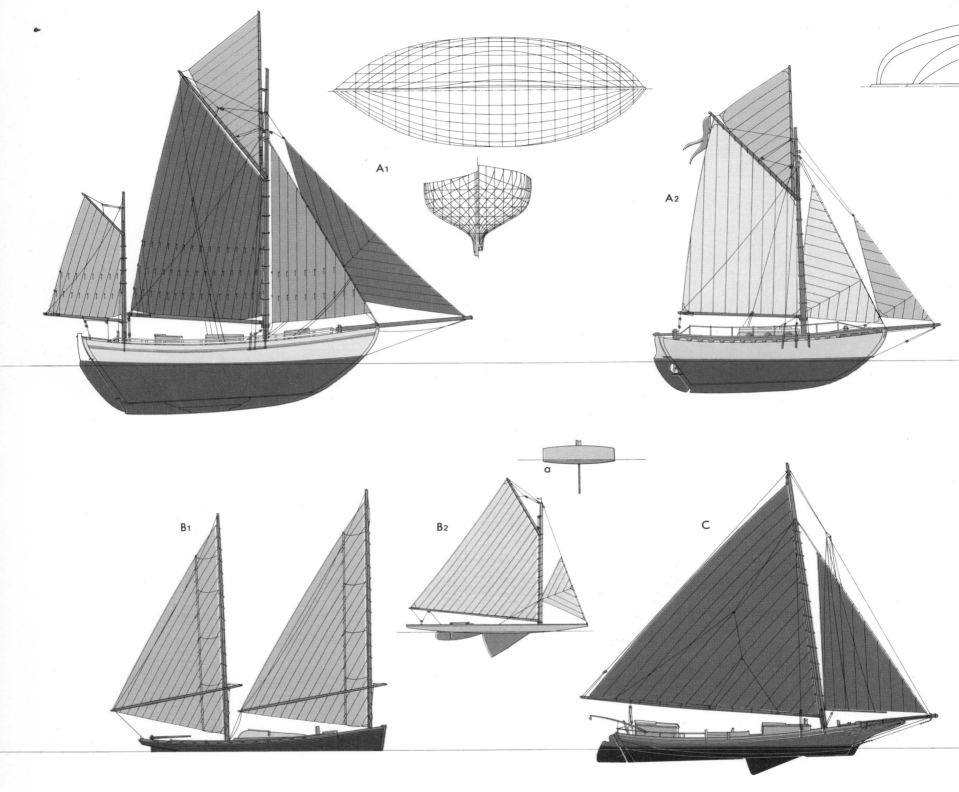

A₁

A₂

a

B₁

B₂

C

A The Norwegian designer Colin Archer made popular a type of heavy, double-ended, beamy cruising yacht (**1**), which became much admired by deep-water yachtsmen. The cutter illustrated (**2**) is a modern GRP version of an Archer design.

B The leg-of-mutton, or Bermudan, sail has never been widely used in work boats; but here we see it in a two-masted New Haven sharpie (**1**), as rigged more than a century ago, with sprit booms and means of brailing the sails. (**2**) An American racing sharpie of 1896 with a gaff rig. (*a*) Midships section.

C The leg-of-mutton sail is also seen on the Chesapeake skipjack, *c.* 1900. Lazy jacks are rigged to allow the mainsail to be kept under control when lowered, without furling. Sometimes used for oyster poaching, the smart sailing qualities of these craft often led to their being converted for pleasure sailing.

D More types of traditional Dutch coastal craft have, with less change, survived into the modern age than any other coastal types. The *Hoogar*, shown here, is clearly identified by the long, straight overhang of its bow.

E The *Bottar* is related in type to the *Hoogar*, having

also a flat bottom and almost-flaring sides which turn into a tumble-home at the gunwale. In both types we see the curved gaff, so characteristic a feature of Dutch rigs, and loose-footed mainsail.

F The American sloops of Friendship, Maine, used to be common in the inshore

fisheries and, like several European types of fishing craft, were often converted into yachts. The smaller Friendship sloops, like that illustrated, had no topmast or topsail. On conversion, cabin-tops were added, and sail-area was sometimes reduced too much.

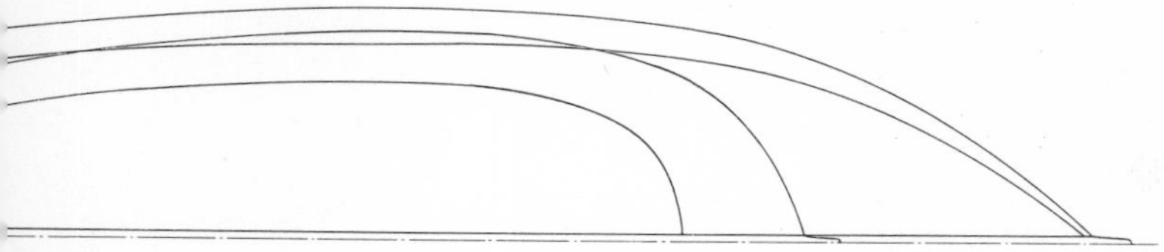

D

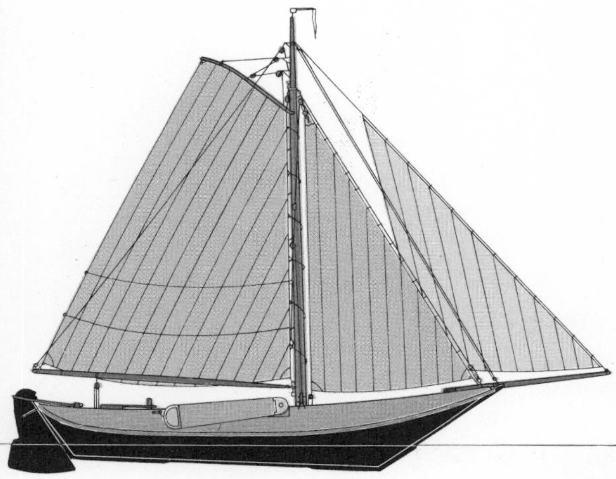

E

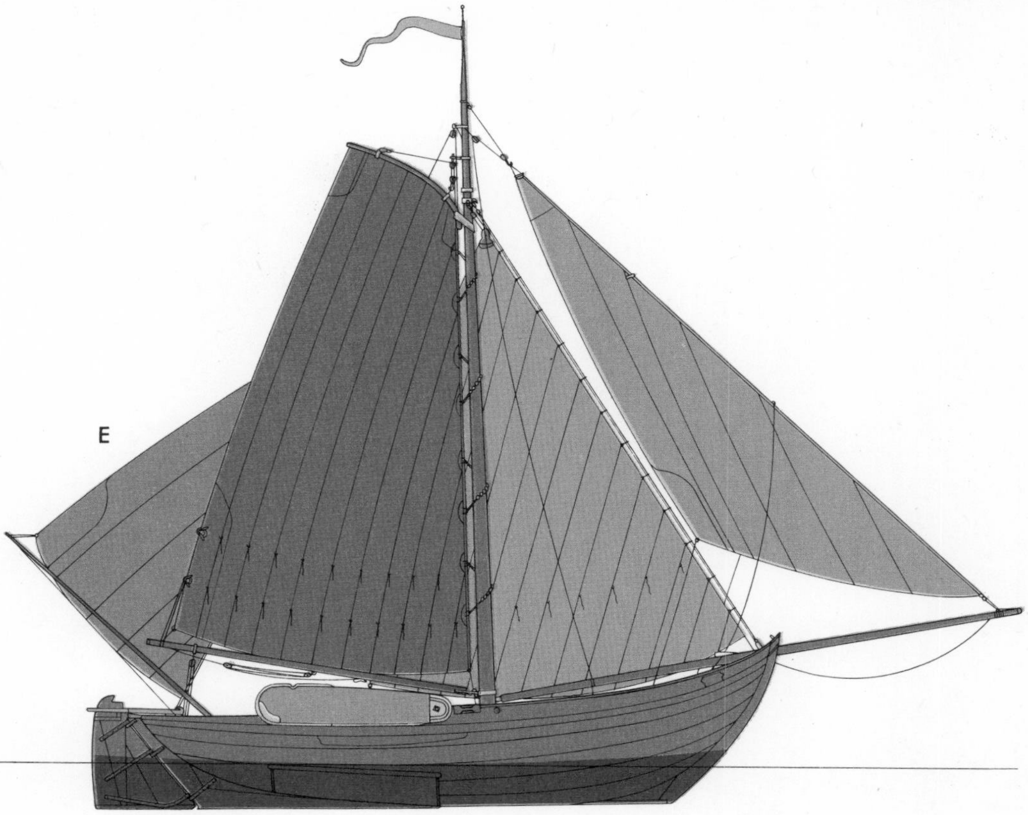

D

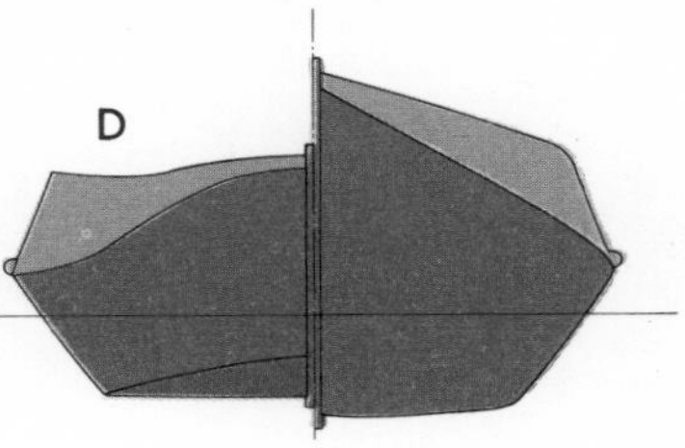

F

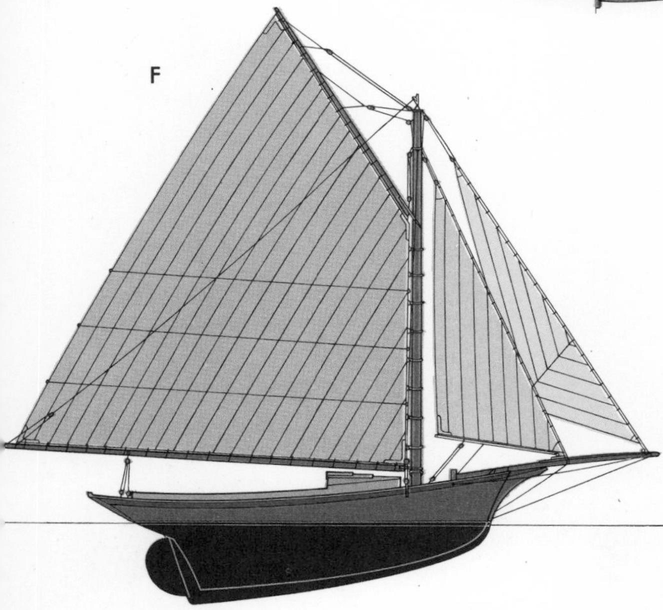

G₁

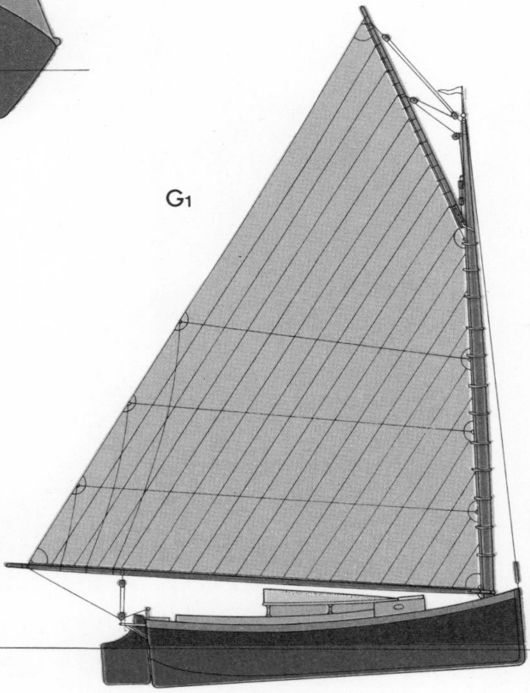

G₂

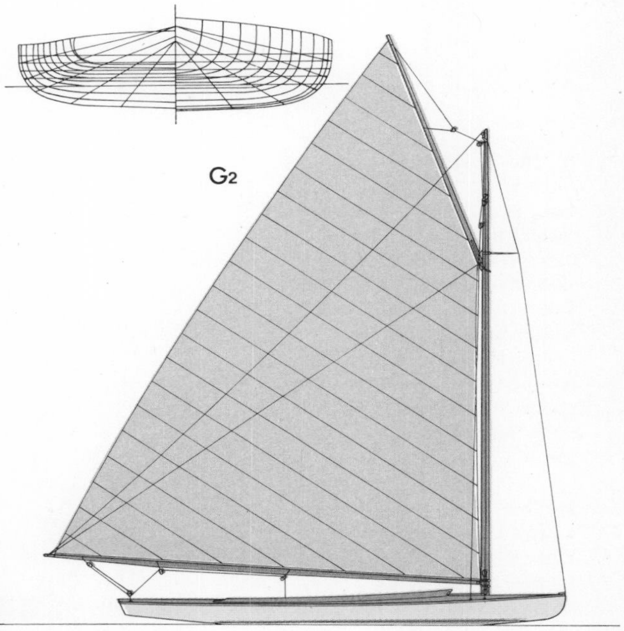

G₂

G A type of single-sail craft called, for reasons unknown, catboat, grew in popularity during the nineteenth century on the New England coast. The hull was shallow, usually with a centre-board, and of extremely wide beam. The working catboat (1) was a reliable and seaworthy craft. As evolved for racing (2), with a still wider beam and excessive sail-area, the catboat became excitingly dangerous.

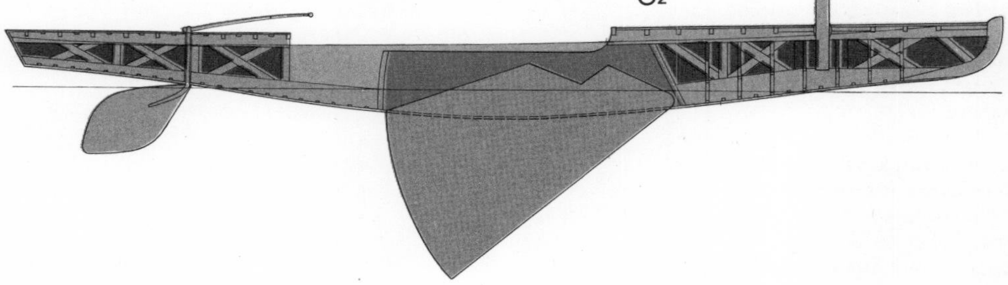

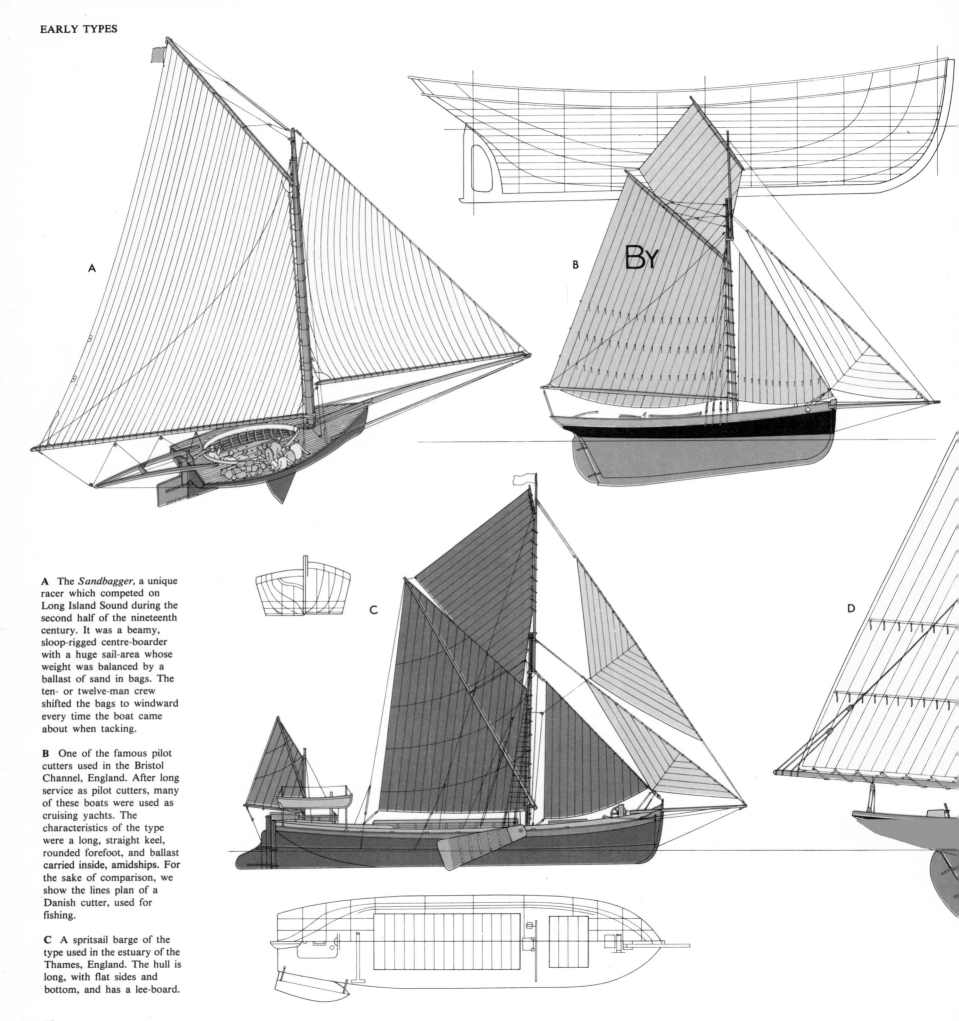

A The *Sandbagger,* a unique racer which competed on Long Island Sound during the second half of the nineteenth century. It was a beamy, sloop-rigged centre-boarder with a huge sail-area whose weight was balanced by a ballast of sand in bags. The ten- or twelve-man crew shifted the bags to windward every time the boat came about when tacking.

B One of the famous pilot cutters used in the Bristol Channel, England. After long service as pilot cutters, many of these boats were used as cruising yachts. The characteristics of the type were a long, straight keel, rounded forefoot, and ballast carried inside, amidships. For the sake of comparison, we show the lines plan of a Danish cutter, used for fishing.

C A spritsail barge of the type used in the estuary of the Thames, England. The hull is long, with flat sides and bottom, and has a lee-board.

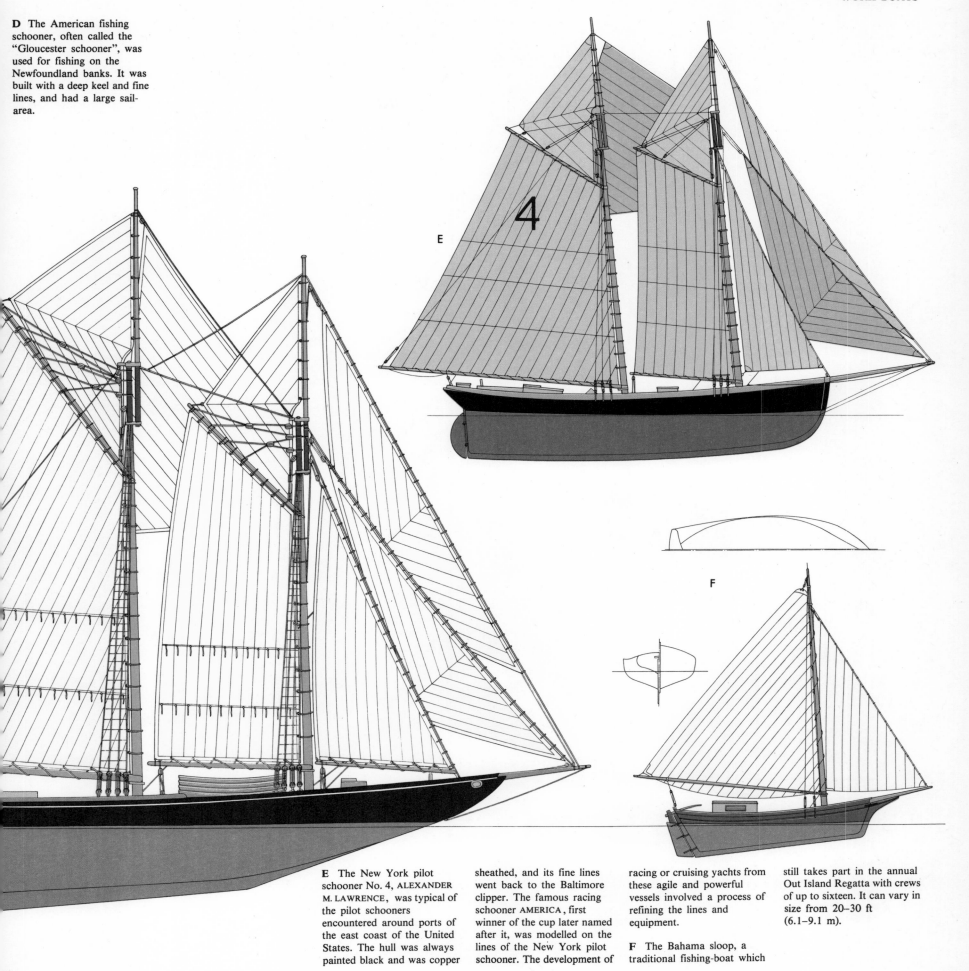

D The American fishing schooner, often called the "Gloucester schooner", was used for fishing on the Newfoundland banks. It was built with a deep keel and fine lines, and had a large sail-area.

E The New York pilot schooner No. 4, ALEXANDER M. LAWRENCE, was typical of the pilot schooners encountered around ports of the east coast of the United States. The hull was always painted black and was copper sheathed, and its fine lines went back to the Baltimore clipper. The famous racing schooner AMERICA, first winner of the cup later named after it, was modelled on the lines of the New York pilot schooner. The development of racing or cruising yachts from these agile and powerful vessels involved a process of refining the lines and equipment.

F The Bahama sloop, a traditional fishing-boat which still takes part in the annual Out Island Regatta with crews of up to sixteen. It can vary in size from 20–30 ft (6.1–9.1 m).

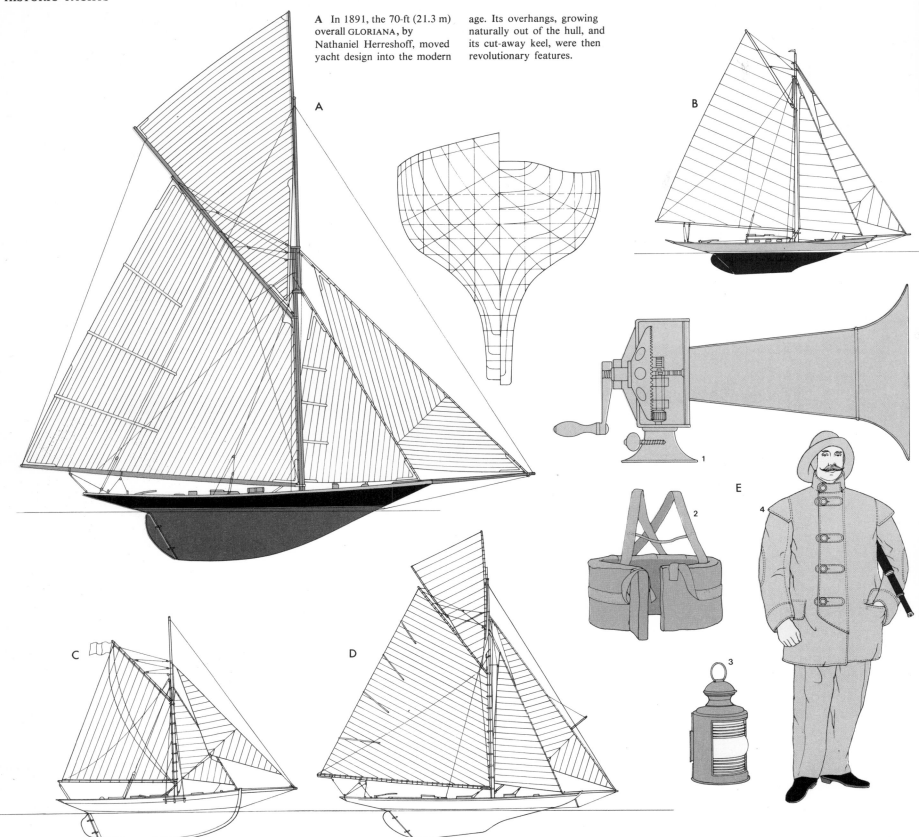

A In 1891, the 70-ft (21.3 m) overall GLORIANA, by Nathaniel Herreshoff, moved yacht design into the modern age. Its overhangs, growing naturally out of the hull, and its cut-away keel, were then revolutionary features.

B During the inter-war period, yachts of the *International 12-, 8-,* and *6-metres* classes were the leading inshore racers in Europe. This Norwegian *8-metres,* 42 ft (12.8 m) overall, shows a late example of the gaff rig.

C Frenchman Alain Gerbault crossed the Atlantic singlehanded in the English-designed and -built cutter FIRECREST during 1923. The voyage was a succession of damages and desperate remedies, as the boat had extremely bad gear.

D In this German-designed *10-metres* R-yacht we see the gaff rig in its final development for inshore racing, just before the introduction of the Bermudan. The topsail, with jackyard and topsail yard, is to be noted.

E Sailing gear from the turn of the century. (**1**) Hand klaxon. (**2**) Lifebelt. (**3**) Running light. (**4**) Foul-weather clothing.

F Of the IYRU classes (see **B**), it was in the smallest, the *6-metres,* that some of the most important design development occurred. CREMONA (1913) represents an early stage in *6-metres* evolution.

G The Universal Measurement Rule was the first to become widely used by clubs in the United States. Boats large and small were catered for. The Q class, boats about 38 ft (11.6 m) overall, were among the smaller.

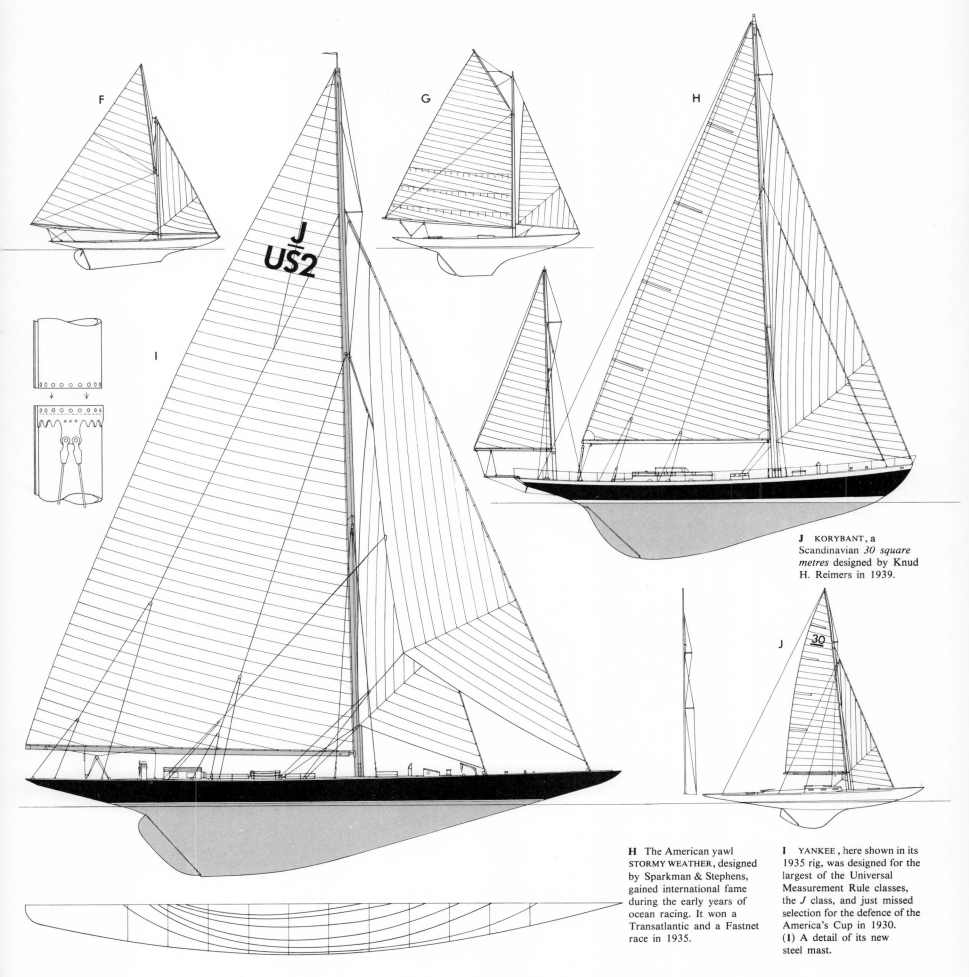

J KORYBANT, a Scandinavian *30 square metres* designed by Knud H. Reimers in 1939.

H The American yawl STORMY WEATHER, designed by Sparkman & Stephens, gained international fame during the early years of ocean racing. It won a Transatlantic and a Fastnet race in 1935.

I YANKEE, here shown in its 1935 rig, was designed for the largest of the Universal Measurement Rule classes, the *J* class, and just missed selection for the defence of the America's Cup in 1930. (1) A detail of its new steel mast.

HISTORY OF POWERBOATING

Curt Borgenstam

The first engine-driven pleasure boats were open ship's boats, designed and built for sailing and rowing, which had been fitted with steam engines. The keel was bored through to house the propeller shaft, and the propeller was placed in a recess in rudder and stern-post. The hull was made of wood or, sometimes, of iron. A simple canvas top provided protection against the weather.

One of the first men to put an engine in a pleasure boat was the German engineer Gottlieb Daimler who, together with his fellow countryman Karl Benz, is otherwise renowned as the "father of the automobile". Daimler designed a light engine which could run at 1,000 rpm, a high speed for its day. From 1886 to 1888, the engine type was installed as a power plant in a motorcycle, a car, a tram, a generating set, and a boat. The boat was demonstrated on the river Neckar in 1888. Its petrol-driven engine had twin cylinders and developed two horsepower at 1,000 rpm. The German authorities were most reluctant to give their permission for the boat to be taken on the river, due to the inflammable nature of the fuel and to the unfortunate choice of name: "explosion motor". In order to get round this difficulty, Daimler hung electric cables on insulators round the vessel to give the impression that it was powered by electricity!

Daimler's boats were copied in practically all countries where car engines were developed and where pleasure boating was popular on rivers, lakes, and other protected waterways. As already mentioned, the hulls of these early boats were almost without exception built of wood. One early attempt to build an aluminium hull might, however, be mentioned. The Swedish inventor Alfred Nobel was among many other things also interested in the manufacture of aluminium, and he co-operated on this with a Swiss company, Escher Wyss. In 1892, he ordered an experimental aluminium boat, MIGNON, from Escher Wyss, and some years later it was demonstrated in Stockholm. The boat was fitted with a steam engine, and a boiler which was fired by oil instead of coal, since Nobel had financial interests in the exploitation of Russian oil deposits. MIGNON was a beautiful little boat, and its lines and layout indicate that it might have been intended as a small-scale prototype for bigger vessels and yachts.

As the reliability and power of boat engines developed, it became possible to go for longer cruises. This created a need for more effective protection against the weather, and two distinct types of boat were developed to meet this need, the saloon boat and the cabin boat.

Amidships, the saloon boat was given a glassed-in structure, not unlike that of the early tram. The engine was placed under a hood forward of the saloon, which was, therefore, relatively undisturbed by engine noise and fumes. In owner-driven boats, the wheel would be placed in the fore end of the saloon. If a special crew was employed, the wheel was placed as far forward as possible, in front of the engine.

The saloon boat was suitable for those who demanded luxury and sailed in fair weather only. It was not a very pleasant vessel in rough weather because of its open forebody, which easily became swamped. The heavy engine and the fact that, in accordance with the vogue of the day, the forebody had fairly sharp lines made the boat respond rather badly to rough seas.

The cabin boat had its weather-protected space forward, beneath either an arched coach roof or foredeck, probably inspired by the design of contemporary torpedo-boats. Cabin boats were especially popular in the Scandinavian countries at the beginning of the twentieth century. Their forward cabins were better suited for spending the night in than were the glassed-in structures of saloon boats.

The motor yacht was a development of the saloon boat, and had a bridge added between saloon and engine-room or, on larger craft, above the engine-room. The larger motor yachts had a cabin forward of the bridge, a characteristic inherited from the cabin boat. This cabin was intended as quarters for the crew and was often small and primitive.

All these boats were relatively slow, with speeds of between seven and twelve knots. Soon, however, power-boat races were arranged, and special racing boats began to be designed. Charles Parsons, an Englishman, was one of the first to experiment with high-speed boats. His TURBINIA, equipped with steam-turbine machinery of 2,000 horsepower, reached over thirty knots in 1897. It was built primarily to draw attention to turbine machinery, and to prove its suitability for high-speed warships and express steamers, and this it did very successfully.

For private use, however, steam turbines were too complicated and difficult to handle. The development of the aircraft and car industries soon provided more suitable power plants in the form of light, high-output petrol engines of 100–200 horsepower. Such engines, in specially designed, long, narrow hulls of 50–65 ft (c. 15–20 m), could produce speeds of twenty-five to thirty knots.

In the first decade of this century, the French Riviera, and especially Monaco, became something of a Mecca to boating and motoring enthusiasts alike. At Monaco, annual regattas were held, and these included powerboat races. As a result of these, much more attention was given to the technical development of powerboats. It was discovered that faster speeds could be attained with less engine power if the boat was virtually flat-bottomed, thus causing it to plane at speed, a principle which, in its purest form, is illustrated by the surf-board and the water-ski. Planing means that the boat, when at speed, is mainly carried by the hydrodynamic forces arising when the water is pressed downwards by the bottom of the boat, running at an angle to the surface. A fairly high power-to-weight ratio is necessary to drive a boat fast enough to start it planing.

In 1909, the American racing-boat designer W.H. Fauber patented a type of boat with a bottom divided into a number of transverse planes or steps. As the boat, at speed, lifted in the water, these steps effectively reduced the wetted surface. The stepped-hull boat was further developed by the British Thornycroft company which, from an early stage, had specialized in fast torpedo-boats and destroyers. One of the company's most successful racing boats was MIRANDA IV, which, during the First World War, became the prototype for a whole series of fast motor torpedo-boats. The fastest of these could reach a speed of nearly forty knots with two 375-horsepower petrol engines.

During the 1920s, powered pleasure boats had their definite break-through. Designers had discovered how hulls should be built in order to suit different speed ranges and demands. Reliable, cheap, and comparatively light engines were now available. The car industry, especially in the United States, had shown the way towards the cheap production of engines in series.

The design of powerboats was to a large extent dictated by the needs of the customers. In the Northern countries, people were able to enjoy pleasure boating even in relatively small and simple craft, due to the abundance of protected waterways such as lakes, archipelagos, and canals. One craft that was particularly popular was the *Pettersson* boat, a type of cabin boat introduced by the Swedish designer C.G. Pettersson who, in 1912, made a much-publicized trip round Scandinavia in his boat VIKING, following the entire Norwegian and Swedish coastline.

Until around 1930, when the world-wide economic slump began, there were still those with money to spend on expensive, luxuriously equipped boats, pleasure yachts as well as extremely fast powerboats. In the United States, a special type of pleasure speedboat was developed. It was fully decked, with two cockpits separated by a decked engine-room. Powered by light, car-type petrol engines of

70 to 150 horsepower, these boats could reach speeds of twenty to thirty knots. The mahogany hull was V-bottomed without steps. This type of boat was, properly speaking, unpractical in several respects. The engine was completely inaccessible when running, and the aft cockpit, which had no means of communication with the fore, was exposed to spray from the bow wave. Despite these drawbacks, the type became very popular, especially among speed-happy youngsters, thanks to its racy lines and elegant finish. It has survived to the present time at one boat-yard only. This is the Italian Riva yard, where such boats are built to serve mainly as harbour commuters for large pleasure yachts. A variety of this type was the American *Dodge* boat, which had a covered superstructure, not unlike a car top, over the front seats. A Scandinavian equivalent was the *Plym cab,* built by the Neglinge boat-yard for the 1930 Stockholm exhibition.

At the end of the 1920s, the outboard engine began to be popular. As early as 1891, the Swedish Vulcan company had produced what might be called an outboard engine, since it was intended to be mounted in the stern sheets of an ordinary rowing-boat. In other countries, the idea was also being developed and, in 1895, the British-built Watamota was introduced. It was hung from a hoop on the transom, and its propeller was driven by a chain transmission. In France at the turn of the century, the "motor oar", Motogodille, was being marketed. A long, inclined shaft, mounted on the transom and driven by a light, single-cylinder, air-cooled engine, drove the Motogodille's propeller.

The first to have any real success with an outboard engine was a Norwegian, Ole Evinrude, who had an engineering business in Milwaukee. The idea for an outboard engine is said to have come to him when, on a hot summer day in 1906, his fiancée coaxed him into rowing a long distance in order to buy her an ice-cream. On the return trip, the ice-cream melted. It must have struck him that a small engine at the stern would have greatly eased the burden of chivalry, and enabled the fair lady to have her ice-cream. He produced a single-cylinder, two-stroke engine with a vertical shaft with a bevel gear at its lower end; the same fundamental principle is still in use today. Evinrude's engine was most successful, but since he did not possess a workshop in which to mass-produce it, he sold the design to a number of engine manufacturers. One of the conditions of sale prohibited him from producing boat engines during the next five years.

In 1921, however, Evinrude re-entered the market with a twin-cylinder, light engine which he named ELTO (Evinrude Light Twin Outboard). Many other makers also switched to two or more cylinders to get a smoother-running engine.

At first, the outboard engine was regarded as auxiliary power for use on rowing-boats, but by the end of the 1920s, boats were being specially designed to carry outboard engines. They were built with more buoyant afterbodies to support the weight of the engine, and their bottom lines were suited for higher speeds. Such boats were often called "camping boats". They were undecked or had a short fore-deck, side-coamings, and a windscreen. Thanks to their inexpensiveness, limited draught, and ease of maintenance, these easy-to-handle craft were eminently suited for shorter trips in protected waters, and they did a

lot to popularize pleasure boating. The outboard engine was started by hand with a crank knob on the fly-wheel or with a starting cord. The engine was often a bit difficult to start, a minor disadvantage when compared to all its advantages.

The outboard engine was also used for racing, usually mounted on 10-ft (*c.* 3 m) long, light boats with stepped hulls built of thin mahogany sheets or plywood, and with decks of canvas stretched over battens. The drivers would usually kneel when racing these boats, which could reach speeds of thirty-five to forty knots. At the beginning of the 1930s, the outboard sport became especially popular in the United States and in Scandinavia, where there were plenty of protected waterways, and on the lakes of Britain, Germany, France, and Italy.

The development of powerboats has always been strongly influenced by powerboat racing, which tries out, under rough conditions, new constructions, materials, and designs. Today, it is often difficult to distinguish between racing boats and pleasure boats, partly because the powered pleasure boats have become much faster, and partly because speed races for ordinary family powerboats are now being arranged regularly. During the 1920s and 1930s, however, differences were much more pronounced. High speeds were, in reality, the prerogative of an exclusive group of speedboat owners with the right combination of money, love of speed, and interest in engines.

Something of a tug-of-war developed during the 1920s between the United States and Great Britain. As early as 1903, Sir Alfred Harmsworth, later Lord Northcliffe, had donated a trophy for international powerboat races for boats no more than 40 ft (12.2 m) long and powered by engines built in the same country as the boat.

At the beginning of the 1920s, the Harmsworth races were dominated by Gar Wood from the United States. All his boats were named MISS AMERICA and numbered in succession. They were powered by powerful Liberty or Packard aeroengines, which could be bought after the First World War at low prices. Wood's last boat, MISS AMERICA X, was, for instance, equipped with four Packard engines with a total of 7,800 horsepower, an enormous amount for such a light hull, only 38 by 10 ft 6 in (11.6 by 3.2 m).

Logically, the British boats were named MISS ENGLAND and numbered from I to III. MISS ENGLAND I and II were driven by the well-known racing-car driver Sir Henry Segrave. But when Segrave died in a boat accident, Kaye Don took over. The first boat was powered by a 950-horsepower Napier Lion aeroengine of the same type as the one used in Segrave's racing car, "Golden Arrow". MISS ENGLAND II and III were both equipped with two 1,750-horsepower Rolls-Royce engines.

In 1928, the world speed record was held by MISS AMERICA VII at 92.7 mph (149.2 km/h). Two years later, Segrave reached a speed of 98.7 mph (158.8 km/h) in MISS ENGLAND II. During a further attempt by Segrave, the boat collided with a floating object, capsized, and sank. Segrave and one of his mechanics were killed.

In 1932, the record was recaptured by Gar Wood in MISS AMERICA IX at 111.7 mph (179.8 km/h), but it was broken anew by Kaye Don in the British boat, MISS ENGLAND II, which had been salved and repaired. Shortly afterwards, Gar Wood retaliated with a new speed record.

Lord Wakefield, who had financed MISS ENGLAND II, now sponsored MISS ENGLAND III, which was built by Thornycroft. With Kaye Don at the wheel, the boat attained a speed of 119.8 mph (192.8 km/h), whereupon Gar Wood squeezed 124.9 mph (201 km/h) out of his MISS AMERICA X. In the course of five hectic years, the record had been broken seven times. Five more years were to pass before another attack was made on it.

The initiative then lay in the hands of Sir Malcolm Campbell, who had broken the land speed record time and again with his *Bluebird* cars. In 1937, Fred Cooper built him a *Bluebird* powerboat equipped with the same 2,150-horsepower Rolls-Royce engine that had powered his latest record-breaking car. Whereas Gar Wood had concentrated mainly on getting the highest possible total power from his boats, *Bluebird* was designed to have a favourable power-to-weight ratio.

In 1938, Sir Malcolm Campbell managed to raise the speed record for boats to 130.9 mph (210.7 km/h). It seemed as if the boat could be driven even faster, but it became impossible to control at these high speeds, despite the fact that the runs were made on absolutely calm water. The bottom of *Bluebird*'s hull consisted of two planes, separated by a step, and the frame curves were slightly concave. At top speeds, the boat lifted and balanced on the central parts of the planes. This allowed the boat to lean a little to one side or the other, but it caused dangerous yawing tendencies. This problem was also common among many other racing boats. The solution was found by Arno Apel, who worked at the Ventnor boat-yard in the United States in the mid-1930s. He introduced the three-point boat whose fore plane was divided into two wing-like sponsons. Since the speeding boat was now carried by three points instead of two, it had a much greater lateral stability and could, therefore, be driven even faster.

In 1939, Commander Peter Du Cane of the British Vosper boat-yard decided to apply this principle to a new *Bluebird*. Its engine and machinery were transferred from the earlier boat. Sir Malcolm Campbell's young son, Donald, christened the new *Bluebird* on Monday, August 14, 1939, and by the following Sunday the speed record had been raised to 141.7 mph (228 km/h). Soon after this, the Second World War broke out, and the powerboat builders of the world had to devote their skills to other tasks, such as the development of motor torpedo-boats, gunboats, and air-sea rescue boats.

Up to the outbreak of war, practically all pleasure boats had been built of wood. During the war, however, a new material called glass-reinforced plastics (GRP) was introduced. True, plastics had been used for some time for lighting and electrical fittings, etc., but by reinforcing it with glass fibres, a much tougher, elastic material was produced. This material proved to be ideal for the manufacture of hulls. It was strong and elastic; proof against water, rot, and ship-worms; it could be moulded into practically any shape; and it was suitable for mass production in long series.

Today, GRP has become the dominating material used for boats of up to about 50 ft (*c.* 15 m). For larger boats, GRP has not been a competitive material so far; such boats are built of wood, steel, light metal, or ferrocement. One reason for this is that the usual method, to shape the hull in an outer mould, is best suited for boats built in long runs, and few—if any—large hulls are in that big a demand. Experiments are, however, being made that aim at finding other plastic-hull building methods more suitable for big hulls.

Since the Second World War, considerable advances have been made in improving the power-to-weight ratio of boat engines. This has been, to a great extent, the result of the research and development work that has gone into the adaptation of autoengines for use in powerboats. The powerboat industry has always been fortunate in that it has benefited from the advances made in the autoengine field, where the tremendously long series have motivated and defrayed costs.

Earlier, inboard engines always transmitted their power to the propeller via a propeller shaft running through the bottom or through the keel. At the beginning of the 1950s, however, the Volvo-Penta company in Sweden introduced the inboard-outboard (IO), or stern, drive, and many other manufacturers soon followed suit. Although the engine is placed inboard, next to the transom, the transmission unit is placed outboard. The propeller is driven via an upper bevel gear, a vertical shaft, and a lower bevel gear in a submerged gear housing, as on an outboard engine. The upper gear is connected with the engine by a short propeller shaft and two universal joints, which allow the drive unit to be swivelled laterally and tipped upwards, so that the propeller is accessible. Usually, a reverse gear-shift is built into the top part. It is common for an IO drive unit to be mounted to the engine via a flange joint, but the engine can also be mounted separately, especially if it is large and heavy.

IO drives have become very popular, especially when combined with light-weight engines of up to 150 horsepower. True, the IO drive is more complicated and expensive than the simple system with a straight propeller shaft, but this is compensated by the fact that it is easier and quicker to install. There is no need for the time-consuming aligning of the engine and the propeller shaft.

Another advantage is that the motor unit is placed in the stern, so that there is more space on board for interior fittings, etc. Furthermore, the light petrol engine provides enough weight aft to reduce water resistance when the boat planes, but it is not so heavy as to cause the afterbody to settle too deeply in the water. On the other hand, the IO drive is less suitable with diesel engines, which are usually almost twice as heavy per horsepower as are petrol engines, and this makes the boat too stern-heavy.

Thanks to the development of light, efficient inboard and outboard engines, high speeds at sea are nowadays within reach of a much wider range of boat-owners than before. Fast boats are no longer something exclusive, and they are used not only for racing but also as ordinary pleasure boats. This is one reason why designers are now trying to combine speed and seaworthiness in these boats.

These two qualities, speed and seaworthiness, were very much sought after by designers of motor torpedo-boats which were required to hold high speeds even in rough seas. The solution to this was to design planing hulls with relatively sharp V-shapes forward, which lessened the impact in a head sea. The after body, however, was given flattish bottom lines in order to create low resistance at planing speeds.

Similar hull shapes were used for fast pleasure boats of the planing type until the end of the 1950s, when Ray Hunt introduced a new bottom shape, which was for a long time called the "Bertram bottom", after the American company that first launched the idea. The new feature was that the hull's bottom had a deep V-shape, not just in the forebody, but along the whole length. In order to maintain good lateral stability at speed, the bottom was fitted with a number of longitudinal spray rails, arranged so that the cross spray from the bow wave was forced downwards by the rails, thus causing stabilizing lifting force.

The Bertram hull quickly became a success, especially for sports boats, for which new racing classes were organized. The many racing successes of boats with the deep V-shape made the design trendsetting, and it has been used even for slower powerboats, where it is little justified.

A deep V-shape with longitudinal spray rails can nowadays be found on almost any boat that lays claim to being speedy or sporty, from 10-ft (c. 3 m) runabouts with twenty-horsepower outboard engines to the most costly offshore racers with, say, two engines of up to five hundred horsepower each, together capable of speeds of about sixty knots.

Since the Second World War, outboard engine development has been concentrated mainly on increased power and reliability, and lower weight. Power has been increased so much that even ordinary standard engines can be used for racing, the only modifications necessary being to gear housings and propellers.

In the 1930s, surface propellers were used for the sea sleds built by Hickman in America. The sea sled actually looked like a snow sled, and consisted of two parallel keels, or runners, with the hull, a concave V-shape, in between. The two counter-rotating propeller shafts penetrated the transom, not the bottom, and were fitted with surface propellers, which work half-submerged, with the boss at the surface and the upper half above water.

In the early 1950s, the surface propeller was revived for use on speedboats. It was realized that, apart from its axial thrust, the surface propeller also produced a considerable lifting force. This force was utilized on three-point racing boats for lifting the after body out of the water. Thus, the after bottom was no longer used as supporting point; instead, the propeller boss was used, and such boats became generally known as "prop-riders". Ordinary propellers had to have slender shafts and shaft brackets, which were often prone to vibration problems, but surface propellers could have sturdier shafts and brackets, since they would be lifted clean out of the water at high speeds.

On June 26, 1950, Stanley Sayre's SLO-MO-SHUN, a three-point prop-rider, recaptured the world water speed record for the United States at a speed of 159 mph (256 km/h), despite the fact that the boat was not really intended for speed-record attempts; it had been built for circuit racing. It was powered by an 1,800-horsepower Allison aeroengine. As was the case after the First World War, practically unused, high-powered aeroengines could be had cheaply as surplus material after the Second World War. Such engines offered an ideal power plant for speedboat designers and builders.

Great Britain had pioneered the use of jet engines in aeroplanes, and attempts were also made to use such engines in powerboats. In 1952, John Cobb, who already held the world land speed record with his Napier-Railton car, had a three-point boat, CRUSADER, built at the Vosper shipyard. Powered by a De Havilland Ghost turbojet engine, the boat was supported at speed by a "reversed" three-point system. The supporting areas were arranged one forward, under the streamlined hull, and two aft on sponsons. At the first attempt, Cobb broke the world speed record with miles to spare, attaining a speed of 207 mph (333 km/h) but, having covered the measured distance in one direction, his craft was forced into a fore-and-aft pitching motion by the wash of a passing boat reflected off the shore. This pitching rapidly increased until the boat dived, and Cobb was hurled out and killed.

Sir Malcolm Campbell's son, Donald, carried on the family tradition when he ordered a new Bluebird car, which was to be equipped with a Bristol Proteus gas-turbine engine. In this car, he beat John Cobb's world land speed record. Donald Campbell then had the *Bluebird* boat converted from propeller to jet propulsion. During trial runs, fore-and-aft pitching was observed long before record speeds had been approached. Bearing John Cobb's recent death in mind, Campbell decided to interrupt the trials. He had a new *Bluebird* boat built, also on the three-point principle, but with two supporting points forward on sponsons, and with the third supporting point aft on the hull centre. The boat looked like a giant lobster. With a Metropolitan Vickers Beryl jet engine in this craft, Donald Campbell set a new world record at 202 mph (325 km/h) on July 23, 1955. Later, he raised the record several times: on November 10, 1958, to 249 mph (401 km/h); on May 14, 1959, to 260 mph (418 km/h); on New Year's Eve, 1964, to 276 mph (444 km/h). In 1966, a more powerful engine was installed, a Bristol Orpheus with twice the thrust of the earlier engine, and Campbell now set his mind on being the first man to exceed 300 mph (483 km/h). However, during a trial run on January 4, 1967, *Bluebird* started to weave from side to side, became airborne, tumbled over backwards, and dived. Donald Campbell was killed.

During the 1950s and 1960s, there was an enormous increase in the number of pleasure boats built. In the United States, with its high standard of living and plentiful access to cheap fuel, powerboating became a national leisure-time activity. The dominating boat types were fast, planing vessels with deep, V-shaped hulls, developed to sizes of about 30 ft (c. 10 m), and with comfortable interiors. Reaching planing speeds, 20–30 knots, was no problem, since the boats could be powered by large but light, twin V8 auto-type engines, each developing 200–300 horsepower. The high fuel consumption caused no worries, since petrol was still an inexpensive commodity. It was also in the United States that a plenteous flora of gadgets designed to facilitate life on board was developed—galley equipment, refrigerators, toilets, and so on. Now that more and more people are spending their leisure time at sea, safety on board has become the concern not only of boating people, but also of the authorities. Design and construction of pleasure boats have long been based on practical experience and the demands of the market. Of late, however, there has been a tendency on the part of the authorities of several countries to establish boat-construction regulations in an attempt to increase the safety of boats, crews, and passengers.

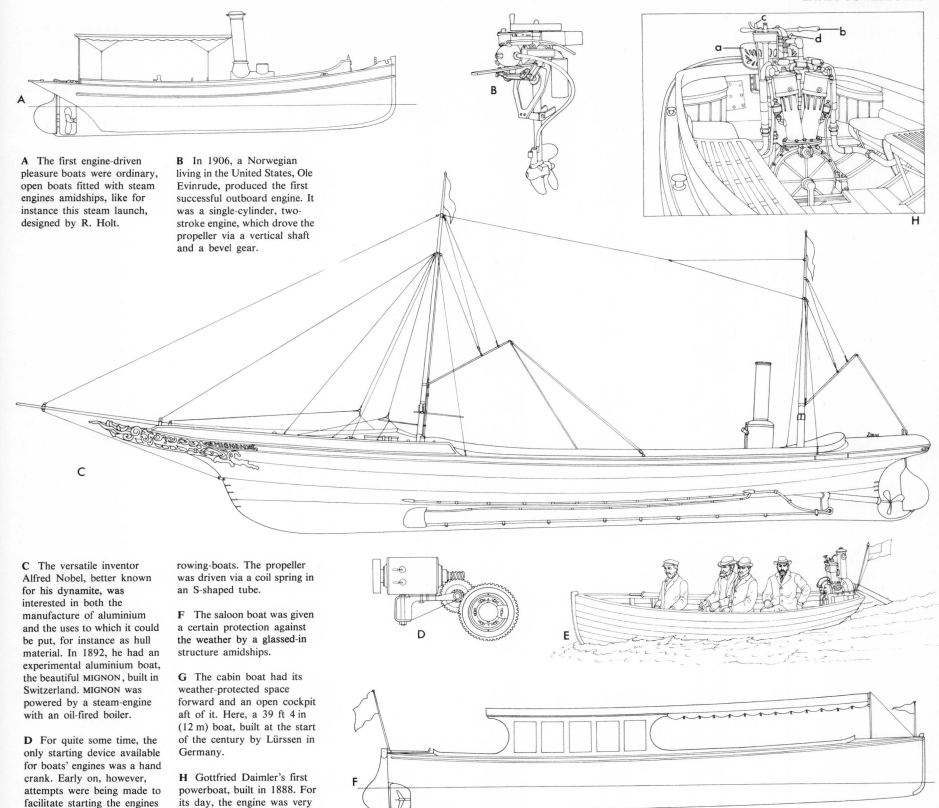

A The first engine-driven pleasure boats were ordinary, open boats fitted with steam engines amidships, like for instance this steam launch, designed by R. Holt.

B In 1906, a Norwegian living in the United States, Ole Evinrude, produced the first successful outboard engine. It was a single-cylinder, two-stroke engine, which drove the propeller via a vertical shaft and a bevel gear.

C The versatile inventor Alfred Nobel, better known for his dynamite, was interested in both the manufacture of aluminium and the uses to which it could be put, for instance as hull material. In 1892, he had an experimental aluminium boat, the beautiful MIGNON, built in Switzerland. MIGNON was powered by a steam-engine with an oil-fired boiler.

D For quite some time, the only starting device available for boats' engines was a hand crank. Early on, however, attempts were being made to facilitate starting the engines of at least the more expensive boats with a special starter motor. Shown here is an electric starter motor from 1913, and its connection to the flywheel via a worm reduction gear.

E In 1891, the Swedish Vulcan company manufactured a series of engines which could be mounted in the stern sheets of rowing-boats. The propeller was driven via a coil spring in an S-shaped tube.

F The saloon boat was given a certain protection against the weather by a glassed-in structure amidships.

G The cabin boat had its weather-protected space forward and an open cockpit aft of it. Here, a 39 ft 4 in (12 m) boat, built at the start of the century by Lürssen in Germany.

H Gottfried Daimler's first powerboat, built in 1888. For its day, the engine was very light and high-speed; it developed two horsepower at 1,000 rpm. (*a*) Helmsman's seat. (*b*) Steering lever. (*c*) Reversing lever. (*d*) Handle for adjusting the air-fuel mixture.

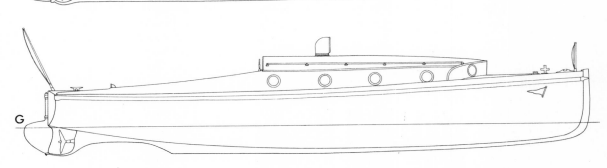

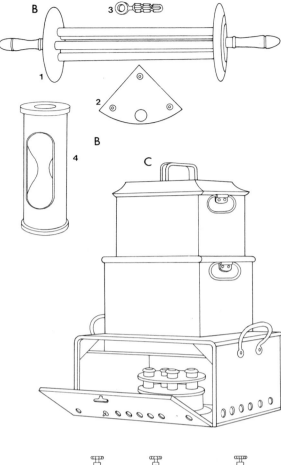

At the start of the twentieth century, larger yachts and motor cruisers often had costly and comfortable interiors. Such boats travelled rather slowly, say, 7–12 knots, and they were best suited for trips in calm weather.

A The elegant saloon in the American motor yacht KOSOGAAS, built in 1907. The wooden details of the interior fittings consist of beautifully carved, brightly varnished mahogany. Light wicker chairs and leather-covered cushions.

B At this time, the hand log was the most common instrument with which the speed of a ship could be determined. For pleasure boats, except for the very biggest yachts, it was, however, too difficult to handle. (**1**) Log reel. (**2**) Log chip. (**3**) Peg. (**4**) Log glass.

C Several types of boat stoves were developed, such as for instance this example from 1907. They were fired with paraffin or petrol. On larger, heavier yachts, coal-fired iron stoves sometimes occurred, used for heating and cooking.

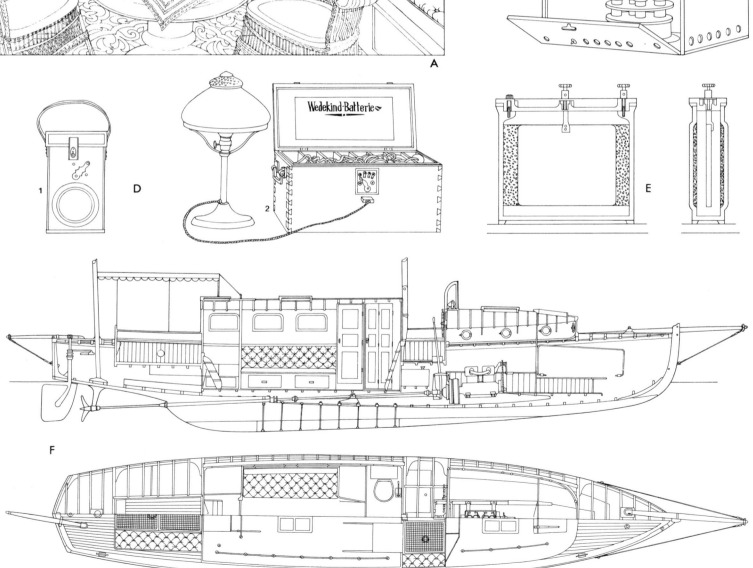

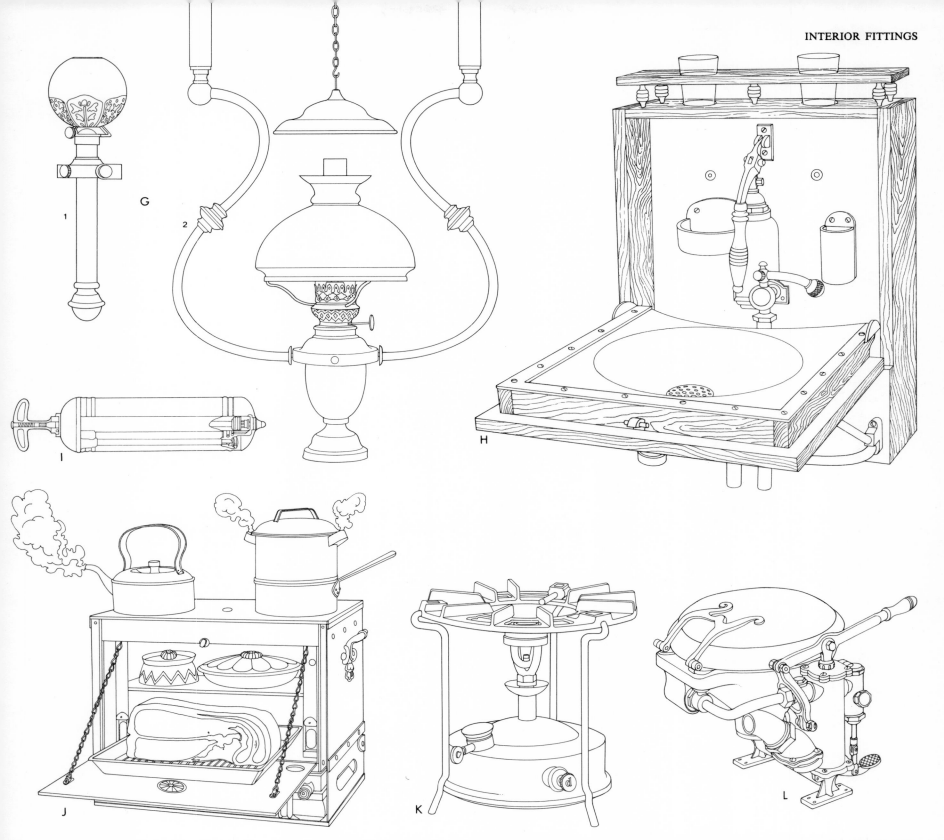

D In the first decades of the twentieth century, electricity made its debut on board boats as well as in the home. On board, dry cells, as in this hand lamp (**1**), or heavy lead accumulators (**2**), were used. A lead accumulator could be used to power the electric starter motor, and it would be charged when the boat was running by a dynamo, powered by the engine.

E Section of a lead accumulator.

F German motor sailer from 1910. Forward of the saloon are the wheel, the engine, and a fairly primitive cabin for the crew.

G Lighting appliances other than electric lamps were, of course, the candle—here in an elegant candle-stick, fixed to

the wall (**1**)—and the petroleum lamp (**2**), both from 1910. Acetylene lamps were also used.

H On large yachts, the same types of covered-up wash-stands were provided as those used on shore, but where the space was limited, one had to be content with a wash-stand which could be folded close to the bulkhead.

Water was pumped up straight from the main tank with a small hand pump.

I Fire hazard was great in wooden boats powered by petrol engines, especially if they were also lighted by petroleum lamps. It was rapidly discovered that petrol fires could not be extinguished with water, and chemical fire extinguishers were

introduced some time before, the First World War. This one is British, from 1913.

J A British patent stove from 1907. It was intended for smaller yachts than the one shown at **C**.

K The Primus stove, the simplest possible form of stove.

L Many interior fittings were smaller counterparts of those occurring on big luxury steamers. One example is this water-closet.

27

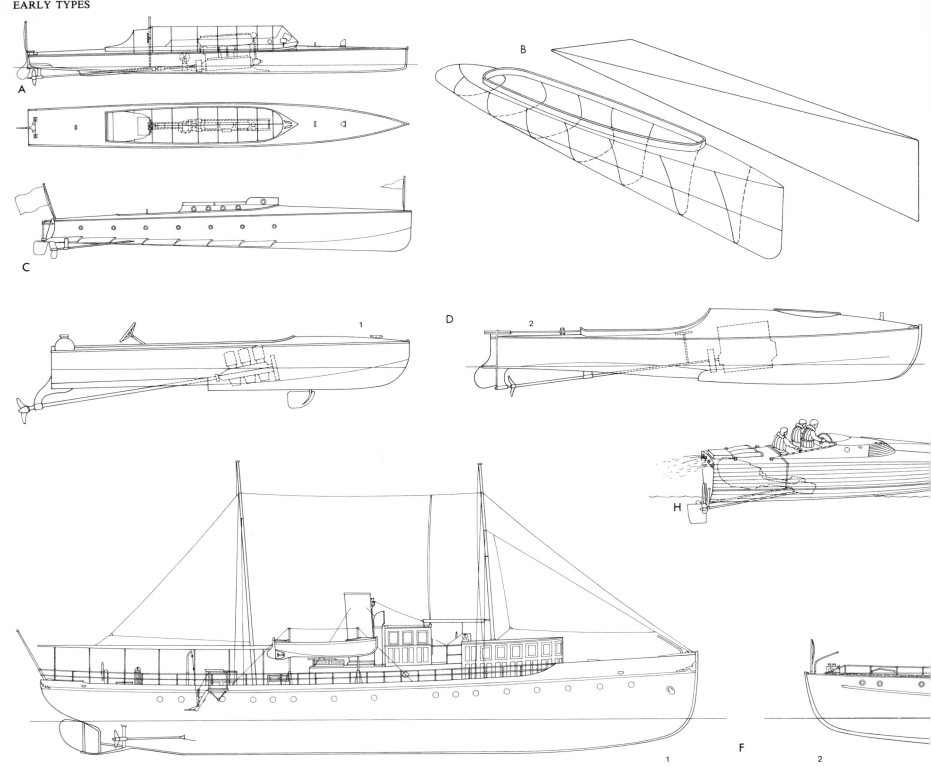

A Extremely long and narrow racing boats were built in the early stages, in imitation of the torpedo-boats and destroyers of the time. An example of this is ZARITZA, designed by H. Teckel and built in 1912 by the Howaldtswerke in Kiel, Germany. The hull resembles a canoe with a large, heavy petrol engine amidships. The open engine-house and cockpit are protected against breaking seas by means of a light cloth cover.

B These long and narrow hulls were given a sharp forebody but a flat stern, so that the water would "let go" of it. Hence, the shape was often referred to as a "double-wedge".

C However, at high speeds it turned out to be more advantageous to have a more or less flat-bottomed hull, so that the upward pressure from the water current underneath the boat could be utilized; so-called planing. The best effect was reached if the bottom was divided into several steps, as in Fauber's patent, which is shown here.

D Examples of step-boats: MARGRET III (1) and Thornycroft's MIRANDA IV (2) from 1912.

E The Coastal Motor Boats built in England by Thornycroft during the First World War were developed from MIRANDA IV. Some of the CMBs, such as this one, were later converted into fast pleasure boats. Nowadays, the step principle has been generally abandoned; instead, hulls are constructed with more or less V-shaped bottoms.

F Slower motor yachts, however, have always been designed with round bottoms. Examples of these are the large pleasure yacht FIORA (1), designed by M. H. Bauer in Berlin, and KUST (2), designed by the Swede Ruben Östlund.

G The motor yacht RIVIERA of c. 15 tons, designed by Juan Baader, New Zealand. Length: 60 ft (18.3 m). A speed of 18 knots can be reached with two 300-horsepower diesel engines.

H In order to combine high speeds with good seagoing qualities, the Americans Ray Hunt and D. Bertram developed the deep V-shaped

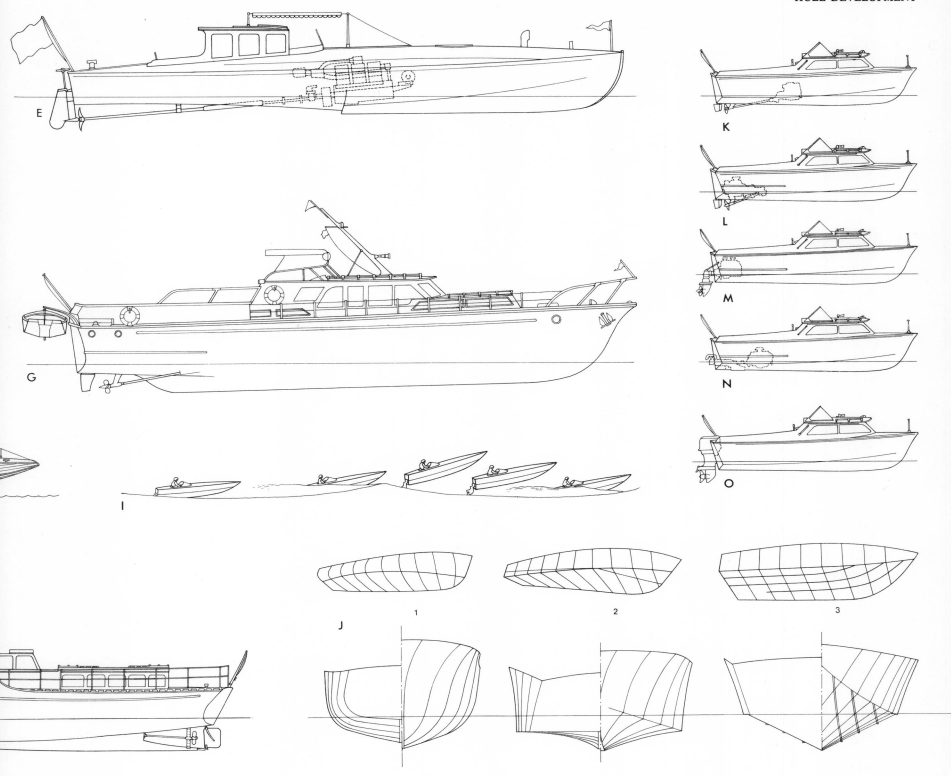

hull at the end of the 1950s. This hull shape has come into extensive use, especially on fast offshore racers like the one shown here, FLYING FISH.

I The great advantage of a deep V-shaped hull is that the boat can be driven at high speeds even in rough seas, without being subject to severe blows. Even if the boat becomes airborne, it can land gently on any part of its bottom.

J Thus, on today's powerboats, three categories of bottom shapes are mainly used: (**1**) round bottom, (**2**) V-bottom, and (**3**) deep V-bottom.

K "Ordinary" arrangement of engine/propeller, in this case coupled via an offset reduction gear. The engine occupies valuable space at the middle of the boat. The propeller has to function at an angle to the water flow, and it is exposed to damage should the boat go aground. The propeller cannot be changed while the boat is afloat.

L The V-drive was a commonly used way—before the advent of the stern drive—to move the engine further aft to be more out of the way.

M The stern, or inboard/outboard, drive, was developed by Volvo Penta in the mid-1950s. It is mechanically complex but has the great advantage of having the engine far aft, where it is more out of the way. No

The V-gear could be a separate unit connected to the engine via a cardan shaft. It could also, as shown here, be flanged to the engine.

rudder is needed, as the boat is steered with the gear. The drive unit can be tilted up.

N Water-jet propulsion means that the engine drives a water pump instead of a propeller. The pump sucks water from a bottom intake and discharges it through a movable nozzle. The main advantage is the absence of vulnerable projections under the hull.

O Outboard engines are specially suited for small, light boats. They occupy no space on board and can be easily removed.

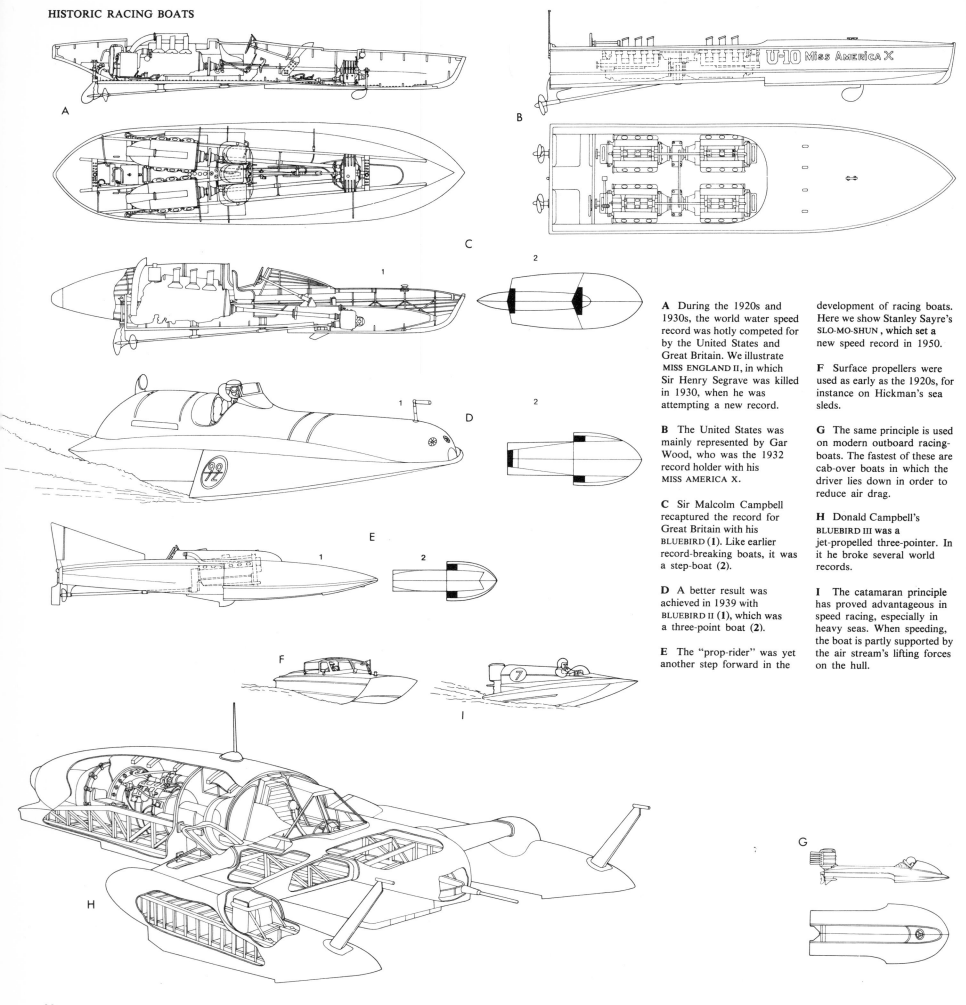

A During the 1920s and 1930s, the world water speed record was hotly competed for by the United States and Great Britain. We illustrate MISS ENGLAND II, in which Sir Henry Segrave was killed in 1930, when he was attempting a new record.

B The United States was mainly represented by Gar Wood, who was the 1932 record holder with his MISS AMERICA X.

C Sir Malcolm Campbell recaptured the record for Great Britain with his BLUEBIRD (1). Like earlier record-breaking boats, it was a step-boat (2).

D A better result was achieved in 1939 with BLUEBIRD II (1), which was a three-point boat (2).

E The "prop-rider" was yet another step forward in the development of racing boats. Here we show Stanley Sayre's SLO-MO-SHUN , which set a new speed record in 1950.

F Surface propellers were used as early as the 1920s, for instance on Hickman's sea sleds.

G The same principle is used on modern outboard racing-boats. The fastest of these are cab-over boats in which the driver lies down in order to reduce air drag.

H Donald Campbell's BLUEBIRD III was a jet-propelled three-pointer. In it he broke several world records.

I The catamaran principle has proved advantageous in speed racing, especially in heavy seas. When speeding, the boat is partly supported by the air stream's lifting forces on the hull.

BOAT TYPES AND EQUIPMENT

Göran Petersson

Sail racing has been part of every Olympic programme since the first modern Olympic games took place. During the first Olympiads of the twentieth century, competitors raced in very large boats which, with reference to their sail-area, were of the *Thirty Square Metres* and the *Forty Square Metres* classes. Nowadays, there are those who advocate the introduction of Olympic offshore racing; otherwise, development within the Olympic classes (rules for these are laid down every four years by the IYRU) has always shown a tendency towards smaller and cheaper boats, as has development in general in the world of boating. At present, however, the IYRU seeks to establish a certain balance at Olympic level between keelboats and centre-boarders, as well as between singlehanded and crewed boats.

The boat that always attracts especial interest in the Olympics is the *Star,* a class which in several respects occupies a place apart. The *Star* was the first international one-design class, designed in 1911 by an American, Francis Sweisguth, at the time employed by the well-known yacht designer William Gardner, who is often named as originator of the boat. At first, the *Star* was gaff-rigged, but in 1921, it was instead equipped with the then modern Bermudan rig, which was slightly modified in 1929 and is still in use. The *Star* retained its rank as an Olympic class until 1968, and it again created a stir by being chosen for the 1980 Olympic events at Tallinn, the first boat ever to recover this position.

During the interwar period, the *10-, 8-,* and *6-Metres* classes were to various extents Olympic as well. The smallest of these classes, the *6-Metres,* was a narrow, deep boat with a displacement of *c.* four tons. Gradually, all these types became extremely expensive to build, and in 1949, the 5.5-Metre rule was introduced. From the 1952 Helsinki Olympic games, the *5.5-Metres* class was Olympic, and it retained this dignity until the 1968 Olympics. By and by, however, the cost of a *5.5-Metres* boat became very high, and one of the reasons for this was that the designs were changed over and over again, in order to adapt them to conditions at the next Olympics. Further, the boats underwent extensive trials in wind tunnels and test tanks, and this made them even more expensive. Therefore, for the 1972 Olympics, the *5.5 Metres* class was replaced by the *Soling,* a three-man keelboat designed by Jan Herman Linge, a Norwegian.

Another keelboat, the *Dragon,* made its Olympic début in 1948. This class, now world-wide, was created as far back as 1928, when the Royal Gothenburg Yacht Club, Sweden, commissioned a Norwegian, Johan Anker,

to design it. Up to the games at Kiel in 1972, the *Dragon* retained its Olympic standing.

During the interwar years, dinghies established themselves in the Olympic events. The first one-design dinghy to be internationally widespread was the *12-foot* dinghy, a clinker-built, lug-rigged boat with centre-board; this dinghy sailed in the 1920 Olympic games in Amsterdam. Sixteen years later, the *International Olympic Class,* a one-man centre-boarder, was raced in the Olympics. After the Second World War, the trend towards Olympic dinghy classes became stronger, and two English dinghies, the *Firefly* and the *Swallow,* were accepted as Olympic classes for the 1948 games.

In 1949, a competition was announced for a new dinghy design, suitable for acceptance as an Olympic class. Despite the fact that it was not ranked with the three winning entries in the contest, however, the *Finn,* designed by a Swedish barber from Uppsala, Rickard Sarby, gained Olympic status. With the *Finn,* general interest in dinghy sailing increased tremendously, and the boat was still an Olympic choice for the 1980 games. Since it carries a mainsail only and has an unstayed mast, it is not unlike the catboats of old and has a reputation of being the toughest to sail and to trim.

The trapeze, developed in the early 1950s mainly in Australia, enables the crew to hang outside the hull with his feet planted on the gunwale. Essentially, the trapeze is a wire attached to the rigging, with a hooking system at its end onto which the crew's trapeze harness can be clipped. The advantage of this arrangement is that the boat can carry considerably more sail than would otherwise have been possible, and this naturally means that it can attain a higher speed.

The first Olympic trapeze dinghy, the two-man *International Twelve Square Metre Sharpie,* sailed at the 1956 Olympics. In the 1960 Olympic games, the *Flying Dutchman* made its début. This centre-boarder was designed in 1951 by a Dutchman, Uffa van Essen, and it is either built of GRP or of moulded plywood. It is equipped with a trapeze and has a very large genoa in comparison to its mainsail. The *Flying Dutchman* was chosen as an Olympic class for the sixth time for the 1980 games.

The *Tempest,* then newly designed by the well-known English boat and rig designer Ian Proctor, made its first Olympic appearance in the 1968 games, which were held in Mexico. The new feature of the *Tempest* was that it had been equipped with both trapeze and a bulbous keel similar to that of the *Star.* However, the boat type did not retain its Olympic standing for long, for with the 1980

Olympic games at hand, it was replaced by the *Star* class, which was thus restored to its place of honour. In 1976, the *470,* a new dinghy class designed by a Frenchman, André Corneau, was added. The *470* carries a spinnaker and is equipped with a trapeze. It is so responsive that, if the crew members hope for success in the class, their total weight should not exceed, say, 300 lb (*c.* 135 kg).

The fastest, series-produced, racing sail-boat in the world is probably at present the *Tornado* catamaran, which was designed in 1967 by an Englishman, Rodney March. This multihull carries mainsail and foresail, and it has a trapeze. Speeds of more than thirty knots have been recorded. The *Tornado* was the first multihull to be accepted as an Olympic class, and it has sailed as such from 1976 on.

During the 1920s and 1930s, even the smallest of the rated yacht classes, the *6-Metres,* became extremely expensive. Several inexpensive one-designs, among them the *Dragon,* were available at the end of the 1920s, but there was still a vast general interest in a rated yacht, if it could be built at reasonable cost. As early as 1929, the International 5-Metre rule was accepted at a meeting in London. The object was to produce a less expensive racing class with simpler rules than those for the *6-Metres* class.

The *5-Metre* class originated in France and is rated, i.e., the individual boats within the class may to a certain extent differ from each other. Length, for instance, may vary from *c.* 27 ft 4 in to 30 ft 6 in (8.3 to 9.3 m), beam from *c.* 5 ft 7 in to 6 ft 8 in (1.70 to 2.05 m). The only measurement all boats must have in common is a draught of *c.* 3 ft 7 in (1.10 m)—probably intended to suit French lakes and rivers. During the 1930s and 1940s, the *5-Metres* was most successful on the race courses of Europe and the United States.

Most sailors learn to sail while they are very young, and there are many light, unballasted boats available today with just such learners in mind. These boats require no great strength for handling sail and rudder, they can be quickly made ready to sail, and they are easy to paddle. An excellent example of a boat for the young beginner is the *Optimist,* designed in 1948 by Clark Mills, an American.

In New Zealand and Australia, the *P* class is a popular beginner's boat. It was designed before the Second World War by Harry Highet, a New Zealander, and it is a singlehanded dinghy like the *Optimist.* In the United States, two popular, singlehanded dinghies for beginners are the *Minifish,* designed by AMF-Alcort, and the *Sailfish,* designed by Jack Carroll. A recently introduced boat of the same size range is the *Bumblebee,* designed by the Englishman Jack Holt. Like most other beginner's dinghies, the *Bumblebee* is well suited for home construction.

More proficient youngsters have a wealth of international classes to choose from, both one-design and restricted. Among the former are such dinghies as the *OK,* designed in 1956 by the Dane Knud Olsen, the *Europe,* which has evolved from the *Moth* class, and the *Laser,* designed in 1972 by Bruce Kirby, a Canadian. The *Laser* is a unique boat in that, according to its class rules, it may only be manufactured by a specific company, and its sails must come from a certain maker. Moreover, the class rules lay down what equipment the boat may carry, which sails may be used, and how often they may be changed for new ones. By the mid-1970s, over 50,000 *Laser*s had been registered. However, the class organization declined a proposal to let the *Laser* be considered for the 1980 Olympics.

Among the advanced singlehanded dinghies must be reckoned the Dane Paul Elvström's *Trapez,* and the *Contender,* designed by the Australian Bob Miller. The *Trapez* was the first singlehanded dinghy to allow the helmsman to sail it while hanging in a trapeze.

One of the first designers to fully exploit moulded plywood to halve the weight of a boat was a New Zealander, John Spencer. His *Cherub* of 1954, a 12-ft (*c.* 3.7 m) dinghy, became very popular in Australia and New Zealand. Later, he designed the somewhat bigger (14 ft or *c.* 4.3 m) *Javelin* and the smaller (10 ft 6 in or *c.* 3.2 m) *Flying Ant.* Spencer did not approve of one-design boats, so all his designs—and they cover the whole range from beginner's dinghies to the *Javelin*—belong to restricted classes.

In connection with his designing the Olympic *Flying Dutchman,* Uffa van Essen also designed the *Flying Junior,* a smaller dinghy equipped with a trapeze. The *Flying Junior* was not dissimilar to the *420,* which was designed in 1960 by the Frenchman Christian Maury, and both these dinghies have become extremely popular among young sailors in Europe. An unusual boat in the same size range is the *Flipper,* a scow designed in 1968 by the Dane Peter Bruun. Over 8,000 *Flippers* had been registered by the mid-1970s. The *Flipper* looks like a smaller, rounded *Fireball,* a dinghy which was designed by an Englishman, Peter Milne, in 1962. His boat created a stir through having several unusual features. With its blunt, low bow, the *Fireball* is exceedingly speedy in a fair wind, but its construction can involve certain disadvantages in a head wind.

The leading precursor of all dinghy sailing is the *International 14-foot* class, which dates from the first years of this century, probably 1901. It is a restricted class. A slightly cheaper version of the *International 14-foot* class was the *National 12-foot* class which, after the Second World War, was the world's most numerous restricted dinghy class. The *International 14-foot* dinghy is still being raced here and there all over the world.

In the United States, no equivalent of the *12-* and *14-foot* dinghies occurred for a long time. Races were held in the *Star* or in the somewhat smaller *Snipe,* a one-design boat, which William Crosby was commissioned to design as early as 1931 by the American boating magazine *Rud-*

der. Without ever having been Olympic, the *Snipe* is one of the world's most popular dinghies; more than 21,000 have been registered. It is comparatively inexpensive, and nowadays it may be built of either GRP or plywood.

In 1938, the world-famous designers, Sparkman & Stephens, designed a dinghy, the *International Lightning.* In size, it resembles the *505,* which was designed in 1954 by the Englishman John Westell. Its name derives from the fact that it is 505 cm (*c.* 16 ft 7 in) long. Both the *International Lightning* and the *505* are advanced dinghies with spinnaker and trapeze, and they make great demands on the skill of their crews. One of the foremost sailors of all time, Paul Elvström, is of the opinion that only those who have sailed a *505* have experienced real dinghy sailing.

A brand-new construction is the 14-ft (*c.* 4.3 m) dinghy *Tasar,* designed by the well-known Australian sailor, Frank Bethwaite, in co-operation with Ian Bruce. This boat is manufactured of the new synthetic material Kevlar, which is stronger and much lighter than the now-traditional GRP materials. The *Tasar* is a two-man dinghy with a centre-board, but with neither spinnaker nor trapeze. It has a narrow, effective sail plan with through-going battens and a very thin, rotating mast. Like the *Laser,* the *Tasar* has a two-piece mast and roller reefing gear for the jib, and it is strictly one-design.

Large dinghies have a limited field of use, and they often demand advanced handling techniques. Therefore, designers have tried to produce boat types which retain the advantages of dinghies, but can still be used both for family day cruising and for club regattas and similar races on a not too advanced level. Such boats also have a wider range of potential buyers, so they can be manufactured in fairly large series. A good representative of this type is the *Efsix,* designed by the Dutchman E.G. van de Stadt. The *Efsix* has good trimming possibilities, and its keel can be raised and lowered to facilitate transport of the boat on a trailer. *Efsix* is a sporty boat with very good sailing qualities and is equipped with a trapeze. In North America, a similar boat called the *Harpoon 5.2* was recently introduced. It was designed by the well-known Canadian company, Cuthbertson and Cassian (C & C). Other boats of this type are the Swedish *Monark 606,* the British *National Squid,* and the Norwegian *Yngling.* These three have fixed keels. All boats in this group are, as a rule, comparatively light and equipped with buoyancy material, which makes them unsinkable.

The next step is boats which can be used for weekend cruising, i.e., they offer simple sleeping facilities. One early design—at the end of the 1960s—in this fashion is the Englishman Ian Anderson's *Hurley 18,* which is still popular and also exists in larger versions. A recent construction, based on the *Nordic Folkboat,* a wooden boat from the beginning of the 1940s, is the Swede Tord Sundén's *International Folkboat.* Both the *Hurley* and the *Folkboat* belong to the more traditional types. In proportion to length, their beams are narrower than those of more modern designs, and their superstructures do not reach all the way out to the rails.

Since the well-known French yachtsman, Eric Tabarly, wanted to put a popular boat of a similar size at the disposal of the French sailing public, he commissioned

Dominique Presles to design the *Pen Duick 600,* which is probably the only mass-produced boat in this size range to be made of aluminium. The *Pen Duick 600* has a very modern design and is a good sailer. It is equipped with a fin keel and an outside rudder. The boat has windows in the sides of the hull, and since it is flush-decked, there is good onboard accommodation. When Pelle Petterson, the famous Swedish sailor, designed his first *Maxi 77,* in 1972, his intention was also to create an inexpensive, roomy family boat with good sailing qualities. Other boats that have since come from his drawing-board are the somewhat smaller *Maxi 68,* and the larger *Maxi 84, 87,* and *95.* All have the same characteristic appearance with their windows located in the dark faking stripe above the rail.

Of all seagoing family cruisers, the one that has had the largest and longest production run is probably the Swedish *Vega,* a one-design by Per Brohäll from 1966. The *Vega* is a long-keeled sailing-boat with an inboard motor, and it has plenty of space aboard for a four-man crew. Over 3,500 *Vega*s have been manufactured so far, and the boat is widespread all over Europe and the United States.

One reason why the *Vega* has had a great deal of attention even in the coastal countries of Europe is its draught, which is 3 ft 10 in (1.18 m), and which it has in common with one of its competitors, the German-built, slightly smaller *Varianta,* designed by E.G. van de Stadt. In order to improve its sailing qualities when beating to windward, the *Varianta* has been equipped with a centre-board, which gives it a draught of 4 ft 3 in (1.30 m). Both the *Vega* and the *Varianta* can be equipped with a spinnaker, and numerous races are arranged for both classes. Because of its construction, the *Varianta* is particularly easy to transport on a trailer.

A somewhat unusual appearance is offered by the Dane Peter Bruun's design the *Spækhugger,* a little double-ender of cruiser-racer type, which has been followed by the slightly larger *Grinde* and *Kaskelott.* Bruun's family boats are all designed on a circular basis.

The rather large, seagoing, production family cruisers are often made in two versions, one for cruising and one for racing. Boats of this size, half-tonners and three-quarter-tonners, are as a rule designed by very well-known yachtsmen. Paul Elvström and his Danish colleague, Jan Kjærulf, have consequently co-operated to design the 39-ft (*c.* 9.8 m) *Elvström Cruiser 32,* and similarly, the Swede Peter Norlin has created the successful three-quarter-tonner *Norlin 34,* which is mass-produced in a cruising version. This trend of well-known yachtsmen designing boats intended for production series also exists in the United States. One interesting new-comer there is the 36-ft (*c.* 11 m) *Ericson Cruising 36,* a comfortable family cruiser designed by Bruce King.

It is an interesting fact that, within the sizes that according to the rules of the IOR belong to the respective ton-groups, well-known and successful offshore racers are often used, with little or no modifications of their designs, as a starting-point for later mass-production cruisers. An excellent example of this is the Finnish Nautor company's new offshore cruiser, the *Swan 47,* which is based on the very well-known contender for the Admiral's Cup BATTLECRY. Of all manufacturers, Nautor is one of those that have had the most success with the production of yachts that are exceedingly good sailers. Their yachts are of the very best quality and equipped with exquisite and expensive woodwork. The name of *Swan* attracted a lot of attention when the Mexican ketch-rigged production yacht SAYULA II, a *Swan 65,* won the Whitbread Round-the-World race after having weathered out extremely bad weather without suffering any severe damage.

Within the three-quarter-ton group, GOLDEN DELICIOUS, designed by Ron Holland and built by the well-known, almost two-hundred-year-old British boat manufacturers, Camper & Nicholson, has served as a model for the new *Nicholson 33.* Doug Peterson's SOLENT SARACEN, which was one of the most successful offshore racing sailers of 1975, has arisen anew in a slightly enlarged version, now under the name of *Contention 33.*

In the size ranges of around 40 ft (12.2 m) and larger, there is a great number of different, very well-equipped yachts intended for cruising. Whether they are powered by sail or by engines, they are all exceptionally good sailers, and the owner and his guests are offered the most comfortable and spacious accommodation possible, with private cabins for at least the owner, and the highest living standard imaginable. Such large cruising yachts thus offer a luxurious setting, such as might be expected in the homes of the potential owners. Boats of this size are commonly ketch-rigged.

The expression "motor sailer" may be popular now, but until relatively recently, it had a not very pleasing ring about it. Some boat-builders have now given up calling their yachts motor sailers, and instead they use expressions like "a cruising yacht with a powerful engine".

The Finnish Nautor company recently introduced its 50-ft (c. 15.2 m) *Nautor 50,* a Sparkman & Stephens design, defined as a motor sailer by its builders, although it does not have the conventional appearance of such a boat. This is partly due to the fact that, for a motor sailer, its deck-house is not very conspicuous, and its fore hull lines are comparatively slender. Above all, however, it is due to the ketch rig with its high aspect ratio, which differs considerably from the arrangements with long foots and short luffs normally expected on a motor sailer. Only when you discover that the sail-area-to-displacement ratio is c. 13 and the displacement-to-length ratio 430 is it self-evident that the correct designation for Nautor's luxury cruiser is "motor sailer".

Another yacht, introduced more or less at the same time as the *Nautor 50,* is Hallberg Rassy's *Rassy 41,* an exclusive cruiser designed by the Swede Olle Enderlein. An interesting detail on this boat is its bowsprit, which doubles as gangway. A further newcomer of the same type is the British *Moody 52,* designed by Laurent Giles. Like the above-mentioned yachts, the *Moody 52* offers luxury and comfort to an almost incredible extent. Also well-known are the German *NAB* boats, which may be had in various sizes: 32, 38, and 44 ft (c. 9.8, 11.6, and 13.4 m). All the above boats have long keels. However, on the French *Amphitrite* which, despite its typically French appearance, has been designed by the English company, Holman and Pye, the keel has almost the shape of a fin keel.

A craft consisting of two hulls kept together by a tunnel is known as a catamaran, if the hulls are of an identical size, and as a proa, if the hulls are of different sizes. If a boat consists of a central hull, with a smaller hull on each side of it, then it is called a trimaran. The multihull has one characteristic in common with the dinghy, namely that it relies on hull shape, not on ballast, for stability.

Catamaran races almost always are performed according to the international rules for *A-, B-, C-,* and *D-Class* catamarans. All are rated classes, and for the *A–C Classes,* length, beam, and sail-area are limited. For the *D-Class* catamarans, length and beam are unrestricted, but the sail-area must be 500 sq ft (46.45 sq m). The *D-Class* catamaran is a three-man boat, the *B* and *C Classes* consist of two-man boats, and the *A Class* is singlehanded. One-design catamarans other than the Olympic *Tornado* are the *Australis,* designed by Graham Johnston, and John Matzotti's *Unicorn,* both of the *A Class.* Most other catamarans in the world belong to the *B Class.* One-designs not internationally belonging to any of these classes are the *Thai IV, YW,* and *Shearwater* catamarans, which therefore are raced between themselves class by class.

In Australia and New Zealand, there are popular catamarans such as the *Quick Cat* (16 ft or 4.9 m), designed by Charles and Lindsay Cunningham, *Kitty Cat* (12 ft or 3.7 m) by Jim Young, and *Paper Tiger* (14 ft or 4.3 m) by Ron Given. Another well-known catamaran is the American Hobie Alter's *Hobie Cat,* a 14-ft (4.3 m) GRP boat with a trapeze but no centre-board. Of the catamarans mentioned here, only the *Kitty Cat* carries a spinnaker. When, in 1976, the IYRU wanted to select a new catamaran for international racing, Rodney March, designer of the Olympic *Tornado,* introduced a new design, which he called *Dart.* This strictly one-design, 18-ft (5.5 m) catamaran has a sail-area of 172.2 sq ft (16.0 sq m). In the *Laser* fashion, the *Dart* manufacturer has laid down in the class rules that parts for the boat can be bought only from the manufacturer or from those companies licensed to make them, and that all parts must be made in compliance with the drawings shown in the class rules. The intention is to keep the price of the catamaran down and to make it popular. From a constructional point of view, the *Dart* has a couple of very interesting details. It lacks a centre-board, and the lateral resistance is instead taken care of by a fin keel, integrated with the hull, which simplifies the manufacturing procedure. Furthermore, March has equipped the *Dart* with a boom-less mainsail; through-going battens are instead used to give the sail its correct shape. The *Dart* is narrow enough to be transported on a trailer, and the boat is also comparatively simply dismantled for transport on a roof-rack.

Most catamarans are built for racing or for pleasure, which makes no demands on accommodation. One notable exception to this is the recently introduced British *Cat Fisher 28,* built by a boat-yard with experience in building motor sailers. The *Cat Fisher 28* is an interesting novelty inasmuch as it is a comfortable cruiser which sleeps seven people in four separate cabins. Multihulls offering accommodation are otherwise usually trimarans, such as Derek Kelsall's recent design, *Tango 32,* and the *Val,* a new 28-ft (8.5 m) trimaran designed by Richard Newick, who has earlier designed trimarans for the Singlehanded Transatlantic race. Both *Tango 32* and *Val* are intended for mass-production. Despite its size, the *Val* can be dismantled, so that transport and storage are facilitated. A trimaran which has been on the market longer than these two is the *Telstar,* which comes in two sizes, 26 and 35 ft (7.9 and 10.7 m) respectively. The *Telstar* offers excellent comfort, and it is a good, safe sailer.

One of the best-known very large trimarans is Derek Kelsall's 80-ft (24.4 m) GREAT BRITAIN III, which has most successfully taken part in transoceanic races.

During the end of the 1950s and the beginning of the 1960s, the outboard engine became more and more widespread all over the world. Development had led to easily handled, reliable, and comparatively inexpensive engines, which could be afforded by practically anyone and could be used for a wide range of boats. At about the same time, GRP made possible the production of light, small, durable boats at a low cost, and these could be propelled by simple outboard engines. One of the smallest boats on the market is the German *Pioneer 8,* which is only c. 8 ft (2.42 m) long and weighs as little as 110 lb (50 kg). Such very small boats are as a rule GRP-built, with a finish that gives them the appearance of being either carvel- or clinker-built. A somewhat longer boat of this type is the Norwegian *Sportsman Junior,* which weighs 165 lb (75 kg). Both the *Pioneer* and the *Sportsman* are powered by outboard engines.

The somewhat larger boats, for instance, the French *Pop 4,* the British *Dory 11,* and the Swedish *Crescent 415,* are sometimes equipped with a console. Usually, boats of this size have no windshield but are completely open. The console will then be often situated a little aft in the boat, but in boats with a windscreen, it is placed right behind the windscreen. Some boats with windscreens in this size range are the British *Arrow 140,* the Swedish *Winth 435,* the American *All American 156,* and the Italian *Pioneer,* which is built by one of Italy's largest boat-yards, Giorgio Adriani.

Day cruisers may be either planing or, like for instance the double-ender, for which the inspiration came from Norway, they may be round-bottomed. One of the better-known double-enders is the 20-ft (6.1 m) powerboat *Saga 20,* which has been followed by the Swedish *Monark 69* and several other, mainly Nordic, boat types. Another popular day-cruiser is the *Shetland 535,* designed by Colin Mudie and nowadays replaced by the *Shetland 536,* which is constructed for an outboard engine of 7–70 horsepower. Boats of up to this size, about 20 ft (c. 6 m), are often equipped with built-in hull buoyancy. Instead of with an outboard engine, the French *Neptune Runabout 560* is equipped with a stern drive. The American company, Reynell, has the same type of drive. Reynell, like most big boat manufacturers, offers a series of different-sized boats. Two of the biggest and best-known Nordic builders of powerboats are the Norwegian Fjordplast company, which offers the *Fjord 21 Weekender* in this size range, and the Danish Botved Boats company, with the *Coronet 21.*

An interesting type of powerboat, at first used as a lifeboat but increasingly popular as a runabout, is the inflatable rubber boat, for instance, the *Avon Semperit* and the *Beaufort.* These boats, which may be fitted with windscreens, comfortable seats, and hulls partly made of plastics, can be used for outboard engines of 40–100 horse-power. Such rubber boats are usually very seaworthy, among other things because they have a special water ballast compartment, which is flooded when the boat lies still and emptied when the boat is under way.

The distinction between those boats just described and those we are now going to discuss is that the latter offer both accommodation and comfort. In this group we find the Swedish-designed *Albin 25,* a trawler-like, 25-ft (*c.* 7.6 m) diesel-powered boat with a cruising speed of about ten knots, and the Norwegian *Draco 2500* and *Fjord 26 Cruiser,* both of which are equipped with stern drives and are very fast. The same goes for the two Norwegian double-enders *Tresfjord* and *Saga 27*; both have aft cabins and are most seaworthy.

One of the best-selling European boats of 30 ft (*c.* 9.1 m) and over is the Dutch *Amerglass 32,* which was introduced in the autumn of 1969. It has been followed by the not entirely dissimilar Swedish-designed *Albin 30* and the British *Moonraker 36.* Boats of this type may often be bought with engines of various powers, depending on the desired speed range and fuel economy, but one thing they have in common: they all offer excellent comfort for a family wishing to spend even long periods out on the sea.

Among the larger boat models, the widest variety—for obvious reasons—occurs in the United States. Such boats offer the greatest comfort possible at sea, and they are seaworthy enough to allow for long passages in the open sea at high speeds. The biggest companies usually offer sizes from about 36 ft (*c.* 11 m) to as much as 70 ft (21.3 m). American manufacturers are well represented on the home market with famous makes such as Trojan, Stamas, Pacemaker, Gulf Star, and Atlantic. Grand Banks, Cheoy Lee, and Island Gypsy offer slightly different boats—roomy and seaworthy trawler types. Naturally, several non-American manufacturers are also established on the American market. Thus, for instance, the Finnish *Admiral Cruiser,* the Swedish *Storö 38,* and the German *Cytra Ambassador 48* compete there.

One of the best-known and oldest American companies is Chris-Craft, which produces powerboats of every size, from the 16-ft (*c.* 4.9 m) ski boat to the 73 ft (22.3 m) ocean cruiser. Chris-Craft boats are renowned for their absolute top quality. Before they are delivered, the boats are run through an elaborate testing programme.

Another top-quality American manufacturer is the Burger Boat Company, a business which was founded as early as in 1863 and which builds aluminium boats of 63 ft (19.2 m) and over. Burger Boat was the first American company to build steel-hulled, later aluminium-hulled, pleasure boats.

The Bertram Yacht Company is known all over the world. It was this company which developed the deep-V hull, and this has made Bertram boats well-known for their ability to give a comfortable ride at high speeds in the open sea. The fact that a boat is extremely luxurious need not necessarily mean that it is a family cruiser or a boat offering comfortable accommodation on long passages. Several of the more famous boat manufacturers also

offer luxury speedboats, well suited for water-skiing and suchlike. Some of the most extreme designs among these speedboats are made by Chris-craft and by the Italian Riva boat-yard (*Riva 2000*); the American Don Aronow's famous *Cigarette* series also features such craft. All these are easily capable of speeds between 40 and 50 knots.

A modern pleasure boat must be comfortable and safe, and the extent to which it is both comfortable and safe depends largely on the equipment.

Masts and spars on most sailing-boats are made of aluminium, although on some dinghies they are still made of wood. Standing rigging is made of steel wire or of steel rods. Stays are attached to the deck with rigging screws or turn-buckles. All stays should have toggles, as they help distribute the load evenly. It is a good idea to protect turn-buckles with plastic hose-like covers. Likewise, spreaders should be covered to protect the foresails from being damaged.

Halyards, the lines used to hoist sails, are made of wire, rope, or a mixture of both. Double-braided Terylene, which has very low stretch and a breaking strength of abouth sixteen times its own diameter, makes very good rope. Halyards can either run down inside the mast and aft over blocks to winches, or go to halyard winches on the mast. Older boats, lacking such winches, needed more hands and the use of tackles (ropes leading round multiple blocks, which provided a mechanical advantage, but at the cost of increased frictional losses, weight, and windage). Smaller boats rely on the unaided strength of the crew to hoist the sails tightly enough. Halyards are secured, as are all adjustable lines, sheets, and such, in cleats or, very occasionally, in jamming stoppers.

Cleats are devices for quickly securing lines. They take many forms. Some grab the rope automatically, some have pivoting jaws which close over the rope, while others require that a line should be led round them in a certain way. The vital thing is that a line should be quickly releasable when under heavy load.

Foresails are fastened to the stem-head fitting, which is usually equipped with jib stay fitting. This must be double if a head foil, or luff profile, is used. The head foil has two luff tunnels, and thus an extra foresail can be set, sheltered by the one which is already hoisted. Naturally, this arrangement calls for double jib halyards.

The standing rigging is adjusted to suit varying weather conditions. The boom is kept at a constant angle to the mast by a kicking-strap, or boom vang, which either consists of a multiple-purchase block or of a stainless-steel rod with a hydraulic lever. The backstay can, if required, be tensioned, thus raking the mast aft. The backstay adjuster can be a rigging screw with a wheel, or else a hydraulic arrangement.

On most sailing-boats, the sheets are of rope. Wool braided with Terylene is an easily-handled material, and its breaking strength is about eight times its own diameter. The genoa sheet runs down to a genoa lead block on a foresail slider in a genoa track. The lead block is equipped with a spring-loaded stopper, so that it can be adjusted along the track. From there, the sheet is led to a winch,

either directly or via a deck block, and from there to a jamming cleat. The main sheet usually has several multiple-purchase blocks and is terminated by a quick-release cam cleat. The main sheet may also be fastened to a track with sliders and stoppers. All sheets should be of dimensions which make them easy to handle even in rough weather.

Among the most expensive and important accessories on a boat are its winches. These commonly occur in diameters of 2.3–3.5 in (59–89 mm). A winch is usually rated according to its power ratio. Thus, a winch with a power ratio of 1:25 is called a "twenty-five". Its gear ratio may then be high, 1:1, or low, 7.5:1. When exposed to higher loads, the conventional type of winch calls for one man to work the winch handle and another to haul in the sheet. The latest winches on the market are self-tailing, i.e., they haul in the sheet on their own. Winches are operated with handles which, for the sake of leverage, should be of a certain length (a common length is 10 in or 254 mm), and which are supplied with or without locking devices.

A boat-hook and fenders are indispensable on any boat, as are mooring lines of suitable thickness and length. For the sake of safety and comfort, a fixed or movable bathing ladder should also be at hand. On sail-boats, it is a good idea to have a boatswain's chair for rig inspection and repairs. All boats should have a fire extinguisher, and all engine-powered boats should have at least two, if possible placed so that they are accessible both from below and from deck, close to where fire can be expected.

Bilge pumps are a vital part of a boat's equipment, and the crew must be able to operate these from the deck as well as below. Less for safety than for comfort, spray hoods and dodgers protect from rain, wind, and splashing seas. In some climates, heaters with or without a thermostat can prolong the boating season considerably.

Instrumentation will be covered in some of the other chapters. However, a brief run-down of the most important instruments is necessary here. Thus, the speed of the wind is measured with a ventimeter, mounted on the masthead. Speed and distance are measured with a log, and depth with an echo sounder. Further, a radio receiver and a radio direction finder (RDF) should be on board. The radio receiver is invaluable for information such as weather forecasts, and a RDF is important to take bearings on various fixed points and on radio beacons.

When using logs, it should be remembered that the usual kinds of logs can give readings which are up to ten per cent out in a rough sea, since the boat's movements up and down in the water will be registered as sailed distance as well.

Equipment available to those who want extremely expensive navigational aids includes radar. Radar helps one discover objects which cannot be seen visually. However, because of the extremely high initial cost involved, such equipment is usually reserved for the largest pleasure yachts.

The choice of equipment and accessories must, in every case, depend on the boat's range of use, economical limits, and the owner's needs and general interest in the various details of accessories and equipment.

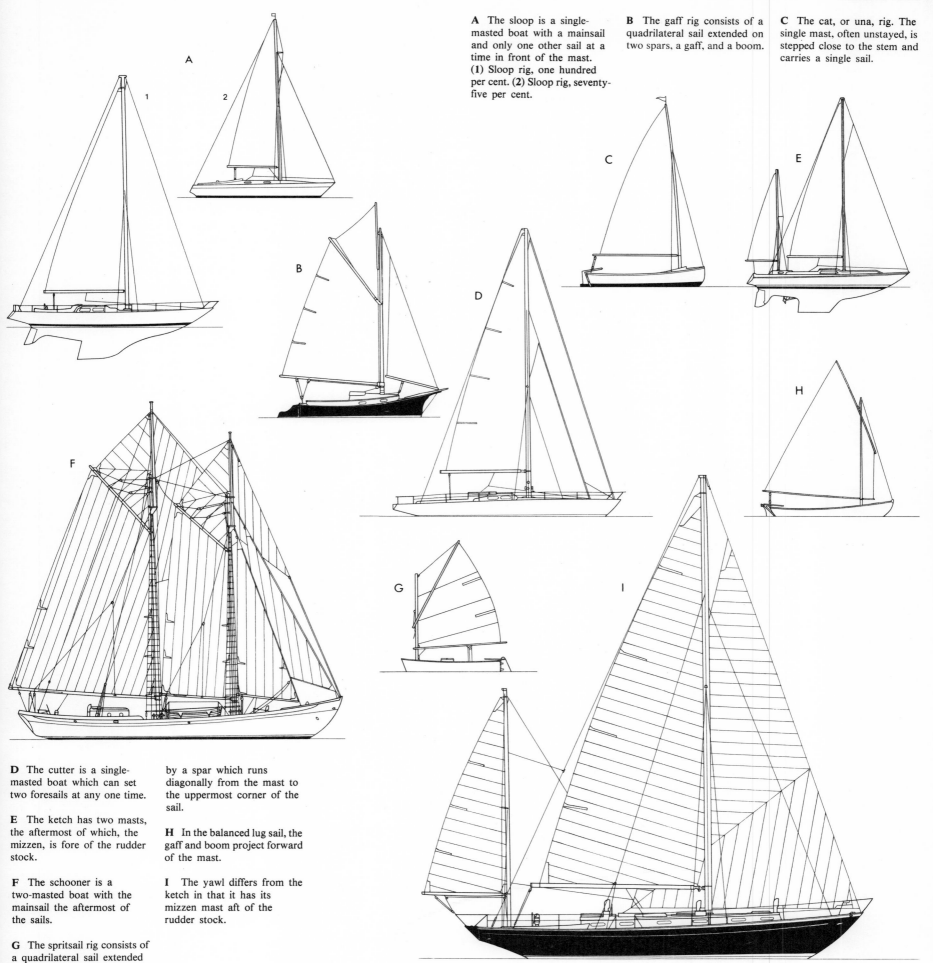

A The sloop is a single-masted boat with a mainsail and only one other sail at a time in front of the mast. **(1)** Sloop rig, one hundred per cent. **(2)** Sloop rig, seventy-five per cent.

B The gaff rig consists of a quadrilateral sail extended on two spars, a gaff, and a boom.

C The cat, or una, rig. The single mast, often unstayed, is stepped close to the stem and carries a single sail.

D The cutter is a single-masted boat which can set two foresails at any one time.

E The ketch has two masts, the aftermost of which, the mizzen, is fore of the rudder stock.

F The schooner is a two-masted boat with the mainsail the aftermost of the sails.

G The spritsail rig consists of a quadrilateral sail extended by a spar which runs diagonally from the mast to the uppermost corner of the sail.

H In the balanced lug sail, the gaff and boom project forward of the mast.

I The yawl differs from the ketch in that it has its mizzen mast aft of the rudder stock.

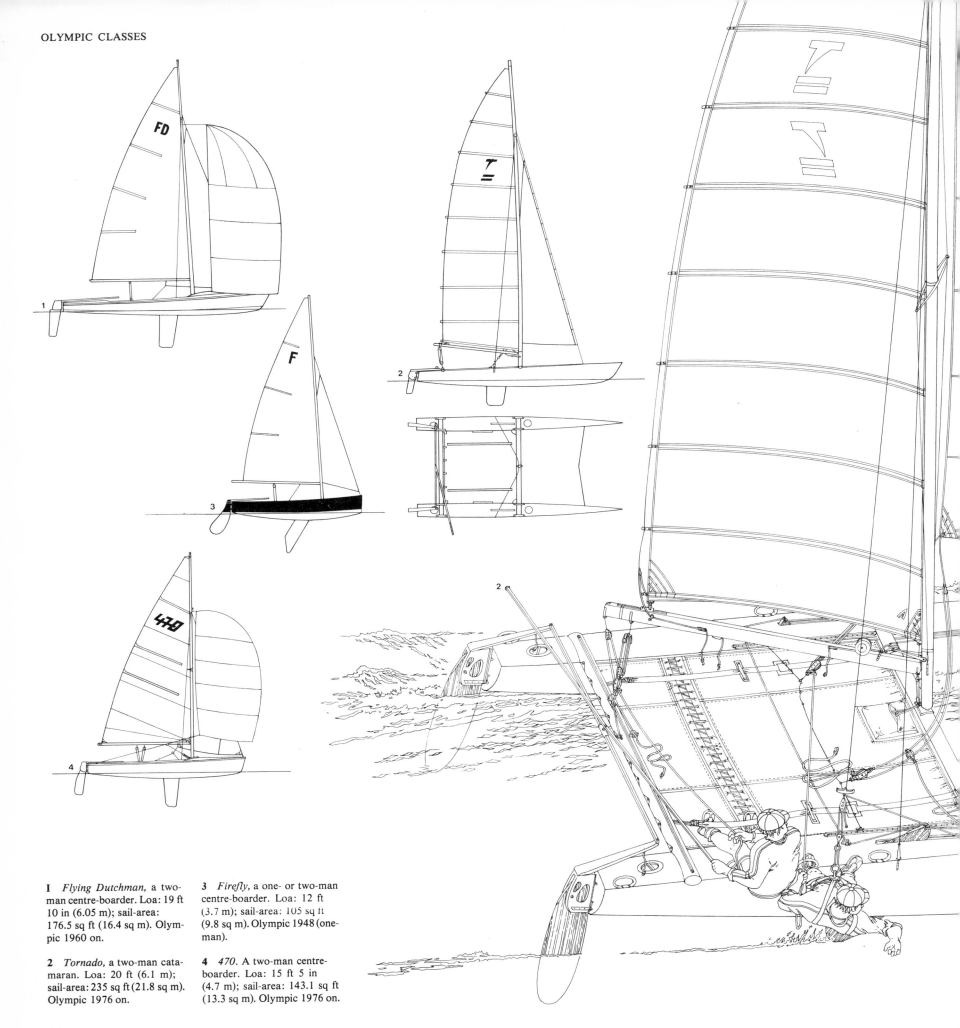

1 *Flying Dutchman*, a two-man centre-boarder. Loa: 19 ft 10 in (6.05 m); sail-area: 176.5 sq ft (16.4 sq m). Olympic 1960 on.

2 *Tornado*, a two-man catamaran. Loa: 20 ft (6.1 m); sail-area: 235 sq ft (21.8 sq m). Olympic 1976 on.

3 *Firefly*, a one- or two-man centre-boarder. Loa: 12 ft (3.7 m); sail-area: 105 sq ft (9.8 sq m). Olympic 1948 (one-man).

4 *470*. A two-man centre-boarder. Loa: 15 ft 5 in (4.7 m); sail-area: 143.1 sq ft (13.3 sq m). Olympic 1976 on.

5 *International 12-foot Dinghy,* a two-man centreboarder. Loa: 12 ft (3.7 m); sail-area: 193.7 sq ft (18.0 sq m). Olympic 1920.

6 *Finn,* a one-man centreboarder. Loa: 14 ft 9 in (4.5 m); sail-area: 107.6 sq ft (10.0 sq m). Olympic 1952 on.

7 The *International Twelve Square Metre Sharpie,* a two-man centre-boarder. Loa: 19 ft 4 in (5.9 m); sail-area: 129.1 sq ft (12.0 sq m). Olympic 1956.

8 *Olympic Monotype,* a one-man centre-boarder. Loa: 16 ft 5 in (5.0 m); sail-area: 107.6 sq ft (10.0 sq m). Olympic 1936.

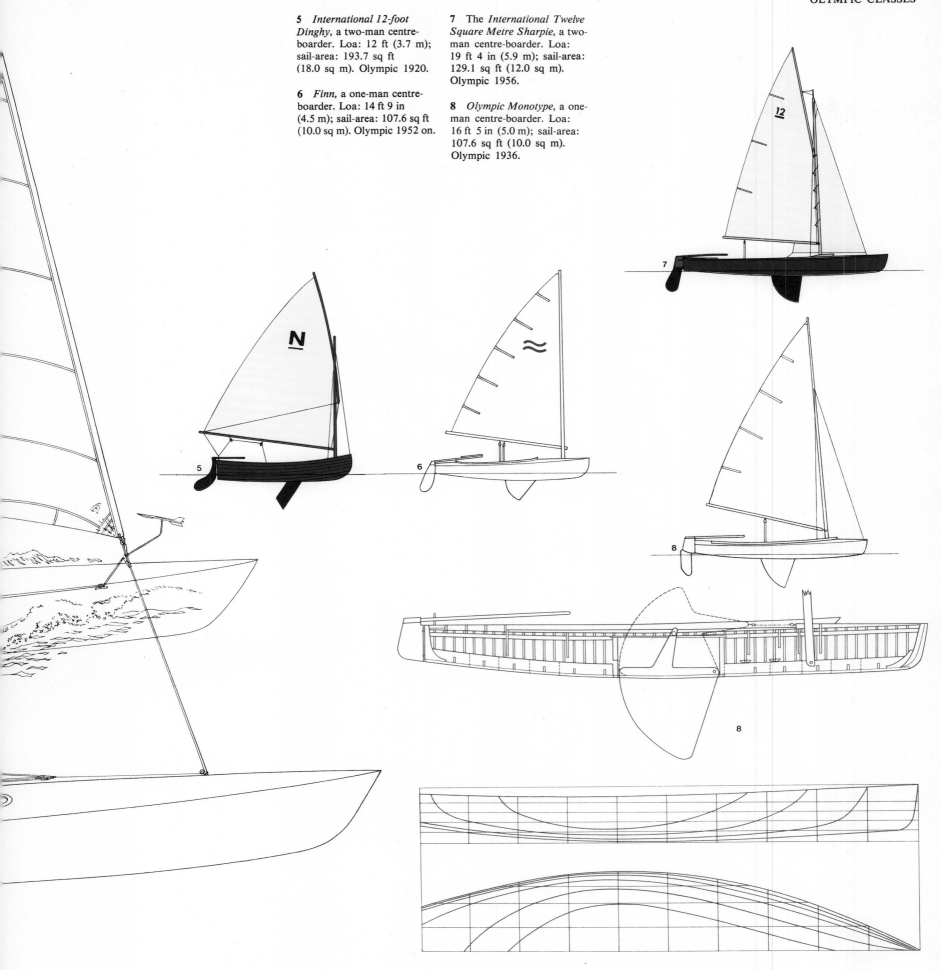

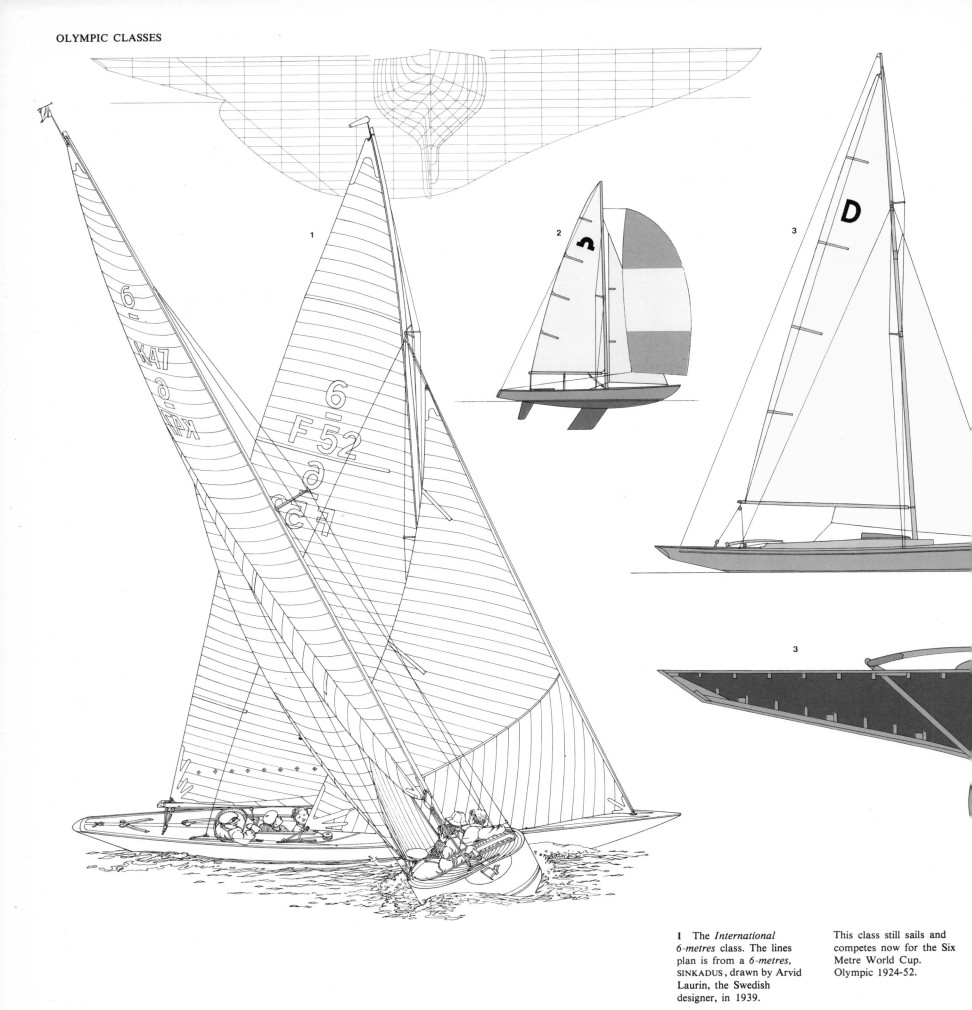

1 The *International 6-metres* class. The lines plan is from a *6-metres*, SINKADUS, drawn by Arvid Laurin, the Swedish designer, in 1939.

This class still sails and competes now for the Six Metre World Cup. Olympic 1924-52.

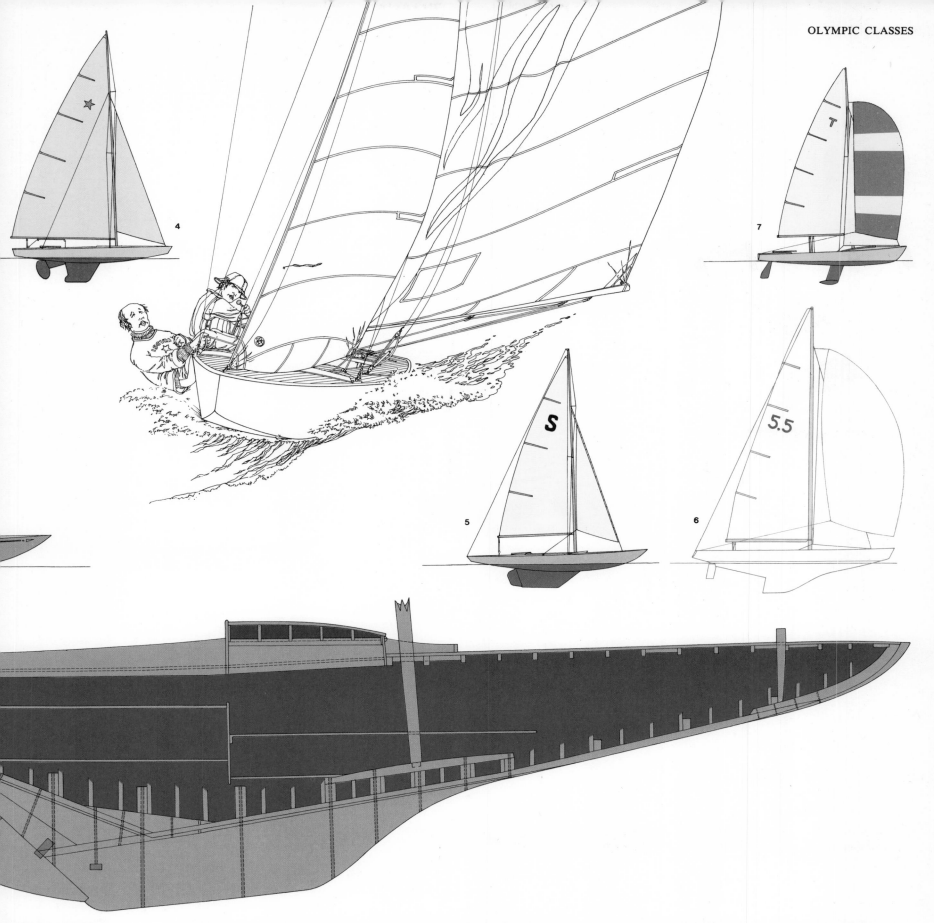

2 *Soling*, a three-man keelboat. Loa: 26 ft 9 in (8.15 m), sail-area: 233.5 sq ft (21.7 sq m). Olympic 1972 on.

3 *Dragon*, also a three-man keelboat. Loa: 29 ft 2 in (8.9 m); sail-area: 235.6 sq ft (21.9 sq m). Olympic 1948-72.

4 *Star*, a two-man keelboat. Loa: 22 ft 9 in (6.9 m); sail-area: 280 sq ft (26.0 sq m). Olympic 1932-72, 1980 on.

5 *Swallow*, a two-man keelboat. Loa: 25 ft 6 in (7.8 m); sail-area: 200 sq ft (18.6 sq m). Olympic 1948.

6 *The International 5.5-metres* class. Loa: 31 ft (9.4 m); sail-area: 300 sq ft (27.9 sq m). Measurements approximate. Olympic 1952-68.

7 *Tempest*, a two-man keelboat. Loa: 22 ft (6.7 m); sail-area: 247.5 sq ft (23.0 sq m). Olympic 1972-76.

1 *Optimist*. Loa: 7 ft 7.5 in (2.3 m); sail-area: 35 sq ft (3.3 sq m). United States.

2 *Piraat*. Loa: 7 ft 10 in (2.4 m); sail-area: 35 sq ft (3.3 sq m). Holland.

3 *Tabur 320*. Loa: 10 ft 6 in (3.2 m); sail-area: 56 sq ft (5.2 sq m). France.

4 *Minifish*. Loa: 11 ft 9 in (3.6 m); sail-area: 64.6 sq ft (6.0 sq m). United States.

5 *Cadet*. Loa: 10 ft 6.75 in (3.2 m); sail-area: 55.5 sq ft (5.2 sq m). England.

6 *Topper*. Loa: 11 ft 2 in (3.4 m); sail-area: 56 sq ft (5.2 sq m). England.

7 *International Moth*. Loa: 11 ft (3.4 m); sail-area: 85 sq ft (7.9 sq m). Australia.

8 *OK*. Loa: 13 ft 1 in (4.0 m); sail-area: 86.1 sq ft (8.0 sq m). Denmark.

9 *Vaurien*. Loa: 13 ft 5 in (4.08 m); sail-area: 87.2 sq ft (8.1 sq m). France.

10 *Pirat*. Loa: 15 ft 5 in (4.7 m); sail-area: 107.6 sq ft (10.0 sq m). Germany.

11 *Triss*. Loa: 13 ft 9 in (4.2 m); sail-area: 100.1 sq ft (9.3 sq m). Sweden.

12 *Flipper*. Loa: 13 ft 5 in (4.1 m); sail-area: 110.8 sq ft (10.3 sq m). Denmark.

13 *Mirror*. Loa: 10 ft 10 in (3.3 m); sail-area: 69 sq ft (6.4 sq m). England.

14 *Flying Junior*. Loa: 13 ft 1 in (4.0 m); sail-area: 100.1 sq ft (9.3 sq m). Holland.

15 *Europe*. Loa: 11 ft (3.4 m); sail-area: 75.3 sq ft (7.0 sq m). Belgium.

16 *420*. Loa: 13 ft 9 in (4.2 m); sail-area: 109.8 sq ft (10.2 sq m). France.

17 *Oslo*. Loa: 18 ft (5.5 m); sail-area: 96.8 sq ft (9.0 sq m). Norway.

18 *Drascombe Lugger*. Loa: 18 ft 9 in (5.7 m); sail-area (main, jib, mizzen): 122 sq ft (11.3 sq m). England.

1 *Windsurfer.* Loa: 12 ft (3.7 m); sail-area: 56 sq ft (5.2 sq m). United States.

2 *Cherub.* Loa: 12 ft (3.7 m); sail-area: 106 sq ft (9.8 sq m). New Zealand.

3 *Enterprise.* Loa: 13 ft 3 in (4.0 m); sail-area: 113 sq ft (10.5 sq m). England.

4 *Trapez.* Loa: 16 ft (4.9 m); sail-area: 166.8 sq ft (15.5 sq m). Denmark.

5 *International 505.* Loa: *c.* 16 ft 7 in (5.05 m); sail-area: 150 sq ft (13.9 sq m). England.

6 *Fireball.* Loa: 16 ft 2 in (4.9 m); sail-area: 123 sq ft (11.4 sq m). England.

7 *Laser.* Loa: 13 ft 10.5 in (4.2 m); sail-area: 76 sq ft (7.1 sq m). Canada.

8 *Snipe.* Loa: 15 ft 6 in (4.7 m); sail-area: 112 sq ft (10.4 sq m). United States.

9 *Lightning.* Loa: 19 ft (5.8 m); sail-area: 177 sq ft (16.4 sq m). United States.

10 *IC canoe.* Loa: 16-17 ft (4.9-5.2 m); sail-area: 107.6 sq ft (10.0 sq m). Open.

11 *Contender.* Loa: 16 ft (4.9 m); sail-area: 120 sq ft (11.2 sq m). Australia.

12 *Loup.* Loa: 18 ft (5.5 m); sail-area: 216 sq ft (20.1 sq m). France.

13 *International 14-foot.* Loa: 14 ft (4.3 m); sail-area: 200 sq ft (18.6 sq m) maximum. Open.

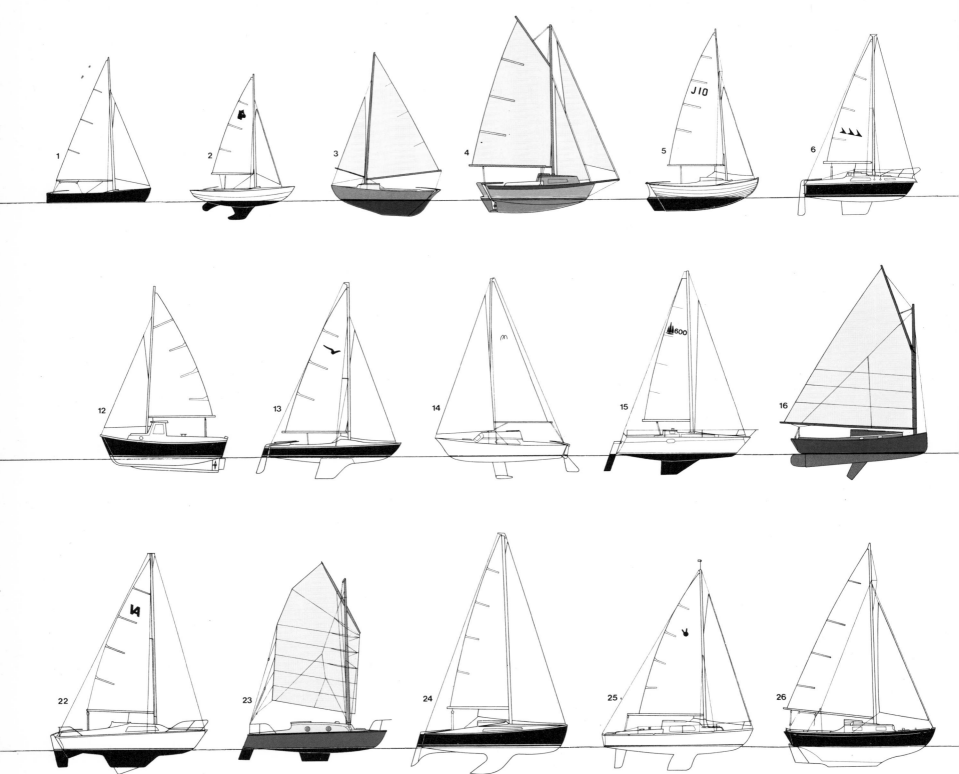

1 *Mercury*. Loa: 15 ft (4.6 m); sail-area: 119 sq ft (11.1 sq m). United States.

2 *Killing*. Loa: 15 ft 7 in (4.75 m); sail-area: 89.3 sq ft (8.3 sq m). Norway.

3 *Bull's Eye*. Loa: 15 ft 9 in (4.8 m); sail-area: 140 sq ft (13.0 sq m). United States.

4 *Saran*. Loa: 16 ft (4.9 m); sail-area: varies from 160 to 270 sq ft (14.9 to 25.1 sq m). United States.

5 *J10*. Loa: 16 ft 3 in (4.95 m); sail-area: 107.6 sq ft (10.0 sq m). Sweden.

6 *Flying Cruiser C*. Loa: 17 ft 9 in (5.4 m); sail-area: 174.3 sq ft (16.2 sq m). Germany.

7 *Alios*. Loa: 18 ft 4 in (5.6 m); sail-area: 161.4 sq ft (15.0 sq m). France.

8 *Stjärnbåt*. Loa: 18 ft 5 in (5.6 m); sail-area: 161.4 sq ft (15.0 sq m). Sweden.

9 *Hurley 18*. Loa: 18 ft 6 in (5.6 m); sail-area: 180 sq ft (16.7 sq m). England.

10 *Listel*. Loa: 18 ft 6 in (5.65 m); sail-area: 170 sq ft (15.8 sq m). France.

11 *KDY Junior*. Loa: 18 ft 8 in (5.7 m); sail-area: 161.4 sq ft (15.0 sq m). Denmark.

12 *Mérou*. Loa: 19 ft (5.8 m); sail-area: 161.4 sq ft (15.0 sq m). France.

13 *Squib*. Loa: 19 ft (5.8 m); sail-area: 173 sq ft (16.1 sq m). England.

14 *Matilda*. Loa: 19 ft 6 in (5.9 m); sail-area: 195 sq ft (18.1 sq m). Canada.

15 *Pen Duick 600*. Loa: 19 ft 8 in (6.0 m); sail-area: 161.4 sq ft (15.0 sq m). France.

16 *Mystic Catboat*. Loa: 20 ft (6.1 m); sail-area: 252 sq ft (23.4 sq m). United States.

17 *Efsix*. Loa: 19 ft 8 in (6.0 m); sail-area: 202.3 sq ft (18.8 sq m). Holland.

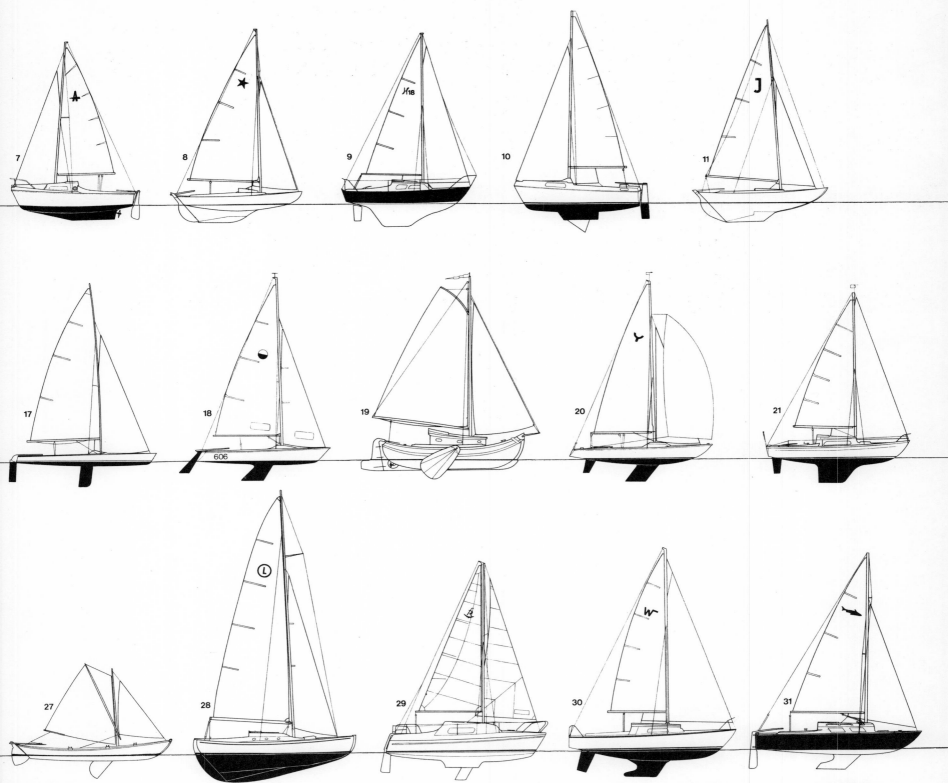

18 *Monark 606.* Loa:
19 ft 11 in (6.06 m); sail-area:
172.2 sq ft (16.0 sq m).
Sweden.

19 *Boyer.* Loa: 20 ft 8 in
(6.3 m); sail-area: 161.4 sq ft
(15.0 sq m). Holland.

20 *Yngling.* Loa: 20 ft 10 in
(6.35 m); sail-area: 150.6 sq ft
(14.0 sq m). Norway.

21 *Splinter.* Loa: 21 ft 2 in
(6.45 m); sail-area: 181.8 sq ft
(16.9 sq m). Holland.

22 *Varianta.* Loa: 21 ft 4 in
(6.5 m); sail-area: 180.6 sq ft
(16.8 sq m). Holland.

23 *Kingfisher 20 Plus.* Loa:
21 ft 7 in (6.6 m); sail-area:
227 sq ft (21.1 sq m).
England.

24 *Piviere 660.* Loa: 21 ft 8 in
(6.6 m); sail-area: 243.2 sq ft
(22.6 sq m). Italy.

25 *Victoire 22'.* Loa:
21 ft 8 in (6.6 m); sail-area:
175.9 sq ft (16.35 sq m).
Holland.

26 *Chub 22.* Loa: 22 ft 6 in
(6.9 m); sail-area: 245 sq ft
(22.8 sq m). United States.

27 *Cape Ann Dory.* Loa:
22 ft 4 in (6.8 m); sail-area:
120 sq ft (11.2 sq m).
United States.

28 *Laurin Double-ender.*
Loa: 23 ft (7.0 m); sail-area:
269 sq ft (25.0 sq m). Sweden.

29 *Rubin 23.* Loa: 23 ft 5 in
(7.15 m); sail-area: 233 sq ft
(21.65 sq m). Germany.

30 *Waarschip Quarter
Tonner.* Loa: 23 ft 9 in
(7.25 m); sail-area: 170 sq ft
(15.8 sq m). Holland.

31 *Shark 24.* Loa: 24 ft
(7.3 m); sail-area: 223.8 sq ft
(20.8 sq m). Canada.

1 *Dufour 24*. Loa: 24 ft 1 in (7.35 m); sail-area: 212 sq ft (19.7 sq m). France.

2 *Spaekhugger*. Loa: 24 ft 5 in (7.44 m); sail-area: 430.4 sq ft (40.0 sq m). Denmark.

3 *Joker*. Loa: 24 ft 7 in (7.5 m); sail-area: 360.5 sq ft (33.5 sq m). Switzerland.

4 *Nordic Folkboat*. Loa: 24 ft 11 in (7.6 m); sail-area: 258.2 sq ft (24.0 sq m). Sweden.

5 *Promenade 760*. Loa: 24 ft 11 in (7.6 m); sail-area: 269 sq ft (25.0 sq m). Italy.

6 *Korneuburg 25*. Loa: 25 ft 1 in (7.65 m); sail-area: 352.9 sq ft (32.8 sq m). Austria.

7 *Tomahawk 25*. Loa: 25 ft 4 in (7.7 m); sail-area: 287 sq ft (26.7 sq m). United States.

8 *Ecume de Mer*. Loa: 25 ft 11 in (7.9 m); sail-area: 258.2 sq ft (24.0 sq m). France.

9 *Waddel*. Loa: 26 ft 5 in (8.05 m); sail-area: 195.8 sq ft (18.2 sq m). Holland.

10 *Loper*. Loa: 26 ft 11 in (8.2 m); sail-area: 263.6 sq ft (24.5 sq m). Holland.

11 *Vega*. Loa: 27.1 ft 8.25 sq m); sail-area: 304.5 sq ft (28.3 sq m). Sweden.

12 *H-Boat*. Loa: 27 ft 2 in (8.28 m); sail-area: 263.6 sq ft (24.5 sq m). Finland.

13 *Tumlaren*. Loa: 27 ft 3 in (8.3 m); sail-area: 215.2 sq ft (20.0 sq m). Sweden.

14 *International 3 metres.*
Loa: 27 ft 3 in–30 ft 6 in
(8.3–9.3 m); sail-area:
204.4–258.2 sq ft
(19.0–24.0 sq m). France.

15 *Yachting World Keelboat.*
Loa: 29 ft 9 in (9.1 m); sail-
area: 269 sq ft (25.0 sq m).
England.

16 *Morgan Classic 300.* Loa:
29 ft 11 in (9.1 m); sail-area:
466 sq ft (43.3 sq m). United
States.

17 *Optima.* Loa: 30 ft 2 in
(9.2 m); sail-area: 389.5 sq ft
(36.2 sq m). Holland.

18 *Half Tonner Miller and
Valentijn.* Loa: 30 ft 3 in
(9.2 m); sail-area: 415 sq ft
(38.6 sq m). Australia and
Holland.

19 *Maxi 95.* Loa: 31 ft 2 in
(9.5 m); sail-area: 301.3 sq ft
(28.0 sq m). Sweden.

20 *Westerly Renown.* Loa:
32 ft 6 in (9.9 m); sail-area:
441.2 sq ft (41.0 sq m).
England.

21 *Elvstrom Cruiser.* Loa:
31 ft 4 in (9.56 m); sail-area:
365.8 sq ft (34.0 sq m).
Denmark.

22 *Panda 31.* Loa: 31 ft 6 in
(9.6 m); sail-area: 554.1 sq ft
(51.5 sq m). Italy.

23 *Ranger 32.* Loa: 32 ft 6 in
(9.9 m); sail-area: 462.7 sq ft
(43.0 sq m). United States.

24 *Phantom 32.* Loa:
32 ft 8 in (9.95 m); sail-area:
359.4 sq ft (33.4 sq m).
Germany.

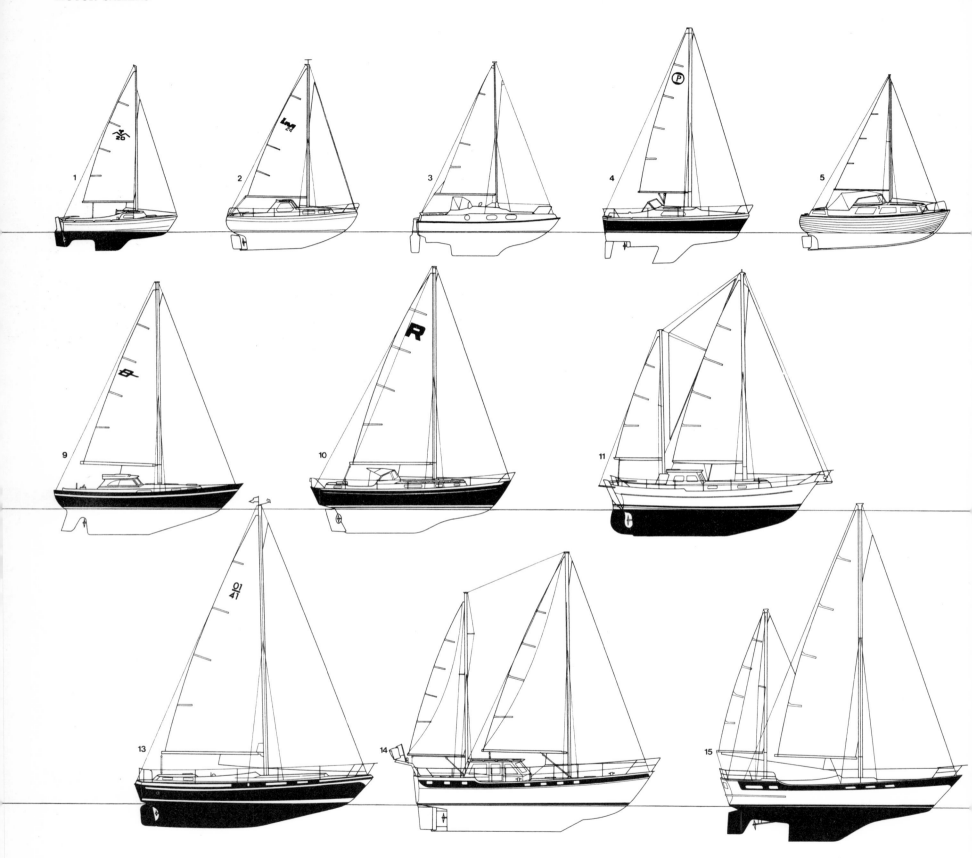

1 *Marieholm MS 20*. Loa: 19 ft 8 in (6.0 m); sail-area: 180.2 sq ft (16.75 sq m). Sweden.

2 *LM 24*. Loa: 23 ft 8 in (7.2 m); sail-area: 247.5 sq ft (23.0 sq m). Denmark.

3 *Medusa*. Loa: 24 ft 11 in (7.6 m); sail-area: 226 sq ft (21.0 sq m). Finland.

4 *Parant*. Loa: 24 ft 11 in (7.6 m); sail-area: 269 sq ft (25.0 sq m). Sweden.

5 *Risörkryssaren 27*. Loa: 26 ft 11 in (8.2 m); sail-area: 182.9 sq ft (17.0 sq m). Norway.

6 *Dartsailer 30*. Loa: 30 ft (9.15 m); sail-area: 399.2 sq ft (37.1 sq m). Holland.

7 *Fairways Fisher 30*. Loa: 30 ft (9.15 m); sail-area: 330 sq ft (30.7 sq m). England.

8 *Evasion 32*. Loa: 31 ft 10 in (9.7 m); sail-area: 371.2 sq ft (34.5 sq m). France.

9 *Fjord MS 33*. Loa: 32 ft 11 in (10.03 m); sail-area: 463 sq ft (43.03 sq m). Norway.

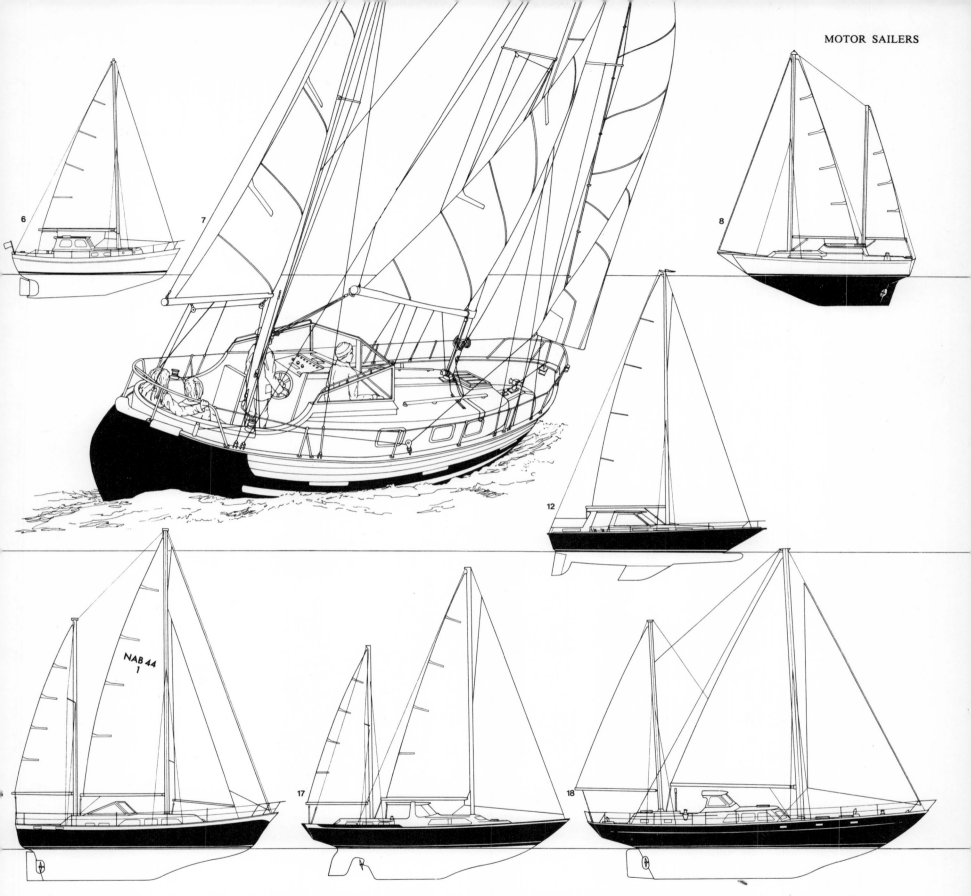

10 *Rasmus 35*. Loa: 34 ft 5 in (10.5 m); sail-area: 484.2 sq ft (45.0 sq m). Sweden.

11 *Sirocco*. Loa: 37 ft 1 in (11.3 m); sail-area: 683.3 sq ft (63.5 sq m). Holland.

12 *Nelson-Elvström 38 Super MS*. Loa: 37 ft 5 in (11.4 m); sail-area: 579 sq ft (53.81 sq m). Denmark.

13 *Morgan Out Island 41*. Loa: 41 ft 3 in (12.6 m); sail-area: 767 sq ft (71.3 sq m). United States.

14 *Suncoast*. Loa: 42 ft (12.8 m); sail-area: 737.1 sq ft (68.5 sq m). Holland.

15 *Amphitrite*. Loa: 42 ft 9 in (13.03 m); sail-area: 774.7 sq ft (72.0 sq m). England.

16 *NAB 44*. Loa: 45 ft 1 in (13.75 m); sail-area: 968.5 sq ft (90.0 sq m). Germany.

17 *Nicholson 48*. Loa: 47 ft 8 in (14.5 m); sail-area: 1,051.25 sq ft (97.7 sq m). England.

18 *Explorer*. Loa: 58 ft 7 in (17.9 m); sail-area: 1,131 sq ft (105.1 sq m). United States.

MULTIHULLS

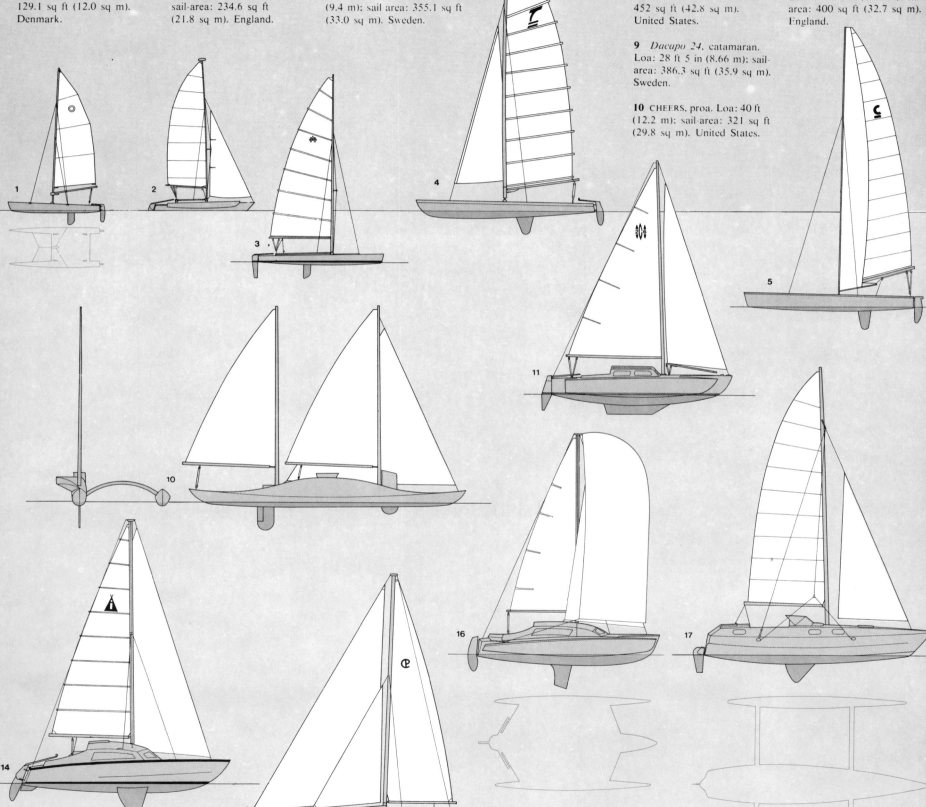

1 *Cat-ya Junior*, catamaran. Loa: 13 ft 1 in (4.0 m); sail-area: 75.3 sq ft (7.0 sq m). Sweden.

2 *Supernova*, trimaran. Loa: 14 ft 11 in (4.55 m); sail-area: 129.1 sq ft (12.0 sq m). Denmark.

3 *Australis*, A-Class catamaran. Loa: 18 ft (5.5 m); sail-area: 149.6 sq ft (13.9 sq m). Australia.

4 *Tornado*, B-Class catamaran. Loa: 20 ft (6.1 m); sail-area: 234.6 sq ft (21.8 sq m). England.

5 *C Class* catamaran. Loa (maximum): 25 ft (7.6 m); sail-area (maximum): 300 sq ft (27.9 sq m). Open.

6 *Linsa, D Class* catamaran. Loa: 30 ft 10 in (9.4 m); sail area: 355.1 sq ft (33.0 sq m). Sweden.

7 *Hobie Cat 16*, catamaran. Loa: 16 ft 7 in (5.05 m); sail-area: 218 sq ft (20.3 sq m). United States.

8 *Val*, trimaran. Loa: 31 ft 2 in (9.5 m); sail-area: 452 sq ft (42.8 sq m). United States.

9 *Dacapo 24*, catamaran. Loa: 28 ft 5 in (8.66 m); sail-area: 386.3 sq ft (35.9 sq m). Sweden.

10 CHEERS, proa. Loa: 40 ft (12.2 m); sail-area: 321 sq ft (29.8 sq m). United States.

11 *Cross 26*, trimaran. Loa: 26 ft (7.9 m); **sail-area: 300 sq ft (27.9 sq m). United States.**

12 *Tangaroa*, catamaran. Loa: 34 ft 6 in (10.5 m); sail-area: 400 sq ft (32.7 sq m). England.

13 *Catalac*, catamaran. Loa: 29 ft 3 in (8.9 m): sail-area: 450 sq ft (41.8 sq m). England.

14 *Iroquois Mk II*, catamaran. Loa: 30 ft (9.1 m): sail-area: 475 sq ft (44.1 sq m). England.

15 *Snowgoose 34*, catamaran. Loa: 34 ft 3 in (10.4 m): sail-area: 500 sq ft (46.5 sq m). England.

16 *Telstar 26*, trimaran. Loa: 26 ft 3 in (8.0 m): sail-area: 298 sq ft (27.7 sq m). England.

17 *Pinta*, trimaran. Loa: 32 ft 10 in (10.0 m): sail-area: 376.6 sq ft (35.0 sq m). Sweden.

18 *Sea Bird*, catamaran. Loa: 44 ft (12.2 m): sail-area: 805 sq ft (74.8 sq m). United States.

19 *Planesail*, trimaran. Loa: 30 ft (9.1 m): sail unit: four rigid 24 ft (7.3 m) aerofoils. England.

20 *Crossbow*, proa. Loa: 60 ft (18.3 m); sail-area: 968.4 sq ft (90.0 sq m). England.

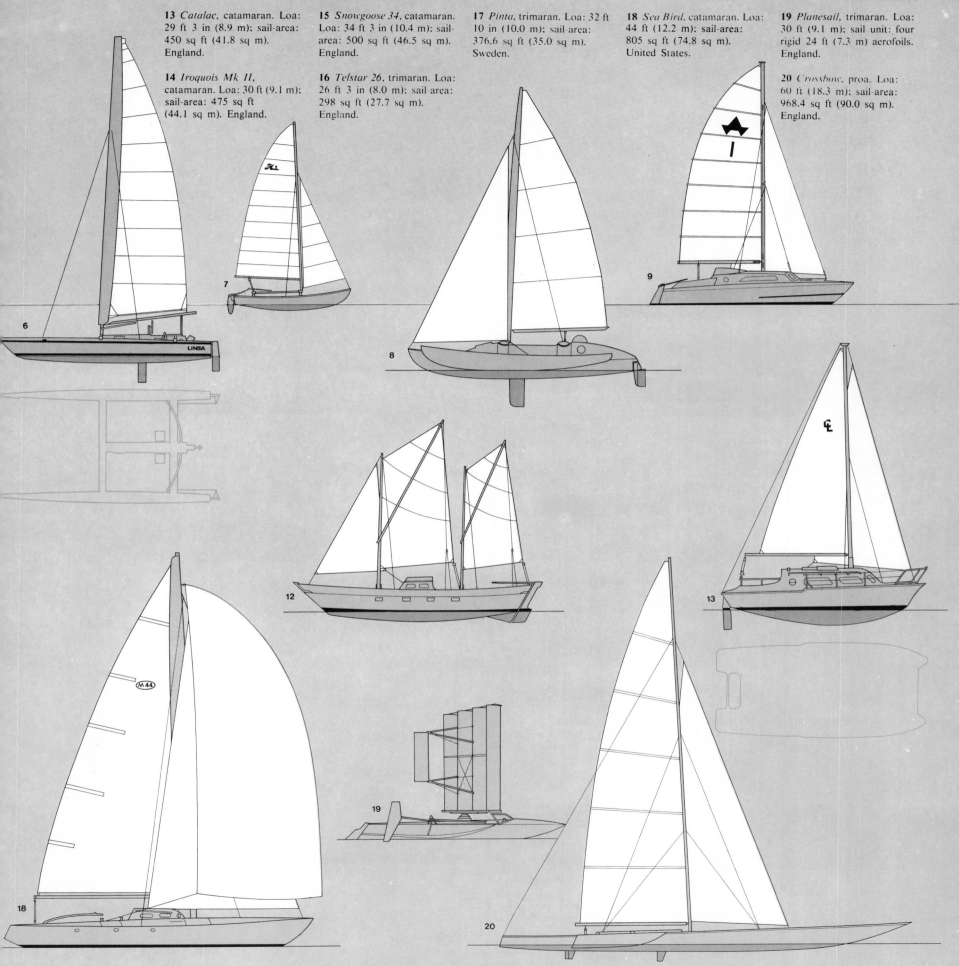

51

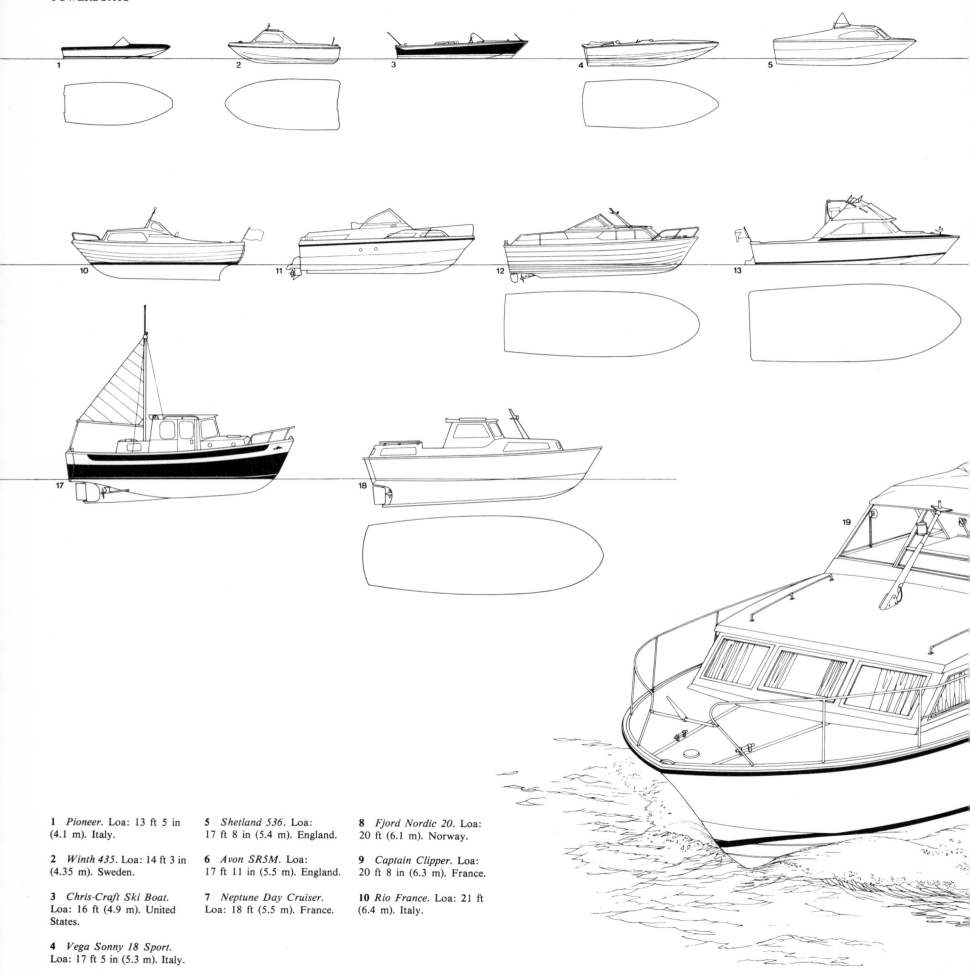

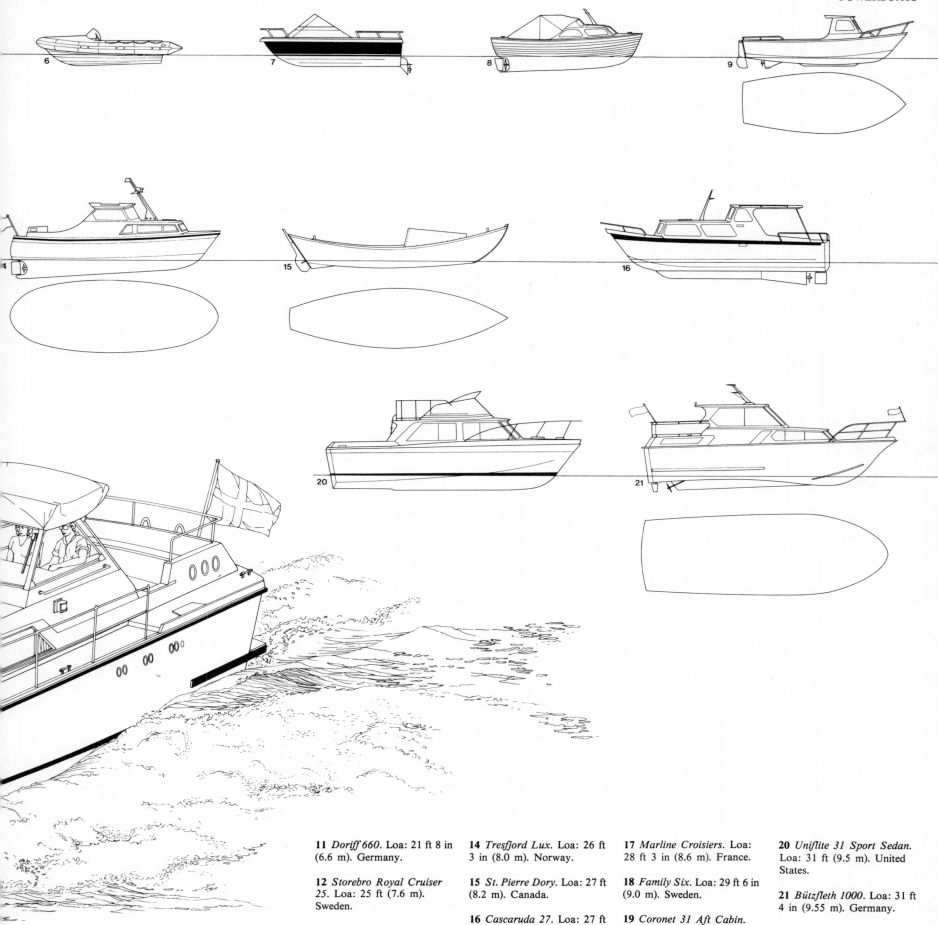

11 *Doriff 660*. Loa: 21 ft 8 in (6.6 m). Germany.

12 *Storebro Royal Cruiser 25*. Loa: 25 ft (7.6 m). Sweden.

13 *Bertram 26' Sport Fisherman*. Loa: 26 ft (7.9 m). United States.

14 *Tresfjord Lux*. Loa: 26 ft 3 in (8.0 m). Norway.

15 *St. Pierre Dory*. Loa: 27 ft (8.2 m). Canada.

16 *Cascaruda 27*. Loa: 27 ft (8.2 m). Holland.

17 *Marline Croisiers*. Loa: 28 ft 3 in (8.6 m). France.

18 *Family Six*. Loa: 29 ft 6 in (9.0 m). Sweden.

19 *Coronet 31 Aft Cabin*. Loa: 31 ft 8 in (9.6 m). Denmark.

20 *Uniflite 31 Sport Sedan*. Loa: 31 ft (9.5 m). United States.

21 *Bützfleth 1000*. Loa: 31 ft 4 in (9.55 m). Germany.

POWERBOATS

1 *Amerglass 32.* Loa: 32 ft (9.8 m). Holland.

2 *Corvette 32.* Loa: 32 ft (9.8 m). England.

3 *Laguna X Metre.* Loa: 32 ft 9 in (10.0 m). England.

4 *Falmouth Fast Fisherman.* Loa: 33 ft (10.1 m). England.

5 *Finnmar Admiral.* Loa: 33 ft (10.1 m). Finland.

6 *Storö 34.* Loa: 34 ft (10.4 m). Sweden.

7 *Tille-Kruiser 1050.* Loa: 34 ft 6 in (10.5 m). Germany.

8 *Grand Banks 36.* Loa: 36 ft (11.0 m). United States.

9 *Galloper 36.* Loa: 36 ft 1 in (11.0 m). Holland.

10 *Arcoa 1100.* Loa: 36 ft 1 in (11.0 m). France.

11 *Cheoy Lee Trawler 36*.
Loa: 36 ft (11.0 m). Hong
Kong.

12 *Riva 2000*. Loa: 37 ft 1 in
(11.3 m). Italy.

13 *Chris-Craft 38'
Constellation Saloon*. Loa:
38 ft (11.6 m). United
States.

14 *Palma 40*. Loa: 39 ft 4 in
(12.0 m). Holland.

15 *Baltic 41*. Loa: 41 ft
(12.5 m). Sweden.

16 *Hatteras 42*. Loa: 42 ft
6 in (13.0 m). United States.

17 *Andromeda 13*. Loa: 42 ft
6 in (13.0 m). Italy.

18 *Bertram 58' Convertible*.
Loa: 58 ft (17.7 m). United
States.

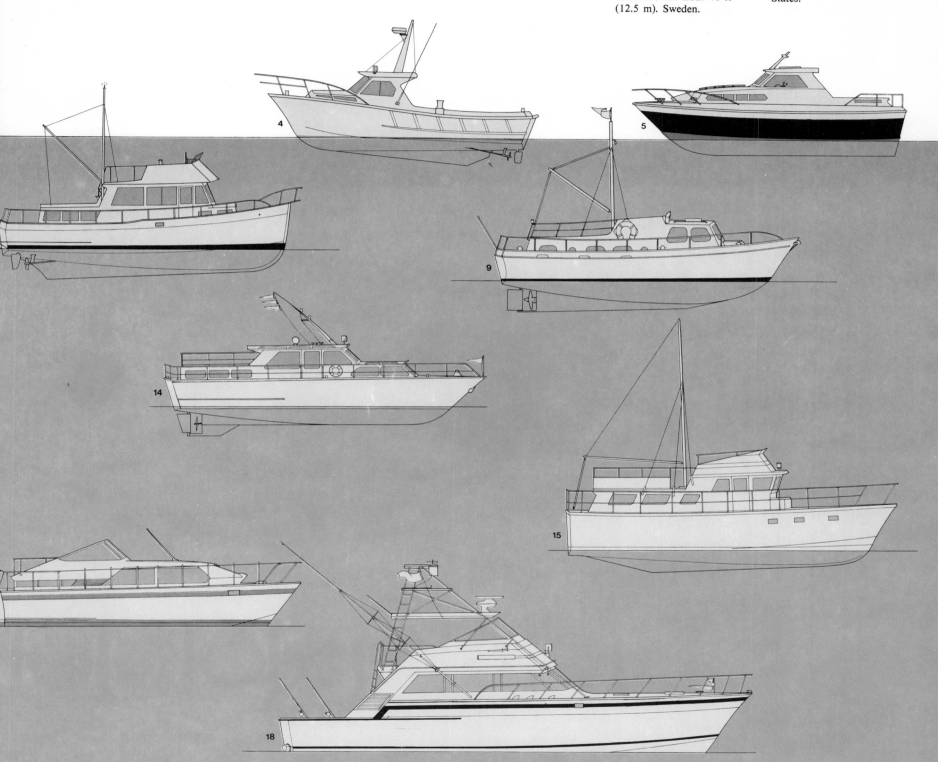

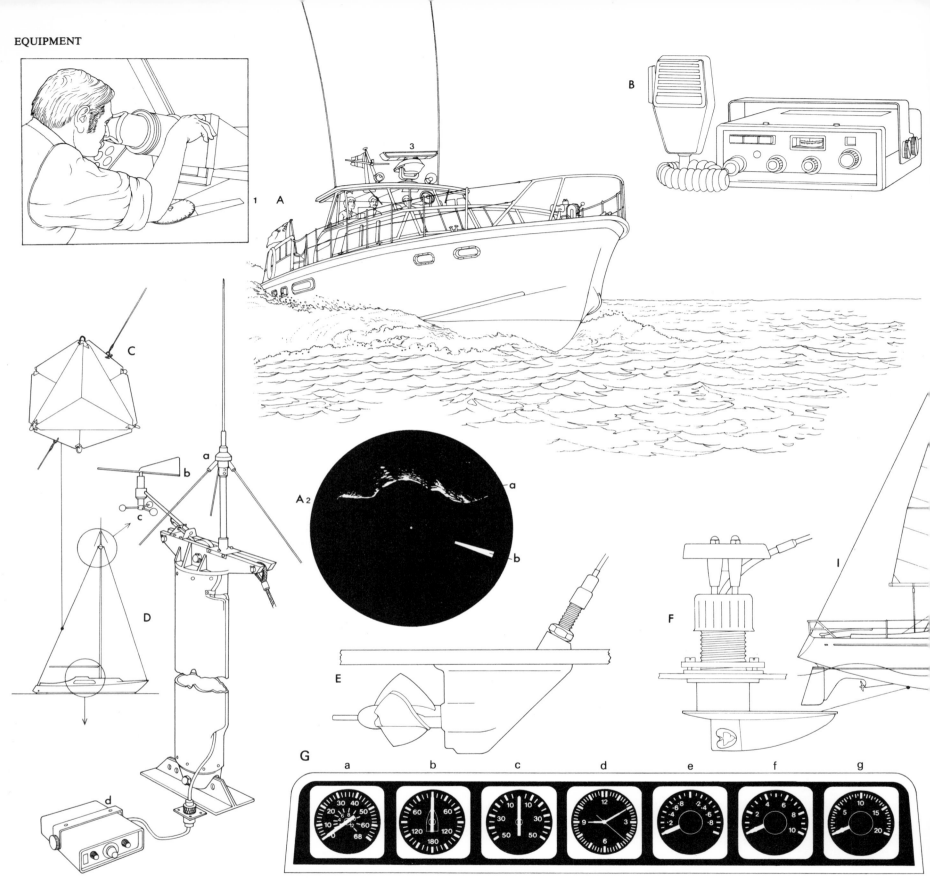

Most communications and electronic equipment on board pleasure boats today are the result of the development of the standard equipment found on ships and aircraft. Advances in electronics over the past twenty years have made it possible to make, for instance, a merchant ship's wieldy radar equipment in small enough sizes to fit on pleasure boats.

A Radar is an invaluable night-time and poor-visibility navigational aid. Nowadays, it can be acquired as a compact and relatively light system with a display unit (**1**), which clearly displays on its screen (**2**) any coastline (*a*), radar beacon (*b*), other craft, or suchlike. (**3**) The scanner unit is small enough to be mounted on a deck house or a mast.

B A two-way radio telephone or communications radio is an important piece of safety equipment. Apart from providing access to regular weather forecasts, it allows the boat to communicate with other vessels and with radio stations on land. In emergencies, a radio can be a life-saver. Here, we show a five-watt communications radio with a sea range of up to thirty-five miles.

C A good big radar reflector is a must on all boats that are planning to sail any distance away from sheltered waters.

D Masthead fitting and equipment on a sailing-boat. (*a*) Aerial. (*b*) Wind-direction finder. (*c*) Anemometer for measuring the speed of the wind. (*d*) Radio unit.

E A mechanical log which can be mounted on the bottom of the hull.

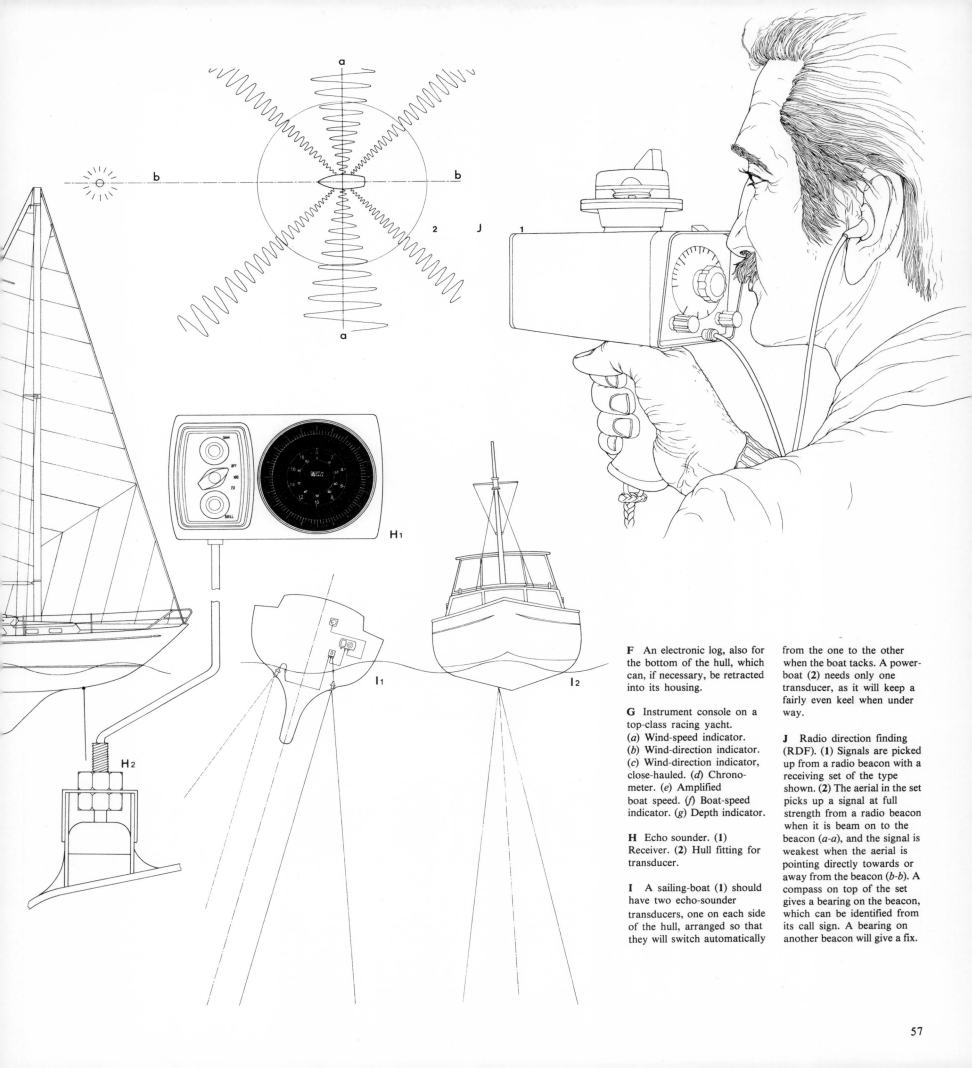

F An electronic log, also for the bottom of the hull, which can, if necessary, be retracted into its housing.

G Instrument console on a top-class racing yacht. (*a*) Wind-speed indicator. (*b*) Wind-direction indicator. (*c*) Wind-direction indicator, close-hauled. (*d*) Chronometer. (*e*) Amplified boat speed. (*f*) Boat-speed indicator. (*g*) Depth indicator.

H Echo sounder. (**1**) Receiver. (**2**) Hull fitting for transducer.

I A sailing-boat (**1**) should have two echo-sounder transducers, one on each side of the hull, arranged so that they will switch automatically from the one to the other when the boat tacks. A powerboat (**2**) needs only one transducer, as it will keep a fairly even keel when under way.

J Radio direction finding (RDF). (**1**) Signals are picked up from a radio beacon with a receiving set of the type shown. (**2**) The aerial in the set picks up a signal at full strength from a radio beacon when it is beam on to the beacon (*a-a*), and the signal is weakest when the aerial is pointing directly towards or away from the beacon (*b-b*). A compass on top of the set gives a bearing on the beacon, which can be identified from its call sign. A bearing on another beacon will give a fix.

57

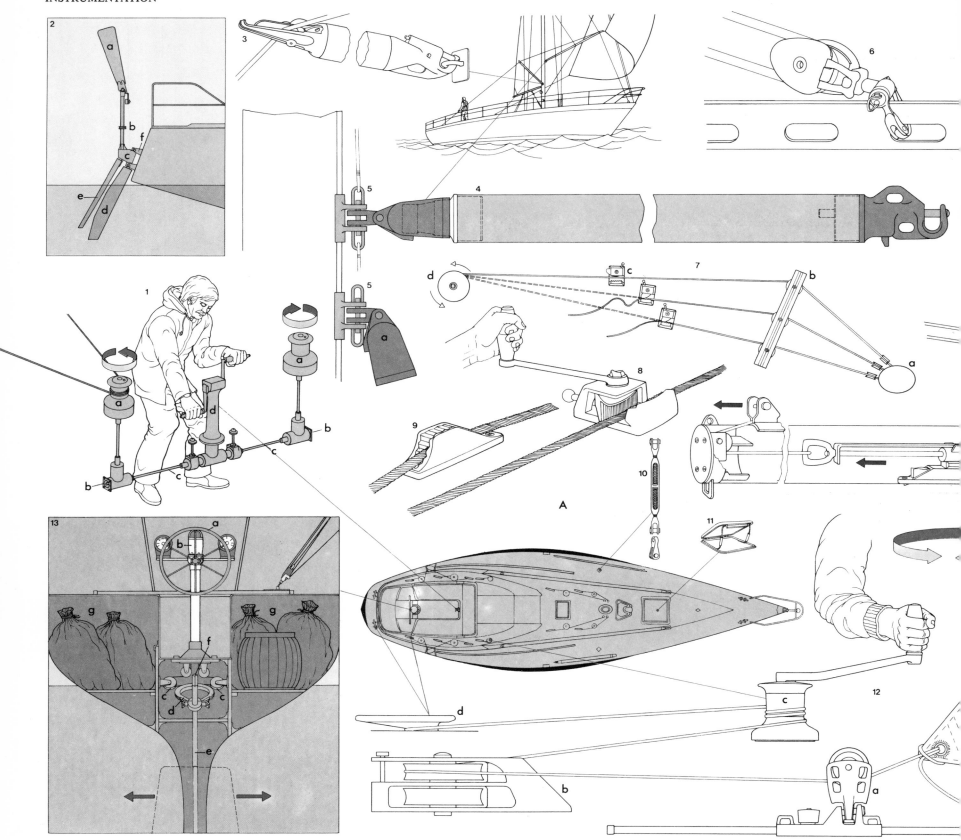

On these two pages are illustrated equipment and fittings. The *Swan 38* is used as an example to show the positioning of various of the pieces of equipment.

A The deck plan of the *Swan 38*. (**1**) A coffee-grinder winch system. (*a*) Winches. (*b*) Gear boxes. (*c*) Drive shaft. (*d*) Remote drive pedestal. (**2**) A modern self-steering system. (*a*) Dual-axis wind vane. (*b*) Vane control wheel. (*c*) Housing. (*d*) Auxiliary rudder. (*e*) Servo-oar. (*f*) Mounting brackets.

(**3**) Spinnaker reaching strut, or jockey pole. (**4**) Spinnaker boom. (**5**) Spinnaker track. (*a*) Spinnaker cup. (**6**) Snatch block attached to toe rail. (**7**) Sheets and halyards can be led from the mast heel (*a*), through a number of deck blocks (*b*) and sheet stoppers

(*c*), to a winch (*d*). (**8**) A power sheet-jammer. (**9**) Clam cleat. (**10**) Rigging screw with toggle. (**11**) Deck hatch. (**12**) Foresail sheet passes through the sliding traveller (*a*) to a foot block (*b*) and then to a winch (*c*), ending up at a cleat (*d*). (**13**) An Edson steering

system. (*a*) Steerer. (*b*) Pedestal with compass. (*c*) Sheave. (*d*) Steering quadrant. (*e*) Rudder post. (*f*) End of rudder post is machined to take an emergency tiller. (*g*) Stowage lockers.

B Side view of the *Swan 38*. (**1**) Main boom equipped with remote outhaul. (**2**) Jiffy, or slab, reefing system. (*a*) Mainsail hoisted. (*b*) Sail reefed. (**3**) Boom-mounted roller reefing system. (**4**) Through-mast roller reefing system. (**5**) Mast fittings. (*a*) Mast step. (*b*)

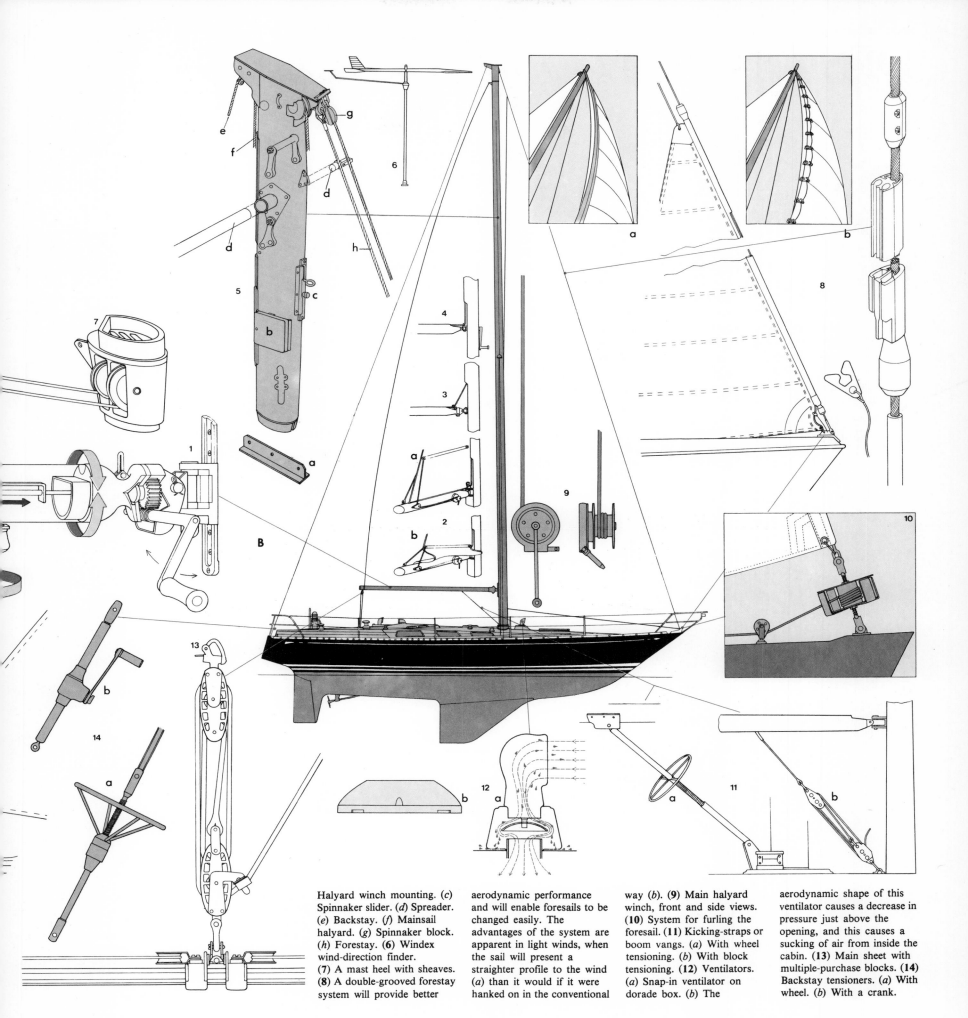

Halyard winch mounting. (c) Spinnaker slider. (d) Spreader. (e) Backstay. (f) Mainsail halyard. (g) Spinnaker block. (h) Forestay. (6) Windex wind-direction finder. (7) A mast heel with sheaves. (8) A double-grooved forestay system will provide better aerodynamic performance and will enable foresails to be changed easily. The advantages of the system are apparent in light winds, when the sail will present a straighter profile to the wind (a) than it would if it were hanked on in the conventional way (b). (9) Main halyard winch, front and side views. (10) System for furling the foresail. (11) Kicking-straps or boom vangs. (a) With wheel tensioning. (b) With block tensioning. (12) Ventilators. (a) Snap-in ventilator on dorade box. (b) The aerodynamic shape of this ventilator causes a decrease in pressure just above the opening, and this causes a sucking of air from inside the cabin. (13) Main sheet with multiple-purchase blocks. (14) Backstay tensioners. (a) With wheel. (b) With a crank.

DESIGN AND CONSTRUCTION

Colin Mudie

Early boat-builders were severely constricted by the materials they had to hand and by the tools they had to work them. The most obvious and simplest material must be the tree trunk, either alone or lashed together with several others to make a raft. This is not quite such an easy task as it might look at first sight as, in the absence of good, powerful saws, the method relies on a supply of tree trunks of the right size. Bamboos are obviously right for rafts, and it is thought that the Chinese were using flat bamboo rafts as early as the beginning of the Stone Age, about 4000 BC. Another excellent material for building a straightforward raft is the wood of the balsa tree. This is so soft that primitive tools can shape it, and so light that it is both easily handled and extremely buoyant. It was on a balsa-wood raft that Thor Heyerdahl crossed the Pacific when demonstrating possible early migration routes.

Once sail power is applied to a simple, rectangular raft, the speed through the water shows up the deficiencies of such a shape. The wave formed by the blunt front starts to get excessive, and the overturning moment of the sail makes the lee bow dip into the bow wave, causing a simple capsize or even pitch-poling. It is necessary to extend the front centre of the raft to improve this characteristic, and even the famous KON-TIKI was built with a rudimentary pointed bow. For this reason, log rafts took a step towards a shape we would recognize as being of general boat form. The wood rafts used until quite recently on the Coromandel coast of India consisted of groups of logs with the longest in the centre. Even more interesting is Homer's description of the craft which Odysseus built for himself during his voyaging. It seems to have been a raft built of some twenty squared-up trees to a boat-shaped plan. On this, Odysseus set up ribs like fence-posts and added some side planking. The hull was further fenced with lattice bulwarks and lined with brushwood.

Many early boat-builders made use of bundles of reeds lashed securely together. The Egyptians, with one of the world's finest waterways to build for, had only small trees like sycamore and acacia, but they had great quantities of papyrus reed. Reeds absorb water down their length from the cut ends, and the Egyptian boats were therefore built from bundles of reeds formed in a crescent, with the ends lifted well clear of the river. The bundles were secured in this position by a rope between the points, somewhat in the manner of a bow string. This form of boat generally consisted of two or more bundles of reeds, made as wide as possible for stability, and on top of these another bundle was placed to keep the passengers and crew dry. Reed

boats of this kind are still used in Lake Titicaca and the upper Nile, and until recently also in Tasmania.

Another material freely available was the skins of animals. Undoubtedly, inflated animal skins have been used as lifebuoys from the earliest days, but the first records of skin being deliberately stretched over a basket framework go back to a model dug up at Eridu, between the Tigris and the Euphrates, and dated approximately 3500 BC. The early Scandinavian peoples also used skin boats, and there are records of such craft from as early as 2000 BC. The skin boat has persisted right up to the present day with the Eskimo *umiaks* and kayaks, the Irish currachs, and the British and Welsh coracles, although the skin has been replaced by canvas. In Scandinavia, the boats were probably used by mainly nomadic peoples, who would have had to take their boats with them on their travels. It is an interesting feature of these particular, skin-clad craft that they were built with an external skid, strongly resembling a sled runner. The Irish currach was produced in the face of a need to get out into deep waters for the fishing. However, the light weight is also a very desirable characteristic in craft which have to be taken ashore every night and hauled well clear of the great breakers, which come in from the Atlantic in bad weather.

The third major ancestor of present-day boat-building is the dug-out, a tree hollowed out so that the crew and load can be set inside, where they are more protected and the stability greatly improved. Once a tree was cut down, the tools for producing a dug-out were principally fire and water, with a bit of axe-work and some wedging and shoring. The dug-out is, perhaps, the natural starter boat for any society with trees. The ancient Minoan civilization was blessed with great trees, and these were probably the foundation of that empire. Scandinavia also has good trees, and literally thousands of dug-outs have been found all over the Northlands. Some dug-outs are lashed together side by side, not unlike modern catamarans, while others are equipped with outriggers and floats on either side of a main hull, just as in modern trimarans. Another method of improving the carrying capacity of a dug-out is to fit plank coamings or wash-boards on either side of the "cockpit". This requires more sophisticated tools, but pictures of this form of construction have been found on fragments of an Aegean vase, dated as far back as 2800 BC.

There is considerable conjecture that this adding of planks to a central log is the basis of the modern planked constructions. The famous Viking type of craft was built outwards from a fairly elaborately shaped and hollowed

keel. Plenty of long, straight timber was available for the planking. The important principle of the northern construction was the fastening of the overlapped planks, which were riveted or clenched, one to another, in what is now called a clinker construction. This made for a very strong and light hull, well suited for use in an area where all the ships had to be manhandled from the water before winter. The Vikings further had to rely on manpower for a great part of their ships' propulsion in the long fjords.

In the south, the first records of fully planked hulls date from Egypt at about 2800 BC. These hulls were apparently planked with short lengths of local timber. However, Cheops' tomb of 2700 BC was found to contain the dismantled remains of a complete, planked vessel, no less than 140 ft (42.7 m) in length, built of Lebanon cedar.

Mediterranean vessels were generally planked over a framework, shaped as a general outline of the boat. The planks were fitted side by side and pegged to the framework. When the hull was completed, the seams were caulked to complete the watertightness. This form of construction has come down to us as carvel planking. In Mediterranean boats, keels are of little importance and, for instance, on the Nile, where every inch of draught must be utilized and craft are rarely hauled ashore, the keel is often omitted altogether.

The next significant step in boat construction was, as always, directly related to the supply of suitable materials. Through the industrial revolution, first iron, then steel, and later aluminium became available in shapes and at costs which could be considered for ships and boats. At first, sheet iron was used only as sheathing material for wooden ships, but in a very short time the advantages of its very thinness, as compared with that of wood, made it extremely attractive for cargo ships, since much greater capacity could be had with the same external dimensions. In addition, the start of the steam age, coupled with the seaman's traditional and pathological worry about fire on wooden ships, brought forward the development of the new metal ships. At first, they were almost exclusively made along traditional boat-building lines, with a series of frames and a basic substructure, plated with iron or steel to form the watertight skin. Later, it was appreciated that metal construction did not pose the same problems as did wooden construction, and in small craft the importance of framing was much reduced. Instead, the skin was allowed to bear a great proportion of the overall hull stresses.

Originally, iron or steel clench bolts, in this context called rivets, were used in the all-metal constructions. The plates were overlapped and riveted to each other and to the internal framework. The joints were then caulked by hammering the plate edges up tight to each other. More recently, welding with butt jointing has allowed a simpler and very much lighter construction to be used.

Aluminium was extremely expensive when first produced and, although the advantages of the material, particularly in terms of weight, were soon appreciated as being attractive for boat-building, it was not until the introduction of the aluminium-magnesium alloys that the problems of electrolysis in salt water were controllable. The first all-aluminium powerboat was, as has already been referred to, built in Switzerland in 1892 by Escher Wyss for use on the lakes, but it is not until comparatively recently that aluminium has become a natural material for the construction of pleasure boats, both power and sail.

Wood is, in itself, a pleasant material to live with. It repays and complements craftsmanship and care. Wood grain is a natural decoration which, scrubbed, varnished, or polished, enhances its surroundings. One of the material's most pleasant characteristics, however, is the ability to bend in sweet curves. In fact, it is difficult to bend wood to look ugly, and it is only now, when we look back on the discipline of wood construction from an age of plastics, that we realize that wood as a material had quite as much influence on the beauty of yachts as had the eye of the designer or builder.

There are many differing desirable qualities in the woods used for boat-building. Keels, for instance, need a timber which will take side and end fastenings, grown frames need a timber with a grain which follows fairly closely to the required shape, steam-bent frames require wood which will bend easily without cracking or splitting, and planking must be resistant to alternate wetting and drying. With each type of wood, the method of sawing the planks out of the logs for different purposes will vary, and it is an essential part of the craft of the boat-builder to use the different swelling and drying characteristics of the wood used for each part of the hull to positively lock the structure together.

Although many of the tools to be seen in museums and even in some of the few remaining wood-building yards look peculiar and special to boat-building, they are really little more than the standard implements of all workers in wood of a century or so ago. They persisted longer in the boat-building trade, because it was an area of individual skill where it was difficult to introduce machinery. One of the two principal features of the boat-builders' work was the need to shape solid timber into the complex, ever-changing shapes of, say, the faying surfaces of keels, stems, or grown frames. For this, the axe was more or less replaced by the much more controllable adze and by the drag knife, which was extremely efficient, especially for shaping thin planking. The other major difference from the work of the house-builder or joiner lay in the pulling of planking and frames into broad curves. For this service, the boat-builder invented a whole host of clamps and developed enormous skill with blocks and wedges.

For many parts of some hulls, such as knees, frames, or the curve of the stem, it was desirable to avoid the weakness of short grain. Timber in which the natural grain followed the required curves was necessary. In the old ship-building days, the shipwrights would go into the forest with templates of their requirements, looking for actual trees with the requisite bends of trunk or branches. A considerable industry flourished in supplying oak "crooks", ready-grown for just this purpose. In lighter boats, the smaller members involved could sometimes be bent to shape from straight-grained stock. The wood was softened by steam generated in a rudimentary boiler.

The main defence of a wooden hull against the entry of water through its myriad of seams is actually the swelling of the wood, caused by that water. Well-fitting, close seams can be swollen to be completely watertight but, in more open seams and in seams in planking with less water absorption, a layer of caulking must be hammered in between the planks. The swelling of the wood and the wedging effect of the caulking would, of course, just push the planking further apart, unless it was firmly strapped against the strain. This is the prime function of most framing, especially of the light, steamed, strapping frames to be seen in lighter hulls. In clinker planking, where the planks overlap, the main watertight load is on the plank fastenings, but the same strapping is necessary in case the inter-plank loads should actually split the planks themselves.

Only in quite small craft can the wood of the planking or even of the keel be long enough to run full length. Wood is usually joined lengthways by scarfing, and the ends are then secured together with fastenings. A straight-forward diagonal is used for planking, relying purely on the fastenings for its strength lengthwise. In all main framing likely to carry loads, the scarf is elaborated. If purely compression loads are expected, the scarf is blunt-ended but, where loads may vary, it is usual to add a hook in the centre of the joint as well. Where large wood members are to be fitted to each other, the normal wood tenon joint is often used, sometimes modified to form a shallow mortice in each member with a hardwood tenon piece introduced between them. The same approach is occasionally used where a double dovetail plate of hardwood is let flush into adjacent faces of members which are later to be clad, possibly with planking. The dovetail joint is extensively used for holding together the deck components, beams, carlings, etc. However, for boat-building, the joint is strengthened by arranging for the whole of the beam to be housed in its partner before the actual dovetail cutting occurs.

Knees in various forms are to be found at every point where corners have been strengthened: breasthooks and transom knees at the ends of the vessel, hanging knees where the frame is coupled to beam connections in order to stop the hull from wracking in one direction, and lodging knees under the deck planking, fitted horizontally to reduce wracking in the other direction. Large knees, called floors, are fitted across the keel. Their prime function is to hold the two sides of the boat together, but they also reinforce the hull to enable it to carry ballast keel loads and to help it resist the impact of a possible grounding.

Hulls are usually fastened with metal fastenings, although wood nails or treenails were used until quite late in the day. A hull is always moving slightly, either from the stresses of its life afloat, from various onboard loads, or from the very swelling and drying of its woodwork. The fastenings have to be strong and not brittle and are usually of iron, bronze, or copper. The old boat-builder normally made up his own fastenings from metal rod or bar. The copper was used for clench fastenings with the inner ends riveted down over washers. The iron or bronze fastenings were usually in the form of nut-and-screw bolts.

The main causes of deterioration in a wooden ship were rot and the electrolytic decay of fastenings. Perhaps the dreaded ship-worm and the gribble should also be mentioned. Dry-rot is a considerable enemy of all timber construction not exposed to air, and the best defence against it lies in the choice of timber. Some species, such as teak and some cedars, are more or less immune. Lacking these, it is necessary to rely on very good ventilation, and it is a basic principle for all good wooden boat-building that there should be passage for an air-flow past every part of the structure. Electrolytic decay not only affects the actual metal of the fastenings, but can also assist in the deterioration of the wood around the fastenings, so-called nail sickness.

Wherever they are found, the ship-worm and, to a lesser degree, the gribble have been the bane of shipowners. One a mollusc and the other a crustacean, they attack any bit of bare wood exposed to their greedy grasp. Heavy, oily woods, again such as teak, are not to their liking and are almost immune to attack. The classic defence for other timbers was to give them an overall sheathing of copper plates but, in some parts of the world, an external layer of planking was applied to the hull over a coating of heavy bitumen. This outer planking was fitted entirely for the feeding of ship-worms, in the hope that they would be content with this and not attack the structurally more important timber underneath.

The traditional wood boat-builder was not solely concerned with binding structural timbers into miracles of efficiency, for ships and boats were valued also for the amount of decoration which they carried, and the boat-builder counted among his skills the ability to turn out handsomely carved and painted figure-heads, trail boards, and stern carvings.

The arrival on the boating scene of waterproof, resin-based plastics in the middle of the twentieth century was, in its way, as cataclysmic an event as was the arrival of radio, electricity, or even of flying. Centuries of know-how became irrelevant almost overnight, and whole new horizons opened up for boating. Plastics, either in the form of adhesives for other materials or as constructional materials in their own right, meant that, for the first time, sizable hulls, which were effectively one single piece, could be produced in a wide range of sophisticated shapes.

It took perhaps twenty years for the full impact of this new technology to become clear. At first, the waterproof glues were used as a handy aid to traditional building, often as no more than a substitute for white lead bedding-compound. Marine plywood, however, which had been a very despised and ineffective boat-building material, was now accepted gladly and without reservation. With the advent of the new adhesives, it had suddenly changed, almost overnight, into a material universally used for bulkheads and joinery. The advantages of plywood for quickly and economically sheeting over large areas of hull, topsides, bottoms, and decks led to a vogue for hard-chine hulls, which coincided very conveniently with a good supply of cheap and powerful engines. Thousands of plywood runabouts as well as sailing dinghies were built, and the advantages of plywood hulls for even sizable yachts came to be appreciated.

When used for boat skinning, plywood was often wrapped round a structure of frames, stringers, and so on, in the conventional style used for a planked hull. There was, in fact, no need to hold the planks together against swelling and caulking, and in a high-speed boat the frames and the rows of fastenings to them were a definite structural disadvantage. Plywood is best used as a stressed-skin material in its own right, and modern plywood constructions are very different from the conventionally-built wooden boats. Plywood is supplied in flat sheets, a fact which severely limits the range of hull forms. Most plywood hulls, therefore, are flat-surfaced with a chine bilge. Some more sophisticated constructions have a form of inverted clinker planking, designed in direct conjunction with the internal structure, and plywood is often used as a composite, with glass-fibre connections laid over the joints.

Nearly every yard building in wood nowadays laminates such components as keels, stems, and sternposts into major subassemblies. The further development is to laminate up the hull skins themselves, making them in effect of a very similar construction to plywood sheets, but built up to the exact shape required for the hull. Extremely light and efficient hulls are produced by this method, and the designer is able to vary not only the thickness and number of laminations, but also the type of wood, to meet the differing stress requirements in different areas of the hull. The most popular method is called cold moulding, after the cold-setting adhesives employed. A wooden framework is set up in the required shape, and the major framing is set into it to be bonded directly to the skin. The first skin, of thin and comparatively narrow planks, is usually laid diagonally from keel to deck-edge and secured to the internal structure. The next layer is glued and secured over this; staple guns are often employed to keep the planks close. When the glue is dry, the staples are removed and another layer is put on. In this manner, a skin is built up of perhaps eight or nine layers, often finished with fore-and-aft veneers to give it the appearance of a traditional hull.

In hot moulding, the hull is built up in the same general manner as for cold moulding, then wheeled into an autoclave where pressure is applied by a vacuum- or pressure-operated rubber skin, and where the setting of the glue is triggered off by heat.

The boom in boat numbers is undoubtedly due to the introduction of hulls completely built of synthetic materials suitable for large-quantity production. Of these, the chief is still glass-reinforced polyester resin, and a hull of this material has all the virtues of the one-piece hull and needs little maintenance. Such a hull is usually built up in a mould from successive layers of resin and glass-thread material, integrated to a structural skin. Reinforcements and framing are added and, when dried and set, a more or less complete hull is removed from the mould. A moulded deck and, perhaps, a moulded interior are added, together with fittings and fit-out, and a production rate can be achieved which far outstrips the wildest dreams of most boat-builders of earlier years.

GRP is a comparatively heavy hull material and the resin, an oil derivative, is necessarily expensive. Competi-tion over prices among manufacturers has coincided with a yacht racing rule which tends to favour light-weight craft, and these combined pressures have put enormous emphasis on the production of ever cheaper and lighter hulls. GRP as a structural material has good strength but only modest rigidity, and a plain GRP hull has to be thicker than it really needs to be only to attain an acceptable stiffness. It was an obvious step, therefore, to improve this aspect and reduce weight by introducing a light-weight material as a sandwich filling between thin layers of hull skin. That normally used is either one of the foamed plastics, such as polyurethane, or blocks of balsa wood used with the end grain across the sandwich.

The advantages of GRP were originally more or less limited to minimum production runs of about twenty or thirty hulls, over which the high initial costs of the carefully finished plugs and moulds could be amortized. Many one-off hulls have been made without these expensive moulds, using instead a basic set of wooden moulds as employed for a conventional hull. Over these moulds is set some core material, such as foam-plastics sheeting, cedar-wood strip planking, or a sheet material of thin glass rods, to give the basic hull form. The GRP is then applied in layer after layer, finishing with a relatively rough exterior to be sanded and ground, painted and filled back to an acceptable yacht finish. The hull is then taken off the moulds, and a similar skin is applied to the interior. Provided that the adhesion to the core material has been properly catered for, such hulls can prove economic and successful, even for the demands of offshore racing.

The welded metal hull has almost completely superseded the riveted variety. Steel is still the natural material with which to build the bigger hulls, and it can be successful for hulls down to 33 ft (c. 10 m) in length, when these are built by a specialist constructor. Sand-blasting the hull and coating it with zinc spray or epoxy resin have greatly controlled rust, and foam-plastics insulation has made steel yachts more habitable in hot or cold climates. Aluminium is more expensive than steel and requires special inert-gas shielding during welding, but it is a pleasantly clean and light material, which is becoming increasingly popular for yachts and boats. In recent years, the introduction of new welding alloys for aluminium has very much cut down the problems of electrolytic corrosion of the hull. The light weight is of especial value for performance hulls, both power and sail, and the welded metal hull is easily cut and altered for improvements. The lower size limit for the welded hull, either steel or aluminium, lies in the minimum thickness of plating suitable for welding —something of the order of 0.03 in (0.8 mm). However, smaller aluminium boats are built in quantities by stretch-forming sheets over a metal die—a technique taken over from the aircraft industry. Other attempts to produce metal boats include explosion forming inside a hollow die and the draping or vacuum forming of special grades of metal over a mould.

The largest production runs of small boats are made in thermoplastics, such as ABS or polythene. A flat sheet is clamped in a frame and exposed to a battery of carefully controlled heaters until it is soft. Then it is blown into an approximately boat-sized bubble, which is collapsed over a hull former by vacuum. The moulding is then removed, perhaps to be combined with other mouldings and buoyancy material to make the finished hull, with a total production time of perhaps an hour from sheet to finished, saleable boat. The length of boats produced by this process is, at the time being, limited to 23–26 ft (c. 7–8 m) by the available sizes of sheets and machines.

One or two ranges of boats are being produced by rotational casting although, again, the lengths of these boats are limited by the sizes of machines available. In this process, the thermoplastic material is fed in the form of pellets or powder into a double mould, which is then rotated in every direction inside a large heating oven. Through the centrifugal force, the melted plastic is distributed all over the inside of the mould, producing, when cooled, a pair of boat-shaped mouldings.

One of the most desirable assets any boat can have is to be self-buoyant, and the obvious material to use in order to attain this is one of the foamed plastics. Many boats have been produced from this material, but they have generally suffered from extremely vulnerable, soft surfaces which must be protected. Self-skinning foams, where the plastic forms a solid outside skin with a fully foamed interior, have great potential for the inexpensive, mechanically built boats of the future. The foamed plastics are, in any case, here to stay in boat-building, and it is likely that every single production boat contains a good measure of them somewhere in its make-up.

People have been building craft of concrete during all of this century, but only comparatively recently have such craft been built in small sizes. Concrete construction is much more attractive than its name and components would suggest. For commercial hulls it has the obvious advantages of durability and strength, but it is also used a great deal for one-off yacht and powerboat hulls. A basic wire skeleton for the hull form is clad in successive layers of chicken wire bound close to approximately the required finished thickness. The next stage is, however, critical: the whole hull has to be plastered up, with complete integrity, to its final interior and exterior finish in one go. The setting concrete then has to be kept under very controlled conditions of humidity for about two weeks, while it dries slowly and evenly. The initial cheapness of the materials and the ease with which one or two people can, except for the plastering, do all the assembly work make this a very attractive construction, particularly for amateurs.

Until comparatively recent times, sailing-boats were designed by their builders and not by separate and specialist "designers". The change-over to modern designing methods for ships, however, started as long ago as the seventeenth century, when the European navies started to come under the centralized control of government authorities. The numbers of ships involved and the sheer logistical problems of supplies made standardization of ships a necessity. The obvious problem arose of how to communicate the form required for the new ships to numbers of different builders, all hitherto keen to build differently. Models had been widely used for assessment but obviously made a cumbersome method of communication. The architects of the new navies were more or less compelled to spend a great deal of time inventing methods of putting three-dimensional forms down onto paper. This pretty problem obsessed naval architects for a century or more, a fact which may explain why the lines plan for a sailing vessel carries such high and almost mystical regard to this very day.

The standard method of drawing a lines plan consists of making imaginary cuts through the hull form in three or sometimes four planes. By placing the cuts at regular spacings and by fully dimensioning each shape revealed by the cuts, the naval architects made it possible for a builder to draw full-size, in his mould loft, a hull form conceived elsewhere. The drawing of a lines plan so that all the shapes marked lock accurately together is a complex geometrical problem. There are various methods, from a laborious drawing and checking, and re-drawing and re-checking, of each line, by a largely trial-and-error process, to several elegant, heavily controlled methods, which are virtually mistake-proof. The latter are usually based on a very exact grid lattice, cutting the hull form at regular stations fore and aft, on horizontal water-lines, on vertical bow and buttock lines, and on a heavy series of diagonals spreading downward from the centre-line. On this are set the main controlling lines for the proposed hull form. The profile, the mid-section, and the main water-line are more or less standard starting points for designers, together with any local shapes they need for any particular design. From points picked up from the three-dimensional grid of these features, the spots can be marked where the first diagonal must pass. A long, flexible batten can then be held to these spots by means of lead weights, so that this very important curve can be marked in. This, in turn, leads to more spots being available for marking the next curve—perhaps a buttock line—and so on, building up all the time until the last curve to be put in has a very exact and very fair curve spotted out for it by perhaps twenty or thirty points.

It is, of course, a cumbersome process and involves such a degree of labour that we now turn for help to computers. The computer lines plan has been possible for some years and is already being used in many offices. It has the great overriding advantage of allowing a whole range of variations to be checked against the requirements for a single vessel, whereas two or at most three possibilities might have been considered with hand-drawn lines.

Although the work of a modern yacht designer covers all aspects, from electronics to lavatory sea-cocks, it is the shaping of the hull which is supposed to be his prime function. The hull of a sailing-boat is certainly complex in its action, involving the balancing of a whole range of conflicting requirements. The power supply is not reasonably constant as in a powerboat, and therefore it has to be designed for efficiency throughout the yacht's speed range. The action of the wind on the sails and spars causes the yacht to heel over, and as the wind changes speed and relative direction, so does the hull of the yacht in relation to the water. A whole range of speed possibilities may, therefore, occur with the yacht at any angle of heel. Throughout all this, the yacht must be easily controllable, even when plunging in a complicated sea-way.

The biggest overriding factor in the design of sailing-boats is, however, the current racing rules. The great majority of yachts take part in some form of racing and must have a reasonable rating if they are to be successful. When the early racing rules penalized beam, yachts grew extravagantly narrow, with heavy lead keels to hold up their rigs. When the later rules, in the interests of offshore sailing, penalized long overhangs, boats grew short and

dumpy. Now that ballast and overall weight have become important, yacht designers are again looking to light-displacement craft, with great beam to hold up the sail plan. The modern offshore racer is a fairly mettlesome steed, generally to be sailed without relaxation, and its cruising cousins have begun to show some of the same nervous characteristics.

The actual performance of a sailing-boat depends, like that of every vehicle, very much on the power-to-weight ratio. The weight is easily assessed, but the power depends not only on the rig but also on the ability of the hull to hold the rig up. In modern yachts, the hull power comes mostly from beam, leaving the ballast as little more than a safety factor to right the yacht after a knock-down.

When the yacht is travelling slowly, the greatest resistance to its movement comes from the friction of its surfaces in the water, and one of the advances of recent design is to cut this skin friction to a minimum by reducing the keel surfaces. As speed increases, so does wave making, until the wave-making drag is the bigger factor. Top speed is obviously of utmost interest and, in all except the fastest and lightest craft, this is dependent on the position of the resulting wave train in relation to the hull. The maximum speed is reached when there is but one trough between bow and stern, and the second wave is as far aft as will reasonably support that end of the hull. With the boat in this trim, the wave making is heavy but, by filling out the bow and stern or by adding bow bulbs and stern bustles, it is possible both to reduce the wave-making drag and to extend the wave support to a greater distance apart, thereby allowing a higher speed without the stern sinking. Some sailing-boats, such as modern dinghies and some larger craft of related shape, can surf through this wave speed-barrier to reach the state of planing, where the speed is virtually unfettered and controlled only by the power available from the sails and hull.

Thanks to their sailing-rigs, most yachts are comparatively easy in their motion when rolling but are often, in some sea conditions, given to heavy pitching. Something can be done about this by arranging the ballast and other onboard weights to avoid any pendulum motion likely to be synchronous with sea conditions. Many yachts are deliberately designed with widely differing bulks in the ends to dampen out this pitching. Apart from affecting the comfort of those on board, pitching ruins the air-flow through the sail system.

Hull form is also heavily related to the waters in which the boat is to operate. Seagoing boats are generally of moderate proportions in all directions, since they have to be prepared for the extremes of conditions and have to operate in waves. Inshore boats, which are not used in rough conditions, can grow excesses of lengthy ends and delicate rigs. Cruising vessels, on the other hand, have to be fairly bulky to accommodate stores and equipment, and built strongly to take the knocks of commercial harbours.

A great deal of hull and rig development is done before the final lines of a new sailing-boat are drawn. Hull models are put through their paces in test tanks primarily built for steamship models, and sailing-rigs are tested in wind tunnels designed for aircraft. A large and useful science has built up around both forms of trial, and a new design may involve a considerable advance worked out first in the laboratories ashore. In the tank, a model of exact shape,

scale weight, and inertia is run through a range of speeds, leeway angles, and angles of heel, and both the resistance and the side forces are measured, giving a relatively accurate assessment of the full-size worth. The models can also be tried in head seas generated in tanks, but these trials are not really representative as head seas are rarely met under sail. Unfortunately, the costs and complexities of testing models against representative wave directions in a "big-ship" open manoeuvring tank are still too heavy. Tests of radio-controlled models, however, give visual assessments of some worth.

A racing sail-boat is designed to make use of the muscle power of its crew members to the limit of their physical capacity. They are required on board for sail handling and, to a minor extent, for their weight as portable ballast. A boat is only winning races when it is moving as fast as it will go. Tacking and sail-changing time is, therefore, of paramount importance. For the former, bigger and bigger winches are being devised, with interconnected driving systems which now allow practically the whole crew to help in getting the sheet home and the yacht travelling again. There is plenty of time to prepare sails for changing, but the actual time between having, say, two different headsails in full operation must be cut to a minimum. Similarly, with spinnakers and big boy sails, the speed of setting and handing is critical, and large, clear deck-spaces for the working parties are essential.

Cruising yachts, on the other hand, are usually short-handed and not so ambitious in their sail setting. People out cruising are usually prepared to luff up or run off to help get sails in or down. Much more important on a cruising boat are, possibly, the arrangements for reducing sail in a squall and for handling anchors and other items, which put a heavy physical load on a short-handed crew. For this, the cruising boat can put up with the modest aerodynamic inefficiencies of roller-reefing headsails and mainsails set with reef pendants ready rove.

Every hundred years or so, there is a vogue for multihulls. Their advantages—great stability and modest resistance—lead to very high speeds through the water in small craft and to comfortable living, with room to stand upright, in yachts of cruising proportions. Without a general need for ballast to support the sail plan, the overall weight of a multihull is small and, therefore, the size and cost of the rig are reduced. Modern materials now allow for the multihull form to be built at a lower cost than in the past. The designer of such craft has several problems, of which the first may be simply that of accurately estimating the stresses on the hull in a sea-way. As important as anything, however, is the stability which, although very high when the multihull is upright or nearly so, falls off very quickly. In a catamaran, it is obvious that a very fraught balancing act is in progress as soon as the weather hull is lifting. The trimaran has a longer range of positive stability by virtue of the need to submerge the lee float, but either form, once on its beam ends, will quickly capsize, unless it carries ballast keels or stability wings. This in itself is bad enough, but multihulls are also extremely stable upside-down and more difficult to right than they are to turn over. Mast-head floats are frequently fitted to avoid the complete capsize. By careful design of the stability curves, the designer has to give the crew time to cancel out any capsizing forces by, for example, letting sheets go. The wide beam and high athwartships stability are sometimes gained at the expense of fore-and-aft stability, and multihulls are often in need of buoyancy to hold the lee bow up. The designer may fit knuckles above water, and even bulbous bows or semi-submersible forms under water, to achieve the forward lift and buoyancy. There are many views on the spacing and form of the hulls, and this is an area where extensive tank testing has been able to give a good lead. The main enemy of the multihull form, and possibly the reason why it waxes and wanes in the shipping and yachting world, is the simple fact of life that two hulls must cost more to build and fit out than one.

The hull and deck-works of a modern sailing-yacht amount to about a third of its total value in workmanship, materials, and equipment. Chief among the extra costs are those of the sailing equipment, for a modern rig is something of a precision instrument. The cost of a mast, a boom, and an outfit of sails, ropes, cleats, winches, wires, and rigging screws, even in a relatively simple form, adds up to appreciably more than that of, say, a diesel engine giving the same speed. An owner spending freely on a top-class racing boat will nowadays command the best engineering skills and craftsmanship, working to aircraft standards of precision. The fittings for production boats represent the same levels of approach but are geared to multiple output to cover a range of requirements. It is all a far cry from the days of sticks and string and boat-yard blacksmiths, but the results are evident in the thousands of small boats which put out to sea in all weathers without their owners being unduly worried about the rig.

The tree is such an obvious thing for the making of masts (grown by nature, it would appear, especially for the job) that it would seem difficult to replace. Masts were, of course, made from trees for centuries, sometimes from a single tree and sometimes, for big ships, from several trees bound together with iron hoops. Such spars, amply rigged with stays and shrouds, answered all the wind propulsion requirements of ships until the industrial revolution produced iron tubes which were lighter and stronger. Weight aloft, as seen by any simple assessment of balance, is of great importance in ships. In yachts, it is doubly so, because a few pounds of weight saved at the mast-head can be balanced by, perhaps, fifty times as much removed from the ballast, giving a quite disproportionate saving in the overall weight. The tree, in fact, is not an economical spar in a strength-to-weight assessment, since the central core is largely superfluous in strength terms and only carries unnecessary weight high up in the mast. From the earliest days of competitive yachting, attempts have been made to construct more efficient spars, usually with wood built up into hollow sections, but also with riveted aluminium plates and, for bigger sizes, with steel. The arrival of waterproof glues changed the picture, and hollow wooden spars, usually of spruce, became almost universal. The Bermudan rig requires an attachment for the mainsail all the way down the aft side of the mast, and the need for other rigging attachments precluded the employment of hoops, as used for gaff sails. In earlier days, a continuous track of brass bar was fitted, but this was soon superseded by the lighter and more convenient extruded aluminium track with light-weight, sliding luff fittings. It was but a short step to extrude the whole mast section, including the luff track, and such masts were not only light but could also be built to much closer engineering tolerances. Further, the attachment of fittings by riveting and welding was much easier, and the aluminium mast is now almost universally used.

Most sail plans are still designed on the basis of a rigid mast, although the bendy mast is beginning to come into greater use. A mast is largely designed as a simple strut to hold up the rigging, which is calculated both to take the sailing loads and to hold up the mast. There are usually two or more support points for the side rigging but, in a sloop rig, only mast-head support in the fore-and-aft direction. The fore-and-aft dimensions of a mast, therefore, have to be greater than the athwartships dimensions, leading, with aerodynamic fairing, to the typical oval or pear-shaped sections.

The average mast and rigging are designed for a theoretical worst case of wind, strong enough to force the yacht down onto its beam-ends. Worse winds have been known, particularly in the roaring forties, but in normal yachting, mast failure is comparatively rare.

The modern Bermudan rig consists essentially of relatively small sails, stretched tightly into highly efficient working shapes. A quite modest distortion will have an undue effect on the efficiency of the air-flow and, therefore, the shape stability of each sail is of great importance. Early sail materials, such as flax canvas, stretched too much under wind pressure, and sails made of such materials blew into generous curves just when the aerodynamics prescribed that they should be as flat as possible. Cotton sails are lighter and more stable, but they have been overtaken by sails made from man-made fibres. The market for yacht sails has also grown to the point where special cloths, of Terylene or Dacron, are woven for the best values in terms of weight, stretch, and impermeability. The efficiency of sails has risen with extensive wind-tunnel and other research work, but still the principal problem remains the conflict between the differing shapes required of the same sail for best efficiency at differing air-flow speeds. The mainsail is now generally built for an average wind strength and fitted with a wide range of adjustments, zips, cunninghams, bendy booms, etc., so that its shape can be adjusted to a degree while it is set. The bendy mast is another means of adjusting the camber of the sail aerofoil when the yacht is under way, but this involves stresses which are difficult to calculate and are still largely a subject for continued experiments.

Under the current rating rules the spinnaker is only controlled by outline dimensions, leaving great incentive for the sail designer to build in high-lifting balloon forms to allow room for further legitimate canvas to be set below it. This largely uncontrolled area is attractive for use on other points of sailing, and the spinnaker is blossoming in all manner of patent cuts which allow it to be used efficiently when reaching and pointing higher. The interest of designers is concentrated now on spinnaker staysails and light sails, to be set inside a spinnaker to augment the area and to direct the air-flow into it to greater efficiency.

The main control for any sail lies in its sheets and, with the predominantly large genoa headsails to be sheeted home, powerful sheet winches are now essential equipment for every yacht. In the good old days, sails were sheeted home by a large crew, using blocks and tackles. Now, on the short-handed family yacht a winch is used, while on the ocean racer the large crew uses large winches for sheer speed.

The main drive in the development of deck gear comes from competitive sailing, where light weight is important, and strength and reliability are essential. The modern winches, for instance, are largely built from aluminium castings, with high-quality steels for their gearing and, sometimes, PTFE non-stick, low-friction bearings. Because of the need to use full crew energy throughout the sheeting cycle, winches have been two-speed for years and are now often three-speed, with interconnection systems to allow additional crew to be employed. This level of care and attention to detail is to be found in every aspect of deck fittings, with high-efficiency blocks of all shapes and sizes and a wide range of rope-jamming equipment to take the place of many cleats.

Jam cleats and high loadings put very heavy wear on the various ropes in use with the rig. Modern conditions have again put the natural materials at a disadvantage, and the ropes used afloat are no longer the tarred Italian hemp or the Manilas of tradition. Ropes made from polyester strands—the Terylenes and Dacrons—are over twice as strong as the traditional ropes and have low stretch and very good wear characteristics. The polyamide fibres, such as nylon, are even stronger, but they have a very high stretch capacity. This, on the other hand, makes them especially valuable for absorbing shock loads, such as those on anchor cables. Some of the other plastics, such as polythene and polypropylene, can be made into low-cost ropes which float. They are, therefore, especially useful for some mooring problems. Yacht rigging wires are used at quite a high proportion of their normal maximum working stresses, especially when the fore-and-aft rigging is wound up tight to reduce the stretch in the forestay affecting the set of the genoa. So important is this aspect of modern sailing that yachts are often fitted with hydraulic backstay tensioners, whereby the load on the stays can be heavily increased to absorb the stretch. Wire rigging of an essentially spiral construction is bound to stretch and, in the general fight for tight luffs, increasing use is being made of rod rigging of stainless steel, threaded into standard end fittings. The metal bar is smaller and smoother than the wire, though the prime reason for using rod rigging is the reduced stretch. The stainless steel used has, in general, high-ductility characteristics in addition to its high breaking strain, and so the rods are not quite as vulnerable to misuse or snatch loads as they might seem.

Stainless steel itself is a common material for yacht fittings. It comes in several grades of finish, strength, and freedom from rust marks for, although very attractive as a metal, it is not quite as "stainless" as some people expect from its name. Aluminium in marine grades is normally anodized to give it an attractive silver, gold, or black finish. Other materials commonly used are bronze and Tufnol—a cotton fabric, bonded under pressure with phenolic resins to give a material extremely resistant to deterioration in a marine environment.

Powerboats are designed in all shapes and sizes for a wide manner of duties. The two principal influences on their design, after those of size and cost, are the speed requirements and the waters for which the boat is intended. Powerboats can be roughly divided into three distinct types according to their speed ranges. Displacement boats are so called because, throughout the whole range of speeds in which they operate, the hull is supported entirely by its buoyancy, which, of course, is its displacement. In this range the limiting factor is, as for sailing-boats, the position of the stern wave, which reaches its limit in relation to the hull at speeds of 1.4 times the square root of the water-line length in feet (2.44 times the square root of the water-line length in metres). If a normal-shaped hull is pushed any faster, the stern wave breaks away from the hull which, deprived of aft support, takes up a very heavy bow-up attitude. Some stern forms will actually be sucked down, which leads to inundation and, possibly, sinking. Either way, the practical limits of speed have obviously been reached. However, there are boats which do go faster. These have to be shaped so that the moving water itself provides support to lift the stern at these critical speeds. Given enough power to blast the hull completely up the slope of its bow wave, the boat will start to surf, with the support for the hull taken more and more by this planing action, and less and less by the buoyancy effect. Powerboats with this capability are said to have planing hulls. True planing starts at speeds of the order of 3 times the square root of the water-line length in feet (5.5 times the square root of the water-line length in metres), and is a very desirable state for a fast boat. However, for many reasons some vessels have to operate in the intermediate speed range, and these are called "semi-displacement" boats.

The buyer of a boat for use in flat water probably looks for initial stability as its prime virtue. For many people, the feeling of the boat giving under their feet when they step on board is distinctly alarming, and to them, being able to move around the boat while, say, fishing, without everything tipping is a definite advantage. At the other end of the scale, the rough-water seaman positively prefers what he calls an easy motion, with the boat giving gently to every change of crew and sea. A boat with the high initial stability preferred by some people for inshore waters will tend to roll quickly back after meeting a wave. A quick, hard, rolling motion is extremely tiresome if it persists for more than a few seconds, and it can be dangerous enough at sea to pitch crew and equipment clean overboard. On the other hand, a sea boat with a relatively slow motion is very much more comfortable. In addition, a boat in a sea-way may find itself, solely by reason of wave action, at high angles of heel. The self-righting ability of the inland boat tapers off quickly with increased angle, but a wide range of stability is another of the characteristics of what is recognized as being a good sea boat.

As fast powerboats became increasingly reliable, with engines more powerful in proportion to weights and costs, they came to be considered and used for offshore racing and cruising. This meant that the boats had to be designed to be comfortable and safe at sea, if caught out in rough weather. A flat-bottomed, planing hull quickly develops an extremely severe motion, heavy enough to break up any hull, if driven hard in waves. To ease this impact loading, a hull with a deep V-shape was evolved, trading some of the high efficiency of the flat bottom for a softer ride. A paral-

lel development of spray rails meant that high-efficiency edges could be fitted to the actual planing areas, limiting the skin friction and, in fact, restoring the overall situation to a great measure. As compared to the earlier hulls, the deep V-shaped hull is a much more balanced hull form when considered simply as a seagoing hull, and it behaves much better at all speeds in rough water.

In offshore race-boats, for which rough-water speed is as much a race-winning factor as is top speed in sheltered waters, the V-shape has become even more exaggerated and combined with a long, fine hull, reminiscent of the earliest racers. At top speed, these boats plane on a minute area of the bottom, and in rough water, their very small frontal area means soft plunging into waves, while their length gives them a very quick pick-up of the speed lost. "Soft" is something of a comparative term in this context, since impact loads of 30 g have been measured in patrol craft, and even a quite modest offshore race-boat will be built for 12 g decelerations—twice the stress levels used for many military aircraft. Almost all equipment has to be specially built or strengthened for this kind of stress level, and the crew must be protected against the wild ride with thick cockpit paddings and special seats.

The principal factor in the performance of any powerboat lies in the power-to-weight ratio and, given weight, and hull size and type, quite accurate performance estimates can be made for different power installations relatively independent of any niceties of hull form, etc. The centre of gravity of the finished vessel has to be matched longitudinally and athwartships with the centre of buoyancy of the hull, if the boat is to float in the correct trim. The vertical height of the centre of gravity is a critical factor in any estimate of the stability characteristics of the finished boat. An important part of any design is, therefore, a close calculation of the weight and position of every detail of hull, deck-works, joiner-work, tanks and contents, machinery, equipment, and crew. It is a feature of powerboat design that this detailed examination is perhaps twice as important as it is in a sailing craft. The required factors of the design have to be met exclusively from the arrangement of every item on board, without a ballast keel to even up the equations. A power yacht has to float to its marks when launched, and there is little possibility of adjustment, the boat being required to meet speed trials with little chance for revision.

The design of propellers, especially for small, fast boats, is still something more than a science and involves both art and craft in the work of the designer and the metal finisher. Certain basic features, however, have an overriding influence on the final design. One is that there is a theoretical maximum speed for the blade tips beyond which the water-flow breaks down in a state of cavitation, and from which the maximum diameter can be calculated. Another is that the thrust from the propeller has to be carried by the surface of the blades and, again, over a certain blade pressure cavitation occurs. In order to obtain a satisfactory blade loading inside a satisfactory blade-tip speed, the rotation speed is adjusted by fitting reduction gearing between the engine and the stern gear. In fact, some very fast boats make use of the blade cavitation. They are equipped with so-called super-cavitating propellers, which induce cavitation and allow extremely high blade loadings, which in turn allow the use of very small

and light propellers and shafts of low drag, connected directly to high-speed engines.

Powerboats are swift compared with sailing-boats and, consequently, spend very much less time actually at sea. The work-load is small, and the main interests of the crew are in life afloat and in using the yacht as a base for life in a marine environment. Standards of life on board are, therefore, very important, and a quite average vessel will often have, in addition to its propulsion machinery, a generating plant, water heating and pressure sets, a sanitary system, air-conditioning, refrigeration, a deep freeze, and a fire-control system, all of which, when added to the electronic navigation equipment, make for an installation of a complexity somewhere between a house ashore and a small airliner. From the designer's point of view, the operation of the systems is almost as important to the vessel as are appearance and performance.

With the advent of plastics construction came the opportunity for the designer to think again about the actual shapes of boats and in this the powerboat, running as it does relatively upright, offers the greater opportunities. Many shapes which had been tried and appreciated in the past now became economic, and chief among these was the so-called rectangular boat. In a simple barge form, the advantages of stability, capacity, and cheapness of a rectangular box plan are obvious when used for heavy hulls run at comparatively low speeds. By introducing sophisticated and complex hull forms under the basic rectangular plan, however, the advantages of stability and capacity have been retained this time allied with speed. The average, modern, rectangular powerboat hull has two or three keel-type projections making for one or two tunnels under the hull. At speed, the greater part of the bow waves is generated inside the tunnels between these projections and, eventually, the hull rides on these accumulated and well-aerated waves. The motion is relatively soft, until the heights of the waves encountered are too big for the tunnels. The majority of rectangular boats are, therefore, of fairly small dimensions and used extensively for tenders and runabouts, which use the stability, capacity, and sheltered-water riding capability to best advantage.

Power catamarans and trimarans are becoming increasingly used wherever a large and stable working platform is required. Quite sizable vessels are being built for research, fishing, and even for use as yachts. The major problem, after the perennial one of structural loadings, is the relationship of the height of the hull weights to the modest fore-and-aft buoyancy available to support it when pitching. The most promising development in this area lies in the research and the practical trials which are being done with semi-submersible forms fitted under the hulls right forward. These introduce dynamic forces to counteract the pitching loads, and they also act as steadying vanes when the hull is stopped in the water.

There has always been an element of "do-it-yourself" about pleasure boating even if, in past days, it was only a question of touching up the varnish a bit. Until recent years, however, only a skilled amateur craftsman could contemplate building his own boat. The use of specialized boat-yard machinery and tools was not within the scope of the general yachtsman, and the materials needed required a good deal of skill in both selection and handling.

The introduction of marine grades of plywood was, perhaps, the greatest single factor in the growth of "do-it-yourself" building and kit construction. Here was a material which was readily available, of manageable size, and of a reliable and consistent quality. Even without power tools, the amateur felt able to tackle the building of his own boat and, as electric hand tools became usual features of the home workshop, so it became even more simple to handle such a job. Even now that GRP is a familiar material, more amateur-built small boats are probably made in marine plywood than in any other material.

"Do-it-yourself" is now an all-embracing field of boat construction. It is possible to buy boats in every stage of finish, from a bundle of wood and a set of plans to a complete boat requiring only painting. Numerous ranges of standard GRP boats are available for completion, with a choice of bare hull, hull and deck-works, bulkheads, engine bearers, etc., plus a list of equipment from which to choose the completing outfit. These standard boats will normally also have a set of plans prepared especially for the non-professional user. Since the designer cannot presuppose the same degree of expertise from amateurs as he could with the professionals of a boat-yard, the plans usually go into great detail, including sketches and full-size drawings of the more intricate sectors.

The designer preparing plans for amateur use has, of course, particular considerations to take into account. Each boat will in effect be a "one-off", and production machinery, or expensive moulds and frames, cannot be considered. A list of materials and information on how to cut them may be required. Here, the designer must take into account how materials, which must be generally available in the required sizes and qualities, can be used in the most economical way. Allowance has also to be made for probable wastage and errors, since the amateur has not a boat-yard's wood and fittings stores or pile of usable off-cuts to draw on in an emergency. When it comes to the fitting out, the designer must also particularly consider the dangers inherent in requiring the home builder to work with electrics, gases, inflammable fuels, or volatile resins.

The actual choice of boat to construct is one which only the home constructor himself can make, and many take the view that buying and fitting out an existing hull will put them a third of the way forward from the start, and will, hopefully, result in a recognizable end product with a reasonable resale value. Numerically, however, small dinghies are the boats most popular for home construction, probably because they are within the scope of most people and fit better into the home boat-yard area—garage, garden, basement, living-room, or bedroom.

The man whose designs have been built by more people in more parts of the world than any other is probably Jack Holt. He was a pioneer of home-construction design, and his *Cadet*, for instance, has probably set more sailors off on the road to the sea than has any other boat. The lineal descendant of the *Cadet* is the *Mirror* dinghy, also designed by Jack Holt, of which over 50,000 have been sold all over the world. This is a 10 ft 10 in (3.3 m) sailing, rowing, or outboard dinghy, which can be assembled by anyone, from teenager upwards, using quite commonplace tools and a method, devised by Barry Bucknell, employing modern materials to "stitch" a boat together in a manner which is, basically, one of the oldest in boat-building. The pre-cut kit of plywood parts is laid out, without frames, and tied together with short lengths of copper wire. There are only six main parts in the hull and, once these have been sewn together, the joints are covered in resin and glass-fibre tape to make them rigid and watertight. As with most kits, the *Mirror* comes with a step-by-step, illustrated guide to the building, and the constructor has the added bonus of being able to obtain a measurement certificate for his boat from the class association; a useful selling point, should it be required.

Following the success of the *Mirror*, the same team produced a larger boat, modestly called the *Miracle*, in an even more advanced form of the construction. This is a 12 ft 9.5 in (3.9 m) long boat which, in kit form, comes in a set of parts accurately machined to size and ingeniously arranged to fit together in jigsaw fashion. The bulkheads and frames, which form part of the finished boat, are held to the skin panels with mortice-and-tenon joints, so that the whole assembly stays together while the stitching and gluing, as for the *Mirror*, are done.

Kits such as these, which provide exercise of sufficient skill to give satisfaction while still offering every chance of a finished boat to a good general standard, are the backbone of the home-construction market. If he wants to, the amateur can also make his own spars, from scratch or from packs of parts, and sew his own sails, either from patterns or from a bolt of cloth and a detailed sail plan.

There are still people who will seek the experience of building the whole boat from the beginning, from wood, foam plastics, reinforced concrete, or GRP, but, for the less ambitious, the home-construction kit can be quite as satisfying in its way, if less onerous.

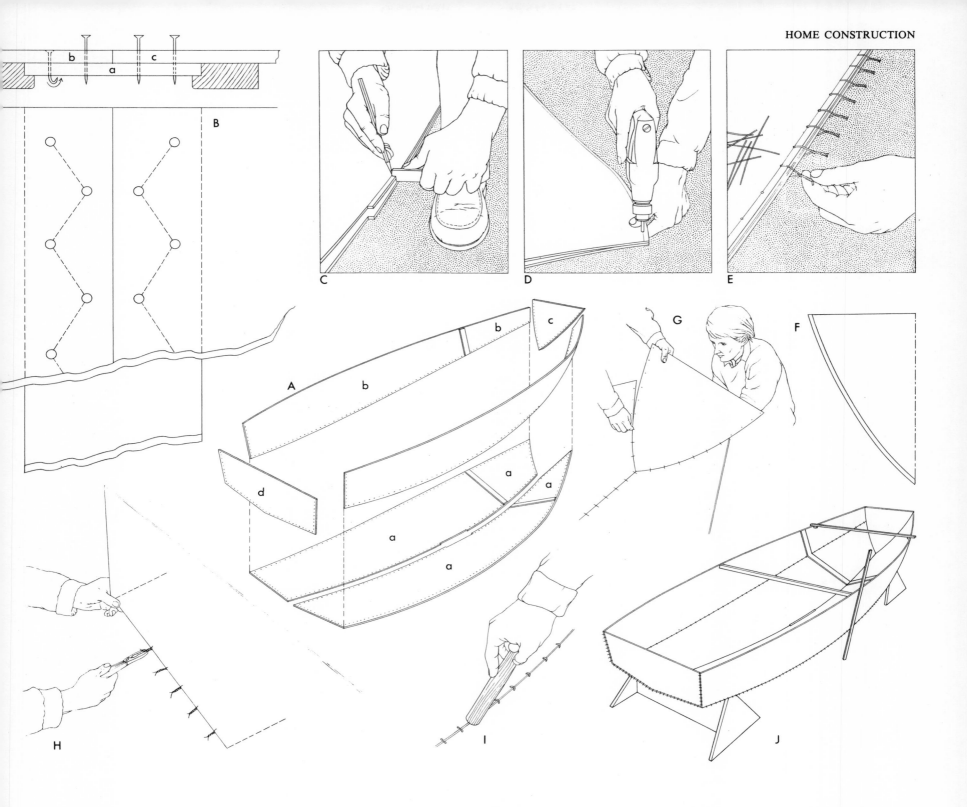

The *Mirror* one-design dinghy is one of the most popular boats available for home construction. An assembly kit with all the parts is provided.

A The main parts of the hull. (*a*) Bottom panels. (*b*) Side panels. (*c*) Fore transom. (*d*) Aft transom.

B Each of the side and bottom panels comes in two separate pieces, which must be joined together, end to end, by means of a butt strap (*a*). The two pieces (*b* and *c*) are placed end to end, with the butt strap along the join. Both pieces are then copper-nailed and glued to the butt strap. The copper nails are best hammered in a zigzag pattern, and their protruding ends are bent over, clipped off almost flush with the joined panel, and hammered flat on the panel. The projecting ends of the butt strap are sawn flush with the long ends of the panel, and the edge of the butt strap which will join the bottom section of the hull is bevelled to ensure a good fit between the side and bottom panels.

C Marking where the "stitching" holes will be. Each hole on a panel must be exactly opposite its "companion" hole (with which it will be stitched) on the adjoining panel.

D The holes are drilled. A hand drill may also be used.

E A piece of copper wire is threaded through each matching pair of holes, and its ends are twisted together.

F The fore transom is marked with a vertical line through its centre on both sides so that this can be matched to the hull's centre-line. The same is done with the aft transom.

G Fitting the fore transom.

H Pliers may be used to twist the wires on the bottom and side panels of the hull.

I Each loop of wire on the inside of the hull must be flattened against the hull by pressing against the loop with, say, a piece of wood.

J The alignment of the hull, using shaping cross struts and vertical props on either side of the longest cross strut.

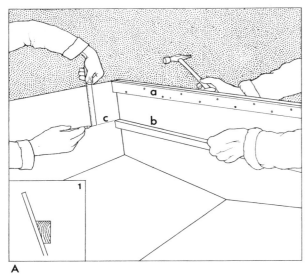

A

B

C

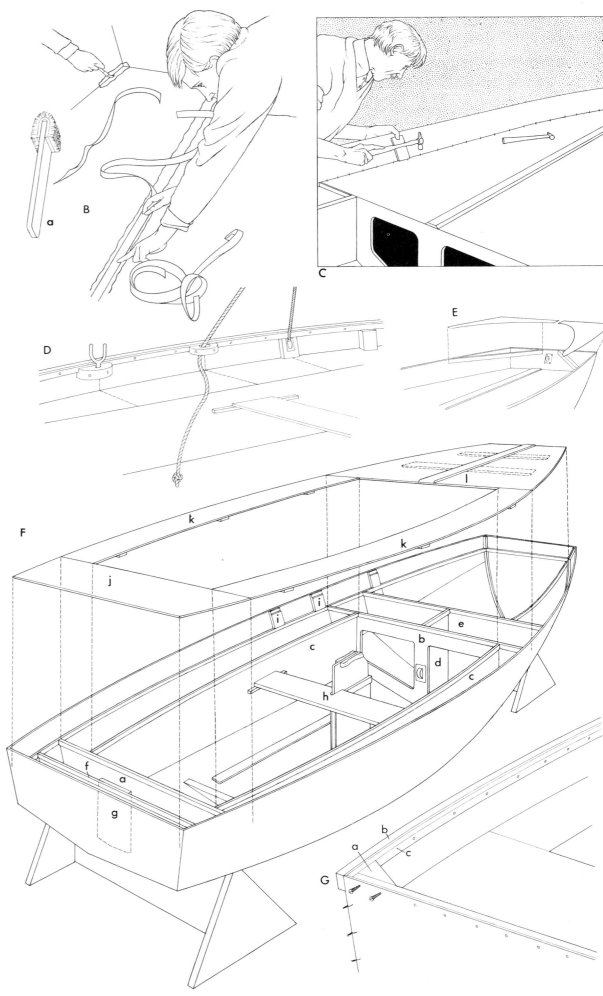

D

E

F

G

(Continuing the home construction of the Mirror *dinghy from the previous page.)*

A The transom top (*a*) is glued and copper-nailed to the inside of the aft transom, so that it is flush with the top of the transom. The two holes in the transom top should, after the top has been fixed in position, be continued out through the ply of the aft transom itself. The apertures serve to drain off any water taken aboard during sailing. The aft transom riser (*b*) is now brass-pinned and glued to the inside of the transom. Guide-lines (*c*) for the stringers are pencilled along the insides of the side panels, and the stringers are fitted in the same way as the aft transom riser. Lastly, the fore transom riser is fastened along the inside of the fore transom, thus making a complete line round the inside of the hull with the stringers and the aft transom riser. (**1**) A cutaway shows the side panel and the stringer, which must have its wide face uppermost.

B Before applying resin to the seams, the alignment of the hull must be checked. The seams are resined, using a spreader of the type shown here (*a*). It is simply a piece of wood with a small piece of carpet nailed to the head. Webbing sealing strips are then laid along the joints and

pressed into the shape of the hull. More resin is applied when the webbing is in position, and it is pressed down into the weave of the webbing.

C Fixing the fore deck in place. The two pieces which form the fore deck should be butt-strapped together by the same technique as before. When the deck is finally in position, the butt strap will lie on the top of the deck. The fore deck is first pinned with brass pins and then glued along the stowage bulkhead, matching in to the forward ends of the side decks. The centre-line of the deck should match those of the fore transom and of the stowage bulkhead.

D The positioning of the rowlock, the fairlead, and the two shroud blocks.

E The assembly of the bow shape.

F A partly exploded view of the *Mirror*, showing the order in which the various parts are assembled. (*a*) Aft bulkhead. (*b*) Stowage bulkhead. (*c*) Side-tank side. (*d*) Mast-step web. (*e*) Fore bulkhead. (*f*) Aft deck beam. (*g*) Aft deck beam support. (*h*) Thwart. (*i*) Shroud block. (*j*) Aft deck. (*k*) Side deck. (*l*) Fore deck.

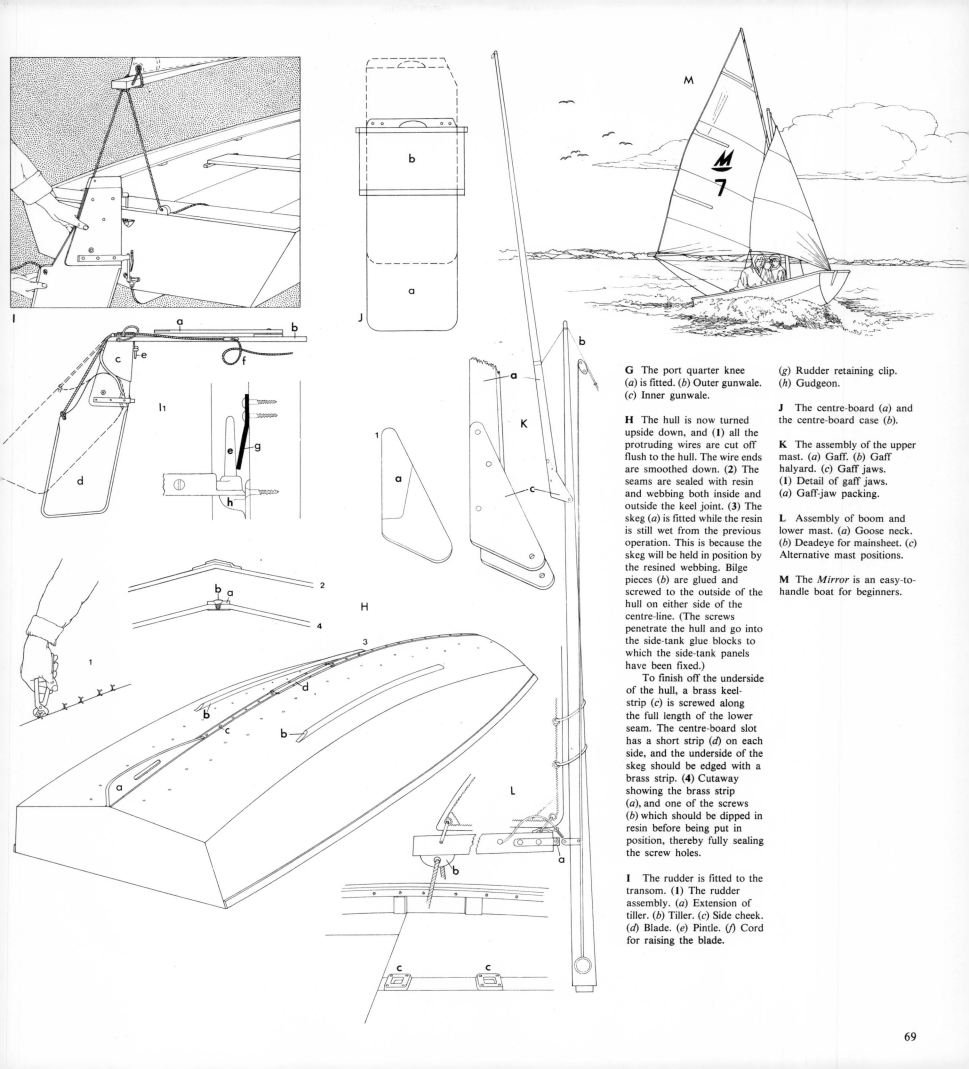

G The port quarter knee (*a*) is fitted. (*b*) Outer gunwale. (*c*) Inner gunwale.

H The hull is now turned upside down, and (**1**) all the protruding wires are cut off flush to the hull. The wire ends are smoothed down. (**2**) The seams are sealed with resin and webbing both inside and outside the keel joint. (**3**) The skeg (*a*) is fitted while the resin is still wet from the previous operation. This is because the skeg will be held in position by the resined webbing. Bilge pieces (*b*) are glued and screwed to the outside of the hull on either side of the centre-line. (The screws penetrate the hull and go into the side-tank glue blocks to which the side-tank panels have been fixed.)

To finish off the underside of the hull, a brass keel-strip (*c*) is screwed along the full length of the lower seam. The centre-board slot has a short strip (*d*) on each side, and the underside of the skeg should be edged with a brass strip. (**4**) Cutaway showing the brass strip (*a*), and one of the screws (*b*) which should be dipped in resin before being put in position, thereby fully sealing the screw holes.

I The rudder is fitted to the transom. (**1**) The rudder assembly. (*a*) Extension of tiller. (*b*) Tiller. (*c*) Side cheek. (*d*) Blade. (*e*) Pintle. (*f*) Cord for raising the blade.

(*g*) Rudder retaining clip. (*h*) Gudgeon.

J The centre-board (*a*) and the centre-board case (*b*).

K The assembly of the upper mast. (*a*) Gaff. (*b*) Gaff halyard. (*c*) Gaff jaws. (**1**) Detail of gaff jaws. (*a*) Gaff-jaw packing.

L Assembly of boom and lower mast. (*a*) Goose neck. (*b*) Deadeye for mainsheet. (*c*) Alternative mast positions.

M The *Mirror* is an easy-to-handle boat for beginners.

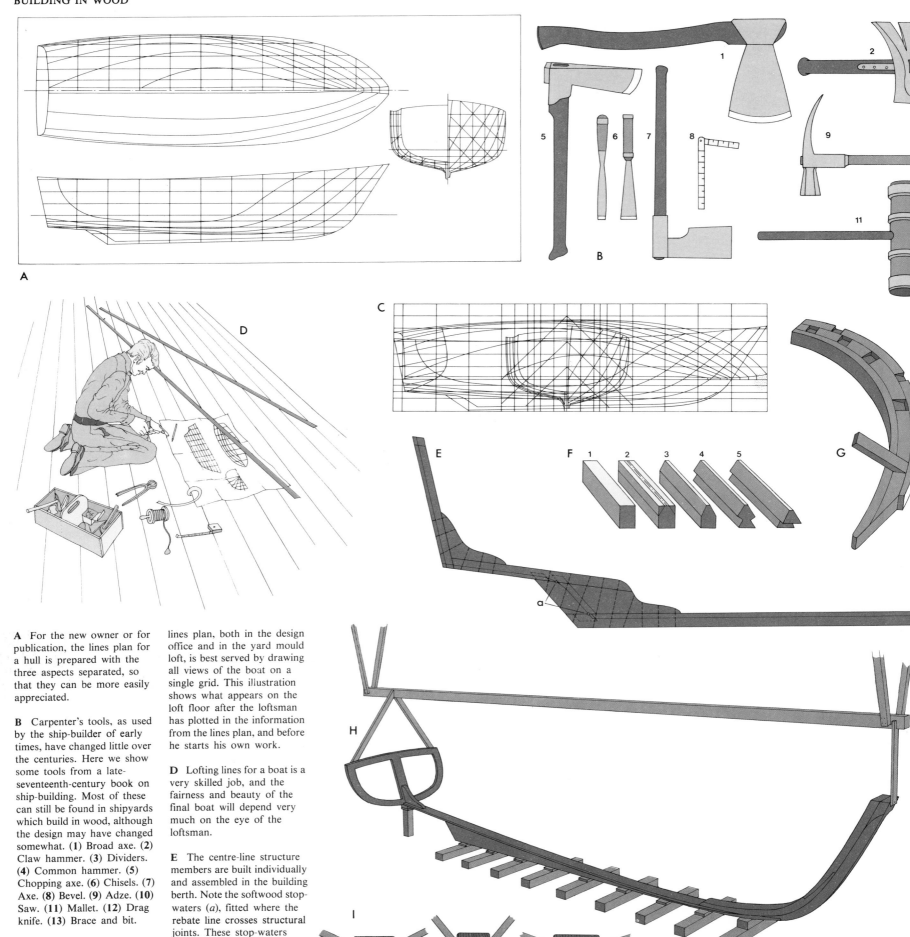

A For the new owner or for publication, the lines plan for a hull is prepared with the three aspects separated, so that they can be more easily appreciated.

B Carpenter's tools, as used by the ship-builder of early times, have changed little over the centuries. Here we show some tools from a late-seventeenth-century book on ship-building. Most of these can still be found in shipyards which build in wood, although the design may have changed somewhat. (**1**) Broad axe. (**2**) Claw hammer. (**3**) Dividers. (**4**) Common hammer. (**5**) Chopping axe. (**6**) Chisels. (**7**) Axe. (**8**) Bevel. (**9**) Adze. (**10**) Saw. (**11**) Mallet. (**12**) Drag knife. (**13**) Brace and bit.

C The need for great accuracy in the drawing of the lines plan, both in the design office and in the yard mould loft, is best served by drawing all views of the boat on a single grid. This illustration shows what appears on the loft floor after the loftsman has plotted in the information from the lines plan, and before he starts his own work.

D Lofting lines for a boat is a very skilled job, and the fairness and beauty of the final boat will depend very much on the eye of the loftsman.

E The centre-line structure members are built individually and assembled in the building berth. Note the softwood stop-waters (*a*), fitted where the rebate line crosses structural joints. These stop-waters inhibit the entry of water through that joint.

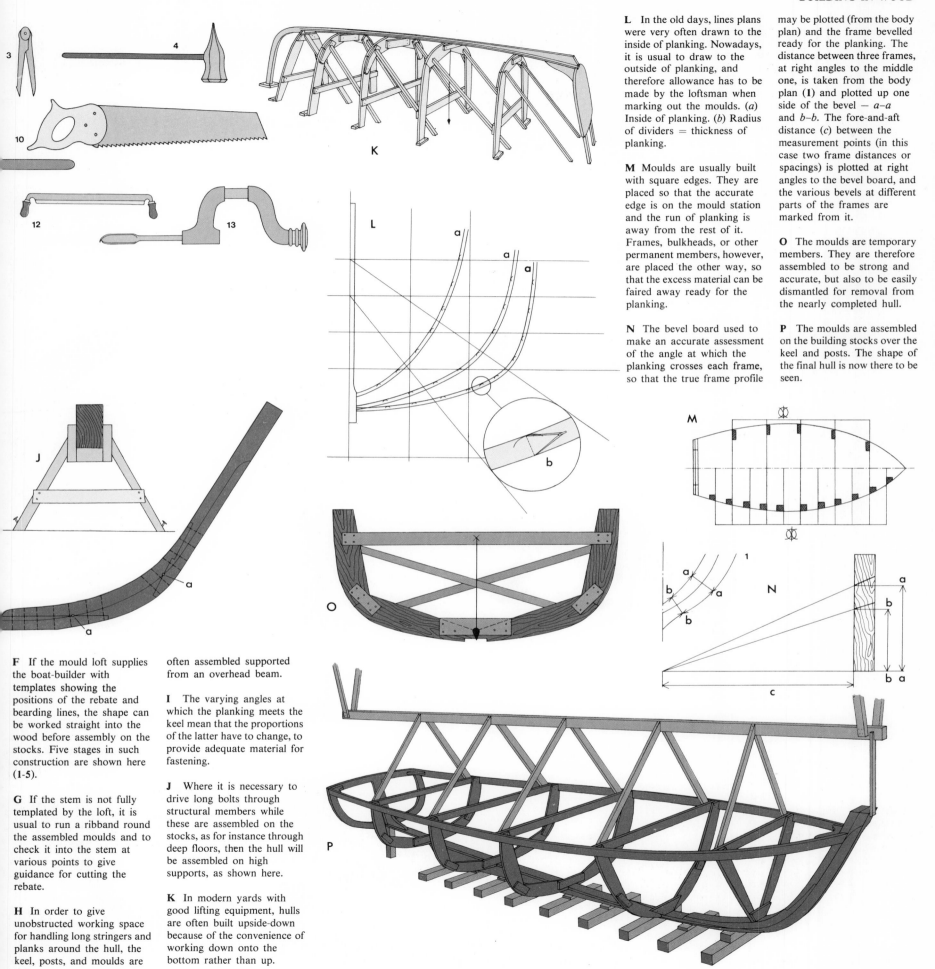

L In the old days, lines plans were very often drawn to the inside of planking. Nowadays, it is usual to draw to the outside of planking, and therefore allowance has to be made by the loftsman when marking out the moulds. (*a*) Inside of planking. (*b*) Radius of dividers = thickness of planking.

M Moulds are usually built with square edges. They are placed so that the accurate edge is on the mould station and the run of planking is away from the rest of it. Frames, bulkheads, or other permanent members, however, are placed the other way, so that the excess material can be faired away ready for the planking.

N The bevel board used to make an accurate assessment of the angle at which the planking crosses each frame, so that the true frame profile

may be plotted (from the body plan) and the frame bevelled ready for the planking. The distance between three frames, at right angles to the middle one, is taken from the body plan (**1**) and plotted up one side of the bevel — *a–a* and *b–b*. The fore-and-aft distance (*c*) between the measurement points (in this case two frame distances or spacings) is plotted at right angles to the bevel board, and the various bevels at different parts of the frames are marked from it.

O The moulds are temporary members. They are therefore assembled to be strong and accurate, but also to be easily dismantled for removal from the nearly completed hull.

P The moulds are assembled on the building stocks over the keel and posts. The shape of the final hull is now there to be seen.

F If the mould loft supplies the boat-builder with templates showing the positions of the rebate and bearding lines, the shape can be worked straight into the wood before assembly on the stocks. Five stages in such construction are shown here (1-5).

G If the stem is not fully templated by the loft, it is usual to run a ribband round the assembled moulds and to check it into the stem at various points to give guidance for cutting the rebate.

H In order to give unobstructed working space for handling long stringers and planks around the hull, the keel, posts, and moulds are

often assembled supported from an overhead beam.

I The varying angles at which the planking meets the keel mean that the proportions of the latter have to change, to provide adequate material for fastening.

J Where it is necessary to drive long bolts through structural members while these are assembled on the stocks, as for instance through deep floors, then the hull will be assembled on high supports, as shown here.

K In modern yards with good lifting equipment, hulls are often built upside-down because of the convenience of working down onto the bottom rather than up.

BUILDING IN WOOD

A If the framing has to be notched into the keel or stem, the notch is tapered, not only to maintain the keel strength, but also to give good drainage to avoid rot.

B The frames (a) are held together across the keel (b) by a large wooden member called a floor (c). The planking (d) is attached to the frame. (e) Garboard strake. (f) Chock under frame leaves waterway, or limber hole, along heel.

C Floors fitted to small frames have to be fitted right up to the planking in order to give proper room for the fastenings. In this example, the waterways will be carved in the bottom of the floors or

in the keel, and the ship-side gaps filled with tar.

D Steel plate or wrought-iron floors are frequently used in place of wood. In this example, a double-plate floor (a) is fitted with a keelson plate (b) to balance the fastening to the keel (c) evenly.

E There are many varieties of steam box, but they all have a basic boiler pouring steam into an enclosed space, in which the timbers are heated for bending. (1) End view.

F In delicate boats or where framing is very heavy, it is sometimes necessary to bend the hot steamed frames over a jig.

G The hot frame is finally snugged down into its final shape and held by clamps to the ribbands.

H The hot wood is brought as fast as possible from the steam box and carefully bent into the hull framing.

I The bent frames are here being assembled in conjunction with the boat's final gunwales and temporary ribbands to give the required shape.

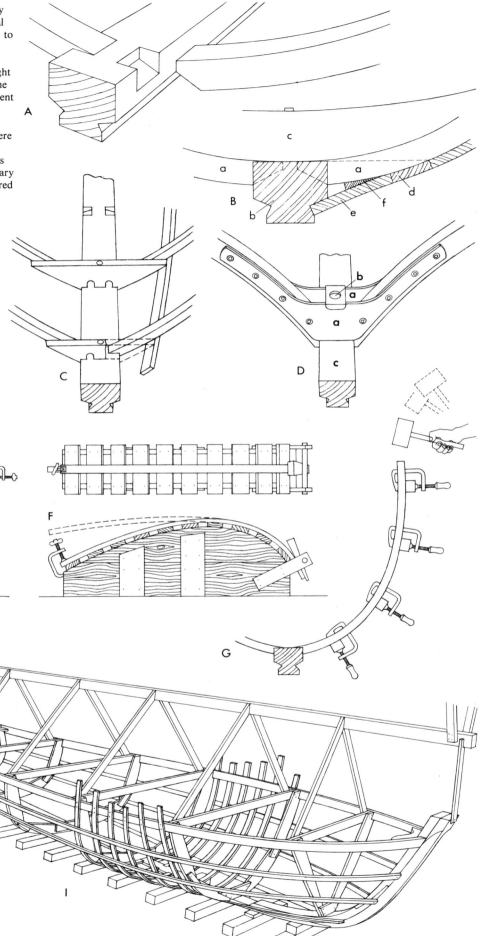

72

O The plank ends are rebated into the stem with plenty of wood for the fastenings.

P The ends of clinker planking have to be delicately rebated to each other, so as to lie smoothly in the stem rebate.

Q On a large hull, planking may be started at the garboards and at the gunwale at the same time. The last plank to be fitted is called the closure.

R Basically, in clinker planking, one plank is fastened to the next through the overlaps, but each is also fastened to the frames. Copper nails are riveted in place over copper washers or roves.

J The heavy grown or sawn frames of **1** form the main framing of the hull and contrast with the light steamed frames of **2**, which are used principally to strap the planking together.

K This section shows the relationship of the members used in a grown frame construction. (*a*) Frame. (*b*) Planking. (*c*) Hanging knee. (*d*) Deck beam. (*e*) Deck planking. (*f*) Bilge stringer. (*g*) Floor. (*h*) Wood keel. (*i*) Lead keel.

L Planks are added one at a time, and wedges are used to close each plank tight to the previous planking.

M Strip planking is a very simple method of boat-building often used by amateurs. The planks are fastened directly to each other and, therefore, caulking is not necessary.

N The lengths of wood for planking are often not long enough to reach from end to end of the hull. They are usually joined by butt straps as shown.

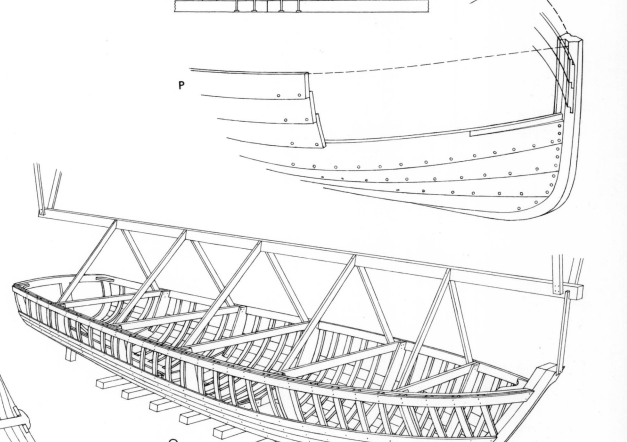

GRP CONSTRUCTION

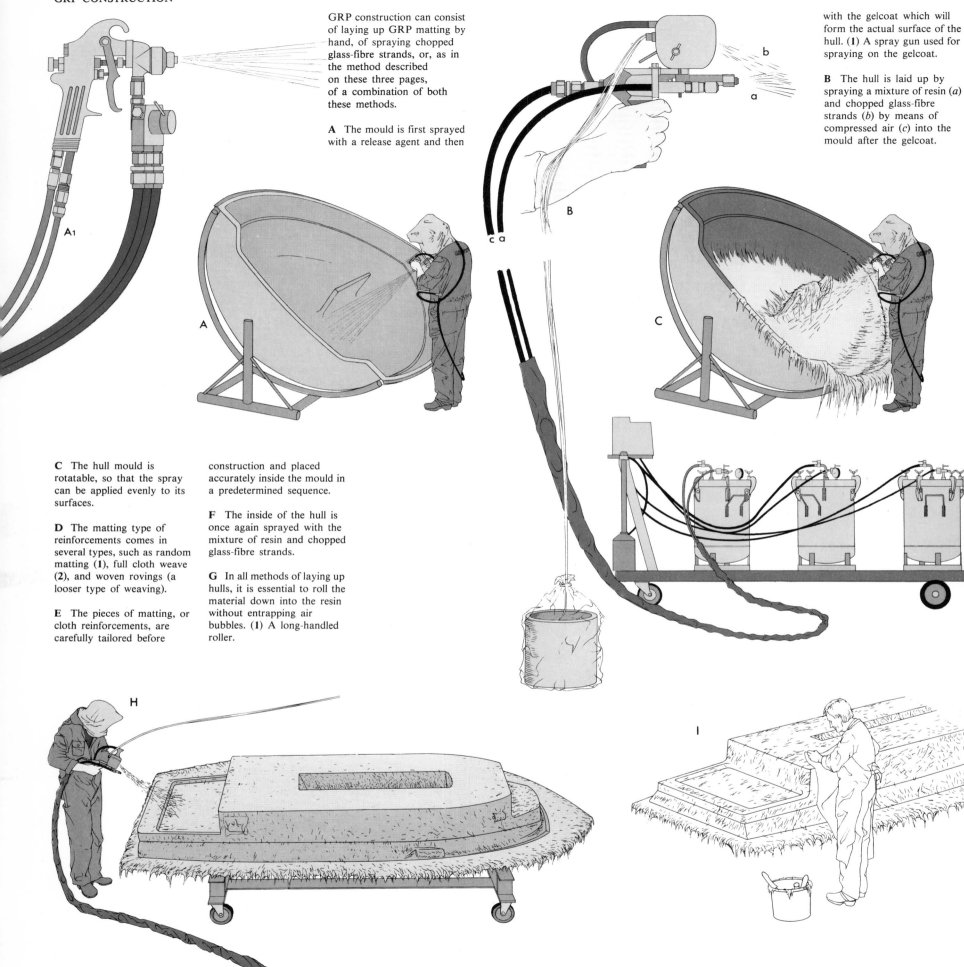

GRP construction can consist of laying up GRP matting by hand, of spraying chopped glass-fibre strands, or, as in the method described on these three pages, of a combination of both these methods.

A The mould is first sprayed with a release agent and then with the gelcoat which will form the actual surface of the hull. (**1**) A spray gun used for spraying on the gelcoat.

B The hull is laid up by spraying a mixture of resin (*a*) and chopped glass-fibre strands (*b*) by means of compressed air (*c*) into the mould after the gelcoat.

C The hull mould is rotatable, so that the spray can be applied evenly to its surfaces.

D The matting type of reinforcements comes in several types, such as random matting (**1**), full cloth weave (**2**), and woven rovings (a looser type of weaving).

E The pieces of matting, or cloth reinforcements, are carefully tailored before construction and placed accurately inside the mould in a predetermined sequence.

F The inside of the hull is once again sprayed with the mixture of resin and chopped glass-fibre strands.

G In all methods of laying up hulls, it is essential to roll the material down into the resin without entrapping air bubbles. (**1**) A long-handled roller.

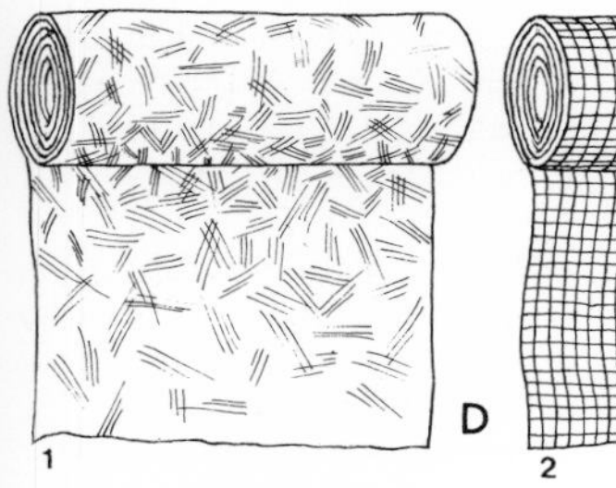

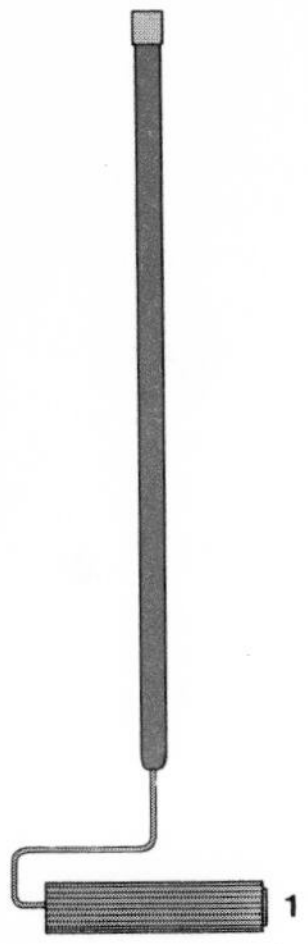

D

J Wood blocks (*a*) are added to the mouldings to give local strength or to provide securing points for fittings. The blocks are then matted in with special rollers (**1** and **2**), used to make certain that the matting is fully rolled into the detailed shapes required without trapping air bubbles.

K Sometimes, tubing of plastics (*a*) or even of paper is used to form reinforcements on the inner skin of mouldings by covering the tubing with several layers of matting reinforcement.

L After the mouldings have set hard and before they are joined together, the stray glass strands are cleaned from the surfaces and the joining edges are sanded to give good adhesion. Typical small sanding machines used for this are shown here (**1** and **2**).

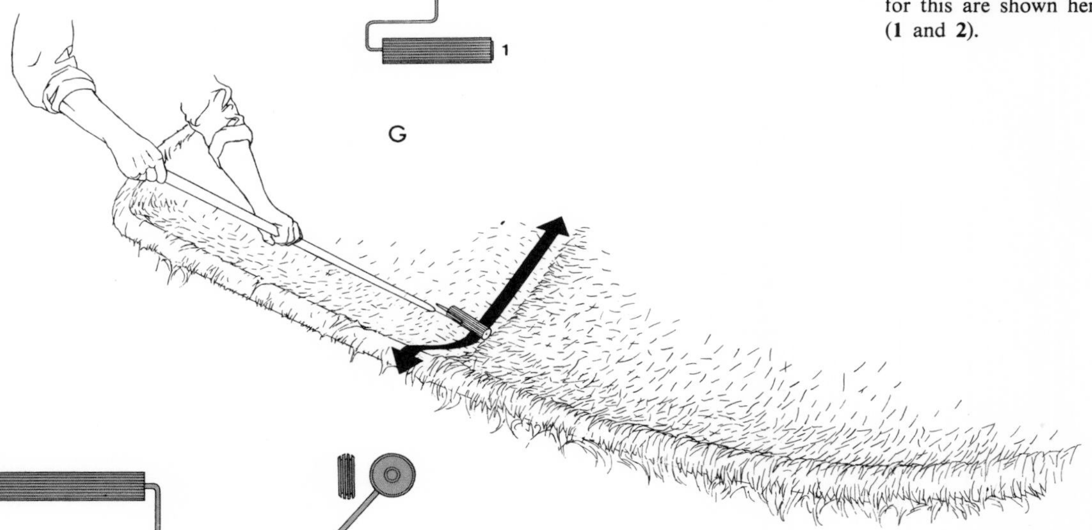

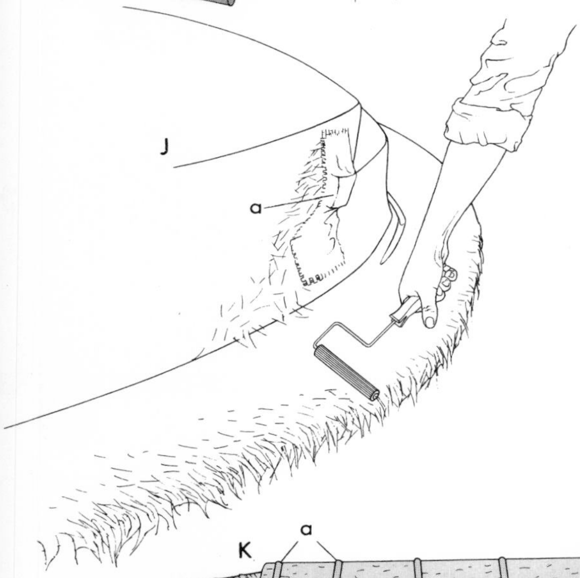

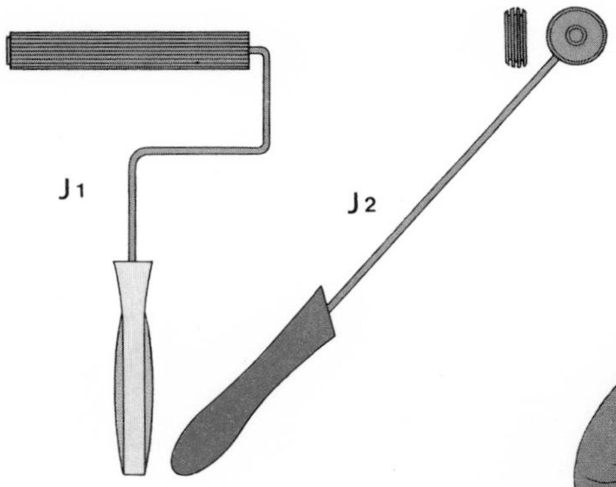

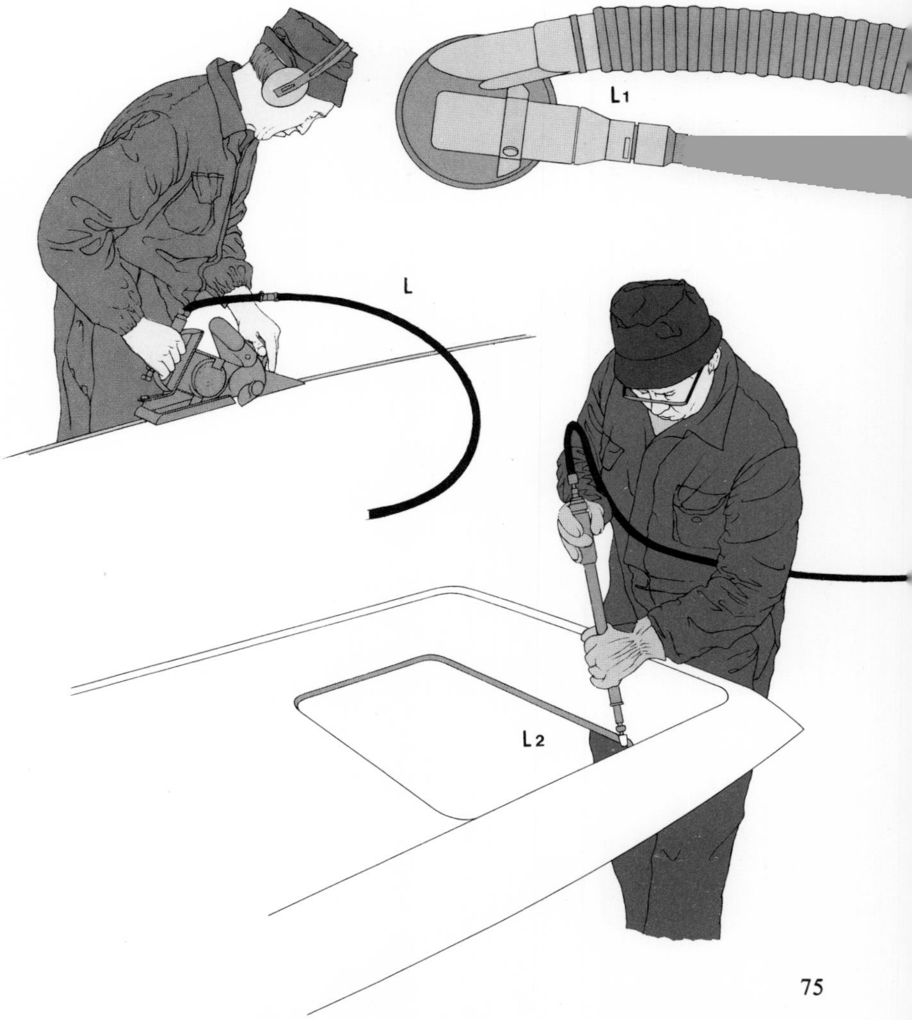

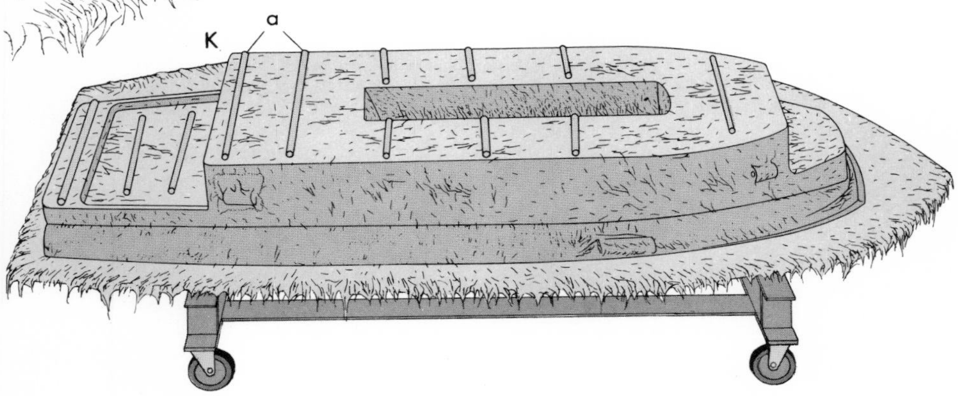

F

G

E

J

a

J 1

J 2

K

a

L

L 1

L 2

H The deck, complete with minor details, is formed over a mould in the same way as the hull. This shows a spray lay-up in progress.

I The tailored lay-up of matting is more difficult over the complexities of some deck moulds.

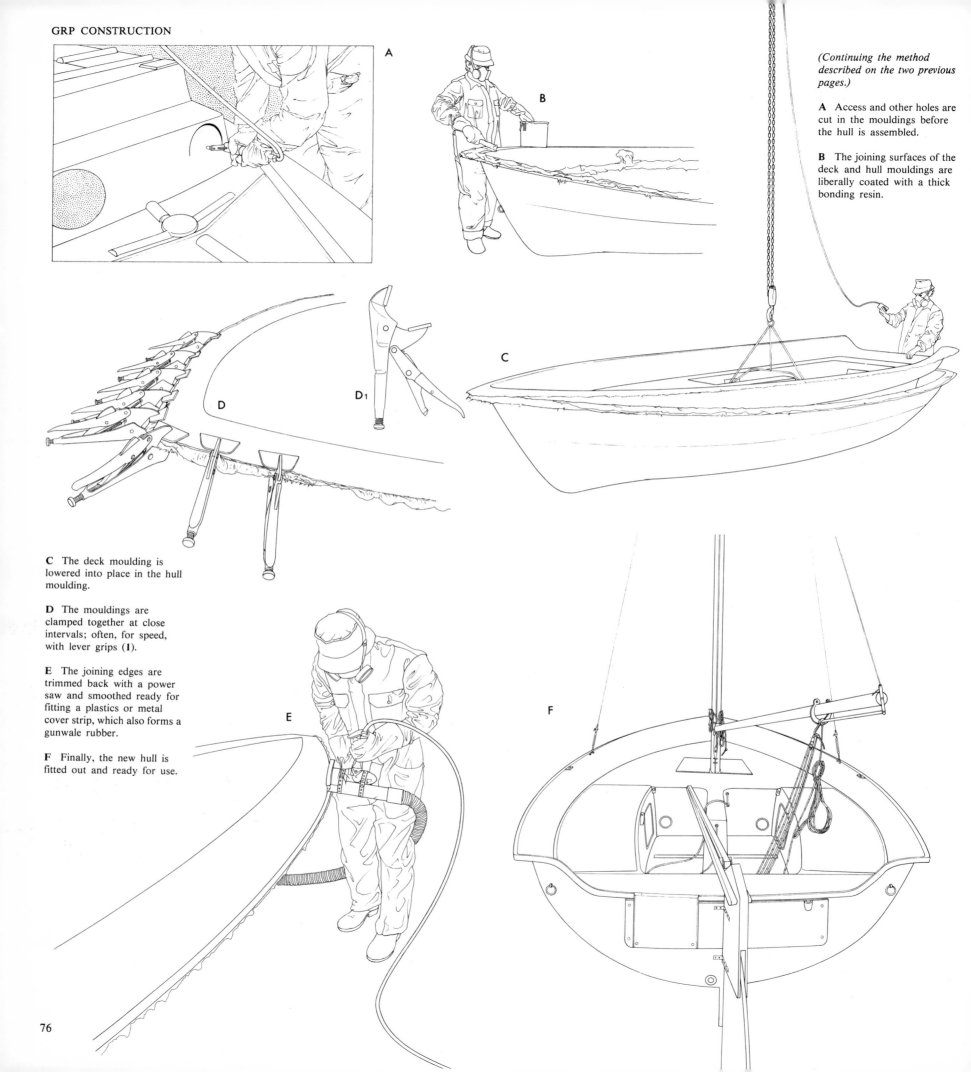

A

B

(Continuing the method described on the two previous pages.)

A Access and other holes are cut in the mouldings before the hull is assembled.

B The joining surfaces of the deck and hull mouldings are liberally coated with a thick bonding resin.

C

D

D₁

C The deck moulding is lowered into place in the hull moulding.

D The mouldings are clamped together at close intervals; often, for speed, with lever grips (1).

E The joining edges are trimmed back with a power saw and smoothed ready for fitting a plastics or metal cover strip, which also forms a gunwale rubber.

F Finally, the new hull is fitted out and ready for use.

E

F

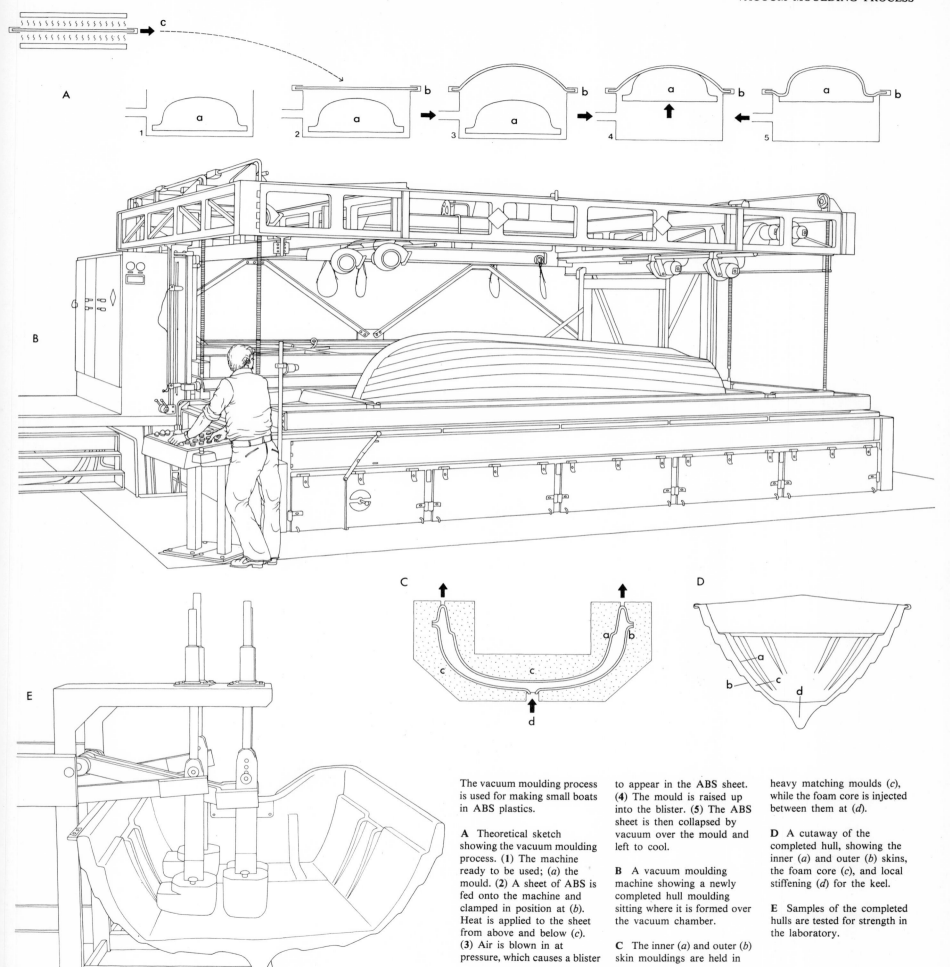

The vacuum moulding process is used for making small boats in ABS plastics.

A Theoretical sketch showing the vacuum moulding process. (**1**) The machine ready to be used; (*a*) the mould. (**2**) A sheet of ABS is fed onto the machine and clamped in position at (*b*). Heat is applied to the sheet from above and below (*c*). (**3**) Air is blown in at pressure, which causes a blister to appear in the ABS sheet. (**4**) The mould is raised up into the blister. (**5**) The ABS sheet is then collapsed by vacuum over the mould and left to cool.

B A vacuum moulding machine showing a newly completed hull moulding sitting where it is formed over the vacuum chamber.

C The inner (*a*) and outer (*b*) skin mouldings are held in heavy matching moulds (*c*), while the foam core is injected between them at (*d*).

D A cutaway of the completed hull, showing the inner (*a*) and outer (*b*) skins, the foam core (*c*), and local stiffening (*d*) for the keel.

E Samples of the completed hulls are tested for strength in the laboratory.

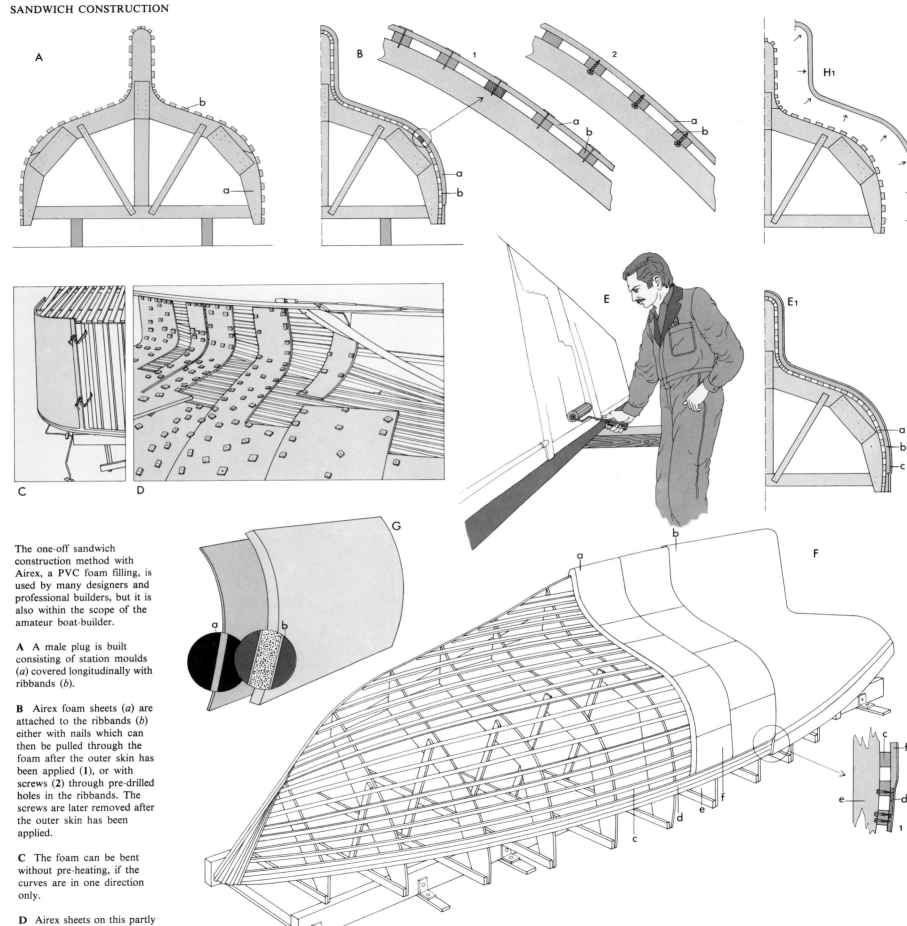

The one-off sandwich construction method with Airex, a PVC foam filling, is used by many designers and professional builders, but it is also within the scope of the amateur boat-builder.

A A male plug is built consisting of station moulds (*a*) covered longitudinally with ribbands (*b*).

B Airex foam sheets (*a*) are attached to the ribbands (*b*) either with nails which can then be pulled through the foam after the outer skin has been applied (**1**), or with screws (**2**) through pre-drilled holes in the ribbands. The screws are later removed after the outer skin has been applied.

C The foam can be bent without pre-heating, if the curves are in one direction only.

D Airex sheets on this partly finished hull have been tacked onto the ribbands. The small pieces of wood protect the material.

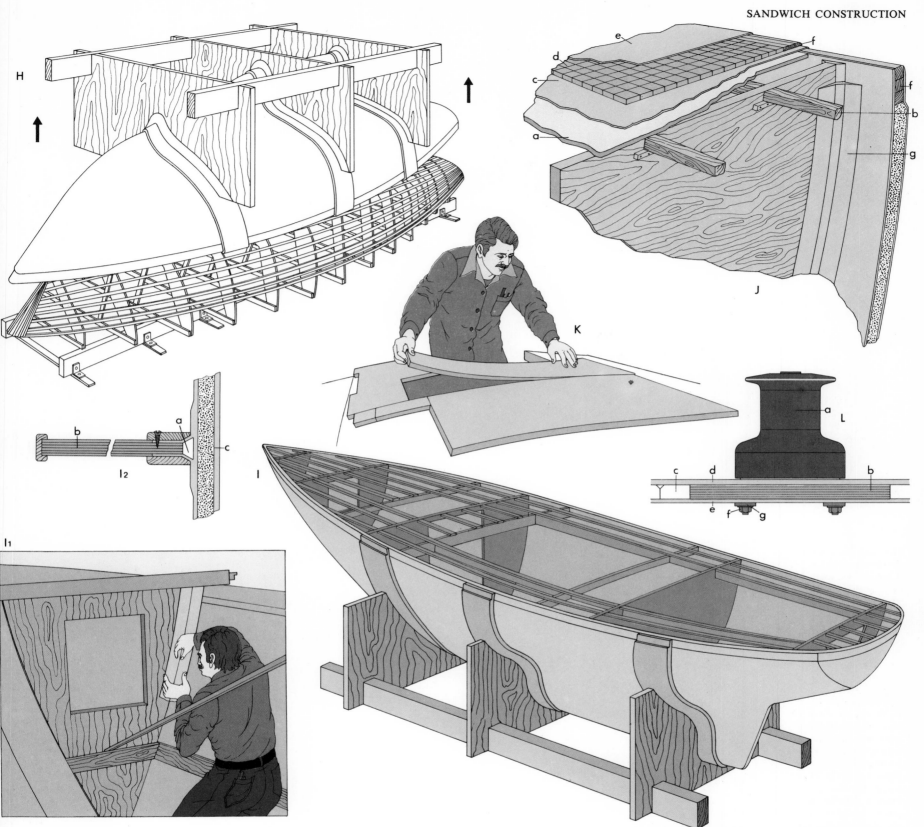

E The outer GRP skin is applied in the usual way, and a primer coat of paint or gelcoat is added. (**1**) Cross-section view. (*a*) Ribbands. (*b*) Airex. (*c*) Outer GRP skin.

F The Airex planking in the keel area (*a*) is covered with a parting agent to allow for the Airex there to be removed, thus producing a solid GRP layup. (*b*) Outer GRP skin. (*c*) Ribband. (*d*) Mahogany sheer planks. (*e*) Mould. (*f*) Airex planking. (**1**) Cross-section view of the sheer planks and Airex, showing the temporary screws through the ribbands.

G A comparison between a single-skin GRP hull section (*a*) and a section of an Airex sandwich hull (*b*).

H Prior to the hull being turned over, a receiving cradle is built on top (**1**). The hull can then be lifted easily off the plug.

I The hull, now right side up, is given a GRP shell on the inside, and the bulkheads are inserted. (**1**) A bulkhead is bonded to the hull with GRP. (**2**) A section of the hull and a bulkhead, seen from above. A trapezoidal piece of Airex foam (*a*) between the bulkhead (*b*) and the hull (*c*) prevents the formation of a hard spot.

J When the bulkheads are installed, a false deck of masonite (*a*) is built, and temporary longitudinals (*b*) between the bulkheads are erected to carry the false deck, which is covered with polyester resin and a mould-release agent. The deck is then constructed, first the inner GRP skin (*c*), then Airex (*d*) and finally the outer GRP skin (*e*). (*f*) Mahogany sheer planks. (*g*) Glass-fibre matting attaching bulkhead to hull.

K Laying up the deck.

L Where deck hardware is to be installed, the Airex is removed and replaced with plywood or solid GRP. (*a*) Winch. (*b*) Plywood. (*c*) Airex. (*d*) Outer skin. (*e*) Inner skin. (*f*) Through bolting. (*g*) Washer.

FERRO-CEMENT CONSTRUCTION

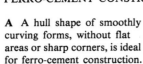

A A hull shape of smoothly curving forms, without flat areas or sharp corners, is ideal for ferro-cement construction.

B The main framing is made from steel piping, bent accurately to full-sized lofted lines.

C Each frame is set up on the building berth, trued up, and fixed.

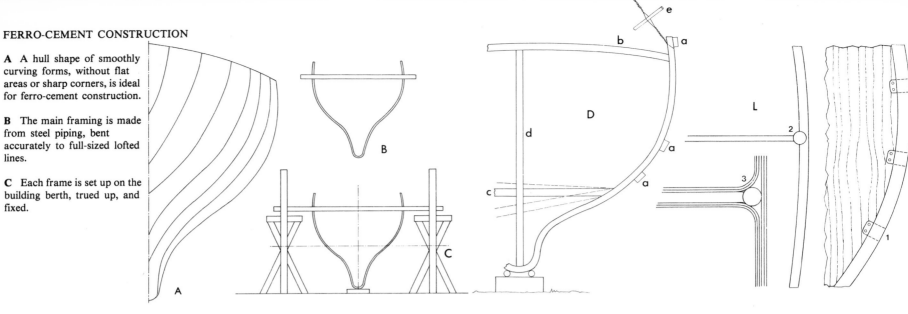

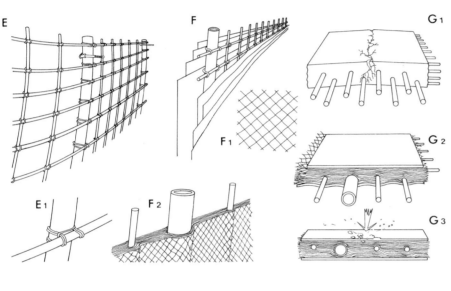

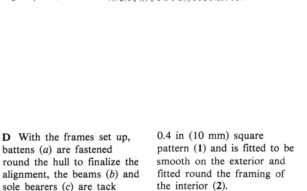

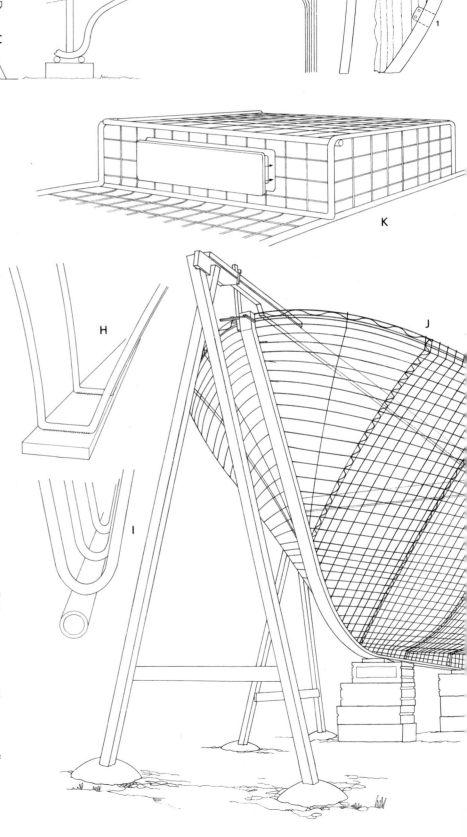

D With the frames set up, battens (*a*) are fastened round the hull to finalize the alignment, the beams (*b*) and sole bearers (*c*) are tack welded in place, and an upright (*d*) is fitted to take the weight of the wet cement deck, together with wire braces (*e*) which also support the edges.

E A secondary framework of steel rods is fitted over the pipe frames at about 3-in (75 mm) spacing. The rods are either welded to the frames or may be wired to them as shown (**1**).

F Many layers of wire mesh are then wired onto the hull framework, perhaps eight or ten layers. The mesh is about

0.4 in (10 mm) square pattern (**1**) and is fitted to be smooth on the exterior and fitted round the framing of the interior (**2**).

G Ordinary reinforced concrete (**1**) will crack, despite the rod reinforcement, but the addition of the close-packed wire mesh (**2**) makes it exceptionally strong, suffering only minor local damage on heavy impact (**3**).

H A steel plate keel is often used to form the basic backbone, to which the frames are welded.

I A steel tube is also used for the backbone, especially for the stem.

J The wire mesh is added progressively to the framing, until the hull is ready to be concreted in one operation.

K The framing for deckworks is usually more complicated than that for the hull, and provision has to be made for windows and hatches, etc.

L Bulkheads have to be positioned in line with pipe frames. In (**1**), a plywood bulkhead is secured to welded lugs. (**2**) and (**3**) show ferro-cement bulkheads, built exactly as part of the main hull, with the wire mesh carried through the hull to the bulkhead.

80

M The hull cementing usually has to be carried out as a single non-stop job and therefore has to be carefully planned, with plenty of labour. Unskilled help mixes the cement and carries it to the hull, where it is pushed through the mesh (**1**) from inside, ready for the really skilled work to achieve a good outside finish.

N Small fittings can be rawl-plugged into place, provided they are clear of main framing.

O A wood deck can be fitted to a ferro-cement hull by bolting a wood beam shelf (*a*)

through the moulding. (*b*) Beam. (*c*) Deck.

P Where a skin fitting is required, a tapered wood plug is fitted before concreting, ready to be knocked out later.

Q For the first few days after concreting, the hull is very vulnerable to any strains and should be left untouched (**1**). For several weeks, it must be protected from hot sun and allowed to dry very slowly, with constant damping sprays if necessary (**2**). During the whole drying period, the shores and supports must stay in place, in case their removal sets up strains.

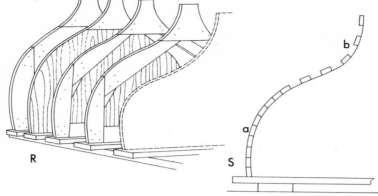
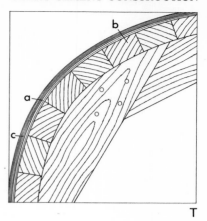
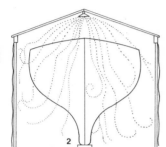
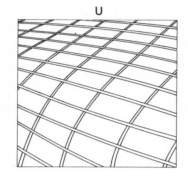
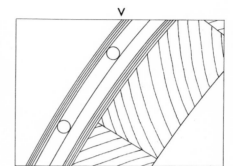
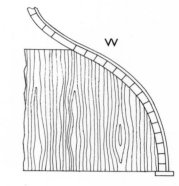
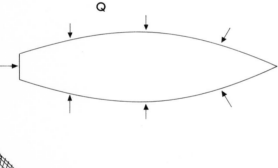

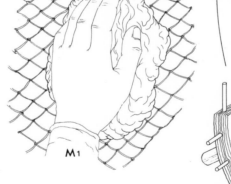

R Some ferro-cement builders prefer to build a plug in wood, using conventional moulds.

S The wood moulds are completely planked in wood battens throughout the accommodation (*a*), where they will eventually form a wood lining to the hull. Elsewhere (*b*), only sufficient battens to support the ferro-cement structure need to be fitted.

T Layers of tarred paper (*a*) are fitted over the woodwork (*b*) to keep out the damp, and these are covered with, say, four layers of wire mesh (*c*).

U A first layer of rods is stapled directly to the wood, and the second is laid across them and secured by staples or wire ties.

V The matching skin of wire mesh is then added to the outside of the rod framing, and the hull is ready for cementing, using a vibrator to get full penetration of the cement.

W The wood lining makes for simple fitting of bulkheads and interior joinerwork.

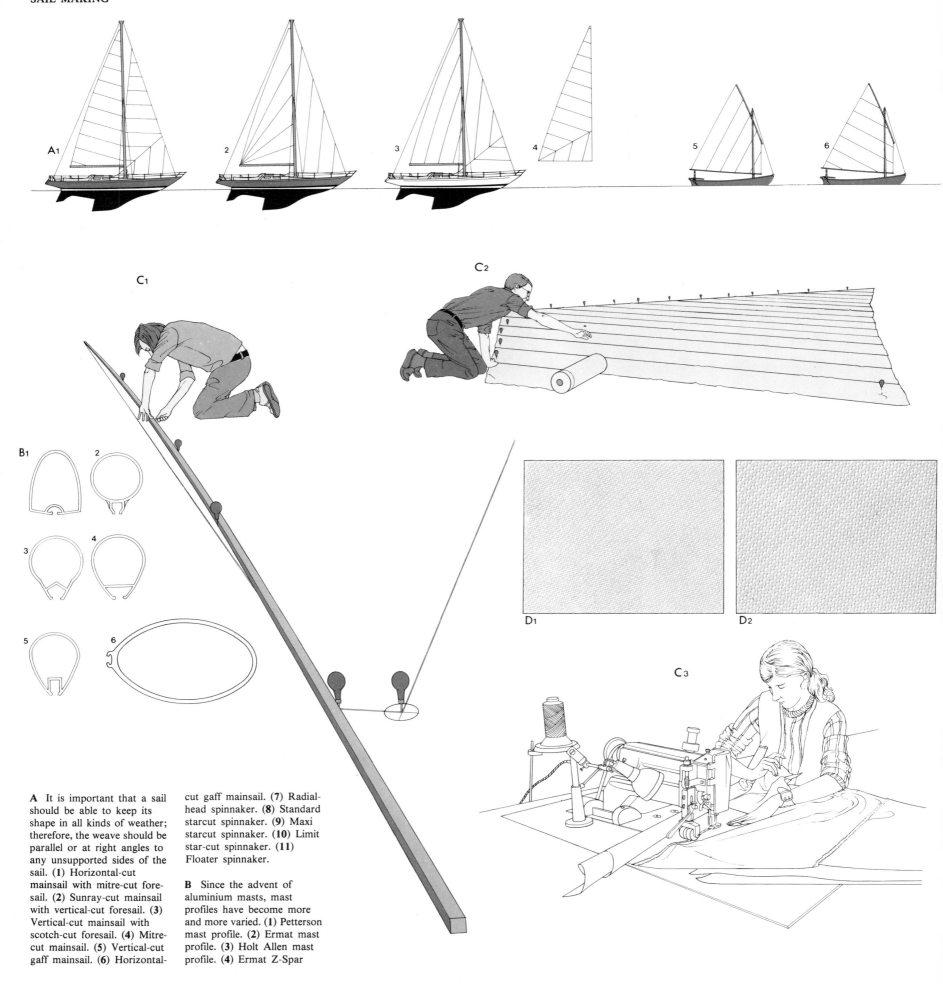

A It is important that a sail should be able to keep its shape in all kinds of weather; therefore, the weave should be parallel or at right angles to any unsupported sides of the sail. (**1**) Horizontal-cut mainsail with mitre-cut foresail. (**2**) Sunray-cut mainsail with vertical-cut foresail. (**3**) Vertical-cut mainsail with scotch-cut foresail. (**4**) Mitre-cut mainsail. (**5**) Vertical-cut gaff mainsail. (**6**) Horizontal-cut gaff mainsail. (**7**) Radial-head spinnaker. (**8**) Standard starcut spinnaker. (**9**) Maxi starcut spinnaker. (**10**) Limit star-cut spinnaker. (**11**) Floater spinnaker.

B Since the advent of aluminium masts, mast profiles have become more and more varied. (**1**) Petterson mast profile. (**2**) Ermat mast profile. (**3**) Holt Allen mast profile. (**4**) Ermat Z-Spar

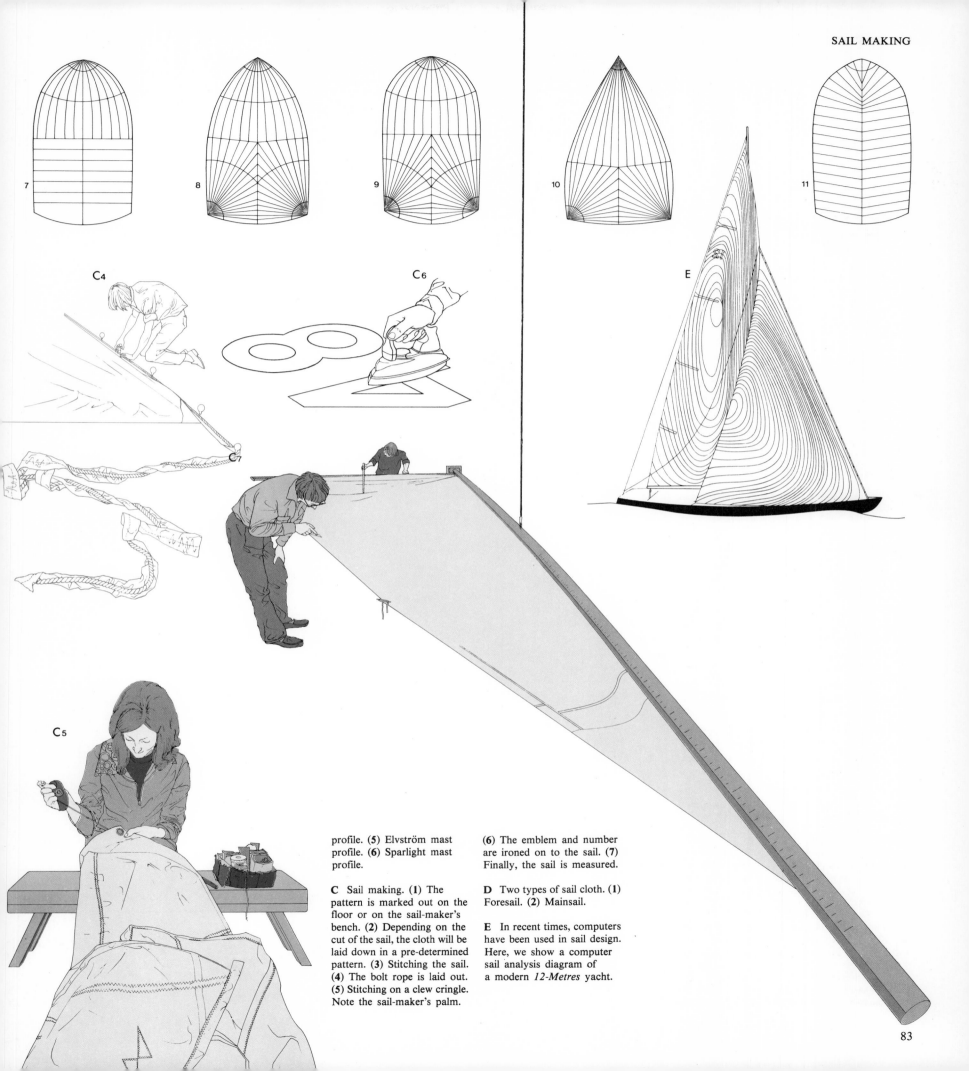

7 8 9 10 11

C4

C6

E

C5

profile. (5) Elvström mast profile. (6) Sparlight mast profile.

C Sail making. (1) The pattern is marked out on the floor or on the sail-maker's bench. (2) Depending on the cut of the sail, the cloth will be laid down in a pre-determined pattern. (3) Stitching the sail. (4) The bolt rope is laid out. (5) Stitching on a clew cringle. Note the sail-maker's palm.

(6) The emblem and number are ironed on to the sail. (7) Finally, the sail is measured.

D Two types of sail cloth. (1) Foresail. (2) Mainsail.

E In recent times, computers have been used in sail design. Here, we show a computer sail analysis diagram of a modern 12-Metres yacht.

83

MAINTENANCE

Per Brohäll

A properly maintained boat is a source of both pride and confidence to its owner; not only will it look good, but it will also be able to stand up to the strains which the environment will impose on it. Furthermore, maintenance and care prolong the life of a boat and keep its second-hand value at a high level.

The marine environment, with its high air humidity, bottom fouling, salt, rain, wind, water pollution, and even sun glare reflected off the surface of the water, exposes a boat's material and paint to great strains. In order to protect your boat from all this, a certain knowledge of boat-building materials is necessary. You must know what demands you can make on the materials in your boat and how they should be treated.

Some woods resist rot more easily than others. However, every kind of wood used on a boat should be treated with preservatives before being painted or varnished. As a rule, heart-wood is stronger and more resistant to rot than is sap-wood, or laburnum. This is particularly true of pine and oak.

All wood used in boat-building must be high-quality, without flaws, and as dry as possible (especially if it is to be glued). When drying, wood shrinks; when damp, it swells. The rate of shrinkage and swelling is about twice as high tangentially (along the annual rings) as it is radially. This is why, for instance, wood for planking should be sawn so that the annual rings are perpendicular to the surface. If this is not done, the boat will not stay watertight in the long run. If, for some reason, the wood is not sawn in this way, the heart side ought to face outwards.

When choosing a wood with which to make a repair or replacement on a wooden boat, you must always take account of how seasoned the wood is. A mitre-cut corner joint may not remain tight if the wood shrinks or swells. Tight-fitting drawers or doors will jam if the wood expands. Coamings, hatches, and other details, which are joined together with cross-beams and corner-pieces at right angles to the wood grain, may warp and split if the wood dries.

Marine plywood is still used for planking and decks on small to medium-sized boats and is an excellent material for these purposes, being light and strong. Today, however, plywood is mainly used for cabin joiner-work in

Wood type	Elm	Ash	Oak	Redwood	Gaboon	Mahogany	Douglas Fir Oregon Pine	Pitch Pine	Spruce	Teak
Coamings and rails	–	2	3	4	–	1	2	–	–	1
Spars	–	–	–	2	–	–	2	–	1	–
Cabin joiner-work	2	2	2	2	2	1	2	–	–	1
Planking *clinker*	–	–	3	2	–	1	2	–	–	–
Planking *carvel*	–	–	3	1	–	1	2	2	3	1
Planking *strip*	–	–	–	2	4	2	2	–	3	–
Deck	–	–	–	3	–	–	1	2	3	1
Deck beams	2	1	2	1	–	2	–	–	3	–
Stringers and carlings	–	–	2	1	–	1	1	–	2	–
Frames *grown*	2	–	1	3	–	–	–	–	–	–
Frames *steamed*	2	1	1	–	–	–	–	–	–	–
Floor timbers	2	–	1	–	–	–	–	3	–	1
Keels, stems, sternposts	2	–	1	3	–	–	–	–	–	–
Shrinkage % *radial*	2	2.5	2	2	2	1.5	2.5	2	2	1.5
Shrinkage % *tangential*	4	4	4	4	3.5	2.5	4.0	3.5	3.5	2.5
Rot resistance	high	low	medium/high	medium	low	medium	medium/high	high	medium	high
Approx. weight by unit volume	0.7	0.7	0.75	0.5	0.45	0.6	0.55	0.7	0.45	0.8

This table shows the most usual kinds of wood used in boat-building, their weight, their shrinkage from wet to room-dry wood, and their suitableness for the various parts of the boat. The figures indicate in which order the various woods should be chosen.

GRP boats. Due to its construction, marine plywood does not swell or shrink to a noticeable degree.

Be very careful when buying plywood for use on your boat. In Great Britain, marine plywood is stamped WBP (Weather and Boil Proof) while, in the United States, the corresponding quality is branded EXT DFPA (Exterior Grade, Douglas Fir Plywood Association). Fir plywood is as strong and tough as most of the plywoods made from tropical woods, but its surfaces usually need more filling and sanding in order to obtain a good finish. Birch plywood should be avoided, even when correctly bonded. Gaboon, or okoumé, plywood is often sold as mahogany, but it is brittle and should only be used below deck, for parts which are not exposed to stress.

Cold-moulded plywood boats are, as mentioned in the previous chapter, very light and strong. They are constructed of thin veneers bonded together over a mould. Damage to plywood planking of this kind should be repaired by gluing new layers of the veneer over some kind of a temporary, inside mould.

Wood rot is caused by certain species of fungus which feed on the cellulose in the wood. The spores of these fungi are carried by the wind and lodge on the wood, where they need moisture and oxygen in order to grow. Because of this, fungi cannot attack dry wood. Properly seasoned wood has a low moisture content and, therefore, a high resistance to rot. Wood entirely immersed in water is hardly attacked at all, as there is not enough oxygen in water to allow the fungi to grow. The inner veneers of plywood are protected from fungi by the layers of bonding glue but, sometimes, the fungi can creep in through butt ends and edges. The appearance of pine is often effected by a blue discolouration which is caused by these fungi. This may spoil the wood's appearance, but it does not affect its strength. However, blue stains are a warning that the wood is subject to the same conditions which cause rot. These disfiguring blue stains may sometimes be slightly bleached by means of oxalic acid, dissolved in water.

The best way to protect your boat from rot is, firstly, to choose the right type of wood (see the table for information on rot resistance). Secondly, the wood must be impregnated with a wood preservative and then painted or varnished. Finally, you must see to it that the boat is well ventilated all over, and that no water from leaks or from condensation is allowed to accumulate anywhere. Good ventilation also prevents mildew. Check that there are limber holes in the floors, and that water can drain away through or past longitudinal stringers, bulkheads, and shelves.

Many repairs and minor jobs can be carried out on the woodwork of a boat with simple carpentry tools but, for more complicated repairs, a more complete set of tools, with different saws, planes, drills, clamps, and so on, may be necessary. As a general rule, before you start doing a more comprehensive job, such as replacing a timber, always figure out how it should be done. The general routine for such a job is the following:

1. Remove the damaged part. This is sometimes difficult to achieve without damaging the wood beside it.
2. Measure or make a template of the damaged part.
3. Select the right type of wood for the purpose, and remember that the wood's annual rings and structure will dictate how it should best be used.
4. Shape and insert the new part.
5. Impregnate and paint or varnish it.

The metals most commonly used in boats are steel (including stainless steel), copper, ordinary and red brass (both are alloys of copper and zinc), different kinds of bronze (alloys of copper and, for example, tin, aluminium, or silicon), and aluminium and aluminium alloys.

As a boat-owner, you should know about the strength of the different metals and their resistance to corrosion, so that you do not use the wrong metal to replace a fitting or fastening.

Steel is strong and inexpensive, but it corrodes in a short time. Galvanized, or zinc-plated, steel is more durable, and hot-dip galvanized steel lasts longest. Stainless steel is strong and resistant to corrosion, and the best acid-proof quality provides a very fine, resistant surface, which polishes easily.

Copper is considerably weaker than steel, but it is resistant to corrosion and easily worked, which is why it is used a lot on wooden boats, especially for nails and rivets.

Brass is a copper-zinc alloy, in which the zinc has a considerable strengthening effect on the copper. Its resistance to corrosion is good enough for fittings which are not exposed too much to the elements. In ordinary brass, i.e., with about sixty-five per cent copper, the zinc has a tendency to precipitate, especially when exposed to salt water. After a time, this causes the material to become fairly brittle. Brass with a higher proportion of copper (80–90 per cent copper) is much more lasting but is not readily available.

The various bronzes are strong and very durable. Silicon bronze is an excellent material for nails, bolts, and screws.

If two different metals, damp or immersed in salt water, are placed near each other, they form a galvanic element, and one of them will be consumed (will corrode). Which one of them, will depend on their relative positions in the galvanic series: gold, 18/8/3 Mo stainless steel, silver, copper, stainless steel, brass, tin, lead, nickel, iron, aluminium and aluminium alloys, cadmium, zinc. The more noble the metal is, the higher it is ranked in the series. The further from each other in the series two metals are, the greater will be the corrosion of the less noble metal. For example, ordinary iron bolts will not do to fasten a lead keel, as they will rapidly corrode to breaking point. If iron and zinc are combined, the zinc will corrode. Zinc is a true protective metal for iron and steel, i.e., the zinc must be consumed before the iron or steel starts to rust.

Galvanic action may also occur if currents from an electric system leak to a metal hull or fitting. A boat battery has its negative pole (the cathode) earthed to the engine, and thus also to the propeller shaft and propeller, if any. Should the positive pole (anode) be connected—by mistake, faulty insulation, or a short-circuit—to the metal hull or to some through-hull fitting, such as a sea-cock or a log, then there will be a stray current, which can cause severe corrosion to the exposed object, as it will turn into a "protective" anode.

In the battle against corrosion, it is most important to choose the right metal for each purpose and to avoid mixing different metals—do not, for instance, use a brass sea-cock for a steel or aluminium hull. Galvanized fittings should be fastened with galvanized screws, bronze fittings with bronze screws, aluminium fittings with stainless-steel screws (if possible, insulated with glue, paint, or grease) and, naturally, stainless-steel fittings with stainless-steel screws and bolts. Cast-iron keels and steel or aluminium hulls must be covered with anti-corrosion primer and paint. Follow the paint manufacturer's instructions. All electric fittings must be properly installed, so that no stray currents can occur.

Bronze propellers on stainless-steel shafts, and other underwater fittings, which are necessarily of dissimilar metals, can corrode in next to no time in salt or polluted water. The corrosion may be reduced or even prevented if a protective zinc anode is attached near the fitting, but it must be made of pure zinc, suitable for the purpose, and it must not be covered by paint. Engine manufacturers will supply you with a proper anode and assist you with good advice. Outboard engines and IO drives can be especially susceptible to galvanic corrosion.

A more sophisticated method, used on some ships, is also available for pleasure boats. This system, called "cathodic protection", can "read" the electric potential of the hull and, when necessary, will apply a direct current, so that the potential is reduced to a safe level. In special cases, a system like this can be well worth the expense.

It is actually little more than thirty years since the first GRP boats were made in the United States. Since then, GRP boat-building has spread all over the world and, today, GRP is the dominating material used for the construction of pleasure boats. Relative to weight, GRP is stronger than wood or steel. It is not affected by fungi or vermin and absorbs very little water. GRP is extremely durable and easily repaired, and it does not cause corrosion to fittings, propellers, and so on.

GRP boats are easy to maintain. Neglect will not cause the material to decay but, without maintenance, the gelcoat will age, the boat will look unattractive, and its value will be reduced. All that is needed to keep it looking its best is a once-a-year cleaning, waxing, and polishing. Use normal synthetic detergents. Non-skid patterns can be cleaned with a dry, stiff brush and some scouring-powder, but this method must never be used on smooth surfaces, where it will cause scratches. Very dirty surfaces may be cleaned with one of the degreasing detergents used for cars. Soap, alcohol, petrol, paraffin, white spirit, and thinner can also be used. Acetone and carbon tetrachloride may be used, but with caution. Avoid strong soda solution, ammonia, trichloroethylene, paint removers, and any detergent which does not label its contents.

Surfaces with scratches, blemishes, and dull patches can be restored by polishing or burnishing. There are several special polishes and creams available, and all that you need with these is a lot of elbow grease.

If a properly-cleaned surface is waxed and polished annually, the gelcoat will be well protected and will repel dirt. The boat will look much better, and you put off the day when you must repaint the boat for appearance's sake. Use car or floor polish to polish the boat, and remember that it is best to use a solid wax. There are also special boat polishes available. All these polishes contain silicone, and when repairing or painting your boat, you must clean and sand all the polished surfaces thoroughly, so that no silicone is left to spoil your job.

Minor damage to GRP can usually be repaired by applying gelcoat putty, as long as the laminate has not been penetrated. Shallow surface scratches on the laminate may sometimes be filled with a two-component epoxy or polyester putty. Gelcoat putty is a type of top-coat, i.e., the gelcoat contains wax, which rises to the surface, thus causing the putty to set in the correct way (ordinary gelcoat hardens against a mould surface).

Sometimes, it can be difficult to match the original colour when repairing the gelcoat, although some boat manufacturers will supply a repair kit with gelcoat putty of the correct shade when they deliver a boat. Repair kits can also be bought in paint shops, but their assortment of shades is, naturally, limited.

Before you start repairing your boat, remove all dirt from the damaged area, which must then be sanded with a fairly rough abrasive paper. Wash off the dust with acetone. The damaged area must be completely dry before you apply the filler. Use the gelcoat putty according to the manufacturer's directions. Normally, a small amount of the hardening agent is well mixed with a suitable quantity of putty on a piece of hardboard or suchlike. The putty is then applied with a putty knife of wood or steel. Do not work too slowly because, at 64° F (18° C), the putty will gel (harden) in fifteen to twenty minutes. Apply a little more putty than necessary, as some of it will be lost when sanding and polishing, and as it will shrink somewhat during hardening. This is best done by fastening masking-tape round the damaged spot and applying the putty up to the level of the tape.

When the putty has hardened, sand it down to the correct level with a No. 220 abrasive paper. Continue sanding with a wet No. 400 paper and, later, with a No. 600. For a really high gloss, finish off with a No. 800 or with an even finer paper. Use a sanding block, and be very careful not to damage the surrounding gelcoat. Finish by burnishing and waxing the repaired area. Hands and tools can be cleaned with acetone.

GRP hulls sometimes develop blisters in the gelcoat below the water-line. This seems to occur more frequently in fresh water, and if the gelcoat is coloured. The reason is probably that the gelcoat is too thin or too soft and lets in water. Minute cavities underneath get filled with water, which dissolves a small amount of the chemicals present in the laminate. Through osmosis more water is drawn in, so that the blisters swell and sometimes even burst. This is no threat to the strength of the GRP hull, but it increases water resistance.

If you remove the blisters and fill in the cavities as described above, new blisters may develop in between the repaired areas, but not to the same extent as earlier. There is no simple, unfailing remedy. An impermeable layer of two-pot polyurethane paint on top of the gelcoat may reduce its tendency to develop blisters. The most radical remedy is to sand down the gelcoat, and then apply top-coat or polyurethane paint. In addition to this, the bottom must be painted with an antifouling paint which is as impermeable as possible.

The handy boat-owner may well manage the minor laminating jobs, such as attaching some detail or other by lamination, or repairing light keel or hull damage where the laminate has not been completely penetrated—even holes in the hull, if they are not too large. More extensive damage, however, is better left to an expert, not so much because it would be any more difficult to repair it, but because the consequences of a non-professional repair job (if it does not *stay* repaired!) can be serious, if the damage is to a vital part of the boat.

For laminating jobs, you need thixotropic, pre-accelerated polyester resin, and catalyst. If you use a separate accelerator, beware of mixing it with the catalyst—this can cause an explosion. Further, you will need glass-fibre mat of $1-1\frac{1}{2}$ oz/sq ft (300–450 g/sq m), a metal roller, a stiff brush, acetone to clean tools and hands with afterwards, self-adhesive tape, abrasive paper, a rasp or coarse file, a pair of scissors, paper cups or tins in which to mix the resin and, perhaps, hack-saw blades and a steel-wire brush. For minor repairs, you will also need a two-component epoxy or polyester filler. If necessary, the filler can be reinforced with glass fibres. Thixotropic polyester resin, ready-mixed with glass fibres, is also available and is useful where a complete lamination is not required. All the types of resin required can be bought in the larger paint shops. Be sure to study carefully the manufacturer's directions for mixing, use, and time of hardening.

First of all, the laminate around the damage should be sanded with coarse abrasive paper, and then washed clean with acetone. In most cases, small notches can be filled and then painted. If the damage is more than skin-deep, the filler should be reinforced with pieces of glass-fibre matting. If lamination is necessary, the damaged area should be coated with polyester resin. A suitable piece of glass-fibre matting is then applied. Roll it with a metal roller or dab it with a stiff brush, so that all of it sticks to the resin and so that all air pockets are removed. Add another layer of resin and work it in thoroughly until the matting is saturated. Continue like this, layer after layer, until the lamination is thick enough.

When the uppermost layer is set but not completely hardened, all superfluous material can be cut off with a sharp knife. When the surface has hardened, the repaired area is sanded, filled if necessary, and coated with polyurethane paint or top-coat.

Traditionally, the major part of boat maintenance consists of scraping, sanding, washing, and painting or varnishing. This does not apply to GRP boats. For them, it is mainly a matter of painting the bottom and oiling or varnishing the wooden details.

The most important thing in painting is to prepare the surface well. No amount of paint will ever hide shoddy preparatory work. A lot of elbow grease is necessary—scraping, sanding, filling, and sanding again. A triangular scraper can be used, for instance, on a rusty iron keel (for which you will also need a wire brush). Great caution must be used if the triangular scraper is employed elsewhere on the boat, as its points can score surfaces badly, if it is carelessly handled. The best kind of scraper is the one which presents a blade flat to the surface. Usually, the blade can be taken out for sharpening and can also be

replaced with a serrated-edge blade for removing rough paint.

If you are going to paint new wood, you must sand it first, and then again between the first coats. Ordinary dry sand-paper will do. Start with coarse paper No. 3 and go on to the finer-grade papers, down to No. 0. Carborundum paper is more expensive but is, at the same time, more effective. For the best results, sand by hand. If you must use a power tool, get an oscillating one, but be very careful that you do not work too deep or burn the surface. Before you add the final coat of paint, sand the surface with wet paper, and do this by hand. Use a fine abrasive paper (Nos. 120–220).

Old bottom paint must always be wet-sanded in order to avoid raising clouds of poisonous dust from the paint. You can start sanding with paper No. 80. If you dry-sand, whether by hand or with a machine, you must wear a protective mask against the dust. Painting the bottom of your boat is important for two reasons: it prevents fouling, and it gives a smooth surface, which reduces frictional resistance. It is mainly the forward part of the hull which dictates the amount of frictional resistance, and this is why you should spend as much time sanding and polishing the forward third of the bottom, keel, and/or centre-board, as you do on the other two thirds together. For racing yachts, a hard bottom paint which can be polished is commonly used in order to obtain the smoothest possible bottom surface.

There are many different anti-fouling paints, and some are more suitable for certain types of waters than others. Choose a type which has proved its worth in your home waters. Study the paint manufacturer's leaflets, and ask the advice of experienced boat-owners.

Modern two-pot polyurethane paints are extremely durable, but they are more troublesome to apply and a lot more difficult to sand down than the conventional and one-pot polyurethane paints. For GRP boats, a two-pot paint is best. Sooner or later, the gelcoat of a GRP boat will be so scratched and unsightly that it must be painted. Two-pot paint is as durable as gelcoat, which is why a painted GRP boat does not need annual repainting.

Before GRP surfaces are painted, all polish, silicone, and mould-release agent must be removed with white spirit or thinner, and the surfaces must be wet-sanded, so that the paint can adhere properly. Never use paint removers or a blow torch on fibre-glass laminate.

A brush will do for many painting jobs, but large areas are more rapidly coated with a roller or a spreader (a cushion of foamed plastic, covered with mohair). Whatever you use, make sure that it is right for the kind of paint you have. For instance, there are special rollers and spreaders for two-pot paints. A rolled surface easily gets somewhat granulated, like orange rind, unless you smooth it immediately after application with a broad, flat brush.

Common solvents are white spirit, thinner (sometimes of a special type), alcohol, petrol, and acetone. The directions for use on the paint-can normally indicate the correct solvent to use.

For wood there are three types of glue suitable for marine use. Urea-formaldehyde resin glue is not entirely waterproof, and the glue lines must be protected by a layer of paint. Phenolic resin and resorcinol resin glues are perfectly weather-proof and should be used where heavy demands are made on the joins. The bond between old or rough wooden surfaces will not hold as well as that between smooth, clean surfaces. Therefore, always plane or sand-paper all wooden surfaces before spreading glue on them. Use plenty of screw clamps to hold the two parts together under pressure while the glue hardens, or screw or nail the two parts together. The higher the pressure, the stronger the bond will be.

Epoxy-resin glue is so strong that you can even use it for gluing metal fittings to plastic surfaces, but not to thermo-plastics. For safety's sake, however, use screws as well. A drop of epoxy-resin glue on their threads will make them grip extra strongly. Always keep a small pack of epoxy-resin glue on board the boat, as it may come in handy for minor repairs.

There are special glues for most purposes. If you want to cover something with insulating material, for instance, you can either use a glue which does not bond immediately, or a contact glue, in which case you must see to it that the joint is perfect at once, since the glue bites instantaneously. Cellular polystyrene, used for insulation or buoyancy, needs a special contact glue, as some glues dissolve cellular plastics.

Pleasure-boat engines rarely wear out. Instead, they are ruined by corrosion, lack of lubrication, or other types of neglect. When you buy an engine, read the operating and installation manuals thoroughly, as each engine type has its own peculiarities.

All boat engines need regular lubrication and anti-corrosion treatment. Make it a habit to check often the oil level in both engine and reverse gear, and see to it that the amount of grease or oil in the propeller-shaft stuffing-box or gearbox is adequate. Your engine should always be neat and clean; when necessary, touch it up a bit with motor paint. Use anti-corrosion oil on all metal parts which are not covered by paint, including those of the electrical system.

However, outer corrosion is no serious menace to your engine. It is visible and thus easily controlled. The real danger to your engine is the one you cannot see, i.e., inner corrosion, and this can cause severe damage. When your boat is in the water, never allow the engine to remain unused for long periods. At least once a fortnight, it should be started up and run until it has reached its normal working temperature. This is necessary to keep the inner parts of the engine lubricated. If you know that you will not have the opportunity to run the engine for, say, a month or so, you should lay it up, or "winterize" it. Naturally, you must also do this when you lay up the boat for the season.

Water-cooled engines are easily damaged by frost. Far too many engine blocks crack because the water in the cooling systems has frozen solid during the winter (in places where winter invariably means below freezing-point temperatures). If your boat is still in the water when autumn comes and temperatures threaten to fall below freezing point, close the sea-cock which supplies salt water to the system and drain all the water from the engine, the exhaust system, and—if water-cooled—the reverse gear. If the engine has a fresh-water cooling system, i.e., equipped with a heat exchanger, make sure that the whole system is drained and that both fresh-water and sea-water circuits are empty. Anti-freeze can then be added to increase the engine's protection against frost. Drain cocks are frequently obstructed by rust and dirt, so if no water runs out when you open a cock, clean it out with a piece of steel wire.

Before draining the cooling system, you should flush it thoroughly with fresh water to remove all traces of salt and dirt. This can be done by closing the sea-cock, loosening the hose and lengthening it with an extra bit of hose, which is then planted in a bucketful of fresh water. Start the engine and rev it for ten minutes, or until the bucket is empty. Drain all water from the engine, the reverse gear, and the exhaust system. Then restart the engine, and run it in neutral for not more than one minute, with a brief spell of revving, so that all the remaining water is blown out of the exhaust system. If you keep the engine running any longer than one minute without cooling water, it may seize, or the water pump may be damaged.

Where salt water is used for cooling, the engine should be protected against frost by filling the system with anti-freeze through some opening near the top (for instance, through the thermostat connection). After rinsing out the system with fresh water, reconnect the cooling-water intake hose, but leave the sea-cock closed. Then close the engine's drain cocks and fill up with anti-freeze (which ought to be able to withstand temperatures of down to −31° F [−35° C]). The anti-freeze also works as an anti-corrosion agent inside the cooling system. Occasionally, if the engine is an old one, the hoses or pump parts can be attacked by anti-freeze, so check that these are sound before adding the anti-freeze.

Preferably, the fuel system should be empty when your boat is laid up; otherwise, the fuel may form deposits of resin and these can foul the fuel pump or the carburettor. Open the carburettor's drain cock to drain any remaining fuel. Clean the fuel filter, or exchange it for a new one.

The electrical system easily corrodes. Spray the inside of the distributor head, the starting motor, the generator, relays, and all switches and cable connections with anti-corrosion oil. While you are at it, give all other unprotected metal surfaces in the engine a good coating as well. Dismount the battery, and store it away from frost. During the off-season, it is a good idea to have the battery recharged.

The internal protection of your engine will be increased if you run it at varying speeds for at least thirty minutes on fuel mixed with anti-rust oil. This should be done immediately before you take care of the cooling system. Up to 5 per cent of a suitable preservative oil can be added to petrol; 33 per cent to diesel fuel. Left-over anti-rust and fuel mixture can be kept for use at the beginning of the next boating season.

If your engine has a carburettor, spray some anti-corrosion oil into the air intake just before switching the engine off or until the oil "kills" the engine. Remove the sparking plugs and pour a few drops of motor oil over the pistons. Even better, spray a generous dose of anti-corrosion oil onto the cylinders. Then turn the engine over a few times, either by hand or with the starting motor, so that the oil is spread all over the walls of the cylinders, top of the pistons, valves, and so on. Replace the sparking plugs if they are in good shape and have the correct spark gap. While the engine is still hot, the motor oil should be changed. Change the oil filter before you use the engine again.

Fire on board is often caused by faults in the fuel system, and this is due, in most cases, to shoddy installation work. This is especially true for petrol-driven boats. When you fill the tank, no fuel must be allowed to escape into the boat. The fuel filler cap must be situated on the deck, and the "breather pipe" must run out as high as possible on the outside of the hull. Portable tanks should be lifted out of the boat before being filled. Hose clips and pipe nipples should be regularly checked and tightened, and the carburettor must be equipped with a flame guard.

If petrol fumes or other combustible gases do escape into the boat despite all precautions, they are usually ignited by faulty electrics or by sparks from the starting motor. This is why it would be less risky to keep a petrol-driven engine running while refuelling than it would be to start up a newly refuelled boat without previously ventilating the engine-room thoroughly, preferably with an extractor fan.

Faulty exhaust pipes, which leak carbon monoxide into cabins, have been the cause of some tragic deaths and many narrow escapes. Keep an eye open for potential leaks in the exhaust system, especially if your boat is decked.

To ensure that your engine keeps working properly, you must check regularly that there is enough oil in both motor and reverse gear, and enough grease in all the bearings. Follow any special lubrication instructions, and see to it that oil and fuel filters are cleaned or changed, and that the acid level in the batteries is about 0.4 in (10 mm) above the plates.

Nowadays, working sails are almost exclusively made from polyester fibres—Terylene, Dacron, Tergal, Tetoron, etc., are all trade names for more or less identical synthetic materials. Spinnakers are usually made from nylon, which is more elastic.

Sails will usually keep the shape given to them by the sail-maker, unless they are subjected to exceptional strains. Still, it is wise to break in new sails in moderate winds without sheeting too hard. Never put an excessive load on your sails; do not, for instance, let the leech carry the entire weight of the boom when you are hoisting the main.

It goes without saying that your sails need maintenance. What will ruin them is, above all, chafing, flogging, overstretching, folds and creases, dampness, dirt, salt, mildew, and direct sunlight. Heads and clews, batten pockets, and the areas which chafe against shrouds and spreaders are particularly exposed to wear. The seams are especially susceptible, as the thread does not sink into the stiffish cloth. Any tear should be repaired before it gets a chance to become bigger. You can mend a sail temporarily with a special adhesive tape. First of all, however, you should find out the cause of the damage, and try and prevent it from happening again. A sharp split pin should be bound with tape, sheeting can be arranged differently, shrouds or spreaders can be given protective coverings, and the sails can be reinforced where they are most likely to be chafed.

As flogging spoils sails, wet sails should be taken down and spread out on the ground to dry. However, in a very faint breeze they may be allowed to dry while hoisted. Creases and sharp folds reduce the efficiency of a sail and may damage it, so do not just carelessly cram your sails into their bags. Preferably, a sail should be folded parallel with the foot, and then loosely rolled around the luff into a neat bundle, which goes easily into its bag. In this way, the sail-bags will be less bulky than they would be if the sails had just been crammed into them. If the sails are to be stored for any longer period of time, they must be dry. Salt makes them heavy and also attracts moisture, which will make them even heavier. Rinse the salt away with fresh water. A good shower of rain will rinse away salt from hoisted sails.

Synthetic sails are fairly resistant to sunshine, but they age faster in the sun than out of it. This is a good reason for using a sail cover, or stowing sails below deck.

Dirty sails can be washed in lukewarm water with a mild detergent. Grease spots may be removed with trichloroethylene, but be sure to rinse thoroughly afterwards. Even a mild detergent must be carefully rinsed away. When you put your sails away for the season they must be intact, clean, dry, and loosely rolled in their bags. Store in a dry, well-ventilated place.

At the end of the season, when you unrig your boat, inspect every single detail of the standing as well as the running rigging, and attend to any defects you find. Aluminium masts and booms should be washed and rinsed with fresh water to get rid of the salt. It is a good idea to rinse the inside of the masts as well. The lower part of the mast is particularly exposed to corrosion, and it must, therefore, be cleaned extra well. If you are going to wrap the mast in plastic sheets, it must be completely dry. When stored, the mast must be well trestled, otherwise it may bend.

If you have a wooden mast, sand and varnish it before stepping it at the start of each season. Aluminium masts should be treated with liquid paraffin or water-free lanolin in order to protect their surfaces.

All details susceptible to corrosion, as well as all adjustable parts, should be greased before the boat is laid up. Electrical connections are particularly susceptible and should be sprayed with an anti-corrosion oil. Deck plugs can be taken apart and filled with vaseline. Rigging screws, winches, sheaves, shackles, and piston hanks should be oiled and greased. Water-resistant propeller grease may be used, but lanolin is "cleaner". Many sailors make it easy for themselves by simply spraying it all with an anti-corrosion oil. Sail tracks and other sliding surfaces are best rubbed with solid paraffin. If you want to fasten new fittings to an aluminium mast you should use plastic, aluminium, or stainless-steel fittings. Brass and other copper alloys will cause severe corrosion. In order to avoid this, insulate all fittings from the mast. Plastic sheet laminate, zinc chromate primer, or vaseline, are useful for this. Fasten the fittings with bolts or screws of stainless steel or with Monel pop rivets. Epoxy glue adds to the strength of the fastening and may be used on bolt- and screw-threads to insulate and lock them. Self-tapping screws increase corrosion risks and should be avoided. The points of screws can also jam halyards inside the mast.

Wooden surfaces below deck can be maintained with ordinary furniture polish. Bare teak surfaces should either be treated with special teak oil or with raw linseed oil, diluted with white spirit. Wipe away any excess oil with a soft cloth, dampened with white spirit.

Textiles can pose problems. Curtains can usually be washed in a washing machine; but, to be on the safe side, all cushion covers and other textiles should be dry-cleaned or foam-cleaned, unless you are absolutely convinced that the materials used are washable in water. Salt and bird droppings on canvas cockpit covers or awnings are best removed with fresh water and a brush, as detergents and solvents will ruin the water-proofing. If you wash the canvas with a detergent—and if you do, a soap detergent is to be preferred—then you have to reproof it. Paint shops market water-proofing in spray bottles. In order to avoid shrinkage, wash and dry canvas cockpit covers when they are pitched.

Cockpit covers made from polyvinyl-chloride (PVC) coated fabric can be washed clean with fresh water and a mild detergent. Washing agents containing acetone or ammonia will make the plastic brittle and brown.

Sea-cocks can corrode, so give them a drop of oil and try them out every now and again. Toilets must also be lubricated. A few drops of oil on the pump lever may be needed, and a spoonful of salad oil, poured into the toilet bowl, may make the valves and so on work better. Avoid strong cleaning agents which might harm hoses, rubber packings, and valves. When you lay up your boat at the end of the season, the toilet should be pumped out and cleaned. Usually, there are drainage plugs so that the system can be emptied; if not, you have to add anti-freeze, if you live where frost is expected. Naturally, the fresh-water tank, if any, must be emptied as well before you lay up the boat.

The end of the season draws near, and the time has come to lay up your boat. It will probably have to spend a number of months on land, which is why there is every reason for you to make sure that it does not have a rough time.

A sailing-boat must be unrigged before it is laid up. Large masts are best unstepped by means of special derrick cranes. Different clubs and ship-yards use different methods to lift and launch boats, but usually a boat cradle or a crane is employed. As a rule, a foreman or crane operator will be in charge to help and guide the inexperienced boat-owner. You should know the approximate centre of gravity of your boat, as well as its underwater shape, so that you can assist in placing the boat correctly on the cradle or can fix the lifting slings in the right position. As soon as the boat is out of the water, scrub the bottom clean of barnacles, seaweed, and anything else that might have fastened there during the season. If these fouling organisms are allowed to dry in, you will have a tough job to get rid of them. Usually, a scrubbing with a stiff brush, and a hose-down with detergent and water will do, unless the boat is heavily overgrown with barnacles, in which case you may have to resort to a scraper.

When a boat is laid up for the winter, it must be placed on a sturdy cradle or trestle, so that it will not budge even in a rough storm. The hull must be properly blocked and shored, so that its shape changes as little as possible.

Before covering the boat, remove everything that is portable and clean the below-deck area thoroughly. Any expensive equipment whatsoever should be dismounted and stored in your home. It is also a good idea to take home anything which has to be repaired, overhauled, varnished, or painted during the off season. Finally, see to it that your boat is well ventilated when laid up. This is very important. Floor boards should be lifted, and all cupboards, boxes, and drawers left open. Naturally, all hatches and ventilators must remain open too—another good reason to remove all valuables and portables. Ensure that the bilges are clean and dry.

Boats can be covered in many ways, from a whole boat-house to a simple cover. Wooden boats should be completely covered, so that rain, hail, or snow cannot get in. GRP boats are less susceptible and, for them, a simple tarpaulin, covering cockpit and openings, will do. However, it is vital that the cover does not prevent the boat from being ventilated. If you use a PVC plastic-sheeting cover, be careful not to let if fit too tightly to a dark-pigmented GRP hull. Condensation under the tarpaulin may penetrate the gelcoat and make it patchy. This usually disappears by and by, as the damp evaporates, but the pigment can also be permanently discoloured.

Another thing to do is to make a note of all the defects that must be attended to during the winter, and of all spare parts and jobs to be ordered. It is usually better to see to these things during the off season. When the time comes to launch the boat again, you may be too busy to attend to them all.

Fitting out a wooden boat mainly consists of cleaning, sanding, and painting. Save varnishing of the deck, cabin, and coamings until your boat is afloat, since surroundings then will be comparatively dust-free. For a GRP boat, it may suffice to paint the bottom and polish the topsides before launching. Everything else can be taken care of when the boat is in the water. All the remaining jobs then follow successively: rigging, functional tests, test-running of the engine, taking aboard all equipment, etc.

When your boat is in use you have plenty of opportunity to look after it well and, as has already been stated, the main things are to keep it clean, to maintain painted or varnished surfaces, to polish GRP surfaces, and to fight corrosion. Apart from tools and spare engine and rig parts, you should thus carry on board detergents, an oil can, grease or lanolin, anti-corrosion oil, teak oil, wax, varnish, solvents, and so on, so that minor damages can be touched up and the boat be kept shipshape.

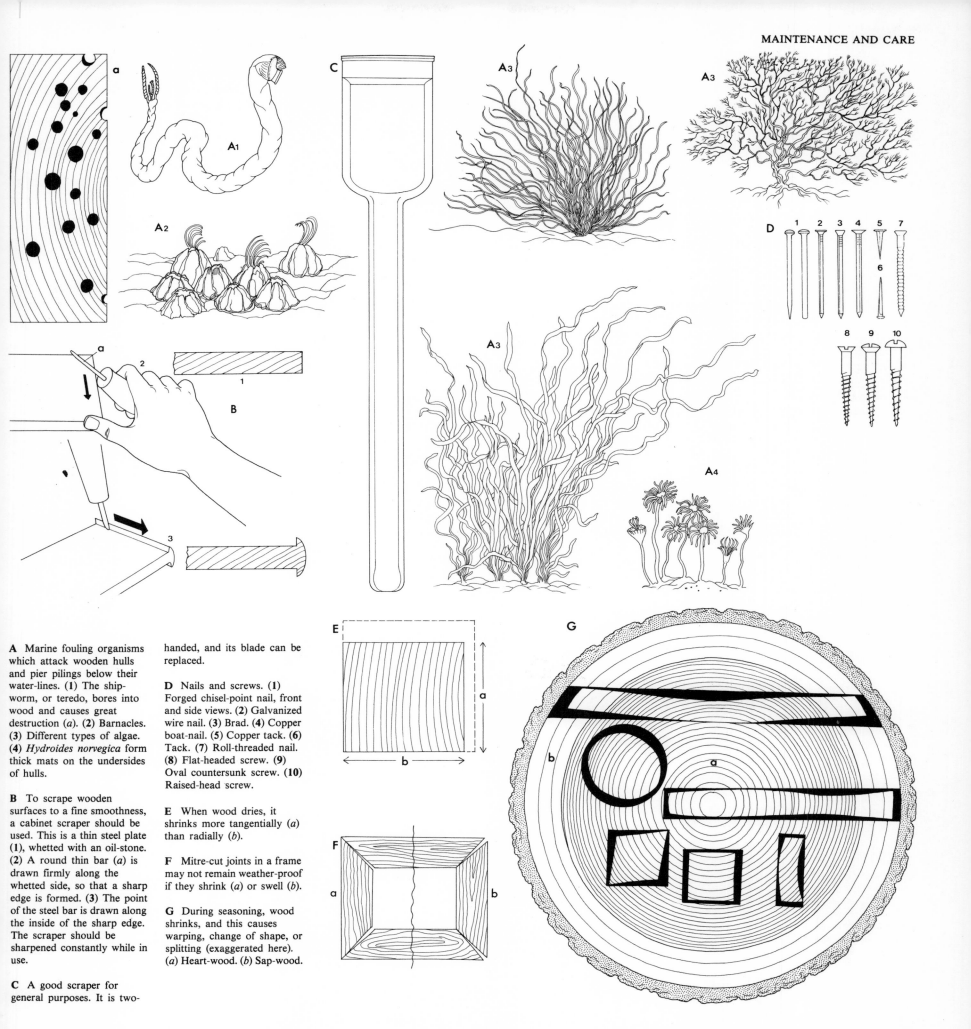

A Marine fouling organisms which attack wooden hulls and pier pilings below their water-lines. (**1**) The ship-worm, or teredo, bores into wood and causes great destruction (*a*). (**2**) Barnacles. (**3**) Different types of algae. (**4**) *Hydroides norvegica* form thick mats on the undersides of hulls.

B To scrape wooden surfaces to a fine smoothness, a cabinet scraper should be used. This is a thin steel plate (**1**), whetted with an oil-stone. (**2**) A round thin bar (*a*) is drawn firmly along the whetted side, so that a sharp edge is formed. (**3**) The point of the steel bar is drawn along the inside of the sharp edge. The scraper should be sharpened constantly while in use.

C A good scraper for general purposes. It is two-handed, and its blade can be replaced.

D Nails and screws. (**1**) Forged chisel-point nail, front and side views. (**2**) Galvanized wire nail. (**3**) Brad. (**4**) Copper boat-nail. (**5**) Copper tack. (**6**) Tack. (**7**) Roll-threaded nail. (**8**) Flat-headed screw. (**9**) Oval countersunk screw. (**10**) Raised-head screw.

E When wood dries, it shrinks more tangentially (*a*) than radially (*b*).

F Mitre-cut joints in a frame may not remain weather-proof if they shrink (*a*) or swell (*b*).

G During seasoning, wood shrinks, and this causes warping, change of shape, or splitting (exaggerated here). (*a*) Heart-wood. (*b*) Sap-wood.

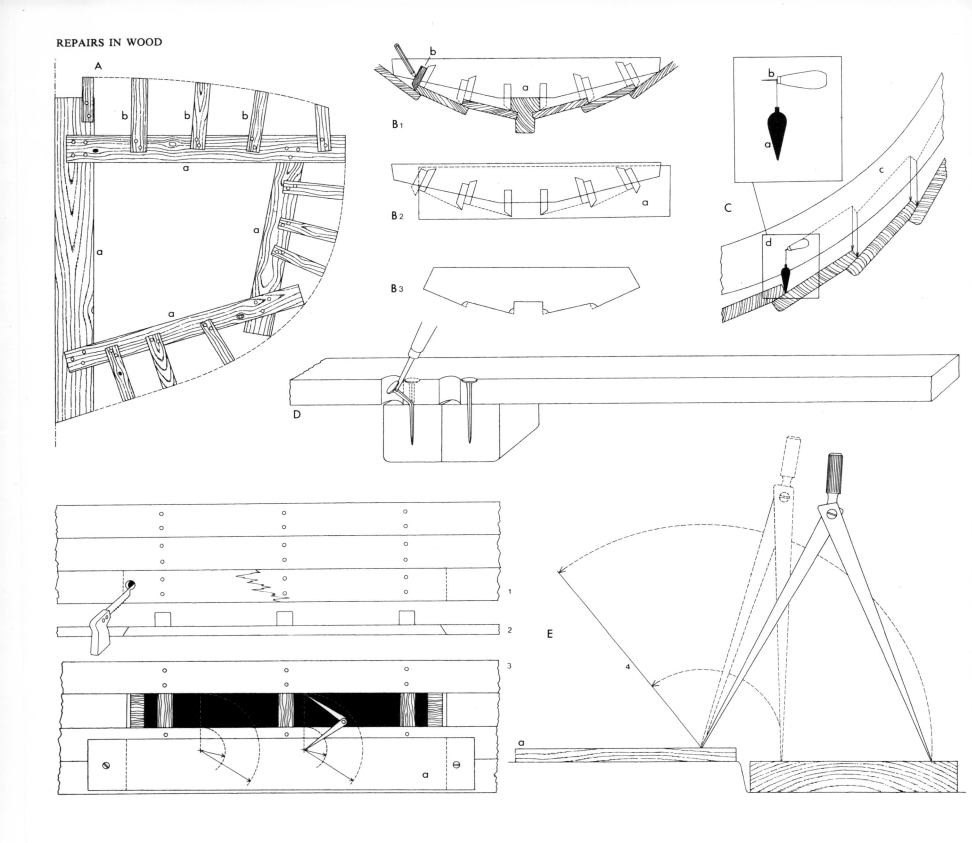

A When a damaged bulkhead is being replaced, a mould of the bulkhead can be made in the following way. On a frame of thin boards (*a*), nail small laths (*b*) so that their outer edges mark out the contours of the bulkhead. These contours can then be transferred to the material for the new bulkhead.

B When making a mould of a floor timber which must be replaced (**1**), take a suitably thick piece of wood (*a*), shaped roughly to fit along the bottom where the new floor timber will go. A small piece of wood with a distinct shape (*b*) is held against the contour to be modelled, and a mark is made on the inner side of the piece of wood, wherever an irregularity occurs in the hull shape. (**2**) The marked mould is now laid on the wood for the new floor timber (*a*), and the marking procedure is reversed, the other end of the small piece of wood being marked, thus tracing the shape of the floor timber on the new wood. (**3**) The completed floor timber is finally fitted in position. Note the limber holes.

C In clinker-built boats, a little plumb-line (*a*) attached to a sharp awl (*b*) can be used when tracing moulds. The roughly shaped piece of wood (*c*) is put into position. The plumb-line is held so that its point just touches the surface of the inside of the hull (*d*), and the awl is pressed into the wood. This is done at each irregularity in the hull, thus tracing the required contour. This can be done on both sides of the piece to be shaped.

D When removing a damaged part, an old screw or nail is often difficult to move. Drill a hole beside it, and knock it to one side with a hammer and punch.

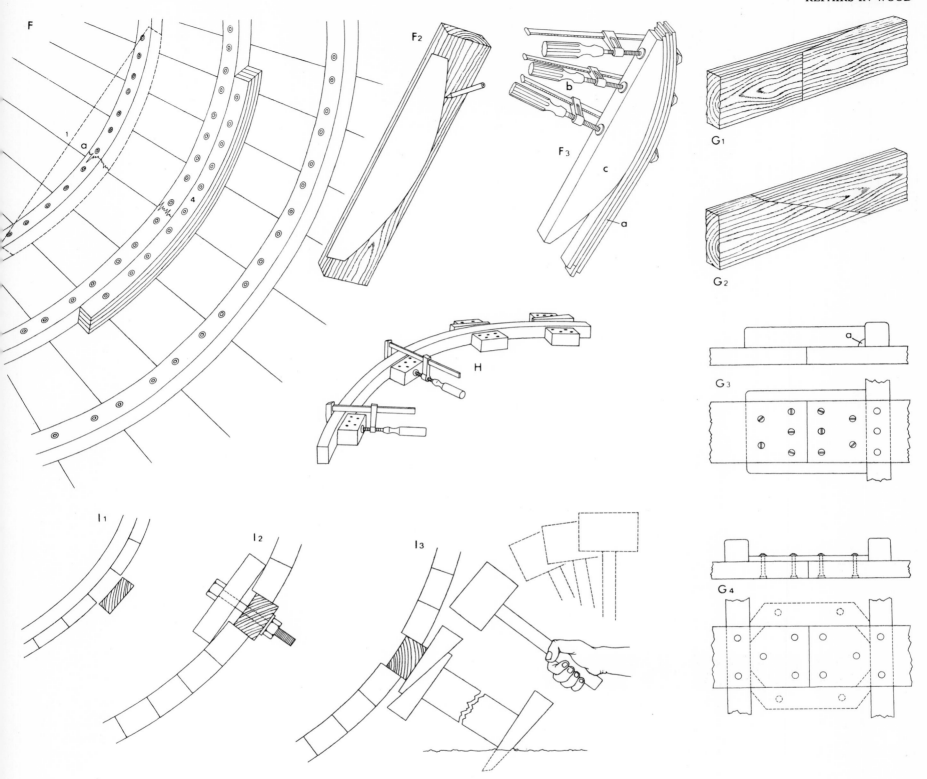

E To replace part of a plank in a carvel-built boat, (**1**) the damaged part must be removed by drilling holes and sawing it out. (**2**) The ends are sawn diagonally, when seen from above. (**3**) A spiling batten (*a*) is screwed onto the hull beside the hole, and the exact shape of the plank is transferred to the spiling batten with dividers. (**4**) This shape is then transferred to the new planking (*a*), which is then shaped accordingly, inserted, and scarfed.

F How to strengthen a damaged rib. (**1**) Make a mould of cardboard (*a*). (**2**) From this, shape a stout wooden mould. (**3**) Glue 1.5-in (3.8 cm) strips (*a*) of oak or ash together, forming them with clamps (*b*) on the wooden mould (*c*). When the glue has hardened, the strengthener is screwed or riveted (**4**) beside the damaged rib.

G Planking is scarfed with either a diagonal or a butt scarf. A diagonal scarf used in clinker building is cut across the broad face of the plank (**1**), while that used in carvel building is cut across the edges of the plank (**2**). In a butt scarf, a butt-block, or butt-plate, of wood (**3**) or metal (**4**) is used. If the butt-block lies against a frame, a limber hole (*a*) should be made. If the butt-block is wider than the planking, as in **4**, the construction will be much stronger.

H Frames can be bent or laminated as shown. The blocks of wood are nailed to the floor.

I A new plank, or part of a plank, should be shaped on the inside, so that it fits flush with the other planks. The outside can be planed after the plank has been inserted (**1**). The new plank can be pressed into place by the nut-and-bolt method shown (**2**), the bolt hole being plugged later. The plank can also be pressed in with wedges (**3**).

GRP REPAIRS

When a boat built from GRP is badly damaged, the repairs should be carried out by a boat-yard. However, the handy amateur can repair some types of light damage to GRP laminate by himself.

A Few boat-owners escape hitting a pier or running aground some time or other. When a grounding occurs, the parts most liable to damage are the stem and keel. Should you hit a pier, it will probably be some part of the hull above the water-line which will be damaged, and usually the damage will be only skin-deep, in which case it can be

repaired with epoxy or polyester resin and then coated with gelcoat or bottom paint.

B Shallow surface scratches in the gelcoat are repaired with gelcoat putty. (**1**) The putty (*a*) is mixed with *c.* four per cent hardener (*b*). (**2**) Masking-tape (*a*) is fastened round the damage, and a steel putty knife (*b*) is used to apply the putty up to the level of the tape. (**3**) As the putty hardens, it shrinks a little. (**4**) When it has hardened, the tape is removed, and the putty is sanded down to the correct level.

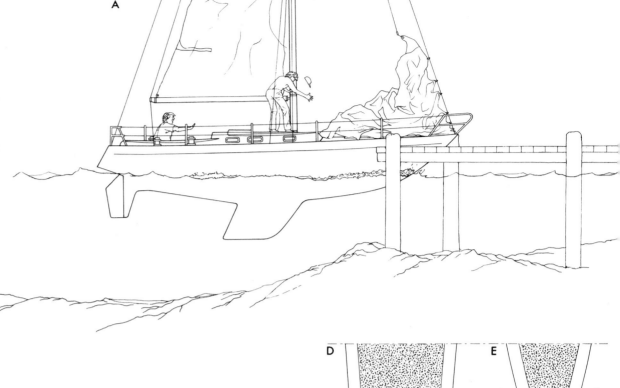

C For repairs to laminate, you need, besides GRP matting, the following tools and materials. (**1**) Pre-accelerated polyester resin is mixed with one to three per cent of the appropriate catalyst (**2**)—follow the manufacturer's instructions. The catalyst is measured in a graduate (**3**). Acetone (**4**) is used to clean tools and hands. Tools that are not properly cleaned, rapidly become useless. Soak your tools in acetone (**5**) during any breaks in work. Suitable amounts of resin and catalyst are mixed in a tin or in a thermoplastic bowl (**6**)—hardened left-overs can be removed easily from these. The resin is applied with a brush or, if it is a large job, with a paint-roller. Cheap throw-away brushes can be

made easily from suitable lengths of wood and pieces of nylon-pile carpeting—"coaters" (**7**) for applying the resin, and "dabbers" (**8**) for saturating the GRP matting with resin, and for removing air pockets.

D Keel damage which results in a deepish cavity in the filling material (*a*) can be filled with pieces of GRP matting, and polyester resin or putty (*b*). Before work begins, the surface around the damage must be trimmed or sanded, and then cleaned, leaving a fresh surface as a base for the repair. When the cavity is filled, the job is finished by laminating a few layers of matting (*c*) over the cavity and the surrounding area (*d*). When the lamination has

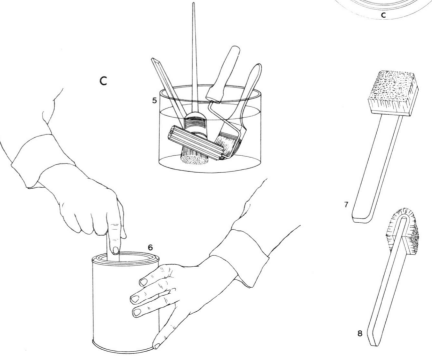

hardened, it is sanded down and painted.

E A cracked fin or rudder can be repaired by filling the cavity with putty (*a*), and by screwing across the crack with a self-tapping screw (*b*). If extra reinforcement is needed, the gelcoat (*c*) around the damage is sanded down, and the area is laminated with matting and polyester resin (*d*).

F If the hole penetrates the hull and is accessible from the inside, the damaged laminate is sawn off with a hack-saw or ground away with a power grinder. (**1**) The edges of the hole are then filed as shown. (**2**) The hole is covered on the outside with a backing piece (*a*) of some material which will not stick to polyester, such as masonite, plywood, or cardboard covered with plastic or aluminium foil. A small backing piece can be fastened with tape, whereas a larger one is best screwed on (*b*). If the repair will be visible above the water-line, a layer of gelcoat is first applied. When the gelcoat has hardened, the lamination can start (**3**).

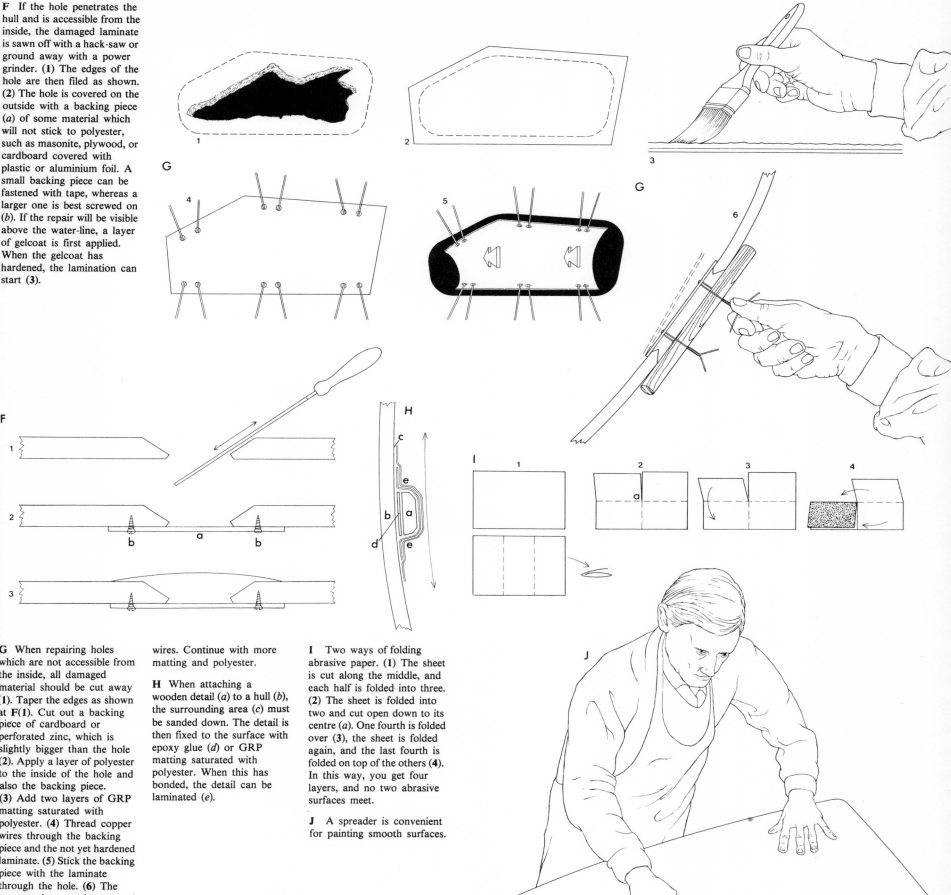

G When repairing holes which are not accessible from the inside, all damaged material should be cut away (**1**). Taper the edges as shown at **F**(**1**). Cut out a backing piece of cardboard or perforated zinc, which is slightly bigger than the hole (**2**). Apply a layer of polyester to the inside of the hole and also the backing piece. (**3**) Add two layers of GRP matting saturated with polyester. (**4**) Thread copper wires through the backing piece and the not yet hardened laminate. (**5**) Stick the backing piece with the laminate through the hole. (**6**) The copper wires are then wound round wooden sticks on the outside. Leave to harden for about one hour; then remove the sticks and the copper

wires. Continue with more matting and polyester.

H When attaching a wooden detail (*a*) to a hull (*b*), the surrounding area (*c*) must be sanded down. The detail is then fixed to the surface with epoxy glue (*d*) or GRP matting saturated with polyester. When this has bonded, the detail can be laminated (*e*).

I Two ways of folding abrasive paper. (**1**) The sheet is cut along the middle, and each half is folded into three. (**2**) The sheet is folded into two and cut open down to its centre (*a*). One fourth is folded over (**3**), the sheet is folded again, and the last fourth is folded on top of the others (**4**). In this way, you get four layers, and no two abrasive surfaces meet.

J A spreader is convenient for painting smooth surfaces.

A When unstepping or stepping a mast with a derrick crane, a noose (**1**) should not be used—for one thing, you may end up with the lifting point wrongly placed, and for another, when you step the mast at the start of the season, it may be difficult to loosen the noose. Instead, you should use a rope, bent with a bowline hitch to a large eye, which is placed round the mast underneath the spreaders (**2**). The rope should be long enough for you to reach one end from deck.

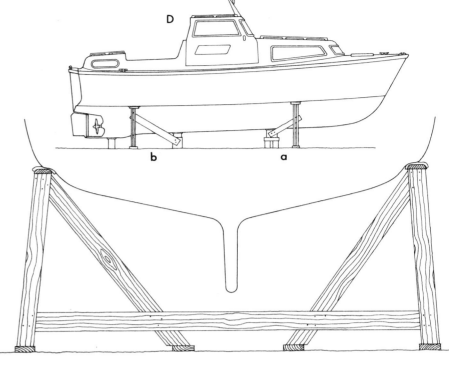

D Supporting frames for the forebody (*a*) and the after body (*b*) can be nailed together from, for instance, 4 × 1 in (100 × 25 mm) wood. Stays secure the supporting frames to the trestling blocks underneath the keel.

E If the boat is equipped with an IO drive, a supporting frame should be placed under the after body (**1**). If the engine is placed in the middle of the hull, a supporting frame should be placed under there (**2**).

F Larger powerboats may need two sturdy frames under the stern.

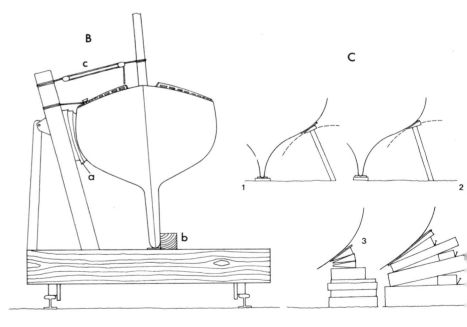

B When being laid up on a boat wagon, a keelboat should be so placed and secured that it cannot slip or turn over. Protection against chafing (*a*), a beam (*b*) which stops the keel from slipping to one side, and lashings (*c*) between the boat wagon's stanchions and the mast, a sheet winch, or some other stronghold, are necessary.

C A laid-up boat must be securely trestled so that it does not budge during winter storms. A stanchion must not be so short (**1**) that it falls down if a wedge works loose—if this happens, the stanchion should instead wedge itself underneath the hull (**2**). Wooden blocks and wedges must not be too loosely stacked (**3**), but should preferably be nailed together (**4**).

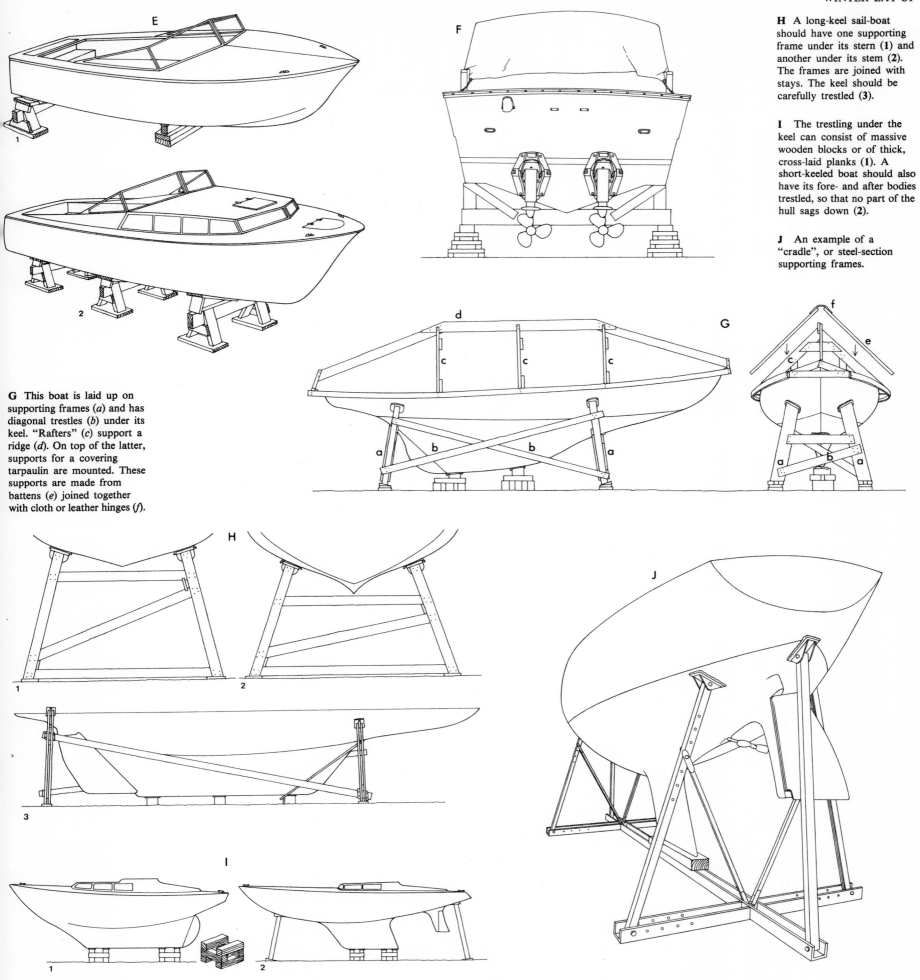

H A long-keel sail-boat should have one supporting frame under its stern (**1**) and another under its stem (**2**). The frames are joined with stays. The keel should be carefully trestled (**3**).

I The trestling under the keel can consist of massive wooden blocks or of thick, cross-laid planks (**1**). A short-keeled boat should also have its fore- and after bodies trestled, so that no part of the hull sags down (**2**).

J An example of a "cradle", or steel-section supporting frames.

G This boat is laid up on supporting frames (*a*) and has diagonal trestles (*b*) under its keel. "Rafters" (*c*) support a ridge (*d*). On top of the latter, supports for a covering tarpaulin are mounted. These supports are made from battens (*e*) joined together with cloth or leather hinges (*f*).

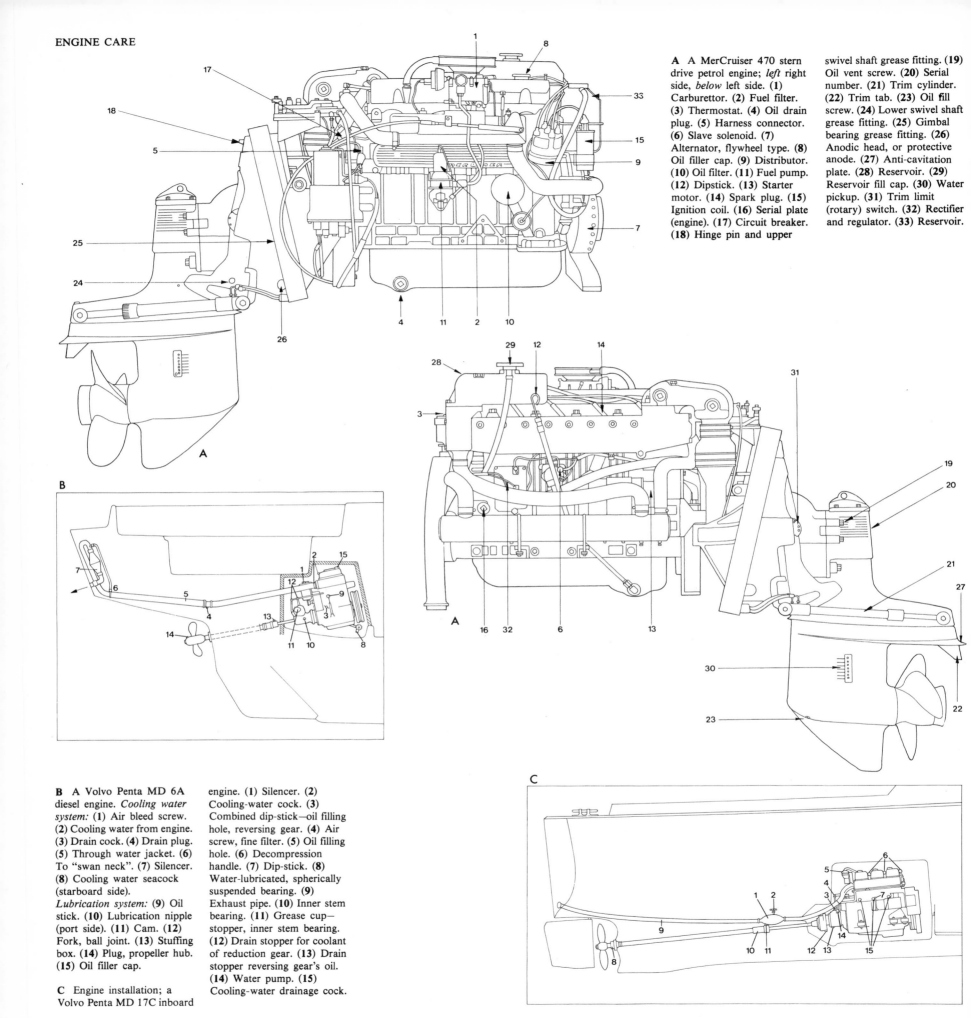

A A MerCruiser 470 stern drive petrol engine; *left* right side, *below* left side. (**1**) Carburettor. (**2**) Fuel filter. (**3**) Thermostat. (**4**) Oil drain plug. (**5**) Harness connector. (**6**) Slave solenoid. (**7**) Alternator, flywheel type. (**8**) Oil filler cap. (**9**) Distributor. (**10**) Oil filter. (**11**) Fuel pump. (**12**) Dipstick. (**13**) Starter motor. (**14**) Spark plug. (**15**) Ignition coil. (**16**) Serial plate (engine). (**17**) Circuit breaker. (**18**) Hinge pin and upper swivel shaft grease fitting. (**19**) Oil vent screw. (**20**) Serial number. (**21**) Trim cylinder. (**22**) Trim tab. (**23**) Oil fill screw. (**24**) Lower swivel shaft grease fitting. (**25**) Gimbal bearing grease fitting. (**26**) Anodic head, or protective anode. (**27**) Anti-cavitation plate. (**28**) Reservoir. (**29**) Reservoir fill cap. (**30**) Water pickup. (**31**) Trim limit (rotary) switch. (**32**) Rectifier and regulator. (**33**) Reservoir.

B A Volvo Penta MD 6A diesel engine. *Cooling water system:* (**1**) Air bleed screw. (**2**) Cooling water from engine. (**3**) Drain cock. (**4**) Drain plug. (**5**) Through water jacket. (**6**) To "swan neck". (**7**) Silencer. (**8**) Cooling water seacock (starboard side).
Lubrication system: (**9**) Oil stick. (**10**) Lubrication nipple (port side). (**11**) Cam. (**12**) Fork, ball joint. (**13**) Stuffing box. (**14**) Plug, propeller hub. (**15**) Oil filler cap.

C Engine installation; a Volvo Penta MD 17C inboard engine. (**1**) Silencer. (**2**) Cooling-water cock. (**3**) Combined dip-stick—oil filling hole, reversing gear. (**4**) Air screw, fine filter. (**5**) Oil filling hole. (**6**) Decompression handle. (**7**) Dip-stick. (**8**) Water-lubricated, spherically suspended bearing. (**9**) Exhaust pipe. (**10**) Inner stem bearing. (**11**) Grease cup—stopper, inner stem bearing. (**12**) Drain stopper for coolant of reduction gear. (**13**) Drain stopper reversing gear's oil. (**14**) Water pump. (**15**) Cooling-water drainage cock.

THEORY OF BOATING

Jaap A. M. Kramer

Manoeuvring a yacht can be learnt from a textbook, from a boating friend, or from an instructor at a club, and from any of these you will be able to acquire a good grasp of the standard manoeuvres. Once under way, however, you can easily find yourself in a situation with which you have not learnt to cope, such as rough weather, perhaps combined with nasty tidal streams and shallows, or with seagoing traffic. In such circumstances, you will have to make your own plan for your manoeuvres. Therefore, you must be in a position to evaluate the situation, to decide what to do, when and how to do it, and to carry out your plan, all within the space of some minutes. In cases of acute danger, there is often only a split second available.

It is, therefore, vital to have a thorough knowledge of boating theory—why your boat behaves the way it does, how it reacts to the different forces of water and wind, and where the dividing line is between "possible" and "impossible" in handling your boat.

It was Archimedes who, when taking a bath, discovered the upward pressure of water. He found that every object, partially or totally immersed in liquid, is subject to an upward force equal to the weight of the displaced amount of liquid. The floating boat, therefore, is supported by the water which presses against its hull from below.

In conformity with the law of gravity, the weight of a boat is directed vertically downwards. Nevertheless, the boat does not sink but settles in the water down to its water-line, which is where the upward force of the water equals the downward force caused by the weight of the boat. This equilibrium is reached when the weight of the boat equals the weight of the water displaced by it.

Thus, in fresh water, the displacement in volume-tons of 1,000 litres will be the same as the boat's weight in weight-tons of 1,000 kilos.

When a boat's equilibrium is disturbed, for instance by filling a tank with fresh water, bringing on board clothes, food, and equipment, and boarding with a crew, the boat will sink deeper into the water so that the displacement is increased by the additional weight which has been brought on board, and a new equilibrium is created.

When floating, a boat will have its hull partly above and partly below the surface of the water. When under way, it is moving through the boundary layer of two media: water and air. Operating under these conditions often presents great difficulties in the form of waves, created either by passing vessels or by the wind.

When a flat, thin plate is moved longitudinally through water, frictional resistance, called skin friction, will occur. This is created because the water particles closest to the plate more or less adhere to it. When the plate is moved, a thin layer of adhering liquid is thus moved along with it. This first layer will set another, adjacent layer in motion, though at a lower speed, and so on. The greater the distance from the plate, the lower the speed of these layers.

If the surfaces of the plate are very smooth, only a limited number of layers of water will be dragged along. If the surfaces are very rough, many more water particles will be set in motion by the plate, and these in turn will drag along more layers. The more water dragged along, the greater is the frictional resistance.

If all these layers are neatly arranged parallel to each other, the result is called "laminar flow". In the case of a very rough plate and/or a high speed through the water, the various layers get entangled, and turbulence occurs. The immediate result is a resistance much greater than in the case of laminar flow.

Turbulence may also be created when a smooth plate, even if moved at moderate speed, is rather long. Towards the aft end of the plate, the laminar flow of the water layers will change into turbulence. Consequently, the after part of the plate will be subject to a frictional resistance which is considerably higher than that experienced by the forward part.

In the same way, the immersed part of a boat is subject to frictional resistance. The outer surface of the immersed parts—hull, rudder, and (if applicable) keel or centre-board—is called the "wetted surface". The greater and rougher this wetted surface, the greater the frictional resistance. The designer, therefore, tries to keep the wetted surface as small and as smooth as possible. When a boat with a smooth wetted surface moves through calm water, the flow around the forward part of the hull will be laminar, while, towards the stern, it will turn into turbulent flow.

When a boat moves through the surface of the water, waves are formed. The boat not only forces an opening in the water but also pushes it aside and up and down. The water pushes up a bow wave which is followed by troughs and crests along the length of the hull. Another wave crest is formed at the stern where the water pushed down by the hull rises to join that forced sideways.

This wave pattern runs along with the boat and spreads along its sides. Such waves, stimulated by the motion of the boat, cause additional resistance, known as wave-making resistance or, as it is largely connected with the form of the underwater body, form resistance.

A wave is a motion, progressing in the water, in which the individual water particles undulate around the true level of the water's surface. The energy required to develop a wave system around a moving boat is provided by the boat, which is driven by the propulsive force of propeller(s), sail(s), or oars. Since most of the waves roll away from the boat, nearly all of the energy put into them is lost. Waves, therefore, are a waste of energy, which is why they should be kept as small as possible. A wave is a physical phenomenon with quite distinct properties. In relatively deep water, a wave moves horizontally. The water particles, however, predominantly move in a circular manner.

There is a correlation between wavelength and wave speed. A wave with a length of about 33 ft (10 m)—measured from crest to crest—moves at a speed of 7.7 knots, whereas a wave of about 66 ft (20 m) travels at around 10.8 knots. Conversely, there is only one possible wave speed for any given wavelength.

When a boat moves through the water, the bow and stern waves move at the speed of the boat and, after the boat has been moving for a short while at a certain speed, the matching wavelength will be developed at either side of the boat. At low speeds, short waves are built up. When the boat moves faster, the wavelength increases until, finally, the bow wave is followed by a long trough, and the next crest appears behind the boat, nearly or exactly coinciding with the stern wave, which in the latter case will be extra high. Most of the boat is then in the trough, and the water-line of the boat is lower than the average water level.

The wave system which an ordinary boat develops cannot have a wavelength greater than the distance between the bow and stern waves. Further, the speed of the boat cannot be higher than the speed allowed by that wavelength. If, for instance, a boat with a very powerful engine is suddenly given more throttle while in the trough between the bow and stern waves, the hull will not be capable of making a longer wave. Consequently, the wave speed cannot be increased, and the boat starts climbing up the back of its own bow wave. Additional power is necessary to get it up the back of its own bow wave, but the boat will not actually go any faster, despite this extra power.

But if the boat does not go any faster, what has happened to the additional power? It goes into the wave system. The bow wave grows higher, the trough behind it deeper, the aft sinks deeper still, and the stern wave becomes higher. Since the wavelength remains the same, the waves get steeper. This can be unpleasant for nearby boats, even dangerous for the smaller among them, and destructive to the shallow banks of rivers and lakes.

A very lightly constructed boat, with a fairly wide, flat-bottomed aft body and a flat stern, and with a high power (either engine or sail)-to-weight ratio, is, however, capable of climbing up to the crest of its own bow wave.

Freed from the suction of its wave trough, the boat can suddenly go much faster; it shoots forward, and the wavelength increases simultaneously with the new speed. The wave height, however, is reduced: the propulsive power is no longer wasted on the formation of steep waves but is transformed into a higher speed. Better still, part of the energy of the bow wave is utilized to lift the boat, whose water-line is lifted above the water surface, thus reducing the frictional as well as the form resistance of the hull.

The stern wave is now far behind the stern. It is a long, fast wave which is low and, therefore, cannot do much harm. The wavelength of a planing boat frequently amounts to twice the boat's water-line length. The wave-length of a perfectly designed hull, which is planing particularly fast, may be as much as eight to ten times the boat's water-line length. When a speedboat starts planing on its own bow wave, it becomes evident that the resistance has been reduced: the boat can be throttled down without losing any of its speed.

At low speeds, a boat creates only small waves, and the wave resistance is also small. The frictional resistance, however, then largely depends on the wetted surface and on the roughness of the underwater surface of the boat. At increasing speeds, the frictional resistance increases only slowly.

Thus, at low speeds, the frictional resistance is by far the dominant one. This is often very noticeable in sailing-boats. In light airs, a boat with a small wetted surface can be faster than one with a larger wetted surface, all other things being equal. In one-design classes, a well-smoothed underwater hull will go faster in light airs than a rough or scruffed hull.

If there is only a slight breath of wind, the helmsman of a light boat may sit far forward, so that the bow is depressed into the water. At the bow, the wetted surface is only slightly increased, and a considerable part of a wide underwater aft body can thus be lifted above the water-line, so that the frictional resistance is reduced.

At relatively high speeds, however, when the length of the created waves is half or more of the water-line length, these waves make up the largest part of the overall resistance, and the amount of wetted surface and the roughness of the hull become less important. For this reason, the hulls of relatively fast boats should be designed so that they develop as small waves as possible. Until some time ago, it was generally considered that everything was fine if the lines of the hull were fair and pleasing to the eye. Many designers, therefore, first made a scale model of a hull and then prepared a lines plan based on the model. Research carried out in recent years, however, has shown that, for each type of boat and for each speed, there exists an optimal distribution of the displacement over the boat's length, resulting in minimal resistance. A good rule-of-thumb is: for low speeds,

slender ends and full sections near the middle of the boat; for high speeds, full ends and rather straight lines in between. A correct distribution of the displacement has proved to be of much greater importance than beautiful lines, and that should put an end to the old-fashioned practice where the designer worked on sight, without preceding calculations.

As soon as a boat is pushed ahead by a propulsive force, it will accelerate in the direction of that force. From the moment the boat starts moving in the water, it experiences frictional resistance, and a pattern of short, low waves is built up. In the course of acceleration, the wave-length increases, as does the total resistance. As soon as the total resistance equals the propulsive force, an equilibrium is reached, the acceleration will stop, and the boat will proceed at a constant speed.

As the throttle is opened wider, the engine delivers a greater propulsive force via the propeller. The boat accelerates again, and the resistance increases, as does the wavelength, until once more the total resistance is matched by the propulsive force. As before, the boat will then continue at a constant speed but, of course, a higher constant speed than previously.

Therefore, cruising at a constant speed always means equilibrium between propulsive force and resistance. A propulsive force greater than resistance results in acceleration, while a propulsive force less than resistance results in slowing down.

When one steps onto the side deck of a boat, the boat sinks deeper into the water and inclines slightly. It is then in a new equilibrium of floating, because the form and the weight of the hull itself prevent the boat from listing any further. If one steps back onto the jetty or quay, the boat will come back to its original, upright position.

This resistance to the heeling forces and ability to return to the original state of equilibrium are together known as stability.

A flat, rectangular piece of wood will float because it is supported by the upward force of the water. This force consists of numerous small forces acting upwards on the wood. In practice, these forces are assumed to be concentrated in one big force acting on one spot, known as the centre of buoyancy (CB); this force acts vertically upwards.

In a similar way, the weight of the piece of wood can be considered to be concentrated on one single point, its centre of gravity (CG). This force works vertically downwards.

When the flat piece of wood floats in a horizontal position, the forces acting on the centres of buoyancy and of gravity are balanced, being equal in size and working in opposite directions along one and the same line.

If the piece of wood is inclined by means of some external force, the centre of buoyancy is shifted to the more deeply immersed side of the block. The forces working on the centres of buoyancy and gravity are not now working along one line, but along two parallel lines, spaced a certain distance apart. The two forces now form a couple and together exercise a righting action. The strength of that action, known as the righting moment, is equal and opposite to that of the external upsetting force,

and is the product of the heeled displacement and the length of the righting arm.

Thus the extent of the righting moment, or stability, depends on two things, namely, the weight of the boat and the length of the righting arm. As a rule, the weight of the boat will not change very much in the course of a voyage. The length of the arm depends on the shape of the boat, because that determines the shift of the centre of buoyancy, and on the position of the centre of gravity.

Because of the rectangular form of the piece of wood, the length of the arm is considerable even at very small angles of inclination. Therefore, the initial stability is large. Beyond a certain angle of heel, however, the situation changes and, at increasing angles of heel, the righting arm will gradually shorten until, at 90°, it will have disappeared. At angles of over 90°, the forces working through the centres of buoyancy and gravity act to form a capsizing moment instead of a righting moment, with the consequence that the piece of wood will capsize.

The stability of this block of wood is predominantly governed by the form of its immersed part; it is therefore called form stability.

The situation would be quite different for a wooden cylinder floating in water. No matter how one turns the cylinder, the centre of buoyancy stays below the centre of gravity; thus, the length of the arm is zero, and there is no couple. The cylinder consequently will remain in the position in which it was placed in the water.

While an external force, such as wind in the case of a boat, cannot develop a couple with a cylindrical object, the addition of ballast will change the situation. The centre of gravity of cylinder and ballast together will not be situated on the axis of the cylinder, but will have dropped somewhat lower, towards the ballast. If we now incline the ballasted cylinder, a righting couple will be developed. The cylinder has been given stability by the attached ballast weight; in this case, we speak of weight stability. At small angles of inclination, the righting arm is small, producing low initial stability. The arm will have its greatest value at 90° inclination, when the righting moment also reaches its peak.

Pure weight stability thus gives small initial stability and is most effective at 90° inclination.

No single boat has the form of the flat or cylindrical pieces of wood taken as examples. That is why no boat has either pure form stability or pure weight stability, but rather a combination of the two.

A better insight into the stability of a boat can be found if its stability is presented in the form of a curve. Such a stability curve helps one to understand how the boat should best be handled. To be able to use the stability curve of any particular boat, all that is necessary is a clinometer. This shows where on the stability curve a boat is at any given moment.

For instance, a yacht, whose stability is largely composed of form stability, may continue to carry all its sails in a strong wind, while comfortably sailing along at a small angle of inclination. But the skipper should not be tempted to delay reefing, for, when a hard gust strikes, the top of the curve may be passed, and the righting moment will start to decrease rapidly. At this stage, or shortly afterwards, an open keelboat will take in water and sink. A yacht with a curve crossing the horizontal axis before 90°

can capsize if, in a gust of wind, the boat is very steeply heeled. Only if the righting moment at 90° is sufficient to withstand the effect of the wind pressure against the bottom of the boat will the boat be considered as self-righting and be relatively safe in strong winds.

It can be breath-taking to sail at the top of the curve in a small catamaran, balancing with one hull just above the water. It demands complete control of boat, muscles, and nerves, but it offers in return unbelievable speeds and a feeling of great exhilaration. Do not, however, try to go past the peak of that curve with a cabin-catamaran, as the curve probably falls steeply after this. With such a boat, you should always reef in time, before the windward hull lifts out of the water.

The curves can help us predict what is going to happen. A wind force which gives a yacht with more form than weight stability a heel of approximately 20° may give a yacht of identical size, but with more weight than form stability, a heel of 40° or more. Even if this is less comfortable, there is no danger of capsizal, as the righting moment is still on the increase and the top of the curve is still far off. Sailing at an angle of 40° is not only less comfortable, but it also reduces the propulsive efficiency of the sails, since these catch far less wind at such an angle, and part of the wind is blown out of the sail at the top. The underside of the hull, sticking out of the water, catches more and more wind, and this causes more leeway, which the keel, being tilted at such an angle, has great difficulty in opposing. When the boat was upright, the water-line was symmetrical, but now that the vessel is heeling, the waterline has become strongly asymmetrical. On the lee side, the bow is pushed away by the bow wave, whereas the aft is sucked to leeward, and this causes the yacht to luff up. While this is not dangerous, it would nevertheless be wise, for reasons of speed as well as comfort, to reef.

The stability curve of a powerboat may provide its owner with valuable information about the boat's intended area of use. It is often possible to judge from the curve whether a boat is designed for inland waterways or for the open sea.

In order to determine the position of the centre of buoyancy for an adequate number of angles of inclination, lengthy calculations used to be required. Nowadays, with the help of computers, the exact position of the centre of buoyancy can be quickly found for any draught at any angle the operator or yacht-designer desires. Thus it is now rather easy to obtain the stability data of the hull form.

The exact position of the centre of gravity must be known before one can calculate the length of the righting arm. To find the centre of gravity, the weight of every part of the hull, superstructure, interior, machinery, rigging, equipment, and so on must be determined, as must their separate centres of gravity and their distances from the horizontal and vertical axes, and that is still a time-consuming job.

When the centre of gravity has been pinpointed, stability curves can be drawn for various positions of the centre of gravity with, say, full tanks and supplies for a long journey on board, or with empty tanks and no provisions, but with a dinghy on deck.

In designing small yachts, data obtained from earlier designs or from experience are frequently used, instead of data obtained from new calculations. Despite this, if one has had an expensive yacht designed or if one orders one from a series, one should always ask for the boat's stability curves, as these provide useful information regarding the behaviour of the boat in the water and, thus, about the way in which the boat should be handled.

An important thing to remember is that the cabin openings, portholes, hatches, ventilator cowls, and so on must be watertight when closed, as even the "safest" curve may suddenly change into that of an open keelboat, should water be allowed to flood into the cabin through any of these openings.

When a boat is under way, water flows from beneath the hull along the rudder. If the tiller is pushed to one side, the water streaming past the rudder is also pushed sideways. On one side of the rudder, an area of high pressure is created, on the other side, an area of low pressure. These combined pressures exercise a force, K, perpendicular to the rudder blade. That force can be imagined as being composed of two other forces, R, which works parallel to the sailing course, and S, which works perpendicular to it.

The force S is the steering force. It tries to push the stern sideways. It would even push the entire boat sideways, if the underwater body did not resist such a movement. As soon as the hull moves sideways, it experiences great resistance from the water, which opposes the movement. This pressure of the water against the hull, D, forms a couple with the steering force S, and this makes the boat alter course.

When the rudder is turned to one side, the stern and sometimes the entire hull is shifted to that side before the water offers sufficient resistance to make the boat turn. A good example of this is a pram or barge with a flat bottom. When the rudder is turned, the stern swings far out. The boat then moves in a decreasing circle, with considerable side slip. This is in contrast with the turning radius of a car where, as soon as the front wheels are in the desired position, the car draws a pure arc of a circle.

A sail-boat with a short, deep keel has great transverse resistance; it will slip sideways only very little and can be quickly steered into a small turning circle.

One of the components of the force on the rudder blade is R, which works parallel to the sailing course. That force is directed aft and is thus a braking force. This can be clearly seen when the rudder is put over hard. The steering force, S, is immediately reduced, while the braking force, R, increases.

The arm between the steering force of the rudder and the side force of the water against the hull is the horizontal distance between the centres of attack of these forces. The steering moment is equal to either of these forces multiplied by the length of the arm.

When rudder and keel form an integrated, streamlined unit, the arm of the couple is rather short, and the steering moment is small. Since the stock of the rudder on such a design is not vertical but inclined slightly, the rudder force, K, will be directed obliquely instead of at 90° to the blade, and up to one third of the steering force may be lost. Even if the height of the rudder compensates for this, quite a lot of blade area is required to provide good steering properties. When a yacht with a rudder of this kind starts turn-ing, the transverse water pressure will be shifted towards the front part of the keel, thus moving D forward and increasing the arm of the couple, and with it the steering moment.

Many people think that a long, streamlined keel with the rudder aft is ideal for cruising, because it would facilitate holding course. This may often be the case in quiet waters, but that this would also apply at sea is nothing but a myth. Each time the yacht starts to sheer, the point of attack of water pressure, D, is shifted forward, resulting in an even more pronounced sheering effect. Thanks to the simultaneously increasing arm of the steering couple and the large, streamlined rudder blade, the helmsman can do a lot to correct the sheer; it is the helmsman who is opposing the sheer, not the hull form itself. The large, wetted surface of the long keel does not of itself give the boat better course-holding ability in rough seas.

A short keel with a rudder hung some distance behind it provides a long arm for the steering couple at all times. When the keel is short and well streamlined, then the point of attack of force D will always be on the forward half of the keel at all times, so that, when sheering or yawing, this point can never shift very far. For this reason, a boat of this type generally offers better steering properties than the long-keel type, both in quiet and in rough water.

The spade rudder often has a small part of the rudder area in front of the rudder stock. On this small part, the water exercises a relatively high pressure, and this can balance the rudder loads around the rudder stock; most are not completely balanced, as the helmsman likes to have a slight pressure on the rudder, so that he can feel every change of course he makes.

A combustion engine produces energy through the explosion of a mixture of fuel and air. This energy is normally transferred in turn to the piston, the propeller shaft, and the propeller, finally ending up by pushing the boat ahead. That is quite a long and wasteful way for the energy to go.

A turbine installation works more directly. Expanding steam or a combusted and expanding fuel-air mixture causes a jet stream to hit blades mounted round the circumference of a wheel, thus turning the wheel and with it the shaft which drives the propeller. A turbine, not surprisingly, employs energy more efficiently than does a combustion engine.

In contrast to the engine, sails do not produce energy, but they withdraw it from the wind and convert it into propulsion directly.

Centuries of experience have taught us how to use sails in the most effective way, and that is, strangely enough, not by stopping the wind, for then a lot of turbulence is created in which wind energy is lost, but by changing its direction slightly, so that it blows along the sail without creating turbulence.

If air flows along a curved sail, thus changing its own direction slightly, the mass of that air develops pressure at the concave side of the sail and suction at the convex side. Because of this, small forces are working everywhere on the sail, practically perpendicular to it. In practice, all these small forces can be considered as one overall force, known as the wind force, which acts almost perpendicularly to the chord of the sail, that is, the line connecting the two ends of the curved sail profile. As soon as a boat is un-

99

der way, the wind will seem to come from a somewhat different direction than it does ashore. This is due to the sailing speed. In calm weather, a head wind would be felt, coming right from in front with a speed equal to the speed of the boat. The wind as it is felt on board, the apparent wind, is the result of the true wind and the created head wind. The apparent wind comes in from further ahead than the true wind, as a result of the speed of the boat. When speed is increased, the apparent wind comes in from even further ahead. Reducing speed has the opposite effect.

When sailing before the wind, the head wind and the true wind oppose each other, less wind than there is in reality is felt on board. When sailing into the wind, the true wind is increased by the head wind, and on board it seems to blow much harder than is, in fact, the case.

Sailing down wind in winds of up to wind Force 5 or 6, many yachts can carry all their sails. But in a winding fairway, when they may have to sail to windward from time to time, it may seem as if the wind suddenly gets much stronger at these times, causing considerable heeling. This is not because the true wind has become stronger, but because the apparent wind has increased.

The apparent wind blows along the sail and exercises a force on it, at about right angles to the chord. The wind force that propels a boat along a certain course rarely works in that direction. The propelling wind's force can be divided into two different forces: a force forward in the direction of the course, and a transverse, or side, force at right angles to the first. The forward force is the propulsive one; it wants to push the boat straight ahead.

Sailing on a broad reach, the propulsive force is rather strong and it produces a good speed, because the transverse force is then weak. When sailing to windward, however, the propulsive force is small and the transverse force a multiple of it. The more the boat is steered into the wind, the smaller the propulsive force, while the transverse force remains strong. If one sails too close to the wind, the propulsive force becomes less than the wind resistance of boat and rigging, so that the boat stops moving ahead and may get out of control.

What, meanwhile, is the transverse force doing? It works on the sail, across the fore-and-aft axis of the boat, and tends to push the boat sideways. The underwater part of the hull has little resistance to forward motion, but quite a lot to sideways motion. In order to increase even further that sideways resistance, a keel or centre-board can be fitted to the boat. Boat and keel together oppose the undesirable side-slip, which will only be marginal. Consequently, the transverse force on the sails will cause the boat to heel.

Although there are a lot of dinghies which, because they are one-man boats, have only one sail, most yachts have at least two sails, a mainsail and a jib, because, for one thing, two small sails can be handled more easily than one large sail. The main reason, however, is that two sails, properly trimmed, can together produce a better propulsive force than one sail with the same overall area.

This is the result of the action of the slot, the narrow opening between the jib and the mainsail. The wind is compressed as it flows through the slot, and it starts working like a sort of mini-jet at the suction (lee) side of the mainsail. The low pressure at that side decreases further,

thereby increasing the difference between it and the pressure working on the windward side of the mainsail, and thus the wind force on the sail increases. However, for this to occur, the width of the slot between the two sails must be correct. Only when the width has been accurately set will the wind be compressed sufficiently to create at the lee side of the mainsail the mini-jet situation referred to. With both sails trimmed correctly, mainsail and jib jointly can divert the air-stream, without causing additional turbulence, much more efficiently than can one large sail. In this way, more propelling force can be won from the same amount of wind.

Should the sheets be eased too much, the sails will start flapping at the luff. Should the sheets be too tight, the wind will strike the sails at such a broad angle that it cannot follow their curves. Although the wind will then be more compressed on the windward side of the sail, it will break free from the leeward side, thus causing considerable turbulence rather than the required suction. The propulsive power will be reduced, while the transverse force will remain strong and press the sail to leeward.

In defining wind force, mention was made of all the minor forces, developed by the wind on each side of the sails, being combined into one overall force, acting on one point on the sails. In designing sail plans, a practical way of finding this point has been adopted. It is assumed that the total wind force attacks at the geometric centre of area of the projected sail, as it is seen on the sail plan. This point is called the centre of effort (CE). When there is more than one sail, the overall, common centre of area is calculated, and this then becomes the common centre of effort.

As we have seen, it is the transverse force on the sail which pushes the boat to leeward. The form of the underwater body is such that it can counteract this to some degree but, on its own, that is not sufficient. In order to reduce this sideways drift, a fin may be fitted under the hull of the boat. This fin has very low resistance to forward motion and a high resistance to being pushed sideways.

When that fin is pushed sideways during sailing, a situation arises similar to that described for the rudder blade and sails, namely the creation of high pressure on one side of the fin and low pressure on the other. The result is a transverse force against the fin, which opposes drifting. What would happen if the boat did not have such a fin can be seen when, for instance, a powerboat with a high superstructure cruises at low speed in a strong beam wind. The wind pushes this boat to leeward, off the steered course. The angle between the course steered and the course actually travelled is called leeway. Leeway is not a distance or a course, but an angle between two courses.

While one mainsail has an outline shape very much like another, an enormous inventiveness has been displayed in the designing of fin profiles. They all have two features in common, however: a high resistance to sideslip, and a low resistance to moving in a forward direction. Regardless of the shape, however, there must always be some side-slip in order to allow the water to strike at the oblique angle which is necessary in order to produce a transverse force on the fin.

This transverse force on the fin is composed of, again, a large number of minor forces, distributed over its sur-

faces. As in the other cases, these small forces can be considered to be concentrated into one central force. Once more, the question arises as to where the point of attack of that central force is located.

As far as its form is concerned, the underwater body is even more complicated than a sail. It may consist of part of the hull, together with the fin and the rudder. The assessment of the real centre of attack of the transverse force is extremely complicated, so that in this case, too, we must resort to a calculation "trick". Take the transverse projection of the underwater body, that is, the profile below the water-line, and then determine its geometrical centre. The handiest way to do this is illustrated on page 114. The geometrical centre of the underwater profile is called the centre of lateral resistance (CLR).

The transverse force induced by the side-slip is of the same sort as that working on the rudder—when giving helm, the hull wants to pivot round the CLR.

A good sail balance has been acquired when the boat follows a straight course without the need for correction with the rudder. A line drawn vertically through the centre of effort (CE) to the water-line should be between five and fifteen per cent of the total water-line forward of a line drawn vertically through the CLR, if there is to be a good sail balance. What the exact percentage should be largely depends on the form of hull and fin, and on the type of rig.

When the CE is too far forward of the CLR, the bow tends to swing to leeward. When, on the other hand, the CE is not far enough forward of the CLR—not to speak of it being behind that point—the bow tends to turn to windward. In either case, course correction will have to be made with the rudder, but this, as has been mentioned, means creating additional resistance. On a centre-board boat, the sail balance can often be restored by adjusting the height of the centre-board. In the case of fixed-keel boats, better balance may be achieved by altering the rake of the mast, which changes the position of the CE. Raking the mast forward brings the CE forward and causes the bow to be pushed more to leeward. Raking it aft causes the stern to be pushed to leeward and the bow towards the wind.

We have to bear in mind that the CLR is also shifted when the boat is trimmed fore or aft. When a fore-peak is stowed with stores for a long trip, the CLR is shifted forward; with numerous crew members sitting near the stern, the CLR is moved aft. Especially at the start of a long cruise, it is well worth the effort to bring the boat into the best possible sail balance. The reward will be higher speed, since less use need be made of the rudder.

As we have observed, the wind exerts a transverse force on the sail, causing leeway. As a result, the water reacts with a transverse force on the keel. When the yacht has a constant leeway, these two forces are in equilibrium. Together, they form a couple, the length of whose arm is the perpendicular distance between the CE and the CLR. The product of the transverse force and the length of the arm is the heeling moment.

The yacht will sail with a constant angle of heel when there is a balance between the righting moment and the heeling moment, that is, when both moments are equal and working in opposite directions.

As can bee seen in the illustrations of righting moments on pages 108–109, the length of the righting lever is very small in comparison to the length of the heeling lever. To obtain a righting moment equalling the heeling moment, the transverse force working on the sail must be very small in relation to the weight of the yacht. This explains why a heavy-displacement yacht can carry a large sail-area, while another yacht of the same length but with a smaller displacement has to have a smaller sail-area in order to be able to sail with an acceptable angle of heel. Fortunately, because of its smaller displacement, the lightly constructed yacht requires less propulsive force to reach the same speed than does the heavy yacht.

Perhaps it is now clear that a sail-boat is not at its fastest when running down wind. Because of the speed of the boat, the apparent wind is not as strong as the true wind. Secondly, the apparent wind is blowing from astern, and the sails will not be efficient, as there will be hardly any decrease in pressure on the lee side of the sail due to turbulence on that side.

Usually, the highest speeds are obtained when the apparent wind comes in approximately a-beam; it is then stronger than the true wind, and the forces working on the sails nearly point in the direction of the desired course. For a given wind-speed, a speed diagram can be constructed to show the speeds which the boat can reach with the true wind coming in at various angles. Such a diagram has to be made from the results of trials, and this is time-consuming but, once it is made, the skipper can determine quite accurately how fast he will cover a certain distance in the prevailing wind conditions.

In a speed diagram, one can also read the limits of the boat's possibilities. By drawing a horizontal tangent at the top of the curve, we find the optimal course for cruising up wind; when we tack to port and starboard within that angle of the wind, we will reach our destination fastest.

As one sails closer and closer to the wind, the boat's speed falls until there is not enough speed left to steer the boat effectively. From the curve of a speed diagram, the skipper can judge how close he can sail in order to stay safely clear of, say, a protruding spit of land, even if this would be at the expense of speed.

For boats capable of planing, the curve will have a sort of protuberance. From the point where the protuberance starts to the point where it ends, the boat will plane.

Each wind speed has its own speed diagram. Besides wind speed, the boat's performance is also dependant upon the length and height of the waves encountered.

The cross-section of a propeller blade has a kind of wing profile. Normally, the aft side is almost straight, and the forward side convex. The same pressure phenomenon occurs when the blade of a propeller is pushed through water as when wind strikes a sail at a small angle of attack; pressure is built up on the flat side and falls off on the convex side. All these pressures form one main propulsive force, known as lift.

As with wind force, the lift of the propeller is made up of two components: the propulsive force in the direction of the course, and a transverse force, the torque. The first pushes the boat ahead, while the torque is the resistance of the propeller to rotation (the engine has to provide a rotative force, equal to the overall resistance of the blades, in order to keep the propeller turning and to allow the water to flow along the propeller blades). The energy required for propulsion is equal, therefore, to the energy required to overcome the resistance of the blades, the torque.

When a propeller turns, it moves through the water. This can be best explained by comparison to the screwing of a nut onto a bolt. Each time the nut is given a full turn, it will advance the same distance along the threads. This distance is called the pitch. If the diameter of the threads is kept the same, and the pitch increased (thus increasing the distance covered by the nut during one complete turn), the threads must be more inclined to the axis of the bolt than was previously the case. Of course, the nut would progress by the same amount if the pitch is kept constant and the diameter of the threads is increased.

The propeller has the same pitch at the boss as it has near the blade tip, because, in one rotation, both boss and blade tip cover the same distance. The diameters of boss and blade tip, though, differ quite a bit. The boss has a small diameter and the cross-section of the blade near the hub has, therefore, a considerable angle of advance, or twist in the blade. At the blade tip, the diameter is large, and very much less blade twist is needed to achieve the same forward motion in one revolution. From boss towards blade tip, therefore, the blade has lessening degrees of twist, since the tip has to turn through a much greater arc than does the blade near the boss.

Here, again, we can make a comparison with the sail. At the mast-head, the wind speed is higher than at just above the water surface, which explains why the top of the sail makes a larger angle to the centre-line of the boat than does the lower part.

The diameter of a propeller is measured to the outer edges of the tips. A propeller with a large diameter does not always deliver a greater propulsive force than one with a smaller diameter, having the same pitch. Propulsive force, or propeller thrust, depends partly on the blade area. Fast boats normally use fast-turning propellers with small diameters and relatively large blade areas—seventy to eighty per cent of the area of a circle of the same diameter as the propeller is quite normal. The powerful engines of these fast boats can deliver adequate thrust over the entire blade area.

For slower motorboats, propellers which turn more slowly and which have relatively small blade areas are used; this has been found to give the best propulsive efficiency. As on fast boats, three-bladed propellers are normal, though one can come across two-bladed or even five-bladed propellers. The latter type runs especially smoothly, provided the boat is suited to such a propeller. A four-bladed propeller is seldom used on a yacht, since it might cause more vibration on board than a three- or five-bladed propeller. A very small blade area is adopted for the propellers of auxiliary motors on sail-boats, so that the least possible resistance is offered when the boats are under sail-power alone.

A propeller can turn right-hand (clockwise) or left-hand (anti-clockwise), seen from astern. There would be no need to pay further attention to the transverse force of a propeller if it did not depend on the position of each blade during a revolution. The pressure on the blades depends on their depth under water. The blade in the highest position is working in the lowest pressure; that in the lowest position is working in the highest pressure, thus developing a greater thrust than the top one. The same applies to the transverse forces. Consequently, the propeller as a whole exerts a transverse force on the propeller shaft; the propeller wants to roll off to one side as if it were a wheel. Going ahead, this is hardly noticed, because the propulsive force is usually many times greater than the transverse force, and the latter is largely counteracted by the rudder, acting in the accelerated water of the propeller race. But if the race is not acting on the rudder, for instance, when just leaving a mooring, and especially when going astern, the rudder will not be working efficiently and the transverse force of the propeller will become clearly noticeable. For efficient manoeuvring, it is therefore necessary to know what type of propeller the boat has, left- or right-hand. The direction of rotation also has an influence on the turning circle. A boat with a right-hand propeller, going ahead, will have a smaller turning circle when turning to port than when turning to starboard. When turning to port, the transverse force of the propeller will be working together with the steering force of the rudder but, when turning to starboard, it will oppose the rudder action.

As we have seen before, the water flowing along a keel can exert a transverse force only if the keel presents an angle of incidence to the water. The same applies to a propeller blade; it can develop lift only if it is not going straight through the water but is inclined slightly forward, so that a pressure side develops. The angle between the straight line and the actual direction of movement is called the slip angle. Since slip is a necessity for obtaining lift, no propeller can do its job if it does not slip.

When a propeller blade is set at a considerable angle to the shaft, thus having a large pitch, the lift force developed by the blade does not act directly along the course taken by the boat. The gain in propulsive force is, thus, relatively small compared to the gain in torque, so a more powerful engine is needed to turn the propeller than would be needed if the propeller were set at a lesser angle to the shaft. But, at each revolution of the propeller, the boat moves ahead over a greater distance than it would if it had a propeller with a smaller pitch.

For a very light, planing boat, only a small propulsive force is needed to develop a high speed. In such a case, a propeller with a large pitch is used.

A boat with a relatively large displacement needs great propulsive power. In order to waste as little of the engine output as possible, the transverse force must be kept as small as possible, and that is why a propeller with a small pitch and a large diameter is used. The further it is from the boss, the more efficiently the section of a propeller blade works. However, the diameter of a propeller is limited by three main factors: the height of the propeller aperture, the strength requirements for the blades, and the danger of cavitation.

As we have seen, the transverse force on the lower propeller blade is greater than that on the upper blade, and this causes a transverse force on the propeller shaft. The larger the propeller diameter in relation to the size of the underwater body, the more pronounced the effect of that force will be. For instance, the helmsman of a tug with a big, slowly turning propeller must take this force into account, while the helmsman of a speedboat with a small, fast-turning propeller need not worry so much about it.

At full speed, the propeller pushes a strong flow of water past the rudder, and this makes for good steering capability; only very small changes of rudder angle are necessary to keep the boat on course.

When a boat must be manoeuvred at very low speeds, a good water-flow past the rudder can be achieved by first turning the rudder to the desired angle, and then giving a short, sharp burst on the throttle so that a useful pressure is built up against the side of the rudder.

Going astern, the propeller blade has the wrong section (convex at the high-pressure side and flat at the low-pressure side), and the efficiency of the propeller is, therefore, low. In addition, the underwater shapes of most boats provide greater resistance when going astern than when going ahead. For these reasons, speed astern is much lower than speed ahead. When a propeller reverses, the rudder has, at first, very little effect, because it misses the strong propeller stream which is now directed forward, away from the rudder. Once the boat is moving astern, the rudder can again begin to work.

Because the propeller stream, in reverse, flows against the skeg, the CLR will shift aft at the moment the boat starts to yaw. At this stage, the arm of the steering couple is getting smaller, and a fair amount of rudder angle will be required to oppose the yawing, if this is, in fact, at all possible. Especially on powerboats with a short skeg just forward of the propeller, steering astern can be virtually impossible, and the boat will often end up with the stern facing the wind.

If the CLR is kept sufficiently far forward to maintain a fairly large steering lever, the boat can be steered astern. However, going astern on a straight course may only be possible if the boat heads at an angle to the destination, because transverse force on the propeller must be compensated for by the transverse forces on rudder and hull.

On a sail-boat with an auxiliary engine, a propeller with a large blade area creates a lot of resistance when sailing; hence the frequent use of two-bladed propellers with narrow blades, whose propulsive efficiency is much lower than that of three-bladed propellers with larger blades, but whose resistance during sailing may be cut by up to half. Not only can a higher speed during sailing be attained, but also steering will be more effective, as less turbulent water from the propeller will flow past the rudder.

Another solution to this problem is to install a propeller with variable pitch, i.e., adjustable blades to suit the conditions. If the boat is heading up wind and against the waves, a small pitch is best; sailing down wind, more pitch is required. Without changing the direction of the propeller's rotation, the boat can be made to go astern by simply adjusting the propeller blades. This means that a reverse gear is not needed, and that one also has the advantage of having efficient blade section while going astern. The transverse force always works in the same direction. In neutral position, when the blades are transverse to the shaft, there is no propulsive force, although a small transverse force does exist.

A second version is a propeller whose blades, during sailing, are pushed into a feathered position by the force of the water-flow. As soon as the propeller shaft is rotated under power, either to go ahead or astern, the blades swing again to the required angle.

Even less resistance during sailing is caused by a propeller whose blades swing backwards and fold together. When the engine is started, the blades are swung open by the centrifugal force; going forward, the water pressure opens them up until they cannot go any further; going astern, it is the centrifugal force only which keeps the blades out and, therefore, a high rate of revolutions is needed. The same applies, of course, in a situation where the boat is still moving forward but is in the process of being stopped.

In the water-jet, a propeller sucks water through a wide tube and presses it out through a somewhat narrower tube. If the same amount of water is to go out through the narrow tube as came in through the wide one, then the speed of flow in the former tube must be higher. According to the principles of mechanics, the kinetic energy of a mass in motion is proportional to the square of the speed. Thus, the outgoing flow of water has considerably higher energy than has the incoming flow. That difference in energy pushes the boat.

Water-jet propulsion has many advantages. The small, enclosed propeller can turn at a high rate of revolution with less danger of cavitation, and it can thus have a small pitch and work efficiently. Because of the high rate of revolution, the engine can drive the propeller directly, without any need for reduction gearing. To go astern, a deflector behind the water-jet can be turned, reversing the stream and thus the direction of the propulsive force. The propeller can, therefore, always rotate in the same direction, utilizing fully the blade's sectional profile. No reverse gear is needed, nor is an ordinary rudder, as steering is carried out by means of the above-mentioned deflector. Finally, under the hull there are no vulnerable protrusions, propellers, rudders, brackets, and so on which can be damaged by hitting the bottom in shallow water or by collision with floating or submerged objects.

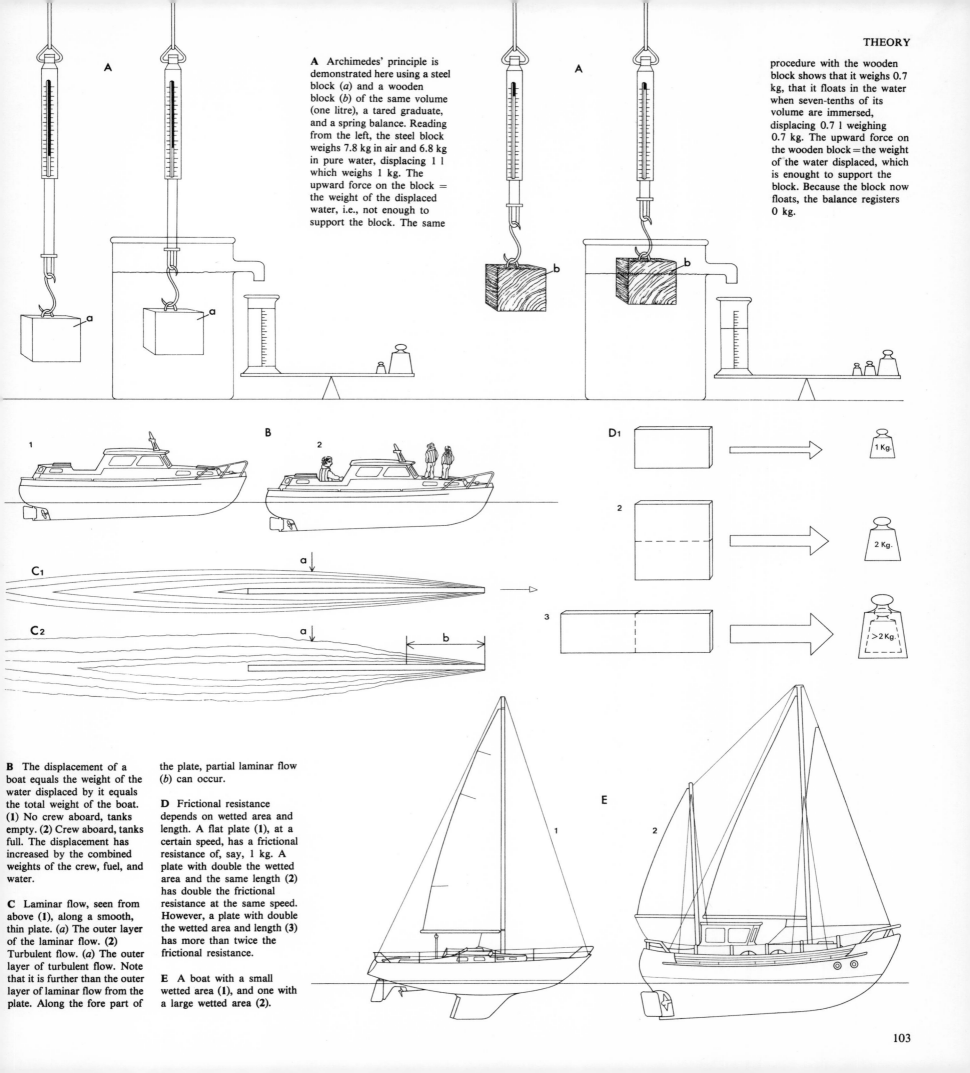

A Archimedes' principle is demonstrated here using a steel block (*a*) and a wooden block (*b*) of the same volume (one litre), a tared graduate, and a spring balance. Reading from the left, the steel block weighs 7.8 kg in air and 6.8 kg in pure water, displacing 1 l which weighs 1 kg. The upward force on the block = the weight of the displaced water, i.e., not enough to support the block. The same

procedure with the wooden block shows that it weighs 0.7 kg, that it floats in the water when seven-tenths of its volume are immersed, displacing 0.7 l weighing 0.7 kg. The upward force on the wooden block = the weight of the water displaced, which is enought to support the block. Because the block now floats, the balance registers 0 kg.

B The displacement of a boat equals the weight of the water displaced by it equals the total weight of the boat. (**1**) No crew aboard, tanks empty. (**2**) Crew aboard, tanks full. The displacement has increased by the combined weights of the crew, fuel, and water.

C Laminar flow, seen from above (**1**), along a smooth, thin plate. (*a*) The outer layer of the laminar flow. (**2**) Turbulent flow. (*a*) The outer layer of turbulent flow. Note that it is further than the outer layer of laminar flow from the plate. Along the fore part of

the plate, partial laminar flow (*b*) can occur.

D Frictional resistance depends on wetted area and length. A flat plate (**1**), at a certain speed, has a frictional resistance of, say, 1 kg. A plate with double the wetted area and the same length (**2**) has double the frictional resistance at the same speed. However, a plate with double the wetted area and length (**3**) has more than twice the frictional resistance.

E A boat with a small wetted area (**1**), and one with a large wetted area (**2**).

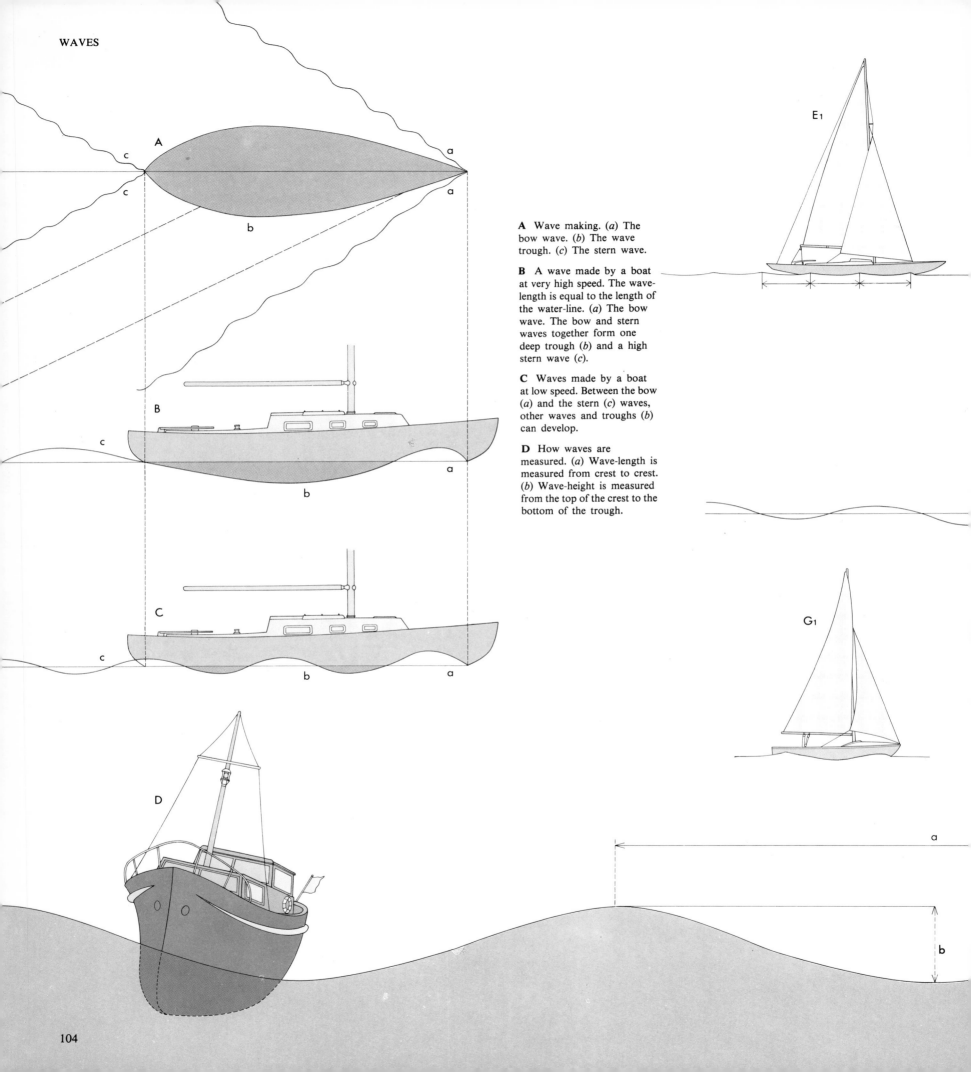

A Wave making. (*a*) The bow wave. (*b*) The wave trough. (*c*) The stern wave.

B A wave made by a boat at very high speed. The wave-length is equal to the length of the water-line. (*a*) The bow wave. The bow and stern waves together form one deep trough (*b*) and a high stern wave (*c*).

C Waves made by a boat at low speed. Between the bow (*a*) and the stern (*c*) waves, other waves and troughs (*b*) can develop.

D How waves are measured. (*a*) Wave-length is measured from crest to crest. (*b*) Wave-height is measured from the top of the crest to the bottom of the trough.

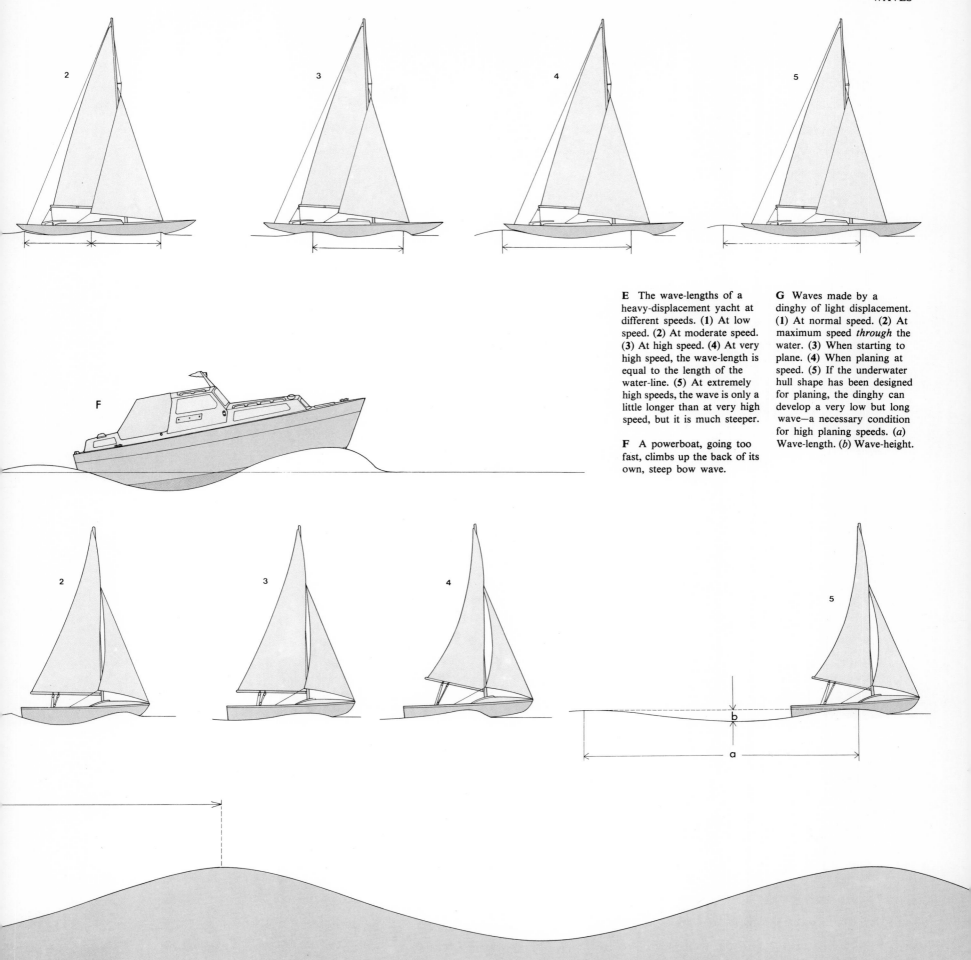

E The wave-lengths of a heavy-displacement yacht at different speeds. (**1**) At low speed. (**2**) At moderate speed. (**3**) At high speed. (**4**) At very high speed, the wave-length is equal to the length of the water-line. (**5**) At extremely high speeds, the wave is only a little longer than at very high speed, but it is much steeper.

F A powerboat, going too fast, climbs up the back of its own, steep bow wave.

G Waves made by a dinghy of light displacement. (**1**) At normal speed. (**2**) At maximum speed *through* the water. (**3**) When starting to plane. (**4**) When planing at speed. (**5**) If the underwater hull shape has been designed for planing, the dinghy can develop a very low but long wave—a necessary condition for high planing speeds. (*a*) Wave-length. (*b*) Wave-height.

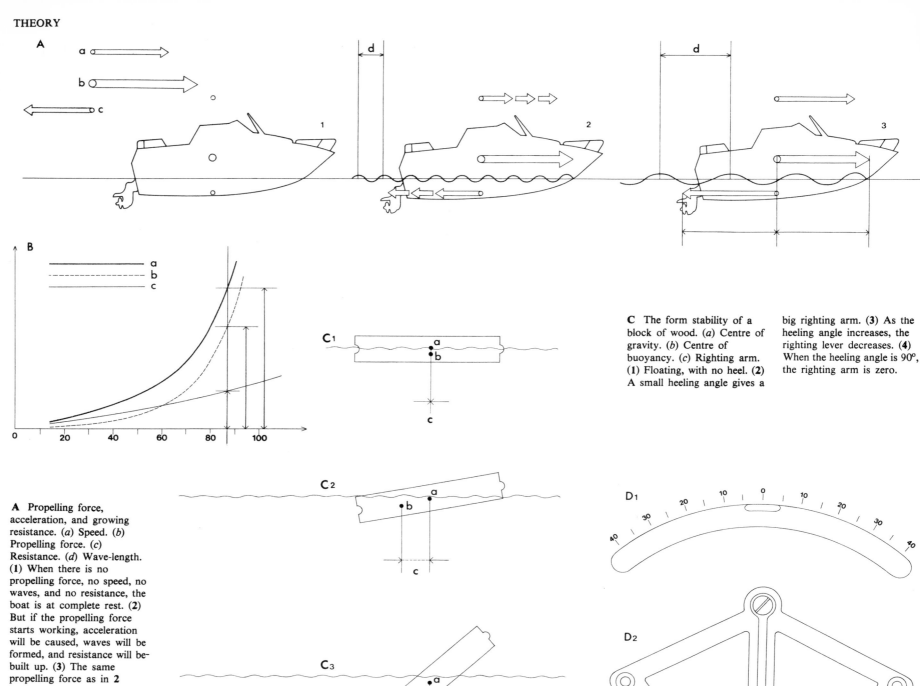

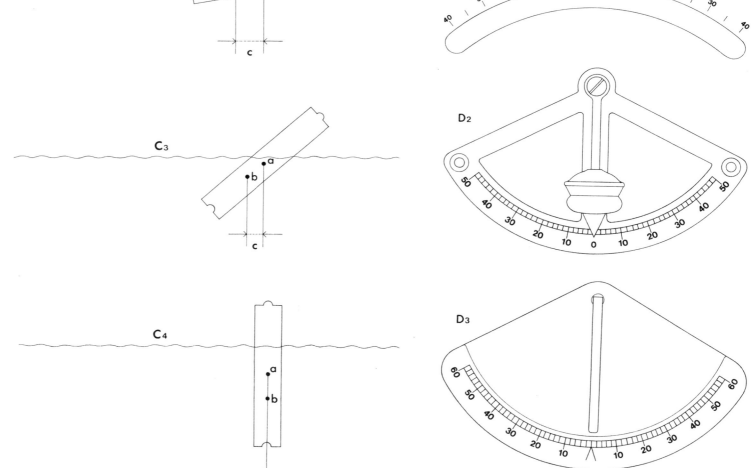

A Propelling force, acceleration, and growing resistance. (*a*) Speed. (*b*) Propelling force. (*c*) Resistance. (*d*) Wave-length. (**1**) When there is no propelling force, no speed, no waves, and no resistance, the boat is at complete rest. (**2**) But if the propelling force starts working, acceleration will be caused, waves will be formed, and resistance will be-built up. (**3**) The same propelling force as in **2** produces, after acceleration, a constant speed at which the propelling force is equal to the resistance. (**4**) To get a greater propelling force, the throttle must be opened. (**5**) This greater propelling force means, as in **2**, acceleration and an increase in resistance and wave-length. (**6**) All the forces are in balance again, producing a constant speed. The propelling force, wave-length, and resistance are much greater than before, while the speed is only a little greater.

B A resistance/speed graph. The vertical axis is resistance, the horizontal speed. (*a*) Total resistance. (*b*) Wave-making resistance. (*c*) Frictional resistance. At any particular speed, $a = b + c$.

C The form stability of a block of wood. (*a*) Centre of gravity. (*b*) Centre of buoyancy. (*c*) Righting arm. (**1**) Floating, with no heel. (**2**) A small heeling angle gives a big righting arm. (**3**) As the heeling angle increases, the righting lever decreases. (**4**) When the heeling angle is 90°, the righting arm is zero.

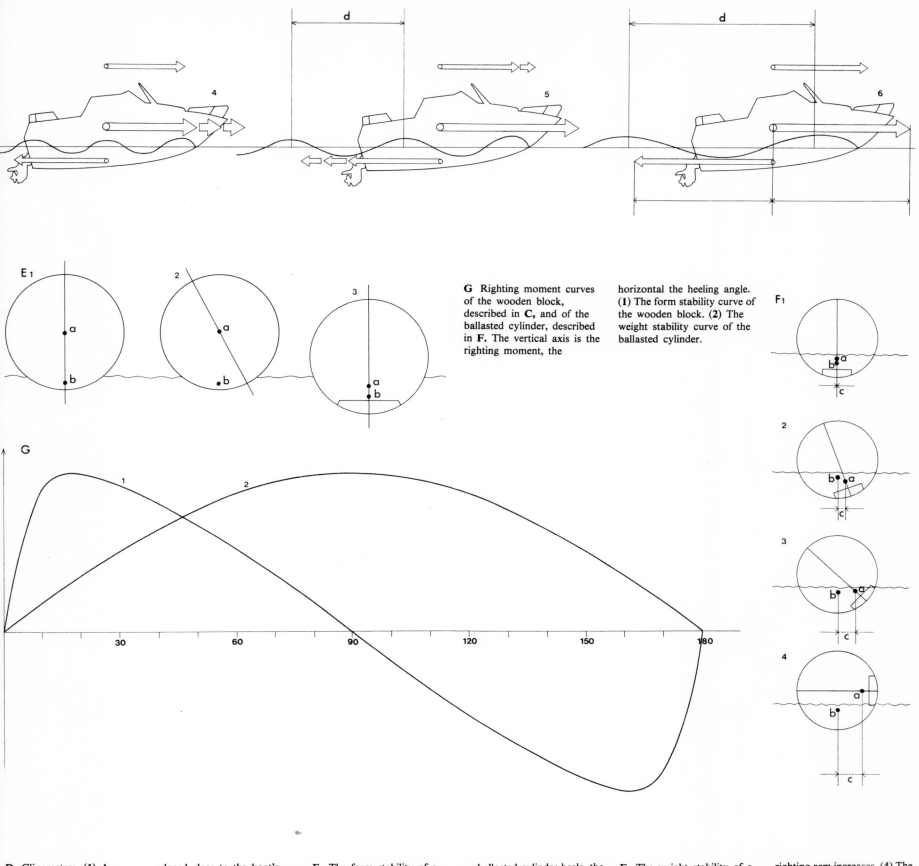

G Righting moment curves of the wooden block, described in **C,** and of the ballasted cylinder, described in **F.** The vertical axis is the righting moment, the horizontal the heeling angle. (**1**) The form stability curve of the wooden block. (**2**) The weight stability curve of the ballasted cylinder.

D Clinometers. (**1**) A curved glass tube with fluid and an air bubble. This registers heeling rather slowly, but it is not affected by the wind, and only a little by gravity. (**2**) A clinometer with a brass pendulum must be placed close to the boat's centre of gravity, otherwise the pendulum may swing as the boat rolls. (**3**) This type, with an uncovered, plastic needle, is not recommended, as the needle can be moved by the wind.

E The form stability of a cylinder, without and with ballast. (*a*) The centre of gravity. (*b*) The centre of buoyancy.
(**1**) Without ballast, the centre of gravity lies in the centre of the cylinder. (**2**) When the unballasted cylinder heels, the centres of gravity and of buoyancy stay as they were. There is no stability, and the cylinder stays in its heeled position. (**3**) When ballast is added, the centre of gravity is lowered.

F The weight stability of a ballasted cylinder. (*a*) Centre of gravity. (*b*) Centre of buoyancy. (*c*) Righting arm. (**1**) When floating upright. (**2**) At a small heeling angle, there is a small righting arm. (**3**) As the heeling angle increases, the righting arm increases. (**4**) The maximum righting arm is achieved when the heeling angle is 90°.

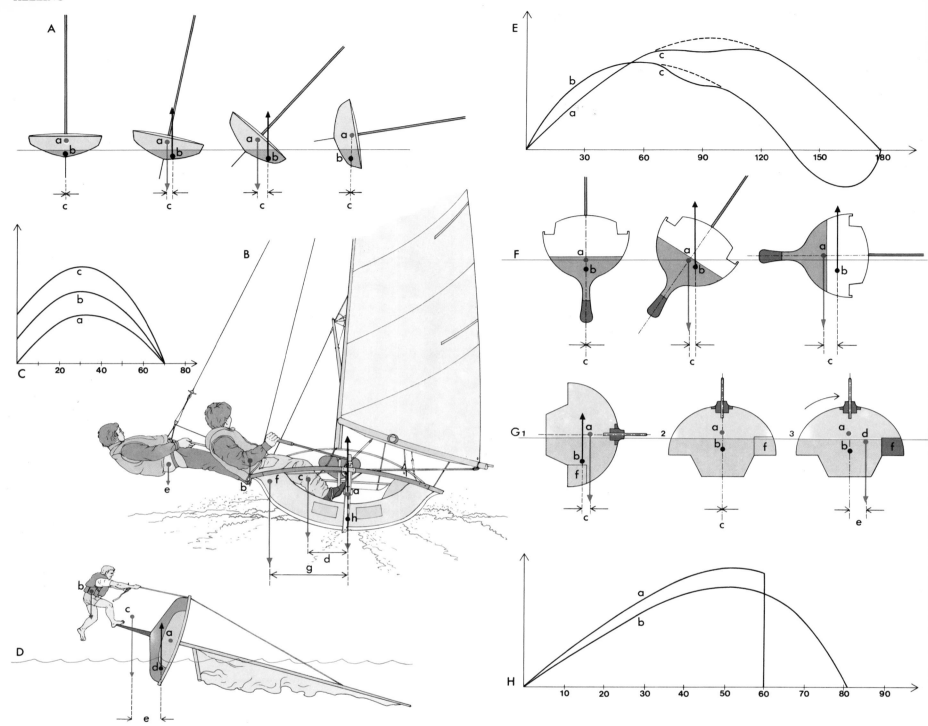

A A centre-board dinghy is one of the strangest combinations of weight and form stability, because it has a movable ballast: the crew. Most dinghies capsize at 70°–80° heel. (a) Centre of gravity (CG). (b) Centre of buoyancy (CB). (c) Righting arm.

B With the helmsman hanging on the side deck. (a) CG of dinghy. (b) CG of helmsman. (c) CG of dinghy and helmsman. (d) Righting arm. With the helmsman hanging in the trapeze. (a) CG of dinghy. (e) CG of helmsman. (f) CG of dinghy and helmsman in trapeze. (g) New righting arm. (h) CB.

C Stability curves for a dinghy. Vertically, we have the righting moment, horizontally the heel angle in degrees. (a) The curve with the helmsman in the centre of the cockpit. (b) With the helmsman hanging on the side deck. (c) With the helmsman in the trapeze. Curves b and c show a positive righting moment at a heel angle of 0°, which means that the dinghy can sail upright in spite of wind pressure on the sails.

D When the dinghy has capsized but has not turned over too much, the "ballast" can be moved to the tip of the centre-board to create a new righting couple. (a) CG of dinghy. (b) CG of helmsman. (c) CG of dinghy and helmsman. (d) CB. (e) Righting arm.

E The stability curve (a) of a keel yacht like F is very like that of a ballasted cylinder. Initial stability is low, but the yacht is stable over the whole range, up to 180° heel. The bulge (c) in the curve is where the side deck comes into the water; at that stage, the righting moment will start to increase more slowly at increasing heel.

A keel/centre-boarder's stability curve (b) shows the same bulge as that of the keel yacht. The righting moment at 135° heel is zero, and it then becomes negative. From 135°–180°, the boat will be stable upside-down.

F A yacht with deep ballast keel, narrow beam, very round bilges, and tumble-home. (a) CG. (b) CB. (c) Righting moment.

G At 90° heel (1), a keel/centre-boarder has a small righting arm (c). When upside-down (2), it is stable. If it is equipped with a side tank (f), which fills automatically with water (3), it is given a new CG (d), and a righting

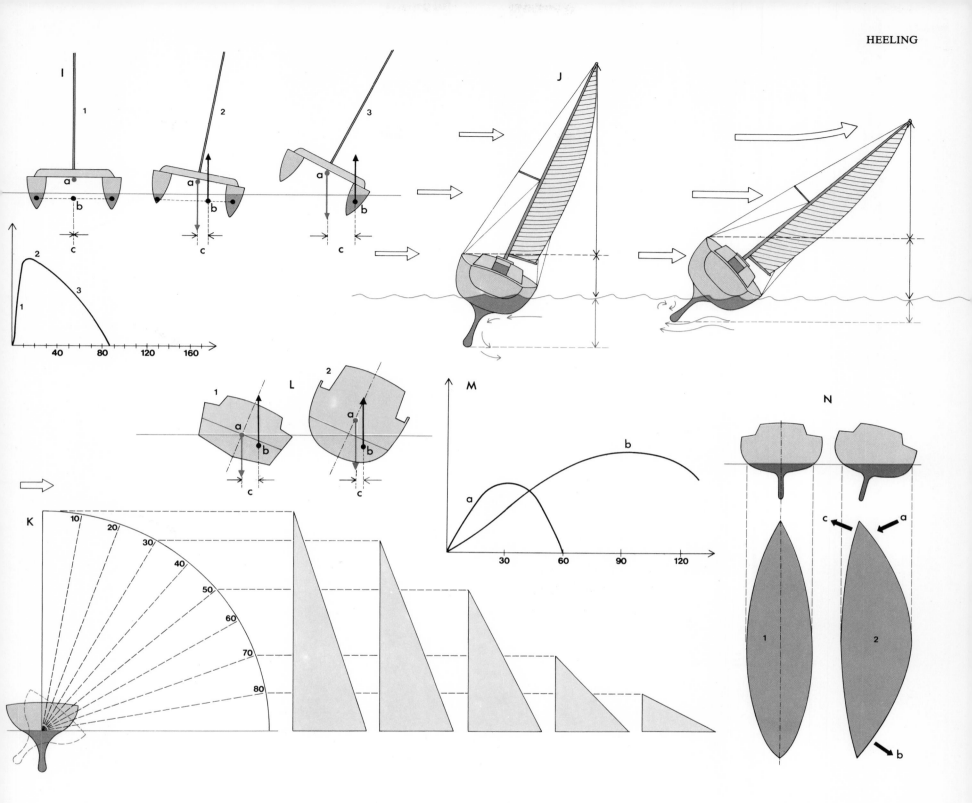

arm (e) which will turn the yacht back beyond a heel of 135°, where the hull regains its own stability. (a) CG. (b) CB.

H The stability curve of a half-open keelboat (a). At about 60° heel, the boat will fill with water and sink. Stability curve b is that of one of the many small "seaworthy" yachts with self-bailing cockpits. Many of these yachts are only stable

until water comes over the side into the cockpit, and that often happens before a 90° heel!

I The catamaran is an extreme example of form stability. The curve (below) shows at **1** an enormous initial stability at small angles of heel until the windward hull is out of the water (**2**). After that, the stability decreases rapidly (**3**). (a) CG.

(b) CB of both hulls together. (c) Righting arm.

J Excessive heel means more wind pressure on the hull and less effect of the keel, and this results in a lot of leeway. The wind flows upwards, out of the sails.

K Here we show the decrease of effective sail area with increasing angles of heel.

L The fairly rounded bilges and rather high CG (a) of a motor yacht (**2**) together make the righting arm (c) grow only slowly when the heel increases. The boat will, therefore, move easily in the waves, without sudden jerks. The high freeboard gives ample stability at large heeling angles. (b) CB.

A motor-cruiser (**1**) with a shallow V-bottom has great initial stability, which

is agreeable when one steps aboard. But the fast-increasing righting arm (c) means that the boat will move from one side to the other with every wave from the side. If the righting moment disappears at a heel of about 60°, then the boat should not be taken out from sheltered waters.

M The stability curves of (a) a motor-cruiser for sheltered

waters and (b) a bigger, seaworthy motor-yacht.

N The symmetrical water-line (**1**) of a yacht becomes asymmetrical (**2**) when the yacht heels, thus causing more resistance. (a) Water pressure of the bow wave. (b) Suction at the stern. (c) Luffing tendency due to the underwater shape.

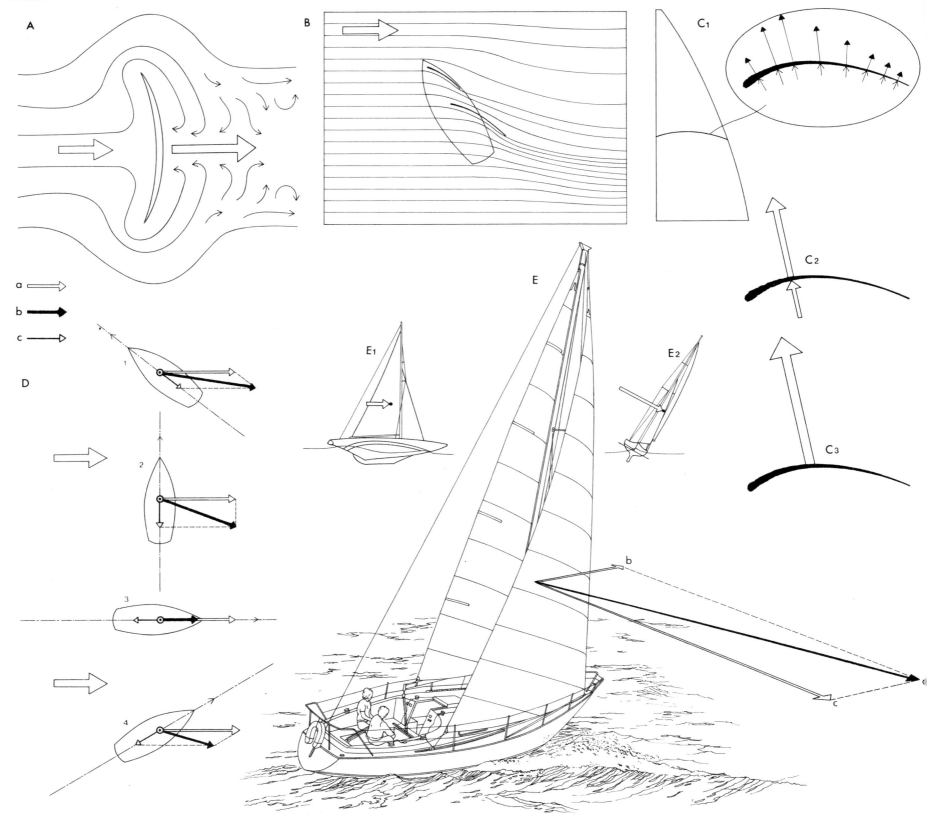

A The force of the wind, striking a sail directly from the side, causes turbulence on the other side.

B More efficient use of wind energy is made by bending slightly the flow of air past the

sail, if possible without causing turbulence.

C When the wind blows on a sail, it creates pressure everywhere on the concave side, and suction everywhere on the convex side (1). All

these different, small pressures can be assumed to form one main suction force (2). The suction force can be about twice the pressure force. Together, the suction and pressure forces form one big force (3).

D True wind and apparent wind on different courses: (1) close reach, (2) reaching, (3) running, (4) broad reach. True wind = a; apparent wind = b; speed wind = c.

E The apparent wind develops a force (a), which acts at almost right angles to the sail. This force can be divided into a forward force (b), in the direction of the yacht's course, and a transverse force (c), at right

angles to it. The small forward force causes speed (1), while the larger transverse force causes heel and leeway, or side slip (2).

F When reaching, the wind energy is used most efficiently

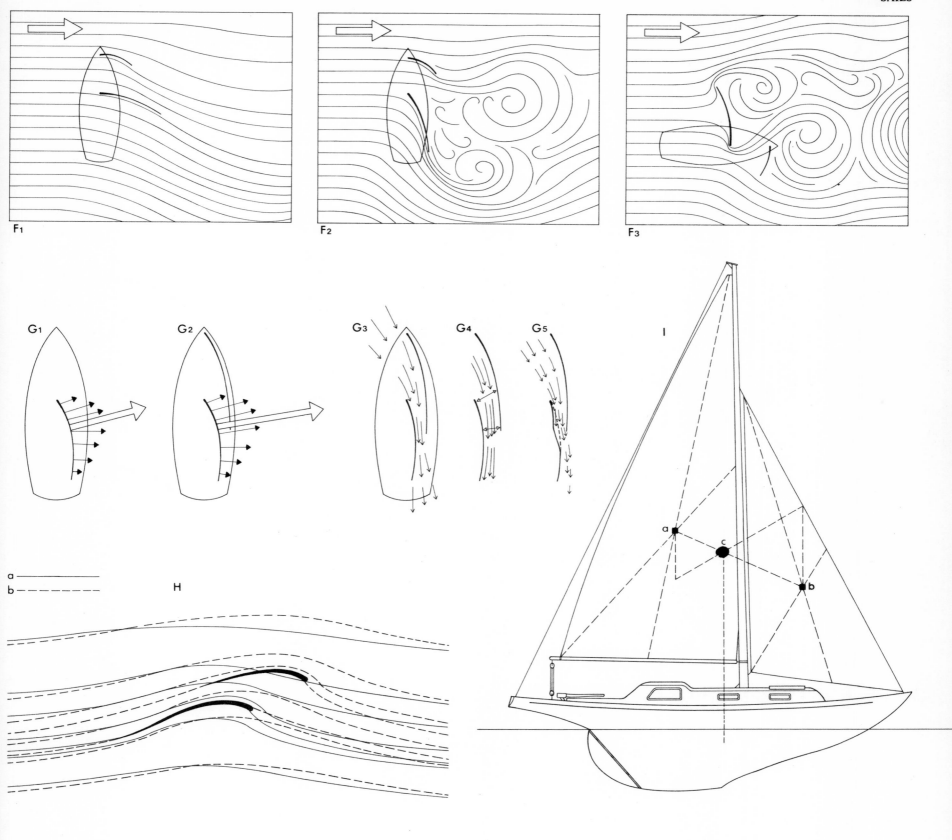

F₁

F₂

F₃

G₁ G₂ G₃ G₄ G₅ I

a ————
b − − − − −

H

(thus giving good speed) if the air-flow is bent smoothly (**1**). Sheeting in too hard on a reach (**2**) causes the sails to stall and turbulence on their lee side, resulting in loss of wind energy and, thus, of speed. When running, the rather low speed is caused not only by the low apparent wind speed, but also by the loss of most of the wind energy through turbulence in front of the sails (**3**).

G If a yacht develops a certain wind force in the mainsail (**1**), this force can be increased in the mainsail by hoisting a foresail (**2**), but only if there is a correct interaction between the sails. If the slot between the sails is correct (**3**), a jet-stream and a strong suction will be created on the convex side of the mainsail. If the slot is too wide (**4**), there will be no extra acceleration of the wind, as it is not "squeezed" enough between the sails. If the slot is too narrow (**5**), the foresail will press the wind into the mainsail.

H Mainsail and foresail together give a sharper bend to the air-flow than does the mainsail alone. (*a*) Air-flow with mainsail only. (*b*) Air-flow with both sails.

I Finding the centre of effort (CE). (*a*) CE of mainsail (the geometric centre of area). (*b*) CE of foresail. (*c*) Overall CE.

111

KEELS

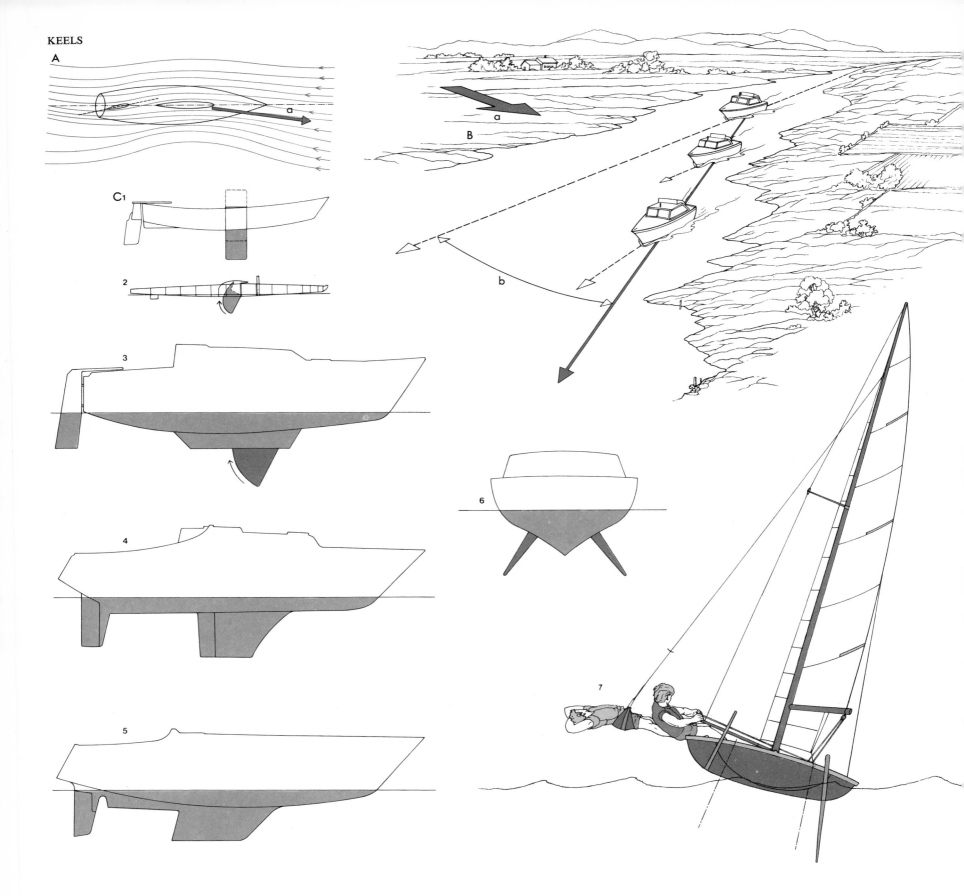

A Water-flow round keel and rudder. (*a*) Leeway is the angle between the course steered and the course sailed.

B A boat with a high cabin and no keel is subject to great sideways slip in a strong wind.

(*a*) Direction of wind. (*b*) Leeway.

C Centre-boards and keels. (**1**) Dagger-board. (**2**) Swinging centre-board. (**3**) Keel/centre-board. (**4**) Fixed keel with trim tab. (**5**) Fixed

keel. (**6**) Twin keels. (**7**) Two retractable bilgeboards.

D A lee-board for deep and tidal waters. The length is about four times the width, for high aspect ratio. The sections under the water function like a

wing and develop "lift", i.e., side force. When sailing, only the board on the lee side is down. (**1**) As seen from above. (**2**) Side view. (**3**) When fully down, the lee-board makes an angle of 2° to 4° with the centre-line of the yacht in

order to develop maximum side force when sailing close-hauled. (**4**) When reaching, the angle is only 1°–2°. (**5**) On a broad reach, the lee-board is parallel to the centre-line.

E A lee-board mounted on a gunwale with "tumble-home". When the boat heels, the lee-board is almost vertical in the water.

F A lee-board for very shallow inland waters. The

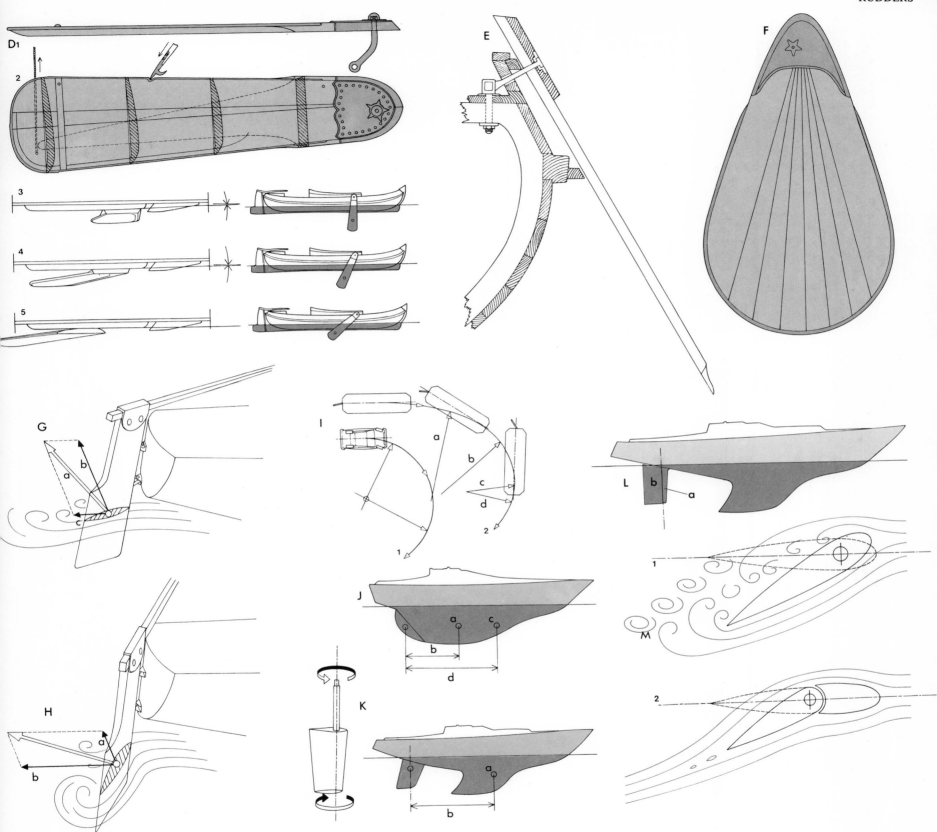

length is only twice or even less than twice the width.

G Rudder action. (*a*) The force created on the rudder blade by the deflected water stream. (*b*) The steering force. (*c*) Added resistance.

H If there is too much helm the rudder will act as a brake. (*a*) Decreased steering force. (*b*) Increased resistance.

I The turning circle of a car (**1**), in which the radius is equal, is here compared to the turning circle of a flat-bottomed pram (**2**) in which the radius decreases (*b* is less than *a*). The pram then turns further in a real circle, in which the radii (*c* and *d*) are equal.

J In a boat with a long keel and an attached rudder, we have the centre of lateral resistance (*a*), and a relatively short steering arm (*b*). When the boat turns, however, the CLR moves forward (*c*), and there is, consequently, an

increase in the steering arm (*d*).

K A boat with a short keel and a spade rudder. (*a*) CLR. (*b*) Long steering arm. (*c*) Spade rudder.

L A boat with a skeg rudder has a fixed skeg (*a*) and a movable rudder blade (*b*).

M A spade rudder (**1**) can stall more easily than a properly designed skeg rudder (**2**).

A The centre of lateral resistance (*a*) can be found in the following way. Project the underwater shape onto a piece of cardboard (*b*) and balance this on the sharp side of a knife or on a ruler. Draw a line along the balancing edge. Now balance the cardboard along a new edge, and draw another line. The CLR is where the two lines cross each other.

B When the centre-board is moved, the CLR is also moved. (*a*) Original CLR. (*b*) New CLR.

C For good sail balance, the centre of effort (*a*) should be between five and fifteen per cent of the water-line length forward of the CLR (*b*), depending on the form of the hull and sails.

D The CE can be displaced by raking the mast aft or forward. (*a*) Mast raked aft. (*b*) Mast plumb. (*c*) Mast forward. (*d*) CLR.

E When the CE is too far forward of the CLR, lee helm is necessary (**1**). When both centres are in their proper place, we have a balanced helm (**2**). When the CE is behind the CLR, strong weather helm is necessary (**3**). (*a*) Sail force. (*b*) Lateral resistance. (*c*) CE. (*d*) CLR.

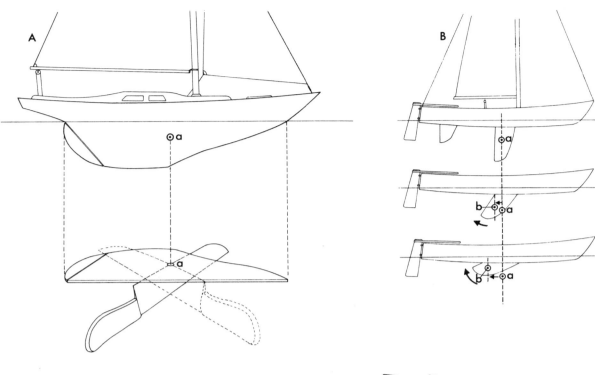

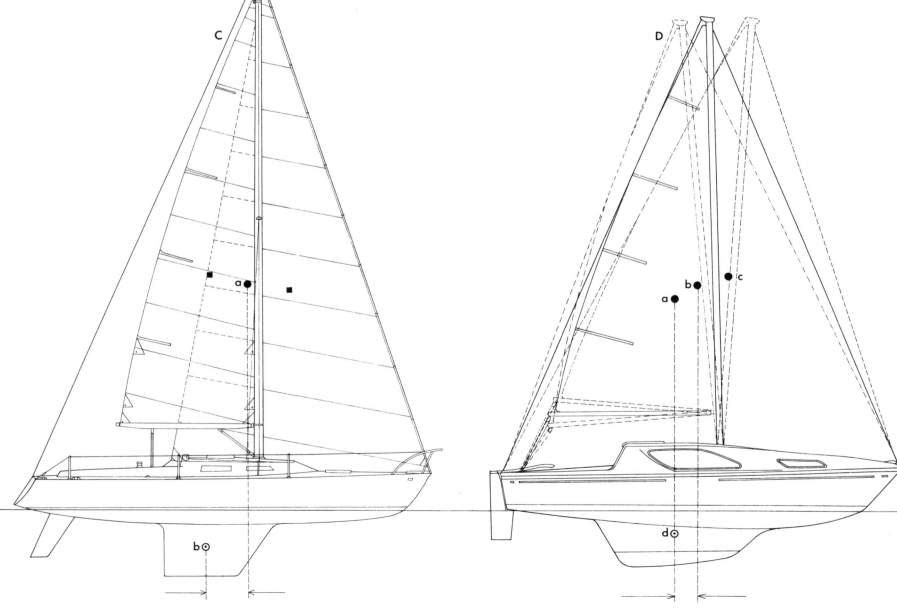

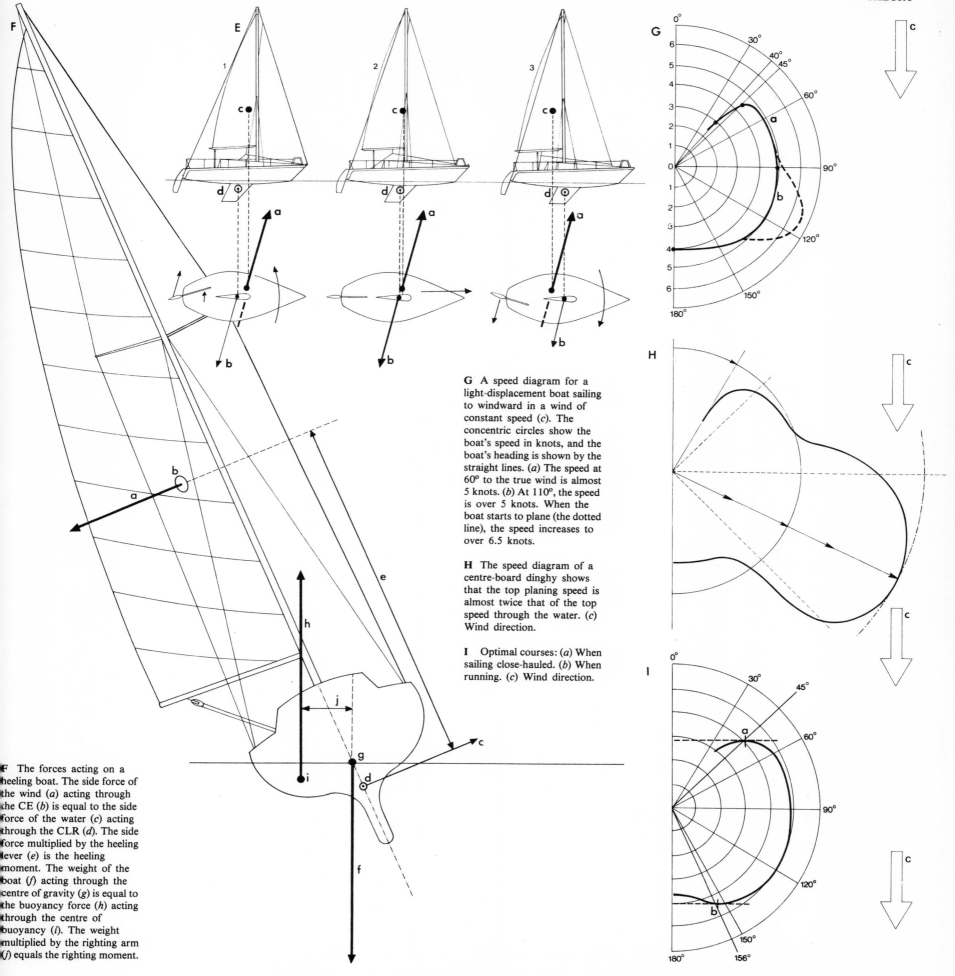

G A speed diagram for a light-displacement boat sailing to windward in a wind of constant speed (*c*). The concentric circles show the boat's speed in knots, and the boat's heading is shown by the straight lines. (*a*) The speed at 60° to the true wind is almost 5 knots. (*b*) At 110°, the speed is over 5 knots. When the boat starts to plane (the dotted line), the speed increases to over 6.5 knots.

H The speed diagram of a centre-board dinghy shows that the top planing speed is almost twice that of the top speed through the water. (*c*) Wind direction.

I Optimal courses: (*a*) When sailing close-hauled. (*b*) When running. (*c*) Wind direction.

F The forces acting on a heeling boat. The side force of the wind (*a*) acting through the CE (*b*) is equal to the side force of the water (*c*) acting through the CLR (*d*). The side force multiplied by the heeling lever (*e*) is the heeling moment. The weight of the boat (*f*) acting through the centre of gravity (*g*) is equal to the buoyancy force (*h*) acting through the centre of buoyancy (*i*). The weight multiplied by the righting arm (*j*) equals the righting moment.

115

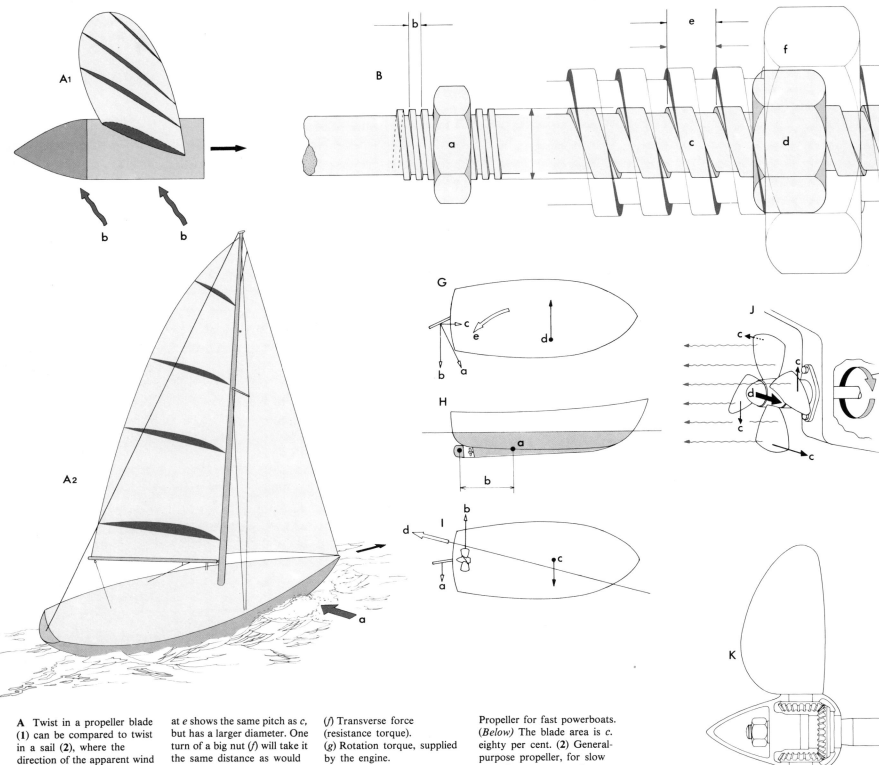

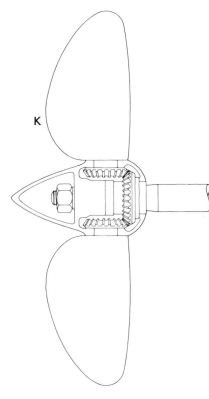

A Twist in a propeller blade (**1**) can be compared to twist in a sail (**2**), where the direction of the apparent wind (*a*) can be likened to the apparent angle of entrance of the water (*b*), when the propeller is moving forward.

B Pitch and diameter of a screw thread. One complete revolution takes the small nut (*a*) round the threads with a small pitch (*b*). The thread at *c* illustrates a big pitch on a small diameter. If the nut (*d*) has the same pitch as *c*, one revolution will take it the length of the pitch. The thread

at *e* shows the same pitch as *c*, but has a larger diameter. One turn of a big nut (*f*) will take it the same distance as would one turn of the smaller nut (*d*).

C The forces operating on a rotating blade. (**1**) Small pitch means big thrust and small torque. (**2**) A smaller blade and bigger pitch mean less thrust, more torque, and more slip. (*a*) Direction of advance of the blade through the water. (*b*) Propeller slip (can be compared to the leeway of a keel). (*c*) Blade angle. (*d*) Lift force, developed by the water. (*e*) Forward force (thrust).

(*f*) Transverse force (resistance torque).
(*g*) Rotation torque, supplied by the engine.

D The pitch and diameter of a propeller. (*a*) Pitch. (*b*) Propeller diameter. (*c*) Propeller hub trace. (*d*) Propeller blade tip trace. The pitch is the same at the hub and at the blade tip, but the diameters are quite different.

E Blade angles at tip (*a*), centre (*b*), and hub (*c*).

F Areas of propeller disc on various types of propellers. (**1**)

Propeller for fast powerboats. (*Below*) The blade area is *c*. eighty per cent. (**2**) General-purpose propeller, for slow powerboats, motor sailers, etc. (*Below*) Blade area *c*. forty per cent. (**3**) Propeller for a sailing-yacht's auxiliary. (*Below*) Blade area *c*. twenty per cent.

G Rudder action when going astern. (*a*) Rudder force. (*b*) Steering force. (*c*) Resistance. (*d*) CLR. (*e*) Direction swinging astern.

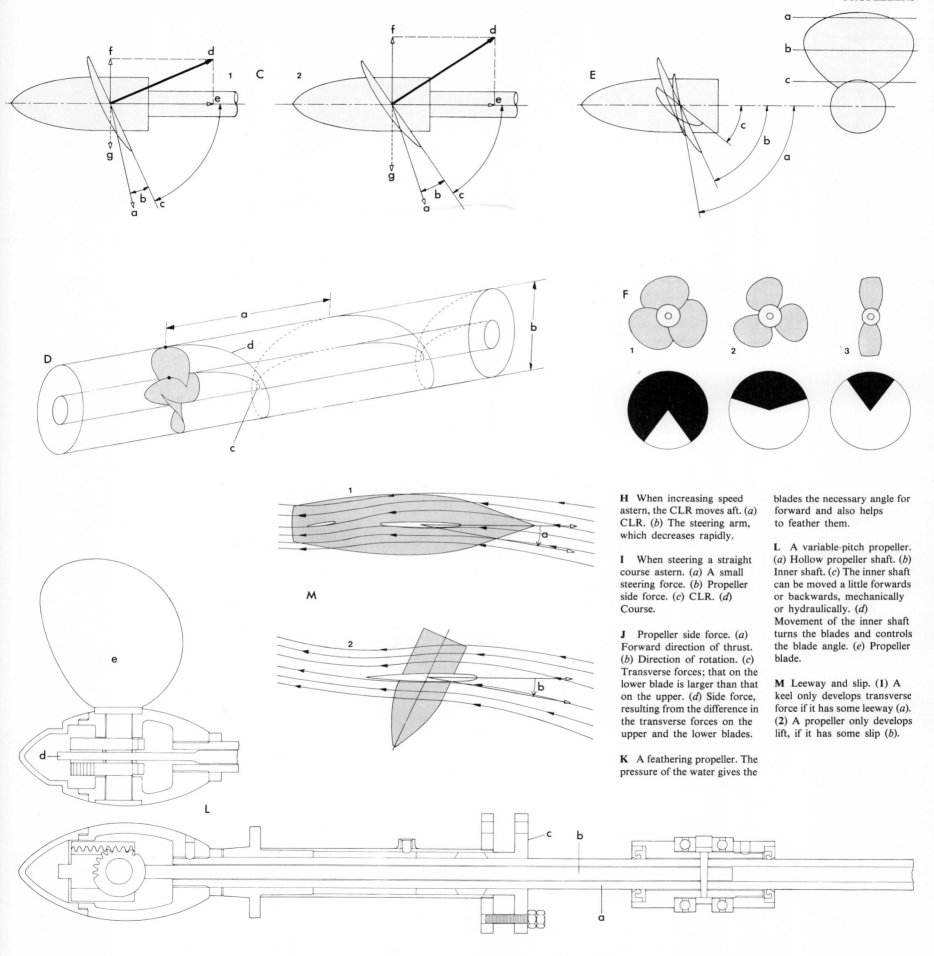

H When increasing speed astern, the CLR moves aft. (*a*) CLR. (*b*) The steering arm, which decreases rapidly.

I When steering a straight course astern. (*a*) A small steering force. (*b*) Propeller side force. (*c*) CLR. (*d*) Course.

J Propeller side force. (*a*) Forward direction of thrust. (*b*) Direction of rotation. (*c*) Transverse forces; that on the lower blade is larger than that on the upper. (*d*) Side force, resulting from the difference in the transverse forces on the upper and the lower blades.

K A feathering propeller. The pressure of the water gives the blades the necessary angle for forward and also helps to feather them.

L A variable-pitch propeller. (*a*) Hollow propeller shaft. (*b*) Inner shaft. (*c*) The inner shaft can be moved a little forwards or backwards, mechanically or hydraulically. (*d*) Movement of the inner shaft turns the blades and controls the blade angle. (*e*) Propeller blade.

M Leeway and slip. (**1**) A keel only develops transverse force if it has some leeway (*a*). (**2**) A propeller only develops lift, if it has some slip (*b*).

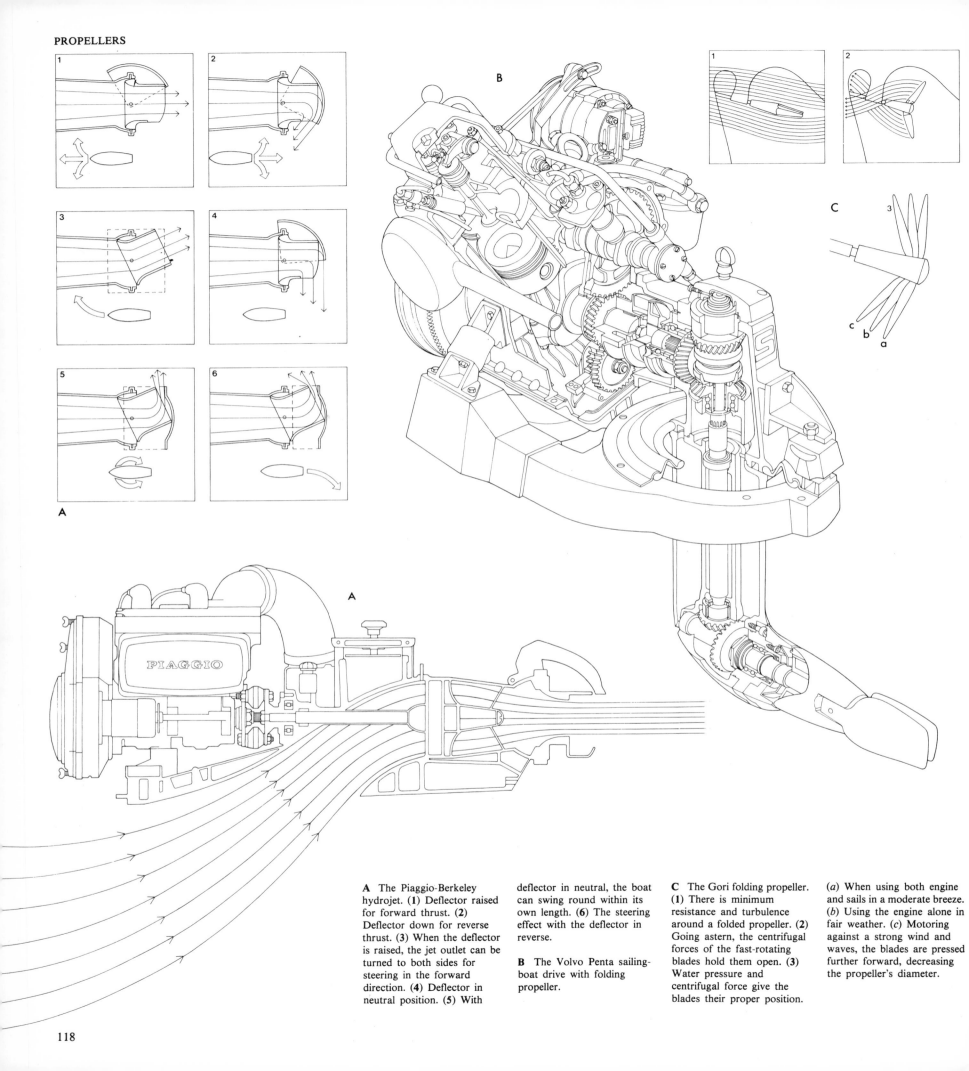

A The Piaggio-Berkeley hydrojet. (1) Deflector raised for forward thrust. (2) Deflector down for reverse thrust. (3) When the deflector is raised, the jet outlet can be turned to both sides for steering in the forward direction. (4) Deflector in neutral position. (5) With deflector in neutral, the boat can swing round within its own length. (6) The steering effect with the deflector in reverse.

B The Volvo Penta sailing-boat drive with folding propeller.

C The Gori folding propeller. (1) There is minimum resistance and turbulence around a folded propeller. (2) Going astern, the centrifugal forces of the fast-rotating blades hold them open. (3) Water pressure and centrifugal force give the blades their proper position.

(a) When using both engine and sails in a moderate breeze. (b) Using the engine alone in fair weather. (c) Motoring against a strong wind and waves, the blades are pressed further forward, decreasing the propeller's diameter.

SAIL-BOAT HANDLING

Jack Knights

The actions which permit a boat to sail, those of wind over sail and of water over hull and keel, are very complicated when explained by scientific theory (as in the previous chapter). The theory of sailing is more difficult to explain than the theory of flight, as it involves both air and water, while flight involves only one medium, air.

So you will be relieved to learn that practical sailing turns out to be far easier than the theory would suggest. Many excellent and able practical sailors know nothing of the scientific theory, yet they sail their boats as fast and as safely as others who may be better grounded in the science.

When a boat is running before the wind, it is easy to understand how it moves through the water. The wind hits the sails and forces them to move in the direction it is going, in just the same way as it carries a falling leaf, a rain cloud, or smoke from a factory chimney.

To help the wind, when running before it, the sailor will extend his sails to catch as much of it as possible. This means putting them at right angles to the wind—and at right angles to the boat. For the same reason—to maximize the wind's effect—the sails are given a baggy shape, and are then known as "full-cut". This explains the shape of the special running sail called the running spinnaker. It is shaped like a ball to reach out and grab as much wind as possible and, having grabbed it, to retain it as long as possible.

When square running like this, the wind enters the sail, eddies about and finally spills out around one or other of the edges of the sail. Ahead, behind, and around the boat will be large areas of air turbulence. It is easy to see that it is quite impossible to sail faster than the wind when running before it. The air turbulence, the drag and weight of the boat, and the friction of the water ensure that, in fact, the boat can never go as fast as the wind.

It should also be easy to see that, when running, the boat has little tendency to heel, as the forces are all being applied from aft, in a forward direction. If a designer knew that his boat would always run before the wind, he could reduce the ballast or the width (which increases sideways stability). Because the wind is not trying to push the whole boat bodily sideways, the designer could also leave off the keel. The ideal running boat would be a long, slim, lightweight craft. The length increases speed because of wave action, and also because it resists the tendency of the wind, pushing from behind and striking the sails high above the deck, to force the bow downwards until, in extremes, the craft can somersault, with the stern lifting up and over the bow.

Since, when running, the speed of the boat will reduce the velocity of the wind as it strikes the sails, more sail can be carried in this mode than in any other. This helps to explain why yachts can carry such large spinnakers when running and, in certain cases, other extra sails such as big boys (otherwise known as bloopers) and spinnaker and mizzen staysails.

Though there is little heeling tendency when running, a hard-pressed hull may show other forms of instability, scarcely less worrying. One is the tendency to roll. If a hull is being driven so hard that it wants to go faster than its length and shape allow, the surplus energy must be somehow allowed to escape. Light hulls may pick up out of the water and begin to skim the waves by surfing and planing. Heavier hulls cannot do this and, as their bow and stern waves increase in magnitude, there will be a noticeable tendency to roll from side to side. This special kind of rolling is self-generating so, if the wind force continues, the degree of roll may build up. Today's wide, flat hulls with their small keels and rudders become very difficult to steer straight when heeled excessively, and the helmsman's efforts to hold his boat straight may only serve to increase the rolling.

In extreme cases, when a sailing-boat heels excessively away from the wind, it will round up uncontrollably into it; and, similarly, when heeling excessively into the wind, it will bear off uncontrollably. Thus, when a boat is rolling rhythmically one way and then the other, it may also twist and turn, first one way and then the other. When the turning forces are beyond control, the boat broaches. It may lean right over, until the mast-head is close to the water and one side of the deck is in the water.

Rhythmic rolling of this kind can be very disconcerting, but it may be overcome in several ways. Firstly and most obviously, the sail may be reduced, so that the boat is being no longer over-driven. Take in your spinnaker first, since this will be your biggest, lightest, and least controllable sail. If the boat is still over-driven, you can then reef your mainsail.

Rolling may be reduced by removing the twist in jib and main. Imagine looking down the sail from the mast-head towards the deck. The top of the sail will be at a smaller angle to the wind than will the bottom. This "screw" effect generates its own rolling tendency, particularly if the top of the sail is beyond 90° to the wind. To "detwist" the sail, you must sheet it down more, pulling it down harder towards the deck. There is a special piece of rigging called a kicking-strap, kicker, or boom vang, which has been devised for just this purpose.

When running, a boat will balance better if the sails are set forward and the rudder as far aft as possible; then it will tend to run straight, naturally wanting to follow the wind.

A running boat is easily controllable, as long as it continues to go straight before the wind. It is when it finds itself veering off course and angling across the wind in heavy weather, that the trouble starts.

Angling across the wind is called reaching, and this occurs on any course where the angle of the apparent wind (the wind actually hitting your sails) is more than about 45° aft of the bow, or more than about 45° forward of the stern. If it is less than 45° aft of the bow, you will be beating to windward. If less than 45° forward of the stern, you will be running, as described above.

When you are reaching, the wind will be, or should be, meeting the sail at its forward edge, flowing smoothly over both sides of the sail and leaving, as smoothly as possible, from the sail's after edge. Thus, a regular air-flow will have been established, similar to the air-flow over the wing of an aircraft in flight. The most important part of this flow is that over the lee side of the sail. It is here that the air is forced to increase velocity, thus reducing pressure. This pressure reduction, as has been explained in the previous chapter, leads to most of the forward sailing force.

When reaching, there are easy, practical ways of judging the best sail angle to the wind. Broadly speaking, you must watch the forward edge, or luff, of the sail. Ease out your sheet until this edge just begins to flutter; then haul the sheet back in, decreasing the sail angle, until the fluttering just disappears—no more. If you pull it in much more, there will be a danger of stalling.

In recent years, people have begun to attach small wool tufts to the leading edges of their sails. These tufts indicate air-flow perfectly, when the air is flowing smoothly across the sail from front to back, as the tufts then trail back steadily. When the flow begins to break down and be turbulent, the tufts begin to jump around. When the flow breaks down altogether, the tufts begin to flow forward.

In practice, these wool or, sometimes, ribbon lengths give a better indication of air-flow across the jib than across the mainsail. The reason for this is easy to see—the air-flow over the leading edge of a jib is not hindered or complicated by the proximity of a mast. The mast makes some turbulence over the luff of a mainsail inevitable. For this reason, the tufts should be placed further aft, at least one third of the chord back in the mainsail and about one tenth aft in the case of a jib.

The important tufts are those to leeward. Luckily, most sail fabrics are transparent enough to allow a dark-coloured tuft to be seen through the fabric.

The basic wind-tuft rule is: adjust the sail angle so that both tufts, windward and leeward, are flowing back steadily. If the windward tuft is becoming turbulent or curling forward in a jib, the wind angle is too fine, so tighten the sheet, thus causing the sail to increase its angle to the wind (in the case of a mainsail, some forward flow on the windward side is almost impossible to eradicate, so pay more attention to the lee side). If the leeward tuft is breaking and turbulent, the angle is too coarse, and it will be necessary to ease the sheet, thus decreasing the angle of the sail to the wind. In practice, since the wind is always varying in some degree and the waves always changing the attitude of the boat, it will be necessary to adjust your sheets constantly.

With the wind exactly on the beam—at right angles to the boat—the sails will be aligned at an angle of about 45° to the hull. The wind tufts and the luffs of the sails will give a more exact guide to the correct angle.

It goes without saying that, as you turn the boat towards the wind, the sails will need to be sheeted more closely to the centre-line, or else the fluttering at the luff will increase until the whole sail flutters like a flag. Conversely, as you turn away from the wind, the sheets must be eased and the angle to the centre-line increased, otherwise the flow will break down, become turbulent, and reverse itself, making the sail stall.

The aim, first and last, is to encourage and promote a regular and smooth air-flow over your sails. The reason that the rigs of boats are divided into small units—jibs and mainsails—is only partly because this makes them easier to handle. A more important factor is the assistance of the jib in promoting a more powerful and smoother air-flow over the lee side of the mainsail (in much the same way as the leading-edge flap or slot in an aircraft wing helps to "bend" the flow around the wing).

Reaching is the most efficient and fastest point of sailing. When close reaching on smooth ice, ice yachts can attain speeds many times the velocity of the wind. Of course, as speed is increased in this manner, the apparent wind will move sharply forward, calling for the sails to be sheeted harder and harder in. It can be easily seen that, as the apparent wind moves forward, the sideways forces on the boat as a whole will increase. These will have to be resisted by an efficiently shaped fin or keel and by increased stability in the form of broadness and flatness of hull form, of live crew weight on the windward side, or of ballast placed low in the hull or, even lower, in the keel appendage.

Spinnakers have been developed to function well when reaching. These are cut much flatter than running spinnakers and are much like jibs, except that they present a far larger area to the wind. Such sails are used almost exclusively for racing, and it is likely that the cruising sailor will be happy to reach across the wind under his normal working sails.

As with running, uncontrolled twist will hurt reaching performance as well, for it should be obvious that, if the sail angle is correct for the apparent-wind angle at one point in a much-twisted sail, it will be incorrect at another point.

Here again the kicking-strap, or boom vang, is tightened to prevent the boom end from rising. In light airs, care should be taken not to over-tighten the kicking-

strap. In fact, all sail controls should be handled gently in light airs.

When it is necessary to sail closer towards the wind's direction than the wind will permit without causing the sails to flutter ineffectually, your only recourse will be to tack—to attack the wind obliquely by zigzagging towards it in a series of tacks. Tacking is also called "sailing to windward" or "beating". (The manoeuvre of changing from one tack to another is also called tacking or putting about.)

Windward sailing is commonly regarded as the most difficult and testing of all points of sailing, the moment when a helmsman's skill is most likely to show. The scope—for good and bad judgement, and good and bad technique—is wider here than elsewhere.

Here again you must be guided by the flutter in the sail luff and by the wool tufts, which we recommend you fit, even if you do not race. Broadly speaking, the main-boom angle for sailing to windward will be at 8°–15° to the boat's centre-line, depending on wind strength, boat type, rig type, sail cut, and other factors.

As you luff (turn towards the wind), you haul in your sheets until the sails assume the close-hauled position (about 12° off the centre); you then approach the wind until your sail luff, or front edge, begins to flutter, and then bear off a trifle until the fluttering disappears; you are now close-hauled. With the average boat, you will be about 30° off the apparent wind and about 42° off the actual wind (which you will not be able to estimate because you are moving). Since the boat will be crabbing sideways slightly as it moves forward (making leeway), a phenomenon which even the most efficient, modern sailing-boat cannot escape entirely, your angle of progress to the actual wind will be something in the order of 48°. You are thus slicing obliquely towards the wind. By tacking or turning onto the contrary tack, sailing close-hauled in the same way but with the wind now on the opposite side, you will be making up into the wind, or beating to windward.

Since the sideways forces are greater than the resultant forward forces, your keel, hull, and even rudder perform a vital function when beating, both in countering leeway and in maintaining stability. A boat's actual windward speed is often directly related to its ability to withstand the heeling effect of the wind. In a given wind, you may be able to carry a spinnaker when running and full plain sail when reaching but, when you come on the wind, you may find you need to reduce sail, either by changing to a smaller jib or by reefing the mainsail. This is because the speed of the apparent wind, since it is coming from ahead of the beam and since the boat is moving forward, will be greater than the actual wind speed.

When beating to windward, the good sailor will be able to sense and feel the behaviour of his boat. He knows when he ought to sail a little freer—further off the wind—because, at a higher angle, the rough seas may be preventing the boat from giving its best speed. He will be able to respond quickly to small wind-angle changes, by constantly luffing or bearing off a degree or two at a time. Though every action of the rudder will tend to slow the boat, it is an observable fact that the best windward sailors, when beating to windward in average conditions, keep turning their boats very slightly all the time. They

find the best route over and across the waves, respond to the wind, feather the boat up slightly to ease it through a heavy squall, and bear off, easing the sheets fractionally when the wind eases.

This is what makes sailing in general, and sailing to windward in particular, such an absorbing business. Your boat will never be correctly trimmed and angled for more than a few moments. Small changes to rudder, sheets, and so on will be constantly needed. Thus it is that sailing requires your fullest attention.

Of course, any old boat will make its way through the wind without this degree of care and skill, but it will not be performing as well as the attentively sailed boat and, if sailing is worth doing at all, it is worth doing well.

We have now considered running, which is the simplest form of sailing; reaching, which can be the fastest; and beating, or tacking, which is the most demanding. Of course, a normal day's sailing, a race, or a cruise will involve a blend of all these points of sailing, and it will be necessary to change from one to the other.

The two turning manoeuvres in sailing are called "gybing" and "tacking". You gybe when you turn so far away from the wind that its direction moves across your stern from one side or quarter to the other. Thus you gybe when you are running.

The tack is the opposite of this and is performed by turning towards the wind, passing the bow of the boat through the eye of the wind, and so changing from one tack to the other.

Gybing is a sudden thing. Your sails will want to flick (or even crash) across from one side of the boat to the other with some force and, since the sails when running will be fully out, they will be moving through an arc of up to 180°. The speed and suddenness of gybing require anticipation and quick reflexes. You will need to learn to anticipate the feel of a sail that is about to flip across, and you must begin hauling in quickly on the sheet to help it across in a controlled manner instead of letting it crash across wildly. If your boat is a light, racy type, you will soon discover that, when you gybe in a fresh breeze, you will need to use the tiller, and possibly your live weight too, to counteract the sudden forces of the gybing sails and pivoting spars. Gybing calls for more practice than any other sailing manoeuvre.

Tacking is gentle by contrast. This is because, turning through the wind's eye, the boat is slowing as it goes. In fact, some boats, such as catamarans, can come to a complete stop in the middle of tacking. When tacking, the sails will flap and flutter across gradually. They will not crash suddenly, as when gybing in a fresh wind. The one thing you must be careful to watch for is that the sheets do not hang up as the sails change sides. (There are two jib sheets in the normally-rigged boat, one led to port and the other to starboard; as you tack, you must release one and haul in the other.) If, when tacking, one jib sheet should foul on an obstruction or not be released, it will pin the jib to windward, and this will cause the bow of the boat to spin around quickly. In a hard wind, this can capsize an unballasted dinghy or multihull.

Perhaps this may be the time to say a little about steering. A rudder is at its most effective, as a turning instrument, when the boat is moving fastest and when the rudder blade is turned no more than about 20°. If you turn the rudder too much, you will only slow the boat and make it even less willing to turn further. All turning should be done smoothly, progressively, and with a minimum of rudder angle. When tacking, you will need to turn the rudder more and more as the boat comes head to wind (slowing as it pivots). Then, as the boat begins to fill away on the new tack, you will find that a contrary checking of the rudder will be necessary to prevent the boat from turning through too large an angle.

This is quite different from steering a car, where you apply a definite amount of wheel and the car describes a definite radius. Boat steering is less exact and geometrical—much more like steering a horse and, consequently, more fun.

Before you can find yourself out in open water and sailing along, it will be necessary to rig your boat and hoist your anchor, slip your moorings, or launch from the beach.

There are no mysteries or any particular difficulties about doing any of these things. What is needed, most of all, is common sense and a feel for the wind and its direction (and for the tide, too, if there happen to be tidal currents or streams).

Sailing-boats do not have brakes. The only way to stop them is to point them head to wind. Then the wind will catch them and hold them up, before beginning to push them backwards. Normally, all sailing is started and finished from the head-to-wind position, with the sails fluttering powerlessly like flags. It is when you try to stop without turning head to wind, or try to hoist sail to start without first making sure that you are pointed head to wind, that trouble can start. Even when you are hoisting sail on a small dinghy on the beach before launching, you must take care to see that it is pointed head to wind.

Think of a weathercock, one of those pivoting wind indicators which people fit to the tops of masts and poles in their gardens or on the roofs of buildings. Think of it in the form of a model sailing-boat. When the model is pivoted on a vertical axis close to its keel, which is normally the case, you can understand that the mainsail will be tending to turn the model towards the wind, while the jib, in front of the pivot point, will tend to make it spin away from the wind. To make it function properly as a weathercock, the mainsail will need to be larger than the jib, so that the model will keep pointing into the wind.

This is the case with a real sailing-boat—the rig is proportioned and positioned in relation to the keel in such a way that, without anybody holding the tiller, the boat will tend to "weathercock" towards the wind. This is an inbuilt safety factor, because if control is lost, for some reason such as the helmsman falling overboard, the boat will turn into the wind and remain there more or less motionless, with its sails fluttering.

This type of balance is called "weather helm" and is to be found in all but a very few boats. It means that the centre of effort of the sails is a little way aft of the centre of lateral resistance of the hull. Obviously, if you drop your jib and keep your mainsail up, the balance will be altered and the weather helm increased.

The rare boats that tend to turn away from the wind are said to have "lee helm". This may be acceptable in some racing craft but is otherwise unseamanlike, since the untended boat will turn away from the wind and increase speed. Lee helm may be caused by setting too big a jib with too small a mainsail, by moving or raking a mast forward too much, by partly raising a hinged drop keel, or by moving a keel bodily aft.

For a proper understanding of sailing, it is important to have a grasp of the principles of balance. It explains why, for instance, when hoisting sail (having ensured, first of all, that your boat is head to wind), you begin by hoisting the after sails, usually the mainsail first. In this way, the boat will weathercock automatically, while you get on with the business of hoisting your sails.

Before a boat is to be sailed away from its mooring or anchorage, it is important (as has been said) to ensure that it is lying head to wind. The procedure will go something like this: If lying to a single mooring, first of all make the mooring easy to throw overboard. Prepare and hoist the mainsail, taking care to see that the sheet is free to run. Now bring the jib on deck and attach it to its stay, sheets, and halyard. Cast off the mooring, making sure that the head of the boat swings off in the desired direction. Haul in the main sheet, and gain speed and steerage way. Finally, at your leisure and when you have sea-room, hoist and then sheet your jib.

The jib may be hoisted before leaving the mooring, but it will often impede the man whose job it is to drop the mooring.

The drill is similar if you are recovering an anchor but, in this case, it may be better not to bring the jib on deck until the anchor has been hoisted, cleaned, and stowed. Otherwise, the jib may be soiled. In a large craft, it will be necessary to sail the boat towards the anchor to enable the anchor cable to be hauled in. The mainsail should be sufficient for this purpose. If not, the auxiliary engine may be employed. The boat should be sailed up to and over its anchor at the same speed as the cable hauler or haulers are able to take in the cable.

When a dinghy or other small boat is to be launched from a beach, the same rules apply. The boat should be pointed head to wind before any attempt to hoist sails is made. You may hoist sails with the boat still high on the beach, then carry it or trolley it into deep water, or you may carry it afloat first and then hoist sail, but in both cases make sure the boat swings head to wind before you hoist sail. To make a good job of launching a dinghy from an open beach, you must be prepared to get wet, particularly if the wind is blowing onshore, thus raising waves. If you try to stay dry, you may well damage the boat. Boats must be taken into fairly deep water in order that their rudders can be fitted and centre-board lowered enough so that the boat can claw off the lee shore into still deeper water.

In the common case of a two-man dinghy, both will carry the boat afloat. The forward hand, or crew, will then move to the bow to hold the boat, while it swings head to wind. The skipper will climb aboard to fit the rudder and hoist sail. When everything aboard is ready, the crew in the water will swing the boat's bow away from the wind in the direction of deeper water and will then swing himself aboard, as the boat begins to move past him. The higher the waves, the more difficult these manoeuvres and the wetter the sailors will probably get, but the principles remain the same.

Life gets slightly more complicated if, for some reason, your moored or anchored boat is not lying head to wind. This may be because a contrary tidal current is stronger than the wind, or because your boat, being moored alongside a dock or another boat, has a fixed position. In these cases, sails will fill with wind as soon as they are hoisted, and it will be difficult to prevent the boat from gathering way before you have thrown off its restraining ropes or hoisted the anchor.

The rule here is to unmoor the boat first, and then quickly make some sail (and thus some steerage way), while you may take your time making full sail. The normal method is to have all sails cleared away for hoisting. Then, as the anchor is recovered or the moorings freed, the jib is quickly run up and sheeted home. You then sail into clear water, luff head to wind, and hoist your mainsail.

So it is, too, with picking up moorings or anchoring. You must first of all decide (by observation of other moored craft) which is stronger, the wind or the tide. If the craft already moored are tide rode (riding to the tide), you must approach your anchoring point or mooring against the tide, even though you will then be with the wind. You reduce sail progressively as you approach; in fact, you can usually drop your jib, bit by bit, as you approach within a few yards of your mooring. Your plan must be to come to rest at your mooring.

If, as will more often happen, the boat will be wind rode on its mooring, the manoeuvre will be easier. Approach the mooring upwind by tacking towards it, and then lower your jib and get it out of the way before your final approach. Tack towards the mooring, luff head to wind when still some distance away, judging speed and momentum so that your boat comes to a halt at the mooring. Then moor up or anchor with the boat head to wind and the sail flapping. Lower the mainsail in your own good time.

Care is needed when approaching a beach in a dinghy. It is important, first of all, to make sure that the waves are not running dangerously high. If the wind is blowing onshore, you must round up while still in water of sailing depth; then one of you jumps overboard to hold the craft head to wind, while the other lowers sail and unships the rudder. If the wind is blowing offshore, there will be less of a problem, since the water will be smoother close to the beach and, when luffing head to wind, you will be pointing towards and not away from the beach itself.

The success of all these manoeuvres will depend upon your ability to judge the behaviour of your boat; to judge, for instance, how long it will continue to move forward through the water after the sails are emptied of wind. Light boats like dinghies and catamarans stop very quickly. Heavy keelboats, particularly narrow racing craft with deep slim keels, will carry their momentum for many boat-lengths. You must get to know your boat and its special characteristics, so that, in a tight corner, it will not surprise you.

This is particularly necessary in today's crowded anchorages and marinas. It is unseamanlike to sail into a marina and then discover that the space is too small to allow you to turn head to wind and cut your speed. On the other hand, it is brilliant seamanship to sail into one of these places, spin round on a dime, dropping your sails as you go, and then nudge alongside your berth at the very moment that your momentum drops away to nothing.

Today's modern sailors usually regard discretion as the better part of valour; they switch on their auxiliary engines well outside harbours, drop their sails, and then motor up to their moorings.

All the same, you must be prepared for the time when your engine refuses to start. Then you will really need to know the way your boat behaves under sail and what you can expect of it.

We have written of leaving and approaching moorings but have not said much of the technical aspects of anchoring and mooring. To function properly, an anchor ought to be as near-horizontal as possible. This tends to drive the anchor blades, or flukes, into the sea bed.

Therefore, the anchor line will need to be three times as long as the depth of the water at high tide, and it will help if it is heavy, so that it will sag in a curve or "catenary". Modern light-weight lines may be encouraged to do this in two ways, either by fitting a length of chain, which will drag on the sea bed, next to the anchor itself, or by fitting a weight to the middle of the anchor line. Full-length chain is best but is prohibitively heavy and expensive for many of today's sailors.

To restrict the full, large-diameter swing of a single anchor, it may be necessary (though this is rare today) to drop a second, smaller anchor, known as a kedge. First, drop the main or "bower" anchor, then let out at least twice as much cable as you will end up with, so that the boat falls back. Then drop your kedge anchor and pull back in on your main cable until the boat is exactly between the two anchors.

If you suspect that the sea bed may be foul, so that there is a risk that an anchor may catch and so be difficult or impossible to hoist, you should fit a "scowing" line. Make fast a lighter line to the lower part of the anchor, seize this line with a light, breakable seizing to the head of the anchor, and then lead it loosely back to the boat. If the anchor fouls, this line is tightened and the main cable is let out. The seizing should break and then the anchor may be recovered upside-down with the lighter line.

A permanent mooring is better, because its line will be shorter and the moored boat will take up less room when responding to wind and tide.

The mooring buoy is normally attached to the mooring line by a secondary light rope which enables the heavier line to sink to the sea bed. So when mooring up, the light line must be fully recovered, and the boat is then attached to the heavy line or chain. The buoy should be hung in the rigging to indicate that your boat is lying to a mooring.

Many modern boats do not have well-designed stemhead fittings for the reception of anchor and mooring lines. These fittings, or fairleads, should be equipped with rollers to minimize chafe and should be designed to prevent the line or chain from jumping out, when the boat is pitching in a sea.

When mooring alongside another boat or a dock, the object should be to prevent the boat from damaging itself where it rubs alongside. This means that it should be restrained from moving backwards and forwards, and should not be pulled inwards towards the object alongside which it is lying.

First, there must be good fenders at the points where the boat would otherwise rub. Old car tyres are adequate, but proper fenders are better, because they do not leave stains. The bigger they are, the better (though over-large fenders are difficult to stow).

Second, the bow and stern lines should be taken as far apart as possible, to accentuate the longitudinal pull.

Third, spring lines should be rigged fore and aft. These counter the pull of the bow and stern lines and so limit the backwards and forward movement. These should be as long as possible.

If mooring alongside in tidal waters, try to moor up against a floating object which will go up and down with the tide. If not, make sure you know at what state of tide you are mooring, and that you have arranged for adequate line lengths to take care of the vertical movement. If possible, place planks between the fenders and the object against which you are mooring, so that the fenders are protected from being chafed.

If the boat is to take the ground at low tide, be sure that weights are placed on the inside side deck or that a line is taken ashore from the mast, so that the boat cannot fall outwards, as the water level drops.

If the wind is blowing onshore, take out a kedge anchor, so that you can lead a line to pull your boat off the dock, to diminish the rubbing, chafing tendency. Often, you will be able to pick up a mooring, which is so placed that your stern will fall back towards the shore, thus enabling you to embark by the stern even though the boat does not actually touch the shore or dock itself. This is a common method in small harbours.

Mooring lines are usually of nylon or polypropylene fibre. These materials stretch a great deal and, thus, absorb shocks instead of transmitting them to cleat and mooring bollards. But do not use polypropylene (which floats) for anchor lines.

Knowing your boat, its abilities and its limitations, is an essential part of seamanship. In this, the amateur can never hope to surpass the professional seaman, because he spends so much less time at sea, but he must get to know his boat as thoroughly as time allows. Good seamanship is a mixture of prudence, common sense, sailing knowledge, weather lore, and, in extremes, resistance to fatigue, cold, and seasickness. Those who know least about the rigours of gales at sea are the most likely to be caught out in them. Some beginners imagine that if a sister-ship of their own yacht has made an Atlantic crossing or come through a hurricane unscathed, then they will be safe attempting the same in their own craft.

But the truth is that the people fail before the boat. Gales test people more searchingly than they test boats. The boats which founder are usually the ones which their crews have lost full command of—maybe the bilge pumps are not worked hard enough, hatch covers are allowed to get adrift, or sail is carried for too long in a rising wind so that a mast collapses overboard, where it bumps into and holes the hull. Little troubles can lead to greater.

The good seaman is the man who gets an accurate weather forecast before attempting a lengthy crossing and decides not to sail until a bad forecast improves. The good seaman is the man who regularly inspects his gear and replaces chafed halyards and rusting shrouds, before they can lead to serious troubles.

The good seaman is the man who dresses in warm clothes, before he gets wet, who wears wind-proof foul-weather gear, and who takes anti-seasickness tablets an hour or more before leaving harbour.

Seamanship is, of course, more than a matter of surviving extreme weather; it is being at home afloat, blow high or low, night and day. A good seaman will retain his footing on deck in rough water when others will be thrown about and feel unsafe (but he will also rig a personal lifeline, just in case a wave takes him by surprise).

The good seaman is the man who works his tides and arranges his sailing life round them instead of round his clock. For instance, he may set sail at four in the morning in order to catch six hours of fair tide, instead of rising at a more normal hour and losing the best part of a day's passage, because he spends his time fighting an adverse tide and getting nowhere.

Certain basic skills are, of course, required of the good seaman. He must be able to tie certain knots—reef, bowline, sheetbend, round turn and two half hitches, sheepshank, clove hitch, figure of eight—and he should be able to splice fibre rope and do a whipping (or at least remember to heat the ends of synthetic ropes, so that they cannot unravel). More important, the good seaman is constantly looking over his boat and gear, maintaining and repairing, making and mending. This is called "ship's husbandry", and it has always been an essential part of the sailor's life. True, modern materials have reduced the degree of maintenance required, but the need for watchfulness remains.

Dinghies, keelboats, and multihulls are three very different boat types which require different handling techniques and understanding of their various capabilities.

Because it has no keel, the dinghy, or centre-boarder, is light and lively. If well-designed and hard-driven, it will lift out of the water, when sailing off wind, and will plane over the surface like a fast powerboat. It will also surf waves, moving down the wave crest at the speed of the moving water. In these conditions, the dinghy is not subject to the same speed limitation as the keelboat, whose speed is governed by the height of the waves it makes at bow and stern.

Size for size, therefore, the dinghy is faster than the keelboat. But it depends, to a large degree, for its safety and speed on its crew's ability. It will not look after itself like a keelboat. Its handling requires greater mental concentration and physical co-ordination on the part of the crew.

The dinghy's stability depends partly upon the hull shape (flatness and width improve stability), partly on the live weight of the crew. This is why some classes allow the crew to use trapeze wires hung from the mast, one on each side, and clipped to a harness which permits the man to hang right out of the boat with only his feet in contact with the hull. A few classes have sliding planks for the same purpose. All high-performance dinghies have toe, or hiking, straps, under which the crew put their feet, so that they can lean back further without toppling over backwards.

In fresh winds, the further you can move this live weight to windward and the larger this weight is, the faster the boat will go.

In light airs, this weight may be moved inboard or even down to leeward to induce a degree of heel.

Off wind, the dinghy will raise its centre-board and, sometimes, even raise its rudder blade partly. This decreases wetted surface, which is not needed at all when running square and is needed less when reaching than when beating to windward.

The live weight of the crew is also used to adjust fore-and-aft trim to suit the prevailing conditions. In light airs, the weight is usually moved forward in the boat to depress the bow and raise the flat stern-sections. This, too, reduces wetted surface. In fresh breezes, and particularly when off wind, the weight is moved aft to prevent the bow from burying.

The dinghy is at its most stable when upright, with the mast vertical. This stability decreases with heel until, at angles of 50° or more, the dinghy will topple over in a capsizal. This is by no means uncommon with today's high-performance racing dinghies and, since they are all fitted with buoyancy compartments and self-draining devices, they may be easily righted by their crews and can usually continue in the race. (Because the dinghy has no heavy ballast keel, it will float when filled with water.)

The dinghy is the sports car of the sailing world, lively, quick to respond, dependent for its ultimate performance on the ability of its crew. It is also, of course, smaller than other sail craft, and it appeals more to younger sailors.

The keelboat is the serious seagoer, the boat that can look after itself in a gale, that may be sailed across oceans by an automatic steering device. Keelboats carry ballast (nearly always in the keel appendage, in order to obtain the lowest possible centre of gravity, but sometimes some or all of the ballast may be inside the hull). The stability of a keelboat increases with heel angle until a maximum is reached when the mast is horizontal. This means that a well-designed keelboat will bounce upright again after the most violent broach, with the mast-head almost in the water and the spinnaker beneath the water.

There are many recorded cases of keelboats being caught by huge waves and being turned through 360° before coming upright again, sometimes with smashed spars and deck gear.

The keelboat is, compared with the dinghy, at its best to windward. Because of its extra weight, it cannot rise up and plane or surf like a dinghy down wind. There are, of course, hybrid types, lightly built and with light keels, which do perform in dinghy style. All the same, their sail-area-to-weight ratios cannot match those of high-performance, unballasted centre-boarders.

Keelboats tend to be slimmer and deeper in hull form than dinghies, such a shape being a more efficient way of disposing of the comparatively greater displacement. They carry their momentum better and are, therefore, easier to steer, to tack, and to gybe. Some light dinghies stop very quickly while being turned through the eye of the wind when tacking.

Except in the largest sizes, the live weight of the crew is also useful to the ultimate performance of a keelboat. Thus, in fresh winds to windward, it helps if the crew moves to the weather rail, but the effect is much less marked than in the case of the dinghy.

In fact, modern design trends have seen the keelboat approach the dinghy in type and proportions, at least in racing. Keels have become shorter and deeper, more like centre-boards. Hulls, under the influence of rating rules, have tended to become flatter and wider—more like dinghies. Construction has become lighter. Yet many serious cruising yachtsmen still prefer the old, traditional type, with a long keel and of heavy displacement. They believe that such a type is easier to steer, will look after itself better when left unattended, and will be easier to slip for a scrub in some remote harbour. Also, it will last longer, will make a better floating home, and be more comfortable in its motion at sea.

The multihull is a third distinctive type, developed first in the South Seas where, over two hundred years ago, examples were capable of going many times as fast as the ponderous European vessels with which explorers such as Captain Cook were opening up the Pacific.

The multihull has one thing in common with the dinghy—it depends for its stability on hull form, not on ballast, but it achieves far greater initial stability than the one-hulled dinghy. Because of this great initial stability, their light weight, and their ability to set even more sail than dinghies, multihulls are the fastest sailing-craft going. This is because the extreme narrowness and fineness of line of their individual hulls reduce the harmful wave-making effect, so that they escape from the rule that limits conventional, non-planing hulls to speeds of around 1.4 times the square root of the water-line length in feet (2.44 times the square root of the water-line length in metres). Well-designed modern multihulls easily exceed the speed of the wind.

Unfortunately, when heeled to extreme angles the multihull will topple over in a capsize, just like a dinghy. Unlike a dinghy, however, it will then prove very difficult to right again, because when floating upside-down it is in a very stable position. In practice, fit crews can right day-sailing catamarans and trimarans of not more than 20 ft (6.1 m). The capsizing danger remains the big and very real obstacle to the general acceptance of larger cruising multihulls for deep-sea work. Some cruising multihulls have floats fitted to the mast-head to prevent inversion. Some designers have arranged for self-righting by means of the flooding of part of one hull. Yet, in the extreme conditions in which capsizing is likely to occur, none of these methods has yet been fully proven.

Most of the deep-sea multihull enthusiasts are, interestingly, concentrated in the Pacific, the historic home of the type, and they reckon that the risks are acceptable, saying that, though a car will skid off the road if cornering too fast, that risk is generally accepted. Though a well-designed multihull may overturn in extremes, a proficient crew should be able to prevent this from happening by reducing sail in good time, and by proper handling.

Multihulls are usually cheaper than keelboats to build, but it is difficult to obtain comparable internal accommodation—up to a certain size. Over about 40 ft (c. 12 m), the accommodation suddenly becomes very good. A multihull's great width makes it unpopular in marinas and in tight mooring areas. Some designers and builders are tempted to increase a multihull's weight unduly, as they strive to provide more and more creature comforts inside. The essence of any multihull is its lightness. When you take that away, you kill its verve and spirit. A slow multihull is a nothing.

Sooner or later, every sailor is going to encounter heavy weather. Therefore, every sailor must be prepared for it. Except in specialized racing types, it is usual practice to reduce sail as the wind increases. Jibs are changed to others of smaller size, mainsails are reefed, either by rolling round the boom, by tying in reef points, or with lashings. In the cases of boats with more than one mast, such as schooners, ketches, and yawls, sail reduction can be more easily made by dropping individual sails altogether.

It will always be possible to carry more sail off wind than up wind. Yet, sometimes, boats can be unwittingly over-driven when running before the wind (your speed will decrease the apparent wind).

The average well-designed sailing-cruiser of about 33 ft (c. 10 m) will usually be able to carry full sail up wind in wind-speeds of up to fifteen knots. From fifteen to twenty knots, the big jib will need replacing with the working jib, and the full mainsail can still be used. From twenty to twenty-five knots, the working jib and one reef in the main will be needed. From twenty-five to thirty knots, the storm jib and two reefs in the main will be called for.

Over thirty knots, we are talking of the various kinds of gale. In open sea, a boat of about 33 ft (c. 10 m) will find it difficult to continue sailing to windward in much over a constant thirty knots but, if it is to do so, it will certainly need its smallest jib and another reef in its mainsail (reducing this sail's total size by over half). Most modern boats will be able to sail to windward under a small jib only. This is a better rig than a close-reefed main alone. Trysails, the small sails which are used in storms to replace mainsails, are not as widely used as once they were. Usually, they only come into use when a mainsail is damaged.

In sheltered waters, it should be possible to continue sailing this size of boat to windward in winds of up to forty knots, providing that sail has been prudently reduced.

In open water, if there is sea-room to leeward, there will come a time when a skipper will decide that the boat will punish itself less, if it is turned down wind to sail with the wind and waves. If this is done, care must be taken not to let it go so fast that it begins to surf uncontrollably down the faces of the waves, so the sail-area must be kept small and, in order to ease steering, should be set in the front part of the boat, in the form of storm jib or foresail.

In very big seas, some experienced sailors have found that a boat's behaviour is much improved by streaming warps or sea anchors (drogues) behind the boat. These reduce speed still further.

The dangers of running before a gale in this way are twofold: lack of sea-room to leeward and "pooping", or overwhelming, by a wave coming up from behind and breaking against the stern of the boat. Modern designs, with their clean shapes, reduce the latter risk, but it is none-theless a real one, particularly in areas of shallow water or strong tides (such as off a headland), where the waves may be more liable to break. Therefore, all hatches must be securely fastened, cockpits must be fitted with adequate drains, and crew members must wear harnesses and life-jackets.

In a real storm with really big seas, running before the wind will become too risky. Then the boat must be rounded up—and this manoeuvre must be carefully timed to coincide with a period of smaller waves—so that it is made to heave to.

Heaving to consists of letting the boat head on something like a close-hauled course, with its tiller fastened to leeward. Sail is either taken off altogether or reduced to a minimal rag of jib, and usually the crew go below and batten down all hatches. Sometimes, a sea anchor is let out on a strong warp from the bow, in order to slow down drift and to hold the bow towards the wind.

Many modern boats seem to prefer being left to their own devices in really extreme conditions. All sail is taken off and they are left to "lie ahull", which will normally mean that the wind will be about on the beam. They will then rise and fall with the seas as these come up on one side and pass under the hull.

Well-found boats should be able to survive all storms except for tropical hurricanes and tornadoes—providing they have plenty of sea-room and providing their crews do not let them down by making errors of judgement. A boat is always safer in deep water than when trying to run for shelter, as the latter can end up in the boat being smashed on rocks near the mouth of a harbour or caught on a lee shore onto which it is helplessly driven.

Providing that it is not breaking, the vastest wave will not harm even the smallest boat but, if a wave is, say, 25 ft (7.6 m) high and the depth of water is only about 30 ft (9.1 m), there will be a tendency for the wave to begin breaking, and a breaking wave is dangerous if the top should fall aboard the boat.

Boats in high seas must be kept dry to preserve their full buoyancy, so pumping will need to be regularly repeated, if not done continuously, and this may prove difficult if the crew is seasick or fatigued.

Food and drink should continue to be taken, if at all possible, and watches should be worked to enable rest to be taken. You have to remember that even the worst storm passes over in time. Each passing hour is a victory over the elements!

When sailing in semi-sheltered waters in strong winds, it will soon be found that waves taken from ahead tend to throw spray over the boat, and that waves taken from behind are much dryer. You must try to steer your boat so that you give it the easiest time. When sailing to

windward, you must luff towards the extra big wave to slow your boat a little and to enable it to give with the wave instead of crashing against it. Then you must bear off to gain speed again. In hard winds, a boat must be kept moving, otherwise it will make a dangerous amount of leeway as each successive wave drives it bodily sideways. Leeway increases sharply with wind strength and sea height.

Heavy weather calls for stamina and, sometimes, for courage and nerve. (It is easy to become unnerved by the very sight of the waves and by their sound and fury.) Light weather calls for quite different qualities—patience, sensitivity, lightness of touch.

The driving forces in light winds may be measured in a few kilos or even less, so they must be treated gently. The tiller must be held lightly with the finger tips, so that the "feel" of the rudder is transmitted. Sheets must be held lightly, too. Sails will need to be fuller, halyards not so tightly hauled out, and clew outhauls eased so that the sails assume a bigger camber.

The boat should be heeled to leeward, away from the wind. This will help the sails to fall into their natural shape, without the wind having to waste its remaining energy on pushing them there. A heel angle will also help to reduce wetted surface. For the same reason, most boats will sail better in light airs with their bows down and sterns up. To windward, the boom angle will need to be wider than in average breezes (wider to the centre-line of the boat), and the boat itself cannot be sailed so close to the apparent wind. The important thing in light airs is to keep the boat moving. Do not worry too much about the course being made good. Watch the water surface for the catspaws which indicate extra puffs of wind. Watch the sky for gathering clouds. Watch other sailing-boats nearby.

Naturally, light-weight sails will fill out better than heavy ones but, sometimes, there will not be enough wind to fill a spinnaker, which will be better left on deck than hanging dead in the rigging.

Finally, here are some basic seamanship rules; most of them are based on common sense. Approach any other boat, obstacle, obstruction, or dock from either down wind or down tide, whichever is stronger. This means you will be approaching the leeward side of the object where the

sea may be expected to be calmer and, because you will be moving against wind or tide, you will be able to stop when you want to. This could prove vital when ranging alongside another boat in a bad sea to take off a sick person, for instance.

In difficult conditions, always proceed slowly, with just enough speed to maintain steerage way.

If you need to go astern, remember that your helm must be reversed.

Plan ahead; think out any complicated manoeuvres before putting them into execution.

When towing another boat, tow from the centre of your boat's stern and use a long length of tow-line. The worse the sea-state, the longer the tow-line. If the towed boat is a dinghy, make sure that its centre-board is retracted and, if possible, tow from low down on its bow (so that the pull is slightly upwards). The towed boat should be steered, if at all possible.

If coming alongside another boat in a sea-way, stand off at a distance of some yards, then throw a line. Do not come straight alongside (this also applies to docking in a sea-way).

If accepting a tow, lead the line from a fairlead at your bow to an extremely strong, make-fast point, such as the base of your mast or a genoa sheet winch.

When leaving a vessel alongside a quay, make quite sure beforehand that a dropping tide will not leave it high and dry.

Even if you always use an outboard in a dinghy, learn to row proficiently and, if possible, learn also to scull with a single oar over the stern—one day you may lose one oar.

When at sea and working on deck, use a harness (attached to your body and clipped to a handy point on the boat). This is absolutely essential if you are singlehanded. Remember the old sailor's axiom: "One hand for yourself and one hand for the ship".

Remember, when turning, that your stern will move in the opposite direction to the turn. Therefore, do not try to turn away from a dock or another boat when very close to it. Instead, wait until your boat is two or more yards clear of the obstruction, or else reverse away from the obstruction first.

Heading with the wind, a boat will have its sails fully extended to catch the wind. In this mode it is said to be running (**1**). When a boat heads up slightly towards the wind's direction, it is broad reaching (**2**), and to prevent the sails from flapping, it will be necessary to haul them in slightly. Spinnakers may still

be carried. When a boat sails across the wind it is reaching or beam reaching (**3**). In light winds it may be possible to carry a flat spinnaker. The other sails will be roughly at 45° to the boat's centre-line. Coming up into the wind still more—"luffing" so that the wind is about 60° off the bow—the boat is close

reaching, or fetching (**4**), and the sail must be hauled in still more. Spinnakers cannot be carried. Luffing still more it will be necessary to haul in the sails quite tight. Now you are close-hauled, or beating or tacking to windward (**5**). This is how a boat sails against the wind, by tacking or zigzagging.

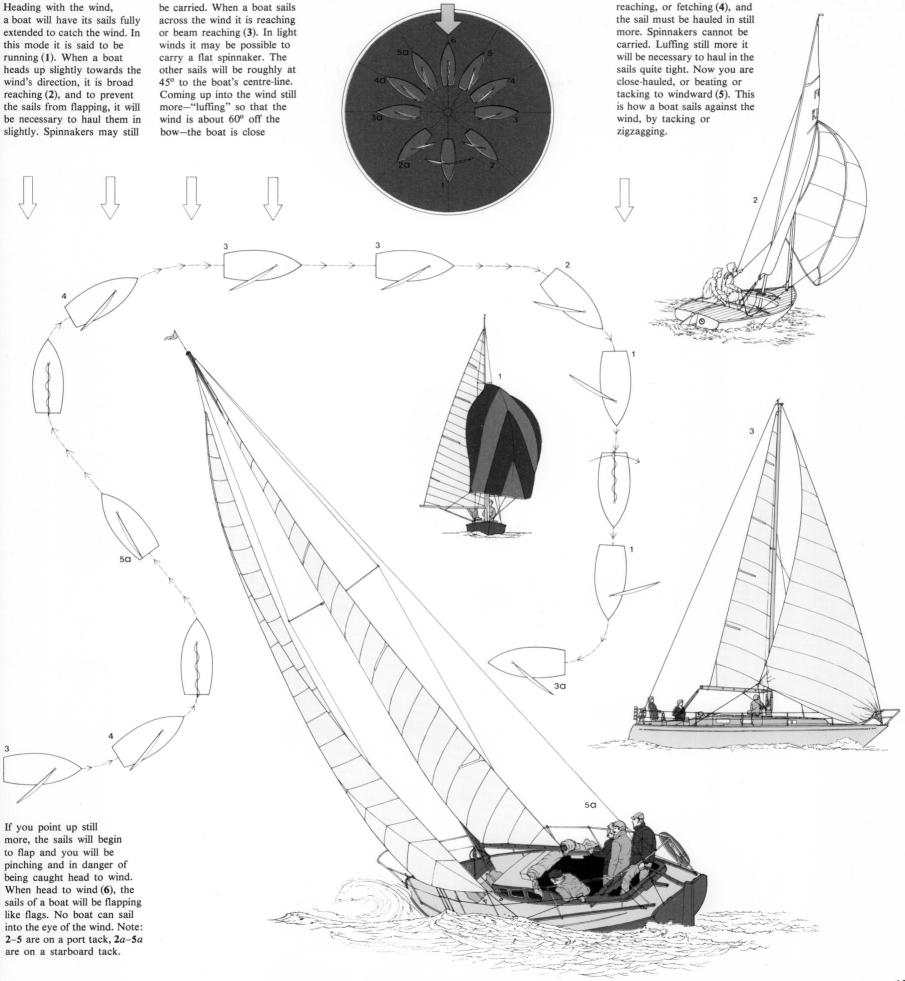

If you point up still more, the sails will begin to flap and you will be pinching and in danger of being caught head to wind. When head to wind (**6**), the sails of a boat will be flapping like flags. No boat can sail into the eye of the wind. Note: **2–5** are on a port tack, **2a–5a** are on a starboard tack.

SAIL SETTING

Hoisting sails on a *505*. Before attempting to hoist sails, ensure that the boat lies head to wind. This will allow the sails to go up without filling with wind. They will, instead, flutter like flags. It is normal to hoist the mainsail first and the jib second. In this way, the boat will tend to weathercock into the wind.

A Hoisting the mainsail. (**1**) Stretch the foot of the sail along the top of the boom. The foot rope will normally fit into a special boom slot or groove (*a*). Fit from forward, aft. (**2**) Secure the tack of the sail to the front end of the boom. (**3**) Secure the clew to the outer end of the boom. Sometimes, the clew can be attached to an adjustable outhaul line (*a*). (**4**) Fit battens into appropriate pockets along the leech of the sail.

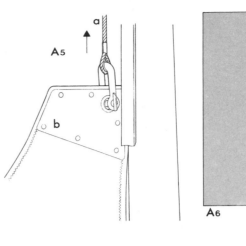

A5

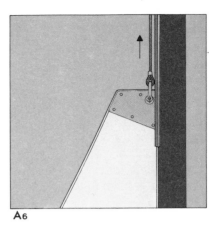

A6

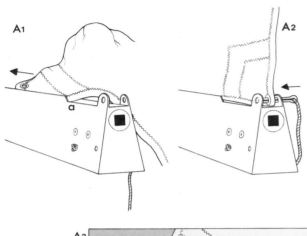

A1

A2

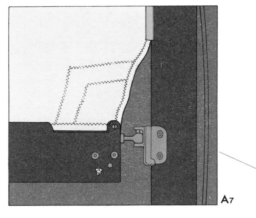

A7

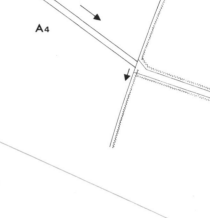

A4

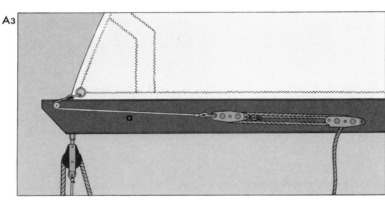

A3

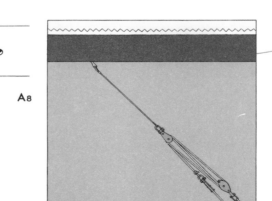

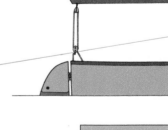

A8

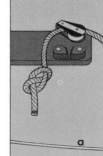

(**5**) Fit the top of the bolt rope, which is attached to the luff of the sail, into the opening in the mast groove on the aft side of the mast, above the point of attachment of the boom. Slide the bolt rope upwards a little. Shackle the main halyard (*a*) into the headboard of the sail (*b*). Make sure the halyard is not twisted round the mast or other rigging. (**6**) Hoist the main halyard and continue feeding the bolt rope into the mast groove. (**7**) As the sail approaches the top of the mast, fit the front of the boom onto the mast. Be sure, as you hoist, that the main sheet is slack. (**8**) Attach the kicking-strap. It is often attached with a keyhole attachment (*a*).

126

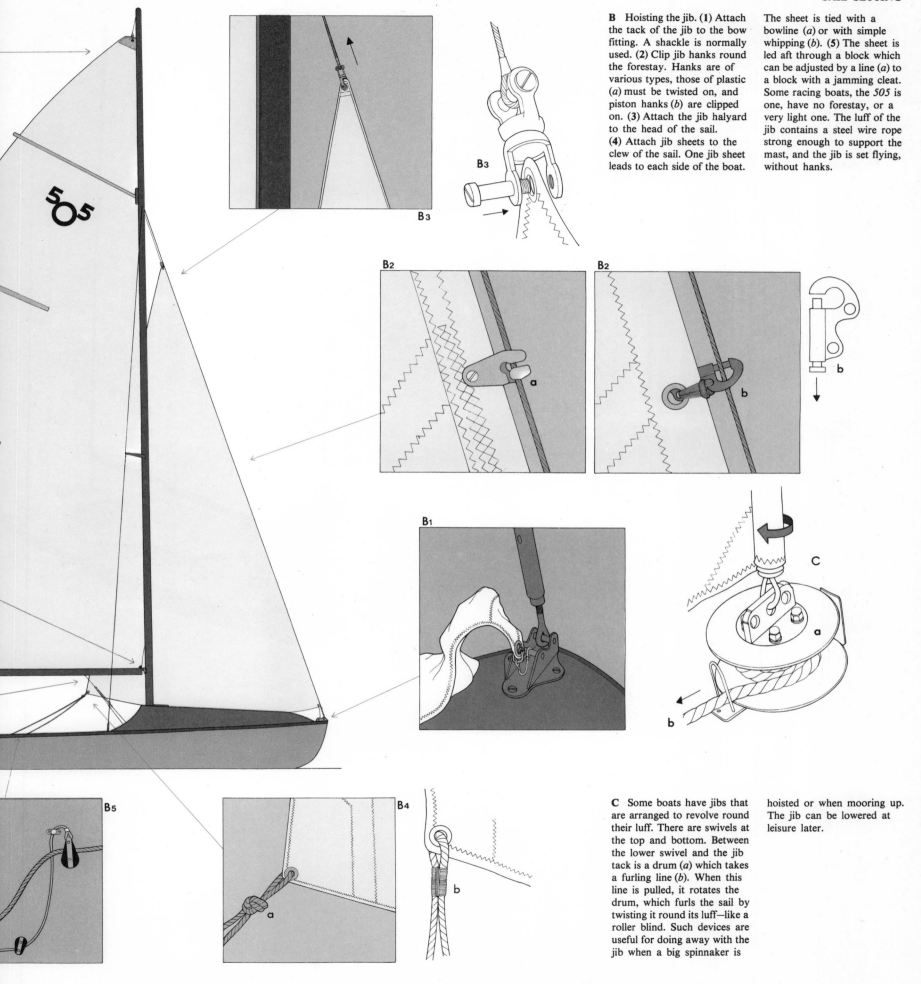

B Hoisting the jib. (**1**) Attach the tack of the jib to the bow fitting. A shackle is normally used. (**2**) Clip jib hanks round the forestay. Hanks are of various types, those of plastic (*a*) must be twisted on, and piston hanks (*b*) are clipped on. (**3**) Attach the jib halyard to the head of the sail. (**4**) Attach jib sheets to the clew of the sail. One jib sheet leads to each side of the boat. The sheet is tied with a bowline (*a*) or with simple whipping (*b*). (**5**) The sheet is led aft through a block which can be adjusted by a line (*a*) to a block with a jamming cleat. Some racing boats, the *505* is one, have no forestay, or a very light one. The luff of the jib contains a steel wire rope strong enough to support the mast, and the jib is set flying, without hanks.

C Some boats have jibs that are arranged to revolve round their luff. There are swivels at the top and bottom. Between the lower swivel and the jib tack is a drum (*a*) which takes a furling line (*b*). When this line is pulled, it rotates the drum, which furls the sail by twisting it round its luff—like a roller blind. Such devices are useful for doing away with the jib when a big spinnaker is hoisted or when mooring up. The jib can be lowered at leisure later.

LAUNCHING FROM A BEACH

A With a light boat that may be carried into the water, it is best to carry it close to the water's edge (**1**), place it head to wind, and hoist the sails. (**2**) Making sure that the sheets are eased, carry it into water deep enough to permit the helmsman to climb aboard, ship the rudder, and lower at least part of the centre-board. (**3**) The crewman turns the bow away from the wind and climbs smartly aboard. (**4**) He pulls in the lee jib sheet (*a*) while the helmsman takes hold of the tiller and hauls in the mainsheet (*b*). They are away. The crew leaves the windward jib sheet slack. It will not be used until they put about onto the other tack.

B If the wind is blowing offshore, the bow must be facing up the beach. It will be unnecessary to drop the centre-board, but the boat will have to be turned round as the crewman climbs aboard.

C If starting from an anchor, with a keelboat, see if the boat is lying head to wind. If it is, hoist the mainsail, with the sheet loose. Have the jib ready for hoisting. Haul in the anchor and, as the boat moves forward, have the helmsman steer it one way or other. As the anchor comes aboard and the boat's head moves away from the eye of the wind, the mainsheet may be hauled in. With the anchor out of the way, hoist the jib at leisure.

D If the tide is stronger than the wind, so that boat heads away from the wind, first shorten in the anchor cable. Then hoist the jib, break out the anchor, sheet home the jib, and sail away before the wind. Hoist the mainsail at leisure, when there is room to luff up into the wind.

E If leaving a dock onto which the wind is blowing, it will be necessary, first of all, to take the anchor out far

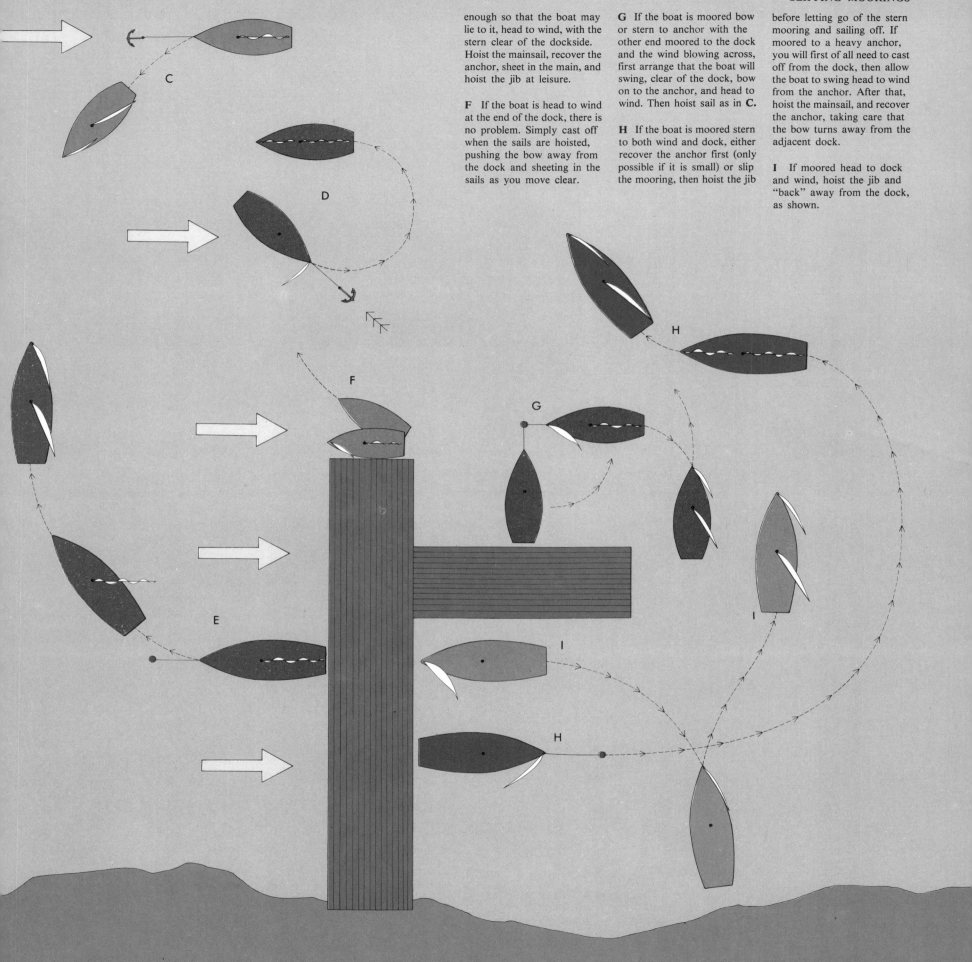

enough so that the boat may lie to it, head to wind, with the stern clear of the dockside. Hoist the mainsail, recover the anchor, sheet in the main, and hoist the jib at leisure.

F If the boat is head to wind at the end of the dock, there is no problem. Simply cast off when the sails are hoisted, pushing the bow away from the dock and sheeting in the sails as you move clear.

G If the boat is moored bow or stern to anchor with the other end moored to the dock and the wind blowing across, first arrange that the boat will swing, clear of the dock, bow on to the anchor, and head to wind. Then hoist sail as in **C**.

H If the boat is moored stern to both wind and dock, either recover the anchor first (only possible if it is small) or slip the mooring, then hoist the jib

before letting go of the stern mooring and sailing off. If moored to a heavy anchor, you will first of all need to cast off from the dock, then allow the boat to swing head to wind from the anchor. After that, hoist the mainsail, and recover the anchor, taking care that the bow turns away from the adjacent dock.

I If moored head to dock and wind, hoist the jib and "back" away from the dock, as shown.

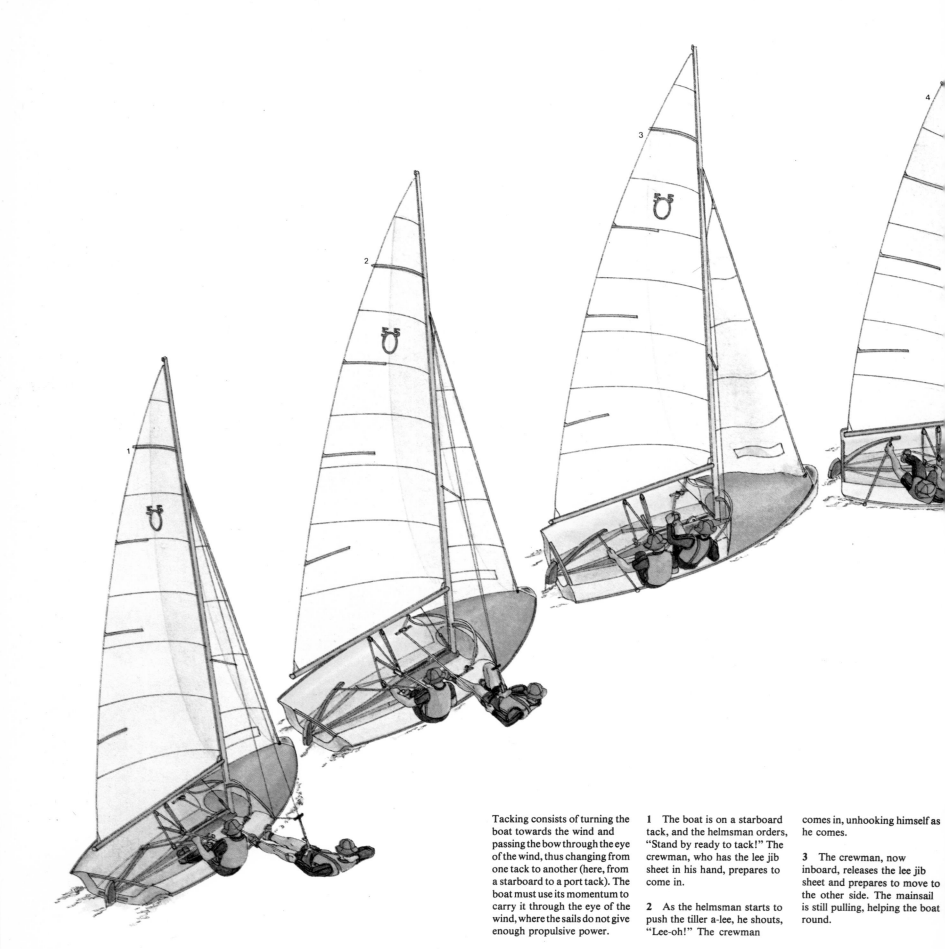

Tacking consists of turning the boat towards the wind and passing the bow through the eye of the wind, thus changing from one tack to another (here, from a starboard to a port tack). The boat must use its momentum to carry it through the eye of the wind, where the sails do not give enough propulsive power.

1 The boat is on a starboard tack, and the helmsman orders, "Stand by ready to tack!" The crewman, who has the lee jib sheet in his hand, prepares to come in.

2 As the helmsman starts to push the tiller a-lee, he shouts, "Lee-oh!" The crewman

comes in, unhooking himself as he comes.

3 The crewman, now inboard, releases the lee jib sheet and prepares to move to the other side. The mainsail is still pulling, helping the boat round.

4 The boat is in the eye of the wind. The crewman crosses the centre-board, avoiding the kicking-strap and grabbing the other jib sheet. The helm is now hard a-lee, and the mainsail is moving over due to the starboard heel.

5 The helmsman moves over the centre-line, while the crewman sheets in the new jib sheet and hooks himself onto the trapeze.

6 The main sail is now full and pulling. The helmsman sits down and changes hands on tiller and mainsheet. The

crewman goes out on the trapeze.

7 The boat is now on a port tack and begins to pick up speed. A really well-trained crew can complete the entire manoeuvre in as little as four seconds.

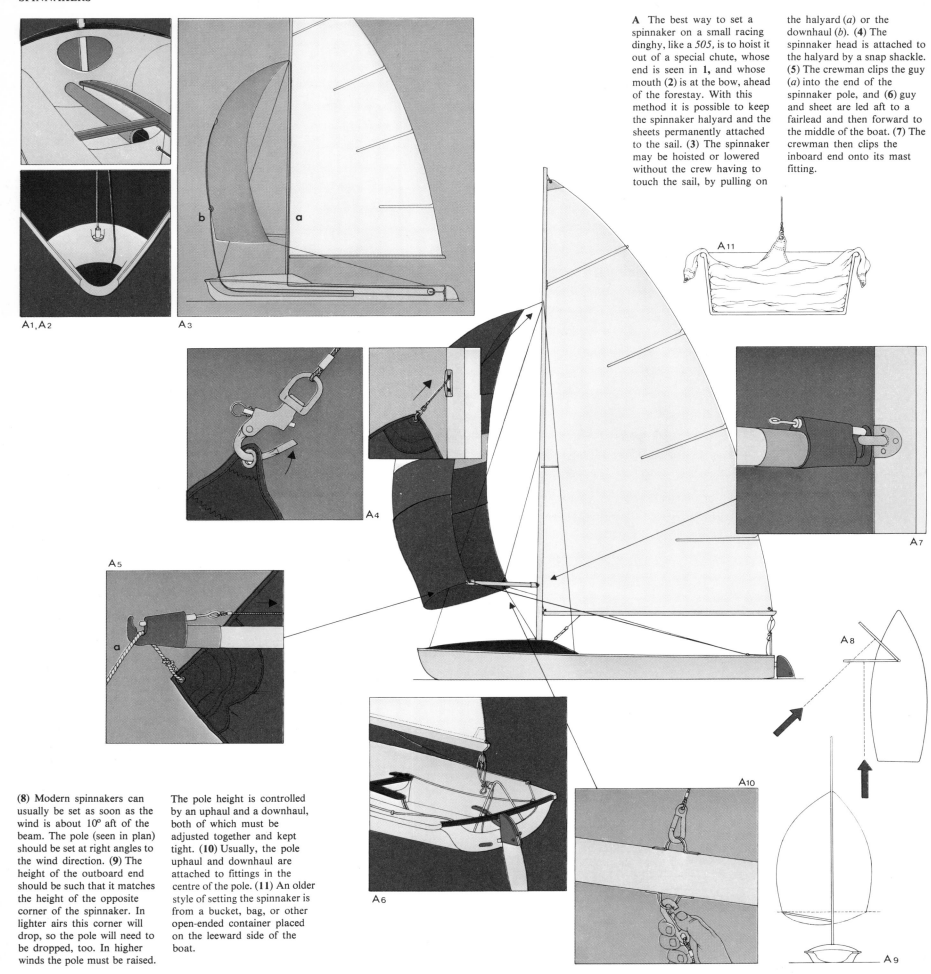

A The best way to set a spinnaker on a small racing dinghy, like a *505,* is to hoist it out of a special chute, whose end is seen in **1,** and whose mouth (**2**) is at the bow, ahead of the forestay. With this method it is possible to keep the spinnaker halyard and the sheets permanently attached to the sail. (**3**) The spinnaker may be hoisted or lowered without the crew having to touch the sail, by pulling on the halyard (*a*) or the downhaul (*b*). (**4**) The spinnaker head is attached to the halyard by a snap shackle. (**5**) The crewman clips the guy (*a*) into the end of the spinnaker pole, and (**6**) guy and sheet are led aft to a fairlead and then forward to the middle of the boat. (**7**) The crewman then clips the inboard end onto its mast fitting.

A₁,A₂

A₃

A₄

A₅

a

A₆

A₇

A₈

A₁₀

A₉

A₁₁

(**8**) Modern spinnakers can usually be set as soon as the wind is about 10° aft of the beam. The pole (seen in plan) should be set at right angles to the wind direction. (**9**) The height of the outboard end should be such that it matches the height of the opposite corner of the spinnaker. In lighter airs this corner will drop, so the pole will need to be dropped, too. In higher winds the pole must be raised.

The pole height is controlled by an uphaul and a downhaul, both of which must be adjusted together and kept tight. (**10**) Usually, the pole uphaul and downhaul are attached to fittings in the centre of the pole. (**11**) An older style of setting the spinnaker is from a bucket, bag, or other open-ended container placed on the leeward side of the boat.

B₁ B₂ B₃ B₄ B₅ B₆ B₇ B₈

B In a large keelboat, the spinnaker is handled differently. Usually, the sail is first carefully stowed in a large, open-ended container, such as a big plastic bucket. The three corners are uppermost, with the head in the centre. Care must be taken to see that the sail is not twisted when folded into the container, which is then taken to the bow and lashed (**1**) or clipped to the pulpit. Next, the spinnaker halyard is clipped to the head of the sail, and the sheets are clipped to the other corners. (**2**) Care must be taken that these sheets lead outside everything—other sails, lifelines, sheets—on their way aft from the sail to their fairleads. (**3**) The outer end of the pole is controlled by an uphaul and a downhaul (known as the "foreguy") attached to the outer end. In smaller keelboats the dinghy type of uphaul/downhaul, attached to the centre of the pole, is often used. It is normal to set the pole of a large yacht before the spinnaker is hoisted. (**4**) As with a dinghy, the windward sheet, or guy, is led through the outer end of the pole before the sail is set. (**5**) The spinnaker pole is too big and heavy for the crew to handle manually. Normally, there is a track on the fore side of the mast. The inboard end of the pole is clipped to a traveller which slides up an down this track. The traveller is pulled upwards by an uphaul line.

Be careful not to pull on the sheets, thus filling the sail with wind, before the sail is fully hoisted. If it fills prematurely, it may be impossible to haul it up the rest of the way. To guard against this happening, the spinnaker is often formed into a long, thin, sausage shape, and secured with thin pieces of line or with elastic bands which will break once the sail is hoisted and the sheets are pulled. This is called "stooping" a spinnaker (**6**).

The rules used for setting dinghy spinnakers apply here, too, but the sheets, halyard, and pole up- and downhaul will be led round and handled by winches. When hoisting the spinnaker (**7**), the foresail is usually up. When the spinnaker is hoisted (**8**), the foresail can, if required, be taken down.

Gybing consists of changing tacks by turning so far away from the wind that its direction moves across the stern from one side or quarter to the other. Here, we show how a boat with a spinnaker gybes.

1 The boat here is on a starboard tack, with the crewman out on the trapeze and the helmsman sitting out, his feet under the toe straps.

2 The helmsman goes inboard, changes hands on the tiller, and bears away. The crewman starts moving in, unhooks himself from the trapeze, frees the spinnaker guy from the fairlead on the gunwale, and makes fast the windward jib sheet. He checks that the centre-board is correctly trimmed and adjusts it, if necessary.

3 The mainsail starts to back, and the helmsman assists it by grabbing the main sheet and swinging the boom across, at the same time putting the tiller over and shouting, "Gybe-oh!" Both duck to avoid the boom, which swings hard over.

4 The boat is now on a port tack. The crewman lets go of the jib sheet, which will blow over to starboard, where it will

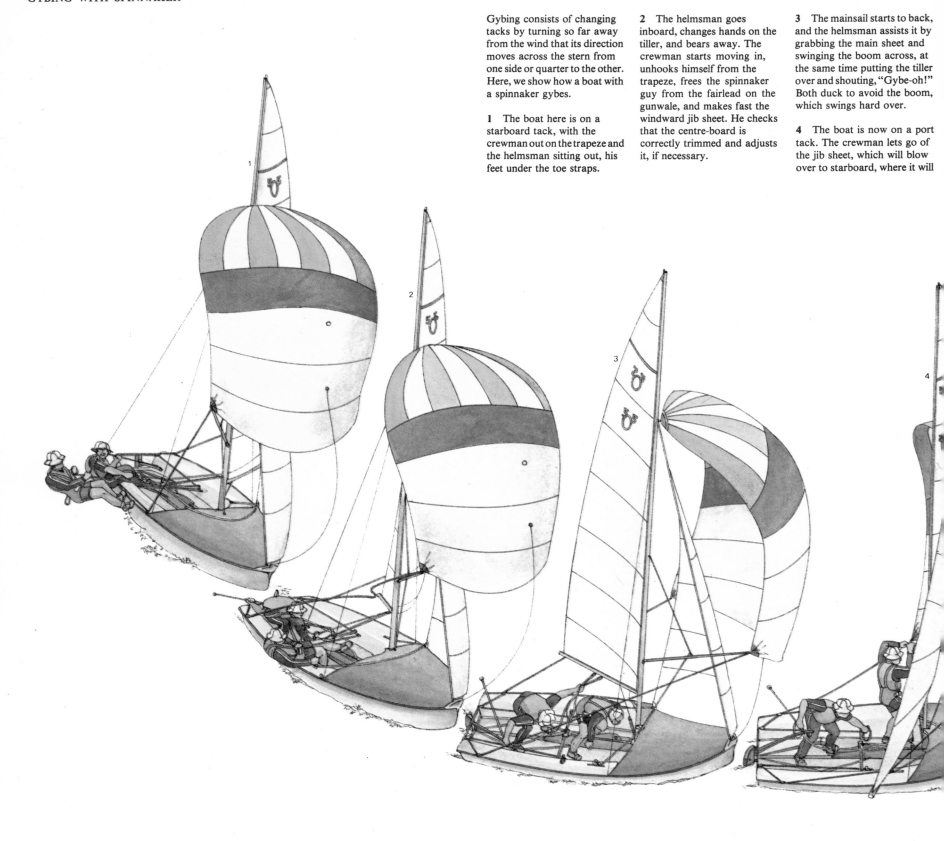

be checked by the windward (now lee) sheet made fast in **2**. The helmsman counters the luffing tendency with the rudder, while the crewman unclips the end of the spinnaker boom from its mast fitting, and fastens it to the new spinnaker tack. The spinnaker boom is now supported by the topping lift and the spinnaker's clew and tack.

5 The helmsman alone is now keeping the boat trimmed laterally by using the rudder. He steers with the tiller between his legs, and trims the guy and sheet. The crewman unhitches the boom end from what was the spinnaker tack, and clips that end to the mast fitting.

6 The helmsman gets his feet under the toe straps and sits on the side while the crewman passes the guy through a fairlead on the gunwale, hooks himself onto the trapeze, and goes out. The helmsman can now luff up.

7 The helmsman is sitting out, while the crewman hangs in the trapeze. Manoeuvre successfully completed.

REEFING

If a boat has the right amount of sail for light winds, it will become over-pressed as soon as the wind starts to increase. Therefore, all seagoing sailing-boats have provision for reefing and for replacing a larger sail with a smaller.

A Roller reefing consists of rolling up the sail by rotating the boom. The roller-reefing system can be either boom-mounted, as shown here, or fitted with a through-mast action.

B In jiffy reefing, the lower part of the mainsail is brought down to the top of the boom and fastened there. (**1**) A mainsail with reefing pendant (*a*) and luff pendant (*b*). With reefing pendant only (**2**), the luff is taken down by hand. (**3**) Most mainsails have three sets of reefing points. If you need a second or third reef, simply pull down on top of the first. Here we show the first reef already taken in.

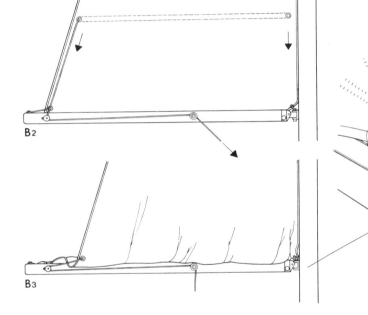

B1

B2

B3

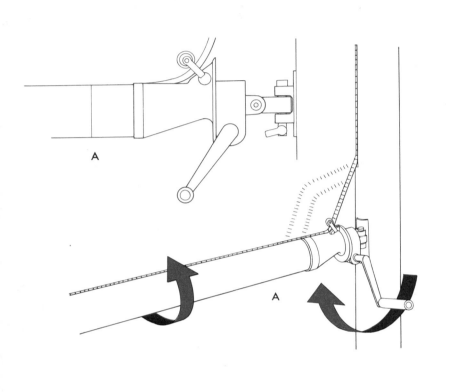

A

A

C

With jiffy reefing, the correct sequence is important, if the sail is to set well. First of all, if there is a topping lift fitted, make it take the weight of the boom. Then ease the mainsheet, ease the halyard, and haul down the luff. Either hook the eyelet over the special hook provided above the goose neck, or secure it with a lashing. Then tighten the reefing pendant, the halyard, and the mainsheet (in that order). Continue sailing. It should be possible to reef without losing much speed.

C The older style of reefing, hand reefing, is still seen on cruising yachts and is similar in principle to jiffy reefing, but instead of leaving the sail to flop round the boom, the sail is secured at intervals, either by endless lacing round the boom or by separate, short lashings called reef points, which are permanently attached to the sail. Hand reefing takes longer but is neater and keeps the sail quieter.

In gale-force winds, cruising yachts will stow the mainsail and replace it with a strong, small sail called the "trysail" or "storm trysail". This is set loose-footed, the main boom being stowed and secured, with the mainsail furled on top of it.

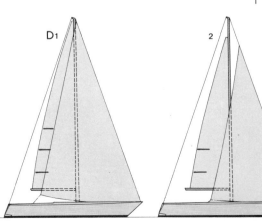

D1

2

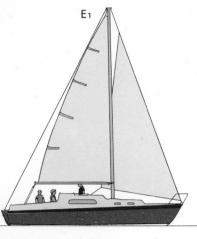

E When changing foresails. (**1**) Ease the jib sheet slightly. (**2**) Start lowering the jib halyard. If only one man is available, he can take the end of the halyard forward with him. He then pulls down the sail with one hand, while lowering the halyard with the other. Lower a bit at a time. Ease the sheet progressively as the sail comes down on deck. It helps to have the sail gathered in along its foot as it comes down, otherwise it may get into the water. (**3**) When the sail is fully lowered, detach its halyard and clip it to the lifeline. (**4**) Unhank the luff of the sail from the forestay. (**5**) Detach the sheets. (**6**) Unshackle the tack of the jib from the stemhead fitting.

When hoisting the replacement sail, bring the sail on deck and fasten the tack to the stemhead fitting. Clip the hanks over the forestay, checking that none are accidentally reversed. Then attach the jib sheets and halyard. Hoist the halyard and sheet the sail in.

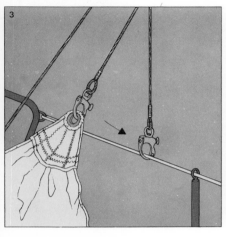

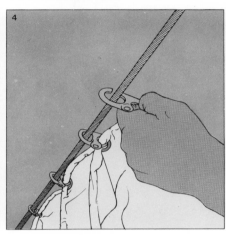

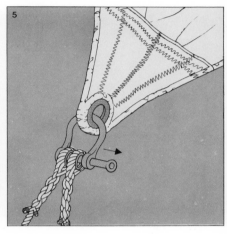

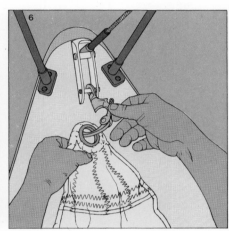

D The modern sailing-yacht has a comparatively small mainsail and a large fore triangle (the area between mast and forestay), in which a variety of different-sized jibs is set to match the weather and the point of sailing. (**1**) For light-weather sailing, to windward and reaching, a large genoa, the No. 1, is used. The clew of this sail extends aft of the mast. (**2**) In moderate wind this will be exchanged for a No. 2 genoa. This will be slightly shorter on the foot, luff, and leech, and will usually be balanced by a single reef in the mainsail. (**3**) The racing yacht will have a still smaller, No. 3 genoa. Others will have a normal working jib (shown here), cut higher than a genoa, to keep it above the waves. This will probably be accompanied by a second reef in the mainsail. (**4**) If the wind increases still further, a storm jib is set, matched by a third reef in the mainsail. (**5**) In extreme circumstances, the mainsail is replaced with a trysail.

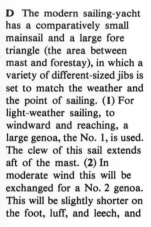

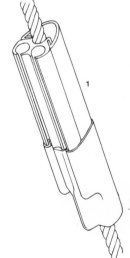

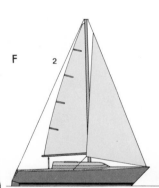

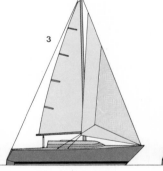

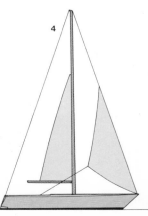

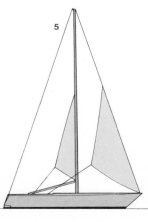

F Changing jibs with a headfoil is becoming increasingly common. The headfoil (**1**) comes in various types, but the best has twin keyhole-sectioned grooves. The front edges of the jibs are fitted with a special plastic beading which fits into one of the grooves. There must be twin halyards. The changing sequence is the following.

Take the spare jib halyard and attach it to the head of the new jib. Feed the head into the unused groove in the headfoil. Hoist the new sail a bit up the stay and attach a second set of sheets to the new sail. Hoist the new sail and, as it nears the top, its tack may be attached to the stemhead fitting. Sheet home the new sail. Ease the sheets of the old jib and lower it. As it comes down out of the groove, detach its tack from the stemhead fitting and pull the sail down through the forehatch, otherwise it may blow overboard. Detach sheets and halyard. (**2**) Old jib set. (**3**) Old and new jibs set. (**4**) New jib only set.

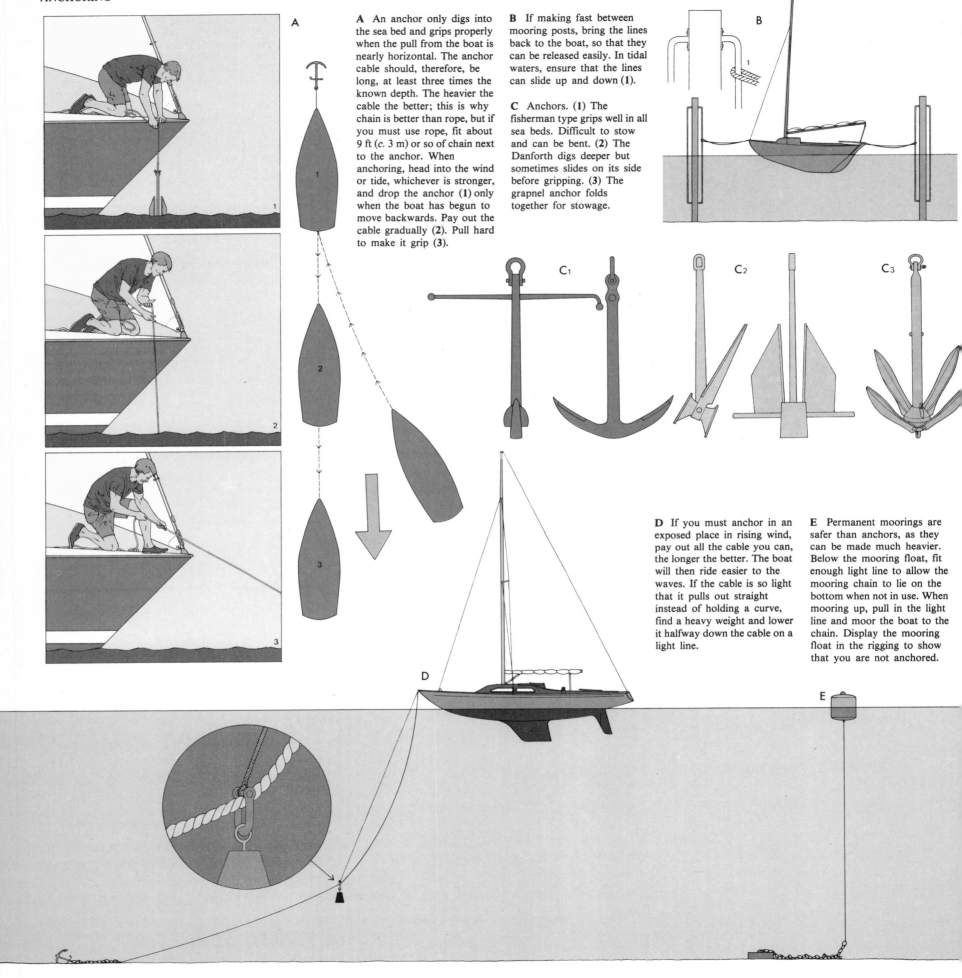

A An anchor only digs into the sea bed and grips properly when the pull from the boat is nearly horizontal. The anchor cable should, therefore, be long, at least three times the known depth. The heavier the cable the better; this is why chain is better than rope, but if you must use rope, fit about 9 ft (*c*. 3 m) or so of chain next to the anchor. When anchoring, head into the wind or tide, whichever is stronger, and drop the anchor (**1**) only when the boat has begun to move backwards. Pay out the cable gradually (**2**). Pull hard to make it grip (**3**).

B If making fast between mooring posts, bring the lines back to the boat, so that they can be released easily. In tidal waters, ensure that the lines can slide up and down (**1**).

C Anchors. (**1**) The fisherman type grips well in all sea beds. Difficult to stow and can be bent. (**2**) The Danforth digs deeper but sometimes slides on its side before gripping. (**3**) The grapnel anchor folds together for stowage.

D If you must anchor in an exposed place in rising wind, pay out all the cable you can, the longer the better. The boat will then ride easier to the waves. If the cable is so light that it pulls out straight instead of holding a curve, find a heavy weight and lower it halfway down the cable on a light line.

E Permanent moorings are safer than anchors, as they can be made much heavier. Below the mooring float, fit enough light line to allow the mooring chain to lie on the bottom when not in use. When mooring up, pull in the light line and moor the boat to the chain. Display the mooring float in the rigging to show that you are not anchored.

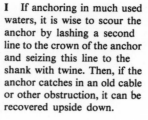

I If anchoring in much used waters, it is wise to scour the anchor by lashing a second line to the crown of the anchor and seizing this line to the shank with twine. Then, if the anchor catches in an old cable or other obstruction, it can be recovered upside down.

J In crowded tidal waters, it is necessary to drop a second, or kedge, anchor. When the wind or tide changes, the boat will ride to the kedge instead of drifting the full length of the main anchor cable.

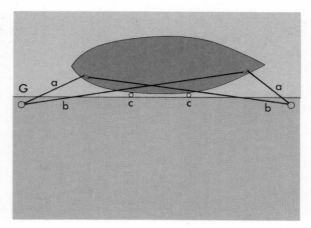

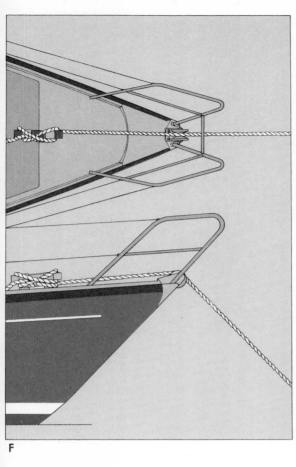

F The proper cruising yacht has a bow fitting which takes mooring and anchor cables without chafing them.

G When moored alongside, spread your head and stern cables (*a*) as far apart as possible. Fit spring lines (*b*) to limit the boat's movements. Too many lines are better than too few. The same goes for fenders (*c*).

H When alongside a wall or posts in tidal waters, make absolutely sure that the boat cannot fall outwards as the tide drops. Put heavy weights on the inside deck, and lead a line from the mast to the shore. Be sure that no one walks on the outer deck.

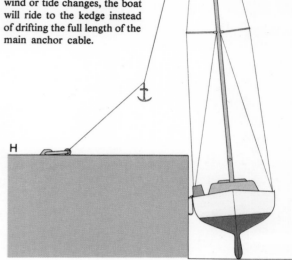

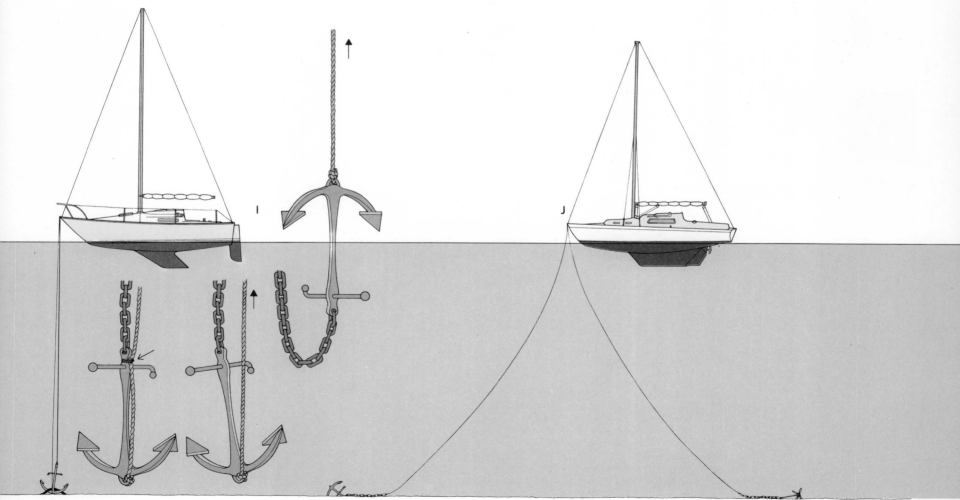

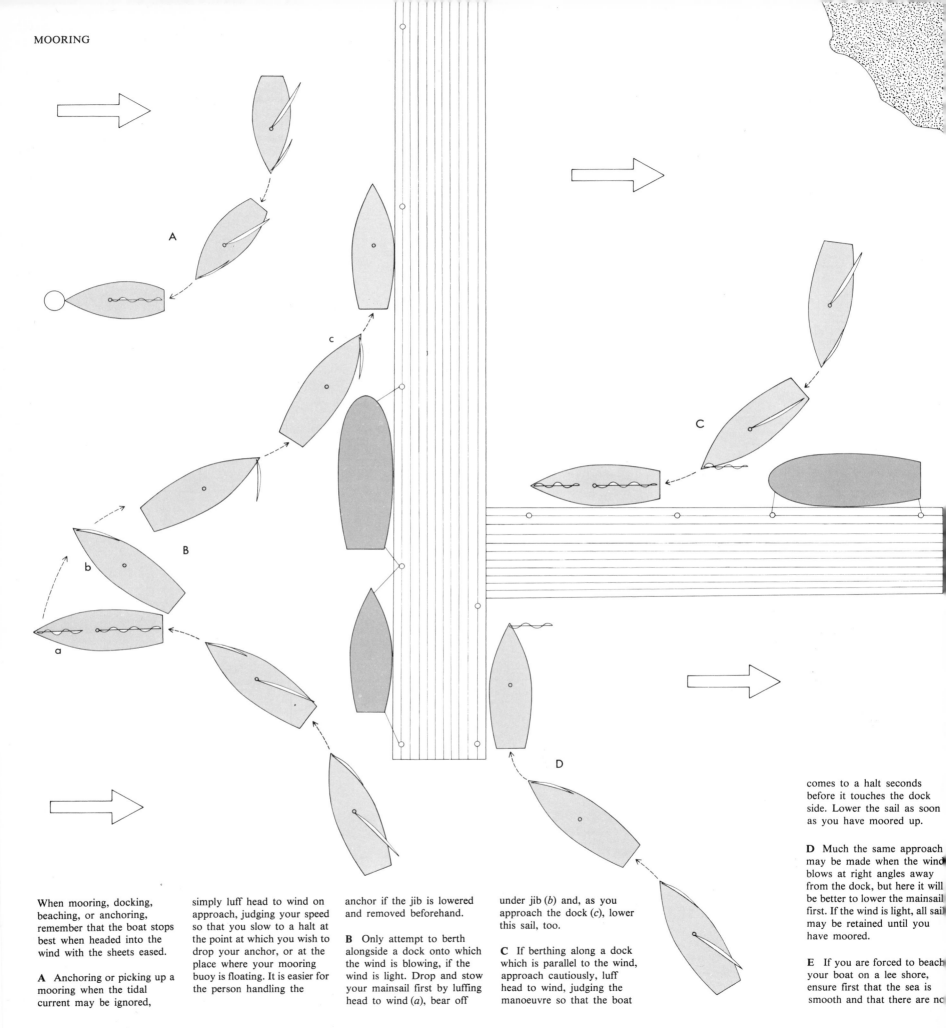

When mooring, docking, beaching, or anchoring, remember that the boat stops best when headed into the wind with the sheets eased.

A Anchoring or picking up a mooring when the tidal current may be ignored,

simply luff head to wind on approach, judging your speed so that you slow to a halt at the point at which you wish to drop your anchor, or at the place where your mooring buoy is floating. It is easier for the person handling the

anchor if the jib is lowered and removed beforehand.

B Only attempt to berth alongside a dock onto which the wind is blowing, if the wind is light. Drop and stow your mainsail first by luffing head to wind (a), bear off

under jib (b) and, as you approach the dock (c), lower this sail, too.

C If berthing along a dock which is parallel to the wind, approach cautiously, luff head to wind, judging the manoeuvre so that the boat

comes to a halt seconds before it touches the dock side. Lower the sail as soon as you have moored up.

D Much the same approach may be made when the wind blows at right angles away from the dock, but here it will be better to lower the mainsail first. If the wind is light, all sail may be retained until you have moored.

E If you are forced to beach your boat on a lee shore, ensure first that the sea is smooth and that there are no

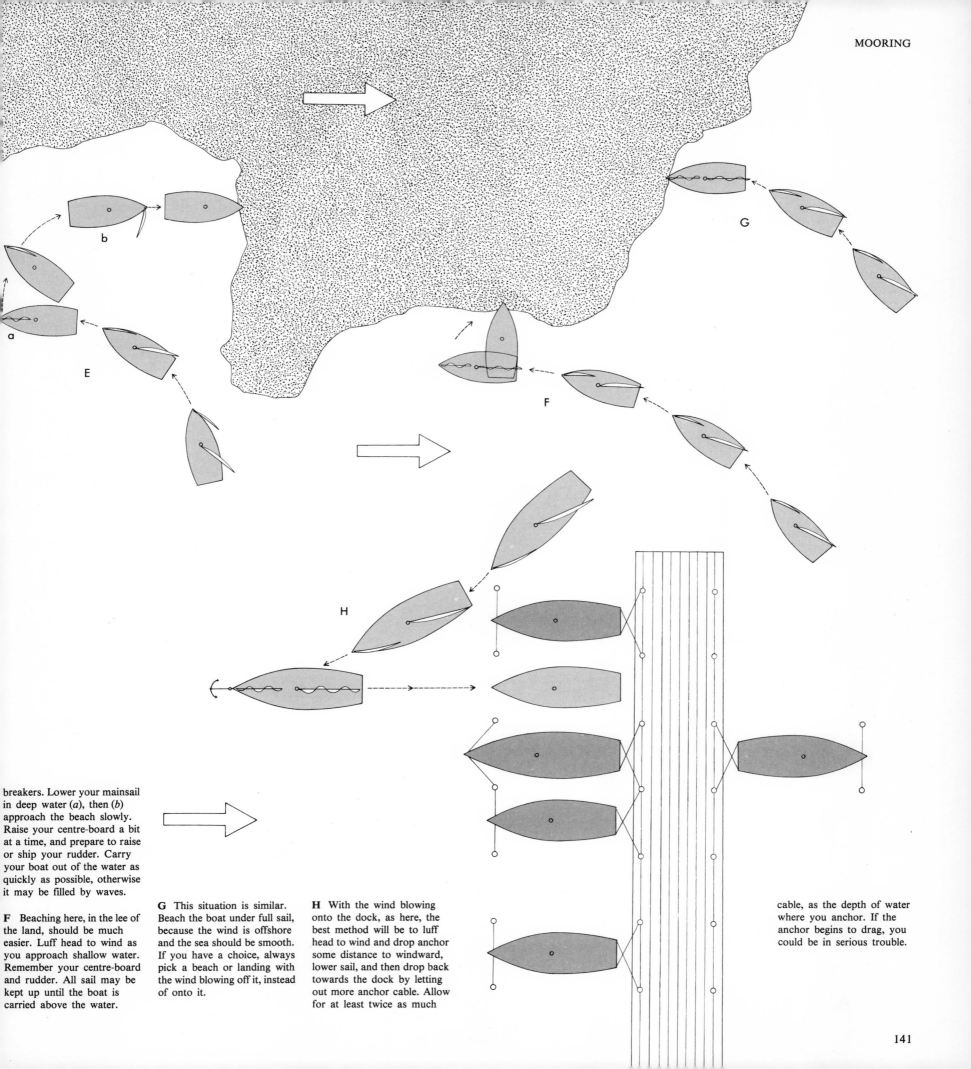

breakers. Lower your mainsail in deep water (*a*), then (*b*) approach the beach slowly. Raise your centre-board a bit at a time, and prepare to raise or ship your rudder. Carry your boat out of the water as quickly as possible, otherwise it may be filled by waves.

F Beaching here, in the lee of the land, should be much easier. Luff head to wind as you approach shallow water. Remember your centre-board and rudder. All sail may be kept up until the boat is carried above the water.

G This situation is similar. Beach the boat under full sail, because the wind is offshore and the sea should be smooth. If you have a choice, always pick a beach or landing with the wind blowing off it, instead of onto it.

H With the wind blowing onto the dock, as here, the best method will be to luff head to wind and drop anchor some distance to windward, lower sail, and then drop back towards the dock by letting out more anchor cable. Allow for at least twice as much

cable, as the depth of water where you anchor. If the anchor begins to drag, you could be in serious trouble.

GOING AGROUND

Sooner or later, everybody goes aground. When it happens to you, act fast. First, decide whether the tide is ebbing or flowing. If the tide is ebbing, then every second lost will make getting off more and more difficult.

A If there is a powerboat nearby, give him a line from your mast. This will heel the boat most quickly. Use a long line to absorb shocks.

B Take out an anchor as far as you can, and try to haul the boat off with this.

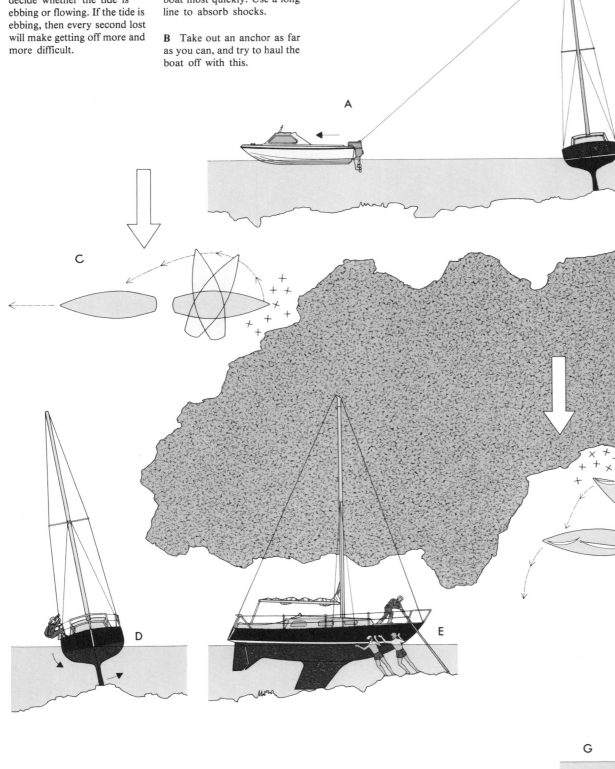

C Modern boats with short keels are easier to get off, because they can swivel on their keels. Use the sails to swing the boat round so that it points into deeper water.

D Try to heel the boat as much as possible (crew leaning to leeward, sails pinned in, etc.). The more it heels the less water it will draw.

E If the boat's draught permits it, get some of the crew to jump overboard. They will be able to push, and the boat, relieved of their weight, will float higher.

F In an up-wind situation, the boat can sometimes be got off by backing the jib, with the crew's weight to leeward.

G A long-keeled boat can be made to draw less water by getting the crew to move to the bow.

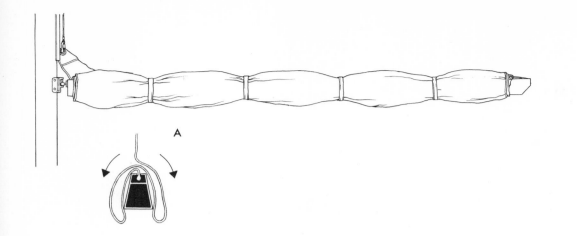

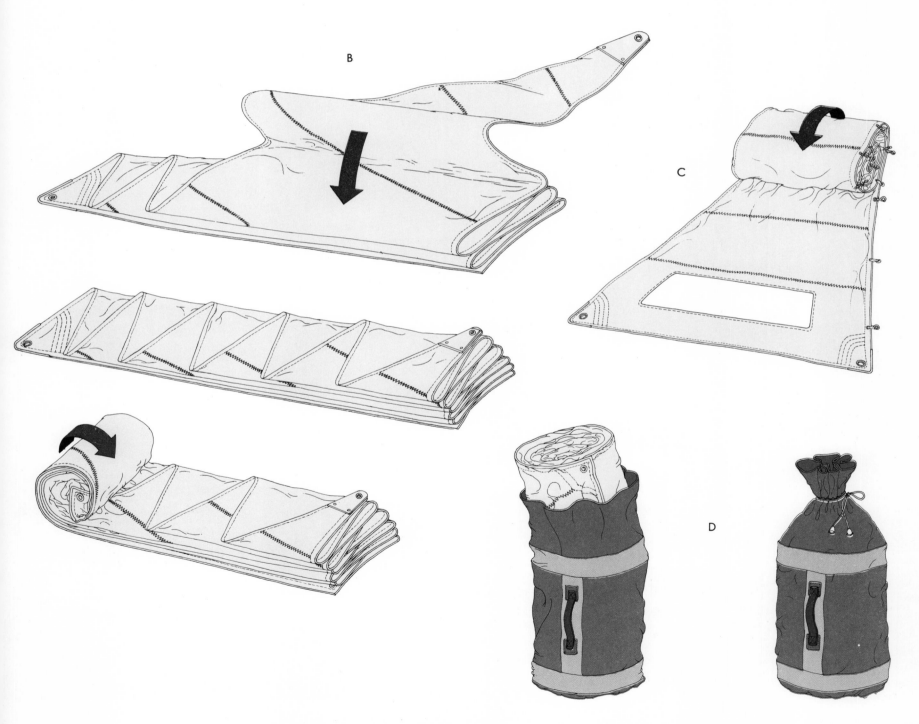

Sails are expensive, so they repay careful stowing. This is particularly true of stiff, racing sail-cloths which contain resin "filler". Wash down with fresh water before folding, if you have been to sea.

A If you must keep your mainsail on the boom, flake the sail down on top of the boom, stretching it out fore and aft as you go. Fit a sail cover, as the sun's rays weaken synthetic fabrics.

B It is better to remove the sails from the boat after use. Before folding, make sure that they are dry. Flake mains and jibs as shown here, smoothing out all creases as you go.

C Tall, narrow sails, such as working jibs, can be rolled from head to foot. By rolling, you do not cause creases, which can come from repeated folding.

D Sail bags should always be large enough to take a sail without squeezing.

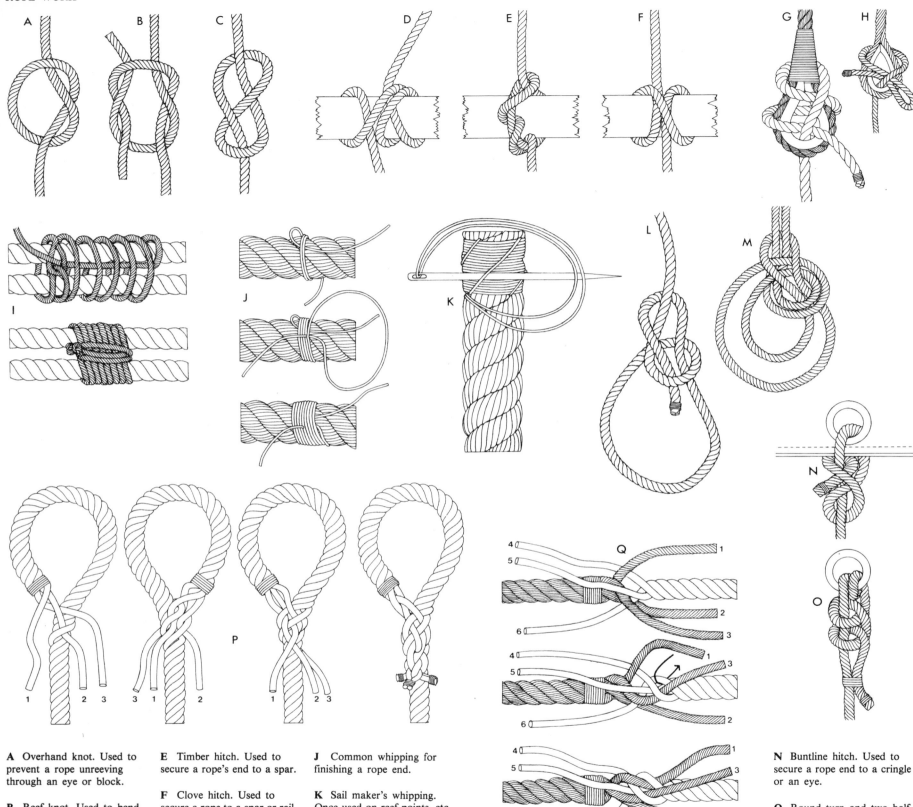

A Overhand knot. Used to prevent a rope unreeving through an eye or block.

B Reef knot. Used to bend together ropes of similar size.

C Figure-of-eight knot. Same use as **A**.

D Rolling hitch. Used to connect a rope to a spar when the pull is expected to be from the one side or the other.

E Timber hitch. Used to secure a rope's end to a spar.

F Clove hitch. Used to secure a rope to a spar or rail.

G Double sheet bend. Used to secure a rope end to an eye.

H Slip sheet bend. A quick-release knot.

I Flat seizing. Used for light work where the strain is equally divided between the two ropes to be seized together.

J Common whipping for finishing a rope end.

K Sail maker's whipping. Once used on reef points, etc.

L Bowline. The most useful knot for making temporary eyes in ropes of all sizes.

M Bowline on the bight. Used for lifting a man out of the water. The short bight is placed under his arms and the long one under his buttocks.

N Buntline hitch. Used to secure a rope end to a cringle or an eye.

O Round turn and two half hitches. Used to secure a heavy load to a spar or ring.

P Eye splice. Used to make a permanent eye in a rope end.

Q Short splice. Used to join two ropes together.

POWERBOAT HANDLING

John Teale

Before any sensible remarks on powerboat handling can be made, the action of the propeller, and the hull's reaction to this, must be considered. As has been mentioned in chapter five, propellers can be right- or left-handed, the former turning clockwise when looked at from astern. This direction of rotation will initially be decided by the rotation of the engine, and then by the combination of gears in the gearbox. Generally speaking, a direct-drive gearbox—that is, one where the propeller shaft turns at the same speed as the engine crankshaft—will allow the propeller to rotate in the same direction as the motor, while a reduction box (where engine revolutions can be reduced by a ratio of, perhaps, 1.5:1 or 2:1 in the gearbox) may well reverse the rotation.

On a twin-screw craft, the propellers are often arranged to turn in opposite directions. These are then called "handed" propellers. The usual scheme is where the propellers are "outward turning", with the starboard propeller right-handed and the port one left-handed. A right-handed propeller on the port side and a left-handed on the starboard side are termed "inward turning", which for certain specialized vessels may be the best arrangement. Most of the problems of manoeuvring a powerboat occur in confined spaces—harbours, marinas, jetties, etc. Therefore, a knowledge of what happens to a boat with any one of the above propeller arrangements is essential when manoeuvring. Most boat-owners know their own boats and react to the quirks of the propeller arrangements almost instinctively, but it is important to know the theory behind these these arrangements. You never know when you may be called upon to pilot a strange boat.

As a propeller turns it, in effect, "walks" across the ground, so that a left-handed propeller will "walk" to the left, pulling the stern of the boat across to the left, or port, and swinging the bow to the right, or starboard. This action is greatest with large, slow-turning propellers, and when the boat is stopped or nearly so. Thus, if the craft is slowly manoeuvring into a berth, a sudden opening of the throttle will tend to swing the bow one way and the stern the other. Obviously, a sudden burst of the engine going astern will have the opposite effect. Thus, if we assume that we are approaching a landing stage in a twin-screw boat with handed, outward-turning propellers, the craft can be allowed to approach the stage at an angle. Going hard astern on the outboard (outward) engine would swing the stern in towards the stage as well as stop the boat, and this would achieve a most satisfactory landing.

Remember that the outward-turning propeller will be turning inwards in reverse. So, if the jetty was to starboard and the port engine was put astern, the action of the propeller would be to "walk" inwards, or towards the stage. Actions of this kind become automatic when you have become used to your boat. If a little more thought were given to propeller effect, fewer dramas would probably be seen in the modern, crowded marinas.

When, for instance, the starboard engine on a twin-screw vessel with outward-turning propellers is shut down, the only power remaining is on the port side, and this tends, regardless of the handing of the propeller, to push the bow to starboard, since the drive is to one side of the centre-line. This tendency is increased by the fact that the port-side propeller is left-handed and "walks" across to port, causing the bow to swing to starboard. Thus everything is working to swing the bow round, and it is a battle to steer a straight course. In fact, some boats with small rudders cannot be handled at all in such situations. So if one had a craft with twin screws, and if it were likely that the vessel would have to operate in the normal course of events under one propeller only, then the propellers should be inward-turning. Such a boat might be, for instance, a twin-screw fishing or lobster boat, where it was desirable to stop the propeller on the side of the boat from which pots or nets were being worked.

As indicated earlier, a sudden thrust from an engine will swing the stern one way and the bow the other. Much the same thing occurs when steering by rudder. If you want to turn to starboard, starboard rudder is given and the first thing that happens is that the whole boat skids out to port. This action is most pronounced on lightly loaded vessels—or those with more boat above than below the water—and it is worth remembering when, say, meeting an empty oil tanker in a narrow channel. If the tanker has to turn, it may drift initially sideways for a distance at least equal to its beam, and the clear passage past it that looked so safe may suddenly be filled with many thousands of tons of steel, travelling at an unnerving pace. In addition to this drift, the stern will swing across at an angle to the turning circle. Every boat will make this crab-like progress when turning, though those with deep draught will perform in a less extreme manner.

Towing procedure is best learned *before* you come across a dismasted yacht or a motor vessel whose engine has broken down in deteriorating weather and rough seas. Clearly, the first thing to do is to get a line aboard. If the usual method of throwing a line does not succeed, then it might be possible to float one, tied to a lifebuoy or lifejacket, down to the crippled craft. In this case, the line should be a very light one, tied to the main tow-line which can be hauled across later. If the weather is really bad, then the anchor chain can be used, for its weight will help

to iron out the "snatch" which will occur as the towed boat is held back by a wave and the cable tightens suddenly. If the tow is down wind, with waves tending to accelerate the towed vessel up to the rescuer, then an iron bucket with a strong handle, a tyre, or even a very long length of rope, let out in a loop, should be dragged behind the towed boat to slow it down.

The tow-line should be led, if possible, to some point on the centre-line of the tug. If this cannot be done, the cable should be secured to the middle of a rope running across the stern. Make this rope as short as possible, otherwise the strain of towing will come alternately on one side and the other, making it difficult to steer a straight course. The tow-line must be very stoutly secured on the boat being towed to safety, preferably at two points. Thus, it might first be fastened to the anchor winch and then led back and fastened to the mast. Ensure that it will not be unduly chafed as it passes through a fairlead or over the edge of the deck. If in doubt, wrap a rag round the rope at this point and tie it securely in place.

It goes without saying that, if it is at all possible, the rescued boat should have someone aboard to steer. As long as some pre-arranged system of signals has been agreed between the two craft, so that the tug pilot knows when he is being asked to slow down, speed up, or stop, all should now be well. If the rescued boat is a small one, then its occupants should sit in the stern and lower the outboard, if there is one, into the water. Both these actions will make the craft easier to tow.

If towing is necessary in calm water, it is often easier to tow alongside. In such a case, the main tow-line is taken from the bow of the tug to the stern quarter of the towed boat, and further lines are lead across both boats' bows and sterns, simply to keep them running in the same line. On a single-screw towing vessel, the direction of rotation of the propeller decides on which side the rescued craft should be placed. A boat on the starboard side, for instance, will tend to cause the tug to turn to starboard because of the extra resistance on that side. If the tug has a right-hand propeller, the bow will swing to port, counteracting the effect of the towed boat.

Most recommendations on what to do in a man-overboard situation apply to sailing yachts, and many consider that a good method of rescue is to come up to the windward of the man in the water. He would then be in the lee of the hull and in comparatively sheltered conditions. Unhappily, this is rarely practical on a modern powerboat, for these craft have comparatively little hull under water and tend to blow sideways when stopped or going very slowly. They would thus blow down on the man in the water, who would then be in a perilous situation, further aggravated by a propeller working far too close to him for comfort. In most powerboats, if one stops the engines there will be very little control left. In strong winds, the answer, if the man is still capable of helping himself, is to circle him and let a line with one end tied to an empty fuel tin, a lifebuoy, or similar, blow down on him. The line should be a light, floating one so that the action of wind and waves will push it to the swimmer. He can then grab it and be hauled alongside. At this stage, the engines can be stopped or, at least, put into neutral. However, it is not much use having an exhausted man hanging onto a bit of rope with no means of heaving him aboard. Make the boarding ladder ready, or have a rope with a loop in which he can sit. It may be necessary for someone to go in the water to help him, but even he will be of no use if no arrangements have been made to get them both aboard—a point worth remembering!

Far too many powerboat owners think that, by opening the throttles wide and steering a compass course, they have done all that is necessary for them to reach their destination. But visibility can be drastically reduced by fog or heavy rain, the port of destination might for some reason be inaccessible, or another boat might need towing assistance, thus making it necessary to head for an entirely different harbour at such a low speed that tides and wind must be considered in plotting a course. In each of these situations, and in many others like them, a firm grasp of the techniques of navigation can be vital, and should be acquired by all boat-owners.

Within limits, it does not matter to the sailing man how long it takes him to get from A to B, and he knows that, if the wind dies, it will spring up again eventually and waft him to port. The powerboat man, on the other hand, has only a certain quantity of power available and, when this is exhausted, he is in real trouble. So the first thing that should be done on acquiring a powerboat is to draw out some curves of speed plotted against engine revolutions, and then another curve of engine revolutions plotted against fuel consumption. The results can be interesting and, occasionally, life-saving.

There is no particular difficulty in plotting these curves. Let us assume that the engine's maximum speed produces 2,400 rpm, while the lowest rpm at which it still runs happily is half that figure. The object is now to find speed at, say, 300 rpm increments between those two. Thus runs would be made and timed over a measured distance at 1,200 rpm, 1,500 rpm, 1,800 rpm, 2,100 rpm, and 2,400 rpm. Ensure that the effects of wind and tide are cancelled out by going over the measured distance each way and average the results. Times and distances can now be converted to speed and plotted against rpm.

Measuring fuel consumption is not easy without specialized equipment, but it is usually accurate enough to take the engine manufacturer's consumption curves for this purpose. These will normally be presented as litres or gallons per hour at various rpm, but may be given as litres or gallons per horsepower per hour. In that case, look further in the manufacturer's curves, and see what power is being developed at the required rpm, then multiply by the consumption figure to find the answer in consumption per hour. Some companies also show consumption curves in grammes per horsepower per hour. In such cases, and

whenever there is a query, or sufficient information is not provided to calculate a curve in readily understandable terms, write to the makers of the engine. It is in their interests that you use their products to the best advantage, and curves showing a weight of fuel consumed rather than a liquid measure are not worth much on a dark and stormy night with the tanks dangerously low. Also make sure that, where gallons are mentioned, you know what sort of gallons these are! There is a considerable difference between British gallons (4.5 l) and American gallons (3.8 l).

These curves can save lives if, for instance, you have headed out into the blue with what you thought was plenty of fuel and bad weather has slowed you down. Your destination is seventy miles away, and there is an estimated 50 gallons (60 US gallons or 227.3 l) of fuel left in the tanks. (Note that dip-sticks will give an accurate guide to the amount of fuel in a tank, while gauges are often unreliable.) A glance at your curves shows that at, say, twenty knots, fuel consumption is fifteen gallons (18 US gallons or 68.2 l) per hour. To do seventy miles at twenty knots and 2,400 rpm will take 3.5 hours, and in that time the engine will have burnt $15 \times 3.5 = 52.5$ gallons ($18 \times 3.5 = 63$ US gallons or $68.2 \times 3.5 = 238.7$ l). In other words, you will not make it. But suppose speed was dropped to eight knots. Then the curves would show, perhaps, that fuel consumption was four gallons (4.8 US gallons or 18.2 l) per hour. Seventy miles at eight knots will take 8 hours and 45 minutes, and $8.75 \times 4 = 35$ gallons ($8.75 \times 4.8 = 42$ US gallons or $8.75 \times 18.2 = 159.3$ l) of fuel will be burnt. Thus you should be home and dry with a bit in reserve. Always plan on a reserve for all cruises. Bad weather can play havoc with calculations. Trials on trawlers have shown that maximum speed, compared with that in calm water, drops by twenty-five per cent when steaming into a head sea in a Force 6 wind, and by fifty per cent into a head sea in a Force 8. A trawler is a big and powerful craft compared with the average boat, whose speed would drop much more dramatically, though the amount of fuel consumed would remain constant. These trials were conducted with full throttle throughout, with the result that if, say, 100 gallons would take you 120 miles in calm waters, it would take you considerably less than half that distance if heading into a Force 8 gale.

Other experiments carried out on trawlers in bad weather were made to determine rolling angles at different wave headings and at two different ship speeds. The first conclusion, and one that every experienced offshore sailor would know without telling, was that the faster the boat travels, the less it rolls. At four knots, as might be expected, waves from the beam produced the worst roll angle. Surprisingly, however, at thirteen knots, the greatest roll occurred with the waves coming in at 45° on the aft quarter. With a working knowledge of the amount of roll caused by different wave headings, a course can be plotted to bring the boat to its destination without taking seas at their worst heading. In really bad conditions, this is important, for fierce rolling can cause breakages and, perhaps most serious of all, tire out the crew. A tired crew is an inefficient crew and one that can make silly mistakes.

Sometimes, entering harbour can be the most hazardous part of a cruise. In rough weather, the harbour mouth can be an awe-inspiring sight, and this is one occa-

sion when you can take no evasive action. In really bad conditions, there are two options open. First, and here we are assuming that waves are running into the entrance, not across it, and that yours is a boat capable of at least twenty knots, you can match speed with the waves. Watch the wave pattern, as the harbour is approached, and attempt to assess when a smaller-than-usual wave is likely to occur. Position the boat to anticipate its arrival and, just as it overtakes your vessel, accelerate to maintain position in the trough behind it. The water here will be calm and relatively still, so that the boat will answer readily to the wheel. Great concentration is needed, for it is not advisable either to overtake or be overtaken by the sea. As you sweep into the harbour, the water should become calmer, and it should be relatively easy to manoeuvre into the required berth. This is a pretty spectacular method of entering port, and it needs considerable boat speed. Another way is to slow the vessel right down by some artificial means, such as by dragging a drogue or sea anchor astern or trailing a very long warp made into a bight, or loop. The idea here is that the throttles can be kept open, thus allowing a good flow of water past the rudders, and this gives good manoeuvring powers while the boat is travelling fairly slowly, being overtaken by waves rather than being picked up and carried forward by them.

All craft, whether propelled by wind or motors, are liable to broach when running with the seas. This can happen in two ways. The first, and this is particularly applicable to power craft, occurs when the vessel overtakes a wave and runs its bows into the back of the wave ahead. This slows it down abruptly, and the following wave is then likely to catch up and, because the boat will probably not now be exactly in the same line as the wave, to swing it round broadside on. This is an unhappy, unsafe, and potentially very wet angle to be in. Modern, fast vessels with fine bows and very fat transoms are most likely to suffer this ignominious fate. The second usual method of broaching occurs when a boat is picked up by a following wave and hurled forward. Because boat and water are then moving at roughly the same speed, there will be little response from the rudder. Eventually, the wave will break up and collapse (few waves exist as individual units for more than twenty seconds or so), or will rush ahead. In both cases, the boat will be left wallowing in the trough at the mercy of the next wave along, which can swing it round broadside once again. The moral is to steer a course that runs slightly diagonally to the seas or, again, to tow a drogue or warp so that the propeller, turning hard, will be giving a good flow of water past the rudder.

Even in quite moderate seas, all powerboats, but especially the medium- and slow-speed types, are liable to fierce rolling. The usual relieving measure is to set a small area of steadying sail on a mizzen mast, but this is normally fairly useless. It may help in bringing the boat's bows up into the wind, which can be valuable in certain gale conditions, but that is about all. Better damping against rolling is provided by anti-roll stabilizers, or "flopper-stoppers", which originated on the west coast of America and consist of a pair of paravanes, towed one on each side of the vessel. These reduce speed a little, because they absorb a certain amount of power, but they are effective if properly designed and installed. The vanes themselves are available commercially in various sizes to suit different boat lengths.

The details of the supporting booms and guys depend to quite an extent on the layout of the boat, but it is reckoned that the vanes should tow at a point some thirty per cent of the length of the water-line forward of the transom. For those who regularly make long cruises offshore in suitable powerboats, these stabilizers would seem to be a worthwhile investment.

Handling powerboats is mainly a matter of common sense, as is all boat handling, and a determination not to become flustered at moments of crisis. A few seconds' thought will probably solve the problem that has arisen, and there are not many situations where a decision to act has to be instantaneous. Always remember that, for manoeuvres to be precise on a powerboat, there must be a good flow of water past the rudder, probably given by a swiftly-turning propeller. On craft with outboard or out-drive power there is, of course, no rudder, and then no manoeuvres at all can be made without the aid of the engine and propeller. Offshore, the object is that you remain in command of your vessel and that the waves do not take over. Beam seas can cause dangerous rolling and following seas possible broaching. Steer courses to avoid these situations in bad weather, and slow down as it seems proper. If necessary, tow something behind to achieve this. Always maintain a good look-out, and do not imagine that the niceties of navigation can be ignored just because you have power and speed available (for limited periods). If your boat is taken to sea, ensure that it is suitable for that task. A chart table is a "must". So are easily-accessible fuel filters. A big anchor and sensible anchor cable are often missing—make sure you have them. Powerboat deck fittings are often flashy but feeble. Equip your craft with rugged bollards and fairleads—remember that, one day, you may have to be towed to safety, and the strains on them can be enormous. A sea anchor is probably of more use on a motor vessel than on a sailing yacht, and it needs to be stoutly made.

It is impossible to see out of a wheel-house at night if there is no way of eliminating artificial light. If you step outside on deck, your vision will be much improved. Can you do this without making a circuit of various bits of saloon furniture and consuming valuable seconds in the process? Imagine yourself in unpleasant situations; ponder how you would deal with them; and then make sure that the solutions are practical on your boat.

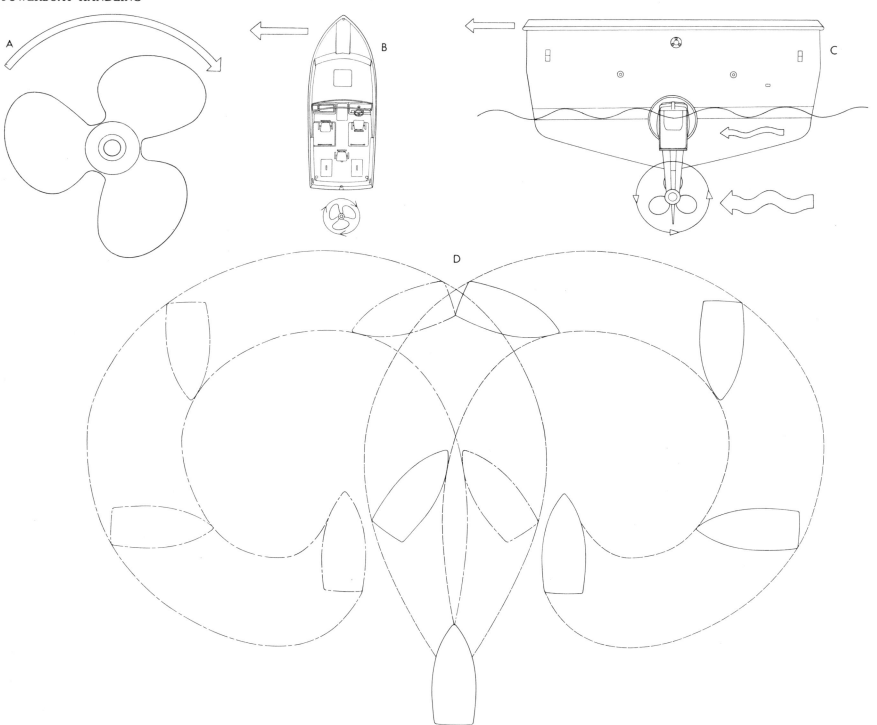

A A right-handed propeller, like this one, turns clockwise when viewed from astern. A left-handed propeller does the opposite, of course. Handed propellers on twin-screw craft turn in opposite directions—normally outwards, with a right-handed propeller on the starboard shaft and a left-handed propeller on the port shaft.

B A propeller tends to "walk" the stern across in the direction of its rotation. Thus

a right-handed propeller, when the boat is going ahead, will swing the stern to starboard with a consequent swinging of the bow to port.

C When the same boat goes astern, the opposite happens: the stern swings to port and the bow to starboard. This action is most noticeable on boats with slow-turning, coarse-pitch propellers.

D A boat's turning circle commences with the whole

boat drifting bodily sideways, while the stern swings considerably. These space-consuming manoeuvres will be most noticeable on shallow-draught vessels, such as modern, fast cruisers (and unladen oil tankers and bulk carriers, so beware!) Typical, complete turning circles are shown.

E If a boat with a right-handed propeller approaches a jetty, as shown, and goes astern on the engine, the boat

will swing, stern in, towards the jetty.

F But if the same boat approaches the jetty from the other direction, the stern would be pulled outwards, if the engine went astern, so the boat must make a gentle approach, go slow astern, and use the rudder only for the final berthing.

G Letting the wind and/or tide work for you. When approaching a berth in a boat

with a right-handed propeller, put the nose in, make fast, and let the stern swing in, blown by the wind, or go ahead on the engine.

H When leaving the mooring, make the bow fast, go astern on the engine, thus causing the stern to swing out, before finally letting go.

I Approaching a berth in a boat with a right-handed propeller, with the wind coming from the opposite direction, put

the nose in, make fast, and go astern on the engine.

J Leaving the same berth, with the wind in the same direction, take a line forward from the stern, as shown, and let the wind or tide do the work. When the engine is put ahead, be sure to draw in both lines smartly, so that they do not wrap themselves round the propellers.

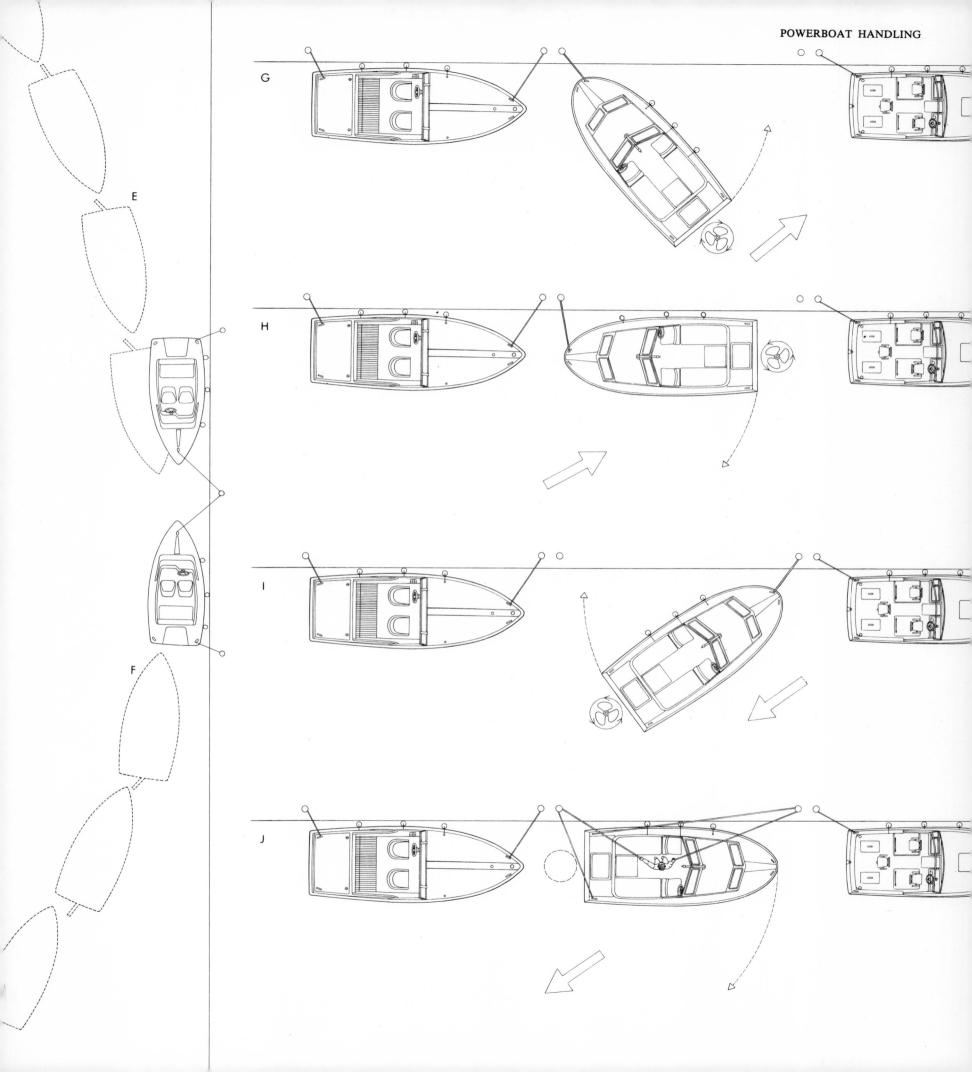

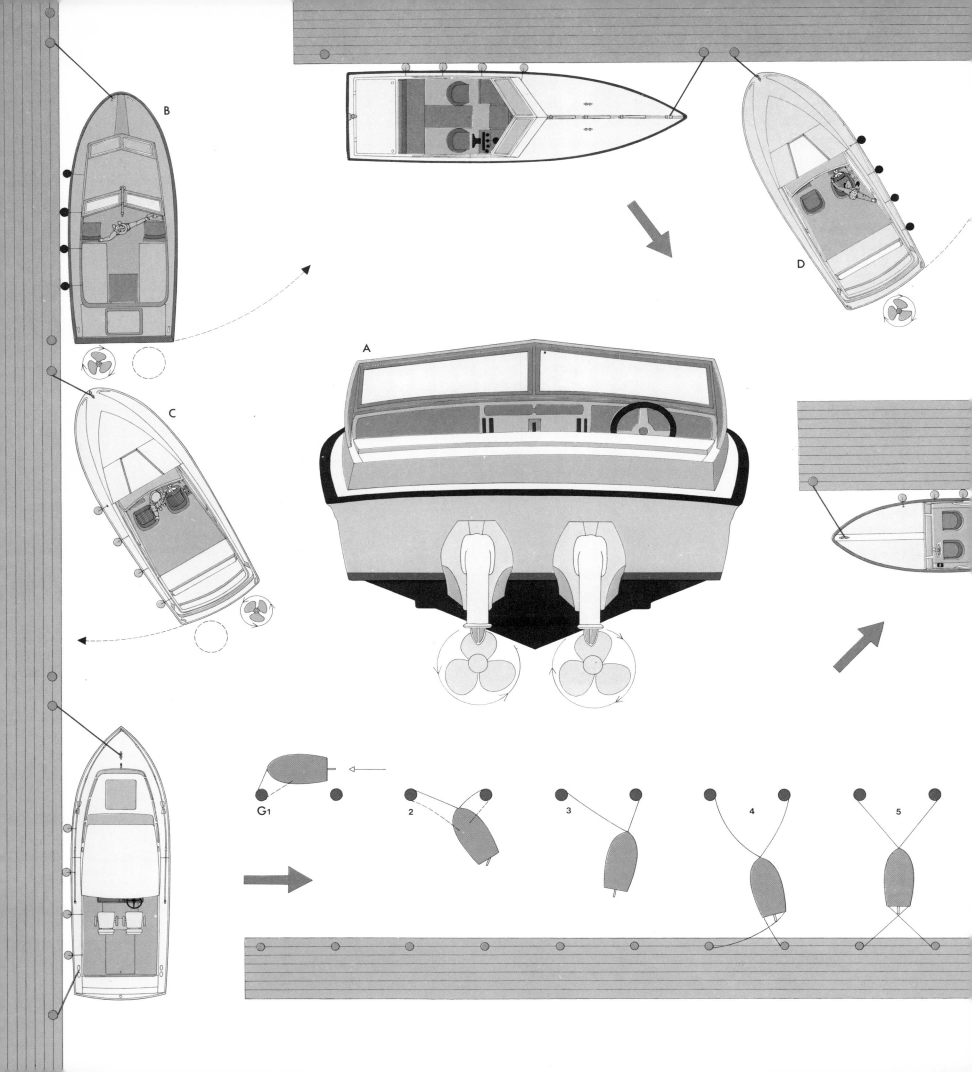

B

D

A

C

G1

2

3

4

5

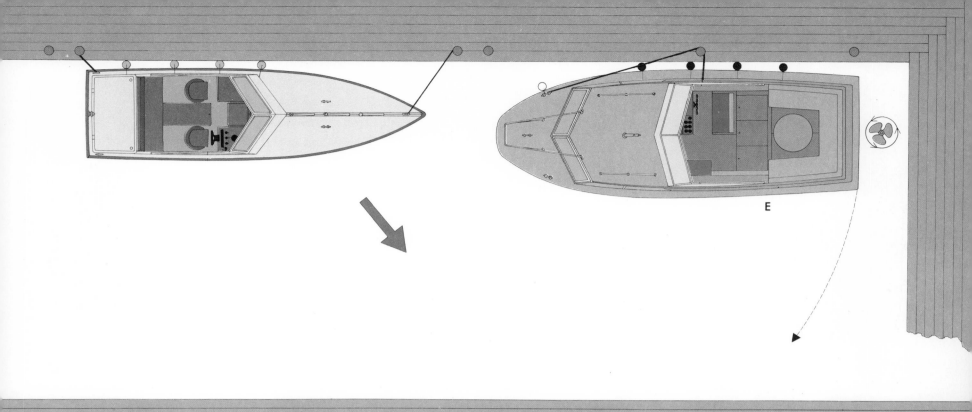

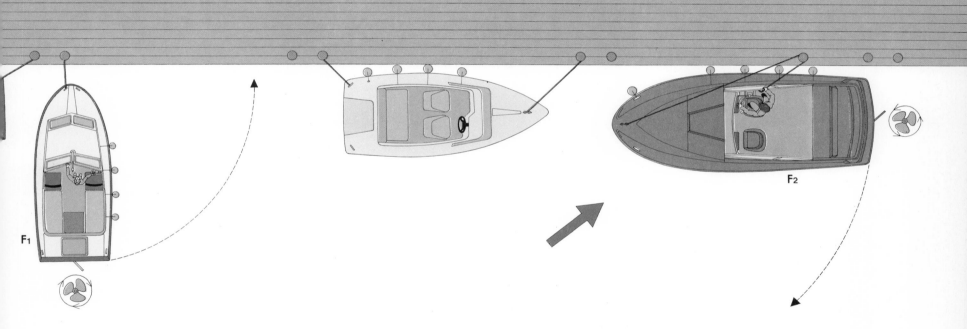

A Conventional outward-turning propellers are good for general handling, but wrong in a boat intended for normal working under one engine only, the second being used mainly in emergencies. Under starboard propeller, for example, its tendency to drive the boat's bows to port would be increased by its right-hand rotation. Inward-turning propellers would be better.

B Life is easier with twin screws. Leaving a jetty with outward-turning propellers, go astern on the inner engine and the stern will swing out.

C The opposite applies when approaching a landing place. Go astern on the outer motor and the stern will swing in. When manoeuvring, place fenders strategically and be prepared to slip mooring lines quickly.

D Always think about the "hand" of a single propeller. With a left-handed propeller and approaching the jetty, nose up to the landing stage and take a line ashore. A burst astern on the engine will swing the stern in.

E When leaving, take a line back from the bows and go ahead slowly. The stern will swing out, but a fender will be needed near the bow.

F The same manoeuvres as in **D** and **E,** but also using the rudder. (**1**) Putting the rudder blade across the main directional stream of water will cause the bows and stern to swing. Thus, when landing and going astern, give starboard rudder and the stern will swing to starboard. (**2**) On leaving, go ahead, and give starboard rudder; the stern will swing to port.

G Warps, as well as wind and tide, are the boatman's best friends. Going into a berth with mooring piles outside, head into the wind and pass a warp round a pile (**1**). Go astern with rudder to port, and pass a warp round the next pile (**2**). Keep both ends free and motor gently astern, using the rudder to counteract the "hand" of the propeller, if necessary (**3**). Take two lines ashore passing them, crossed, round a bollard (**4**). Tighten up on bow lines until the boat is well out from the edge of the jetty, and then make stern lines fast (**5**). The essence of this whole manoeuvre has been to use a post to pivot round; but always check whether the wind or tide is having the greater effect on your craft and plan accordingly.

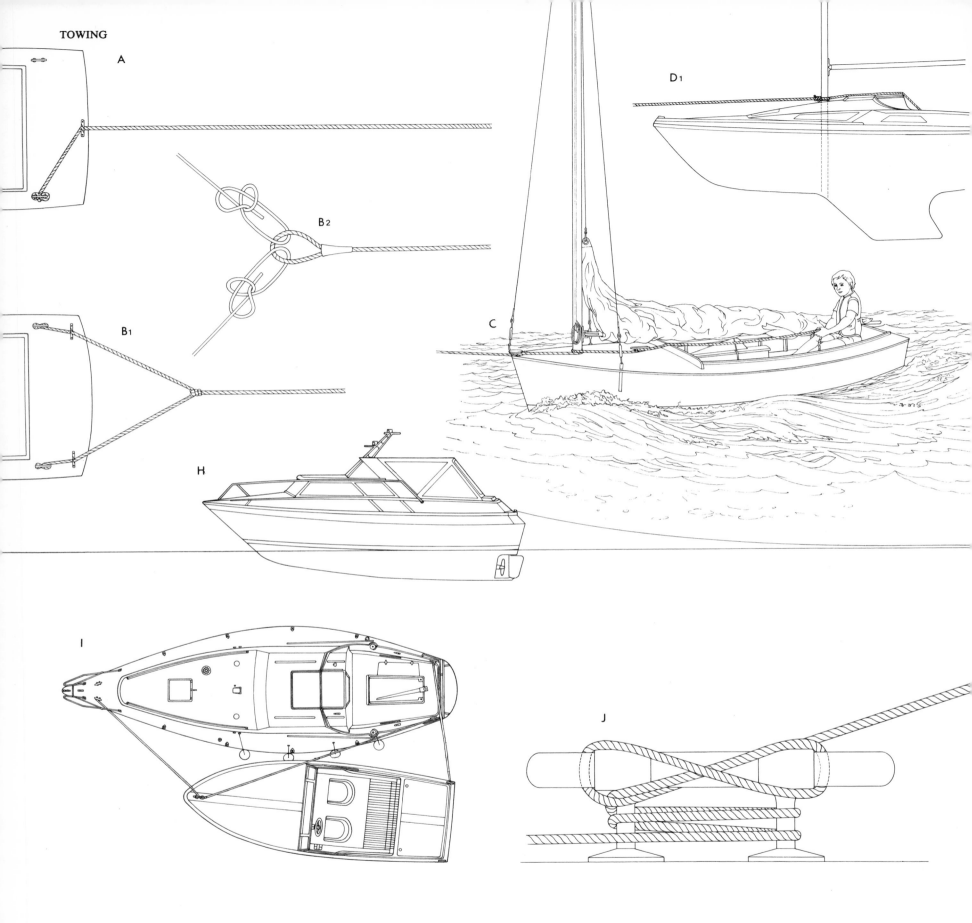

A Always try to arrange a tow from the centre-line, or the towing vessel will be constantly pulled across to one side.

B If a centre fairlead is not available, tow from a warp spanning the stern (1), but keep the warp as short as is practical. Fasten the tow-line with bowline hitches (2).

C Wind the tow-line round as many stout fittings as possible, to allow friction to reduce the final pull.

D On sailing-boats with a keel-stepped mast, the tow-line can be fastened to that, but the load should still be reduced by friction elsewhere. (1) Side view. (2) From above.

E Few craft have strong enough deck fittings for a long tow at sea, but the rope could be taken round the superstructure.

F For a calm-water tow, a stout timber could be placed under the fore-hatch. Pad the coaming to prevent chafe.

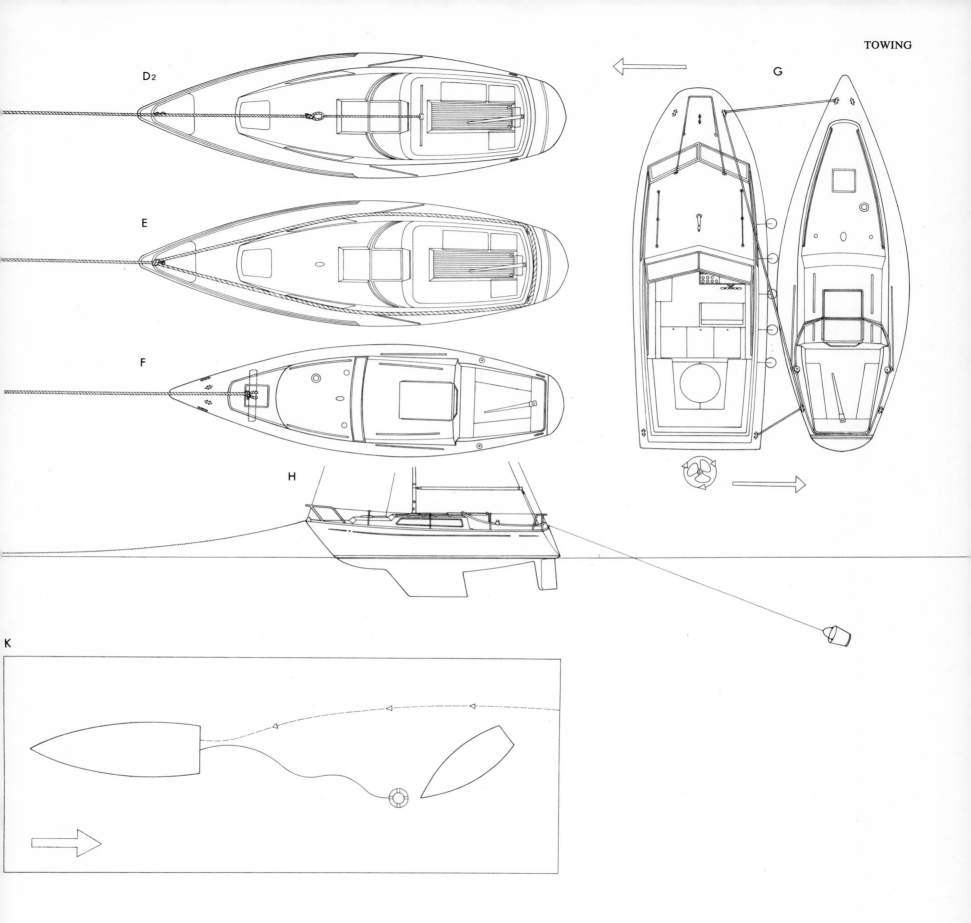

G Allow for the hand of the propeller when towing alongside. A boat on the starboard side will compensate for a right-handed propeller.

H At sea, use as long a tow-line as possible, incorporating the anchor chain from the towed boat to reduce snatching. In a following sea, the rescued craft may tend to run up on the tug. A bucket, towed astern, will prevent this.

I If the towing vessel is the smaller, position it aft and give the towed boat a slight "toe in". Compensate with the rudder.

J Put a couple of round turns on the cleat, followed by as many figure-of-eight turns as are required, but never use half-hitches.

K Rather than go alongside to pass a line, it is sometimes better to float it down on a lifebuoy or an empty jerry-can.

HEAVY WEATHER

A In rough weather, some motor cruisers and many fishing boats set a small emergency sail on a mast near the stern. If this is not practical, it may be possible to devise a sail between the aft end of the wheel-house and the stern. Without that sail, the wind, blowing at the centre of area of the hull and superstructure (*b*), will turn the bows round with it. With sail set, though, the centre of area is further aft (*a*), and the boat is pivoted round so that it faces the wind. (*c*) The pivoting point of the hull.

B Details of setting and handling the sail will vary from boat to boat. Very often, the wheel-house will need strengthening to stand up to the extra strain. Here, the sail is set on an eye-plate (*a*) and two blocks (*b*). Cleats (*c*) are needed when handling.

C For efficient running, a fast boat should have its bows up about 3°, compared with trim at rest.

D When running before the waves, the same boat should adopt a more nose-up attitude, which will give better and safer handling.

E When heading into steep waves, though, a flatter trim will be more comfortable.

F An outboard tilted out (1) tends to drive the stern down and the bows up. Swing the motor in towards the transom (2), and the opposite happens.

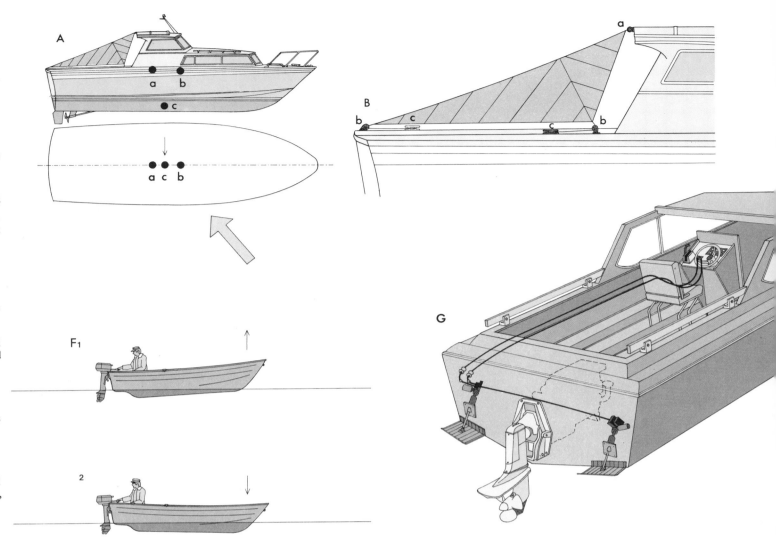

G On inboard craft, electrically or hydraulically operated flaps can be used to depress the bows. These trim tabs are pivoted along the transom and can be pushed down, so that their trailing edges are forced into the water flow. Illustrated are Volvo Penta electro-mechanically operated trim tabs.

H A boat without trim tabs (1) has "stern squat", while one with trim tabs (2) is running at optimum plane, which gives a smoother ride and better fuel economy.

I The most common and simplest way of reducing roll on powered craft is to fit bilge keels. These are flat plates which project diagonally from the turn of the bilges and are most effective on round-bottomed craft. A further measure of roll-damping is provided by adding a wide, flat plate across the bottom of the keel.

J More sophisticated and costly schemes include roll-damping fins. These project from the sides like bilge keels and are electrically or mechanically operated to pivot through an angle of about 20°. As the boat rolls to

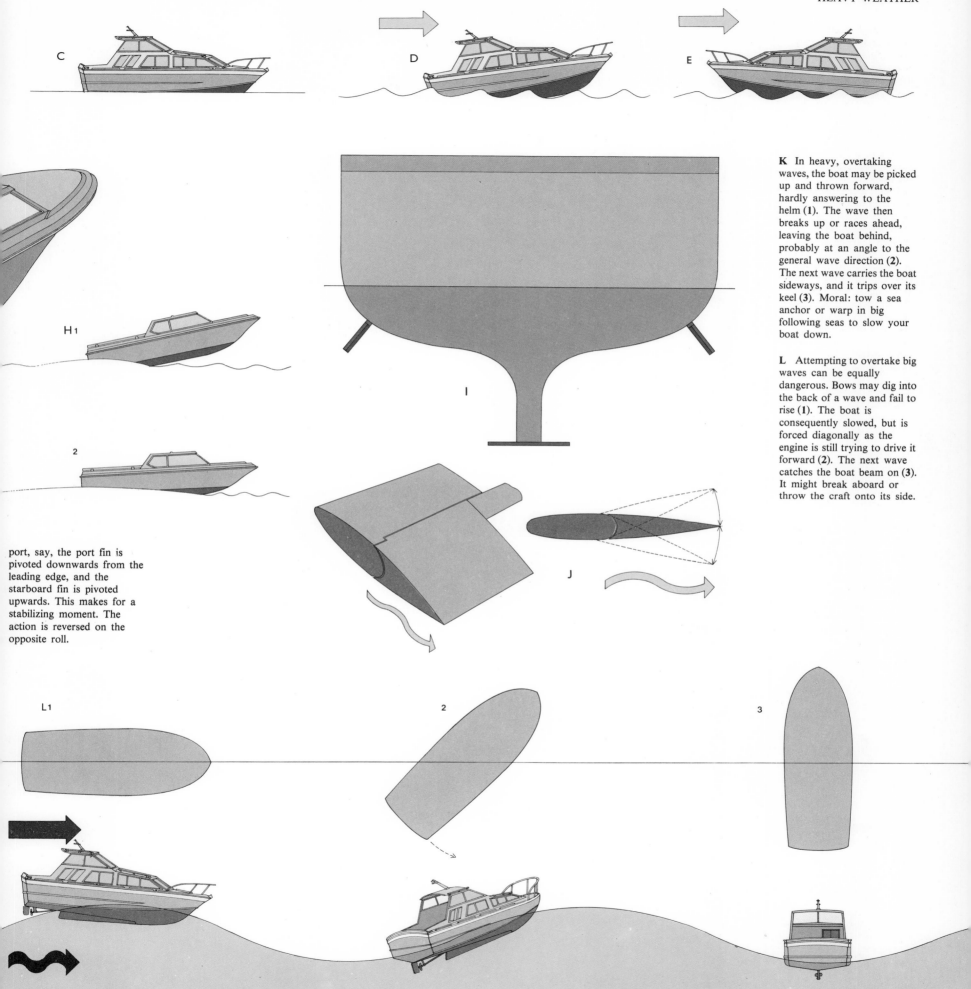

K In heavy, overtaking waves, the boat may be picked up and thrown forward, hardly answering to the helm (**1**). The wave then breaks up or races ahead, leaving the boat behind, probably at an angle to the general wave direction (**2**). The next wave carries the boat sideways, and it trips over its keel (**3**). Moral: tow a sea anchor or warp in big following seas to slow your boat down.

L Attempting to overtake big waves can be equally dangerous. Bows may dig into the back of a wave and fail to rise (**1**). The boat is consequently slowed, but is forced diagonally as the engine is still trying to drive it forward (**2**). The next wave catches the boat beam on (**3**). It might break aboard or throw the craft onto its side.

port, say, the port fin is pivoted downwards from the leading edge, and the starboard fin is pivoted upwards. This makes for a stabilizing moment. The action is reversed on the opposite roll.

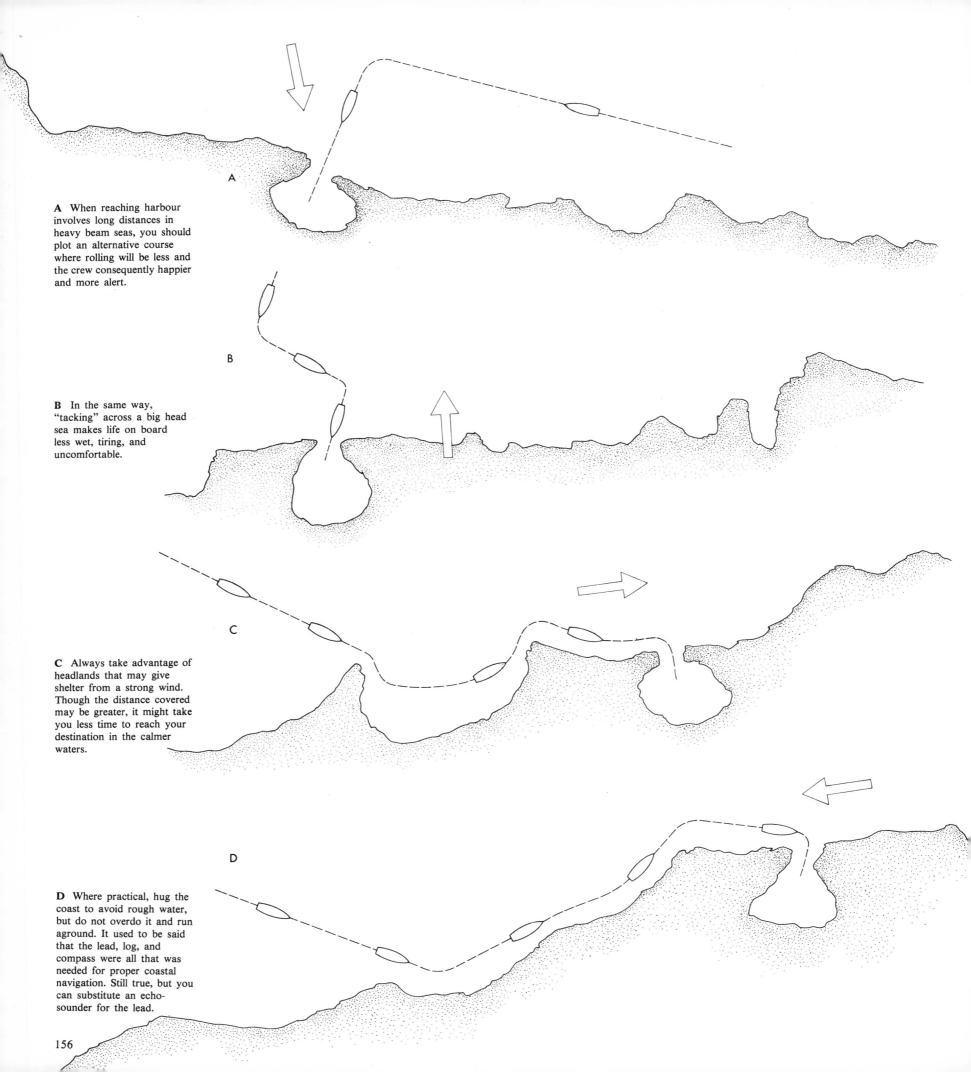

A When reaching harbour involves long distances in heavy beam seas, you should plot an alternative course where rolling will be less and the crew consequently happier and more alert.

B In the same way, "tacking" across a big head sea makes life on board less wet, tiring, and uncomfortable.

C Always take advantage of headlands that may give shelter from a strong wind. Though the distance covered may be greater, it might take you less time to reach your destination in the calmer waters.

D Where practical, hug the coast to avoid rough water, but do not overdo it and run aground. It used to be said that the lead, log, and compass were all that was needed for proper coastal navigation. Still true, but you can substitute an echo-sounder for the lead.

NAVIGATION

Kenneth Wilkes

There is a world of difference between "navigating" a car and navigating a yacht. A car driven along a road has its limits clearly defined by kerbs and white lines. Most roads are signposted and, if one loses one's way, one can usually stop and ask. None of these aids is available to the mariner. A car rides on the road—any obstruction is visible. A boat proceeds in the water and needs a particular depth of water in which to sail safely. While a yacht's echo-sounder will show what depth it is in at that instant, it will not show what the depth will be further on, nor whether it is approaching hidden rocks or shoal waters.

Navigation can be described as the art of directing a vessel from A to B expeditiously and in safety. To do this, and especially to do this in safety, requires the intelligent use of the chart, the compass and, above all, the practised eye. If he is to be effective, the navigator must be in a position to answer three questions at any required time: 1. Where are we now? 2. In which direction should the yacht be headed in order to reach our destination? 3. Is that a safe direction? There is rather more to answering these questions than might appear at first. Let us start with some of the terms we use.

Position can be defined relative to a stated landmark or position, e.g., "Position two miles due east of Eagle Island lighthouse", or by stating the latitude and longitude of the position, e.g., "30°20′ N, 10°40′ W". This is a form of "grid" reference. Parallels of latitude can be drawn, all being parallel to the equator and all running due east and west. In this case, the position is somewhere on a parallel which is exactly 30°20′ north of the equator. Meridians are lines running straight between the north and south poles. Each one cuts all the parallels of latitude at a right angle. The meridian drawn through our position is 10°40′ westward of the meridian passing through Greenwich, 0°, called the prime meridian. Thus, 30°20′ N 10°40′ W precisely defines the position. This method is used when offshore, out of sight of land, or where no clear landmarks are available.

Latitude may be any figure between 0° and 90° and may be north or south. Longitude is measured either west or east from 0°, and can never exceed 180°W or 180°E.

Direction may be expressed: (a) in relation to a stated object, e.g., "Buoy, 25° to the left of lighthouse"; (b) in relation to the direction of the yacht's head, in which case the direction is referred to as a "relative bearing", e.g., "Vessel 45° on the starboard bow" or "Vessel bearing 045° relative"; or (c) in relation to the direction of north, in which case it is essential to specify which "north" is being used. As will be explained, this may be true N, magnetic

N, or compass N, e.g., "Lighthouse bearing 032°T" or "Buoy bearing 280°C".

Distance at sea is always measured in nautical miles. Unlike the statute mile, which is 5,280 ft (1,609 m), the nautical mile has a scientific basis and averages 6,076 ft (1,852 m), which is some 15 per cent longer than the statute mile. By definition, the nautical mile is the distance between two points on the earth's surface which subtend an arc of one minute (1′) at the centre of the earth, or to be pedantic, at the centre of the earth's curvature at that place. Distances on inland waterways, some rivers, and canals are often stated in statute miles or kilometres. Distances on the chart are scaled off using the minutes of latitude on the vertical edges of the chart (*never* the longitude minutes on the top and bottom edges).

The unit of speed at sea is the knot (kn), which is one nautical mile in one hour. (It is incorrect to say "knots per hour".) On inland waterways, mph or km/h may be used.

Charts are the mariner's map, specially drawn to show everything the navigator needs to know about the area in which he may be sailing. An up-to-date chart—and the ability to understand what it shows—is essential for the navigator to be able to answer the three questions: Where are we now? In which direction should we go? Is it safe?

The types of information shown on the chart are:
Water — navigable areas, depths of water;
Dangers — rocks, shoals, types of bottom, areas of rough water;
Navigational aids — positions of lighthouses, buoys, beacons; their distinguishing lights and shapes, and fog signals of each; positions of radio beacons, etc.;
Tides and currents — directions and rates of flow;
Various limits — e.g., "Anchoring prohibited", traffic separation areas;
Topography — position of shore line; features on land of navigational interest, hills, buildings, cliffs, etc.
So much information is packed onto a chart that much has to be indicated by abbreviations, initials, or symbols. It is important to be able to recognize all these, which can be studied in the standard work published officially in every maritime country (in Great Britain, booklet No. 5011; in the United States, HO No. 1).

Navigational buoys are of particular importance. These are placed to indicate the sides of a channel, the position of a bank, shoal, wreck, or other danger. They indicate their purpose in several ways: by day, by their shape, colour, top mark (if any); by night, by the colour of light exhibited and the number and period of flashes. There are two principal buoyage systems: the lateral, to indicate

the respective sides of a channel, and the cardinal, to indicate the position in which the buoys lie in relation to the danger they mark. (Mostly used around off-lying dangers.) In the lateral system, used in most European countries, buoys indicate on which side of a channel they lie, viewed as when entering port or river, or when proceeding in the direction of the main flood stream, thus:
Port hand — can-shaped, painted red or red and white, flashing red or even number of white flashes;
Starboard hand — conical shape, painted black or black and white, flashing an odd number of white flashes.
In North America, the terms used are:
Port hand — "Can", painted black, white light;
Starboard — "Nun", painted red, red light.
Note that the colours are *reversed* from those used in Great Britain.

The scale of the chart is important. We use a large-scale chart when in rivers and estuaries or when passing close to land or any dangers. This should show all the buoys and other marks and give full details of them, such as heights of lighthouses, colours and shapes of buoys, and particularly the characteristics of the light (if any) which each will exhibit at night. For making coastal passages, medium-scale charts are required showing perhaps ten to twenty miles of coastline on one sheet, plus a passage chart, probably to a smaller scale, showing both departure point and destination on a single sheet, so that the whole passage can be viewed.

The scale of a chart is most easily seen by noting how far apart are the minutes (1′) of latitude (= 1/60th of a degree), using the vertical scales on either border of the chart. One minute of latitude is one nautical mile. The small numbers found all over the water areas of the chart are soundings, or depths of water. These are all measured downwards from the level of chart datum (CD). This is the lowest level to which the tide normally falls. At any other time, the water level will be somewhat above the level of chart datum. Put another way, the actual depth of water at a given point will at certain times be somewhat more than the charted depth. For this reason, it is necessary to be able to work out what is the height of tide, that is, the amount by which the level of the water is above the level of chart datum, at any required time in any area. So it will be seen that the depth of water in which you are sailing (shown by the echo-sounder) is very seldom the same as the depth shown on the chart at that point.

We have to be prepared to deal with two types of chart, the older fathoms chart and the newer metric chart. All European continental charts are metric. British charts are gradually being changed from fathoms to metric, and

North American charts will follow suit. British and North American charts which are already in metres are easily distinguished from fathoms charts by being more brightly coloured and by the words "Depths in Metres" printed boldly in magenta on the upper and lower borders. On the fathoms charts, all soundings given in water areas are stated in fathoms, and in depths usually below 10 fathoms, in fathoms and feet, thus 5_4 = 5 fms 4 ft. There are 6 ft (1.83 m) in one fathom. The figure printed against any object which is never covered by the sea (hill-top, lighthouse light, etc.) is given in feet, measured from the level of mean high water spring tides. Positions on the chart, which are periodically covered and uncovered by the tide as it rises and falls, such as banks and some rocks, are called "drying heights". These are measured from the level of chart datum but, of course, upwards. They are shown on the chart in fathoms and feet, the fathoms figure being underlined, e.g., $\underline{0}_4$ = drying height, 4 ft (1.2 m) above the level of chart datum. On metric charts, *all* depths, drying heights, and heights are given in metres. In shallow water, metres and tenths may be given, e.g., 4_8 = 4.8 m (15 ft 9 in).

Before using a chart, look at the title and detail given below the title. This will state the type of projection used (Mercator or gnomonic) and the unit being used for soundings, either fathoms or metres, although on some charts, feet only are used. Notice in the bottom left-hand corner the list and dates of corrections which have been made to the chart. From time to time, alterations have to be made to charts because of changes, such as the repositioning of buoys, the changing of the characteristics of lighthouse lights, the occurrence of fresh wrecks, and the like. All these are listed in officially published weekly notices, which are available from chart agents and from shipping offices, and which contain the data from which authorized chart agents correct all their stocks of charts. It is advisable to take your charts to an authorized chart agent at least once a year, and preferably before a cruise, to have them corrected. Charts are not inexpensive and are worth looking after. Always use soft (2B) pencils and a soft rubber on them. Keep your charts preferably flat and in "folios" or in a large plastic envelope. Put not more than about half-a-dozen charts in one envelope, and stick a label on the outside, listing the charts. When preparing for a passage, arrange the charts in the sequence in which they will probably be required. Buy your charts from a nationally recognized chart agent, if there is one.

The compass is certainly the most important navigational instrument carried on board, and no yacht should go beyond the harbour mouth without one. Buy your compass from a reliable instrument-supplier, and get the best you can afford. A wide variety is now available, many for particular applications, so seek advice before you buy. A steering compass consists of a bowl containing a compass card with the degrees marked on the edge, clockwise from 0° to 360°. Markings vary according to the size of the compass, the larger the compass, the clearer the markings. Many show a mark either every 2° or 5°, with perhaps every 10° marked with the figure. Usually the last digit is omitted, so that the figures can be large. The mark at 150° may be "15" and at 350°, "35".

The compass card has two or more small bar magnets

fixed to its underside, and the whole assembly is carried on a bearing which minimizes friction. The magnets are fixed exactly parallel to the N–S line (0° to 180°) on the compass card. The bowl is filled with a liquid, usually distilled water and alcohol (to resist freezing) in the proportions 2:1, so that the card almost floats, thus having very little friction, and its movements are damped. There is a mark fixed on the inside of the bowl called the "lubber line", so placed that a line through the centre of the card and the lubber line is perfectly parallel to the keel in a fore-and-aft direction. In this way, the lubber line indicates on the card the direction in which the yacht's head is pointing. Any required compass direction is achieved by turning the helm in such direction as causes the lubber line to move round the compass card to opposite the required degree mark. The magnets fixed to the compass card seek to lie parallel to the lines of magnetic force in which the compass happens to be at the time. The principal directing force is the earth's magnetic field. These lines of force do not run exactly between true N and S poles, but "wander" between the earth's magnetic poles. The amount and direction, by which the lines of force and hence the compass N differ from the direction of true N, is called "variation", and is named E or W. In British waters, the variation is between about 6°W and 9°W. On the western seaboard of Canada, variation is about 24°E. It changes as the yacht's position changes. It also changes very slowly over the years.

The variation's amount and "name" (E or W) are given on every chart. Two compass roses will be found, and each shows two concentric circles, both marked (clockwise) from 0° to 359°. The outer, or true, rose is orientated so that a line, drawn through its centre and its 0° and 180° points, is parallel to every meridian, and similarly the 90°–270° line is parallel to every parallel of latitude. The inner, or magnetic, rose is turned so that its 0°–180° (N–S) line makes an angle with the true N–S line of the outer rose. The angular difference, or displacement, is the variation in that locality, and N may be displaced either to eastward (clockwise) or to westward (anti-clockwise). The amount of the variation is also stated within the rose, e.g. "Variation 8°15′ W (1977), decreasing about 5′ annually". Note that not only is magnetic N displaced from true N by the variation shown, but also every bearing taken from the magnetic rose will be different, by the same amount, from the same bearing taken from the true rose. It is sufficient to work to the nearest whole degree of variation.

To convert a course or bearing from true to magnetic, or vice versa, variation must also be applied. This jingle is a sure-fire way of checking that the conversion has been correctly carried out:

Error EAST, compass LEAST   (= less than true)
Error WEST, compass BEST   (= more than true)

e.g.:

Course	045°M	172°M	053°T	162°T
Var'n	+ 8E	− 10W	− 8E	+ 10W
	053°T	162°T	045°M	172°M

If two or more roses are shown on the chart, use the variation given in the rose nearest to the position. Note that the amount and direction of the variation (E or W) depend solely on the geographical location of the yacht and change very slowly over the years.

While the earth's magnetic field is the main directing force, any ferrous or other magnetic material on the yacht near the compass will also exert a magnetic influence and will cause the compass N to be "deviated" from the *magnetic* N. A well-sited compass on a wood or GRP yacht is unlikely to be affected by metal in the yacht's construction (though this may happen). A steel yacht is certain to have its compass markedly affected. The amount and direction by which the compass N is deflected from the magnetic N (the direction it would point if no metal were affecting it) is called "deviation". Thus the difference (if any) between any compass bearing and the equivalent magnetic bearing is deviation.

Deviation can be caused by the engine, by an iron keel, or by a magneto in the outboard motor, if any of them are within 4-6 ft (1.2-1.8 m) of the compass. Tools, a jack-knife, beer cans, etc. can cause deviation, if they are from 1-3 ft (0.3-0.9 m), and a camera light-meter, a loudspeaker, headphones, or even a ferrous buckle on a lifeline harness can cause deviation under 2 ft (0.6 m).

A yacht can be "swung" for deviation, but it is best to employ a compass adjuster. He will take bearings with the yacht heading in different directions all round. He will then fix magnets near the compass in such positions as to cause them to exert an equal and opposite force to that caused by interfering metal in the yacht. He will then either declare the compass free of any deviation or will prepare for you a deviation card. This lists all headings round the compass (probably either sixteen or twenty-four equidistant bearings) with the degrees and name (E or W) of the deviation to be applied when the yacht is heading in any particular direction. Note particularly that, if the compass has any deviation, the amount to be applied is that applicable to the yacht's heading at the time. It is most likely to be different on various headings. The reason for this is that the offending ferrous or magnetic material, being in the boat, moves round the compass card as the boat's head changes direction, while the compass card remains steady, always seeking to point to magnetic N. Deviation (if present) must be applied whenever converting between a true and a compass bearing, course, or heading. The same jingle as before can be used, e.g.:

Course (per chart)	135°T
Variation	+ 8°W
	143°Mag
Deviation	− 5°E
Course to steer	138°C
Course steered	255°C
Deviation	− 4°W
	251°Mag
Variation	− 8°W
Lay off on chart	243°T

Note the sequence in which variation and deviation are applied. Variation is the difference between true and magnetic, while deviation is the difference between magnetic and compass.

When starting on an offshore passage, or on one where few or no landmarks will be visible, it is necessary to study the chart and to decide what compass course to steer to take the yacht along the required track line. To do this, several estimates have to be made. These are the yacht's expected speed through the water, the direction and rate of the expected tidal stream, and the amount of leeway to be expected in the prevailing conditions. This process is called "shaping a course".

When sailing on lakes or inland waterways without tidal stream or current, course may be set, or shaped, by drawing a straight line on the chart from departure point to destination, examining it to see that the line does not pass near any dangers nor areas with insufficient water. This is the track, or rhumb line, required. The direction, or bearing, of the line is determined by protractor, and this bearing, if a true bearing (taken by reference to meridians or to the outer circle of a compass rose on the chart) has to be converted into a compass bearing by applying the local variation, per the nearest rose, and deviation for the required heading taken from the deviation card (if any). This will not give the correct course to steer if the wind is such as to produce leeway, or if there is a current or tidal stream setting across the track.

Leeway is the angle between the direction in which a vessel is pointing and the direction of her movement through the water. If a vessel heading due E (90°) has a stiff breeze blowing from N or NE, its actual direction of progress through the water, or its "wake course", will be somewhat south of due E, perhaps about 100°. It will be pushed slightly sideways. Its wake, or a line of empty beer cans dropped over the stern, will form a line stretching slightly on the windward side of the "dead astern" line, because its forward progress line is slightly to leeward of the direction in which it is pointing. The amount (and direction) of any leeway depends on the relative direction and strength of the wind, the type of yacht, and the state of the sea. Leeway is greatest when the wind is from ahead of abeam, in a yacht without a deep keel and with a large windage area, and in a short, choppy sea. It can vary between 3° and 5° and go up to 15° or more in extreme cases. This has to be estimated and allowed for when shaping a course to steer.

A tidal stream or current causes the whole body of water to be carried in a particular direction. A drifting vessel will be borne a certain distance and direction in a given time by a stream. A yacht, moving or not through the water, is affected by the same amount, and its track, or direction over the sea bed, will be deflected from the direction of its progress through the water (its wake course). This, too, has to be allowed for when determining the course to steer to make good a required track. A "tidal vector" will solve this.

However carefully the course has been shaped, the yacht is unlikely to remain on the required track, or rhumb line, indefinitely. This is because, when we shaped the course, we had to make certain assumptions or predictions as to what we *expected* to happen. We had to estimate the yacht's probable speed through the water, the time at which we expected it would be in a particular area of the sea and hence the tidal stream that would affect its progress over the ground, and the amount of leeway expected.

After we have sailed some distance, we may well find that the yacht's speed has been greater (or less) than an-

ticipated, that we have been in a tidal area earlier or later than expected, that leeway suffered is different. If any of these is different (and they frequently are), we shall not be where we planned to be—we shall be somewhat off course.

For this reason it is essential to keep a record of the yacht's progress, and the prudent navigator never neglects a chance to establish his position by reference to any available landmarks, navigational aids, or by other methods. Methods of position fixing will be discussed later.

On a passage of any length there are often periods—sometimes quite long—when no landmarks are visible and the yacht's true position cannot then be determined. It is still necessary to make the best possible estimate of its position, from time to time, using all the available information. A position so found is called the "estimated position" or EP. This is obtained by keeping careful records of what has in fact happened (as opposed to what we assumed would happen when we shaped the course). These records are kept in the log book.

The log book should be written up at regular intervals, say every hour, whenever the course steered is altered, or on any other event which has a bearing on the subject. Every log-book entry should show date and time, log reading (from the log which records miles sailed through the water), and course steered since the last log-book entry. Columns should be provided for entering the direction and rate of the tidal stream being experienced, preferably a note of the approximate direction and strength of the wind, and the barometer reading. A "remarks" column is useful for additional comments, such as sail changes, etc. Only if the log book is kept accurately written up can the navigator plot the yacht's track on the chart and thus establish his EP.

Entries will usually be made in a deck log, written up by the various helmsmen or watch leaders. The navigator will find it helpful if he transfers all relevant information from the deck log into his own "Navigator's Log Book", ruled up so as to make his chart plotting as easy and certain as possible. Suitable headings are shown on page 169.

To plot the course steered, the following is the procedure. Miles sailed on the last course steered are found by subtracting the previous running miles from the present miles, convert the compass course into wake course true; multiply tidal stream rate by time on that leg or tack to provide drift. From the departure point or from the last EP, draw a line whose direction is the wake course True and whose length is the miles since the last entry. This represents the wake course—where the yacht would have gone had there been no tidal stream. From the end of the wake course, draw a line in the direction of the tidal stream, length equal to the drift. Mark the end of this line with a triangle to show that it is the EP, place a reference letter (or latitude and longitude) against it and note this in the log-book column, "Reference". Each line in the log book will give the data for the next wake course line and stream line to be plotted on from the last EP to give a new EP.

Whenever a position "fix" can be found (from landmarks, etc.) the fix is marked by a dot and a circle round it. The old EP is now abandoned (obsolete), and further courses are plotted on from the fix.

Provided we have an echo-sounder or a lead-line aboard, we can ascertain the actual depth of water where we are at any time (provided we are "within soundings", i.e. the bottom is not "beyond our reach"). But this will not be the same depth as is stated on the chart—the "charted depth"—nor does it say what depth there will be here in, say, two hours' time. This is because the level of the water in tidal waters is constantly changing, and because the charted depths are recorded as depths measured, not from water level now, but from the level of chart datum (CD), which is usually taken as the lowest level to which the tide normally falls. The connecting link between actual depth (per echo-sounder) and charted depth is the height of the tide at the moment we read the echo-sounder.

Official tide tables, published annually, give daily predictions of the times and the heights of tide at a number of standard ports throughout the year. They also explain how to calculate the height of the tide at any time between the times of high and low water. The tide tables also list a larger number of lesser ports for which no daily predictions are given. Instead, these secondary ports are listed, and the differences both in the times of high and low waters and of their heights are given relative to a specified standard port. To find the information for a secondary port we refer to the "Differences" section, find the time and the height at the standard port, and apply the secondary port's differences to them.

It is advisable to familiarize yourself with the tables, and to practise working out heights of tide *before* they are needed at sea.

The prudent navigator loses no opportunity to fix his position whenever he is within sight of land and can see one or more identifiable landmarks. Any object used for fixing the yacht's position must be positively identifiable both visually and on the chart. Make sure the lighthouse you see is the one you find on the chart—check its characteristics most carefully. Your pilot book will describe it for day identification, and will give the exact characteristics of its light at night.

If we can see only one identifiable landmark (lighthouse, buoy, beacon, etc.), we can find its bearing from us by a hand-bearing or other compass. Convert this to true bearing and lay off a line from the landmark, the reciprocal of its bearing from ship. (Reciprocal = bearing plus or minus 180°.) This gives a position line (PL) somewhere on which we must be. If a second landmark can be seen, a bearing of this will provide a second position line. The intersection of the two PLs provides a fix. Where possible, select two landmarks which make a good wide angle of cut (ideally about 90°) as this minimizes the effect of any error.

If a third landmark is visible at the same time, this will give a further PL. All three PLs should cross at a point; they seldom do but form a triangle or "cocked hat". If they form a large cocked hat, then one or more of the PLs must be wrong.

If two identifiable landmarks or beacons are seen to be in line, one beyond the other, they form a "transit" (in the United States, a "range"). A line drawn through them seawards gives a good PL, somewhere on which the yacht must be at the time. Their great merit is that no compass is required, so no compass error can arise.

Some harbours have a pair of beacons or transit marks placed in such a position that, when kept in line (in transit) with each other, they provide a safe line of approach. These may be shown on the large-scale chart or be given in the pilot book. Look up their bearing, and if any doubt exists as to whether the correct beacons or landmarks have been seen, steer so as to get them in transit and check their bearing by compass, convert this to true, and ensure this corresponds with that given. If not, search for other marks which do correspond.

Clearing lines are sometimes given on the chart or in the pilot book. For example, "End of pier kept open of black cliffs leads safely past rocks". If one is able to see the end of the pier beyond the cliffs, one is outside the clearing line. If one steers in too close, the end of the pier will be obstructed or shut in by the cliffs. Again, no compass is required provided both objects have been correctly identified. Quite often it is possible to find one's own clearing lines by studying the chart.

When approaching or departing from a coast at night, if a lighthouse light can be seen just as it rises above the horizon (or on departure, dips below the horizon), the distance from the lighthouse can be found very simply. All that is needed is a table of Rising and Dipping Distances (see Norie's, Reed's, or Bowditch's nautical tables) and the height of the light. This is given in feet or metres on the chart. The table is entered with the two factors, the height of the light and the height of observer's eye above sea-level. The table then gives the distance off, to within about a half-mile. There are two important requisites: correct identification of the light seen and the moment when the light itself pops up above the horizon (or disappears on departing). Preferably the "loom" of the light should be seen first. This is the flicker of the light on the clouds seen shortly before the actual light strikes the eye. Only in this way can one be sure that one has not sailed on a mile or more since the light first "rose".

If a compass bearing of the light is taken at approximately the same time as its distance off is found, a good fix is obtained.

On most coasts where there is a lot of shipping, marine radio beacons are installed which can be used by any yacht having a RDF radio aboard. Most marine radio beacons are arranged in groups of six, and are twenty to sixty miles apart. Those in any one group all transmit on the same frequency, between about 250 and 400 kHz. The first in the group transmits for exactly one minute, then ceases. The next then transmits for one minute, and so on till it is the turn of the first to transmit again. This goes on continuously. If you are within radio range, all six can be heard in a period of six minutes. The message each sends is its call-sign (two letters in slow Morse) repeated for fifteen seconds, followed by a continuous note for forty seconds, then its call-sign again. A RDF set has a directional aerial. A ferrite rod aerial picks up a signal at maximum strength when it is "beam on" to the signalling station, and at minimum strength when parallel to the direction to the station. The position of minimum strength (called the "null") is much more clearly identifiable than that of maximum strength. The procedure is: Tune to the group's frequency to give maximum strength signal. Wait for the next call-sign and identify. As soon as the continuous note is heard, turn the aerial to the point where the signal diminishes to zero. This is the null. Note the direction of the aerial then. This is the bearing of that beacon. Some sets and radio aerials have an in-built compass. With these, the compass bearing of the radio beacon is found direct. Others have a verge ring which will provide the relative bearing. This must be applied to the yacht's heading by compass at the time to provide the compass bearing of the beacon. Both require converting to true for laying off on the chart. A good deal of practice is necessary.

Points to watch are: Select from the chart radio beacons which are well within their listed range. Those beyond about half their listed range are unlikely to give very accurate bearings. Bearings taken between one hour before to one hour after both sunrise and sunset are unreliable at more than about twenty miles' range. Those taken by day are more reliable than those at night. Avoid using beacons whose signal will pass over high ground or makes a small angle with the coast—the line may be refracted. Check for "quadrantal error" (QE) by sailing within sight of a radio beacon and comparing visual bearing with radio bearing, while the yacht is being sailed on various relative bearings from the beacon. If these show discrepancies construct a QE card, similar to a deviation card but with error plotted against relative bearing.

Near some coasts there are aero radio beacons. These also can be used if marked on the chart. Their signals differ from those of marine radio beacons, but all give their call-sign, and most transmit continuously.

Marine and aero radio beacons should not be regarded as a primary method of position fixing due to inevitable errors and difficulties but can be used for corroborating (or otherwise) a position found by other means. They come into their own in fog or when no other means are available, but they should be treated with due caution. Their accuracy increases rapidly when at short range—say ten miles or less.

Other radio aids include Consol, a medium- to long-range system (up to 1,000 miles or so). Any radio covering the long wave 940 m (319 kHz) to 1,150 m (266 kHz) and preferably with a BFO incorporated (on some sets marked "Nav." or "Beacons") can be used, but a special chart overprinted with Consol lattice lines is required. Accuracy is not high—positions can be up to ten miles or more wrong—and Consol must not be used for making landfall or for navigating near dangers. Loran-A and the newer Loran-C are much more accurate but need more expensive equipment. Omega is probably the most sophisticated radio aid and is said to provide positions almost world-wide to an accuracy of a couple of miles. The equipment is expensive and requires a reliable power supply. Decca is used by most commercial and fishing vessels and is extremely accurate at short to medium range. It can only be hired, and is hardly suitable for moderate yachts.

A record of all a boat's passages should be kept, both for personal interest and to meet any legal requirements that may arise. If overnight or more lengthy passages are likely to be made, it will be found better not to try to put all the information into one book, but to keep perhaps three books, viz:

1. Ship's Log Book. This is, sometimes, a handsomely bound book in which the skipper enters the main details of each passage, including dates, times, and ports of departure and arrival, names of crew, and interesting incidents. In short, the story of each passage.

2. Deck Log Book. In this each helmsman or watch leader enters full details of compass courses steered, mileage at every change of course, on which tack, sail changes, details of wind direction and force, and barometer readings. Entries should be regular, routine ones made every half-hour or hour and whenever course is altered for any reason. Only if this is regularly and properly kept up can the navigator keep good track of the yacht's position. This book may be entered up by several people—each successive helmsman—and sometimes may not be too well written. While it is possible for the navigator to plot direct from this record, it will be found a deal easier—and more accurate—if he maintains his own personal log, namely,

3. Navigator's Log Book. In this he enters only the information which he needs to plot his courses and track. This information he will extract from the deck log and the tidal-stream atlas (or tidal information on the chart). The book can be ruled up to give this information in a straightforward and logical sequence, with provision for arriving at wake course and tidal drift.

The skipper can enter his ship's log book from the deck log, the navigator's log book, and from memory, whenever he wishes.

A successful passage, be it short or long, commences long before the yacht leaves its berth. The secret lies in careful preparation, most of which can be done days or weeks in advance.

It goes without saying that no prudent skipper leaves his berth unless he has satisfied himself that both yacht and crew are seaworthy and are equipped and equal to the conditions which may be experienced. If the passage could involve heavy weather or be in any way hazardous, the skipper should consider whether yacht and crew are fully up to it and, if he is in any doubt, should not hesitate to change his plans.

Having satisfied himself on these points, charts should be studied, initial or tentative courses or tracks pencilled in, particular care being taken that the proposed track passes any dangers at a safe distance and in ample depths of water. Having planned the proposed track, a passage list should be drawn up, listing all turning points, headlands, and all navigational marks which should be seen, such as lighthouses, buoys, beacons, etc. The skipper should note the characteristics of each, draw the symbol for each buoy, so that these can be positively identified as each comes in sight, either by day (colour, shape, etc.) or by night (number of flashes, colour and period of every light). This saves hunting on the chart at a time when one may be busy sailing. Distances between each landmark or fresh mark will also be most useful. It will make it simple to calculate the time when the next mark should be visible.

Very shortly before leaving, the skipper should check the latest weather forecast and be prepared to defer starting if heavy weather or fog is to be expected.

One has met people who think that the rules of the road at sea mean, "Keep to the right, and power gives way to sail". There is far more to the matter than that. "The International Regulations for Preventing Collisions at Sea", to give them their correct title, apply to all vessels on the high seas and on all waters connected therewith navigable by seagoing vessels. This includes all yachts when in these waters. The regulations cover very much more than "who goes which side". All watch-keeping officers are required to know all the rules very thoroughly, and a competent skipper of any yacht also makes sure he knows, and understands how to apply, the rules. The rules are given in full in Reed's Nautical Almanac and many other books, and should be mastered. They include rules regarding (*inter alia*):—

steering and sailing, keeping a proper look-out, safe speed, determination of risk of collision, conduct in narrow channels;

conduct of vessels in sight of one another, sailing vessels, overtaking, head-on and crossing situations, responsibilities of power, of sail, of fishing, and of hampered vessels;

conduct in restricted visibility, fog, snow, heavy rain, etc.; lights and shapes to be shown, with types of lights and angles of arcs of visibility, by various categories of vessel; sound and light signals, types, when and by whom used; signals to attract attention, distress signals.

It is not enough to know what *you* should do, you must also know what sort of vessel the other is, his probable intentions, and so on. You need to know all the ways in which *you* can call for assistance, but it is equally important that you can recognize when someone else needs help. Remember it is your duty to go to the aid of any vessel needing it.

The rules are too detailed to include here but are readily available. There are also "teaching books" which greatly help one to remember—and to understand— the rules of the road.

A word of caution: The prudent skipper of a yacht, be it sail or power, does not stand on his rights in all circumstances. When on a possible collision course with a large vessel, even if one is technically the "stand-on" or "privileged" vessel, it is wise to get out of the way, in ample time, and by a substantial alteration of course. Always avoid a close-quarters situation from developing, and do *not* be "right—but *dead* right"!

When sailing within sight of land we can usually fix our position at intervals by reference to landmarks, lighthouses, buoys, or other marks. When sailing well offshore, and certainly when crossing an ocean, we shall be out of sight of land for days or perhaps weeks. There are then no land-marks, but there will be "sky marks" we can use instead. These are, of course, the heavenly bodies. The sun is the principal one, because it is unmistakable and is visible (in clear weather) from dawn to dusk. As we shall see, there are other bodies we can use, which are sometimes equally or more useful than the sun. These are the moon, four planets, and a host of stars. The art of position finding by all heavenly bodies is called celestial or astro navigation.

Many are deterred from studying celestial navigation, because they feel it may be beyond them or will be hard to master. There were some grounds for this attitude when sextants were difficult to read and the tables then available needed a fair amount of figure-work. In the last fifty years, the micrometer sextant, which is much easier to read than the old vernier models, has arrived. During the Second World War, new tables were devised to help wartime, non-professional sailors and airmen to work out their sights in the quickest and simplest way, and with the minimum of study. These are called "Sight Reduction Tables". The work is little more than, and rather like, that needed to plan a cross-country train journey from a railway time-table. It involves looking up some figures in an almanac, using the correct date and time, and finding a result in what amounts to a "ready reckoner".

The only instruments necessary are a sextant and a good clock or timepiece. The only books required are a nautical almanac (for the current year), a set of sight reduction tables (which last indefinitely), a notebook for writing down one's answers, and a chart on which to plot the position. For the occasional user, and certainly for practice, a plastic sextant will provide as good a sight as the most expensive, because the degree of accuracy obtainable in a small yacht is usually determined by the motion of the boat.

The books recommended are a nautical almanac for the current year and Sight Reduction Tables for Air Navigation, Volumes 1-3. Reed's or Bowditch's Nautical Almanac for the current year alone can be substituted for all these, but they are rather slower to use and involve more figure-work. Sight Reduction Tables for Marine Navigation (NP 401 in Britain or HO 229 in the United States) can be used instead of the above-named air navigation tables. They are fractionally more accurate, but this has no practical significance aboard a yacht; also they are not quite so quick to use, and more volumes are required.

The same general principles apply to taking sights of any heavenly body—sun, moon, planet, or star—but for clarity and simplicity we will discuss the sun first. The sextant measures the angle (in degrees and minutes) between two imaginary lines from the observer, one to the sun and the other to the horizon immediately below it. This is the sun's "altitude". We need to know the exact time and date when we make the observation, because the sun is moving very rapidly in relation to any given position on the earth's surface. So we need a chronometer or other accurate timepiece (such as a quartz-crystal clock) which records GMT (accurate to within about five seconds). Such a clock is kept on GMT wherever we are.

As when using a landmark, we must know the exact position of the sun in relation to the earth, at the moment we take our sight of it. Our nautical almanac gives us this. Given the sun's altitude and the sun's position at the moment we observe it with our sextant, we can establish our position line—a line somewhere on which we must be. This is similar to the single observation of a single landmark, which also will give us only a position line but not, by itself, our position along this line.

If we are only using the sun, we must establish a first position line, then sail on till the sun has moved a substantial distance across the sky. We then take a second observation and establish a second position line. We transfer the first PL forward in the direction and as far as we have sailed since the first PL was found, keeping the transferred first PL parallel to the first PL. The yacht's position, when the second PL was established, is where the first PL, transferred forward, crosses the second PL.

The accuracy of our position on the second PL will depend on our having accurately recorded and plotted the distance and the direction of the run between the two observations. For this reason, it is a great help to accuracy if we can observe two (or more) heavenly bodies almost simultaneously. Each observation will provide its own PL, and where these cross, preferably making a good wide angle of cut, is our position, without any error in a run between sights. This is like taking bearings of two or more landmarks. If three or more PLs, obtained from three or more heavenly bodies (stars, planet, or moon), all cross at a point or form only a small "cocked hat", we can have a high degree of confidence in their accuracy—just as with PLs from several landmarks taken at the same time. Note that the exact time, GMT, of each sight, as well as each body's altitude, must be recorded.

Having taken a sextant sight of the sun (or other body), how do we establish a position line from it? Consider first a very distant, high mountain. As we sail towards it, it appears to rise out of the sea. If we measure its "altitude", the angle between its top and the horizon we see below it, we will find this increasing as we approach. This increase in altitude is, of course, partly due to our getting closer to it, but also because we are moving round the curve of the earth towards it. (We cannot disentangle these two components without some very complicated calculations.) Now imagine a line from your eye to the mountain top and extended many millions of miles to a fixed point in space. As you sail towards that point, the line's altitude above your horizon will gradually increase as you move round the curve of the earth. If you sail on for many miles in the same direction the altitude will go on increasing until your fixed point in space is directly overhead— altitude 90°. The position you have reached on the earth's surface is called your fixed point's geographical position (GP).

Now go back to the sun. The point on the earth's surface where the sun, at any given moment, is exactly overhead is the sun's GP. A line drawn from the centre of the earth to the sun cuts the earth's surface at the sun's GP, and the sun's altitude there is 90°. The sun's GP is moving round the earth, always travelling from E to W, very rapidly, making a complete 360° circuit every day (due to the earth's daily spin). The track of the sun's GP is also "tracking" round in a very flat spiral, moving slowly more to the N or to the S, and running N or S of the equator depending on the season of the year (N of equator April to September, S from October to March). The nautical almanac gives us the GP of the sun at any moment required.

To describe a position on the earth's surface, we use latitude and longitude for most purposes. The terms used for the sun's GP are similar but are called Greenwich Hour Angle (GHA), which is like longitude, and Declination (Dec), like latitude. GHA used to be recorded in time—the number of hours and minutes since the sun passed westward from the Greenwich meridian, 0°. Hence the term "hour angle". We now use degrees and minutes instead. The sun moves 360° (a circle) in twenty-four hours, 180° in twelve hours, 90° in six hours, and thus 15°

in one hour and 15' in one minute of time. So GHA may be any figure from 0° to 359° always measured westward from the Greenwich meridian, 0°. Declination is the "latitude" of the sun's GP and, like the latitude of a place, is given in degrees and minutes and is named either N or S, measured from the equator. The sun's declination never exceeds 23°N or 23°S (the tropics of Cancer and Capricorn).

The sun's GP is very seldom on the chart we are using for plotting our position, so we cannot plot the sun's GP and work from it. We therefore tackle the problem another way. We choose a position on our chart, somewhere near where we think we are. We call this the sun's chosen position (CP). This position should be within 30' of the EP found by plotting the direction and distance sailed since the last EP or fix. The term DR is often used loosely to describe the EP.

With the sextant, we measure the sun's altitude at our actual position, the latitude and longitude of which we do not know. Then we calculate what the sun's altitude would be if measured at the chosen position (CP), the latitude and longitude of which we know. We can also find Zn, the direction, or bearing, of the sun's GP from the CP.

We now compare the sun's altitude, found by sextant, at the true, unknown position with the sun's altitude, found by calculation, at the CP, the latitude and longitude of which we know. The difference between these two altitudes, in minutes of arc, is the number of miles the PL is from the CP and is called the intercept.

The bearing of the sun's GP gives the direction of a line which, if drawn from the CP and extended far enough (off the chart) would meet the sun's GP. This is the outer end of a radius from the GP. If we measure the intercept in miles along this line from the CP, we have the intercept terminal point. Draw a line through this point at right angles to the intercept and we have our PL. Strictly, our PL is the circumference of a circle, whose centre is the sun's GP, but this circle is normally so very enormous that a tangent to this circumference corresponds closely to the bit of the circumference on which we are. We get this tangent by our line at right angles to the intercept or radius line. We can calculate the altitude the sun would be at, if

measured at the CP, by trigonometrical functions (haversines and cosines), but our sight reduction tables will do this for us with very little effort. For either method, the data required is the GHA and declination of the sun (we get this from the nautical almanac) and the latitude and longitude of the CP (from the chart).

If we are using sight reduction tables, these only tabulate the answer using round degrees (no minutes) of LHA and latitude. We get LHA by applying CP longitude to GHA (add longitude East, subtract longitude West). Choose a CP whose longitude is such that, when applied to GHA, we get a LHA in round degrees. As said already, the longitude of the CP should not be more than 30' from the longitude of the EP. The latitude of the CP should be to the nearest whole degree of the EP's latitude. Thus: *1976, April 22, at 14h 54m 30s GMT, in DR 50°15'N 19°45'W*
From the nautical almanac, the GHA for 14h 54m 30s is found to be 44°01'. Also from the nautical almanac, the declination of the sun is found to be 12°22.4'N, which is 12°22'N when rounded to the nearest whole minute.

To get the LHA, we subtract from the GHA the longitude of the CP, which is the nearest figure which will yield a whole degree to the longitude of the DR. Thus 20°01' is the longitude of the CP, as it is the nearest figure to 19°45' (the longitude of the DR) to yield a whole degree.

$$\begin{array}{rl} \text{GHA} & 44°01' \\ \text{CP's longitude W} & -20°01' \\ \hline \text{LHA} & 24° \end{array}$$

Enter the sight reduction tables with the LHA, the latitude of the CP, which is 50°N (i.e., the nearest whole degree to the latitude of the DR), and the declination of the sun (to the nearest whole minute), 12°22'N. We then get:

$$\begin{array}{rl} \text{Hc} & 47°12' \\ \text{d } +55 & +20' \\ \hline \text{tabulated altitude} & 47°32' \end{array}$$

The sun's azimuth, Z, is 144°. By applying the precepts

printed on every page of the sight reduction tables, we get

$$\begin{array}{rl} & 360° \\ Z = & -144° \\ \hline Zn = & 216° \text{ (the bearing of the sun)} \end{array}$$

That is, the bearing of the sun's GP from the CP is 216°.

If the true altitude, taken by the sextant, is greater than the tabulated altitude, lay off the intercept from the CP in the direction of the sun's GP. If the true altitude is less, lay off the intercept away from the sun's GP.

The sun's altitude increases moment by moment from sunrise until it crosses the meridian of longitude of our position, wherever we are. There, it reaches its highest altitude for the day and commences to fall. If the sun is observed when it reaches its highest altitude, it will appear to dwell there for a few minutes before starting to fall. This highest altitude is its meridian altitude. Observation of this will give us the ship's latitude very simply and without the use of any tables. All we need is the sun's true altitude and its declination at the time (from the nautical almanac). We subtract the sun's true altitude from 90°, thus getting the true zenith distance (TZD) in arc. To TZD, we add or subtract the sun's declination, and this gives us the boat's latitude. (TZD is the same as the distance between the boat and the sun's GP, and declination is the distance between the equator and the sun's GP. Therefore, TZD ± sun's declination = boat's latitude.)

To determine whether to add or subtract the sun's declination, a foolproof way is to note whether the sun is bearing N or S from the boat (it must be exactly the one or the other), then reverse the name (N or S) of TZD, and apply declination. If both have the same name (both S or N), then add; if contrary (one S, the other N), then subtract the smaller from the greater and name as the greater, e.g.:

true alt	66°25' bearing S *or*	48°10' bearing S
from	90°	90°
TZD	23°35'N (name reversed)	41°50'N (reversed)
Dec	14°15'N	12°27'S
latitude	37°50'	29°23'N

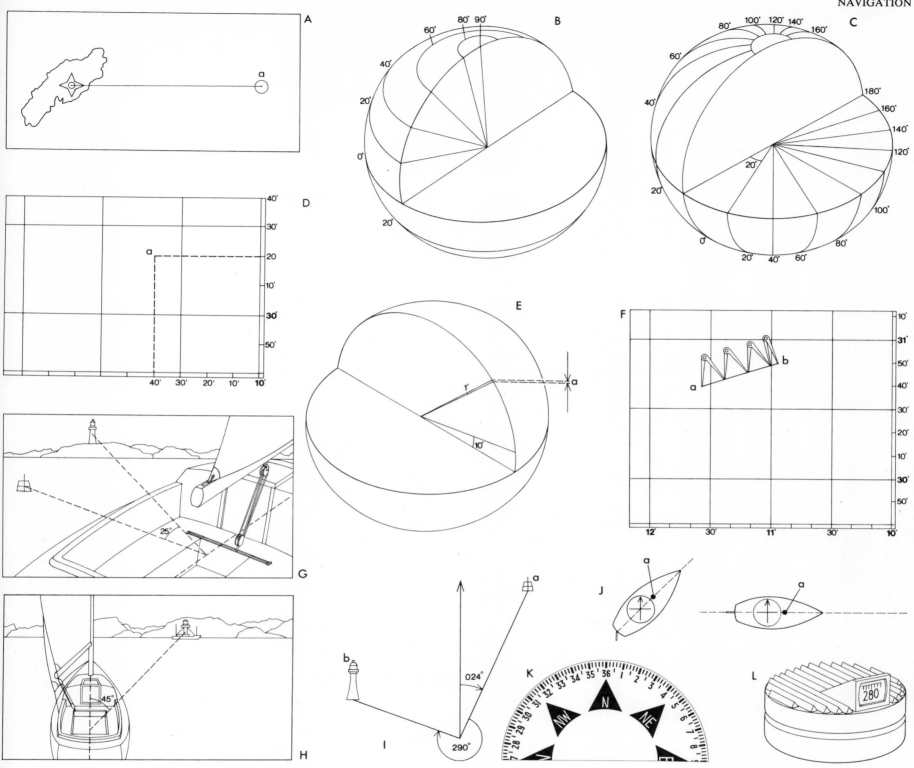

A Position *a* can be described as being a number of miles due E of the island lighthouse.

B The parallels of latitude. All are small circles, except the equator.

C The meridians of longitude. All are great circles.

D Position *a* is 30º20′N, 10º40′W. All meridians run true N–S. All parallels of latitude run true E–W.

E The nautical mile (*a*) is the distance between two points on the earth's surface, which subtend an angle of 1′ (1º/60) at the centre of curvature of the earth.

F On a chart on Mercator projection, the parallels of latitude (horizontal) are spaced further apart towards the nearer pole. The meridians of longitude (vertical) are equally spaced. A straight line on a Mercator chart is a rhumb-line. It crosses each meridian at the same angle. Scale off the distance, using the latitude scale (1′ = 1 mile). The distance from *a* to *b* is, here, 33 miles.

G The buoy is positioned 25º to the left of the lighthouse.

H A bearing expressed in relation to the direction of the yacht's head is a relative bearing. Here, there is a vessel bearing 045º relative, or 45º on the starboard bow.

I The buoy (*a*) is bearing 024º true. The lighthouse (*b*) bears 290º true.

J To achieve the required compass direction (090ºE), turn the bow to starboard so that the lubber line (*a*) moves round the compass card to 090º.

K A white compass card with black notation, marked every 2º.

L A mini prismatic hand-bearing compass.

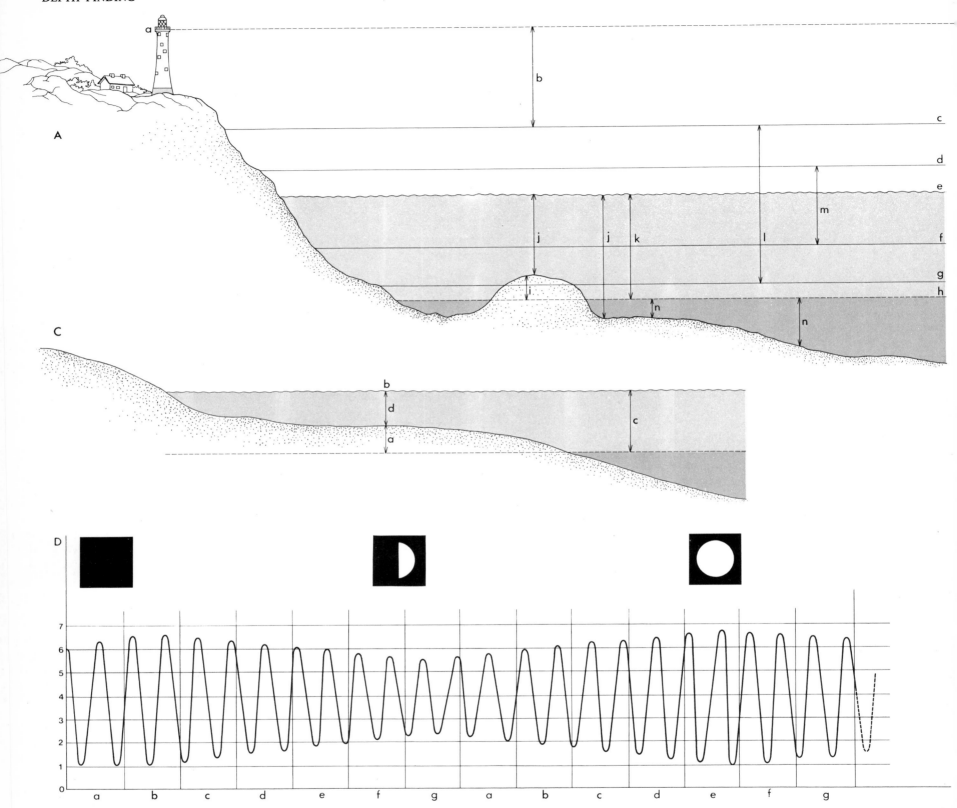

A Charted soundings are all depth to sea bed measured down from the level of chart datum, CD (h). Drying heights are measured upwards from CD. Heights which are never covered (a) are measured upwards from the level of mean high water springs, MHWS (c). To find the depth of water (j), add height of tide (k) to charted depth (n), or subtract the drying height (i) from the height of tide (or vice versa).

To find the height above sea level of, for instance, a lighthouse, add to the charted height (b) the difference between MHWS level (c) and the height of the tide at the time. (d) Mean high water neaps. (e) Level of water at a particular time. (f) Mean low water neaps. (g) Mean low water springs. (l) Mean range springs. (m) Mean range neaps.

B Charts show depths measured from the level of chart datum, CD, which is fixed, usually at the lowest level to which the tide normally falls. The amount by which the level of the water is above the CD is the height of the tide at that time. To find the depth of water at a position for which the chart gives a sounding, one must determine the height of the tide at the time, and add this to the charted sounding. (a) Level of CD. (b) Sea level. (c) Sea level, changed. (d) Height of tide, 2 m. (e) Charted depth, 12 m. (f) Depth of water at b is 12 + 2 = 14 m. (g) Height of tide, 4 m. (h) Depth of water at c is 12 + 4 = 16 m.

C The depth of water over a charted drying height (a) is the height of tide at the time less the drying height. (b) is charted as "drying 2 m". If the height of tide at the time is 5 m (c), there will then be 3 m depth of water (d).

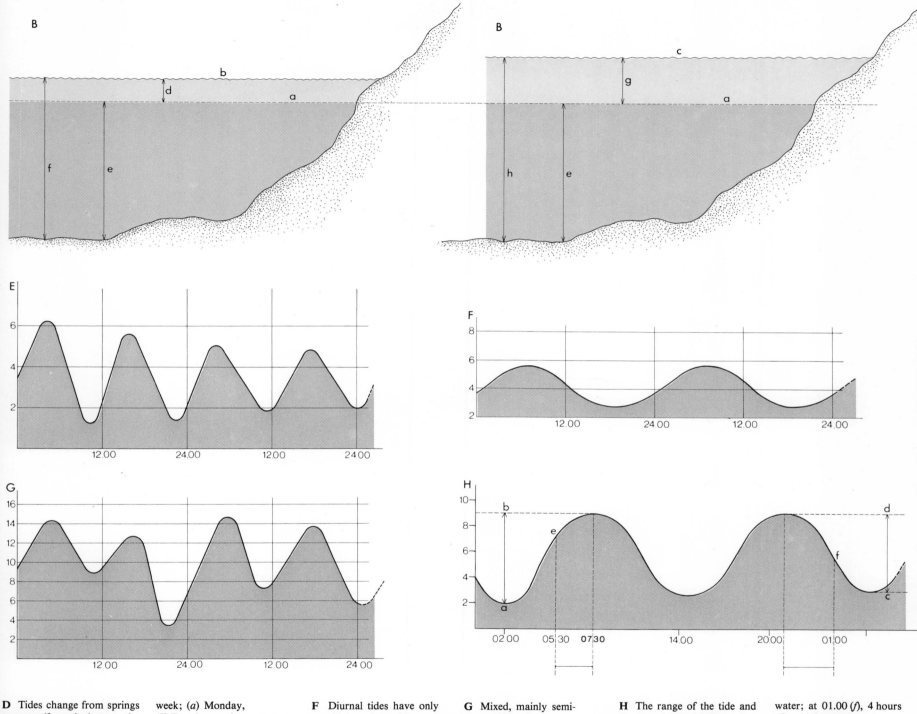

D Tides change from springs to neaps (from the large to the small range on the graph) about every 6½ days. There are two high and two low waters roughly every 25 hours. Illustrated are typical semi-diurnal tides (in North European and British waters). The vertical axis represents height above CD, and the horizontal the days of the week; (*a*) Monday, (*b*) Tuesday, and so on.

E Semi-diurnal tides have two complete oscillations per day. The vertical axis represents the height of tide, the horizontal time.

F Diurnal tides have only one high and one low water per day. Symbols: see **E**.

G Mixed, mainly semi-diurnal tides have two complete oscillations per day, but they have marked inequalities in height and time. They occur, for instance, on the western seaboard of North America. Symbols: see **E**.

H The range of the tide and the time interval before or after high water are the keys to working out the height of the tide at a required time. Vertically, the height of tide in metres; horizontally, the time. The range of the first tide (between low, *a,* and high, *b*) is 7 m, and that of the second (*c–d*) is 6 m. At 05.30 (*e*), the interval is 2 hours before high water; at 01.00 (*f*), 4 hours after high water.

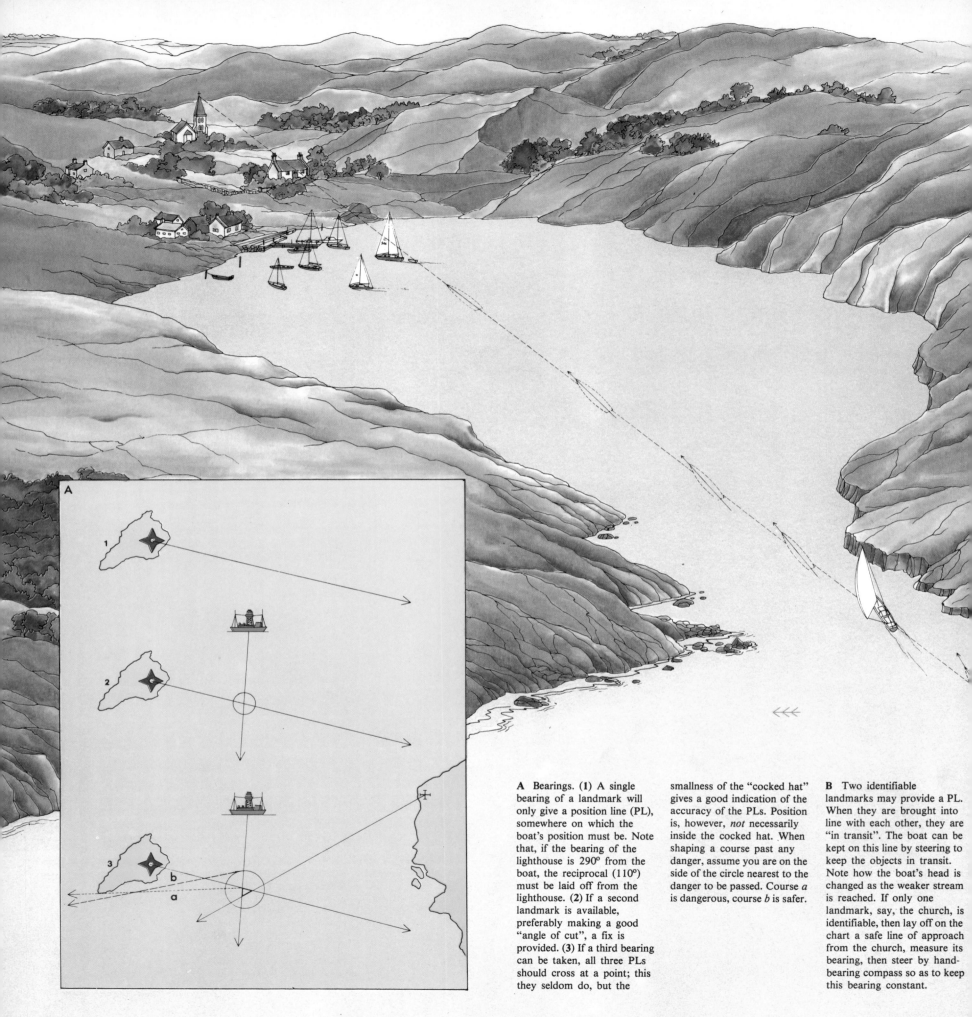

A Bearings. (**1**) A single bearing of a landmark will only give a position line (PL), somewhere on which the boat's position must be. Note that, if the bearing of the lighthouse is 290° from the boat, the reciprocal (110°) must be laid off from the lighthouse. (**2**) If a second landmark is available, preferably making a good "angle of cut", a fix is provided. (**3**) If a third bearing can be taken, all three PLs should cross at a point; this they seldom do, but the smallness of the "cocked hat" gives a good indication of the accuracy of the PLs. Position is, however, *not* necessarily inside the cocked hat. When shaping a course past any danger, assume you are on the side of the circle nearest to the danger to be passed. Course *a* is dangerous, course *b* is safer.

B Two identifiable landmarks may provide a PL. When they are brought into line with each other, they are "in transit". The boat can be kept on this line by steering to keep the objects in transit. Note how the boat's head is changed as the weaker stream is reached. If only one landmark, say, the church, is identifiable, then lay off on the chart a safe line of approach from the church, measure its bearing, then steer by hand-bearing compass so as to keep this bearing constant.

C *Wrong.* If the boat is kept pointing directly at the church and there is a cross-tide flowing, then the boat will not remain on the safe track but will follow a curve, which may lead it into danger.

D When coastal sailing, examine the chart near dangers to see whether there are any prominent features which will form a "clearing line" when brought into transit. (1) Here, if the end of the pier is "kept open" of the headland, the boat is outside the clearing line. (2) Even if there is a cross-current, the boat will clear the danger, provided it is steered so that the headland does not obscure the pier.

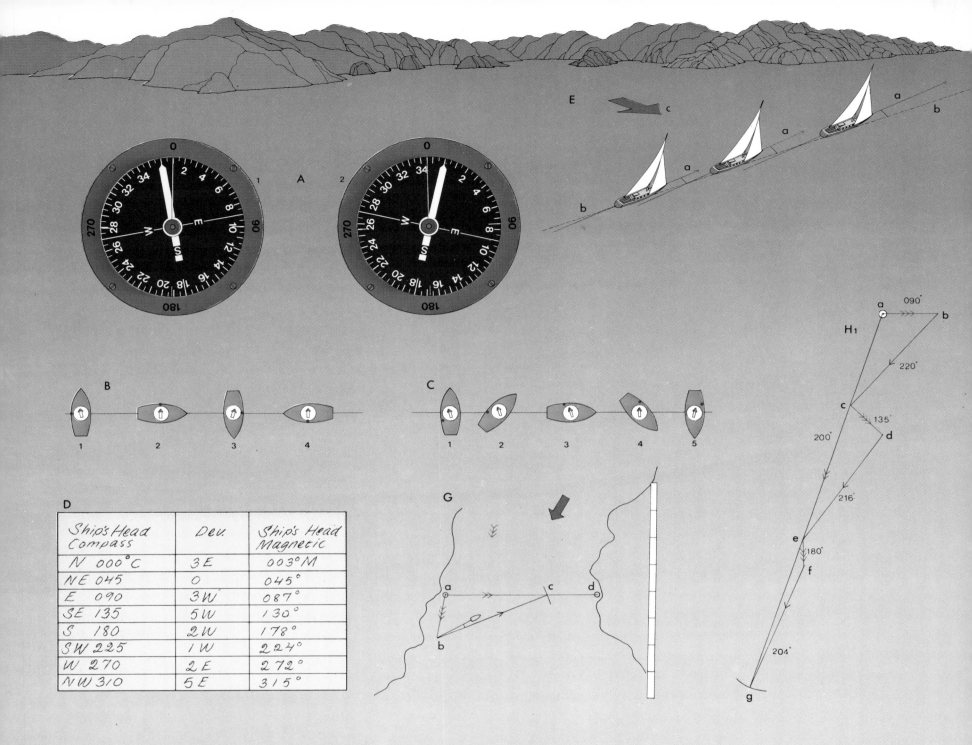

Ship's Head Compass	Dev.	Ship's Head Magnetic
N 000°C	3 E	003° M
NE 045	0	045°
E 090	3 W	087°
SE 135	5 W	130°
S 180	2 W	178°
SW 225	1 W	224°
W 270	2 E	272°
NW 310	5 E	315°

A Variation. The compass is directed by the lines of force of the earth's magnetic field. These lines do not run true N and S, parallel to the meridians (which do), but form "magnetic meridians", which are at an angle to the true meridians, and this angle is different in different places. The difference is called "variation". Thus, the direction of N, indicated by the compass, may be to E or W of true N, according to the locality. The direction and number of degrees of variation are given on the compass roses printed on the chart. Use the variation on the rose nearest your position.
(1) Here, the compass N is 10° to W of true N. Therefore, all compass readings are 10° more than true. The compass is "reading high" or "fast".
(2) Here, the compass N is 15° to E of true N. Therefore, all compass readings are 15° less than true. The compass is "reading low" or "slow".

B Deviation. On this boat, ferrous metal in one of the fixtures is near enough to affect the compass. This example shows the metal attracting the compass N and repelling S. (1) Boat heading N. Metal attracts N.

Maximum deviation is to W. (2) Boat heading E. Metal attracts N but is in line with compass N; therefore, no deviation. (3) Boat heading S. Metal attracts N. Maximum deviation is to E. (4) Boat heading W. Metal repels S, but is in line with compass S; therefore, no deviation.

C As a boat's heading changes, the position of the metal moves round the compass, so the amount and direction of deviation (E or W) varies with the change in heading. (1) Boat heading N. Metal repels S slightly as it is diagonal. There is a small

deviation to W. (2) Boat heading E. Metal attracts N but is in line with compass N; therefore, no deviation. (3) Boat heading S. Metal attracts N slightly, as it is diagonal. There is a small deviation to W. (4) Boat heading SE. Metal attraction is in line with N; therefore, no deviation. (5) Boat heading S. Metal attracts N slightly, as it is diagonal. There is a small deviation to E.

D There may be several sources of attraction or repulsion on board, but they can be resolved into a single

point, which may be anywhere around the compass. Deviation may be eliminated or reduced by a compass adjuster, who places small magnets where they will exert an equal and opposite force to that of the metal. He may provide a deviation card, showing the deviation in different headings. In any case, the boat should be swung and the compass checked against known landmarks' bearings, and, if any of the bearings differs from its real magnetic bearing, a deviation card should be prepared and used whenever finding a course to steer by

compass. For instance, using the deviation card shown here, we can work out the course to steer if the wake course desired were 265°T:

wake course desired	265°T
variation (locally)	+ 6°W
equals	271°M
deviation (card)	− 2°E
equals	269°C

Thus, the course to steer is 269°C. Check whether to add or subtract the variation and deviation by the jingle:
Error West, compass Best.
Error East, compass Least.

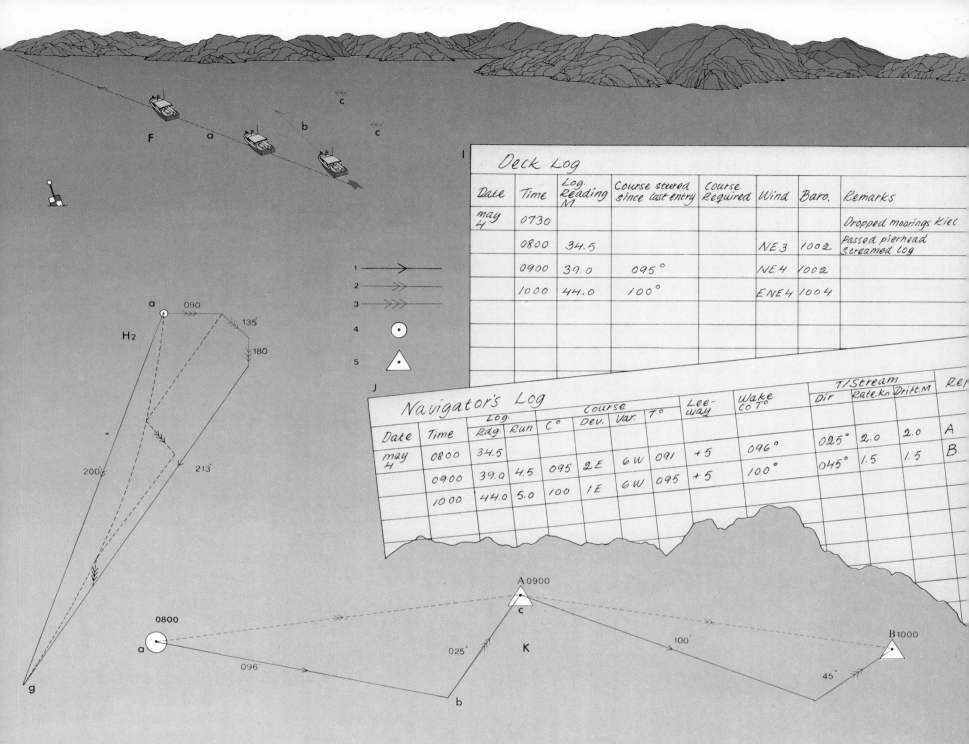

Deck Log

Date	Time	Log. Reading M	Course steered since last entry	Course Required	Wind	Baro.	Remarks
may 4	0730						Dropped moorings Kiel
	0800	34.5			NE 3	1002	Passed pierhead Streamed Log
	0900	39.0	095°		NE 4	1002	
	1000	44.0	100°		ENE 4	1004	

Navigator's Log

Date	Time	Log. Rdg.	Run	Course C°	Dev.	Var.	T°	Lee-way	Wake CO T°	T/Stream Dir	Rate. kn	Drift. M	Ref
may 4	0800	34.5							096°	025°	2.0	2.0	A
	0900	39.0	4.5	095	2 E	6 W	091	+5	100°	045°	1.5	1.5	B
	1000	44.0	5.0	100	1 E	6 W	095	+5					

E When shaping a course, allow for leeway (if any) by making the course to steer up wind of the desired wake course. When plotting the wake course, leeway suffered (if any) must be applied down wind of the heading. (*a*) Course steered. (*b*) Wake course (the direction of progress through the water). (*c*) Wind.

F The effect of any tidal stream or current must be taken into account when shaping a course and when plotting a course that has been steered. (*a*) Direction of track over sea bed. (*b*) Yacht's heading. (*c*) Tidal stream or current.

G To shape a course. Track required, 090°T. Boat's expected speed, 5 kn. Leeway due to N wind, 4° (estimate). Expected tidal stream, 190°; rate, 2 kn. Variation, 6°W. Deviation as per card. *Procedure:* Lay off track required, *a–d*. This is the line required on the chart and over the sea bed. Lay off the tidal stream, length the units of rate, from *a* to *b*. With centre at *b*, strike arc of radius of yacht's speed to cut *a–d* at *c*. Join *b–c*. This is the wake course. (Leeway is not usually plotted.) Determine the bearing of the wake course. To this, apply leeway up wind. This gives the course to steer, 065°T. Convert T° to C° thus:

wake course	065°T
leeway	− 5°
	060°T
variation	+ 6°
	066°M
deviation	+ 1°W
course to steer	067°C

H Two methods of shaping a wake course where several tidal streams will be met. (1) Track required, *a–g*, 200°T. Boat's speed, 5 kn. Tidal stream: first hour, 090° at 2 kn; second hour, 135° at 1.5 kn; third hour, 180° at 1 kn. Three hourly vectors are plotted. Course: 220°T (*b–c*), 216°T (*d–e*), and 204°T (*f–g*). The yacht's track will be very close to the track line required. (2) The second method consists of a single vector, covering the three tidal streams. A single course, 213°T, is steered throughout to bring the boat onto the track line after three hours' sailing. The dashed line shows the approximate track over the sea bed. This saves hourly alterations of course, but should not be used if required track passes near any dangers.

I The deck log is kept by the various helmsmen or watch leaders.

J The course is laid off by the navigator. The symbols used are: (**1**) wake course, (**2**) track (not normally plotted), (**3**) tidal stream or current, (**4**) fix or observed position, (**5**) EP.

K The navigator transfers all the relevant information to his navigator's log book. The following is the procedure to plot the boat's progress from the log book: from the departure point, last fix, or estimated position (EP), lay off a line along the first run, *a–b* (096°T, 4.5 miles long). From the end of the run, lay off a line for the tidal stream, *b–c* (025°T, 2 miles drift; drift=rate time hours on the run, i.e., 2 kn per one hour, 2 miles). Give this EP a reference letter and time (A, 0900). Repeat for each successive run and tidal-stream drift.

Landfall at the end of a day's cruising. The helmsman studies his chart, while the crew keeps a sharp look-out for identifiable landmarks.

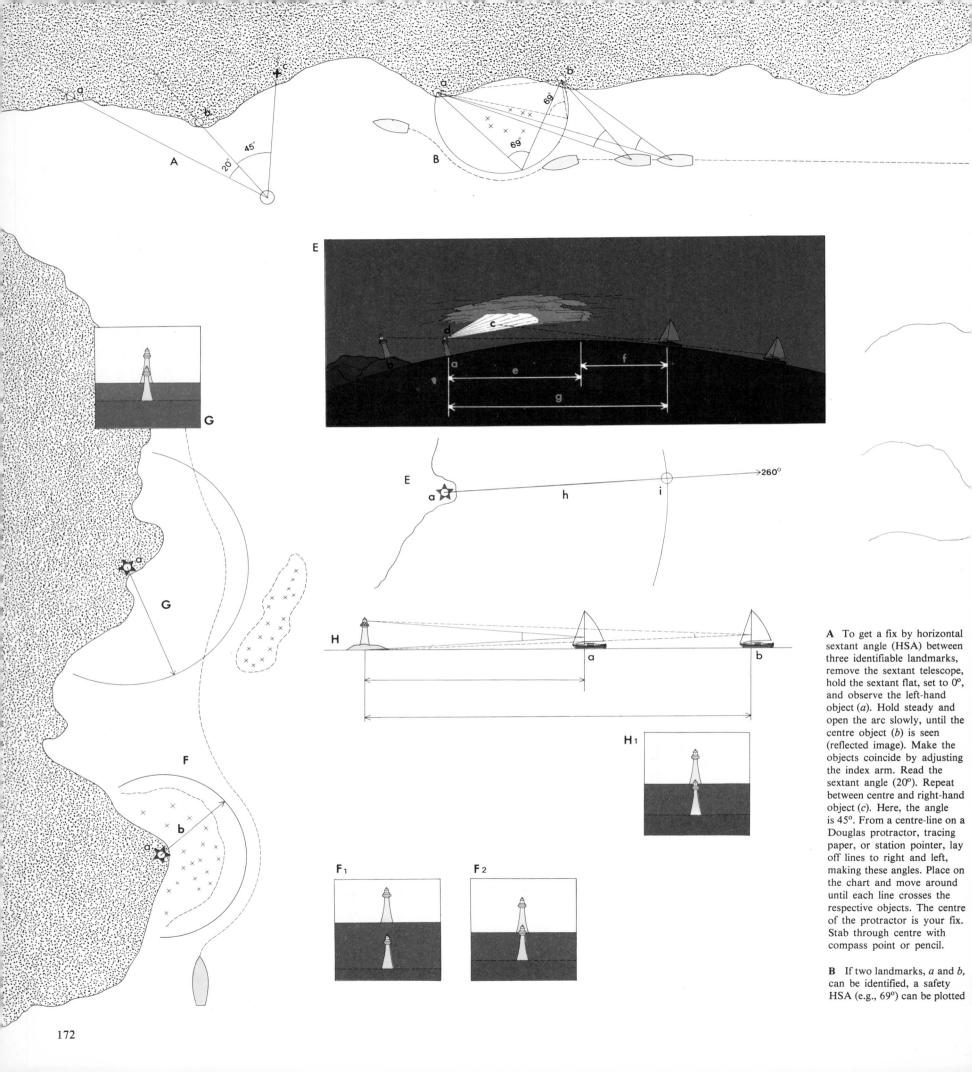

A To get a fix by horizontal sextant angle (HSA) between three identifiable landmarks, remove the sextant telescope, hold the sextant flat, set to 0°, and observe the left-hand object (*a*). Hold steady and open the arc slowly, until the centre object (*b*) is seen (reflected image). Make the objects coincide by adjusting the index arm. Read the sextant angle (20°). Repeat between centre and right-hand object (*c*). Here, the angle is 45°. From a centre-line on a Douglas protractor, tracing paper, or station pointer, lay off lines to right and left, making these angles. Place on the chart and move around until each line crosses the respective objects. The centre of the protractor is your fix. Stab through centre with compass point or pencil.

B If two landmarks, *a* and *b*, can be identified, a safety HSA (e.g., 69°) can be plotted

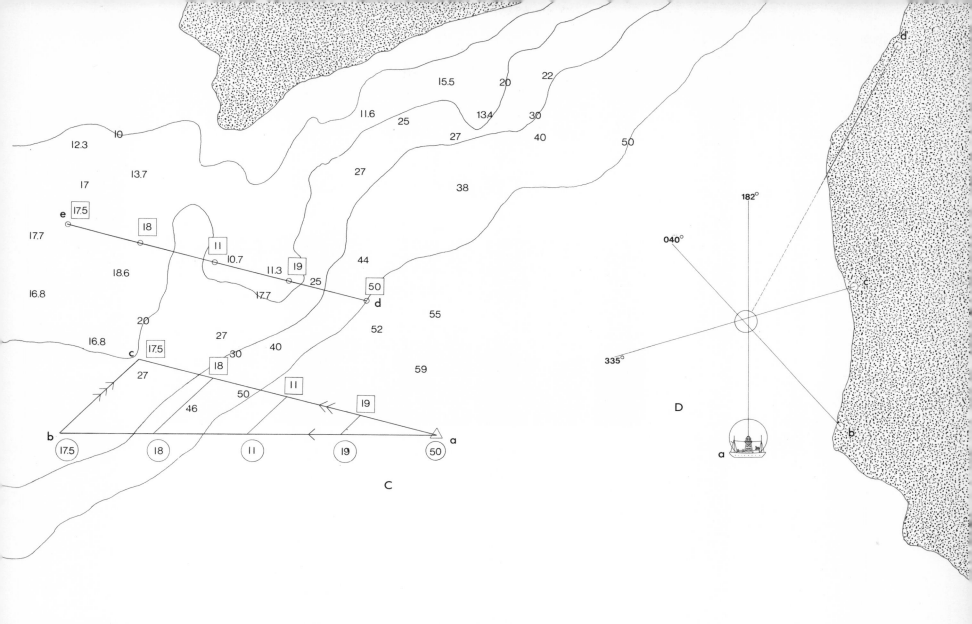

C

D

from the chart and set on the sextant. Watch the objects through the sextant until they coincide, then bear away, keeping them almost coinciding or making a smaller angle than 69° until you are well past the danger area. You will then be outside the circumference of a circle, of which the chord is the line between a and b. All points on this circle make the same 69° angle with a and b. To find the centre of the circle, join a and b and lay off lines from a and b at an angle of 21° (the complement of 69°, i.e., 90° minus 69°). Where they cross is the centre.

C In fog, position can sometimes be fixed by taking a line of soundings at regular intervals, starting at a (DR). Depths per echo sounder are reduced to soundings by subtracting the height of tide at the time. The boat is steering 270°T, tidal stream

setting is 044° at one knot. Lay off the wake course line from a, marking soundings at regular intervals. From the end of the wake course line, lay off the tidal stream line length equal to the drift (b–c). Connect up soundings onto the track direction line (a–c), parallel to the tidal stream line. On tracing paper, mark the soundings the same distance apart as on the track direction line a–c. Keep the tracing parallel to the track direction line, and move around to find where the soundings most closely correspond with those on the chart (see track transferred line d–e). Ensure that there is no other position where soundings also correspond, especially near dangers.

D Radio Direction Finding, RDF, by coastal radio beacons gives fair results, provided that the beacons are

well within their listed ranges, that they are positively identified by their call signal, that the position lines do not make an acute angle from the coast, and that the radio waves do not pass over high ground. a, b, c, and d are radio beacons. d is unreliable, as its waves pass over the hill before being received. A circle of probable position is established by taking bearings on a, b, and c.

E Lighthouse b would have been seen at a greater range than a, because of its greater height. To work out distance off and a fix by the rising or dipping distance of light: when the loom of the light is seen against the clouds (c), watch for the instant when actual flashes are seen on the horizon. The light (d) has then just "risen". Identify it positively by its flashes and period. Enter the table of Rising and Dipping Distances

with the height of the light (e), taken from chart or list of lights, and with own height of eye above sea level. For these the table gives distances e and f which, added, give the distance (g) to the light. The tables give the distance from the light to the nearest half-mile. The same procedure is used when departing from a lighthouse. If a compass bearing (h) is taken as the light rises or dips, a fix is established (i).

F Safety angle. To ensure keeping a safe distance from a landmark of known height (a), for instance, a lighthouse, determine a safe distance off, find height of landmark, enter the Vertical Sextant Angle (VSA) tables with the height of the object and the distance required, and extract the sextant angle. For example, if the height is 120 ft (36.6 m), and the distance required (b) is 0.7 miles, then

the VSA is 1°37′. Set this angle on the sextant. When you are, say, 1.5 miles from the lighthouse, it will appear as in **1**. As you approach, the reflected image will creep up. Before they touch, bear away from the object and keep the images apart (**2**).

G When we are setting a safety angle to pass *inside* a danger, for example, if the distance off the lighthouse (a) is not to exceed one mile, add to the charted height the amount by which the level of the water is below MHWS. This gives the height of the lighthouse above water level— say, 130 ft (39.6 m). Checking against the VSA tables, we get a sextant angle of 1°14′. We must then steer so that the images always overlap (**1**), until we are well past the danger.

H Distance off a landmark of known height can be found by

VSA. Take an observation of the lighthouse so that the centre of the lantern of the reflected image is cut by the sea level below the direct image (**1**). Read the angle, say, 1°8′. Found in the chart or a list of lights, height of lighthouse, 120 ft (36.6 m), is entered in the VSA tables, together with the angle. Distance off is extracted and is 1 mile at position a. At position b, the sextant angle reads 0°34′, and the distance off is 2 miles.

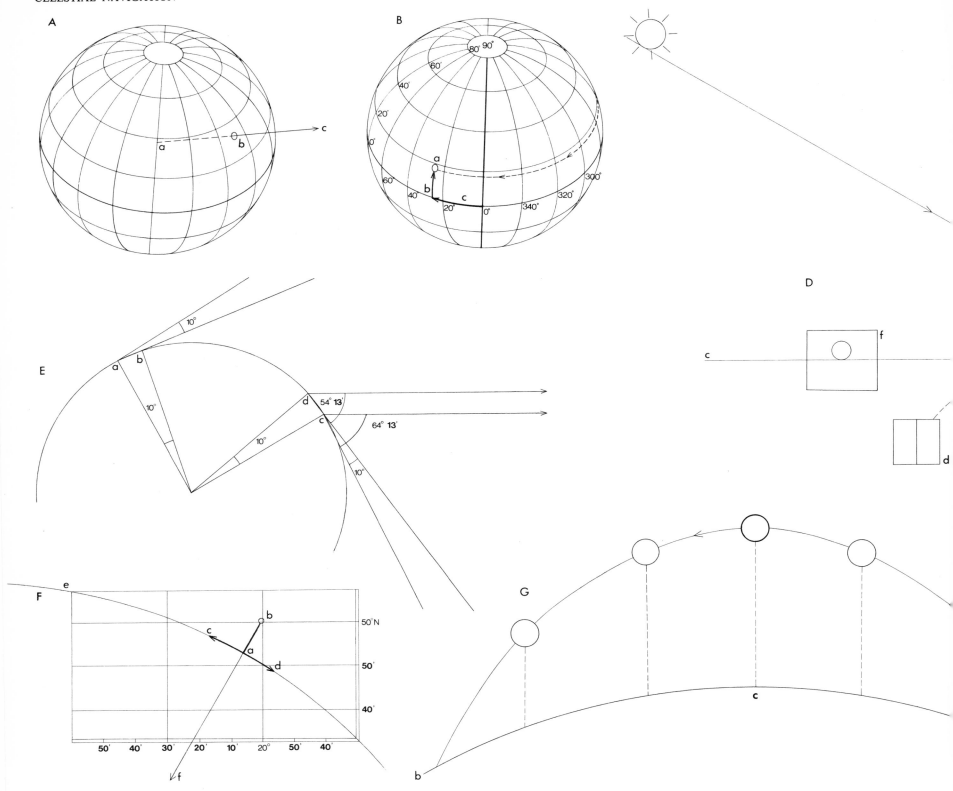

A The sun appears to travel round the world once a day. At any instant throughout the twenty-four hours, there is a spot somewhere on the earth's surface where the sun is exactly overhead. A line drawn from the centre of the earth (*a*) to the sun (*c*) would go through this spot (*b*), called the sun's geographical position, GP.

B The sun's GP (*a*) moves round the earth every twenty-four hours, always westward, and very slowly towards N or S, depending on the season. Its distance from the equator (*b*) is its declination (Dec), which never exceeds about 23°N or 23°S. The distance (*c*) which the GP has moved westward from the Greenwich meridian, 0°, is its Greenwich Hour Angle, GHA.

C The sun's GP is very seldom on our chart, so we choose a position near to where we think we are (*a*). This is our chosen position, CP. Here, it is 50°N (*b*) 20°W (*c*). The Nautical Almanac gives the sun's GP (*d*) at any required moment. Here, it is Dec 18°N (*e*);

GHA 40° (*f*). From this we can arrive at the local hour angle, LHA (*g*)—the angle, or "longitude", from the CP to the sun's GP. Entering the sight reduction tables with the CP's latitude, 50°N (*b*), the sun's Dec, 18°N (*e*), and the LHA, 20° (*g*), gives Hc 54° 17′, which is the true altitude of the sun if sighted at the CP, and the bearing of the sun's GP from the CP, Zn,

214°. We now have the altitude at which the sun would be if we were at the CP, and its bearing from there.

D The sextant measures the angle between the sun and the horizon, i.e., the sun's altitude. One of the shade glasses (*a*) is put over the index mirror (*b*), and you look at the horizon (*c*) through the plain-glass side of the horizon

glass (*d*), which is half mirror, half plain glass. Adjust the sextant with the index bar (*e*) until the reflection of the sun appears to sit on the horizon (*f*). After corrections (see p. 176), this gives the sun's true altitude. (*g*) The arc, known as the limb.
(*h*) Micrometer screw.
(*i*) Clamping mechanism.
(*j*) Telescope.

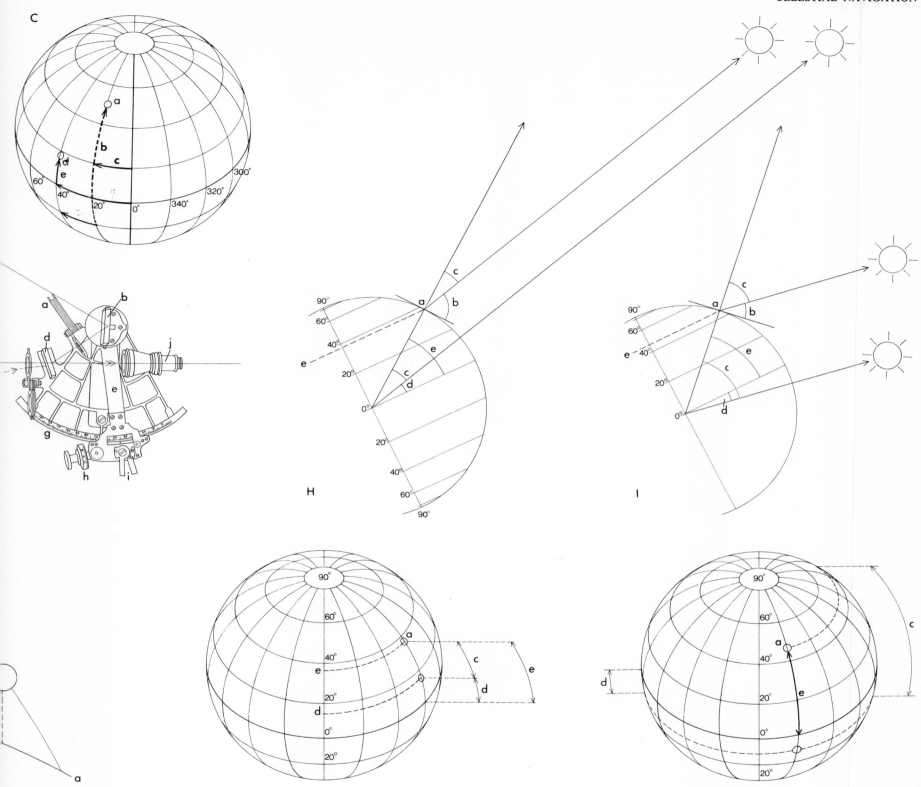

E The horizon seen at *b* makes an angle to the horizon seen at *a*; here, 10°. The angle, expressed in minutes of arc, is the distance between *a* and *b*, by definition of the nautical mile. If the sun's altitude at the true position (*c*) is 64°13′ (by sextant), and its altitude at the CP (*d*) is 54°13′ (by tables), then the "intercept" is 10°; 10° × 60 = 600′ = 600 miles towards the sun's GP.

F Normally, however, the intercept is only a few minutes of arc. Let us assume that the true altitude at ship (*a*), by sextant, is 64°13′. The tabulated altitude at CP (*b*), by tables, is 64°03′. The intercept (*a*–*b*) is then 10′ = 10 miles towards the sun's GP.

If we draw a line (*c*–*d*) at right angles through the end of the intercept, we get a position line, PL. It represents a small portion of the circumference of a very large circle (*e*), whose centre is the sun's GP. True position may be anywhere on this PL, which may be extended either way. (*f*) To sun's GP.

G The sun always rises somewhere towards E (*a*) and sets towards W (*b*). It daily reaches its highest altitude (*c*) as it crosses the meridian on which we are at midday, local time. It then bears exactly S or N of us, depending on the hemisphere. A sextant measurement of this highest altitude, coupled with the sun's declination (from the Nautical Almanac), provides the yacht's latitude.

H Latitude by sun's meridian altitude. At position *a*, the sun's altitude (*b*) is 66°25′, bearing S. Subtract from 90°. This gives us a true zenith distance, TZD (*c*), of 23°35′N (name reversed). If we add the sun's declination (*d*), 14°15′N, we get the latitude (*e*), 37°50′N.

I Here, at position *a*, the sun's altitude (*b*) is 35°00′, bearing S. Subtract from 90°. We then get a TZD (*c*) of 55°00′N (name reversed). The sun's Dec (*d*) is 10°00′S, which gives us a latitude (*e*) of 45°00′N.

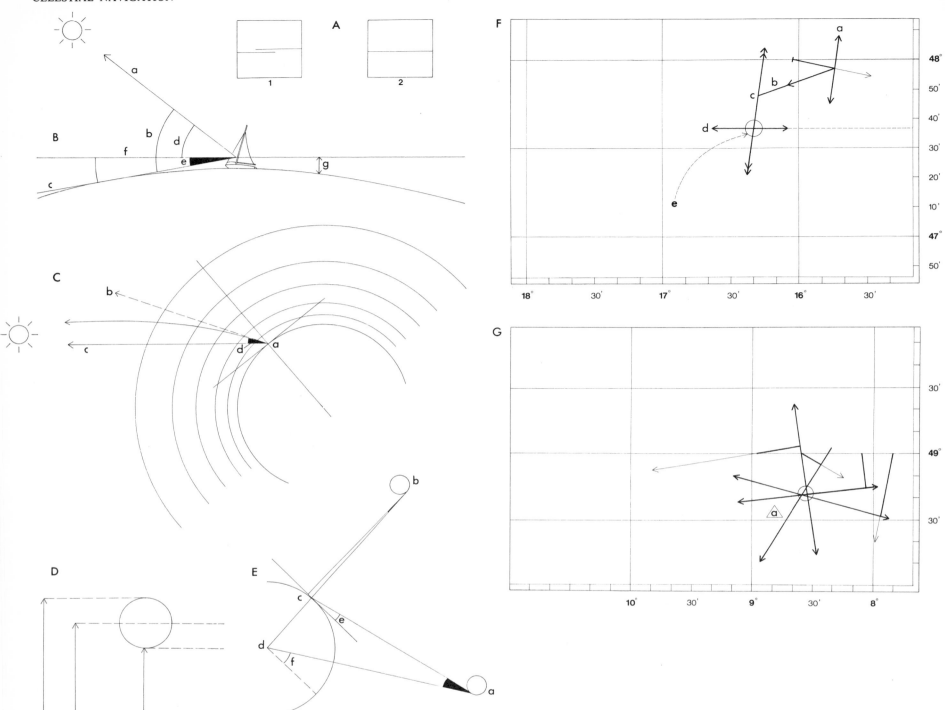

A The angle read on the sextant has to be corrected to arrive at the "true altitude", used for all sights. The index error is found for the particular sextant, and is the amount the sextant is over- or under-registering all angles measured. Set sextant at 0°00′. Sight a clear horizon. If the direct and reflected images do not form a single, straight line (1), adjust the micrometer till they do (2). Read the angle on the micrometer. If the angle is read on the main arc, the sextant is registering high.

Note the error and subtract it from all readings. If the angle is below zero on the main arc, the registering is too low; add error to all readings.

B The angle of dip is the angle between the visible horizon and a line at right angles to the vertical. The amount, always to be subtracted, depends only on the height of the observer's eye above sea level. (a) To sun. (b) Observed angle. (c) Line to observed horizon. (d) Required angle. (e) Angle

of dip. (f) Horizontal plane through eye. (g) Height of eye.

C Refraction is the bending of light-rays entering the earth's atmosphere. It varies with the altitude of the body observed; the lower the altitude, the greater the refraction. (a) Observer. (b) Apparent direction. (c) Real direction. (d) Angle of refraction.

D The sun and moon both have appreciable diameters. We measure altitude to one

limb, usually the lower (c). But the true altitude we need is to the centre (b). The sun is nearest in December and furthest away in June, so the correction for "semi-diameter" varies; always plus when the lower limb (c) is observed, minus when the upper (a) is observed.

E Parallax is the apparent displacement of a celestial body due to altitude being measured at the earth's surface instead of from its centre. Only the moon needs

correction for parallax, because it is so near the earth. Parallax is largest at low altitudes (a) and smallest at high (b). (c) Observer. (d) Earth's centre. (e) Altitude observed. (f) Altitude required. The corrections mentioned in captions C, D, and E are all made with a single correction, given in the Nautical Almanac.

F Plotting a sun-run-meridian altitude. At morning sun sight, PL a is plotted. At midday, local time, course and

distance—the run—taken from the log is plotted (b). PL a is transferred forward to the end of the run (c). Midday latitude is plotted (d). The intersection, e, of c and d is the midday observed position.

G Plotting multiple, simultaneous sights, using, say, the moon, a planet, and two stars. Each PL is plotted from its own CP, which will all be on a common parallel. (a) Estimated position.

METEOROLOGY

K.E. Best

Most of the processes that govern our weather take place within a relatively thin layer of air, called the troposphere, which extends about six miles (10 km) above the earth's surface. Within the troposphere, there are enormous exchanges of heat energy which drive the weather systems around our planet.

The heat energy comes, of course, from the sun, without which the earth would steadily cool by radiation of heat into space. At the equator, more heat is gained by the sun than is lost by radiation, while the reverse is the case at the poles. Nature's way of correcting this potential imbalance creates our weather.

The surface of the earth in the strongly heated equatorial region warms the air closest to it; the air then becomes less dense and rises to the upper troposphere, where it flows north and south, slowly cooling and becoming more dense, so that it sinks back to earth at between about 30° and 40° latitude. Upon reaching the surface again, some of the air returns towards the equator, and the rest flows to higher latitudes.

As the air over the poles becomes progressively cooler, it flows away from the polar regions. When it meets the warmer air from the sub-tropical areas, it undercuts warmer air, forcing it to rise. The boundary area of cold and warm air is called the polar front.

As far as horizontal movement of air is concerned, the polar and equatorial areas are semi-stagnant. These areas, where the air acquires the character of the underlying surface, particularly in terms of temperature, are called source regions.

At the top of the troposphere, the air is always much colder than it is at ground level. This decrease in temperature with increasing height is called the lapse of temperature. As cold polar air spreads over a warmer surface, its lower layers are warmed, and the temperature lapse becomes greater. The reverse happens with air carried away from the equatorial areas; here, the cooling of the lower layers makes the vertical temperature lapse smaller.

Rising air will expand as it moves into the lower pressure prevailing higher up in the atmosphere, and this expansion will cause its temperature to fall. The air will continue to rise as long as its temperature is higher than that of the air surrounding it. These conditions are called unstable. If, on the other hand, the surrounding air is warmer than the rising parcel of air, it can rise no further but will sink to an environment which matches its temperature—this is known as a stable condition. In other words, a greater fall of temperature with height will favour instability, and a smaller will favour stability. Therefore, air originating from a colder region is more likely to be unstable, whereas air from a warmer region is usually stable.

The diagram on page 181 showing the transfer of heat around the world indicates that descending air is associated with high-pressure areas, which normally produce dry, quiet weather, rarely with strong winds. Ascending air is associated with low-pressure areas, where rain and strong winds are likely to occur. Tropical storms are extreme cases of low-pressure systems. These storms develop over tropical or sub-tropical waters when the sea temperature is at its highest, which is why they occur seasonally. A tropical storm is called a hurricane in the Atlantic, a cyclone in the Indian Ocean, a typhoon in most Pacific areas, and a "willy willy" in the waters around Australia.

In the latitudes of the westerlies, the weather is dominated for much of the year by a sequence of lows, which develop on the polar front and are interspersed with ridges of high pressure, thus giving changeable weather. Occasionally, such a ridge will develop into a longer-lasting anticyclone, which produces dry, settled weather for a longer period than usual.

The lows that develop on the polar front are born when a wave forms at the front, and the pressure falls at the tip of the wave, eventually forming a low with winds circulating around it. These winds distort the front even further, so that a tongue of warm, moist air, called the warm sector, is carried eastward. The part of the front ahead of the warm sector is known as the warm front, and the part to the rear of it is called the cold front. The colder air behind the cold front moves faster than does the warmer air in the warm sector, and as a result, the colder air undercuts the warm air near the ground, causing the warm air to be lifted. Where the warm air has been lifted, it is marked on weather maps as an "occlusion". The passing of an occlusion often produces a sequence of weather similar to that occurring during the passage of a cold front. The occluding process normally marks the start of the decay of the low, which will then start to fill. Each of these frontal depressions has its own peculiarities and life span but, typically, it will take five or six days from birth to decay.

The high- and low-pressure areas on a weather map are shown by isobars, which are lines joining places with equal air pressure. Isobars can be likened to the contours on a topographical map, which are closest together where the steepest slopes or gradients occur. The wind is created by the force which tries to equalize the pressure by a flow of air from high- to low-pressure areas; thus the strongest winds are where the pressure gradient is the greatest. Due to the spin of the earth, the air does not flow directly to the low but is diverted to the right in the northern hemisphere and to the left in the southern hemisphere, so that the winds blow along the isobars and are slightly deflected towards the low pressure. The relationship between wind and pressure is summed up in a law stated by the Dutch meteorologist C.H.D. Buys-Ballot in 1857: "If the observer stands with his back to the wind, the lower pressure will be on his left if in the northern hemisphere, and on his right if in the southern hemisphere."

In 1808, a numerical wind scale was devised by Admiral Sir Francis Beaufort; each number on his scale represented how much canvas a man-of-war of the period could carry. In a similar fashion, the modern yachtsman should be aware of how his craft behaves with different

METEOROLOGY

wind speeds, whether he uses the Beaufort force number or the equivalent speeds as a reference.

When planning a passage, the long-distance sailor will have the global wind belts in mind, as well as the winds around high- and low-pressure systems. But the actions of a yachtsman under way will, of course, be dictated by the wind blowing at each particular time and place. Local influences will modify the wind which one would expect on a consideration of the atmospheric pressure pattern alone. Weather forecasts can never include all the variations of wind-speed and direction in an area. A knowledge of the likely behaviour of local winds in a region will help the yachtsman to interpret a forecast properly, thereby enabling a faster passage with greater safety.

The character of the wind depends largely upon the type of air mass obtaining at the time. When the air is stable and a temperature inversion exists, the air is constrained by the inversion, and there is little mixing between the air near the ground and that higher up. When the air is unstable, on the other hand, it will be more buoyant and much more variable. These are conditions under which the racing helmsman under sail will have his reactions tested, while a cruising skipper may prefer to set a constant course, which means that he will not set a course too close to the wind, in case a wind shift puts him in irons. Similarly, when off the wind, the cruising skipper will set a course more broad off, to guard against an unexpected gybe.

Under extremely unstable conditions, and when convection is very vigorous, the wind changes can be dramatic—particularly in the vicinity of showers. The up-draught from an approaching, large cumulus or cumulonimbus can turn the wind through 180°. When these large convection clouds are seen to be approaching, the helmsman can be alerted to the possibility of gusty conditions and may be able to change course in order to avoid the worst of the gustiness. Occasionally, however, showers become concentrated in a line, thus making the resulting line squall unavoidable. The helmsman may then consider it prudent to head into the wind and be prepared to free the sheets.

Obviously, it is in a yachtsman's interest to be able to ascertain whether the air mass is a stable or an unstable one. This he can do by observing cloud types and shapes, which are visible signs in the sky of the likely character of the wind. Intelligent interpretation of weather charts and forecasts can also help in choosing the right sails at the start of a passage.

On many occasions, the strongest winds occur in the middle of the afternoon, and there is often a marked decrease in the wind speed in the evening. This daily, or diurnal, variation in the wind pattern is caused by the changing stability of the air in the lower layers of the atmosphere. During the day, rising temperatures close to the land or sea surface will tend to make the air more unstable and a stronger wind will be brought down from above. Cooling towards and after sunset will have the reverse effect of setting up a temperature inversion at low levels. The diurnal variation is most noticeable when the air mass is generally unstable at daytime temperatures, and when the skies are reasonably clear of cloud, since this will allow greater heating by day and more loss of heat through radiation at night. The diurnal variation is small offshore, where the temperature change from day to night is limited;

it is much more noticeable over and near to land, which responds more quickly to the sun's heating.

A local wind effect that all yachtsmen will have experienced is the sea-breeze, which can be of great importance to the inshore sailor. The sea-breeze occurs when the land is heated by the sun, while the nearby sea temperature is relatively low.

The rising, warm air currents over the land makes the air pressure a little lower at the surface, with a small area of higher pressure at a height of about 1,100 yards (1,000 m). The air flows away sideways from the higher pressure and this causes a minor rise of pressure at the surface offshore, which then causes a returning flow of air on to the land. Thus, a vertical circulation is inaugurated in a fashion similar to the way warm air is taken away from the equator—but, of course, on a much smaller scale.

The on-shore sea-breeze is usually experienced as a modification of the general wind. Since the sea-breeze circulation is small, it can be easily swamped by a larger, more vigorous weather system. As a rule, a sea-breeze will not occur if the general wind is about Beaufort Force 5 or above, because the vertical circulation cannot be initiated.

In tropical and semi-tropical areas, the sea-breeze can occur at any time of the year, but in temperate zones, it is a seasonal feature occurring in the summer and late spring, when the temperature of the land rises higher than does the temperature of the sea.

The sea-breeze effect can also be found on some inland waters. The lakes of North America frequently experience this phenomenon and, even on quite small areas of inland waters, the effect can be detected on hot, sunny days, with little general wind flow.

Since the sea-breeze relies upon sunshine, it is naturally a daytime phenomenon. Typically, it will start during the late morning and reach the peak of its strength in the middle of the afternoon, by which time it will have veered in the northern hemisphere and backed in the southern hemisphere. The sea-breeze fades quickly in the late afternoon and, occasionally, a reverse vertical circulation causes an offshore land-breeze, if the skies are clear. The land-breeze is rarely a significant feature except where the soil of the adjacent land is of a type that will lose its heat quickly, such as a sandy desert terrain.

Although the land-breeze is often a weak feature, another wind which has similarities to it can, in some places, reach proportions which constitute a hazard to small craft. This wind is called a katabatic wind and, like the land-breeze, it is started by the cooling of the land, which lowers the temperature of the air immediately above it. If the land is sloping, the colder, denser air will flow downwards. The wind so caused is most noticeable over water near mountainous country, particularly where the downward flow is channelled through valleys. Strong katabatic winds are often experienced in the Adriatic. Another example is the night-time wind found in some Scandinavian fjords. A katabatic flow can also be caused by the cooling of air overlying sloping, snow-covered or glaciated land.

The opposite of the katabatic wind is the anabatic wind. It occurs when air, warmed by sunheated land, rises up a slope or valley. The anabatic wind can rarely be defined as a separate entity, as it will enhance the sea-breeze which occurs under similar conditions.

A tornado is a local wind of extreme severity. Tornadoes frequently occur in tropical and semi-tropical areas, where the spiralling vortex of very strong winds can cover a path of several miles—the damaging tornadoes of the southern United States are well known. Away from the low to middle latitudes, the tornadoes are much smaller, perhaps 55 yards (50 m) in diameter, and they will occur mainly in the summer in a thundery type of weather situation. They occur only rarely in higher latitudes. Tornadoes should be avoided at all costs. Fortunately, a tornado displays a characteristic warning sign—a dark, funnel-shaped extension which can be seen reaching from the cloud towards the sea, which will have a disturbed appearance. Sometimes, a water-spout will develop and, over land, loose debris will be taken up in a spiral column. Although a tornado moves somewhat erratically, it will travel in a direction similar to that of the general wind.

Up to now, we have considered the local winds that result from temperature changes. Over land and in coastal waters, however, the wind is often changed by topographical features. The main changes that occur to the wind flow are better illustrated than described. From the comfort of an armchair, the changes shown may appear to be obvious but, on a heaving deck, perhaps in bad weather, they can be easily forgotten.

As a general rule, it might be said that air has a distinct tendency towards laziness. Rather than going over an obstacle in its path, it will go round it. Hence the wind will be funnelled through valleys and gaps in mountain ranges. Two good examples of this can be found in the north-west Mediterranean. A north to north-easterly wind over southern France will funnel through the valley of the Rhône, thus giving rise to the notorious mistral. Further east, a ravine wind, blowing through the gap between the Alps and the Apennines, occasionally causes strong winds in the Gulf of Genoa.

When the wind is forced over a barrier, it does not necessarily become lighter on the leeward side. When the barrier is a high one, the air flowing downwards becomes warmer, rather more unstable, and often strong and gusty. This is the case with the föhn wind of central Europe and with the chinook near the Rockies.

Fog is, quite rightly, treated with great caution by yachtsmen, especially when navigating the more crowded inshore waters. Few pleasure craft are fitted with the expensive navigation and radar equipment that reduces to a minimum the risk of collision or running aground.

The weather-wise sailor will be alerted to the possibility of fog when examining current and forecast weather charts, either provided by a meteorological service or constructed by himself. Fog is much more likely to occur in warm, moist air from over warm seas than in air from a higher-latitude source. It is a foolhardy person who takes to the water without first seeking the guidance of a weather forecast, but no forecast will be able to give precise details of the location and extent of the fog. Nevertheless, it is possible, while on passage, to check the fog risk by observation and, also, by taking simple measurements; these are described below.

Let us consider how and why fog forms. In all air, there is a quantity of water in the form of invisible vapour. The higher the temperature, the more vapour can be sustained in the air and, conversely, the cooler the air, the less vapour it can hold. If air is progressively cooled, a temperature will be reached when the vapour condenses into water droplets. In the free atmosphere, these droplets are suspended in the air in the form of fog or cloud, or deposited on the ground as dew or hoar-frost. The temperature at which condensation takes place is called the dew-point. It will vary with time and with different air masses.

For the formation of fog, the temperature of the air must be lowered to its dew-point. At sea, this commonly occurs when warm, moist air is carried over a cooler sea. Indeed, as far as sea fog is concerned, we can say that "when the dew-point of the air is similar to the sea temperature, a potential fog situation exists". In the opposite fashion, sea fog will be dispersed if it is carried over water which has a temperature higher than the dew-point.

Over coastal waters, banks of fog can shift their position with the changes of the tide. Cooler water offshore can bring fog to the beach-lands, while an ebb-tide may take warmer shoal water from estuaries and larger harbours, and disperse fog over the coastal waters.

Inland fog will usually develop at a temperature somewhat lower than the dew-point, because some of the water condenses on the ground. Inland fogs are more common at night and in the early morning, especially with clear skies and light winds, when heat is lost from the ground by radiation. A moderate breeze is normally sufficient to clear or inhibit the formation of fog over land. In comparison, sea fog has little diurnal change. It can form almost as easily during the day, and it can develop or persist in stronger winds—up to about Beaufort Force 6. Land fog that drifts over the sea will usually disperse offshore.

There is one other kind of fog which should be mentioned, although few people indulging in pleasure boating will experience it. It is formed when very cold air, from a frozen continent or an ice cap, condenses the vapour given off by relatively warm, adjacent water. This type of fog has various names; sea smoke, steam fog, ice fog, and Arctic sea smoke are some.

Generally, an intelligent interest in and study of the weather will make pleasure boating safer, more comfortable, and more enjoyable. Many forthcoming general or local changes in the weather have definite symptoms that can be observed. The human eye is the most useful instrument we possess, particularly when it is coupled to an enquiring mind. Every weather phenomenon seen should be accompanied by the question "why?". The answer may not always be known, but the search for an answer will lead to greater knowledge akin to that almost instinctive "feel" for the weather, which is often displayed by fishermen and farmers. The one disadvantage of the eye is that it cannot make a quantitative measurement, and we need a few instruments—not necessarily very expensive ones—to do this.

Any well-found boat will be equipped with a barometer to measure atmospheric pressure. The usual instrument comprises an aneroid capsule, linked to a needle, which indicates the pressure on a circular dial. Traditionally, the barometer is mounted with a matching clock.

For the pressure shown to be as correct as possible,

and thus consistent with weather charts, the barometer will have to be calibrated to mean sea-level. This must be done with the instrument in the boat, which must be afloat; if the instrument is set at a different location and height, and taken aboard later, an error will result. The correct reading to set can be obtained from a local weather office or observatory. The pressure reading at any particular time has only little significance. Instead, it is the changes in pressure that are most important, and so a regular watch should be kept on the barometer. It is good practice to read and note the pressure at every hourly log entry; more frequently, if the pressure is rising or falling rapidly. The pattern of barometric changes can be seen more readily if entries are plotted on graph paper.

A barograph is an instrument which automatically plots the pressure on a paper, revolving over a drum; this is the most convenient method of recording pressure but, unfortunately, it is very difficult to install the instrument so that the boat's movements do not cause the traced record to be too blurred to be useful.

Excellent distant-reading instruments for measuring wind speed and direction are now available. They are rather expensive, but most top helmsmen of larger yachts consider them to be well worth the investment. The instruments are mounted on the mast-head, which is relatively clear of eddies, and they are read from dials mounted in the cockpit, over the navigator's table, or in both places.

It is, however, not essential to have instruments of this high quality. The speed of the wind can be read quite satisfactorily from a hand-held cup anemometer or ventimeter. The wind's direction can be found by holding a hand-bearing compass with a tell-tale outstretched. When the tell-tale is blowing directly towards the observer, the magnetic direction from which the wind is blowing can be read directly from the compass. The readings must be taken on the windward side, and as high as possible, where no objects obstruct the wind.

It is important to remember that the wind thus recorded is the apparent wind, not the true one. When the boat is under way, the apparent wind blows from nearer the stem than does the true wind, which appears stronger than it really is when it blows from forward of amidships, and weaker when it blows from abaft the mast. The wind measured should be, therefore, adjusted to account for the speed and course of the boat, and also for magnetic variation.

As mentioned above, the fog risk at a particular time can be assessed if we know the temperature of the sea and the humidity of the air, expressed as the dew-point. One way of measuring humidity is with two thermometers, one having a piece of dampened muslin around its bulb. As the water evaporates from the muslin, heat is taken from the bulb, thus giving a lower reading on this thermometer than on the other. The difference in the two readings is used to calculate the humidity and obtain the dew-point, usually from a set of tables.

The most convenient way of using this dry-and-wet-bulb method of obtaining the dew-point is with an instrument called a whirling psychrometer. In such an instrument, the two thermometers are mounted in a frame that rotates round a handle—both in looks and method of use, the instrument is similar to a kind of rattle used by some fans at sporting events. Care should be taken that only

clean, fresh water, preferably distilled, is used, and that the readings are made in the open air, away from spray and direct sunshine.

Instruments are available which record air humidity on a dial. These are rarely accurate, and they present problems of exposure and also of calculation of the dew-point, so they are not recommended.

If you use a whirling psychrometer to find the dew-point, a temperature reading is taken at the same time. If not, any thermometer of reasonable quality can be used. It should be mounted in the free flow of air, away from direct sunshine and any local source of heat, such as engines and reflection from decks. The sea temperature is simply measured by taking a bucket of water from over the side and placing a thermometer in it. Make sure that the bucket is not warmed in any way while the thermometer is settling down to a true reading.

No weather forecast can include all the variations of wind, weather, and visibility that can, and often do, occur in an area during the period of the forecast. By sensible interpretation, one can guard against local changes by relating the forecast to one's own observation and experience. It must also be remembered that any forecast is a statement of probability, and although newer techniques and modern methods are helping the meteorologist towards greater accuracy, errors do occur in the forecasts.

If a sailor knows and understands an existing weather situation, he is in a much better position to realize when a forecast is going wrong in some respects, and to make a better judgement on what his course of action should be. This implies knowing what the weather is doing further afield than in the immediate sailing area, and the best way to do this is to construct a weather map. One requirement for the granting of various certificates of competence to the yachtsman, whether he uses power or sail, is his ability to interpret weather maps. The information available to make one's own weather map will vary from one country to another, but the general method is as follows.

First of all, the information has to be gathered in, usually by radio from shipping forecasts, coast-guard services, public service and aviation channels, etc. These forecasts and weather reports are usually broadcast at normal speaking pace, so that the recipient must be prepared to write quickly. This task is made easier if a shorthand form is evolved. It must be unambiguous to the user, who should not vary the abbreviation conventions he has adopted. The internationally-agreed meteorological symbols can be used with advantage. Until some expertise is acquired in taking down the information manually, a tape-recorder can be used, so helping to guard against information being missed. The weather reports are then plotted on a chart, again using some of the international symbols. Using the plotted information, the isobars are drawn and the fronts marked in. It is advisable to use a soft pen for drawing, and an ink or ball-pen for plotting, because many of the lines will have to be rubbed out and adjusted. There is no shame in having to do this. A professional weather forecaster will use a rubber almost as much as a pencil. In many countries it is now possible to obtain charts for making your own weather map.

Of the various weather hazards that affect the yachtsman

and his decision-making, strong winds probably concern him more frequently than anything else. But it is not the wind that represents the main danger (except, perhaps, to the dinghy sailor, who risks capsizal due to windage), but the rough water it causes. The guide to sea conditions given in the Beaufort table is only a rough indication of the effects of the complex interaction that takes place between wind and water. The subject is not fully understood, but with some understanding of what is happening to the water, the yachtsman may be able to seek areas where the motion of the water is less of a menace.

The waves that are generated by the wind in the immediate area of a specific place, say, within a radius of 150 miles, are called wind waves. These small waves increase with a strengthening wind and die down when the wind has abated. A water surface is rarely completely smooth, but when it is, ripples will form as soon as any wind springs up; for no wind is constant, and its variations in speed and direction will impose pressure differences on the water surface. Once a ripple exists, a freshening wind will increase the air pressure on the windward side of the ripple, and a slight suction effect will be created on the leeward side. As the wind becomes stronger, the pressure differences will increase, and waves will develop, become higher, and move in the same direction as the wind. A wave system takes a certain time to develop, and it will only develop fully if the wind is carrying the waves over a longer distance, or fetch. For instance, a thirty-knot wind blowing for twelve hours will produce waves 10 ft (c. 3 m) high over an oceanic fetch of about 150 miles, but the same wind over a shorter sea passage of 50 miles is unlikely to make waves of more than 3 ft (c. 1 m). So, to the mariner, "sheltered water" often means shelter from a long fetch rather than shelter from the wind, and this, as we shall see, may not necessarily mean inshore waters.

There is a certain amount of lore attached to wave formation and, sometimes, dogmas are heard like "every tenth wave is a high one". Although such statements are not accurate, there is, nevertheless, a tendency for waves to collect in groups—perhaps three high waves followed by four shorter ones. When sailing in rough water, it is worth trying to establish the wave-group pattern before changing course, especially if the waves are steep and the manoeuvre entails going beam-on to the waves.

In the open sea, after a reasonably constant wind, waves will advance in a sequence of well-defined lines. Near coasts, however, the pattern is often more confused. One of the reasons for this is the effect of the shallower inshore water, which will shorten the wave-length and slow the wave down. This means that the line of the waves becomes curved or refracted by, perhaps, as much as 90° from its original orientation. The situation can arise where lines of waves approach an island and become curved as they pass the land. By the time the wave lines have passed the island, those inshore on either side have been bent to such an extent that, once they are clear of the land, they will approach each other, which leads to a very confused and sometimes violent sea, but usually only in a limited area. Therefore, it is not necessarily safe to assume that a boat will find shelter everywhere on the leeward side of an island.

Another very important effect is caused by shallower water. The wave motion on the surface also occurs throughout the water, although it diminishes further down, so that, in deep water, the motion is very small towards the bottom. However, in the shallows, there is insufficient depth of water to absorb the energy of the waves, and this energy is transmitted upwards, thus causing a marked steepening of the waves. This is why shoal water and sand bars often have turbulent water with broken crests over

them; they should always be approached with a certain caution.

When waves have been formed and a tidal or other current is flowing, a stream of flow exists, similar to the air-flow above the water. When the direction of the current is opposite that of the waves, the pressure and suction areas are reinforced, so that the waves are higher than they would be if they were caused by the wind alone. Conversely, the waves are made smaller when they are travelling in the same direction as the current. Naturally, this effect is most marked where the current is strongest —for instance, in a tide race.

Large waves are sometimes found, especially in tropical waters, when there is little or no wind. To mark the difference between these and the wind waves, this phenomenon is called "swell". However, like wind waves, swell is also caused by the wind—a wind of considerable strength, blowing from the same direction for a long time. The waves that are caused do not readily die down; they will often travel for thousands of miles, before being finally destroyed when they pound against a distant shore.

On its own, swell has a different appearance to wind waves; it has a smoother, more rounded look. The crest lines are longer, as is the wave-length. Swell also has a greater inclination than wind waves to form into wave groups. Another feature is its persistance; if it moves into an area of strong, opposing winds, it will be reluctant to decay, even if wind waves become imposed on it.

We have looked briefly at how waves are formed, and at some of the most important processes that modify them. Remember that any combination of these processes may occur on any one occasion. For instance, a wind of only Force 5 could make very rough water, should the waves it caused run over a bar in opposition to a strong ebb tide.

This diagram shows the general circulation in the earth's troposphere—how warm air is carried away from equatorial areas and how cool air flows away from the poles. The vertical scale of movement of the air is, of course, greatly exaggerated.

Enormous exchanges of heat energy take place within the troposphere, that part of the earth's atmosphere within which most of our weather processes take place. The troposphere is about 5 miles (8 km) high at the poles and about 10 miles (16 km) high at the equator. (a) Cold air. (b) Warm air. (c) Polar high. (d) Polar easterlies. (e) Lows in the travelling westerlies. (f) Westerlies. (g) Sub-tropical high pressures. (h) North-east trade winds. (i) Equatorial lows (doldrums). (j) South-east trade winds.

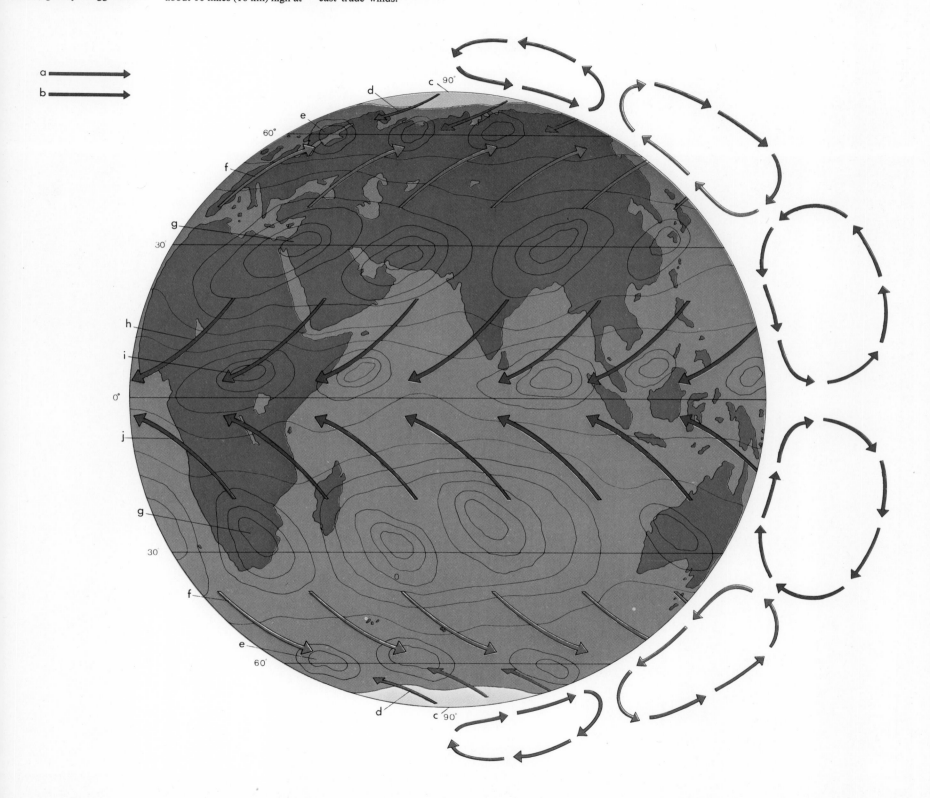

A

C

B

A Cumulus. This cloud has a characteristic, heaped appearance and occurs when the air mass is unstable. At this stage, there is insufficient vertical development to produce showers or gusty conditions, but if this type of cloud is rapidly growing, it may develop into a cumulonimbus, with the rapid wind shifts that the larger convective cloud often produces (see **F**).

B Cirrus. A high, wispy cloud which may be the forerunner of bad weather. The strong winds in the upper air, which are twisting the cloud into "mare's tails", may be quickly bringing a depression or frontal system nearer. If the cirrus is seen to thicken and lower to cirrostratus (**C**), this is added evidence that bad weather could be on its way.

C Cirrostratus. Another high-cloud type, which is stratiform (layered). This cloud frequently causes a halo round the sun or moon. The halo is a good, but not invariable, indicator of approaching bad weather. The solar halo can be seen more easily with sun glasses, which make all cloud observation in bright light easier—never scan a bright sky through binoculars!

D Altostratus, a layered cloud at medium levels, and below it, stratocumulus, which is a low-cloud type. This sky scene could well be a progression from cirrostratus. Along with his personal observations of wind and pressure changes, the sailor can confirm and monitor the approach of a depression or frontal system which weather charts and forecasts have indicated.

E Stratus. A very low, layered cloud; sometimes low enough, as in this case, to cover high ground. This is typical of conditions found after the passage of a warm front, the air being moist and stable. Visibility is rarely good, and rain or drizzle will further reduce it, while sea fog commonly occurs. Stratus is sometimes formed from fog which has been lifted by the turbulent action of the wind.

F Cumulonimbus. The extent of vertical development shows that strong convection is taking place in unstable air. The wind will be variable, especially near showers like the one seen falling on the right, and sudden, strong gusts should be anticipated. The cloud on the left has the anvil-shaped cap of cirrus often associated with thundery weather.

A When air from a cold source (*a*) is carried over a warmer surface, its lower layers are warmed, thus increasing the rate of fall of temperature with height (*b*). The air is unstable when an upward movement, given to the air, is continued (*c*). The air cools as it rises, but in spite of this, it is still warmer and less dense than its surroundings, so the upward movement continues. Vertical axis: height. Horizontal axis: temperature.

B Stable conditions develop in the opposite fashion to unstable conditions. The warm air (*a*) is being modified as its lower layers are cooled (*b*). If a parcel of air is moved upwards (*c*), it will cool, but then, as it is colder and more dense than its environment, it will tend to return to its original position. In the inversion in the lowest layers (*d*), low cloud and poor visibility are often found. Vertical axis: height. Horizontal axis: temperature.

I The first sign of the approach of a warm front is usually thickening cirrus cloud, often with a solar halo (**1**). After that, the cloud lowers and thickens even further, and this is usually accompanied by a gradual backing of the wind in the northern hemisphere and a veering in the southern. Often, there is not a lot of rain,

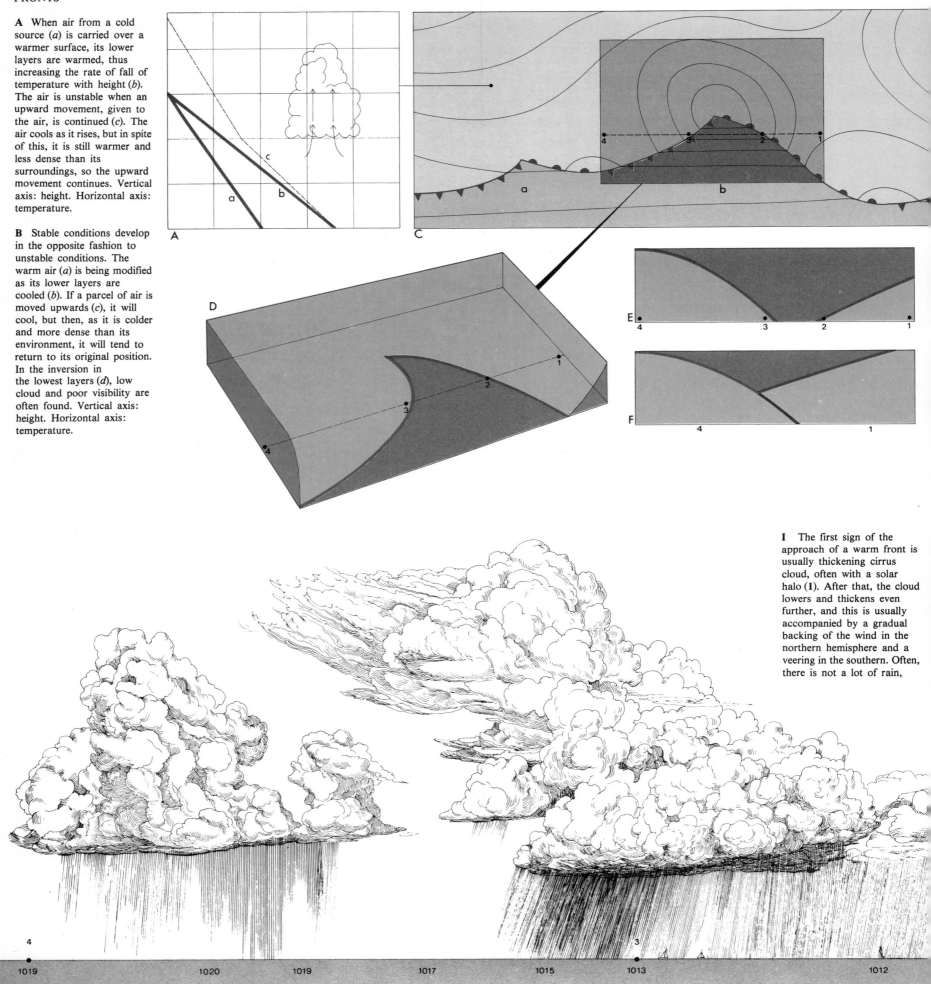

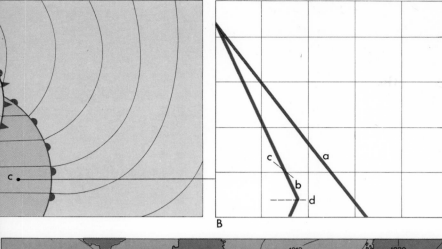

B

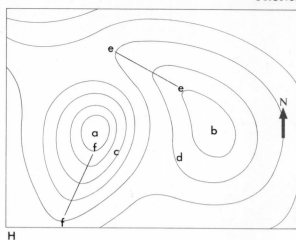

H

C A "family" of depressions on the polar front in the northern hemisphere, each at a different stage of development. The polar front marks the boundary between cold air to the north and warmer air to the south. At *a*, a small wave has developed on the front and, typically, will grow into a depression such as the well-formed and active one seen at *b*. At *c*, an occlusion (*d*) has formed; usually, a depression starts to decay after this. The points marked **1, 2, 3,** and **4** represent the same parts of the depression in illustrations **C, D, E, F,** and **I.**

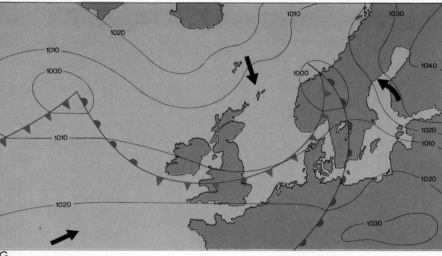

G

D At the surface, the warm front (**2**) marks the forward boundary of the warm sector, and the cold front (**3**) the rear. The air within the warm sector fans out aloft, because it is warmer and less dense than the surrounding air.

E This cross section of a warm sector exaggerates the slope of the fronts. The slope on a warm front is typically 1:200 to 1:300 and on a cold front 1:80 to 1:150.

F When the cold air undercuts the warm sector, an occlusion is formed.

G A warm front is approaching Scandinavia, Denmark, and Germany, while the present depression moves NE through the Norwegian Sea. The cold front is trailing behind in mid-Atlantic, where there is a small wave on it. If a depression develops from this wave, it could well take a similar track to its predecessor, in which event the front would move NE over Great Britain as a warm front, and the cold front would be greatly delayed in reaching France, Denmark, and Germany.

H Isobars are lines joining places with the same mean sea-level pressure, thus showing the location of lows or depressions (*a*) and highs or anticyclones (*b*). Since the strength of the wind depends mainly upon the pressure gradient (shown by the distance between the isobars), the wind will be much stronger at *c* than at *d*. According to Buys-Ballot's law, the winds at *c* and *d* will be between SE and S in the northern hemisphere and between NNE and NE in the southern hemisphere. (*e–e*) Ridge. (*f–f*) Trough.

except near the front itself (**2**). After the front has passed, the wind veers, or backs. Behind the front, one should always be prepared for fog.

If the warm sector is a wide one and the preceding warm front is weak, the cloud may break but will thicken again as the cold front approaches. A cold front (**3**) often passes with heavy rain and squalls, and with a sharp change of wind direction (veering in the northern hemisphere, backing in the southern). In the showery weather after the front has passed (**4**), it is normal to experience a marked improvement of visibility. Atmospheric pressures in millibars are given at the bottom of the illustration.

1012   1012   1013   1015   1017   1   1019

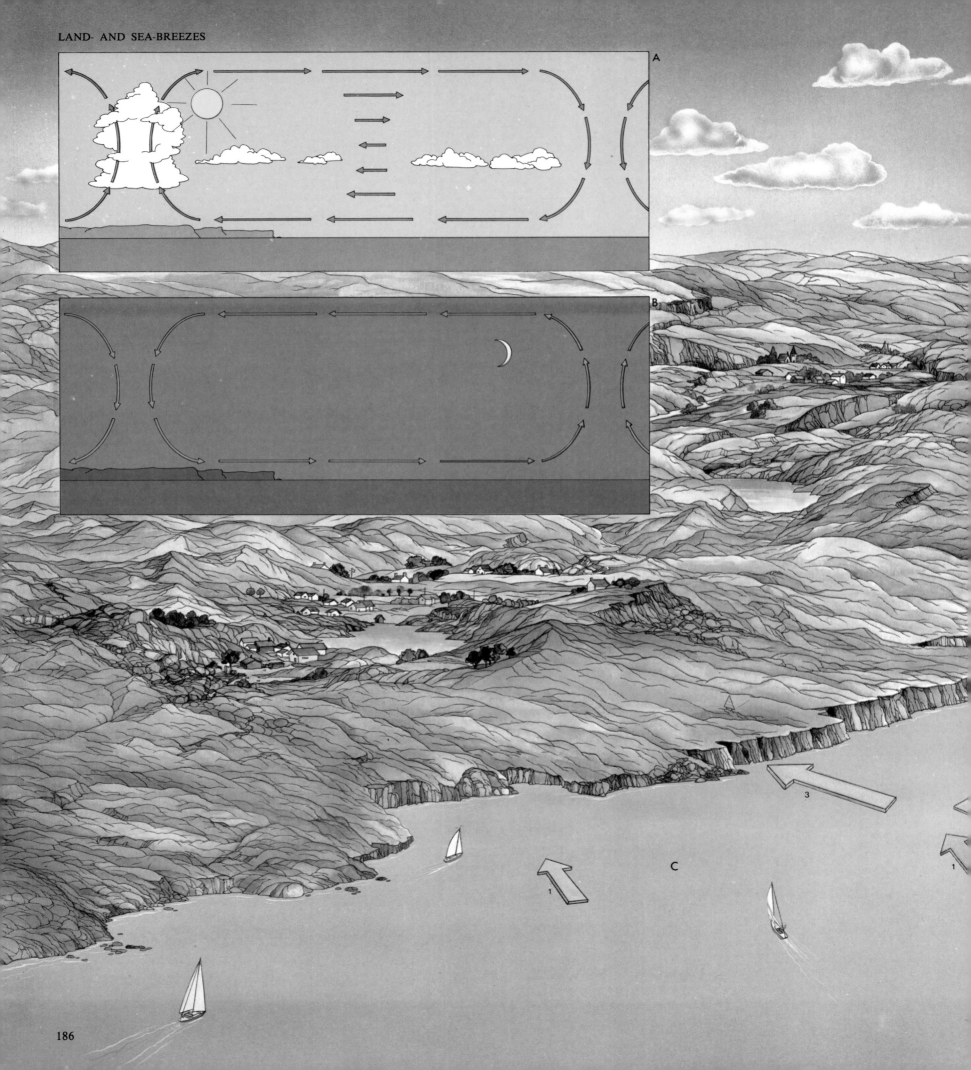

A How the sun-heated land inaugurates a sea-breeze circulation. When the land is strongly heated by the sun, the air close to the land is warmed and rises. Air from over the relatively cooler water will then flow landwards to replace it.

Composed of the wind flow around major pressure systems, the sea-breeze circulation is a weak one and will be destroyed if the general wind is about Beaufort Force 5 or above. Cumulus cloud often develops over land at the edge of the sea-breeze, which will tend to encroach inland during the day.

B The night-time land-breeze is caused by the reverse process. It occurs when the land cools under clear skies and the general wind is light. The land-breeze is usually much less noticeable than the sea-breeze, but the yachtsman should be alert to the possibility of a strong wind off the land, due to katabatic effects.

C The sea-breeze is usually experienced as a modifying effect on the general wind at the time. Here, the on-shore sea-breeze (**1**) sets in from SE, thus changing the general wind (**2**), which is E, to a

stronger ESE wind (**3**). If the general wind has a NNW direction (**4**), the sea-breeze (**1**) will transform it to a much lighter, NE wind (**5**).

D Within and below a cumulonimbus cloud, there are vigorous up- and downward currents, which cause the wind to be gusty and variable in direction in the vicinity of the cloud. Strong down-draughts often fan out from the cloud, particularly where showers are falling. An upward current towards an advancing cloud may give the impression that the cloud is moving against the wind.

A When air cools over land at night, it becomes more dense and will flow to a lower level, if the topography allows it to do so. This flow of air is called a katabatic wind. It is most noticeable where a deep valley opens onto the water, and when the land is cooling under clear skies with little general wind. The effect is enhanced if the land is snow- or ice-covered.

B Because the air is reluctant to rise over a barrier in its path, a wind blowing towards a river mouth will be squeezed between the land on either side of the entrance, and this often leads to a stronger wind. As the wind blows up the river or estuary, it will tend to be constrained between the shore lines, which usually come closer together, and the funnelled wind could well be stronger up river than out at sea.

C The temptation to take a short cut into a harbour or estuary by sailing close to a headland should be resisted. In addition to possible hazards such as outcrops of rock and stronger currents, squeezing of the air-flow is also frequently experienced. Under the lee of the promontory, there will almost certainly be a patch of lighter wind, but the wind may possibly be blowing from the opposite direction at one point where it is part of a horizontally circular eddy (**1**).

D When the wind is forced to rise over a barrier, lighter winds are often found close by, but possibly with vertically circular wind eddies (**1**). No wise sailor will seek those lighter winds with land under his lee, because it may be difficult to sail off again.

The distance from land where the lighter winds occur depends largely upon the wind strength, but as a general rule, the distance will be ten to twenty times the height of the barrier.

E Waves at sea travel in the general direction of the wind that caused them, the water

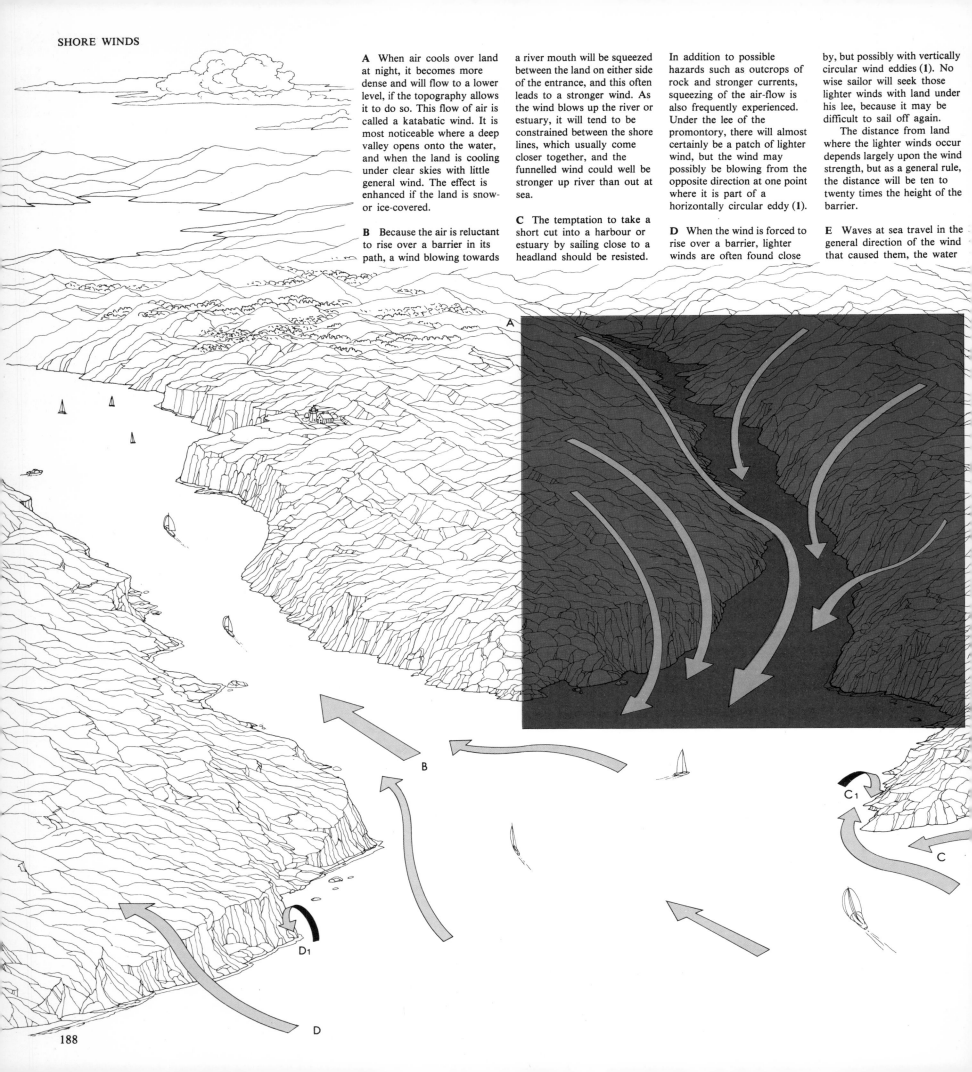

itself making little progress. Thus, waves may be likened to a stretched-out rope, which is given an upward flick—a wave travels along the rope, which itself does not move forward. Each particle of water describes a circular path, the circles diminishing lower down, with no motion at the bottom of deep water. (1) In shallow water, the surface wave energy cannot be absorbed in this way, and breakers result.

F As waves approach land and shallow water, the wavelength decreases and the speed of the waves becomes less. As a result, the lines of waves shown here become curved when travelling on separate sides of the island, so that, off the western end of the island, two sets of waves are approaching each other, causing a confused sea. Over the shallows to the south of the island, tumbling seas can frequently be expected even in calm weather, if the tide is running strongly.

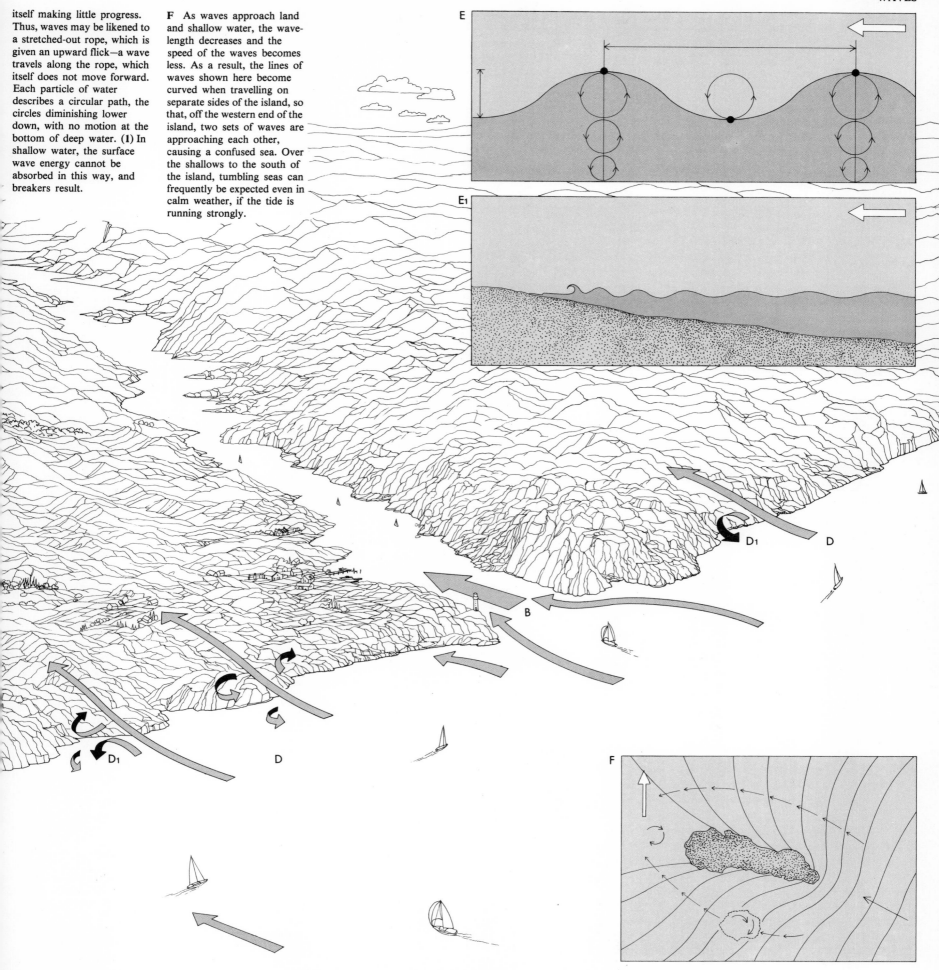

189

Beaufort Number	Speeds for a height of 33 ft (10 m) above sea level		Description of wind	Sea criterion
	Knots	Ft (m) per second		
0	Less than 1	Less than 2 (0–0.6)	Calm	Sea like a mirror.
1	1–3	2–5 (0.6–1.5)	Light air	Ripples with the appearance of scales are formed, but without foam crests.
2	4–6	6–11 (1.8–3.4)	Light breeze	Small wavelets, still short but more pronounced. Crests have a glassy appearance and do not break.
3	7–10	12–18 (3.7–5.5)	Gentle breeze	Large wavelets. Crests begin to break. Foam of glassy appearance. Perhaps scattered white horses.
4	11–15	19–27 (5.8–8.2)	Moderate breeze	Small waves, becoming longer; fairly frequent white horses.
5	16–20	28–36 (8.5–11)	Fresh breeze	Moderate waves, taking a more pronounced long form; many white horses are formed (chance of some spray).
6	21–26	37–46 (11.3–14)	Strong breeze	Large waves begin to form; the white foam crests are more extensive everywhere. (Probably some spray.)
7	27–33	47–56 (14.3–17)	Moderate gale	Sea heaps up and white foam from breaking waves begins to be blown in streaks along the direction of the wind. (Spindrift begins to be seen.)
8	34–40	57–68 (17.4–20.7)	Fresh gale	Moderately high waves of greater length; edges of crests break into spindrift. The foam is blown in well-marked streaks along the direction of the wind.
9	41–47	69–80 (21–24.4)	Strong gale	High waves. Dense streaks of foam along the direction of the wind. Sea begins to roll. Spray may affect visibility.
10	48–55	81–98 (24.7–29.9)	Whole gale	Very high waves with long, overhanging crests. The resulting foam in great patches is blown in dense, white streaks along the direction of the wind. On the whole, the surface of the sea takes a white appearance. The rolling of the sea becomes heavy and shocklike. Visibility is affected.
11	56–65	94–110 (28.7–33.5)	Storm	Exceptionally high waves. (Small and medium-sized ships might for a long time be lost to view behind the waves.) The sea is completely covered with long, white patches of foam, lying along the direction of the wind. Everywhere, the edges of the wave crests are blown into froth. Visibility affected.
12	Above 65	Above 110 (33.5)	Hurricane	The air is filled with foam and spray. Sea completely white with driving spray; visibility very seriously affected.

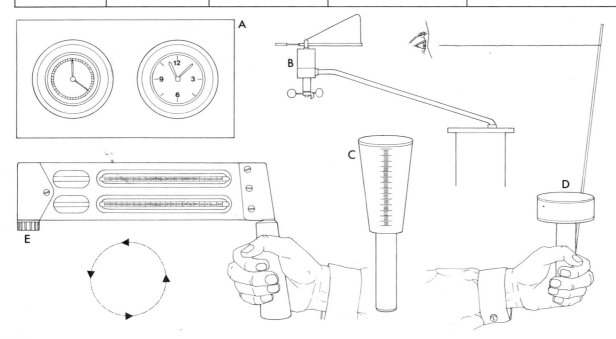

A The chronometer and barometer are traditional instruments which are essential for ocean voyages. It is the weather-wise interpretation of changes in the pressure that is most important. Pressure changes can be readily seen if regular barometer readings are plotted on a graph, perhaps as part of the log.

B Wind speed and direction can be measured with an instrument like this, mounted on the mast-head with indicating dials in the cockpit or cabin.

C A Ventimeter gives a cheap and reasonably reliable method of measuring wind speed, provided that it is held as high as possible to windward.

D Wind direction can also be found with cheap hand-held instruments. As shown, the ship's hand-bearing compass is put to use with a tell-tale. When the tell-tale is blowing directly towards the observer, the direction of the apparent wind can be read directly from the compass.

E Temperature and dew-point can be obtained by using a whirling psychrometer. Tables for obtaining the dew-point with the wet-and-dry bulb method are usually supplied with the instrument.

SAFETY ON BOARD

John Chamier

Safety and seamanship have to do with staying alive. Boats may sink, blow up, catch fire, or be lost by stranding or being run down. In the long term, it does not matter how accidents happen, the important thing is to survive them. For this reason, one starts with personal buoyancy aids in the form of life-jackets. It is not known how many lives were saved among air crews during the Second World War due to the "Mae West", but they were many—and, of its day, the "Mae West" was an excellent life-jacket. Since then, advances in design and material have been achieved. Moreover, governments and various concerned bodies have taken a hand in the matter to ensure that life-jackets are not death-jackets. A death-jacket would, for instance, be one which would float an unconscious man face downwards in the water. Rule One, therefore, is to buy a personal life-jacket which has been manufactured to officially approved standards. An owner of a crewed yacht must ensure that there are life-jackets on board, placed where they can be readily grabbed, for every member of the crew. It is the owner's or skipper's responsibility to see to it that life-jackets are worn when conditions demand it.

Since people drown by being in the water, it is clear that they should be kept on board. In heavy weather, crew members have been lost when working on deck—or, even, in the cockpit—when the yacht has taken a sudden lurch to a wave. A wise seaman will have his own safety harness, a sort of belt-and-braces arrangement of straps, attached to a length of sturdy line with a strong quick-action clip at its end. This harness is worn outside all clothing. It can be clipped on to rigging or lifelines and, should the wearer go over the side as he works, which might be at night in rough weather, he would still be attached to his ship. Again, a seamanlike owner of a crewed yacht will ensure that there are enough harnesses on board for the number of crew he has shipped, and that they are worn.

"Wet suits" do *not* give buoyancy. They are based on the tight-fitting "outer skin" of scuba divers and frogmen and, usually, they are made from foam neoprene. They provide insulation against the killing effect of cold, since water soaked up by the wet suit is warmed by body heat and retained within the insulation. Obviously, wet suits are more relevant to sailors of dinghies and open or semi-open boats than to crew aboard vessels with interior accommodation, where shelter may be found and hot food or drink prepared. Nevertheless, in chilly climates, wet suits can be worthwile even on cruising craft. In such cases, however, they are a matter for personal decision—by no means obligatory, like life-jackets or harnesses, but not a bad idea all the same.

The importance of good seagoing gear cannot be over-emphasized. There are, of course, climates where all that is necessary are a pair of shorts and a light shirt but, in other than sub-tropical conditions, cold and wet can reduce crew effectiveness to an alarming degree. Keep warm—wool and cotton are better for this than are synthetics. Light string undervests are good under shirts and woollen sweaters. Many layers of light clothing are better than a single, heavy sweater, as air in between the garments, warmed by body heat, is more efficiently retained. A heavy sweater can be bulky and irksome when worn under oilskins. Furthermore, layers of clothing can be peeled or added in order to suit conditions more exactly than can a single "heavy". When reefing with reef-points or reef-lines, it is better to take in a number of lesser reefs rather than one big one. One can strip them gradually and as appropriately to improving conditions. The same goes for clothing.

Good oilskins are a first consideration. A suit of jacket and trousers is probably better than an overall type, though I happen to prefer overalls. In a suit, the trousers should have a chest-high bib, and the coat should be long, reaching well below the sit-upon. Much boat work involves bending, and a short coat is useless, as it then leaves the small of the back unprotected. A button/zip-fronted coat should have wide storm flaps. A smock will do but is often difficult to get into or out of. All oilskin clothing should be very loose in order to allow ease of movement. It may have to be worn over layers of underclothing, and a chap in a strait-jacket is not mobile enough to do his job.

Footwear must be safe. Having your feet slide from under you on a wet deck does not help with the work and may be dangerous to life and limb. The maximum efficiency of the patterned rubber sole of a shoe or boot depends on the integrity of the original surface. This will be diminished if sailing footwear is constantly worn on shore, as contact with concrete, tarmac, etc. wears down the rubber pattern—as any motorist will tell you when he goes to buy new tyres. Besides this, these "suction" soles pick up grit and tar, and carry them back on board to the damage of decks. It is best to have footwear which is *exclusively* reserved for sailing. A worn pair will be good enough for shore-side walking and may still be smart, even if their gripping power has lessened. A final point concerning good and sure footwear is that it is expensive. But quality costs, and when really at sea it is quality you want, and not frivolity, however chic and fun-to-wear.

In a way, many of us have been lucky in that we have grown up with our sailing, learning our "trade" as we went along. Newcomers to the sport have no such advantage and have no time to absorb these things, especially if they are on in years when they take it up. It is only sensible, therefore, to spend a little time at a sailing-school, if one possibly can. The basics of personal safety will be quickly learnt, and one can then be confident that all areas have been covered, and not just some of them. In the matter of safety, there ought to be no gaps. Most "sailing" countries have schools, and their addresses can be obtained from the national authority for yachting. The IYRU at 60, Knightsbridge, London S.W.1 will help you here, if you do not know your national authority.

A cruising or racing/cruising yacht will have its own built-in safety precautions. The most obvious of these will be the "pulpit" round the bow and the "pushpit" round the stern—strong, firmly fixed railings which will take a man's weight if he is flung against them. It is absolutely essential that the palms at deck be through-bolted. Screws will *not* do. Stainless steel tubing is the most satisfactory material for these railings. Galvanized steel tubing is also satisfactory but does not look so good. Pulpit rails should not be so low as to trip a man, nor so high that he can slide under them. Offshore Racing Council Special Regulations stipulate that, for a yacht rating 21 ft (6.4 m) and over, the upper rails and associated upper lifelines (of two on each side) be *not less* than "2 feet (60 cm)" above the working deck, and be supported at *not more* than intervals of "7 feet (2.15 m)". The requirements for a yacht rating under 21 ft (6.4 m) are similar, except that a single lifeline may be employed and heights above working deck are reduced to "18 inches (45 cm)" although, if at any point a lifeline is more than "22 inches (56 cm)" above the rail cap, a lower lifeline must be fitted. These regulations can be recommended for non-racing yachts too.

Lifelines, the natural adjunct to pulpits, are wires, supported by stanchions, running around a yacht. Again, the palms of these stanchions must be through-bolted. Mostly, there is an upper and a lower wire. Both must be capable of being tensioned, because wire stretches, and a sagging wire not only looks bad but is also dangerous. Lifelines will keep a man inboard in normal circumstances, and they can also be used to accept the harness clip, about which we have already spoken. The ocean racing regulations which govern wire heights and the distance between supporting stanchions should also be followed by cruisers. Stainless steel is again the favoured material, for reasons of lightness, strength, and appearance. Strength is the major factor. A heavy man, thrown off his feet, arrives at the lifelines with considerable force.

A development of the pulpit of recent years is the companion-way guard. Many modern yachts no longer have "doghouses", and coach roofs are now little more than blisters on the decks. A man emerging from below finds nothing to hold on to, and a sudden heel may throw him completely off balance. In wider areas of the boat, he has a maximum way to fall before coming up against the lifelines, and he may suffer injury. A rail round the hatchways is, therefore, a good safety measure, useful not only for grabbing when off balance, but also for hooking on the harness clip. These guards need to be designed carefully, so that they do not tangle up sheets or snag the ship's working gear. Large yachts may also have a tubular rail around the mast, as crew working in this area may need both hands for the job, thus having none over for themselves.

You can see that one is much concerned with keeping the crew where they belong—inboard, and not swimming for their lives. This brings us to one of the problems with GRP. It is very smooth and becomes slippery when wet. Most deck areas carrying heavy traffic have a pattern moulded in bas-relief in an effort to make them non-skid. Even then, the decks may be very slippery. Some patterns are more effective than others and, in my view, more research is needed here by the manufacturers. My own preference is for a small, irregular pattern, deeply etched, rather than for a shallow pattern that does not clear the water fast enough and, if regular, does not "surprise" the

grip of the sole of the shoe. To increase the deck's foot-holding power, it is a good idea to put down self-adhesive strips or patches of highly non-skid material (like rough sandpaper).

As a second line of defence, a yacht should also carry safety equipment in portable form. The most important of this category is the inflatable life-raft. Not every drama is one of "man overboard". A boat can catch fire, blow up, collide with another vessel or with rocks, even spring a leak and founder. Any of these instances might call for abandoning ship, and notice can be very short. A boat which goes any distance offshore, makes extended passages, or sails at night should carry an inflatable raft with automatic inflation. In fact, ocean-racing regulations require this and, yet once more, the cruising world can do no better than follow suit. A four-man raft is the minimum. In any case, the number of crew must not exceed the capacity of the raft(s), as specified by the manufacturer. In fact, rafts will take an overload, and hand-ropes will support other crew in the sea. Rafts must be stowed where they can be got at in a hurry. The regulations state that the rafts must be stowed so that one person can get one to the lifeline within ten seconds. Also, each raft must have a valid annual certificate, a copy of which must be kept aboard.

Equally important equipment are the pyrotechnics: distress rockets, flares, and smoke candles. There is a wide choice of such "fireworks". Fortunately, the Offshore Racing Council provides guidance on what a boat should carry, and manufacturers produce pyrotechnic packs which conform to ORC regulations. A typical kit will contain four red parachute flares, four red hand flares, four white hand flares, and two orange-smoke day signals. Like the life-raft, the kit should be tested periodically, for instance, at the start of each season. Self-evidently, there is no 100-per-cent way of testing a flare kit except by firing it off and, that done, you need a new kit. But you can do a percentage check by firing off one of the flares. If it fails to ignite, then get rid of the lot. If it lights, then you can take your chance with the rest of the pack—a sort of maritime Russian roulette. The other recourse is the "eyeball test" in which you take a good look at the flare and, if it is "weeping", growing grass, or otherwise looks in poor shape, you should ditch it and its companions. In any case, do not carry a pyrotechnic kit which is over two years old. The most effective flare is the parachute flare, as it burns aloft for some time. It should be fired *down* wind. The pyrotechnic kit should be stowed where it can be quickly got hold of and not in a locker at the bottom of the stock of canned beer.

Lifebuoys or life-rings are pretty standard on most boats of any size. The best is the square-sectioned horseshoe type. It is good practice to carry two in holsters on the pushpit or on lifelines within reach of the helmsman who, by virtue of his office, is the one man on board who hangs on to something most of the time and is to be found at one station. I use the word "holster", because a quick draw and a quick throw to a man in the water may be vital. One of the pair of lifebuoys should have a marker buoy with a light-staff, attached to the end of a line, like a dan buoy. Staff and buoy, manufactured to regulation specifications, can be bought at any chandlery. The staff is telescopic and, when extended, flies a flag at the required

height off the water. In this case, the ORC specifies a height of a minimum of "8 feet (2.45 m)". The staff must be attached to a horseshoe-type life-ring by "25 feet (8 m)" of floating line. Besides the staff arrangement, the life-ring must also be equipped with whistle, dye marker, drogue, and self-igniting, high-intensity water light. These ORC requirements are very sensible and should be followed.

An interesting safety device, which has recently appeared, is the quoit and heaving line. In practice, this is just a rubber ring, like a deck quoit, attached to a long, neatly coiled line. It can be thrown further, and possibly more accurately, than a comparatively heavy lifebuoy. The end of the line is retained on board. An interesting development of this is where a canister, containing the line itself, is thrown to the person in the water. The end of the line is secured to the boat, and the rest is paid out from the canister as it flies through the air. The canister, which is shaped much like a beer bottle, contains about 130 ft (40 m) of 260-lb (*c.* 118 kg) floating line. When thrown by hand, it can cover up to 90 ft (*c.* 27 m). There is no doubt that "throwing a man a line" is a good safety measure and that these "gadgets", properly prepared and packed, are sound value. Whether you indulge in "gadgets" or not, ORC Special Regulations call for a heaving line (floating type) of "50 feet (16 m)" minimum length to be readily accessible from the cockpit.

Anchors are too often overlooked when discussing safety equipment. An anchor is by no means just a method of hooking the boat to the sea bottom in order to have a picnic and a swim. Neither is it just concerned with stopping in some chosen and remote place for a night. An anchor can be used for stopping a disabled boat from being driven ashore. It can, moreover, be used for dragging a boat into sufficiently deep water for it to get under way and under command again. If a craft is properly equipped, there should be a main anchor and a kedge anchor. The main anchor, attached to a chain, is heavy and cumbersome to handle. In choosing this, one can do no better than follow the requirements of Lloyd's Register. The kedge anchor, on a nylon warp with a couple of fathoms of chain at the anchor end, is a satisfactory piece of gear for anchoring in quiet times, and it can back up the main anchor to a remarkable degree, if spread in its holding location in times of emergency. Anchoring can save a ship—as both St. Paul and Nelson knew.

Tools are a *sine qua non*—tools to do with engine problems, as well as tools for the problems which need sudden attention at sea. A skipper without proper tools is sailing his ship short-handed and, when the pressure is on, that is dangerous. All adjustable tools must be free to adjust—you cannot turn a nut with a frozen-up wrench, spanner, or pliers, and you may not have time to free the tool in order to do the job. So far as a boat is concerned, the most important tool is a pair of wire-cutters capable of cutting the largest size of standard rigging wire aboard. The teeth of the jaws must be really tough and not just "putty steel". It may be necessary to cut away a fallen mast before it bashes its way through the hull. A hacksaw with a supply of high-speed blades should also be carried, as there may be rod rigging to cope with.

Navigation aids are clearly a part of a boat's safety equipment. Principal among these is the compass. No boat should go outside the harbour without a reliable compass.

Get the best you can afford, and make sure that you understand fully how to use it. An echo-sounder is also an important navigation aid, which will warn of shallowing water and dangerous shoal conditions beneath the boat. The instrument may also be used in the strict navigational sense, picking up a safe depth-contour and showing how to proceed along it out of harm's way. It can be employed to identify a position, when a succession of recorded depths at a given speed or distance run can be referred to the course sailed and to soundings on a chart. It will also inform about depths in which one can anchor, be it to picnic or to avoid being driven ashore. While speed is relatively unimportant, an accurate knowledge of the distance run is paramount. With log, echo sounder, chart, and compass, alongside a reliable timepiece, one has all the ingredients for safe and intelligent navigation. It is best to have a spare compass and an extra watch or clock.

Radio is another safety aid. At its most basic, a radio receiver will provide accurate time signals, shipping forecasts, and warnings of gales. Coastal stations broadcast characteristic radio signals in a way similar to that of lighthouses sending out characteristic light signals. A receiver with a directional aerial will thus provide bearings on the *known* position of the transmitting station. The reception of signals from one such station will give a position line; from two, a radio "fix". Reception on "domestic" radio receivers, even when equipped with directional aerials, have not proved satisfactory. It is best to invest in proper marine equipment. It is tougher and more reliable in the hostile environment of the sea and it is geared to the job rather than to the latest ravings of pop music or quiz programmes.

With radio, we enter the field of signalling. Many owners now fit their boats with two-way radio-telephones. Some sets can provide almost world-wide communication, but most pleasure-boat skippers will be content with VHF R/T, an extension of the walkie-talkie. It has limited range, but, within that span, it is useful for telling your club that you will be in to dine, or your marina that you will be back to your berth for the night. It is also useful for contacting the coastguard or the lifeboat service to say that you are in trouble—and possibly more effective than burning your shirt at the mast-head. Early appraisal of situations of peril is all-important in matters of aid or rescue. It is, of course, imperative to acquaint yourself with how your set works, but it is perhaps useful to know that Distress Traffic on normal R/T will be answered on 2,182 kHz, and that the radio-silence time-zone must be observed by non-distress traffic, so distress signals get free air. This time-zone is for a period of three minutes, commencing at each hour and half-hour on 2,182 kHz. This restriction is world-wide, since the world is divided into hourly time-zones.

Small-boat radar is a new development in navigation and safety. One is instinctively accustomed to thinking of radar as bulky, heavy, and vastly expensive. This is not the case. In practice, a boat needs no more than a ten-mile radar range. This modest but practical requirement allows considerable miniaturization and cost-saving. An effective small-boat radar costs no more than other electronic instrumentation systems, commonplace today on modern pleasure boats. Radar is used to pin-point channels, buoyage, and coastlines, and as an anti-collision measure, to indicate the presence of unseen traffic in the vicinity.

Among the top of the list of Public Enemies is the boat on fire. Fire is a demon. It can destroy of itself or give birth to an explosion. A boat is a small thing and, if in the grip of flames, will as often as not produce few places to which to run to for safety. It is imperative that fire is tackled with the utmost speed and at its source. This may be quite impossible in the case of explosion followed by fire. But, should there be a fire first, then an explosion can be prevented if the fire is immediately tackled.

There should be two extinguishers on board. Both must be reachable from the deck, as well as be to hand in likely fire-spots in the accommodation, such as around the galley and engine-space areas. One extinguisher should be aft and one forward, since it may be necessary to tackle the fire from both ends of the boat. Powerboats should also have self-contained, automatic extinguishing systems triggered by heat in the engine compartments. Most countries list approved types of extinguishers for marine use. What must not be carried are carbon tetrachloride (CTC) extinguishers. (These are banned in, for instance, the United States.) CTC produces lethal phosgene gas in confined spaces. Unfortunately, such extinguishers are readily available for use in cars and other places which do not have the small boat's ventilation problems. Other extinguishers contain foam or carbon dioxide, but the best type for small or smallish boats is that storing liquid bromo-chloro-difluoromethane (BCF), which turns to gas when released. Always strike at the base of the fire, and strike quickly.

Fire should never be allowed to start. In ninety-nine cases out of a hundred, fire starts because of bad practice. The commonest causes are gas and fuel leaks and spillage due to bad refuelling drill. Be careful when taking on fuel, and do not smoke or operate electric switches, which may cause a spark and ignite vapour. Do not overfill tanks—and diesel is safer than petrol. Leaking joints and splits in fuel and/or gas pipes can turn a boat into a potential bomb. Safety, in this respect, is a matter of installation. Lines between the container and the operating point should never be rigid. Vibration or shock (thumping into a rough sea) can damage the integrity of piping, without anyone being aware of it. Any pipe system carrying gas or fuel should have a flexible length of proper hosing incorporated in it. Fit the proper hose, not any old piece of rubber tube. Keep the number of joints to a minimum. Good ventilation is vital, as the explosive material is gas, which can lurk, ready to ignite, in any unventilated space. Hence, it is good practice to give a cabin boat a thorough airing immediately after stepping on board, before starting up the motor(s), lighting the cooker, or operating electrical switches. Many yachts have removable vent cowls which are taken off at sea, when they may foul the sheets or otherwise get in the way. Replace these cowls when leaving the boat for any length of time, and isolate the gas cylinder at the regulator valve on the cylinder head. Ideally, gas cylinders should be sited externally. If they are kept in a box, this should have scuppers, so that escaped gas can leak away into the open air.

Another Public Enemy is fog, and a very dangerous one it is, too. In fog, collision risk is immeasurably increased. Furthermore, fog can overtake a vessel in a position of some navigational hazard. To minimize collision risk, a skipper should have a radar reflector on board, and in this matter nothing compensates for size. Some radar reflectors sold by chandleries are a laugh and of no more use than a Christmas-tree decoration. If the reflector is of the octahedral type, the Royal Ocean Racing Club's amendments to the ORC regulations prescribe a minimum diagonal measurement of "18 inches (46 cm)". If of another type, for instance the Swedish cylindrical type, an "equivalent echoing area" of not less than 108 sq ft (10 sq m) is required. The regulations also state that the minimum effective height above water is "12 feet (4 m)".

When you hit fog, hoist the radar reflector. Then bring your navigational plot up to date with the time of entering the fog zone, and keep it so at fifteen-minute intervals. It is imperative to know where you are, relative to heavy shipping lanes, tidal races, rocks, shoals, and nearby coastlines. Crossing shipping lanes should be done at right angle to the traffic stream, so as to stay in it for as short a time as possible. If under power, stop engine(s), and "coast along" for two minutes at short and regular intervals, and listen. Your own engine noise may drown out the sound of an approaching merchantman. Everybody should be on deck, life-jacketed, listening, and looking out. The life-raft should be made ready for immediate launching, since there will be little time if you are rammed by a coaster or a tanker on passage. The pyrotechnics, ready to fire, should be in the cockpit, and the white flares should be used first to warn the advancing vessel of collision danger. It is required practice to carry a fog-horn. The Regulations for Preventing Collisions at Sea are detailed enough but, as a rule of thumb, any efficient sound signal at intervals of not more than one minute will suffice. As a final piece of advice, make for tolerably shallow water. Tankers and big cargo ships are not so likely to be encountered there.

Of all maritime dangers, gales are the most feared; yet they are, on a quantitative basis, the danger to be least feared. A sound, well-fitted-out yacht with a cool-headed skipper will, bobbing like a cork, live out most of what the weather will send. In a gale, the skipper's choice is plain. Either he gets into the shelter of a lee, or he goes out to sea to get plenty of sea-room. This is a dilemma, and the judgement must be made according to the prevailing circumstances. If a gale is clearly signalled, and there is a lee conveniently to hand within, say, an hour's sailing, then it is right to seek shelter. If you are caught out, then stay out.

The classic example of recent years is the wrecking of the ocean racer MORNING CLOUD, owned by the then prime minister of Great Britain, Mr. Edward Heath. The yacht was on passage from the English east coast, after a successful week at the international regatta at Burnham-on-Crouch, to Cowes on the south coast, where it was to take part in the end-of-the-season racing. When it put out, the weather was bad but not impossible for a top-class yacht. Off the south coast, the weather deteriorated, but not so much as to cause real anxiety to a competent crew in a well-found vessel. But it was close in and in proximity of shoals, which increased the violence of the sea. There was some seasickness on board. A series of incidents culminated in the breaching of the fore-hatch and the intake of water. The ship had to be abandoned and was driven ashore. A man was lost. There were a number of contributory causes of this disaster, but the prime reason was that MORNING CLOUD was where it was. Another ocean-racing yacht in the vicinity made an offing and came through unscathed.

Calms may sound harmless enough and, as with the rest of the weather, you cannot do much about them. But, in certain circumstances, they can be dangerous. In areas of strong tidal conditions close to shore or rocks, a sailing-boat can be swept into a position of peril, where it can be driven onto a reef or rocky ledge. The obvious thing to do is to start the engine and get clear of any approaching hazard (which could also include a ship). The wise skipper will, therefore, ensure that his fuel tank is not empty, that his filters have not clogged with dirt and water, and that his battery is not flat. He ought to be prepared to anchor, so the "hook" should be accessible, the chain free to run and shackled on. He should know both where he is on the chart and the most likely spot where he can fetch up and hold until the wind comes, the tide turns, or the engine gets sorted out. Remember that a passing merchantman or fishing trawler must be brought to realize that you are dead in the water. The required signal is to hoist two shapes—a rolled-up sail cover, plus anything else which can be bundled up to make a spherical shape, will do. At night, the signal is two red lights, visible all round. In either case, the signal should be hoisted "one over one", each 6 ft (1.8 m) apart.

Like fire, collision should never be allowed to happen. Yacht versus yacht will mostly prove other than mortal, but being hit by a trawler or other commercial vessel can lead to a desperate situation. The golden rule, even if you have right of way, is to keep out of the way and to do so in good time. Do not leave your avoiding action until the last moment. This is particularly important in confined waters and where traffic is bound to be heavy, such as in the vicinity of ports. Night-time increases the danger, since visual range is greatly reduced and, by the time steaming lights have been spotted and correctly identified, a ship may be much closer to hand than one would suppose. So, as well as keeping out of the way, keep a very sharp look-out during the hours of darkness. This means not leaving the helmsman alone in the cockpit or wheel-house. A deck look-out must be on watch, and preferably not behind glass. In spite of these sensible precautions, collision may occur, in which case everyone must move fast, but without panic. The deck crew gets the life-raft "out of its kennel" and ranged on the rail, ready for instant launching. The crew below must be roused (it is incredible what some people can sleep through), and everybody should be on deck soonest, life-jacketed and in oilskins. The flare pack should, in any case, be in the cockpit or at the command position on deck at night. If it is not, some one person must have been previously allotted the job of grabbing it and bringing it with him. Now is the time to look around and take stock before taking further action. There is absolutely no sense in abandoning ship if the boat is not actually sinking beneath one's feet. A collision may mean the boat's being cut in half, in which case nobody may know much about anything any more; it may mean smashed-in topsides, in which case there may be some time in which to beat an orderly retreat; or it may mean dismasting and severe, but not ultimate, hull damage. Keep your cool and remember that this has saved as many lives as have lifeboats.

Apart from colliding with other vessels about their various businesses, there is the matter of colliding with the land. Running ashore can be anything from humiliating to perilous. In heavy weather, small boats and hard land are never good companions. If a boat is disabled in such conditions, the anchor may be the best tool to use to prevent the boat's being driven ashore and wrecked—and it should not be the light "picnic" kedge which is used, but the heavy main anchor, with as much scope of chain as you can give it. Moreover, the inboard end should be secured to a strong point, not just to a screw-fastened pad-eye. The final securing should be by means of a rope lashing which can be cut, should it be necessary to let the "hook" and cable slip, in order to get the boat under way and thrusting out of a position of danger.

Most people who run ashore do so in less dramatic circumstances, and for reasons of, for instance, misreading a chart, cutting corners, or being inaccurate in calculating position. Such incidents, at the outset, are not really questions of basic safety, but they may become so if the weather deteriorates and the yacht is held fast in the trap. For this reason, if no other, one should avoid running ashore. But once there, you can get off and under way by a number of methods. In the first place, it is logical that the best way to get off is the way you came on. You may be able to sail away by heeling the boat and turning around to go back the way you came, possibly with engine power. A powerboat may be able to back off under full power astern. Since most strandings end up on a lee shore, it is important to stop the boat from being driven *further* on by wind, current, or both. A boat or a rigid or inflatable dinghy (not a life-raft) may be used to take out an anchor and warp in the direction from which the boat has come to ground. With this point *established,* it may very well be possible to haul oneself off. The accent is on "established". The hold must be *firm* and, in this context, the longer the kedge warp the better. Give the anchor the best chance of digging in. If you are as good as on top of it, then all you will do, when you put on the strain, is to lift your anchor off the bottom and drive further on.

You may also be lucky. A fellow sailor may happen by and offer you a tow or a pluck to get you off. One must realize that this can impose considerable strains on the boat. There is not only the heave itself to be considered, but also the sudden "snatch" loading. Both on tug and tow, the tow-line should be secured to real strong points and not just to deck cleats, used for mooring in some sheltered marina or yacht harbour. Deck cleats sometimes have a nasty habit of popping out of the deck, taking some of it with them, when asked to do real work. In contrast, the mast (even the stub of a broken mast, if stepped through-deck and onto the keel) can be considered very much a strong point. I would rather trust this than a cleat. Besides, one can get a decent-sized rope around it. A tow-line is likely to be heftier than the ropes of fenders or even sheets.

Capsizing is yet another specific danger. Although keelboats have been capsized or turned over, this is really a matter for dinghies. In the world of dinghy racing, capsizing is taken as a matter of couse. But this is rather different, as one is then in the company of a lot of other boats, and rescue craft are usually out on the course to help, should there be any real trouble, caused through,

say, exhaustion from efforts to right the dinghy or cold from being too long in the water. However, if a dinghy sailing alone capsizes, knowledge and practice in righting are vital. Basically, the drill consists of standing on the centre-board, grasping the gunwale with both hands and heaving. The trick is not to capsize again immediately and over the other way. Then you have to start all over again. It is vital for the crew to stay with the boat, and this is done by grasping anything that happens to be trailing from it. You cannot right a dinghy if you are some distance away from it!

Cruising boats can also be capsized, though this takes a lot of doing, and then only with the help of exceptional wind and sea conditions. There is no "what to do" answer to this. Some have survived the experience, some have not. For a cruiser to capsize, the weather must be extreme, and the boat, perhaps, overdriven. One cannot do much about the first, and about the second one can only remark that a boat, hove-to and under minimum canvas (or indeed no canvas at all), has seldom, if ever, been rolled over. So adequate precautions must be taken ahead of any "crunch-time", if things should be seen to be turning out that badly. These precautions are a snug rig, plenty of sea-room, constant checking of the bilges for evidence of leaking, dry-pumping of the ship, updating of the navigational plot at regular intervals, and the maintenance of an extra-sharp look-out. Indeed, these duties apply *all* the time, and not just in the tough conditions which might precede a capsizing or a roll-over.

Here may be the point to make an observation about multihulls which may not be popular with the devotees of the two and three "boots". Given enough ferocity of weather and sea, multihulls go over "better" than monohulls, as they can do gymnastics both laterally and linearly. By reason of their great beam, the multihulls can stand up to the wind more than can craft of conventional configuration, which lean away from the wind, thus spilling a proportion of its power to drive.

It is my belief, and I submit that the mechanics of the operation support this view, that the only practical method of righting a capsized multihull is to call up either a miracle or outside assistance. A capsizal may finish with the vessel completely upside-down. This presents many problems with the siting of the life-raft, which must be accessible either way up. On the whole, the best place for the life-raft is right aft, in a special cradle on the rearmost cross-bar of a catamaran, on the transom of the centre hull of a trimaran.

The question of "man overboard" has been left to last as it is probably the most important. The accepted drill is to gybe and to sail back on a reciprocal course. This works, but it is the circumstances which will finally dictate the course of action. A modern boat running before the wind with spinnaker (and other sails, such as a big boy designed for this point of sailing) set is likely to be travelling fast, and the attendant gear and cordage will take some time to sort out and be taken off, when a sudden call to reverse course comes. Hence the boat may travel quite some distance after losing a man overboard before being made ready to back-track. There is no reason why a boat should not be put about rather than gybed. Given space and time, the result should be the same, though gybing will tend to bring you back down wind of the man in the water, while going about will bring you up wind of him. The former is to be preferred, as it is better to sail up to him than down on top of him. A life-ring will, no doubt, have been thrown, but one ought not to stop there. A world-famous yachtsman used to carry a telephone directory in the cockpit. His drill was to tear out wads of pages and throw them over the side, thus leaving a paper-chase trail for him to sail back along to his "target". When the "body" is found, it may be wise to put a man on the end of a line into the water alongside him. The guy may be in a state of shock or hurt and not necessarily capable of helping himself. The topsides of the boat are an awful long way up if you are in the water. Oilskins may hold a lot of trapped sea, so that a "body" is much heavier than usual as it is heaved clear of the waves.

There are two final things to be said. Every life-jacket or other personal buoyancy aid should be equipped with a whistle. It has been amply proved that, day or night, a whistle signal is invaluable for helping a rescue ship home onto someone in the water. The second thing is that everybody should have a knowledge of first aid, and that every boat should have a first-aid pack. Obviously, the "kiss of life" procedure should be known, as well as the rudiments of splinting a broken limb. Cuts and abrasions are no different afloat than ashore, but you cannot just ring for a doctor to come around if you are way out to sea. However, of all the mishaps on a boat, burns from galley accidents and seasickness are the most common. And it must be remembered that the crew on any boat is limited in number. One man out of action may reduce the effective crew by twenty or twenty-five per cent, which is an awesome thought.

A foam life-jacket of the type approved by the United States Coast Guard. The quick-draw tapes keep the vest correctly positioned.

B This safety-harness can be made up from the type of safety-belt used in cars. It is simple and effective, and allows freedom of movement.

C A more sophisticated safety-harness in the form of a waist-coat. It can be attached to guard-rails or to the pulpit. The two hooks give either short or long lengths.

D A good, gripping sole on deck shoes or boots makes sound sense. Always be sure-footed. Decks can be very slippery.

E Every life-jacket should be equipped with the type of whistle used by a football referee. Its shrill blast can be heard across a long distance.

F Good foul-weather clothing is light, waterproof, and roomy. "Stay dry and don't restrict the action", is the gospel.

G Buoyancy aid of a type much favoured by dinghy and small-boat sailors. It comes in four ascending flotation capacities, from 110 lb (50 kg).

H An inflatable life-jacket. Note the collar which will keep the head up, the whistle, and the retro-reflective patches which make the wearer more easily seen at night.

I In contrast to the life-jacket just shown, we illustrate a buoyancy aid, again of the type popular on small boats.

This one helps to keep the wearer warm.

J A typical wet suit, of nylon and foam neoprene. Water absorbed by the suit is warmed by the heat of the body.

K A safety harness of heavy-duty nylon webbing. It is especially suitable for small children aboard boats, as it can be attached to both a stanchion and the lifeline. The buckle at chest height gives a safe attitude in a towing situation.

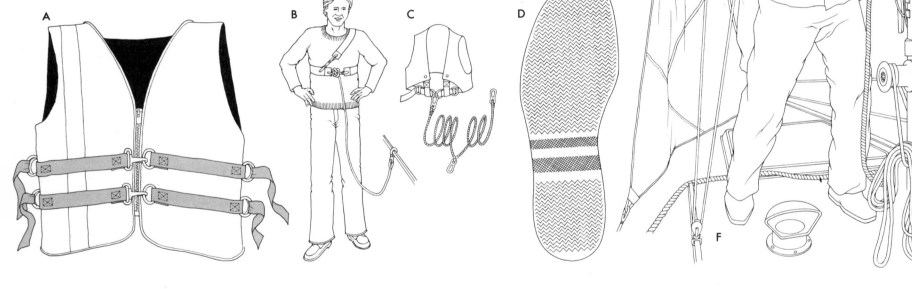

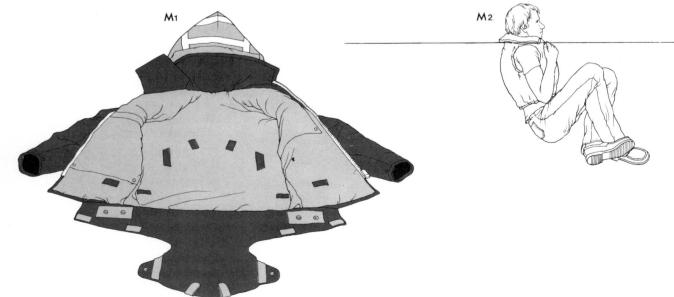

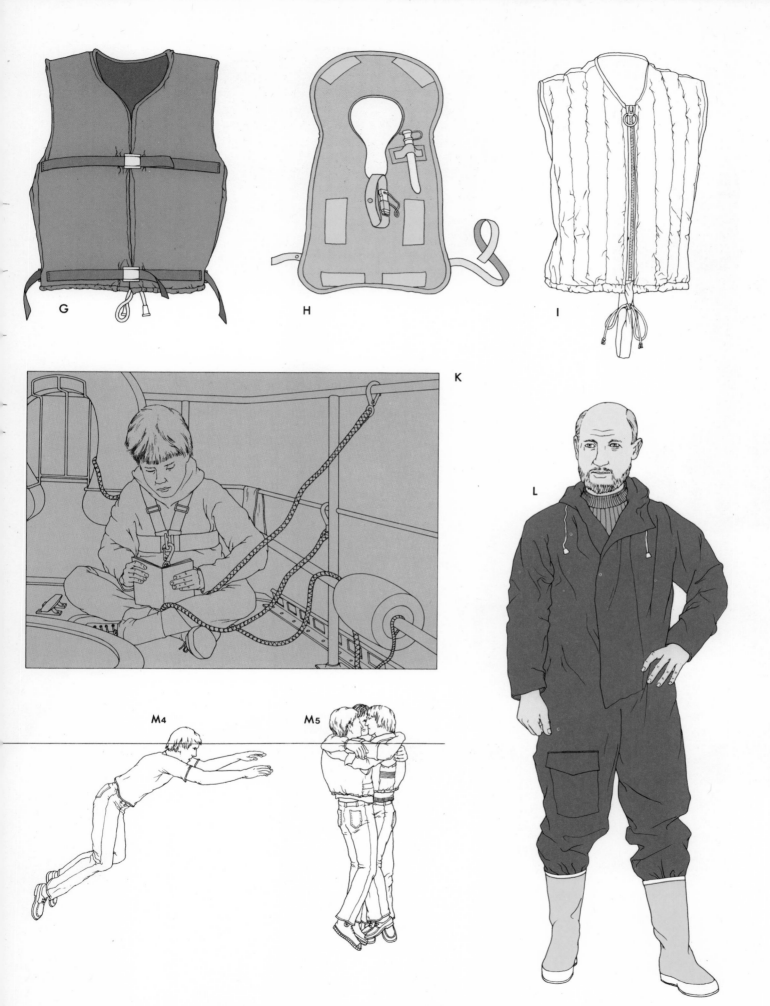

L Overall foul-weather gear. Loose-fitting for freedom of movement. Big overlap on front flap.

M An insulated life-jacket (**1**) which will retain body heat for quite a long time if the wearer falls into cold water. (**2**) To reduce loss of body heat when in the water, curl up, covering the flanks of the torso and the groin. (**3**) Exercise uses up energy, which costs heat to produce. Treading water causes a person to lose body heat thirty-five per cent faster than if he were floating in a life-jacket. (**4**) Floating in the water face down and raising the head every fifteen seconds or so may help one to survive longer. However, the head is a body-heat loss-point and exertion also causes heat loss. This course of action causes heat loss at a rate which is eighty-two per cent faster in 10º C water than if the person in the water is floating in a life-jacket. (**5**) If more than one goes overboard, preserve body heat by floating chest-to-chest. Hug each other.

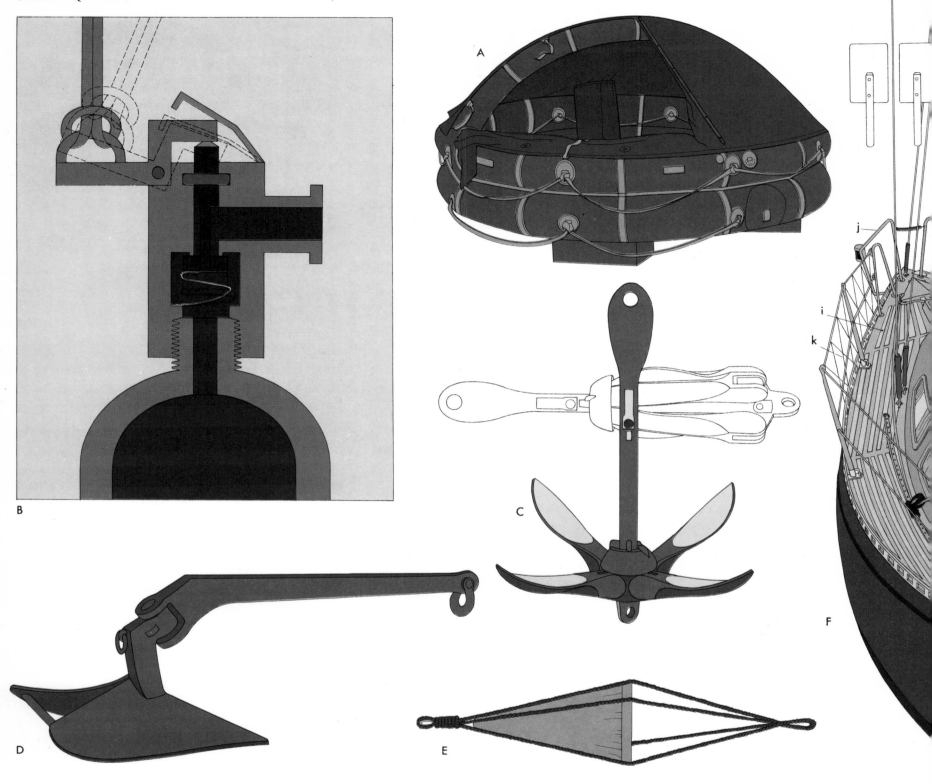

A A typical life-raft configuration, with two inflatable-ring buoyancy chambers under which are integral "drogue" boxes. A protective canopy is supported by an inflatable arch.

B A release mechanism for a life-raft inflation air-bottle.

C A useful "umbrella" kedge anchor favoured for small craft because it is compact and easy to stow. However, this type is unsuitable as a main anchor on larger craft.

D A main anchor of the plough type. Its efficiency depends on its weight and basic design. It has good all-round characteristics, but it

has a tendency to "capsize" in soft sand.

E A sea anchor, or drogue. When streamed from the bow, it will help to hold the boat's heading towards the wind and will reduce the rate of drift.

F A well-equipped boat, from the safety point of view. (a) A transom boarding

ladder. Without one, it is hard to get a swimmer out of the water. (b) A rigid "pushpit", usually of stainless-steel tubing, must be securely fastened with bolts, in order to withstand the weight of a man being thrown against it. (c) Likewise, lifelines, or guard-rails, of wire must be strong and supported by stanchions. Safety harnesses

can be clipped on to lifelines. (d) A man overboard may not be easy to spot in heavy seas. A dan buoy, like this one, has a flag on a telescopic shaft, and is thrown overboard to mark the spot where the man went in. (e) The best type of life-ring, stowed close to the helmsman. Stowage must allow for instant use. (f) The fire extinguisher should be

stowed in a place where it will not normally be cut off by fire, for instance, on the underside of a cockpit-locker lid. A second fire extinguisher should be positioned under the fore-hatch. (g) Good grab-rails are safety essentials, particularly in the companion-way area. A man emerging on deck must have a handhold.

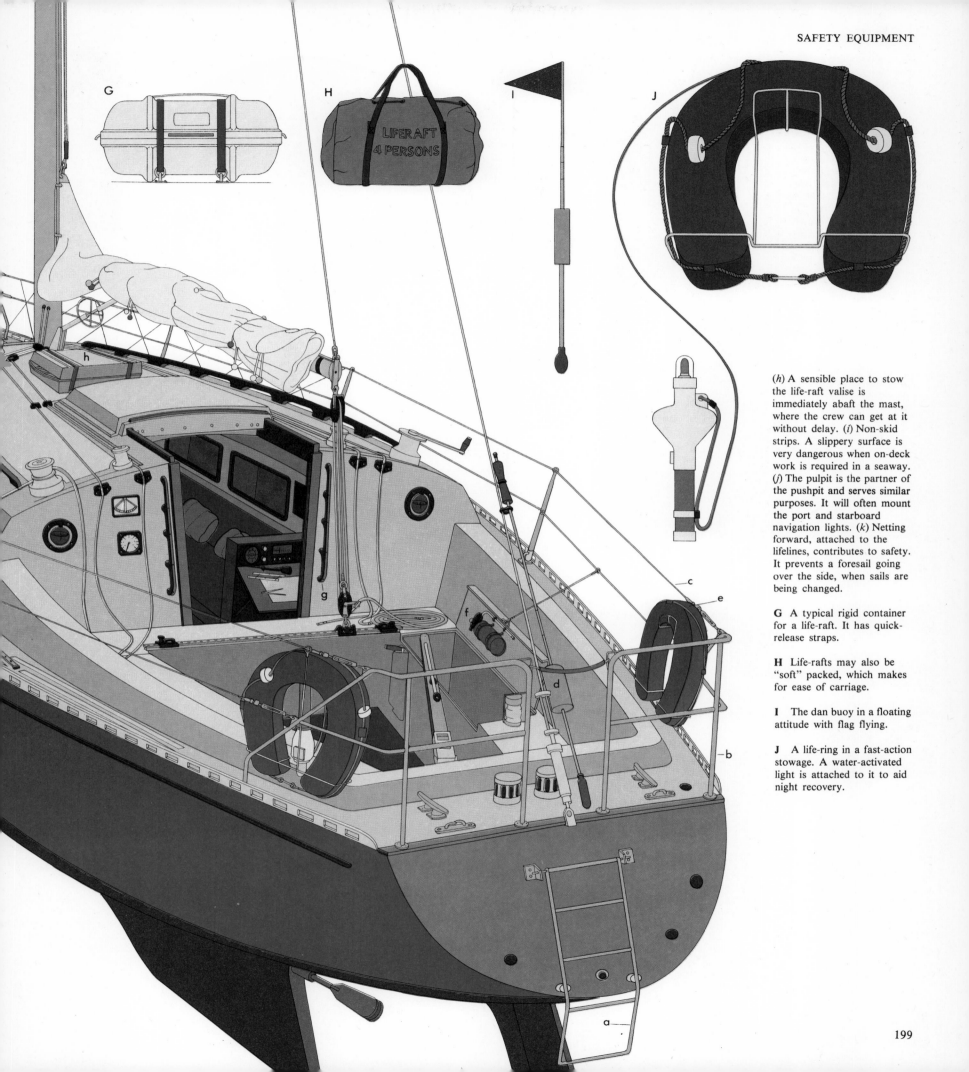

(*h*) A sensible place to stow the life-raft valise is immediately abaft the mast, where the crew can get at it without delay. (*i*) Non-skid strips. A slippery surface is very dangerous when on-deck work is required in a seaway. (*j*) The pulpit is the partner of the pushpit and serves similar purposes. It will often mount the port and starboard navigation lights. (*k*) Netting forward, attached to the lifelines, contributes to safety. It prevents a foresail going over the side, when sails are being changed.

G A typical rigid container for a life-raft. It has quick-release straps.

H Life-rafts may also be "soft" packed, which makes for ease of carriage.

I The dan buoy in a floating attitude with flag flying.

J A life-ring in a fast-action stowage. A water-activated light is attached to it to aid night recovery.

FIRE CONTROL

A Runabouts and sportboats often have fuel tanks (*a*) under the seating. The fuel hose should be grounded with a wire (*b*) from the deck connection to the tank. When the tank is being filled, a "breather pipe" (*c*) allows air in the tank to escape. Ventilation cowls (*d*) should allow air to circulate freely around the tank and the bilges to prevent fumes from accumulating. A valve (*e*) for shutting off the flow of fuel to the engine is important, as are sturdy fastenings (*f*) for the tank.

B Fire may need to be attacked simultaneously from two points, so extinguishers should be sited in the cockpit and fore-hatch areas.

C A portable fire extinguisher containing monoammonium-phosphate-based dry chemical.

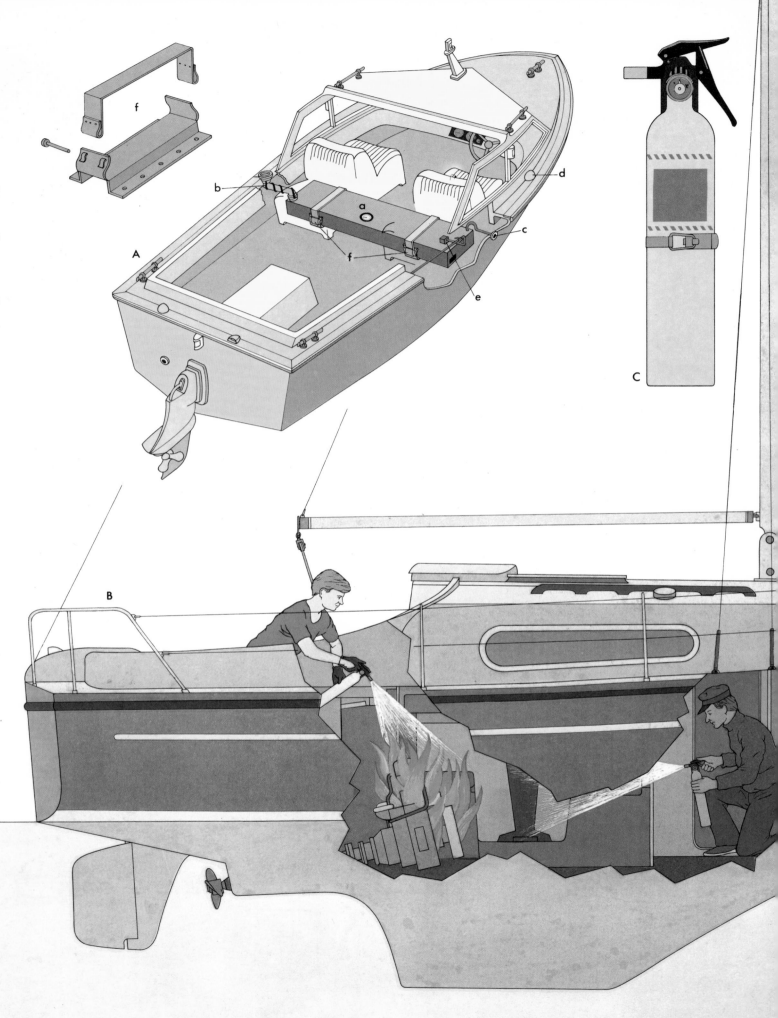

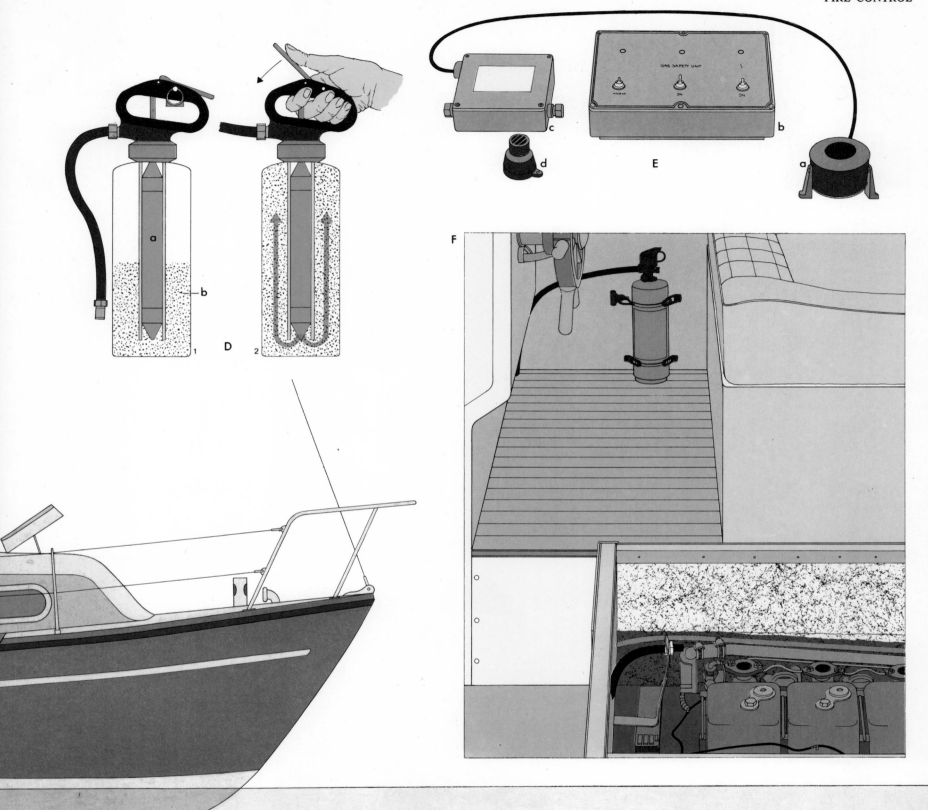

D This type of fire
extinguisher (**1**) contains
a gas cartridge (*a*), which is
replaceable after use, and
powder (*b*). When the
cartridge is punctured, the gas
is expelled and mixes with the
powder (**2**), and the
extinguisher is ready for use.

E This gas safety unit detects
escaped gas, sounds an alarm,
and isolates the source of
supply. It detects petrol fumes
as well as propane.
(*a*) Detector head. (*b*) Control
panel. (*c*) Remote gas valve.
(*d*) Alarm.

F A "remote control"
extinguisher which releases a
shower of powder onto the
engine. The main advantage is
that the hatch cover remains
closed, thus stopping a flow of
oxygen to the fire.

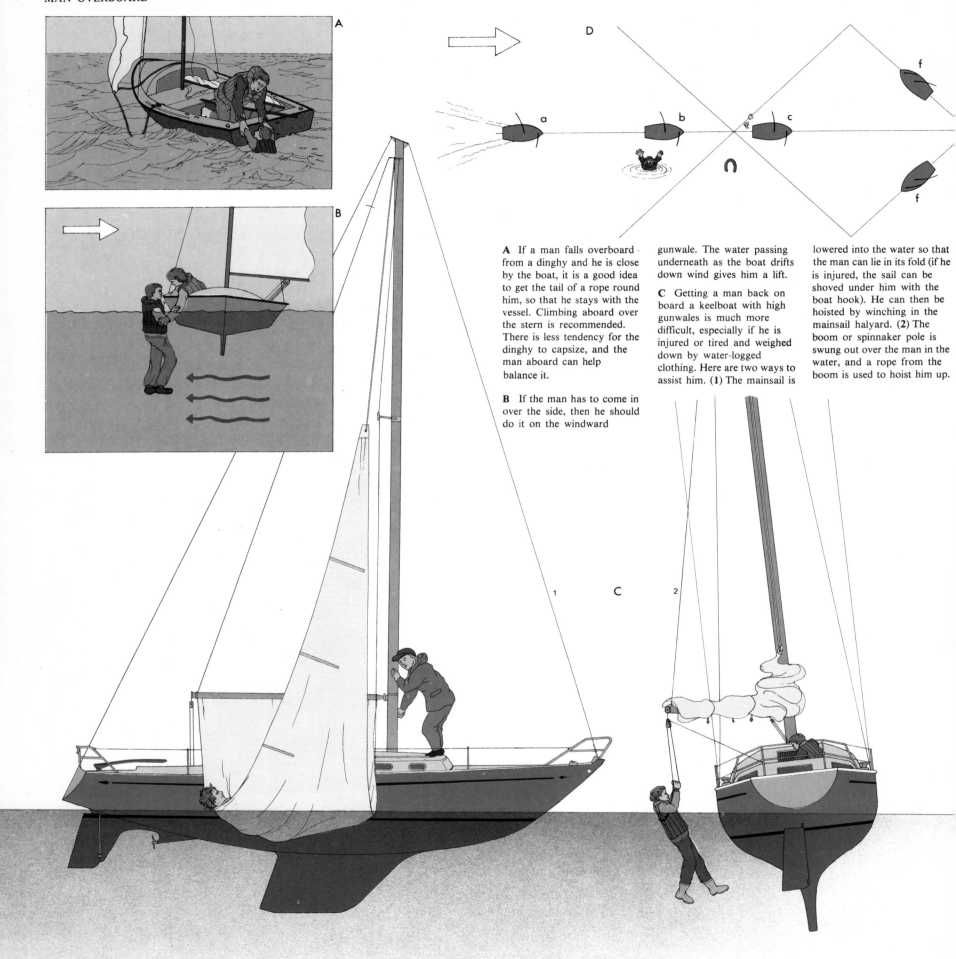

A If a man falls overboard from a dinghy and he is close by the boat, it is a good idea to get the tail of a rope round him, so that he stays with the vessel. Climbing aboard over the stern is recommended. There is less tendency for the dinghy to capsize, and the man aboard can help balance it.

B If the man has to come in over the side, then he should do it on the windward gunwale. The water passing underneath as the boat drifts down wind gives him a lift.

C Getting a man back on board a keelboat with high gunwales is much more difficult, especially if he is injured or tired and weighed down by water-logged clothing. Here are two ways to assist him. (**1**) The mainsail is lowered into the water so that the man can lie in its fold (if he is injured, the sail can be shoved under him with the boat hook). He can then be hoisted by winching in the mainsail halyard. (**2**) The boom or spinnaker pole is swung out over the man in the water, and a rope from the boom is used to hoist him up.

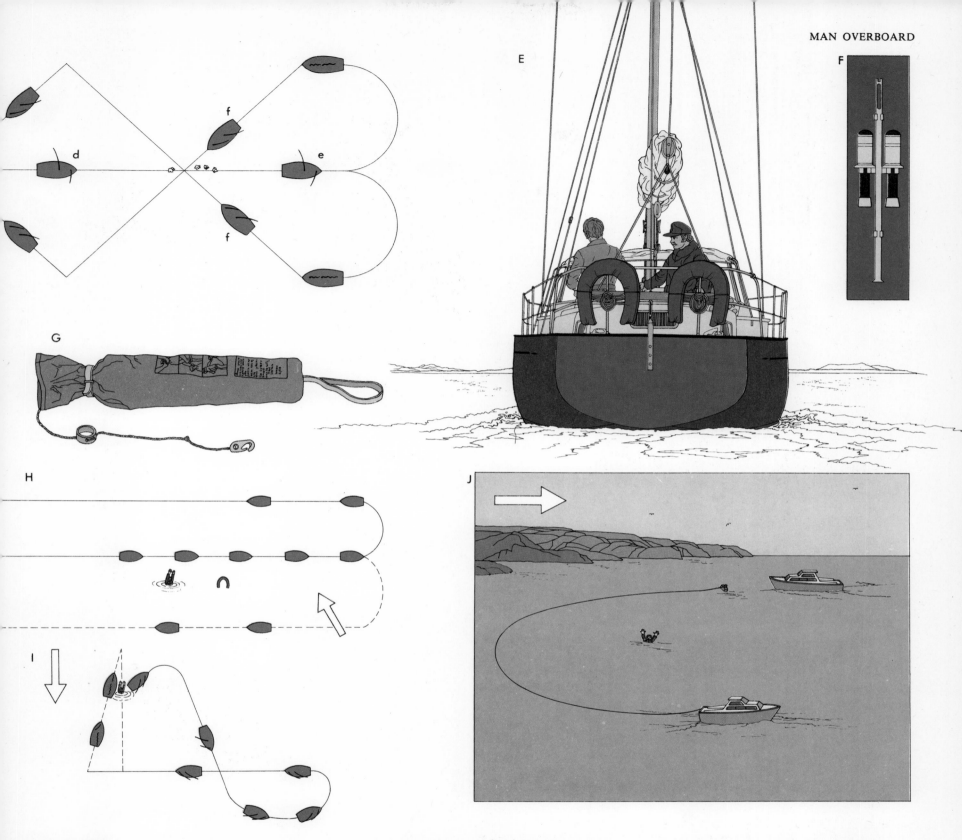

D If the boat is running, with perhaps spinnaker and big boy set, and a man falls overboard, it will take time to get the boat sorted out. Whether the skipper decides to gybe or go about, it will help if floating objects (cushions, paper, etc.) are thrown overboard to show a path back. (*a*) Off-wind track. (*b*) Man overboard. (*c*) Throw life-ring, dan buoy, etc.

(*d*) Prepare crew and boat. (*e*) Execute manoeuvre (gybe or go about). (*f*) Quick tacks.

E Most boats have two life-rings. An automatic releasing device can be fitted whereby the life-ring, floating line, and attached floating quoit are released. The floating line will make it easier for the man in the water to find the life-ring.

F Heaving lines in canisters can be thrown quite far with the help of throwing sticks. The coiled line is inside the canister.

G Another form of heaving line. Place the loop round the wrist and throw the bag. The line runs easily from the bag. Both line and bag float.

H Picking up a man when on a windward course. It is best to gybe and sail back on reciprocal. The man will be to windward, and the skipper may point up head to wind and stop to pick him up.

I Another way is to bear away sharply and sail on the same gybe before the wind for four boat's lengths. Then tack gently and broad reach back for four boat's lengths. Harden up and come head to wind to pick the man up. This is called the "figure-of-eight" technique or the "Q-turn".

J Picking up a man overboard from a powerboat. Approach the man in the water up wind. Before he is abeam, drop a floating object tied to a long floating line. You then have him in a ring of safety, as the line blows down to him on the surface of the water.

203

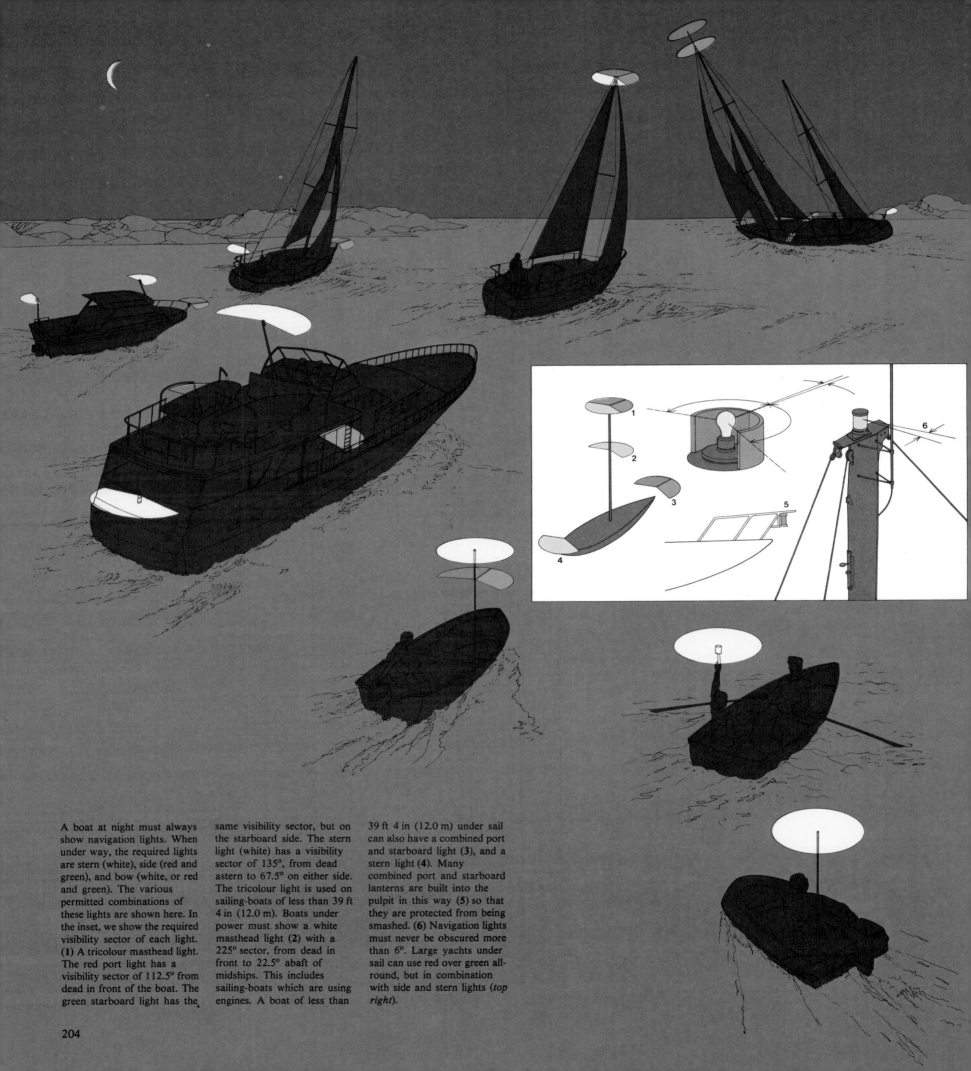

A boat at night must always show navigation lights. When under way, the required lights are stern (white), side (red and green), and bow (white, or red and green). The various permitted combinations of these lights are shown here. In the inset, we show the required visibility sector of each light. (1) A tricolour masthead light. The red port light has a visibility sector of 112.5° from dead in front of the boat. The green starboard light has the same visibility sector, but on the starboard side. The stern light (white) has a visibility sector of 135°, from dead astern to 67.5° on either side. The tricolour light is used on sailing-boats of less than 39 ft 4 in (12.0 m). Boats under power must show a white masthead light (2) with a 225° sector, from dead in front to 22.5° abaft of midships. This includes sailing-boats which are using engines. A boat of less than 39 ft 4 in (12.0 m) under sail can also have a combined port and starboard light (3), and a stern light (4). Many combined port and starboard lanterns are built into the pulpit in this way (5) so that they are protected from being smashed. (6) Navigation lights must never be obscured more than 6°. Large yachts under sail can use red over green all-round, but in combination with side and stern lights (top right).

INSHORE RACING

Jack Knights

It is hardly possible to sail a boat well if you have not raced. Racing, formally or informally, is the best method of measuring your own skill and the speed of your boat against others. For this reason, a far higher proportion of sailors race their boats than motorists race their cars.

The long history of sailing is rich in stories of one ship or boat matched against another. Sometimes, such a race would be from China to the tea markets of Europe; sometimes, it would be between pilot cutters striving to be first out to an incoming ship. One of the reasons that American schooners were so fast was the impetus given to their development by the demand to sail from the east coast to the west, by way of Cape Horn, in order to take part in the gold rush and the development of California.

Unlike other racing forms—car racing, downhill skiing, powerboat racing—there is very little physical danger, though sometimes some physical hardship, in sail racing, which is a sport that may be indulged in by children, by people long past retirement age, and by everyone in between. The sadness of some sports—athletics is one of them—is the short span of a competitor's career. This is not true of sail racing; by selecting your boat type to match your ability, you can keep on racing for decades, and by substituting hard-won experience and judgement for passing physical strength, stamina, and agility, you can keep on winning.

For all of these reasons, sail racing is today one of the world's fastest-growing sports. Countries which, a few years back, had no organized racing are today contending for Olympic medals and giving the established sailing nations a hard struggle. There are scores and scores of different racing classes, some of then numbering over fifty thousand world-wide and increasing by thousands every year.

Because of this expansion, the sport needs planning and control, and happily its international authorities, the

IYRU and the ORC (which supervizes offshore racing), appear alive to the potential problems.

From the very beginning of yacht racing, it became obvious that order and discipline were necessary. The first racing yachtsmen bet one another large sums of money that their vessels were the fastest. It soon became clear that the best way to win such wagers was to buy a larger boat, carrying more sail than one's sailing rivals' craft. When allowed to develop freely, such trends eventually destroyed the sport, because the richest and most determined would always win in the end.

Wise yacht-owners soon saw the need for classes or categories of boats. This, after all, only followed naval traditions, and it ensured that boats of roughly similar performance could race together, safe from being plundered by owners of much faster craft.

At much the same time, attempts were made to give slower craft a chance of winning prizes, if not actual races, against faster craft by the institution of handicapping. As has been mentioned in chapter one, early handicapping systems were over-simple and insufficiently scientific, and it was not difficult for ingenious builders and unscrupulous owners to cheat their intention.

Yet what safeguards yacht racing today as a practical and comparatively inexpensive sport is the continuance of these two first principles: the division of racing craft into classes and the equalization of actual speed by the imposition of handicapping systems. And if you find this talk of organization and discipline tedious, be assured that, without them, sail racing would be almost impossible and would certainly not be seen on the present world-wide, everyman basis.

The first yacht races were between large vessels entirely handled by professionals and, often, the owner himself would be absent during a race, preferring to watch and possibly bet from the sidelines. The first organized races started in England, on the river Thames, and when, many

years later, the Thames became cluttered with commerce, the yacht clubs gravitated to the south coast and the Solent, which has remained the centre of British racing activity ever since. It was to the Royal Yacht Squadron's racing area, the Solent and the waters of the Wight, that the fine American schooner AMERICA came in 1851, winning a silver cup against the combined English fleet, in a race around the Isle of Wight. This was the first bid for international supremacy. AMERICA had been conceived from the outset as the champion of United States yachting on the eastern seaboard. Its success proved what the Americans had long believed—that their sailing craft and sailors were superior to those of the British. The silver cup which the schooner took back to the United States has remained there ever since and has become yacht racing's most famous and most prestigious trophy: the America's Cup.

Today, ambitious yachtsmen outside the United States are still trying to win the America's Cup and are willing to spend millions on a quest that has so far proved fruitless. The Americans, for their part, loyally spend even more heavily to ensure that the cup remains safe in the quarters of the New York Yacht Club. Since 1958, the trophy has been contested in yachts of the *International 12-Metres* class. This Metre formula, which originated at an international meeting held soon after the First World War, allows a designer some latitude in his choice of hull shape, length, depth, width, and weight, as well as in rig. It states absolute limits to such speed-enhancing features as sail-area, height of mast, narrowness of hull, and lightness of displacement, and it places sliding limits on such features as depth of keel and length. Stated in a very simple manner, the formula is length in metres added to the square root of the sail-area in square metres divided by 2.37. The result of this equation must be exactly twelve metres.

This is known as a restricted class, meaning that the

designer is free to design within restrictions which give some safeguard against obsolescence to existing yachts in the class. Over the years, designers have occasionally made important breakthroughs, but usually the gain in speed has been very much less than one per cent at each America's Cup challenge and, more than once, there has been no measurable gain at all.

Other restricted classes which follow this same formula (which dates back to 1919 in its original form) are the *6-Metres* class, which was officially ended by the IYRU fifteen years ago but which shows no signs of dying, the *8-Metres,* which has virtually died, and the *10-Metres,* which only gained a real toe-hold in Scandinavia, and that in the 1930s.

A newer restricted class to a different formula is the *5.5-Metres,* which was used in the Olympic yachting events from 1952 to 1968. This class was planned as a replacement for the too expensive *6-Metres,* but it was turned out of the Olympics when it was considered that it, in turn, had become too expensive for true world-wide competition. What makes any restricted class expensive is the ingenuity of the designer, who continually finds ways, even within the strictest set of rules, to achieve a slightly faster yacht.

It was realized by a few, back in the nineteenth century, that the best way to prevent design obsolescence was to arrange that everybody in a race sailed exactly the same design of yacht. This is the one-design principle which, ever since, has come to have an increasing influence in world yacht racing. Today, there are six classes in the yachting events of the Olympics, and all six are one-design boats. No two vessels can be exactly alike, of course, as there will be slight differences in weight and weight distribution, and possibly larger differences in rig and sails, yet the aim is always to achieve as great a parity as is practicable. The adoption of GRP as a boat-building material, in the 1950s, made it possible to produce better one-designs, since boats built on the same moulds could be expected to be more similar than boats built of wood from different trees. GRP construction still permits of differences, as one man can spread the resin more thickly than another. As a safeguard, new tests have been conceived for measuring the weight distribution within the hull as well as the simple weight of a yacht or dinghy. The principle is that of the pendulum; the hull is balanced and allowed to oscillate back and forth, and the oscillations are timed. A boat with a high concentration of weight in the middle will oscillate faster than one with the weight spread into the ends, and it is known that a boat with light ends will be faster–and possibly dangerously fragile.

In the future, we can look forward to still more similar one-designs, mass-produced in highly automated moulds, with the scope for human error entirely removed.

When they leave the factory, one-designs are carefully measured, weighed, and awarded certificates. When they race in major events, their shape is checked, and details of their sails and rigging are carefully measured. If found to be under weight when built, they must carry corrector weights until remeasured. The one-design idea probably achieved popularity by accident, since it was the result of sales campaigns in the United States to sell plans for lively little sailing-boats that could be easily built at home. Soon, there were large American fleets of such boats as the

Snipe, the *Comet,* and the *Star* keelboat. In other parts of the world, and Scandinavia was a leader, one-design classes came into being as a result of design competitions, which were aimed at finding new, modern, and practical boats which could be cheaply built, raced, and even cruised. For instance, the *Dragon* three-man keelboat came about through a design contest organized by the Royal Gothenburg Yacht Club, the winning designer being Johan Anker of Norway.

Modern yacht racing owes an enormous debt to the one-design principle. One has only to compare the sport with that of powerboat racing, which signally lacks this principle, and which, in consequence, is now conducted mainly by professionals while the amateurs have to watch.

The most popular modern racing classes, numerically speaking, are all one-designs. In the world today, there are over 60,000 *Mirror* dinghies, over 50,000 *Optimists*, a like number of *Lasers* (the fastest-growing class of all), and almost as many *420*s and *Snipes.*

Some criticize the one-design idea because, they say, it prevents the keen owner from achieving greater speed through his own technical ingenuity. They say it is stultifying; yet, in nearly all one-design classes, some scope is offered for detail modification of fittings and, sometimes, rigging. The *Flying Dutchman,* a big two-man centre-boarder, is an example of a loose one-design which allows much scope. Some latitude in hull shape and complete latitude in materials are permitted. The mast may be of any shape, weight, or section and rigged in any way you like. As a consequence, the *Flying Dutchman* is a more expensive class to race than, say, the stricter *505*-class, and the top-level racing life of a *Flying Dutchman* is likely to be shorter than that of stricter classes.

At the other end of the scale is the *Laser* singlehander, a class so strict that all boats are made by one firm, and all sails by another. The choice of fittings is extremely limited. That this is what the world needs is shown by the success of this class, with over 50,000 built in less than five years.

The one-design idea has, not surprisingly, had less numerical success in the larger sizes. The *Folkboat* and the *H Boat* are successful one-designs with cabins, but there is not yet—though many are trying—a truly international, deep-seagoing, one-design class.

A very few racing classes are open in concept. Thus the *International C Class* catamaran limits length to 25 ft (7.62 m) and sail-area to 300 sq ft (27.9 sq m), and that is all. Consequently, the *C Class* has become an extremely fast but complex and fragile craft, which is only used for a very few special events.

Boats do not have to be similar to race against each other. The crews of slower boats can have their chances improved by handicapping. Normally, in handicap races, boats all start together and finish in their own times. Afterwards, the handicap allowances are worked into the finishing times of each boat to evolve the corrected or handicap times. Handicaps can be rule-of-thumb, based on observed performance over a period of time and many races, and subject to slight adjustment in the light of recent performance—rather like a golf handicap—or they can be based more scientifically on an analysis of the various features of a boat which make for speed or tend to rob the boat of speed.

The first type of handicapping is exemplified by the Portsmouth Yardstick method, first used by Britain's Royal Yachting Association and now widely used everywhere for the handicapping of dinghies and similar small craft. As a consequence of a great store of race information, drawn from as many club results as possible, each established class or type is awarded a Yardstick figure, a number. Classes supported by the most thorough information are given Primary Numbers, others are given Secondary Numbers. The Primary Number for a *Flying Dutchman* is 78, that of a *505* is 81, and that of a *Fireball* is 85. Thus if a *Fireball* takes 84 minutes to finish a race which has taken the *Flying Dutchman* 81 minutes and the *505* 82 minutes, the *Fireball* will be placed first, the *505* second, and the *Flying Dutchman* third. Tables are available for the quick calculation of race times.

One should emphasize that, however scientific it may appear, all handicapping is really imprecise. It can never exactly equate every nuance. One boat will have a better chance in one kind of weather, and one in another. Thus handicap racing can never be as fine a form of yacht racing as is level racing, either between one-designs or between yachts designed to rate equally under the same restricted-class rule.

Now let us look at racing boats in another way. They may be divided roughly thus: at the top end are the racing keelboats, the largest of which are likely to have living accommodation. Keelboats have the one great virtue of being uncapsizable (though they may be flooded, in which case they may sink). Because of their extra weight and size they manoeuvre more deliberately, and therefore they need to be handled with more planning and forethought. Some keelboats, such as the *Tempest* and the *Flying Fifteen* both light-weight two-man boats, are halfway to being dinghies, but they still possess the characteristic of being able to bounce upright again after being knocked down by a squall.

The dinghy, by contrast, depends for its stability almost entirely upon the movable weight of its crew, which today is often enabled to extend out to windward on a so-called trapeze wire. For their size, dinghies are faster than keelboats and much quicker in their responses. So they tend to be thought of as young people's boats. Thanks to flotation compartments and similar devices, they are almost always unsinkable. With the help of self-bailing or self-draining devices, they can survive open-water conditions, but they do depend to a great extent upon the strength and energy of their crew and, when that disappears, they are helpless.

In the last Olympics before the Second World War, in 1936 at Kiel, only one of the classes was a dinghy, the others were all keelboats. At present, only two Olympic classes are keelboats, the others are all dinghies. That shows the extent to which the dinghy has predominated in recent years. Of course, it has the great virtues of portability and cheapness.

The third main racing type, more specialized than the others, is the catamaran, which is the fastest inshore racing craft of all. Catamarans derive their enormous initial stability from having two hulls, placed wide apart. Sometimes, as in the case of the *Tornado* class, the stability is augmented by a trapeze for the crew. As a result of this great stability, a cat can carry a bigger higher rig than monohull and, also, a much bigger spread of sail, when seen in proportion to the boat's weight. This, combined with the very slender shape of the hulls, confers great speed on a catamaran, whenever the wind begins to blow a little. The *Tornado* has been timed well in excess of twenty knots. On the other hand, catamarans are slower to turn and generally less manoeuvrable and, in consequence, their racing tends to be less tactical. Winning is more a matter of making your own boat fast, and less a matter of beating the opposition by outwitting it. Whether it be said of catamaran or monohull, it is true that the higher the potential speed of the boat, the less tactical the racing and the more dependent will it be upon sheer "boat speed", by which is meant attention to all those details of rig, sails, trim, hull weight, bottom finish, and keel and rudder shape which, taken together, have such a big influence on performance.

Thus, the *470* class is more tactical than the *Flying Dutchman* class which, in turn, is more tactical than the *Tornado* class. When choosing your racing class, you should try to decide which you prefer: the excitement of a tight battle with other boats or the excitement of travelling fast in a boat you have tuned to perfection. Bear in mind that all boats are faster and better than they used to be. They are lighter but stiffer and stronger, and they are more seaworthy and better able to look after themselves. Sails and rigging stretch less, masts are smaller and lighter yet stiffer and, when they do bend, the degree of bend is controlled and planned for. The sailor himself is better equipped to withstand the elements. His wet suit keeps him warm, his trapeze harness and hiking straps enable him to put his weight to maximum use. His life-jacket (far more common than only ten years ago) makes him safer and, therefore, more willing to drive his boat hard and to take risks. The general standard of both boats and the people who sail them has increased enormously in recent years. It has never been more difficult to win a race.

When planning a course, race organizers follow printed recommendations and regulations. The object is to give a comprehensive all-round test. This means that any single race should give windward sailing and off-wind sailing, both running and reaching across the wind. Since there is always an element of sheer luck in yacht racing, it is normal to score an event over a series of races. It is common, too, to allow for one dropped or discarded race. This allows for gear failure, bad luck with a wind shift, or a bad start that may have been caused by a boat capsizing in front of you. The best thought-out racing regulations and provisions are those of the Olympic regatta, and these are, as nearly as possible, duplicated for all major events.

In the Olympic regatta there are seven races, each crew counting its six best results. There is only one race a day, and halfway through the series, there is a two-day break. Thus nobody can complain that it all happened too quickly, or that any single race became too much of a test of physical stamina.

Each day's race starts late enough in the day—usually soon after noon—to permit the day's wind a chance to settle down and become steady. If one starts at ten a.m., it is quite possible that a sea-breeze will arrive later and cause a 90° change to the wind's direction. This change will almost certainly benefit some more than others.

The present Olympic course is strictly regulated as to length, pattern, and direction. First, there must be a beat, dead into the wind from the starting line to the first mark. The length will depend upon the class raced and will be between 1.5 and 2.2 miles.

The first mark is turned anticlockwise (in sailor's jargon, "the mark is left to port"). There are technical reasons for this which may become clearer later. Then follow two reaching legs, with a mark in between which has to be gybed round. At the end of the second reach is the leeward mark, which also marks the start of the second windward leg.

The windward mark is turned, for the second time anticlockwise. Now comes the square-run leg, reciprocating the windward-leg direction. The leeward mark is turned anticlockwise, and the course finishes with a third and final beat, this time to the finishing line, which is at the opposite end to the start of the course.

This is the conventional Olympic course for all but the *Tornado* catamaran. You will see that it has three long windward legs, two slightly shorter reaching legs, and one long running leg. This reflects the comparative importance of these forms of sailing. It is still widely held that windward sailing is the most difficult and, consequently, most important part of sailing. Yet, in our fast modern boats, it is easier to gain and lose distance off wind.

A further requirement of the course is that every part of it is clear of the influence of the land and as free as possible from tidal streams. In lesser regattas the course pattern is often changed; thus there may be two separate triangles sailed over a slightly smaller course to give the same total distance as has the Olympic course.

This course can only be laid when the wind's direction has been plotted with some accuracy, for instead of a compass course, this is a wind-oriented course. If the wind changes between the course being laid and the start, then the race officer should signal a postponement and have all three marker buoys lifted and dropped elsewhere.

If the wind changes after the race has started, the race officer may, if the rules allow, alter the course during the race. He usually does this by moving the windward mark. But he must, first of all, give warning, by visual and audible signals at the leeward mark on the previous round, that such a change is being made. Usually, he will show the compass course of the new leg on a board. (He will normally have shown the compass course of the original opening windward leg on a board on the committee boat.)

Changing course in mid-race is fraught with difficulty and requires good communications and a reliable boat at each mark. But it does reflect a growing feeling that every race should have its large quota of windward sailing and that a race which does not, is not a good race.

In the Olympic course it is important that the starting line be laid at right angles to the wind (even more important than laying it at right angles to the first leg of the course). If it is not at right angles, one end of it will be unduly favoured, and most alert skippers will plan to start at this favoured point, thus causing a traffic jam, which will usually lead to a ragged and undisciplined start, with many boats crossing the line before the starting gun. If this happens, the race officer has two courses of action: he may note the sail numbers of individual competitors, who cross early, and disqualify them, if they do not return and restart; or, if it is impossible to take each boat's number, he may signal a general recall, bring the entire fleet back, and restart the race.

In today's more popular events it is by no means uncommon to have one general recall followed by another, spread out over two hours or more, while a harassed race officer struggles to get a fleet of more than a hundred over-eager competitors away cleanly. The best safeguard against this indiscipline is a line laid square to the wind. Another safeguard is a strict limitation of numbers. Sixty boats is as much as can be easily started at once.

The requirements of the Olympic course make it essential to start the race from a moored boat, with a movable marker buoy marking the other end of the line. After the start, the boat will lift its anchor, lift the marker buoy, and proceed to the opposite end of the course to make ready the finishing line. The starting line will be down wind of the leeward mark, and the finishing line will be to windward of the windward mark. In this way one class can continue racing while another, ahead of it, is finishing (or maybe one class, behind, is still attempting to get away to a clean start).

The Olympic course is the counsel of perfection. The great majority of inshore races will be sailed over simpler courses. Many are still started from fixed lines, usually from transits erected on a convenient headland or river bank. These starting lines will hardly ever be at right angles to the wind. Consequently, one end of them will always be more favoured than the other.

Clubs that hold their races on narrow rivers and confined waters will not often be able to arrange for the first leg of the course to be to windward. (The idea behind having the first leg to windward is that it is the quickest way of sorting the faster boats from the slower, hence preventing a crush of boats at the first mark.)

To be honest, there is a certain monotony about the Olympic course, endlessly repeated, and there is fun to be had from racing at individual places with their own topographical situations and problems. Thus, at Cowes, the famous Admiral's Cup and Cowes Week are both started from a fixed shore line, made by transits off the Royal Yacht Squadron's castle battlements. Sailors like to complain about this arrangement, but they also enjoy it, for all its shortcomings.

Olympic courses should never be shortened. If the wind is insufficient, the time-limit will be invoked and the race abandoned. The normal Olympic time-limit is five hours, which means that, if the leading boat has not finished within five hours of the start, the race is called off. If it does finish within this time, other boats gain an extension of the deadline, normally one extra hour.

In lesser racing it is normal to shorten a course if the wind drops, or to set a shorter course if the wind is light throughout. The length of a course should be determined by the speed of the competing boats, by the demands made by the boats on their crews, and by the rigours of the conditions. All inshore racing is normally confined to the daylight hours.

The start is the most important part of any yacht race. In today's big and competitive fleets you will never get anywhere unless you can start well, which means crossing the line at full speed within an instant of the starting-gun firing.

Yacht races are started with flying starts. Helmsmen must judge their approach to coincide with the start. To help them in this, there are normally two previous warning guns, the first ten minutes before the start, the second five minutes before the start. Visual signals are made at the same time as the guns are fired (the signals are the important thing, the gun is only to draw one's attention to them and, in the event of a misfire, the signal prevails).

It should be obvious that a perfect start calls for perfect judgement. This calls for a good knowledge and understanding of your boat's speed and handling, an accurate analysis of the starting line itself, and an insight into the likely behaviour of your rivals.

No line is ever laid with absolute accuracy. One end will always be slightly favoured. You can plot which is the better end in several ways; your compass (which every racing boat should have, whether or not it ever sails out of sight of land) is the best instrument for detecting which end is better for you. Many helmsmen, particularly those commanding large craft, like to make dummy starts before the real one, timing themselves over plotted distances. If you start this way, you must beware of last-minute interference by other boats.

The object is to win clear wind for your sails from the start of the race. If you start with other boats already ahead, you suffer not only the disadvantage of having to overtake them to beat them, but also of having their sails shading the wind from your sails and, without the best wind, your sails will be like an engine lacking fuel. So you will fall further behind.

The first racing axiom is: get clear wind for your sails. The second might well be: sail your boat to the best of your ability, and do not look over your shoulder at the others. Axiom number three: never give up until the race is finally won and lost. Axiom number four: when ahead, keep between your most dangerous opponent and the next mark. (This might seem to contradict my second axiom, but it should only be invoked towards the end of a race or series.)

At the ordinary club level of competition, technical ability and tactical experience will win and lose races. At the top level, the characteristics of tenacity, "killer instinct", and sheer physical strength will often be the deciding factor, since all competitors may be presumed to possess adequate technical ability.

The racing rules determine what you may and may not do on the race course. Remember, first and last, that the rules are framed to avoid collision. They are intended to avoid trouble and preserve order, not the reverse. You will find that the best racing sailors usually seem to manage to avoid entanglements in the rules.

The racing right-of-way rules, like everything else, have grown more complicated over the years, but at least we now have a single, world-wide code, though sometimes with local variations. These rules are subject to revision every four years.

There is no space here to consider the minutiae, the intricate little details which so fascinate the sea lawyers. It is, however, essential to grasp, from the beginning, the few corner-stone foundations upon which the whole edifice of the rules is erected.

One boat may not touch another, nor may it touch any of the course marks. The rules are intended to prevent collisions. If two boats touch, one will be in the wrong and should retire from the race, perform a 720° turn, or accept such other penalty as the regatta instructions require. If a boat hits a mark, it must either retire, return and reround the touched mark, or perhaps protest another boat, if it believes that this other boat forced it onto the mark (we will consider protests later).

A boat sailing on the port tack gives way to a boat sailing on the starboard tack. A sailing-boat must always be on one tack or the other, which tack depends upon which side the main boom is—if the boom is to port, the boat is on the starboard tack. It does not matter whether it happens to be beating to windward, with sheets pinned in, or running free, perhaps with main boom on one side and spinnaker pole on the other. The main boom is what decides.

The importance of this rule is that converging boats will normally be on opposite tacks. Given this rule we now know which boat is required to keep clear of the other. The right-of-way boat, for its part, must be careful not to incommode the other as it tries to keep clear. Remember, a port-tack boat is one which has its main boom on the starboard side with the wind coming at it from the port side.

A boat to windward gives way to a boat to leeward. This takes care of the case of two or more converging boats which are on the same tack. The windward boat is the one nearest to the wind.

An overtaking boat keeps clear of the boat it overtakes. This is a common-sense provision. It would be unreasonable to expect an overtaken boat to have to avoid an overtaking boat.

Stemming from this, it is a peculiar but lasting tradition in yacht racing that the overtaken boat has single right of defence. It may luff, head to wind if necessary, to harass a boat which is overtaking it to windward. The overtaken boat may not bear down on a boat which has elected to pass to leeward. It may not alter course at all in this case.

The luffing right is circumscribed by the proviso that once the overtaking boat draws so far ahead that the helmsman, in his normal position, is ahead of the mast of the overtaken boat, the latter must revert to its former course. It is normal for the helmsman of the overtaking boat to hail "Mastline" or "Mast abeam" to signify his claim that this situation has been reached.

It is obviously an advantage to turn inside another when rounding a course mark. Often, this is the easiest way of gaining a place since, if you begin the turn behind but inside, you may easily emerge ahead, when the mark has been rounded.

To prevent disorder when rounding marks, the boat claiming an inside overlap (as it is called) must have established that claim before the leading boat comes within two boat-lengths of the mark itself. In other words, you must not push in at the last moment. In considering overlaps, one takes a line across the leading boat's stern, perpendicular to its centre-line. If the bow of the boat behind cuts this line, it has an overlap. It may be seen that, as soon as the leading boat begins to turn to round the mark itself, it tends to give overlaps to boats behind, which did not previously have them. This is one reason for the two-boat-length proviso—the leading boat will not normally begin its turn until it has come within two lengths of the mark, by which time it is too late to claim an overlap.

This rule leads to much argument and frequent protests. Bear in mind that it does not apply at starts. The boat to leeward can shut a boat to windward out of the starting line altogether. Once the starting gun has fired, the leeward boat may not sail above close-hauled course but is still able to shut out the windward boat, which might otherwise claim an overlap on the buoy or boat marking one end of the starting line.

When two yachts approach an obstruction (which might be another boat, a rock, or other piece of land), the yacht nearest to the obstruction may only claim room to avoid it from the other boats, if it has established an overlap on the other boats before the obstruction was reached. If it did not establish that overlap in good time, it has no right to request "water" (as the term is) and must take other avoiding action. When two boats are tacking towards an obstruction, one boat can hail the other for room to tack away from it. The other must immediately respond but need not itself tack, providing that it can give room for the first to tack in some other way.

The boat on port tack, which decides to put about, or tack, to keep clear of an approaching right-of-way starboard-tack boat, must tack early enough to complete its tack (which means that it must be headed on the new, close-hauled course before the other is forced to alter course in order to avoid it). As soon as a yacht, which crosses the starting line early, begins to return to restart, it loses all of its rights and does not regain them until it has restarted. This means that, in the act of returning, it must keep clear of all others—a difficult business on a crowded starting line.

Nowadays, it is quite common for the sailing instructions to require that an early starter returns round the ends, outside the starting line, and not in between the buoys or boats marking the ends.

A yacht which touches a turning mark must either retire from the race, reround the mark, or protest a boat which it thinks has forced it to hit the mark.

Once you have grasped the above rules, you may go out and race safely. As you go along, you will acquire familiarity with some of the more "recherché", fine details. If you run aground, you are permitted to use your own anchors, oars, paddles, and physical strength to get yourself off. But you may not accept outside assistance, and you must recover all your gear before continuing.

A boat must finish a race with the same crew that was aboard when it started. You may anchor during a race, but you must recover the anchor and cable before proceeding. You may not pick up a mooring. You may not add to your speed artificially, i.e., the boat has to be propelled by the natural action of the wind on the sails, and you must not bring the sails to the wind, roll the boat, or row the rudder. This rule is the source of many protests and arguments since, with small and lively dinghies, it is very easy to augment your speed, particularly in waves, by using your strength and weight. Such use of your body is, indeed, legitimate if the wind is strong enough for you to plane and surf. In 1977, an experimental rule was added which allows limited muscular actions of this kind, if the wind is fresh and a special signal is given.

There is a rule against movable ballast. This has

recently come into increased prominence because of the modern habit of wearing water-soaked sweaters, special heavy jackets, or water-filled jackets to increase one's weight and, hence, the righting moment. For the Olympics, it has been decided that crews may be asked to strip after a race. All their clothing will then be soaked with water, allowed to drain for a minute, and then weighed. If it weighs more than 20 kg (44.1 lb) per person, they will be liable to disqualification.

Mention has been made of protesting. You may already have realized that more than one rule may be involved in any single situation and, often, these rules will appear to conflict. When there is doubt about who was wrong in a collision, a skipper feeling himself to have been in the right will lodge a formal, written protest. This will be considered by a jury. Witnesses may be called, evidence agreed, and a written verdict handed down.

If one party feels that, the evidence having been agreed, the verdict is incorrect, he may, in very special circumstances, lodge an appeal to his national yacht racing authority. A race officer may lodge a protest, and a competitor may protest a race officer. But if you can avoid all this trouble, and you usually can, it is better to do so.

It may be timely here to consider briefly the structure of world yacht racing. At the top is the IYRU. This body writes the racing rules, oversees the racing classes, and coordinates the most important fixtures. It conducts its business through specialized committees, and its members are delegates sent by national authorities who, in turn, represent clubs and national classes.

Tactics are extremely important in racing, since a race is never straightforward but is as subtle as the wind and current are changeable. Every wind shift of more than 5° brings its own tactical opportunities. One should start from the assumption that the wind and the tidal current will be changing. If they were constant, it would be possible—and best—to sail the windward leg in two long tacks, for the fewer times you tack, the less time you lose.

In fact, because the wind will be shifting this way and that, it will be necessary to tack constantly, in order to get on to the gaining tack. First you must understand the terms. A wind that is said to veer changes direction clockwise: thus it might go from south to west (though it is more likely to go from 180° to, say, 190°).

A wind which backs goes anticlockwise; thus it might go from 180° to 165°, from S to SSE.

It is normal for the summer breeze to veer during the day, the magnitude of veer being more marked in the afternoon and evening. Yet this rule is far from being invariable.

When you find that the wind is going more ahead, your boat is said to be headed. If you are tacking to windward, this is the time to think of putting about, because the same wind which heads you when on starboard tack will be freeing you on port tack. A "freeing" wind, or "a freer", is a wind which enables you to luff up and sail higher.

Though a freeing wind may be pleasant to find, it is usually the headers which will help you gain ground when racing to windward, and it is the headers you want to look for, as they permit you to put about and gain on the contrary tack. Sometimes, the land or some other feature will

cause a permanent wind bend, which can be used to advantage on a windward leg.

Because of the changeability of the wind, it is usually unwise to go too far out to one side or other on the windward leg, and it is safer to sail up a cone, towards the weather mark, decreasing the length of your tacks as you approach.

On the reaching legs, though you must guard against boats coming up on your windward side and taking your wind, you should be still more concerned not to luff too far to windward of the next mark. It is better and quicker to hold to the direct-course line. The advantage of this will become apparent as you approach the next mark, as those who have luffed high will have to bear off and will be slowing down; those who have kept low will be holding speed and, maybe, even gaining.

Offwind, use the harder puffs to bear off and get down wind. Use the lighter puffs to luff and keep good speed. Usually, it pays to sail in a series of angles which will be dictated by the wind speed. Often, the wave pattern will lead to further helm changes.

When running before the wind, even with a big spinnaker set, it will normally pay to sail in a series of slants, gybing between each. This is because all boats sail faster with the wind slightly on the beam instead of square over the stern. Catamarans are especially appreciative of being "tacked down wind", as this practice is called. The extra distance sailed is not as important as the extra speed.

We will mention one more tactical ploy: the so-called safe leeward position. This is of great defensive value when you are covering another boat on a windward leg. It may seem safer to cover him to windward, but it is actually far more effective to be to leeward, for in this way the other boat gets the bad wind which bounces off your own sails, and this slows him more than if he were merely in your wind shadow.

Let us agree, then, that yacht racing is usually very tactical, which explains why it appeals to the intellect as much as to the senses, and why some men remain top-class winners long after their youthful vigour and natural quickness have deserted them. Do not worry if you make tactical mistakes. This is bound to happen. What should concern you is that you do not repeat the same mistakes. The capacity to learn is what distinguishes the good sailor from the bad.

We have assumed that yacht racing takes the form of a race or series of races in which several boats take part together, each one racing for itself. But there are other forms, too. The most famous yacht racing trophy of all, the America's Cup, is for match racing, which means that it is competed for by only two boats. Match-racing tactics are quite different from and, usually, even more fascinating than those of ordinary racing. For instance, it does not matter how late one boat in a match race may be in crossing the starting line, providing that it crosses that line ahead of the other line. The problem in match racing is to get ahead of your opponent and, once ahead, to cover him and keep him behind. You can luff him as hard and as often as you like, and tack to cover whenever he tacks, for there will be no third boat to slip in ahead of you both. In the United States, the Congressional Cup, held always in San Diego, is giving wider notice to this interesting, if specialized, form of racing.

Then there is team racing. In the best form of team racing, one team of three or four boats races against another of like number. The point is not for any one boat to come in first but for the team to score more points than the opposing team. You may decide to let an opposing team boat go out ahead and win if, by so doing, your boats, which now outnumber the rest of the winning boat's team, can force it into the last places. This sort of team racing is best when sailed in small and responsive dinghies. Because of the scope for harassment, there are special rules for team racing. It is a sport that has special appeal with school and university sailors and, also, those racing on confined waters.

The Admiral's Cup, now regarded as one of the leading world events in yacht racing, exemplifies another form of team racing. Here, each nation nominates its team of three yachts. All teams race together, and the team that has the most points at the end wins. It may be seen that, in actual fact, the scope for real team tactics is very limited, as each skipper will be trying to score the most points possible for himself and his team.

In the case of an event involving several teams, it is best, from a team-racing point of view, to have one team sail another, a pair at a time, in a round-robin or knock-out system. In this way, the repertoire of team tactics may be given full scope.

Some races are limited to solo sailors, not only races in dinghy classes such as the *Finn, Moth, OK,* and *Laser,* but also in larger craft over much longer distances. The Singlehanded Transatlantic Race is a case in point. A very few races, the Round Britain Race is one, are limited to crews of two.

Some handicap events take the form of pursuit races. The slowest start first and the fastest last, and the first home is the winner. The difficulty with this form of handicapping is that the wind speed, and hence the speed of the boats and the time taken for the race, will have to be guessed at beforehand. Though in most ways a more exciting form of handicap racing, it is by its nature a more rough-and-ready form.

A word about scoring: in the Olympic system the best crew is the one with the least points. The winner of a race gets zero, second home gets 3 points, third home 5.7 points, fourth 8 points, fifth 10 points, and sixth 11.7 points. After that, you get your placing plus 6 points. This is a compromise system which encourages one to take risks in order to win, since the difference between first and second is 3 and between seventh and eighth only one. Yet many series are still won by crews who do not win a single individual race.

How do you begin to go yacht racing? The best way is to find a friend who is already in the sport and persuade him to take you along as crew. This will give you an insight into what it is all about and what sort of yacht racing is likely to suit you best. Failing this, seek out your nearest sailing club. When buying your first racing boat, try to join a proper class which is raced locally. Handicap racing in a variegated fleet is not as much fun. If you can, buy a boat of a well-established, widespread class. Such a class is likely to give the best choice of racing, will permit you to race abroad, and will be likely to sustain the resale value of your boat.

Much of the satisfaction of racing is to be got from

maintaining your boat at concert pitch. You sails, which are your engine, must be examined regularly for signs of stretch. Once they depart from the maker's original shape, they will become slower. The fastest racing hulls are the stiffest. If a hull bends, it absorbs energy, and the distorted shape will cause speed-sapping drag.

Aerodynamic drag, or windage, mainly affects the rig, so it is most important to reduce it to the minimum there. The drag of an over-large mast will hurt you a second time, because it will interrupt the clean flow of the wind over the mainsail as well as cause drag on its own account.

Nothing stops a boat like too much weight. As Uffa Fox, a famous sailor, once said, "Weight is useful only to the designer of a steam roller." Most racing classes have minimum weight rules, and you should strive to get your boat and gear down to this minimum. Better than that, you must work to concentrate that weight as close to the centre of the boat as possible. Weight in the ends is bad, because it induces heavy pitching.

Look to the shape of your rudder and keel or centre-board. When working in deep water, the finish and sectional shape of these are more vital even than the finish of the bottom of your hull. Do not worry about gloss, but take care to eliminate all hollows. Opinions vary as to the best sectional shape of fins. In general, the leading edge should be parabolic and rounded rather than sharp, the trailing edge should be as sharp as is practicable, and the maximum thickness, or chord, should be between one third and one half the distance from the leading edge. Rudder blades which change their working angle frequently can be profitably fatter than keels and centre-boards and can be given a more rounded leading edge.

You may think yourself a very fine sailor—until you have sailed your first race. Once you have got over the humiliation, you will begin to see the great attractions of this sport. Then you will become a keen racing enthusiast, and then, and only then, will you be on the road to becoming a truly fine sailor.

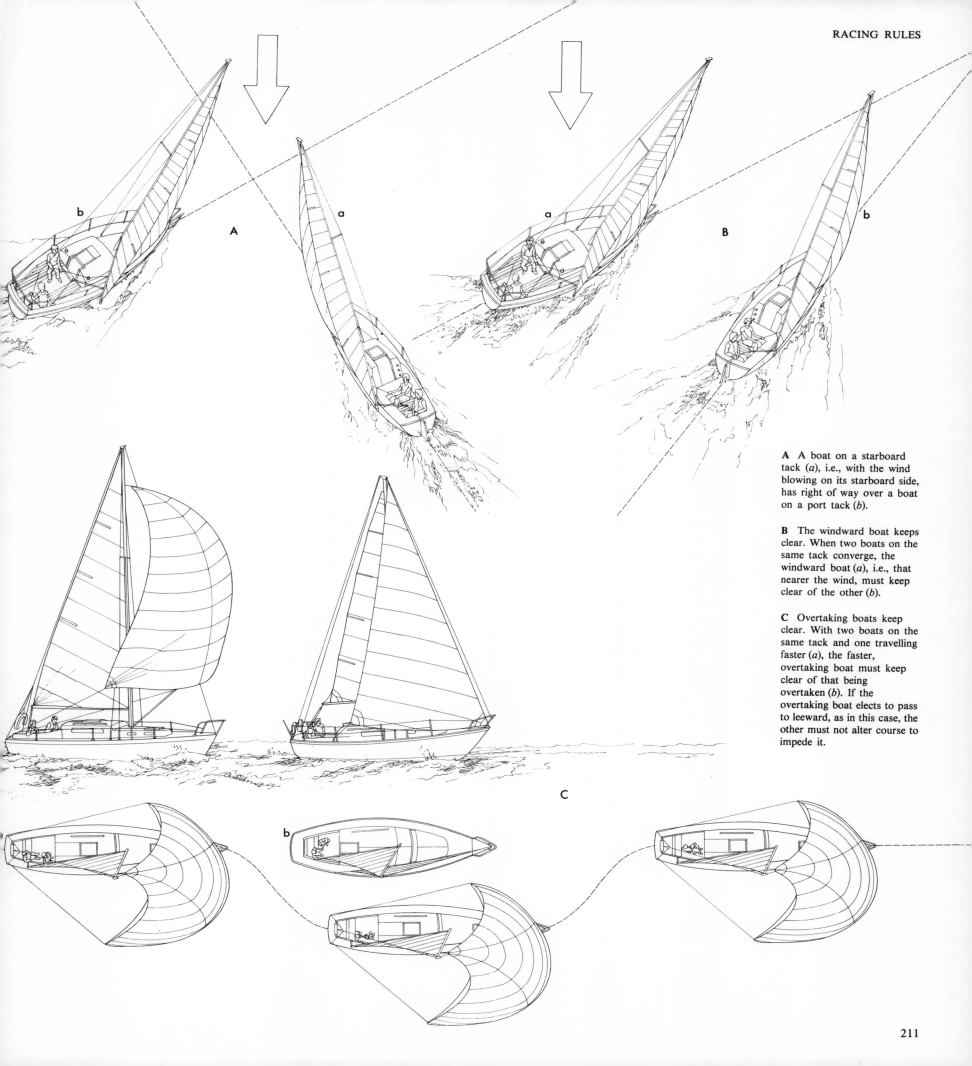

A A boat on a starboard tack (*a*), i.e., with the wind blowing on its starboard side, has right of way over a boat on a port tack (*b*).

B The windward boat keeps clear. When two boats on the same tack converge, the windward boat (*a*), i.e., that nearer the wind, must keep clear of the other (*b*).

C Overtaking boats keep clear. With two boats on the same tack and one travelling faster (*a*), the faster, overtaking boat must keep clear of that being overtaken (*b*). If the overtaking boat elects to pass to leeward, as in this case, the other must not alter course to impede it.

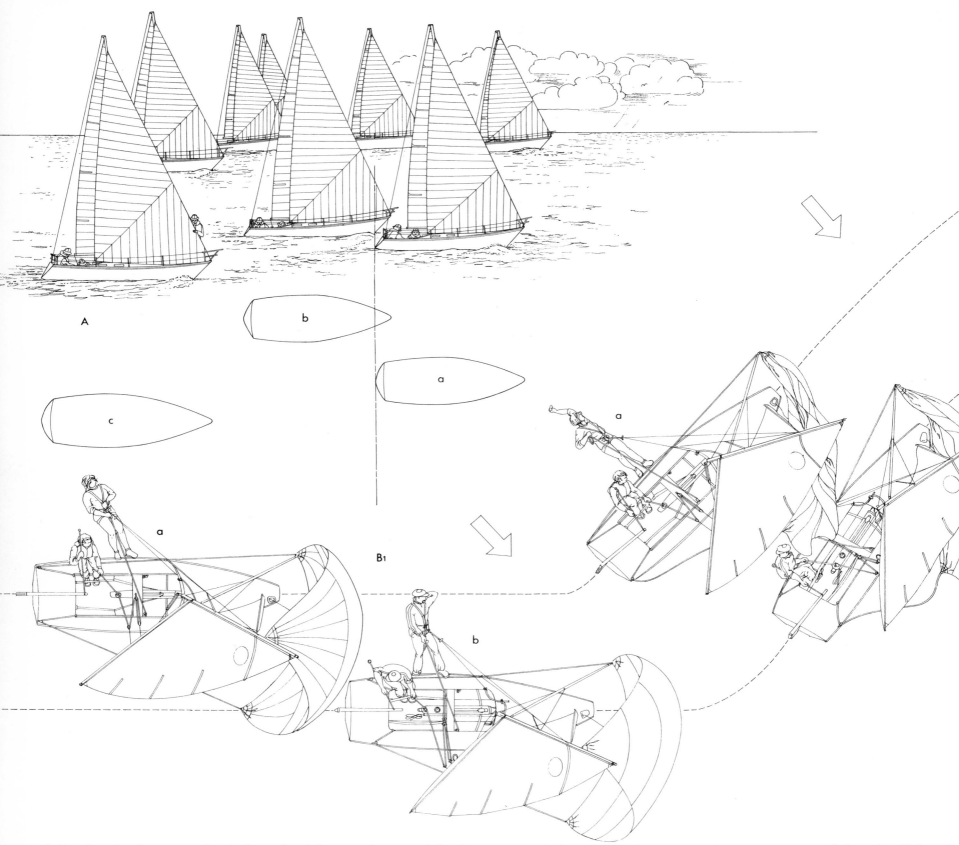

A

b

a

c

a

B₁

a

b

b

A Boat *b* overlaps boat *a*, because a line drawn at right angles across the stern of *a* cuts across the bow of *b*. Boat *a* may, therefore, luff boat *b*, head to wind, if it wishes. Boat *c* is clear astern of both *a* and *b*, and may go where it pleases, there being no overlap.

B These two dinghies, moving fast under spinnakers, show how overlaps work, when one boat overtakes another to windward. (**1**) Seeing that boat *a* is coming up to windward, boat *b* is free to head up, head to wind. Boat *a*, once its bow overlaps boat *b*, must immediately respond. (**2**) The situation changes radically once boat *a* draws up so far that its helmsman, sighting across his boat, finds that he is personally ahead of the other's mast. Once this position has been reached, he is entitled to hail " Mast abeam" or similar words. (**3**) Upon receiving this hail, the other helmsman is obliged to resume the course he was holding before he began to luff to impede the overtaker.

C Two boats are sailing towards a turning mark. If the boat behind, *a*, establishes an inside overlap before the leading boat (*b*) has come within two boat-lengths of the mark, boat *a* is entitled to call for water and may turn inside the other, thus gaining an advantage.

D The fleet is coming in to its start with the windward boat (*a*) overlapping the next to leeward (*b*). All are close-

hauled on a starboard tack, except for boat *a*, which is reaching off wind slightly in order to get to the right side of the race committee's boat (*c*). This is a complex situation which changes with the firing of the starting gun. Before the gun has fired, boat *b* may head close-hauled, even if this means squeezing boat *a* onto the wrong side of the committee boat. After the starting signal, and provided that it had established its overlap beforehand, boat *a* is entitled to room between the committee boat and boat *b*.

A fresh breeze, an international fleet of fast and furious *505* dinghies, and the second mark of the Olympic-style course appears almost before the busy crews are ready for it.

Approaching on the plane on a starboard spinnaker reach, each boat must be gybed, every other boat must be avoided, legitimate buoy overlaps must be requested

and agreed, the others must be decisively rejected.

There is much shouting about such things, and many commands from skipper to crew, with a few protests hurled the other way. The *505* dinghy has an unusually long spinnaker pole which must be somehow unrigged from the starboard side of the mast and set up on the other side, once the sails are across. The *505*'s

hull is inherently unstable, so the helmsman's prime concern, as he pulls his tiller towards him and brings in the mainsheet, must be to keep an even keel. More capsizes occur in a *505* at the gybing mark than anywhere else.

The Americans in US 6847 having gybed neatly, have preserved their lead and, since the forward hand is already fully extended on his

trapeze and all three sails are pulling hard and the hull is already skidding on a plane, they must be pulling away from the others, who are all still struggling with sails and gear, and struggling, too, to avoid one another.

Sailing is more athletic than it ever used to be.

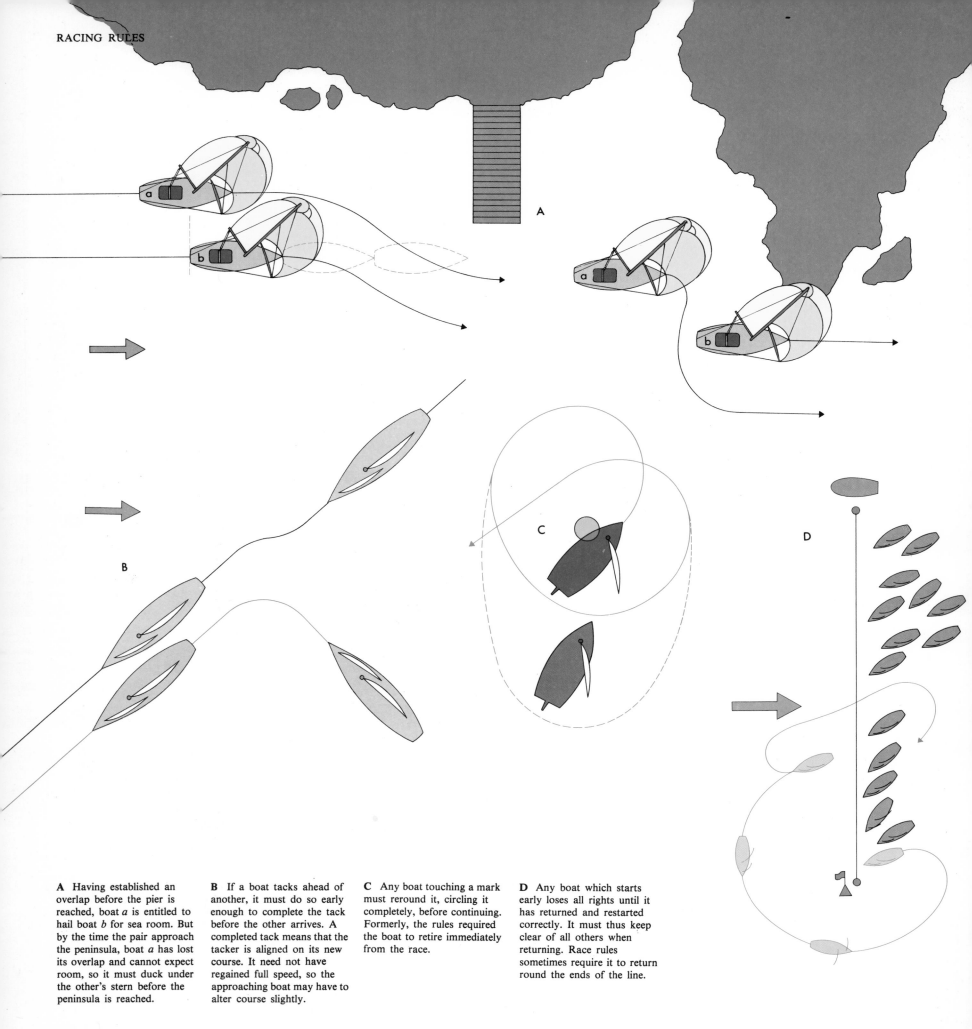

A Having established an overlap before the pier is reached, boat *a* is entitled to hail boat *b* for sea room. But by the time the pair approach the peninsula, boat *a* has lost its overlap and cannot expect room, so it must duck under the other's stern before the peninsula is reached.

B If a boat tacks ahead of another, it must do so early enough to complete the tack before the other arrives. A completed tack means that the tacker is aligned on its new course. It need not have regained full speed, so the approaching boat may have to alter course slightly.

C Any boat touching a mark must reround it, circling it completely, before continuing. Formerly, the rules required the boat to retire immediately from the race.

D Any boat which starts early loses all rights until it has returned and restarted correctly. It must thus keep clear of all others when returning. Race rules sometimes require it to return round the ends of the line.

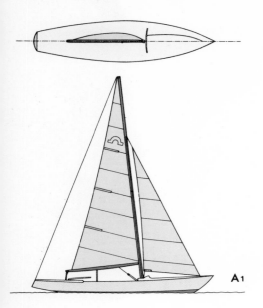

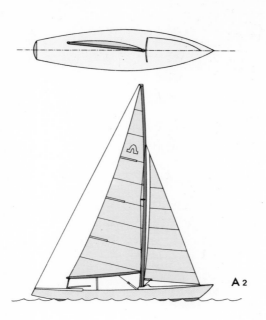

A_1

A_2

A_3

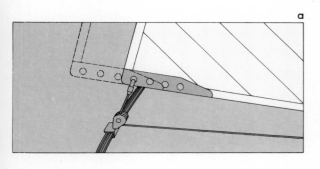

a

A Trimming a *Soling*. (**1**) In light airs to windward, the mast is raked aft but kept straight (unless the sailmaker specifies otherwise). The mainsail clew is eased inwards a little. The jib is sheeted to the aft corner of the clewboard (*a*). Both main and jib are sheeted close to the centre-line (see plan view), but neither sheet is very tight, so the sails are allowed to twist off at the top. (**2**) To windward in more wind, the mast is more upright, but the backstay is tightened to induce bending. The jib sheet is attached to a more forward point on the clewboard. Both sails are sheeted harder and at wider angles. The Cunningham downhaul is tightened. This flattens the camber of the sails. (**3**) Under spinnaker, the backstay is eased, allowing the mast to lean forward. The boom-vang tension prevents the boom from lifting and the mainsail from twisting.

B Trimming a *Flying Dutchman* is different, as there is no backstay. Main shrouds do the backstay's job by being led aft of the mast. The mainsail is flattened for sailing in hard winds by tensioning the mainsheet. The leech of the jib is eased in strong wind by raking the mast. (**1**) In a good breeze, the *Flying Dutchman,* like most dinghies, can be given stability by the righting lever of its crew. The small mast spreader (*a*) controls the bend of the middle of the mast. The mast is allowed to bend to leeward at the top in order to ease the leech of the sail and to reduce heeling pressure.

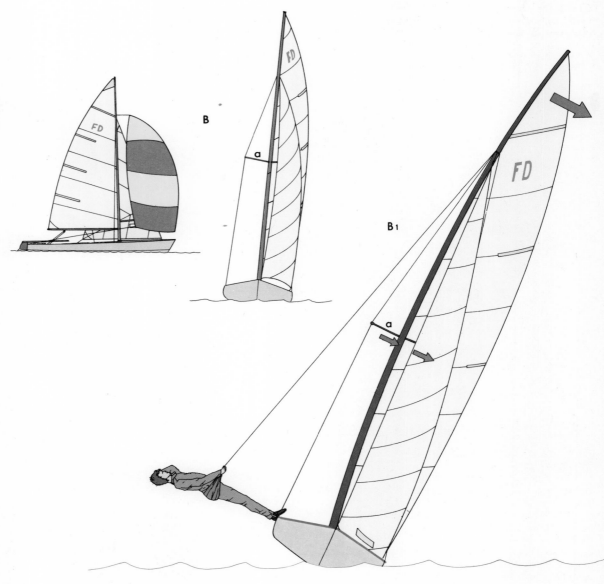

B

B_1

217

A Under the pressure of racing competition, quicker ways of adjusting sails and trim have been developed. Such developments are typified by the Olympic *Soling* three-man keelboat. In this class, it is now possible to make any kind of adjustment, and even to hoist the spinnaker, while the crew is hiking out over the weather rail. (Once one or more has come into the cockpit, stability is reduced, the boat heels more, and speed decreases.)

The *Soling* class was designed by the Norwegian Jan Herman Linge. We show here a *Soling* built and fitted by Paul Elvström, the famous Danish sailor and four-time Olympic gold medallist. The controls of this boat look complicated, because almost every one of them is double-ended (so that it can be adjusted from both sides of the boat).

(1) Quick adjustment for backstay. **(2)** Mainsheet-traveller adjustment (helmsman). **(3)** Spinnaker

halyard. The helmsman hoists while the crew controls sail, guys, and poles. **(4)** Fine, extra-powerful backstay control (helmsman). **(5)** Line for controlling length of toe straps (optional). **(6)** Double-ended mainsheet (helmsman). **(7)** Spinnaker sheet and guy (middle hand). These are led below deck at the stern (*a*). **(8)** Mainsail-clew outhaul (middle hand). **(9)** Mainsail-Cunningham adjustment at tack (*b*), operated by the middle hand. **(10)** Fine adjustment of kicking-strap (optional). **(11)** Jib-sheet adjustment (forward hand). **(12)** Jib-traveller adjustment (forward hand). **(13)** Jib-luff tension (optional). **(14)** Self-tacking jib track. **(15)** Jib-halyard quick-hoist. **(16)** Spinnaker-pole downhaul. **(17)** Forestay tension (tighten when running, and the mast will lean forward). **(18)** Jib-halyard fine adjustment. **(19)** Main halyard. **(20)** Kicking-strap adjustment. **(21)** Spinnaker-pole traveller hoist (goes up inside of mast). **(22)** Spinnaker-pole uphaul.

(23) Spinnaker bins (two to port and two to starboard). **(24)** Spinnaker-pole traveller. **(25)** Halyards, pole uphaul, and pole traveller hoist, all inside the mast. **(26)** Compasses. **(27)** Hinged tiller extension. **(28)** Toe straps for hiking. **(29)** Self-bailer.

B Racing pulley-block. The sheave has a large diameter to lessen friction, and it is made of plastic for lightness.

C Schematic drawing of the stern, showing how the backstay is adjusted. Line *a* is for rapid adjustment and is led to the centre of the aft end of the cockpit (**1** in illustration **A**). The helmsman casts this off to let the mast lean forward, after the weather mark has been rounded. In addition, there are two finer but more powerful controls (*b*), one led to port and one to starboard (**4** in illustration **A**). These owe most of their power to a differential winch (*c*).

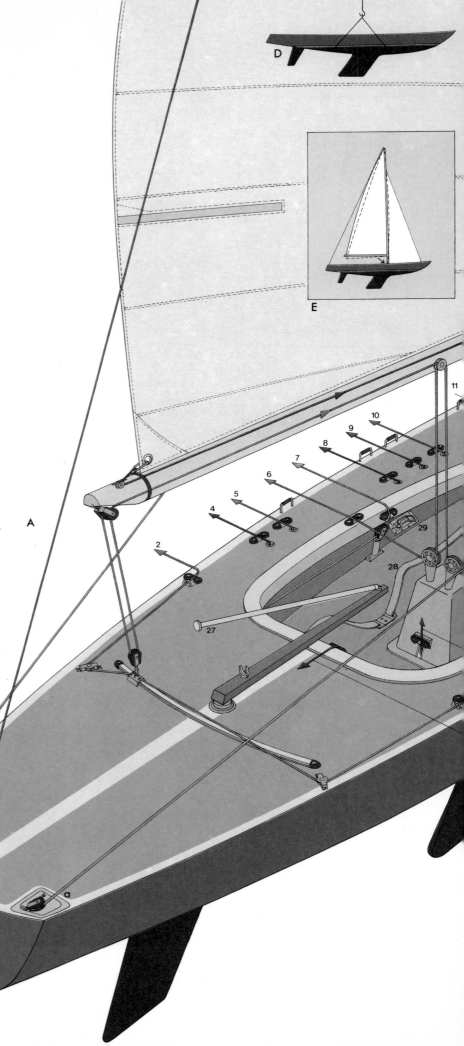

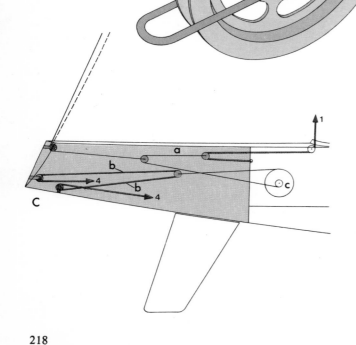

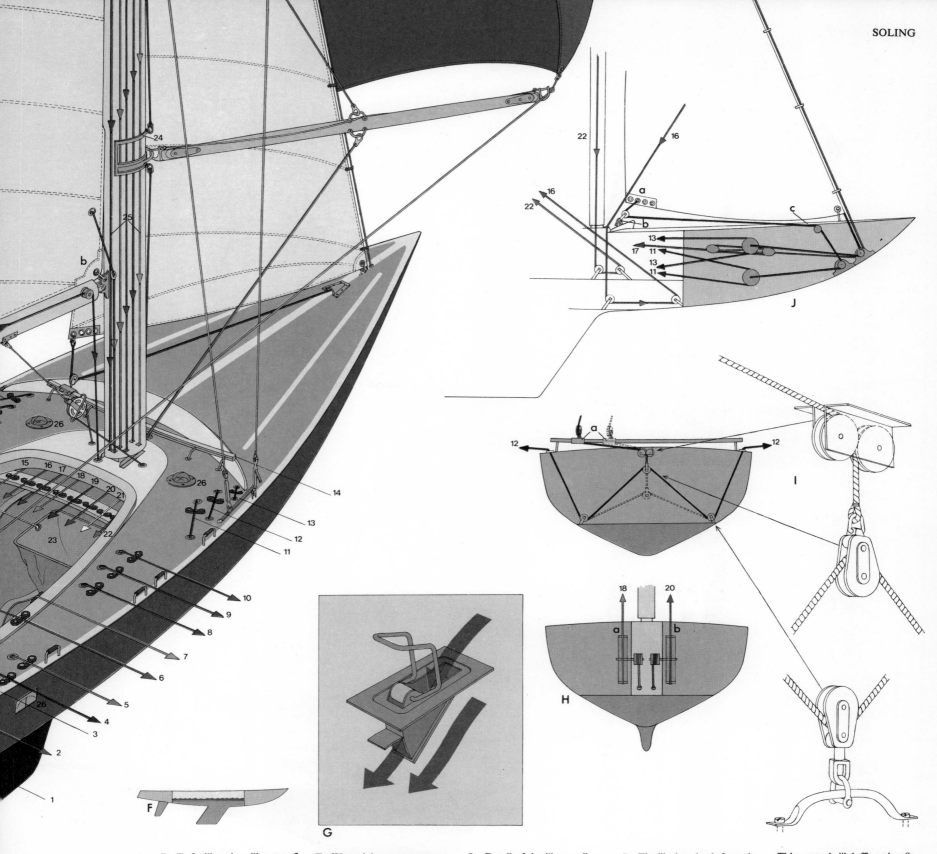

D To facilitate handling out of the water, wire rope bridles are shackled into two eyes fitted to keel bolts, and are then led to the hook of a hoist or crane.

E The kicking-strap is used to prevent the boom from rising, as well as to pull the boom down in order to bend the mast aft.

F Watertight compartments are found under the cockpit floor and at the bow and stern.

G Four self-bailers, two at each side, are fitted.

H A cross section at the mast shows the differential winches for the fine adjustment of the jib halyard tension (*a*) and for the kicking-strap control (*b*).

I Detail of the jib traveller adjustment. Lines led to the forward hand on the port and starboard sides (**12** in illustration **A**) control the distance the jib traveller (*a*) is allowed to slide out from the centre-line.

J The jib sheet leads from the jib clew (*a*) down through the jib traveller (*b*) and forward to just aft of the jib tack, where it goes through the deck at *c*, and back to the control lines to port and starboard (**11** in illustration **A**). A second line leads from the jib tack down through the deck and aft to a block from which control lines go to port and starboard (**13** in illustration **A**).

This controls jib luff tension (it is tightened as the wind freshens).

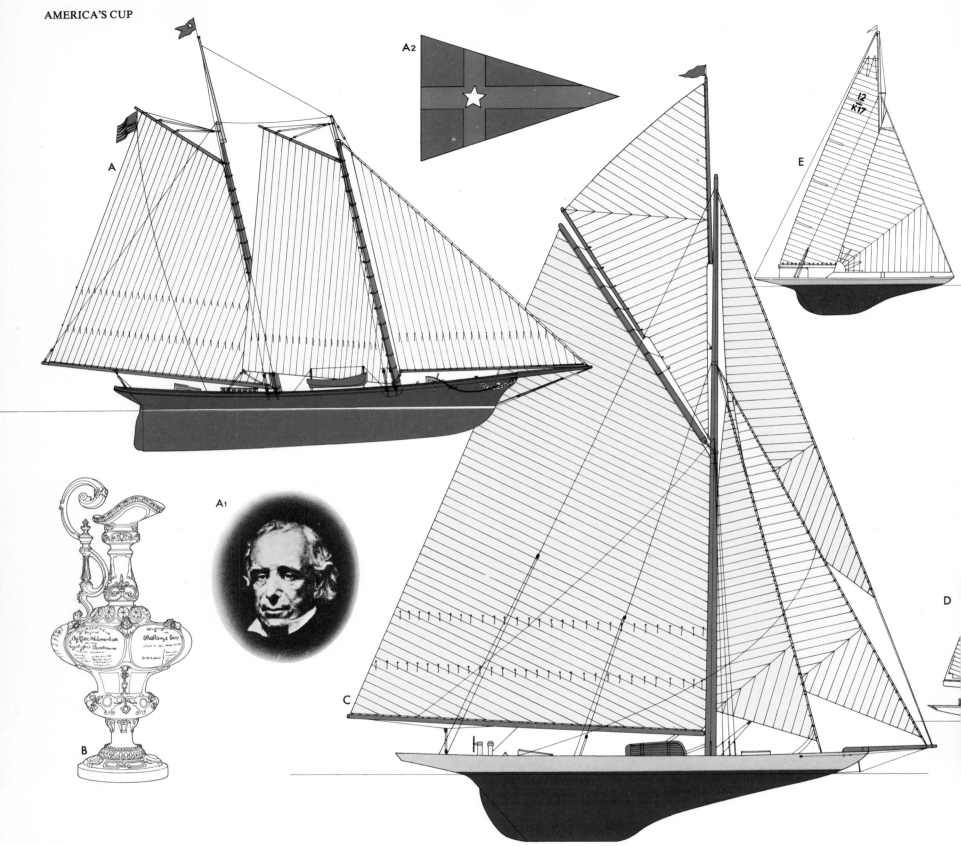

The America's Cup race, held every third year, is the one of the most important, and certainly the most glamorous of all yachting events. Since the trophy was first won by the United States in 1851, no other nation has succeeded in winning it.

A AMERICA, first winner, was owned by a syndicate of six Americans, led by John Cox Stevens (**1**), Commodore of the New York Yacht Club, whose burgee is shown (**2**). In 1851, AMERICA beat a squadron of schooners and cutters off the Isle of Wight to win the trophy.

B The cup itself, first known as the "100 Guineas Cup", was put up by the Royal Yacht Squadron in England.

C RESOLUTE defended the cup in 1920 against the British SHAMROCK IV. This was the first race in which amateur skippers commanded, and the last to be held in New York

waters. RESOLUTE was designed by Nathaniel Herreshoff.

D ENDEAVOUR II, a *J*-class cutter designed by Charles Nicholson, was soundly defeated by the American RANGER, in 1937. This was the final race to be contested by *J*-class boats.

E The first contest held after the Second World War was in 1958, between the *12-metres* yachts SCEPTRE (shown here), for Britain, and COLUMBIA for the United States. Again, the challenge was unsuccessful.

F Modern *12-metres* design is shown by some of the boats

involved in the 1977 America's Cup. (**1**) SOUTHERN CROSS II, one of the two Australian challengers, was designed by Miller and Valentijn. (**2**) One of the two American boats built to defend the cup was ENTERPRISE, designed by Olin Stephens. (**3**) FRANCE II, the French challenger, was

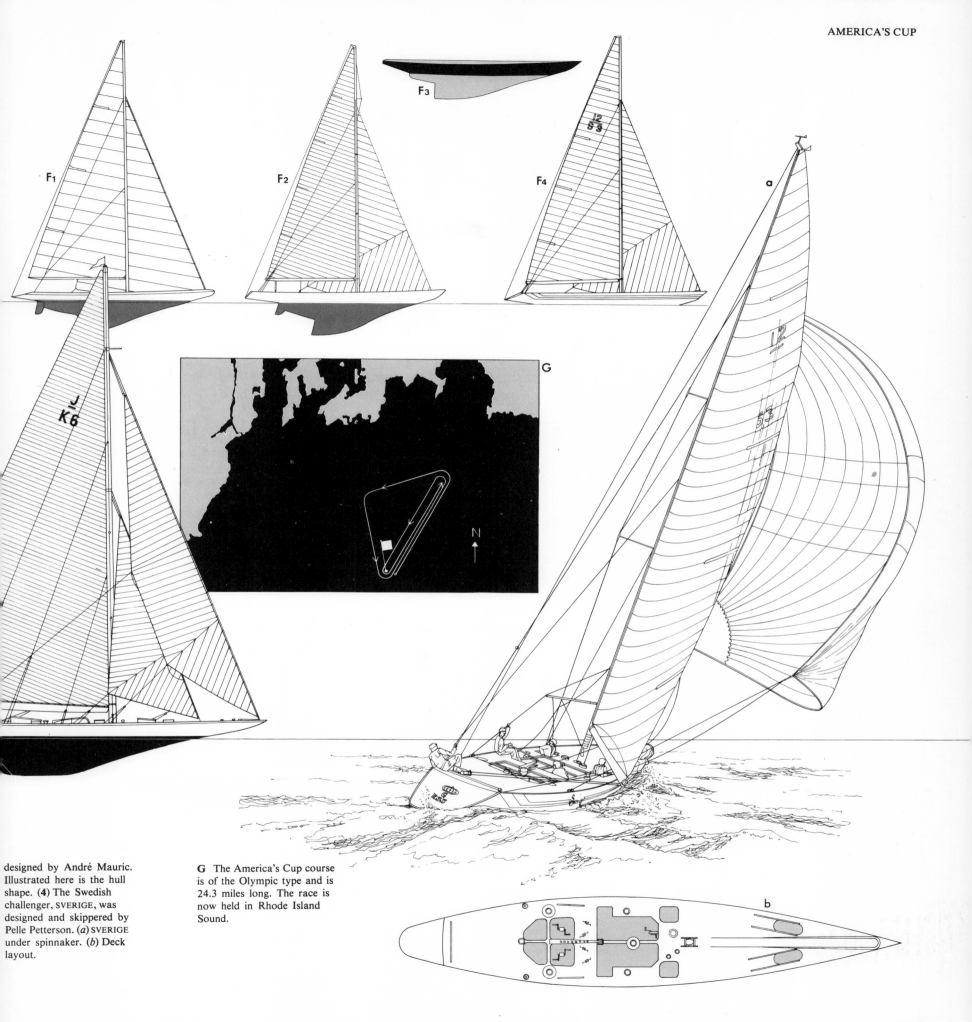

designed by André Mauric. Illustrated here is the hull shape. (4) The Swedish challenger, SVERIGE, was designed and skippered by Pelle Petterson. (a) SVERIGE under spinnaker. (b) Deck layout.

G The America's Cup course is of the Olympic type and is 24.3 miles long. The race is now held in Rhode Island Sound.

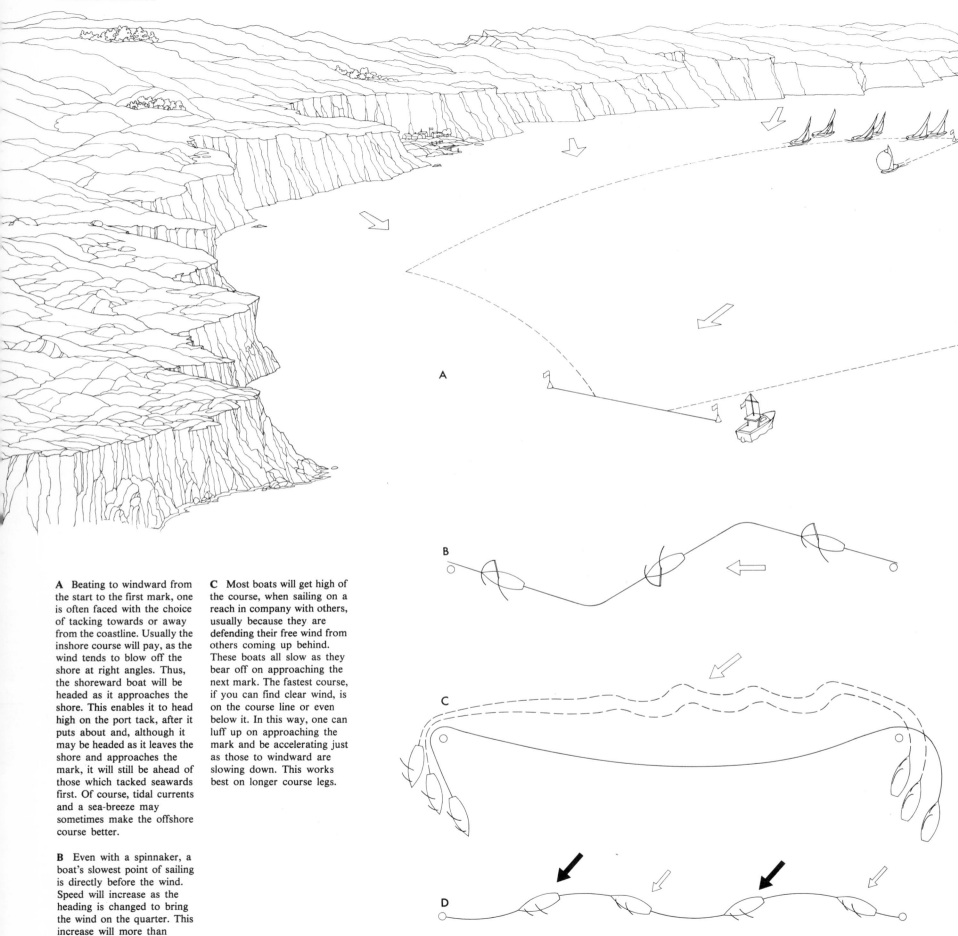

A Beating to windward from the start to the first mark, one is often faced with the choice of tacking towards or away from the coastline. Usually the inshore course will pay, as the wind tends to blow off the shore at right angles. Thus, the shoreward boat will be headed as it approaches the shore. This enables it to head high on the port tack, after it puts about and, although it may be headed as it leaves the shore and approaches the mark, it will still be ahead of those which tacked seawards first. Of course, tidal currents and a sea-breeze may sometimes make the offshore course better.

B Even with a spinnaker, a boat's slowest point of sailing is directly before the wind. Speed will increase as the heading is changed to bring the wind on the quarter. This increase will more than outweigh the extra distance sailed.

C Most boats will get high of the course, when sailing on a reach in company with others, usually because they are defending their free wind from others coming up behind. These boats all slow as they bear off on approaching the next mark. The fastest course, if you can find clear wind, is on the course line or even below it. In this way, one can luff up on approaching the mark and be accelerating just as those to windward are slowing down. This works best on longer course legs.

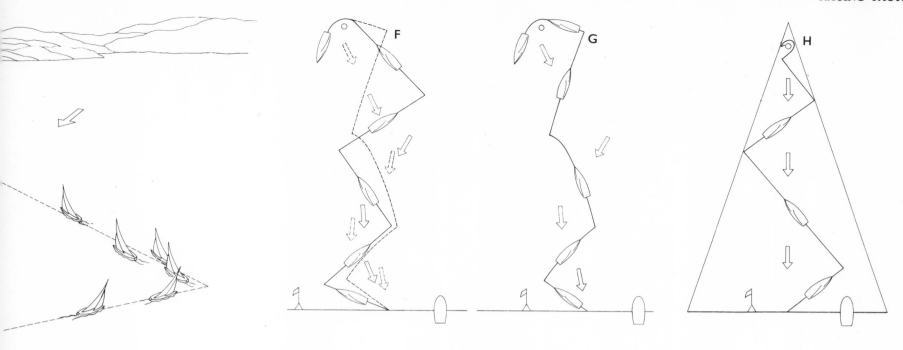

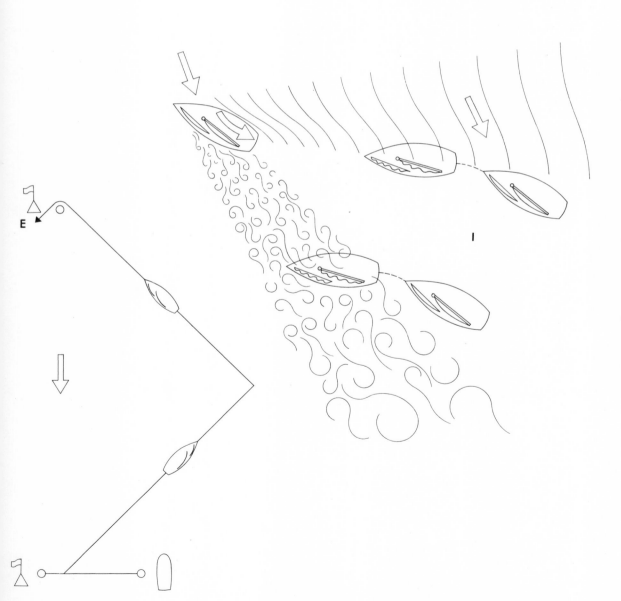

D The wind shifts in strength and direction, as much when one sails down wind as up, but upwind changes are harder to analyse. The main aim is to retain the fastest speed and never mind the heading. To keep speed up, one must luff as the wind drops, and bear off to resume course each time it rises. Bear off, too, if the wind draws ahead slightly; luff up if it draws aft.

E If the wind was constant in direction, the fastest way of sailing the windward leg would be with only two tacks, approaching the mark on the right-of-way, starboard tack. The only difficulty would be in judging the right moment to tack to lay the far-off mark.

F Because the wind is always shifting, it must be exploited properly. Start on the tack that takes you closer to the distant mark. When headed by the wind, tack. On the "dream" beat to windward, you would be headed at regular intervals, enabling you to shorten greatly the distance sailed to the turning mark.

G If the wind should free as one nears the end of each tack, it would take a nightmarishly long time to reach the mark, and would mean a much longer distance sailed (dotted line). In practice, of course, the wind is never completely helpful and hardly ever completely harmful. The skill lies in maximizing the opportunities and minimizing the ill fortune.

H To reduce the risk of overstanding the weather mark and of sailing unnecessary extra distance, it is best to tack up a cone with its apex at the mark, shortening tacks as you approach. Be prepared to break this rule in shifty winds.

I When beating to windward, use the wind from your own sails to harm others, either the back wind (reflected wind which bounces back behind you) or the wind shadow (cast by your sails to your leeward). Those in the back wind or shadow will drop further behind.

A The modern Olympic course is used in most of today's major, inshore events. It consists of a start into the eye of the wind, followed by a windward leg to the first mark (*a*). Then comes a broad reach to the second mark (*b*), where the fleet gybes before going on a second broad reach to the lee mark (*c*).

This first round is followed by a second windward leg to mark *a*, then a square run back to mark *c*.

Finally comes the last leg, which consists of beating into the wind towards the finishing line. Note that the course direction is normally counter-clockwise (because the boats turn the marks on the right-of-way, starboard tack). Note also that the starting and finishing lines are at opposite ends of the course and are normally outside the course itself (to prevent congestion when several races are being held over the same course). If the waters are confined and the legs have to be shortened, the number of laps will be increased.

B When the line is not at right angles to the wind, distance will be saved by starting at the end closest to the next mark, but remember that you will be well advised to start on the right-of-way, starboard tack. Remember, too, that each time you put about you will lose speed and time.

C The race organizer must ensure that the starting line is at right angles to the wind, even if it is not directly down wind from the first mark. This diagram shows that the three different courses are of the same length to a mark, not directly up wind.

D With the line at right angles to a steady wind and with the first mark up wind, any course from any part of the line should take you to the mark equally quickly—except that each tack steals time.

E One way of finding the favoured end of the starting line: luff, head to wind, when you are up to the line. The end to which your bow points is the favoured end for starting.

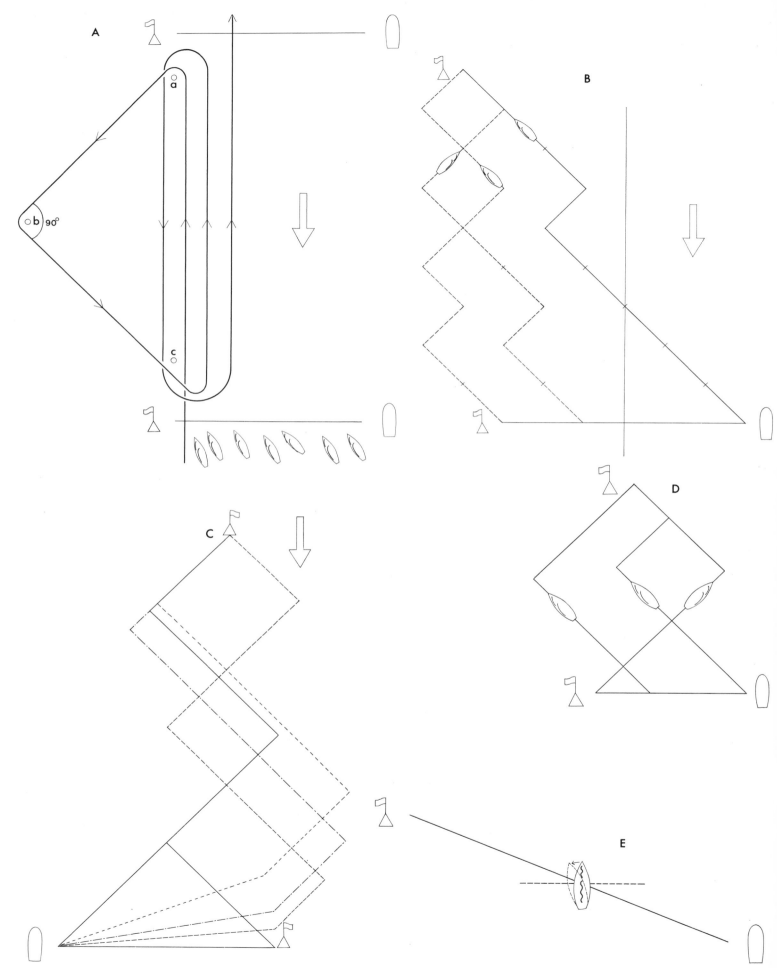

OCEAN RACING

Alain Gliksman

Thomas Fleming Day, editor-in-chief of the American magazine *The Rudder* and passionate advocate of the use of small sailing-boats on the high seas, was the man who, in 1906, organized the first-ever ocean race, from Rhode Island to Bermuda. Two years previously, Day had decided to prove that small boats could be raced safely on the high seas by organizing a race from New York to Marblehead. Contrary to gloomy forecasts, none of the boats was lost, either in that race or in the Bermuda race, and the latter continued to be held every two years, with an occasional lapse when there were too few entrants.

Between 1906 and 1924, five races between San Francisco and Honolulu are known to have been held, with a modest total of twenty competing boats. Only in 1922 was the Cruising Club of America formed, the first American club to be based on an interest in the high seas. From the following year onwards, the Bermuda race was organized by the CCA.

Since 1880, Britain had had the Royal Cruising Club, composed of members who were active small-boat ocean sailors. It might have been expected that, when the time came, the Royal Cruising Club would have taken the organization of ocean races into its own hands. But conservative traditions were too strong and, though the Royal Cruising Club provided the personnel, the organizing function was entrusted to a new body, the Ocean Race Committee, which rapidly became the Ocean Racing Club. Its first official appearance came in 1925, with the initiation of the Fastnet race.

In order to ensure fair competition between different boats, a handicap formula was created—that sacrosanct device, the rating rule. On each side of the Atlantic, the two clubs that together represented almost all active ocean racers, independently developed rating rules, based on slightly different criteria. The two rules were constantly revised and improved, thus becoming more and more complex, but they functioned and, despite a number of trials and setbacks, fulfilled their purpose satisfactorily. The main difficulty, which became more and more obvious as races between boats of the Old and the New Worlds became more frequent, was that boats built to one rule could not be easily adapted to another. Certain characteristics of the hull shape and type would be penalized under one rule, even though they suited the requirements of the other.

On the technical side, the CCA had established a number of basic characteristics relating to length. The differences between the basic characteristics of a boat and its actual dimensions were interpolated as positive or negative values in the calculation of rating, which took the following form:

$E = .95(L \pm Dr \pm D \pm S \pm F \pm IKf) \times$ Ballast $\times$ Propeller factor. L=measured length, Dr=draught, D=displacement, S= sail-area, F=freeboard, and IKf=iron keel factor. Naturally, the basic parameters often needed adjustment, and it was impossible to prevent the rule from influencing the design of boats.

After repeated trials, the following RORC formula was laid down in 1931, and it remained fundamentally unchanged until 1970:

$$R = .15 \frac{L \times \sqrt{S}}{\sqrt{B \times D}} + .2L + .2\sqrt{S}$$

So as not to hamper designers, this formula adhered to the principle of determining rated length irrespective of fore and aft overhang and of the general shape of the boat. Neither was it necessary to lift the boat out of the water to measure or weigh it—as had been necessary using the CCA formula. In 1957, the formula was refined with the addition of: $\pm$ stability factor $\pm$ propeller factor $\pm$ draught correction.

In the 1960s, the disadvantages of having two major competing standards of measurement, compounded by the imperfections peculiar to each rule (which were fully familiar to, if not exploited by, designers), at last wore down the resistance of many to change. After ten years of long-drawn-out meetings and intricate negotiations, an "Offshore Rules Coordinating Committee" created an "International Technical Committee", presided over by Olin Stephens and including, among others, Dick Carter and Ricus van de Stadt, both well-known designers, and David Fayle, the RORC's prime expert on rating rules. In January 1970, after three years' work, this international committee produced an international standard, christened "International Offshore Rule IOR Mark II", which took the form:

$$R = \left(\frac{.13L\sqrt{S}}{\sqrt{B \times D}} + .25L + .2\sqrt{S} + DC + FC \right) \times EPF \times CGF$$

At present, the version in use is IOR Mark III, which contains the addition: $\times$ MAF.

In these formulae, L = length between girths, S = sail-area for rating purposes, B = rated beam, D = displacement, DC = draught correction (positive or negative), FC = freeboard correction (positive or negative), EPF = engine and propeller factor, CGF = centre of gravity factor (positive or negative), and MAF = movable appendage factor, designed to penalize movable keels which, as a result, have practically disappeared from ocean-racing yachts.

This theoretically quite simple formula becomes much more complicated in practice, because it is impossible to relate the basic figures simply to the rating formula. When length at water-line is the criterion for measurement, boats tend to be built with exaggeratedly long overhangs. When overall length is the criterion, they tend to have vertical, awkward-looking ends. As soon as one dimension is selected as a means of determining the rule, designers, always anxious to produce boats with the most favourable dimensions, rush to accommodate their designs to that parameter. The rule is, therefore, determined by calculating certain measurements.

First, the overall length is measured in a precisely defined way. Next, the forward and after girth stations are found. The girth of a hull is its circumference, measured downwards in a vertical plane from a point where the hull meets the deck, round the keel, and up the other side to the corresponding point where the deck and hull meet on the opposite side of the hull. Girth is a measure of the fullness of a hull. It is an important measurement, because hulls with full ends are believed to be faster than hulls of the same length which have fine, pinched-in ends. Since the rule makers wish to encourage wide yachts with ample room inside, they have linked these girth stations to the beam, or greatest width, of the yacht. The after girth station is the point where the girth of the stern of the hull is equal to three quarters of the width of the boat. The forward girth station is the point where the girth in the fore part of the hull is equal in length to one half of the width of the boat at its widest point.

To find a yacht's measured length, or length between girths, the distances from the bow to the forward girth station and from the stern to the after girth station are measured. These two small measurements are added together and then subtracted from the length overall. The resulting figure is the measured length, or length between girths.

In fact, there are numerous small corrections which must be made to this simple equation. Special clauses in the rules take account of unusual bows and sterns. (The rule book is over one hundred pages long and is subject to annual revision.)

Obviously, a boat which is wide in the middle and fine in the ends will have its forward and after girth stations closer together than will a narrow boat with full ends. Therefore, the beamy boat will have a shorter measured length than the narrow boat, a feature which will help it to rate lower and thus have a more favourable handicap. The hull's immersed depth is measured with equal care, so that displacement can be evaluated without actual weighing, which can be an expensive and difficult operation. Freeboards are also measured in various complex ways. A boat with a low freeboard, built for speed, may not be sufficiently roomy inside, or its decks may be subject to constant swamping. Therefore, the low freeboard is penalized. At the other extreme, the formula provides that an excessively high freeboard be automatically awarded a light penalty.

Other factors, intricately woven into the rating formula, produce other small checks and balances. Suppose, for example, that a boat-owner, in order to qualify for a better rating, decides to lighten the ballast in his boat, thus decreasing its displacement and improving its performance in light weather at the expense of its showing when sailing close to the wind in a strong breeze. The boat's stability declines, the centre of gravity factor falls below 1, and a bonus is awarded. At the same time, the freeboards increase, and this can occasion a light penalty. The immersed depth decreases, and this definitely means a penalty, so that, all in all, it is quite possible that the rating will remain the same.

The effective stability of a boat is calculated by the measurer, who uses weights suspended from the outer end of a spar, fixed at right angles to the boat's centre-line. The weight needed to make the boat heel at 1° is measured. A small bonus may be awarded, if stability falls below the norm, but a maximum value is laid down for this correction. Effective draught is related to a base figure, which is one of the few arbitrary parameters in the rule. If the draught is higher than the base value, a penalty is incurred; if it is lower, a corresponding allowance is made, though only down to a certain, specified minimum. Boats with deficient draught lose out in this kind of reckoning.

Sail-area is, obviously, of vital importance in assessing a boat's rating. The mainsail is assumed to be a triangle, and only its width along the boom and its height up the mast are measured.

The dimensions of jibs and spinnakers are checked only to ensure that they do not exceed certain maximum figures which are related to the geometrical area of the boat's "fore triangle" (the triangle formed by the forestay, the fore side of the mast, and the distance between the fore side of the mast at deck level and the point at the bow where the forestay meets the deck). The width of the biggest jib used must not exceed 1.5 times J (the base of the fore triangle). If the jib exceeds this, the boat will receive a rating penalty. Spinnakers, too, are related to J and, also, to I (the height of the fore triangle). The J measurement also controls the length of the spinnaker pole. To discourage unduly-big fore triangles and very small mainsails, there is a special rule which says that, if a mainsail is not a certain proportion of the fore triangle, it will be measured as if it was. The sail-area goes into the formula as the square root, in order to be on the same terms as the measured length of the boat.

Since 1977, there are limits to the number of sails that an ocean racer may carry, and these limits increase with sail size. The idea behind this is to reduce the escalating cost of racing.

Rating a boat has gradually become a complex and rather expensive operation. It involves scores of measurements which have to be accurately taken, both on land and afloat in calm water. Boats must be re-rated each time they are modified or change hands.

The ocean-racing yacht is, by definition, the product of the rating rules. If the rules are defective and favour boats that lack strength, comfort, or seaworthiness, it follows that a boat which satisfies the requirements of the rule will equally be bad. This statement is more than hypothetical. Such unhealthy situations have often occurred in the past, under earlier rating rules. However, the committees which now have the task of developing and revising the rule are well aware of their responsibilities. While taking care not to hamper design development, they try to encourage the design of boats that are reasonably comfortable, durable, swift, and safe.

An ocean-racing yacht will undoubtedly cost more than a similar yacht meant only for cruising, but it will have a longer ocean-going life than the cruiser. After its racing days are over, it will make an excellent, fast-cruising yacht which will retain its resale value for many years, for buyers never fail to appreciate a boat that is well-built, strong, and fast in all points of sailing, especially if, as is often the case, it is elegant to look at as well.

Nowadays, mass production is the only way to prevent yachts from having astronomical price-tags. The need to amortize a set of moulds tends to curb the development of new models, and so do costs for advertising campaigns based on one particular model. To what extent, then, is the ocean-racing yacht affected by these considerations?

Undeniably, the "one-off", designed according to the owner's specifications, is often to be found at the highest level of ocean racing—the One Ton Cup or the Admiral's Cup. This might lead one to think that these custom-built yachts have the edge on standard models. On the other hand, it must be pointed out that owners of one-offs generally are very demanding, have set ideas, and treat a race largely as an opportunity to test their own theories. Evidence shows that production-line boats, when manned by first-class crews, often put up a fine showing in ocean races. The two types of boat have, of course, much in common: as a rule, the production-line boat is the developed version of a design first tested, both in its prototype form and in its variants, by one-offs. Usually, a boat cannot be fully tested or proved during one season. This reduces the difference between a well-tested model and a prototype which has not yet achieved its full potential. Besides, the boat-yards which specialize in production-line racing yachts change their models quite frequently. A production-line boat permits full return on investment in the fields of accommodation and comfort. The use of moulds rationalizes and simplifies production, especially in the case of such fitments as galley and bathroom units, and storage lockers for sails, where good design and weather-resistant materials contribute enormously to easy upkeep.

Almost invariably, rating rules proscribe extremes in yacht construction, and even an old racing yacht is identifiable at first glance, since it will have certain elements, utilitarian or aesthetic, in common with other, more modern racing yachts. For instance, the deck-house is nearly always very low and streamlined, even on light-displacement yachts where a deck-house is the only way of creating internal space. This is because a prominent deck-house presents a bigger surface to troublesome winds.

The deck of a racing yacht is always uncluttered. There is, in fact, usually a flush deck or a false flush deck, rising in a slight hump where the deck-house is. The flush deck provides the crew, when in action, with room to manoeuvre, especially when handling the spinnaker. Generally speaking, the flush deck also raises the freeboard on small and medium-sized boats, so that the interior height is enhanced.

Similarly, the racing yacht has a special kind of divided cockpit. In the large yacht, it is usually placed at the stern to permit the largest possible living area. If the boat is under 50 ft (15 m), however, performance will suffer if the weight of the crew is too close to the stern, and so a little "cheating" is needed.

In the majority of cases, the helmsman remains at the stern, which is both the most sheltered position and the best for getting the feel of the boat's movements (a helmsman amidships is too high up in relation to the pitching axis of the boat). However, the deck plan provides for only two or three work positions at this level. The crew members are grouped near the centre of the boat in a shallow cockpit, which is too squat to decrease the height of the cabin, or else they are posted at different winch sites. The cockpit arrangement of the *Swan* goes one better by providing not only a separate stern cabin for the owner and a cockpit aft for the helmsman, but also a crew cockpit which does not encroach on the volume of the central cabin. This is a model of its type in all ways, and it took over twenty years and the driving force of Olin Stephens to refine. The only disadvantage in the design is that the companion-way is rather steep and placed in the deepest part of the boat.

Nowadays, designers are prepared to place the helmsman right at the stern, because modern yachts, with more modest displacements than their predecessors, lift more in a following sea, and the helmsman is less exposed to the full impact of waves breaking over the stern. Another factor, not unconnected with the first, is the fuller shape of the bow and stern on modern yachts, and the absence of overhang at the stern. A shield, designed to protect the helmsman from the waves, and installed on the stern of PEN DUICK VI during the yacht's first race round the world, proved unnecessary and was discarded on arrival in Sydney.

More and more often, the rail capping on racing yachts is made of light alloy extrusion, perforated at regular intervals. This provides a simple and effective point of attachment for those snatch blocks which, especially on beamier boats, can fulfil so many purposes. Usually, the only way of providing leads for the sheets and running rigging, without allowing the sheets to rub against and chafe each other, is to install one or more turning blocks. The holes in the rail capping also serve as drain holes, which assist the rapid escape of water landing on the decks. Lastly, fenders can be attached wherever necessary along the rail capping, on arrival in a port.

The rule does not bear directly on the length of the overhangs. The tendency is for these to be considerable on wide or heavy boats, while on yachts with a light displacement the overhangs, as one would expect, are a lot shorter.

On the other hand, recent experience has shown that yachts, which are trimmed with their sterns well out of the water and their bows level or slightly low, do better than others in the measurement stakes. This being so, it is no surprise to find that many modern racing yachts have this rather "down-in-the-mouth" look.

The present rating rules, unlike those of recent years, refrain from putting absurd restrictions on sail-area, so that, nowadays, racing yachts no longer tend to be under-rigged. In general, the mast of a sloop or the mainmast of a ketch will rise high above the deck and be about ten per cent longer than the overall length of the boat. Usually, the fore triangle is appreciably larger than the mainsail, sometimes twice as great, although a rule modification on this point by those responsible for the IOR has slowed down this tendency. In most cases, however, the spinnaker boom remains short, and the mainsail has a high aspect ratio.

The low superstructures on ocean-racing yachts provide little room for opening ports; instead, it is usual to have a number of good-sized, transparent sliding hatches, sometimes tinted, which allow the interior to be aired from time to time. These hatches are generally placed near the middle of the boat, so as not to occupy manoeuvring space. The spinnaker poles often seem to be clumsily located, but their position has been carefully thought out, so that the big, heavy spars are easy to handle.

Every now and then, designers try to revise cockpit arrangements. The cockpit on many cruising yachts is situated amidships between two saloons, but this layout is hardly ever adopted on racing vessels, doubtless out of consideration for the helmsman, as mentioned above. However, side cockpits, which allow the crew members to help stabilize the boat without unduly exposing them to the elements, are common. These cockpits are often situated well forward, so as to distribute the weight to the best advantage and to ensure easy access to the spinnaker, although this reduces the protection offered to the crew.

It is in its interior that the one-off racing yacht differs most from the production-line boat. The man who expends much thought, trouble, and expense on the commissioning of a purpose-built yacht tends often to cut corners on the interior, which is usually bare and spartan, in order to save weight, to provide the maximum relaxation area for the crew, and to allow space for a good-sized sail-locker. The bunks usually consist of canvas sheets stretched over tubing, there are no partitions to speak of, and often there is no dining table of the kind that is so useful when the boat is moored. The galley unit and the navigator's table remain sizeable, for they correspond to two of the basic activities of ocean racing, but there is no sign of dressing-tables, comfortable seating, reading lamps, or a luxurious shower-area. Ironically, the owner of one of these racing contraptions often also maintains a more traditional yacht, full of charm and comfort, for his cruises and holidays... By contrast, one of the main advantages of the mass-produced racing yacht is its well-planned and well-appointed interior. Whether performance always suffers from an increase in weight and a lowering of the centre of gravity is not known for certain, for the rating rule keeps an eagle eye on this side of things, too, and a yacht which is a little lighter and stiffer than another will, other things being equal, automatically be given a heavier rating.

Deck equipment represents a significant part of the cost of an ocean-racing yacht. The most expensive items are the large, multi-speed jib winches, which increasingly are of the "coffee-grinder" type (i.e., with an upright column supporting horizontal cranks) and are sometimes linked together. In addition, there are pairs of less powerful winches for the sheets of the spinnaker, the fore staysails, the spinnaker staysails, the big boy, etc. If there are running backstays, these are nearly always operated by a pair of winches reserved for that purpose; backstay levers have almost disappeared. On small boats, halyard winches are fixed to the mast, while on larger boats, they may be placed around the foot of the mast or even mounted on a winch table. The mainsail halyard is usually made of steel rope and led to a drum winch.

Lifelines and pulpits are often arranged so as to facilitate the handling of the genoa, without infringing on the rule that requires the lifelines to form an unbroken girdle around the boat. The height of the lifelines and the spacing of the stanchions are also subject to rule requirements (see chapter ten), and this helps to create a family likeness between all racing yachts.

Most of the successful racing owners seem to have been racing all their lives. Often they are people who started out crewing for their fathers, sailing first in small boats and then, with increasing means and declining agility, rising up the scale from class to class. The bigger and more complicated the boat, the more it provides its skipper with the opportunity to use his experience and to develop his knowledge of boat racing. A bigger yacht can stand up to the elements and can continue racing, when smaller boats are just bounced about in the water.

In certain areas where competition is very keen, owners, tired of meeting endlessly escalating bills, have been known to come to a joint decision to step down a class or two, for they know very well that the main ingredient of an enjoyable race is the existence of worthy rivals, sailing-boats of similar sizes. This downgrading is a recent development, and it has been most noticeable in Italy. However, the overall trend is still for the better-known owners to appear each year or "on" season (the Admiral's Cup takes place every other year, on the Bermuda race's "off" year) with bigger and better boats. In these cases, a skipper will achieve upgrading through a series of careful stages. While sailing his current boat, he may notice some of its weak points or discover loop-holes in the rating rule. He then approaches his designer, who has, in all probability, noticed the same things himself and, together, they produce a better boat. (The skipper can also change designers and engage one who is currently "in the swim". No doubt for a variety of good reasons, each of the top designers enjoys one or two successful seasons and is then eclipsed by a rival.)

While on the subject of ordering new boats, let us suppose, for the sake of argument, that a top-class skipper, who has kept on the sidelines for some years, now finds the time or the means to re-enter the fray. Choosing a boat is obviously one of his first concerns. Apart from the cost, which can be enormous (though to a fortunate few money is no object) several elements enter into the choice of size. There is no doubt that, in the rating scale (from the bottom of class 5 to the top of class 1), certain ranges of ratings are more favourable than others, though these, unfortunately, vary according to the waters raced in, to the prevailing system of handicapping, and to the dominant weather pattern of the season. A skipper may often be tempted to choose a rating near those of the better boats in his part of the world, because competing with them will be more demanding. Another skipper, however, aware of his limitations, will deliberately seek out the classes and sub-divisions of classes where the opposition is less exacting. Sometimes, builders do the same thing, but with a different end in view. By adjusting sails and ballast, they produce a boat with a rating which puts it in a class where the opposition is weak. The boat is then methodically entered in every race in the calendar, with the result that it can be publicized at the end of the season as "the boat which distinguished itself in six international races".

The choice of a new boat may be governed by a number of considerations, such as the possibility of racing in the Half Ton or the One Ton Cup, the hope of being selected as one of the Admiral's Cup team, or perhaps most important of all, which class the owner wants to race in (the difference between the top of one class and the bottom of the next is minimal, so that borderline cases may well be allocated to either class). The type of rigging is almost automatically determined by boat size—sloop rigging for most boats, ketch for the biggest models. Delivery delays may influence the choice of a standard model—everybody wants a boat ready in April! Full racing rig is rarely offered on a standard boat, for this would raise catalogue prices out of all proportion. At the time of ordering the boat, the owner must choose his winches and electronic equipment, and be ready with a definitive deck plan. Certain choices may be deferred until the winter Boat Shows, where prospective owners can see on display the latest internationally available products and can discuss their merits with the manufacturers.

Ordering the sails is a major step. The large international sail-makers make sweeping claims in their publicity about the number and prestige of their clients: "In the latest Admiral's Cup, eight out of ten boats had XYZ sails". The small firms promote the opposite argument: "Deal with us, and you won't be just one in a crowd". In fact, a well-known skipper is fairly sure to receive a perfect set of sails. The situation is a little different for a beginner. His boat is not news, and he may have problems with delays and poor finish due to rushed work. A small sail-making firm will often do meticulous work, altering sails as often as may be necessary, but it may not be able to obtain the best-quality cloth, especially the heavy-weight cloths.

To get safely through this first stage, the skipper not only must order a first-class set of sails, but also must be capable of telling a perfect sail from a faulty one, otherwise he will not have a leg to stand on in his dealings with the sail-maker. He must also have some business experience and a knowledge of human nature, so that the sail-maker he chooses will be sure to keep his promises and finish the job properly.

Once the boat has been delivered and the launching ceremony is over, work begins in earnest. The racing crew must be on the scene right from the beginning, both because tuning the boat needs the help of many skilled hands and because there can never be too much sailing practice undertaken during training. The first sorties are devoted to sorting out details and to making adjustments.

Mass-produced boats have the advantage of being operational much more quickly; on a one-off job, even one from an excellent boat-yard, countless minor alterations are to be expected. Moreover, few boat-yards are sufficiently in touch with racing to be able to adapt themselves spontaneously to all possible racing requirements. Not uncommonly, the boat-yard will quote a price which presupposes the presence of leading crew members during construction, and they will supervize the positioning of the deck fittings, an operation that is becoming more and more complicated all the time.

On practice runs, the crew will note everything which needs rethinking or modifying; such as faulty creases in a sail, halyards spliced badly or wrongly placed, a cleat that needs to be moved, a leak that must be traced, a jib-track with faulty bolts, a defective contact in the electrical wiring—there is no limit to the list. In theory, all these faults should be put right before the boat is taken out for its next run which, in turn, will bring a whole new list of defects.

During these practice runs, it is wise to start tuning the boat itself. First, the correct tension of the various components of the standing rigging must be established by observing closely how the mast behaves under different rigs in different wind and sea conditions. Usually, a small amount of stretching will occur in the rigging at the beginning, even though it has been pre-stretched at the factory, as the stretching does not occur in the wires alone, but also in the end fittings and, sometimes, in the socket in which the mast is stepped. Some parts of the rigging can only be adjusted by a man sent up the mast, and this takes time.

The exact location for the jib lead block has to be found and marked on the deck. Guiding-marks are placed on the spinnaker guys and sheets to make gybing easier; markings are made on sail-bags and sails, and the stowage of sail-bags in the sail-locker is decided upon. The length of strops and pennants needs to be regulated, and ways are found to simplify the work of the crew: specially-shaped spinnaker bags, gadgets for returning jibs to the locker without replacing them in a bag, and so on. Above all, one needs to be on the look-out for anything that sticks or fails to work as it should: an eye splice on the spinnaker guy which jams in the end fitting of the spinnaker pole; the spinnaker pole deck-stowage that comes loose in a heavy swell and, when the boat is tacking, allows the sheet to catch and get jammed or twisted under the pole; a bilge pump that becomes choked or fails when the boat is heeling—anything is possible.

At the same time, sail-handling techniques are finally perfected, some of them by joint consultation, others decreed by the skipper on the basis of his past experience. As it happens, sail-handling techniques follow similar patterns on all boats. Some of the operations need to be carried out with split-second timing, and the crew members need to synchronize their movements in much the same way as a football team.

Up to this point, the crew members have concentrated on themselves and their boat without reference to others but, before completing the tuning and fine adjustment, it is essential to compare the boat's performance with that of other boats. In sailing, a stop-watch cannot be used to reckon performance exactly, so comparison with the performance of other boats is the best solution. The simplest method is to enter the boat in one-day training races, which are organized so that crews can acquaint themselves with their boats. It pays to be extremely methodical at this stage. The wise skipper makes a point of noting everything—weather conditions, swell, wind force and direction, which sails are set, the adjustment of the sheets, the position of the jib leads, the number of people on board, how much water is in the tank, how the weight is distributed, and so on. One never knows which of these points will turn out to be vitally relevant in the end. Naturally, time elapsed between buoys, speed of the other boats over the same distance, and actual and corrected times for each part of the course need to be noted. By taking stock of the other boats and their characteristics, an astute observer will quickly deduce the strengths and weaknesses of his own boat. Trim adjustments of halyards and sheets, made when the boat is close alongside a competitor known for his reliable methods, will definitely do more for the boat's chances than a fortune spent at the sail-maker's or the builder's—what is the use of having three light genoas if one does not know which one to use and how best to use it? Tuning against another boat usually produces very rapid results and can so improve a yacht's performance that it should have no difficulty thereafter in outclassing boats of the same rating. It is for this reason that boats in the One Ton Cup are often put in a special class for handicap races as, in corrected time, they often put up as good a fight as boats with a higher rating.

Instead of, or in addition to, these practice races, ambitious crews go in for test runs on lengthy courses alongside one or more partners, with one of the boats acting as a pace horse.

However, it is worth remembering that, except in level-rating races, a boat may find itself more or less alone from within a few minutes of the start until the end of the race. In these circumstances, it is difficult to get the best out of a boat, if it has not been decided beforehand which sails to hoist and which sheet adjustments to use for every wind speed and change of direction that might occur. Questions will arise all the time, and the answers must be known in advance, otherwise decision-making will sink to the level of guesswork: Is it best to keep the floater or to use a light spinnaker? Should the starcut be hoisted or the reacher retained? Should the mainsail traveller be let out and the sheet tightened, or should the traveller be brought in amidships while easing the sheet? Theoretical knowledge helps one to ask the right questions at the right time, but there is no getting away from the fact that, in most circumstances, the answers will be merely rough-and-ready. Especially on biggish boats, skippers often make the mistake of carrying too much sail when the wind is fresh. All experienced racers can recall an occasion when, after a sheet or halyard had parted, thus putting a sail temporarily out of action, the boat picked up speed instead of slowing down. The racing boat cannot be considered adequately prepared unless a list, giving the correct rig for each wind speed, is pinned up where everyone can see it.

At national level, a team appointed for the Admiral's Cup or the Sydney-Hobart race will often assemble, perhaps appoint a team manager—often one of the skippers—and undergo a self-instituted training programme. Sometimes, the team is not chosen until after a series of heats, but the competition in these is really lively only in Britain, the United States, and Australia, where there are a number of serious contenders for places on the team.

Until recently, crew training has not been undertaken as systematically in ocean racing as in other sports. Ocean racing is still an amateur pursuit. One of the least of the difficulties is assembling a fleet each week for a weekend of competition that starts on Friday morning and often ends on Monday evening.

With practice and the ensuing rise in competence, a level of physical fitness can be achieved and maintained that compares favourably with that attained by a classical athletic training. At present, the critical qualities for the crew of a small or medium-sized yacht are experience, which gives a facility for thinking ahead; correct sheet adjustment and good helmsmanship; the ability to concentrate in spite of heat, cold, and darkness; resistance to seasickness and lack of sleep; and endurance. On large yachts, the crew members work more as a team, with more specialized individual responsibilities; life on board is better organized, and there is more time for rest and relaxation. While one or two top-class helmsmen are necessary, the crew members usually consist of tough and disciplined lads, who make up in team spirit and loyalty what they may lack in experience. Somewhat less is required of them in terms of endurance, but they must be supremely fit and agile so as to be able to handle the heavy sails and operate the big winches.

For a weekend race in a boat with standard equipment and an average crew, the crew members usually assemble the day before the start, or at least some hours beforehand. The boat is taken from its moorings to the travelift or hauling-slip for scrubbing. At the same time, some of the crew go out to buy stores, spares, batteries, a pump diaphragm, or other items which can be needed on board at short notice. When the boat has been returned to its berth, it is stocked up with fresh water, the engine is started to recharge the batteries, and the engine hood is opened to allow air to circulate. The bilge is inspected to make sure that it is dry and in good order, someone goes up the mast to check that all is well, and everyone keeps an eye out for last-minute repairs needed—a loose screw, a bent turn-buckle, or suchlike. The spinnakers are aired so as to get rid of damp, but it is wise to refold them afterwards, for a good crew has no great confidence in something done by someone else. When the boat is ready, the crew takes it out for a short trip if weather permits, to cast a final glance over the sails, to go about a few times, to get the feel of the boat and, if need be, to get their hand in again after a week in the office—gybing the spinnaker needs as much practice as an orchestral score. If the race is scheduled to start very early the next morning, it is sometimes wise to eat and go to bed early rather than to get some more practice in.

The most serious moment is before the actual start of the race. If there is time, the boat is usually sailed over and around the line, while the skipper makes a mental note of the tides, tries out both tacks to see which gives the better course, puts the boat about a few times to see that everything is working smoothly, and checks his own sense of timing at the helm.

The last few minutes before the starter's gun, and the half-hour or hour afterwards, are filled with frantic activity. A lot of things have to be done in rapid succession—tacking, gybing, adjusting the sheets—while the helmsman steers a course to get the boat off to a good start. Once the boat is well under way, watch-keeping begins. Half the men eat and sleep, while the other half work. Usually, the watches are four hours long, with two half-watches of two hours each between 1200 and 1600 hours to break the rhythm and prevent the watch from midnight to 0400 hours from falling always to the same crew members, since it can be very uncomfortable in cold weather. A well-run race is always exhausting for the crew; sail-changing always has to be done at top speed, and the rest of the time is mainly spent adjusting the sails. After each change of jib, the old jib has to be re-stowed in its bag and the bag returned to its allocated position or put under the cockpit seats. Then everything has to be tidied and the ropes re-coiled.

A long race, run against the wind in a high sea, is especially taxing. Whatever the size of the boat, the crew cannot sleep, nor can they eat anything except sandwiches without risk of its being upset by the tossing of the boat. Hatches, lockers, and so on need to be kept shut, because

the deck is permanently inundated, and the interior becomes damp and filled with the unpleasant smell of damp clothes and bedding. If, to cap it all, the boat has to sail round a headland or along a coast against the current, the crew faces the ultimate test, for progress has to be made in very short tacks while keeping to the white water close to the shallows, where the current is weaker. A few hours' work at the winches has been known to get the better of the strongest of crews. Even with the return of good weather or the passing of the headland, the crew members cannot rest. All hands are needed on deck to hoist the spinnaker, shake out the reefs, take in the storm-sails, repair any damage sustained, and generally put things to rights again.

When the boat has crossed the finishing line and the crew members have had their long-awaited showers and a few hours' sleep, duty calls again. Sails have to be taken away to be rinsed in fresh water, dried and maybe mended, other sails have to be stowed away, the boat must be hosed down and made shipshape, topsides cleaned, batteries recharged, and minor repairs made.

In the days when racing boats were heavy and somewhat under-rigged, and the use of a spinnaker was a hit-and-miss affair, skippers could rarely afford to take any but the most direct route. In fact, the boat travelled at more or less the same speed, whatever its sailing rig, and the best way of gaining an advantage was nearly always to cut short the route somehow. Tactics consisted essentially of deciding how and when to tack and, in some cases, of anticipating a shift in the wind.

Today, ocean-racing yachts have sleek, fast hulls and sophisticated sails, and they are capable of spectacular differences in speed, depending on how they are rigged. Thus, present-day tactics are very different from those to be found in books dating back twenty years or so.

One of the greatest advantages of modern boats is the improvement of performance in a light wind. Nobody has an excuse any longer for not knowing how the speed of the boat and the current can affect the apparent wind, the wind that is actually felt by the boat when under way. Sailing close-hauled, it is sometimes best not to go for top speeds but to try to keep to a direct course. In other cases, it may be worth abandoning the direct course in favour of a longer but faster course. When the wind is astern, there will always be the option of running before the wind along the direct route or tacking down wind, and the course chosen will vary from one boat to another.

As a general rule, the navigator will spend most of his time comparing the expected increase in speed that results from a change of heading with the increase in length of the resulting course. In practice, it might often be feasible to deviate 10° or 20° from the direct route (thereby adding between two and six per cent to the distance), with a resulting gain in speed of up to thirty per cent.

The use of spinnakers presents a similar sort of situation: the new spinnaker cut, known as "starcut", can be set very close to a light wind. Usually, a skipper will alter course readily by the few degrees necessary to allow the spinnaker to be hoisted, for this gives him a very advantageous rig, especially when the finishing line is still a fair way off.

There has been a dramatic increase in the windward

performance of modern ocean racers, and this has had a considerable influence on race tactics. Tacticians are now more willing to leave the direct-course line in pursuit of favourable wind shifts and streaks. Because the modern racer is so close-winded, it is essential for it to tack when the wind heads, in order to get quickly on to the favourable tack. The proximity of land and a change in tidal currents will, of course, also have their influence and, for these reasons, a yacht which is sailing to windward will almost always spend more time on one tack than on the other, even though the finishing line may lie to windward.

Now that boats travel so fast and so close to the wind, unsettled meteorological conditions have a more important bearing on a boat's progress. The more precise the measurement rules become, the more boats find themselves on par with regard to top speed, and the more capricious and unfair the weather seems to be. For sailors forever caught in the weather's game of chance, the overriding temptation would be to sail the shortest, most direct course possible without making any attempt to find a good wind or to guard against a sudden unfavourable shift in the wind. But, of course, other elements can also enter into the decision on which is the optimal course. Placings are generally established on the basis of a series of races and, when some of the races have been sailed, it is common that the well-placed boats, during the remaining races, keep each other under close observation or try to avoid each other completely. The leader's main interest during these races is to prevent his rivals from establishing themselves in positions from which they can threaten him.

In spite of its quirks, the weather can be forecast pretty accurately, and navigators are usually very well up in this matter, basing their conclusions on systematic study, comparisons, and attempts to discover recurring patterns in different situations.

Depending on the boat's position as it passes the half-way marker buoys, a choice has to be made between the safe course and the risky one, and it will be based on speculation that there will not be a radical change in the wind conditions. Boat-buyers tend, when choosing a boat from first principles, to pick a light-weather boat for the Mediterranean and a heavy-weather boat for the Channel; nonetheless, there is always a range of winds which the skipper knows will give him a slight edge and, conversely, winds outside that range which will lose him points. Thus a boat with too little sail, or with a spinnaker that is on the small side, will fare badly when running before a direct following wind or before a very feeble wind. Such considerations all enter into the skipper's thinking. If, for example, he knows that, whatever else happens, his chances of winning are lost if the wind does not change, he has nothing to lose if he alters course and "hunts" for a favourable wind.

Of course, the navigator will make thorough use of his knowledge of the elements, but that cannot really be called tactics. It is the least he can do to seek out an off-shore breeze along a coast at sunset, to go out of his way to position the boat in the path of a large cloud, and to wring all the information he can from meteorological bulletins.

Experience has shown that navigation and tactics pose the same problems in long-distance ocean races as they do on much shorter courses. Certainly, the theory of fronts can be reliably applied to the passage of a pressure trough, but it is still difficult to forecast the pattern of winds likely to be encountered in the course of a crossing, or to know whether one should abandon the shortest route in order to circumvent a permanent anticyclone. However, purely tactical decisions, based on plotting the course of other competitors, have every chance of being the most effective ones. For fixed-rating races, such as the One Ton Cup, practically everything goes by the board except the good old principle followed in a regatta: stay close to the other competitors and get to the finish as fast as possible.

The situation in multihull racing today is similar to what it was for monohull racing at the beginning of the century. Opinion about multihulls is split between the majority of sailors, who categorically reject them, and the minority, who are unshakeably enthusiastic. Traditional ocean racing clubs have until now consistently refused to organize competitions for multihulls, which they consider dangerous, so the task has fallen instead to a small number of isolated organizations. Thus there is a fleet of catamarans in California, very fast craft with very competent and highly trained crews. Ironically, not a single capsizal or serious accident has occurred among these boats, which race every two years along a trans-Pacific route from San Francisco to Honolulu. On this fast and tricky course, their speed is phenomenal, faster than that of the biggest and best monohulls which race along the same route every other year.

In Europe, the only race specifically devoted to multihulls has been until now the Crystal Trophy, run over a triangular course in the English Channel and starting early in the summer, in May or June. It is nothing much to speak of but, so far, the main efforts of multihull sailors have been directed towards experimentation and the search for solutions to technical problems rather than towards conventional boat-against-boat competition.

However, a few out-of-the-ordinary races have been held, which have enabled multihulls to meet monohulls on equal terms at top competitive level. One of these is the Round Britain race, for boats with two crew members; this race, although not strictly speaking an ocean race, offers splendid opportunities for testing a boat's seagoing qualities. Another is the Singlehanded Transatlantic race, though on this route the drawback is the very high proportion of up-wind sailing, in which multihulls find it hard to give their best.

The Whitbread Round-the-World race of 1977, for both monohulls and multihulls, should give the latter the opportunity to show off their capabilities. Indeed, other mixed races, with their restrictions on the number of crew members, victimize multihulls, which need a sizeable crew to get the best performance out of them without excessive risk. Too much sail on a monohull usually means some time lost, minor damage, and the odd tear in a sail; on a multihull, it may mean capsizing the boat, with drastic consequences.

The situation should improve for multihulls with the coming into force of the IMOR rule, the equivalent for multihulls of the IOR rule for monohulls. Published only in 1974 by the IYRU, it is still having teething troubles, but at least now there exists a set of regulations that is recognized world-wide.

The IMOR rule is a complex piece of work which is based on three assumptions:

1. Speed under sail is directly proportionate to the ratio of the sail-area to displacement, expressed by the square root of the sail-area in square feet divided by the cubic root of the displacement in pounds.
2. Speed under sail is inversely proportional to the displacement expressed in terms of the ratio of length to displacement, i.e. the displacement in tons divided by the cube of one per cent of the water-line length in feet.
3. Speed is proportional to the square root of the water-line length.

In 1968–69, the first singlehanded race round the world was staged by the British newspaper *Sunday Times* and won by Robin Knox-Johnston. This was essentially a test of human endurance, and there were virtually no rules other than that the voyage must be non-stop. In 1973–74, another race round the world was held, this time for fully-crewed yachts, and according to the racing rules of the IYRU and the IOR measurement rule. This race was a model of organization as well as a natural development of traditional racing, and so looked set fair to become a regular event. The race was run in four legs, with stops at Cape Town, Sydney, and Rio de Janeiro. For the 1977 race, multihulls were allowed to compete, provided the conditions of the new IMOR rules were met.

Parallel with this Whitbread Round-the-World race is the *Sunday Times'* "Clipper Race", which has a single stopover at Sydney.

The numbers of boats and crews seem to be increasing all the time, and there is constant speculation about some new race or other right round, or very nearly round, the world, the latest being the "tea" race, which would be run along the old route taken by tea clippers, to Hong Kong and back. In a few years' time, we shall most probably see a continuous procession of yachts tackling various high-sea routes once frequented by clippers, and thereafter it may not be too long before sailing-boats show up in force at Cape Horn.

The International Offshore Rule contains a vast number of measurements used in calculating a yacht's rating. We show some of the more important hull measurements.

A Measurement of beam (here, of half the beam) is taken at the hull's greatest width, one-sixth of the maximum beam down from the sheer line. (1–2) How different hulls are measured. With extra-beamy hulls, an average is taken (2). (a) Half the measured beam. (b) Half the maximum beam. (c) One-sixth the maximum beam.

B A section at mid-boat depth shows: (a) Beam at water-line. (b) Centre mid-boat depth immersed (CMDI), taken at one-eighth of the measured beam from the centre-line. (c) Mid-boat depth immersed (MDI), taken at one-quarter the measured beam from the centre-line. (d) Outer mid-boat depth immersed (OMDI), taken at three-eighths the measured beam from the centre-line.

C The aft girth station (AGS) is the point where the girth of the stern is equal to three-quarters the measured beam. The after inner girth station (AIGS) is the point where the girth is seven-eighths the measured beam.

D The forward girth station (FGS) is the point where the girth of the fore part of the hull is one-half the measured beam. The forward inner girth station (FIGS) is the point where the girth is three-quarters the measured beam.

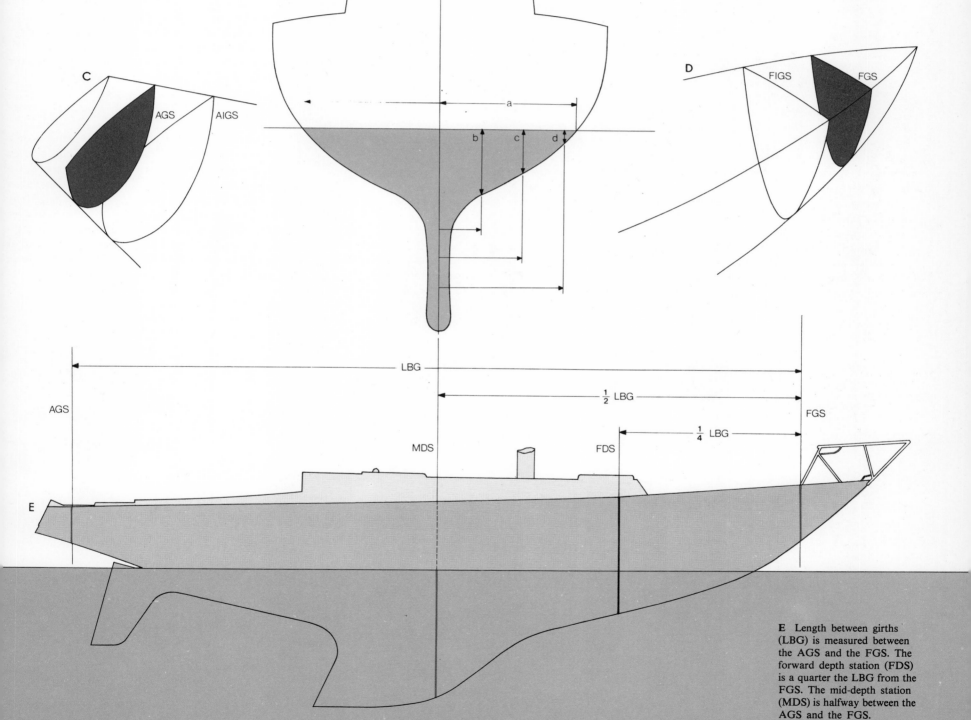

E Length between girths (LBG) is measured between the AGS and the FGS. The forward depth station (FDS) is a quarter the LBG from the FGS. The mid-depth station (MDS) is halfway between the AGS and the FGS.

231

The major ocean-racing competitions involve round-the-clock sailing. One watch sleeps, while the other races.

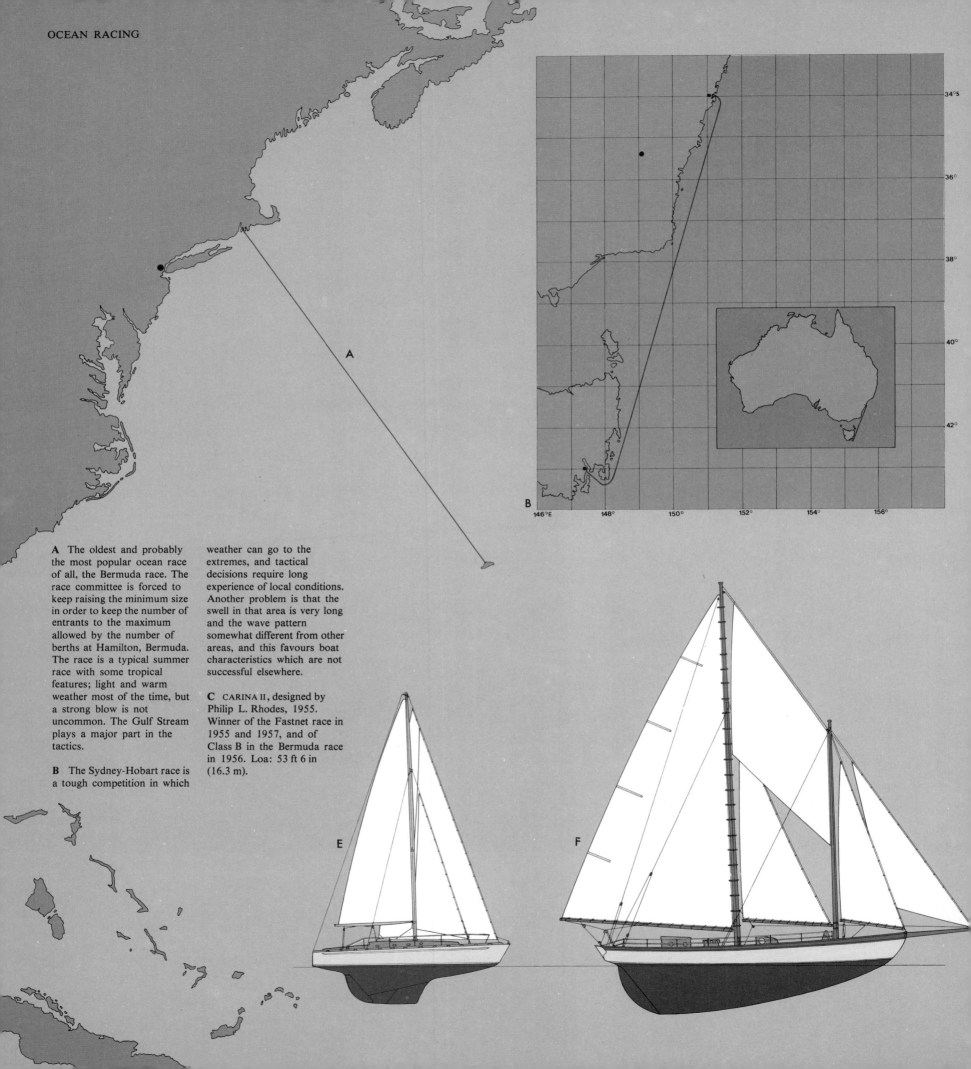

A The oldest and probably the most popular ocean race of all, the Bermuda race. The race committee is forced to keep raising the minimum size in order to keep the number of entrants to the maximum allowed by the number of berths at Hamilton, Bermuda. The race is a typical summer race with some tropical features; light and warm weather most of the time, but a strong blow is not uncommon. The Gulf Stream plays a major part in the tactics.

B The Sydney-Hobart race is a tough competition in which weather can go to the extremes, and tactical decisions require long experience of local conditions. Another problem is that the swell in that area is very long and the wave pattern somewhat different from other areas, and this favours boat characteristics which are not successful elsewhere.

C CARINA II, designed by Philip L. Rhodes, 1955. Winner of the Fastnet race in 1955 and 1957, and of Class B in the Bermuda race in 1956. Loa: 53 ft 6 in (16.3 m).

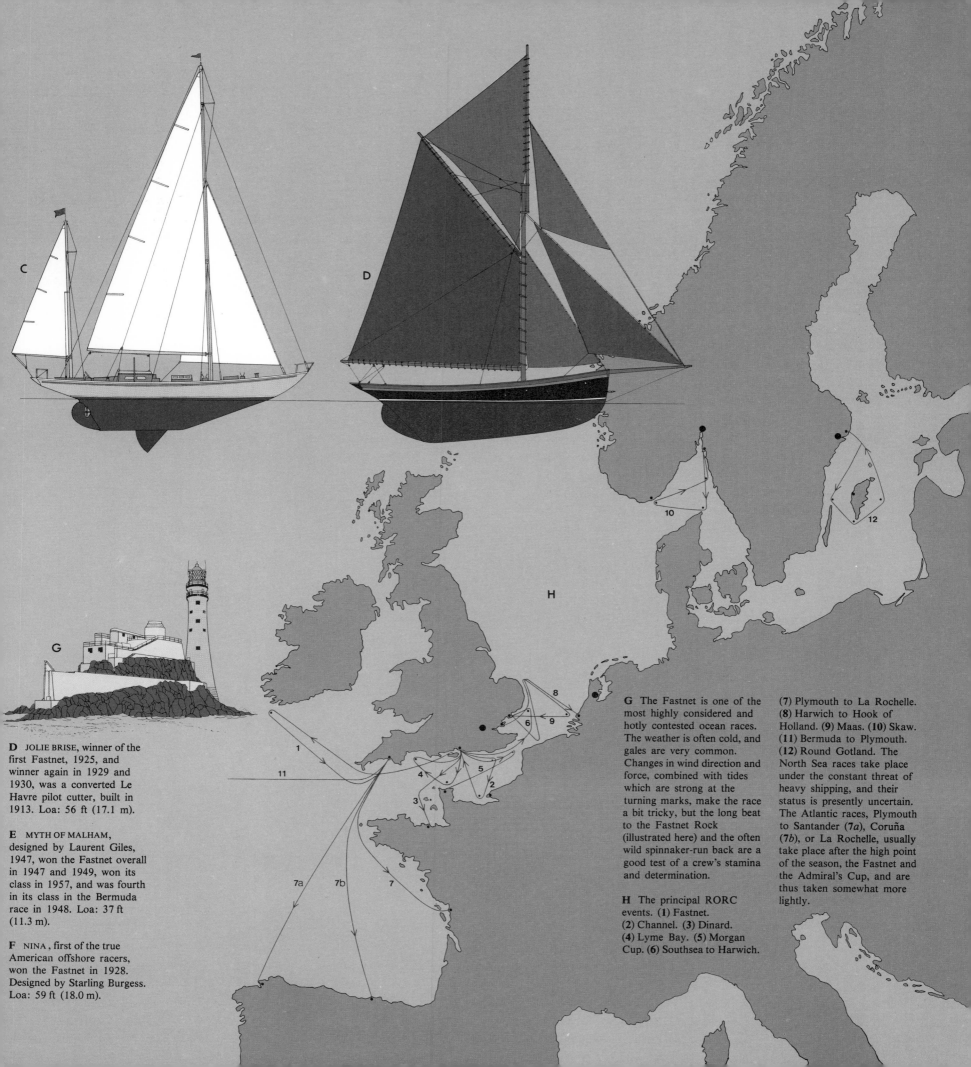

C

D

D JOLIE BRISE, winner of the first Fastnet, 1925, and winner again in 1929 and 1930, was a converted Le Havre pilot cutter, built in 1913. Loa: 56 ft (17.1 m).

E MYTH OF MALHAM, designed by Laurent Giles, 1947, won the Fastnet overall in 1947 and 1949, won its class in 1957, and was fourth in its class in the Bermuda race in 1948. Loa: 37 ft (11.3 m).

F NINA, first of the true American offshore racers, won the Fastnet in 1928. Designed by Starling Burgess. Loa: 59 ft (18.0 m).

G

H

G The Fastnet is one of the most highly considered and hotly contested ocean races. The weather is often cold, and gales are very common. Changes in wind direction and force, combined with tides which are strong at the turning marks, make the race a bit tricky, but the long beat to the Fastnet Rock (illustrated here) and the often wild spinnaker-run back are a good test of a crew's stamina and determination.

H The principal RORC events. (**1**) Fastnet. (**2**) Channel. (**3**) Dinard. (**4**) Lyme Bay. (**5**) Morgan Cup. (**6**) Southsea to Harwich.

(**7**) Plymouth to La Rochelle. (**8**) Harwich to Hook of Holland. (**9**) Maas. (**10**) Skaw. (**11**) Bermuda to Plymouth. (**12**) Round Gotland. The North Sea races take place under the constant threat of heavy shipping, and their status is presently uncertain. The Atlantic races, Plymouth to Santander (**7***a*), Coruña (**7***b*), or La Rochelle, usually take place after the high point of the season, the Fastnet and the Admiral's Cup, and are thus taken somewhat more lightly.

DECK LAYOUTS

A On offshore racers, deck layouts are of the greatest importance, and thus the subject of constant reflection on the part of designers and skippers. The layout must provide good working conditions for the crew and must allow everyone to work undisturbed at the same time. Each crewman must be able to watch the sail he is operating, and the crew weight must be kept in the middle of the boat—if possible, slightly to windward. Hands and feet should be out of reach of the dangerous steel wire, and everyone should be under the helmsman's eye without obstructing his sight of the course and of other competitors. Here, we show two typical layouts.

B HELISARA's deck is a good example of the modern tendency to position the helmsman at the extreme rear, in a "private" cockpit which is uncluttered, and which slightly dominates the scene. The crew weight is mostly amidships, and the crew works under the helmsman's eye.

A

B

C

C HUMBUG XIX. The famous Swedish sailor Pelle Petterson's ocean racer. Note the twin companion-ways, the coffee-grinder low on the cockpit floor, the flush deck, the hydraulic backstay, and the unique chain-plate giving maximum freedom to the

boom on the dead run and to the genoa when close-hauled.

D YEOMAN XX, a relatively small racing yacht but all the more efficient for that, played a major part in the British Admiral's Cup victory, in 1975. Design: Doug Peterson.

E DECEPTION, designed by Gary W. Mull and built in Italy for the Admiral's Cup.

F CORIOLAN, the first Class 1 racer from Paul Elvström, was full of new ideas, costly, and disappointing. The conception of ocean racers is a full-time

HUMBUG XIX
GKSS

job. The slightest detail can spoil a brilliant project.

G MILLER & WHITWORTH 48. Very successful in the highly competitive Australian waters, the Miller designs are original and very fast in certain points

of sailing. In European waters, they sometimes have trouble in adapting themselves.

H NORYEMA X, designed by German Frers for the Admiral's Cup competition. A very fine, aluminium-built ocean racer.

I ENTEARA II, designed by Britten Chance. The rating rule has become more positive to sail-area, and we often see walls or clouds of canvas on down-wind legs, just as in the "good old days".

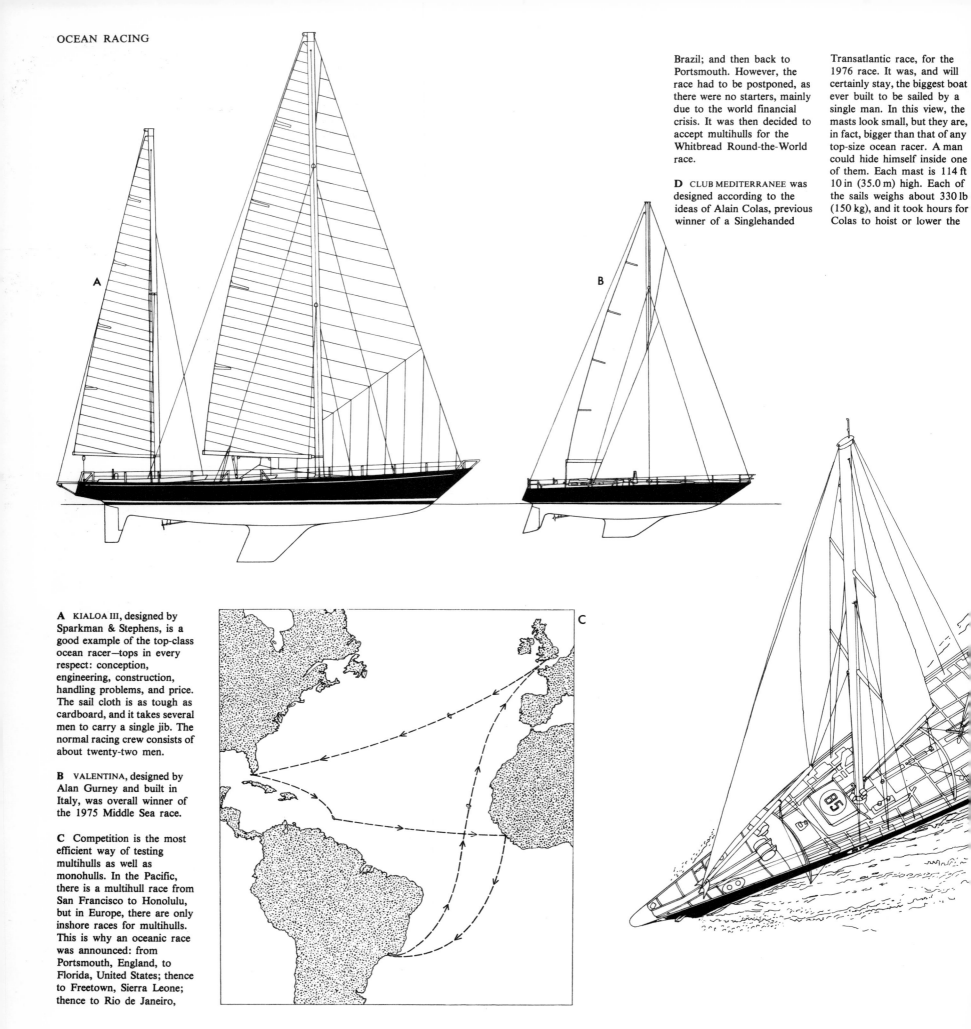

Brazil; and then back to Portsmouth. However, the race had to be postponed, as there were no starters, mainly due to the world financial crisis. It was then decided to accept multihulls for the Whitbread Round-the-World race.

D CLUB MEDITERRANEE was designed according to the ideas of Alain Colas, previous winner of a Singlehanded Transatlantic race, for the 1976 race. It was, and will certainly stay, the biggest boat ever built to be sailed by a single man. In this view, the masts look small, but they are, in fact, bigger than that of any top-size ocean racer. A man could hide himself inside one of them. Each mast is 114 ft 10 in (35.0 m) high. Each of the sails weighs about 330 lb (150 kg), and it took hours for Colas to hoist or lower the

A KIALOA III, designed by Sparkman & Stephens, is a good example of the top-class ocean racer—tops in every respect: conception, engineering, construction, handling problems, and price. The sail cloth is as tough as cardboard, and it takes several men to carry a single jib. The normal racing crew consists of about twenty-two men.

B VALENTINA, designed by Alan Gurney and built in Italy, was overall winner of the 1975 Middle Sea race.

C Competition is the most efficient way of testing multihulls as well as monohulls. In the Pacific, there is a multihull race from San Francisco to Honolulu, but in Europe, there are only inshore races for multihulls. This is why an oceanic race was announced: from Portsmouth, England, to Florida, United States; thence to Freetown, Sierra Leone; thence to Rio de Janeiro,

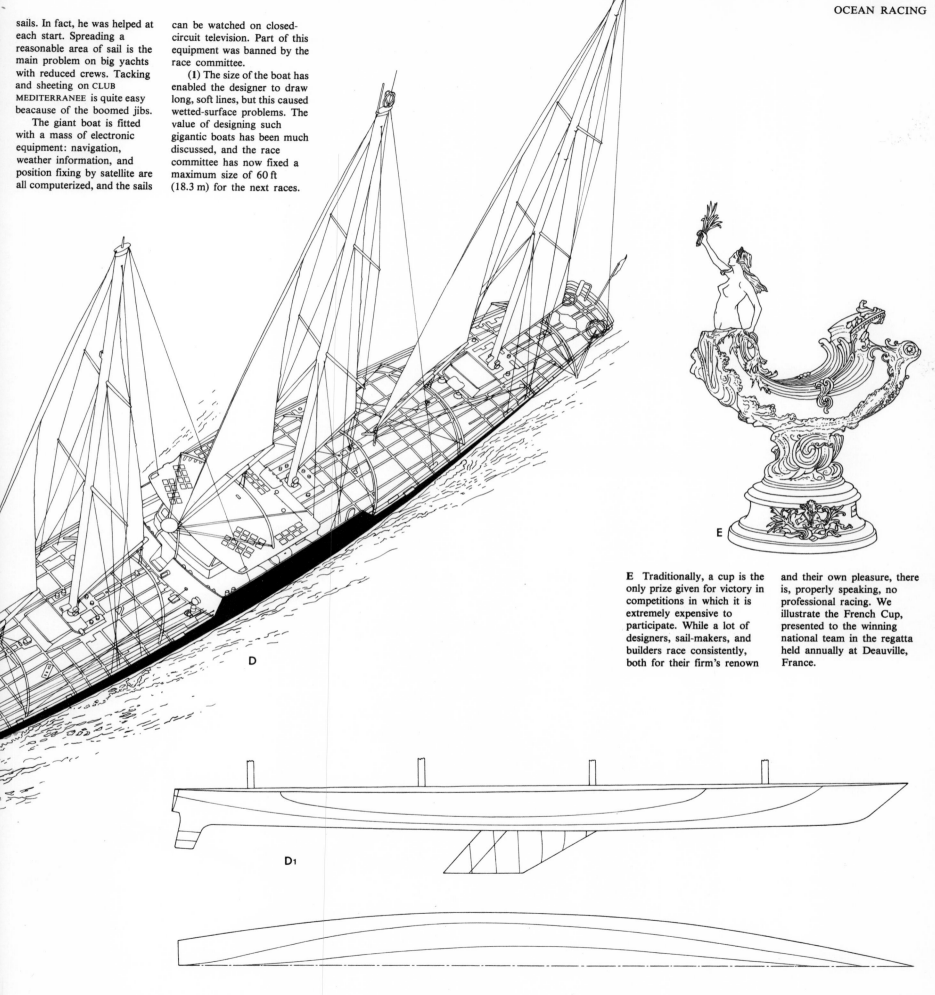

sails. In fact, he was helped at each start. Spreading a reasonable area of sail is the main problem on big yachts with reduced crews. Tacking and sheeting on CLUB MEDITERRANEE is quite easy beacause of the boomed jibs.

The giant boat is fitted with a mass of electronic equipment: navigation, weather information, and position fixing by satellite are all computerized, and the sails can be watched on closed-circuit television. Part of this equipment was banned by the race committee.

(1) The size of the boat has enabled the designer to draw long, soft lines, but this caused wetted-surface problems. The value of designing such gigantic boats has been much discussed, and the race committee has now fixed a maximum size of 60 ft (18.3 m) for the next races.

E Traditionally, a cup is the only prize given for victory in competitions in which it is extremely expensive to participate. While a lot of designers, sail-makers, and builders race consistently, both for their firm's renown and their own pleasure, there is, properly speaking, no professional racing. We illustrate the French Cup, presented to the winning national team in the regatta held annually at Deauville, France.

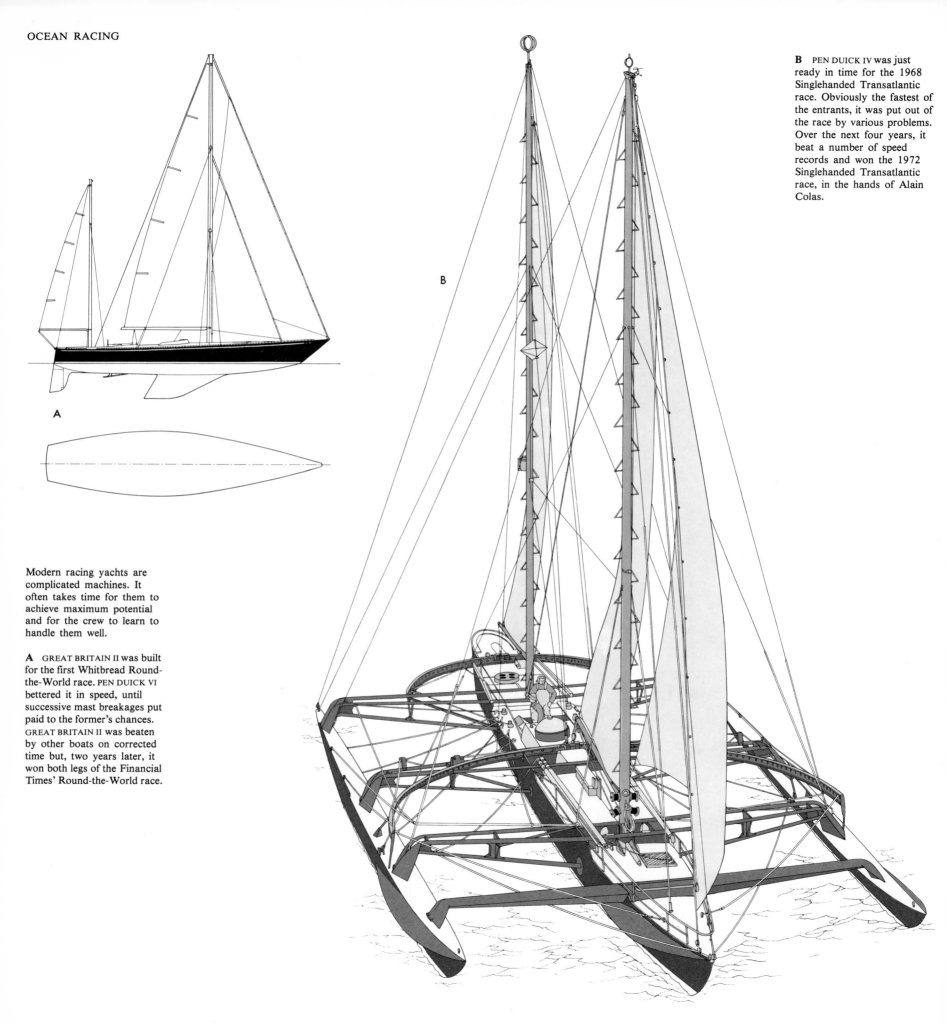

A

B PEN DUICK IV was just ready in time for the 1968 Singlehanded Transatlantic race. Obviously the fastest of the entrants, it was put out of the race by various problems. Over the next four years, it beat a number of speed records and won the 1972 Singlehanded Transatlantic race, in the hands of Alain Colas.

Modern racing yachts are complicated machines. It often takes time for them to achieve maximum potential and for the crew to learn to handle them well.

A GREAT BRITAIN II was built for the first Whitbread Round-the-World race. PEN DUICK VI bettered it in speed, until successive mast breakages put paid to the former's chances. GREAT BRITAIN II was beaten by other boats on corrected time but, two years later, it won both legs of the Financial Times' Round-the-World race.

CRUISING

Jaap A.M. Kramer

Cruising has been called "an escape from the routine or the complexities of everyday life".

The vast world of sailing can be divided into several parts. Cruising is the biggest part; day sailing is another big part; racing is a third and smaller part. For centuries, the big cruising part has seemed to remain hidden behind the racing scene; for racing attracts the most publicity and, many times, has caught the headlines.

For some decades, however, something has been going on. Many ideas have altered and, nowadays, cruising is "in".

Day sailing is sailing around in home waters. Cruising means that home waters are left behind and that the yacht heads for other waters and ports. Cruising is *not* characterized by living on board a yacht. Many cruises are made in day sailers, with the crew sleeping ashore in tents; this is cruising, but not with a cruising yacht. On the other hand, plenty of people live on board their cruising yacht without leaving home waters; though they live on board, they are not cruising.

There are many differences between cruising and racing. In his book *The Sailor's World* (New York, 1973), Arthur Beiser writes, "Racing is the ultimate test of sailing skill". That may be true for one-design classes. For handicap classes it seems more correct to say, "Racing is the ultimate test of designing and sailing skill", and that is only correct if sailing skill and speed are equated. Cruising, however, is the ultimate test of seamanship, and seamanship is much more than sailing skill alone.

A race is only worthwhile when you pass the finishing line within the determined time; and for some people, only when they are the first to pass the finish! But cruising can be worthwhile and enjoyable, whether or not you reach your destination.

In racing, you have to start at the exact starting time and sail as fast as possible to an obligatory destination. And if you are a true racer, you will take some risks to be the first to reach the finish. In cruising, on the other hand, all things, such as time of departure, courses to steer, destination, and speed, are up to yourself, and you can eliminate as many risks as possible.

But there is another, more essential, difference between cruising and racing. Cruising is measuring yourself *against the elements* by means of your boat. Therefore, your boat must be designed to stand up to the strains which will be imposed on it by the elements. Racing, on the other hand, is measuring yourself *against others* by means of your boat and the elements. It is no longer the elements, but rather the other competitors, who are the op-

ponents, whose challenge you accept. With the aid of your boat and the elements, you must be able to compete against those opponents by means of speed and within the limitations of a "rule" to be observed by all participants; a rule whose aim is to eliminate as much as possible the differences between the competing boats.

Last, but not least, cruising is sailing for pleasure. "The purpose of a sailboat is pleasure", writes Arthur Beiser. For racing men—actually only for the winner of a race—the pleasure is victory, maybe after a course full of hazards, risks, and all sorts of hardships. For many racing men, fun means the suspense of gaining or losing half a length or a few seconds.

But cruising means sailing from one port to another, with as much pleasure as possible en route. It is sailing in comfort, in a comfortable yacht, with the elimination of most of the hazards, risks, and hardships. Bad weather? You can delay your departure yourself; you are not dependent upon a race committee. A wind, unfavourable for your planned destination? You may alter your plans and choose another destination. Again, you decide for yourself.

For cruising, you can choose a yacht with the optimal possibilities for sailing in comfort and safety. Speed is not the most important factor, and that allows for the many other properties desirable in a good cruising yacht. Moreover, there is no need to wrestle with the limitations and the consequences of a complicated and continually altering measurement rule.

For true cruising, the two indispensable conditions are a good cruising yacht, and a good cruising skipper and crew, who know how to utilize the yacht's possibilities to the full.

Though cruising is possible in many day sailers and even in racers, the true cruiser has its own specific properties. It can be defined as a sailing yacht which is optimally suited for cruising by a specific cruising sailor.

This definition suggests two kinds of criteria. "A sailing yacht which is optimally suited for cruising" requires universal criteria, which can be applied to every cruising yacht. A yacht not meeting these universal criteria is not worthy to be called a cruising yacht.

"By a specific cruising sailor" refers to specific criteria, partly or completely optional, chosen to suit a specific user and his short- and long-term intentions with this yacht.

Most cruising sailors are not only individualists but, usually, they are also tied to certain circumstances and personal aspirations, which dictate the kind of cruising they do. One may want to cruise round the world, whereas

another—whatever his reason—may aspire to nothing more than to navigate sheltered inland waterways. Inexorable circumstances which limit the cruising man's scope are, often, his financial situation and the amount of time he has available.

If we want to respect the individuality and the personal circumstances of every cruising sailor, there cannot be such a thing as only one, universal, optimal cruising yacht. However, it must be possible to design an individual yacht for every cruising sailor, a yacht which is optimal and ideal just for him, and which possesses all the universal properties of a cruising yacht, but only those specific properties which the owner wants included.

"The one certain thing that comes out of all this is that there is no one kind of boat that can be said to be the best: it all depends on the character of the owner and the kinds of thing he wants to do with the boat", wrote D.M. Desoutter in *Small Boat Cruising* (London, 1963).

Proceeding on this concept, we can formulate a number of universally applicable criteria. These criteria, however, will only be of practical value—both for designing and for testing existing designs—if they are supplemented by specific criteria, based on the owner's circumstances, such as the waters in which he wants to cruise, his crew, finances, etc.

There are five *universal criteria* for any cruising yacht: good sailing ability, comfort, safety, ease of handling, and the ability to be self-supporting (i.e., it should depend as little as possible on shore facilities).

The following four aspects, which depend on the owner's special requirements, could serve as a base for *specific* or *optional criteria:* suitability for certain waters, suitability for certain climatic conditions, planned future (modifiability), adaptability for any special purpose which the owner might have in mind.

Now we can divide the cruising yacht into a number of elements, and we can consider what requirements are made upon a particular element by each of the nine criteria mentioned above. For this purpose, the yacht can be divided into the following nine elements: hull shape; keel and ballast; rudder and steering gear; hull construction; deck, cockpit and superstructure; interior and accommodation; rigging; equipment (also for navigation, safety, etc.); and auxiliary propulsion.

By plotting both the universal and the specific criteria vertically and the yacht's elements horizontally, we can make a block, or grid, scheme. Each block can be filled up with the requirements made upon the element of the yacht concerned by the criterion concerned.

	a	b	c	d	e	f	g	h	i
good sailing ability									
safety									
comfort									
ease of handling									
self-supporting									
for certain waters									
for certain climates									
planned future									
special purposes									

A block, or grid, scheme for evaluating cruising yachts. a=hull shape; b=keel and ballast; c=rudder and steering gear; d=hull construction; e=deck, cockpit, and superstructure; f=interior and accommodation; g=rigging; h=equipment; i=auxiliary propulsion.

Thus, for instance, the criterion "safety" may make the following demands upon the element "hull construction": it must be strong; fire resistant; and have as few holes as possible below water-line, all of them being closable. These are universal requirements, to be made upon any cruising yacht.

The sixth optional criterion, "suitability for certain waters", may make the following demands upon the element "hull construction": it must be unsinkable; it must have buoyancy bags or air tanks; it must have watertight bulkheads; and one must be able to reach the bottom from within. From among these optional requirements a choice may be made, according to the personal wishes or circumstances of the owner. A small yacht, for instance, could be made unsinkable by buoyancy bags, air tanks, or in another way; but in the case of a large yacht, a construction will be chosen in which the hull is divided into compartments by watertight bulkheads. The customer or the yacht designer can choose which is the most suitable, depending on the circumstances.

Thus nearly every block of the scheme can be filled up with few or many requirements, which are made upon the element of the cruising yacht by the criterion concerned.

Finally, these formulated properties have to be "translated" into certain constructions or into exactly measurable technical specifications. Here we encounter one of the greatest problems of the criteria for cruising yachts; namely, that a clear, unmistakable and/or measurable description of the formulated properties is very difficult to make. Thanks to progressing research and modern calculating systems, an increasing number of properties can be expressed in exact specifications. But a lot of things must still be worked out. The cruising sailor wants to measure himself against the wind and the waves; but these cannot always be defined in simple formulae.

If, for instance, a sailor decides to order a one-off cruising yacht, he must first decide which of the details of the optional criteria he wishes to have applied to it by the designer.

Then he must evaluate all the details of the universal criteria and the chosen details of the optional criteria. Different customers can set different values on the details of the criteria which they want applied to their yacht. In the box scheme, therefore, a scale of importance from 1 to 3 may be applied. Little value is put on 1; great value is put on 2; and 3 represents a feature of dominating importance. The customer who wants a yacht for sheltered, inland waters will, for instance, give "good behaviour in a seaway" 1 point, but "manoeuvrability" 3 points. For a yacht intended for long passages, however, these figures may be respectively 3 and 2.

From an evaluation of all the customer's needs, it is possible to compose a set of requirements which is, in fact, the "translation" of the details into constructions, arrangements, equipment, and measurable technical specifications.

Once this set of requirements is ready, it is necessary to assign a certain desirability or priority to each requirement of the set. In practice, it will be convenient to work again with three priorities. The highest priority can be valued with 3, a high priority with 2, and a low priority (for each detail that may be cancelled if necessary) with 1. Consequently, each requirement has to be marked with a value figure.

When the designer has received the set of requirements with every detail valued, he will try to combine as many of the highly valued details as possible in a preliminary design and only sacrifice the lowest valued, if necessary. In this way, the ideal cruiser for that customer may be approached as closely as possible. Theoretically, this design will be ideal, if the addition of the value figures of the details is maximal. In practice, however, this will not always hold true. For a yacht is, like any ship, a complicated compromise between many, largely contradictory, good qualities. It is certainly not a simple addition of independent details.

Therefore, as the preliminary design takes shape, the designer will come upon contradictory demands or wishes. Then he will, with the aid of his professional knowledge and experience, find the compromise himself which, in his opinion, is most in accordance with the customer's ideas, and which will also produce a good yacht, which is a well-functioning unity, a creation he himself can totally support as an expert. It may even conflict with the set of requirements or with the priorities of the customer.

When the preliminary design is ready, the designer and the customer get together for a thorough discussion of all the pros and cons, of why this or that compromise was necessary, and so on. Is the proposed compromise complete in itself and are the customer's demands optimally realized? Only when the customer and the designer have agreed that the preliminary design is the optimal realization of the priorities made, can this phase be completed. Then the preliminary design can be developed into the final design, and the yard can start building.

It may seem to be a long way from the block scheme of detailed, elaborated criteria, via the set of requirements, up to the agreement on the preliminary design. But it is a rather safe way, because both customer and designer are going step by step, both knowing what they are doing. This way of working can prevent long discussions after the event—and a lot of annoyance on the owner's part should he eventually find that the finished yacht does not meet his expectations.

Since the proof of the pudding is in the eating, the customer will only be able to evaluate whether the original priorities and the subsequent compromises have indeed resulted in the cruising yacht that is optimal for him. If so, it is very important for the designer to know that he has fully succeeded in the performance of his task.

Should the yacht prove not to be optimal, the owner will conclude that the priorities made by him might have resulted in another, better compromise—or, while sailing, he may come to the conclusion that it would have been better if he had formulated his priorities differently. These things, too, are of interest to the designer. Furthermore, there may be possible complaints about parts that prove unsatisfactory or do not function adequately; both the designer and the builder would like to be acquainted with them.

This feedback—the passing on of observations and criticisms based on the practical use of the yacht to designer and builder—is important both in one-off and in serial production. In the former, the designer can take advantage of this new information, when he is designing new boats and, in the latter, corrections can be made.

This feedback is only usual from the owners of one-off yachts; if the owner has observations or criticisms, he will pass them on to the designer and/or to the yard.

In serial-produced yachts, this feedback is not much of a success, as the yachts are usually sold through a dealer, and often not in the country where they are built. Reactions from the owner often do reach the dealer, but they are rarely passed on, or only after a long time. Often, small defects are remedied and shortcomings overcome by the dealer himself, usually without informing the builder concerned. Usually, the dealer only contacts the builder when a claim, which he wants to pass on to the builder, has been made upon him. Thus it may easily happen that serial builders, who export most of their production, remain ignorant of the complaints and suggestions from the users of their yachts. Consequently, their designers will remain ignorant of this information as well, and the development of the yachts concerned will stagnate unnecessarily. It is, therefore, desirable that the sellers of serial-built yachts make sure that complaints and wishes of the owners are passed on to the builder and the designer, who can then correct and improve the series concerned.

Studying these criteria helps the cruising sailor to think long and deep about cruising, cruising yachts, and his own personal situation. He must ask himself the following questions. What is the present family situation (if any), and how is it expected to develop over the next five or ten years? What is the normal weekend sailing range required? How far and where does he want to sail during his holidays? What other activities does he want to partake in during or between sailing (such as, swimming, fishing, diving, maintenance, exploring the shore, studying flora and fauna, etc.)? How far can his finances stretch? With the answers to such questions in mind, the block scheme can be filled in, and a set of requirements can be drawn up.

A sailor who intends to buy a new or second-hand yacht can also use these criteria. Generally, he will not be able to check them point by point when comparing several yachts at a boat show or in the water, but he can make a list of those points which he considers most important for *his* future yacht and for *his* circumstances, and check them off. He can also question the broker or salesman about those points which he cannot check himself.

For those who already own a cruising yacht, the criteria may also be very useful, as they can find out whether or not their yacht optimally fulfils their demands and wishes. If it does not, then they may be motivated to have improvements made. Moreover, they may discover properties in their yacht which they have not utilized properly before.

The use of the elaborated criteria may be of great importance for the improvement of communication between customer, designer, and builder, who often do not understand one another clearly, as they do not use the same terminology. In such cases, the designer must be both a psychologist and a detective—listening and discreetly questioning—in order to find out what exactly the customer's demands and wishes are. By means of the elaborated criteria, the customer, the designer, and the builder can learn how to speak the same language.

The remark made above, about one cruising sailor wanting to circumnavigate the world while another may only want to sail on inland or sheltered waters, should perhaps be treated with caution. Many sailors, at first quite happy with navigating sheltered waters, later want to sail on the open sea as well. But, obviously, a cruising yacht which is optimally suited to sailing on sheltered waters will not be the best choice for sailing on the open sea.

Furthermore, the number of crew aboard may increase or decrease with the years. The family may increase; little children may grow up and require longer bunks and more space. Older children may have a small boat of their own, and the parents may then want a yacht which suits just the two of them. Many fathers end their sailing days as involuntary singlehanded sailors or with ever-changing, inexperienced guests as crew. These problems can be solved by the purchase of a yacht which is more suitable to the changed circumstances, but there are also other ways.

Firstly, one can design a yacht that is optimally suited to certain circumstances, while it is, at the same time, adaptable so that it can suit altered or new circumstances. Secondly, a yacht with a "planned future" can be designed. This means that the design and construction of the yacht allow it to be modified so that it suits, for instance, other sailing waters. A ballast keel, for example, may be built with the ballast weight placed very low. Above the weight can be a removable section of a certain height. When sailing in shallow, sheltered waters, the draught can be reduced by removing the intermediate section. The consequent reduction in stability is not a setback in sheltered waters. When navigating on the open sea, the removable section may be replaced, thus lowering the ballast and making the yacht more stable. The greater draught is usually an advantage at sea.

Planned future should also mean that there is enough room for other modifications in the future, for instance, for an extra fresh-water tank or for the installation of a radio-communications system.

Finances may also be another motive for designing boats with a planned future. A cruising sailor who, at a given moment, cannot afford to buy the yacht of his choice has three possibilities: he can wait and save up the necessary money; he can borrow the money; or he can buy the yacht in a partly completed condition and finish it in the course of time. Saving money takes time and is not a very attractive proposition in these days of inflation. Borrowing, on the other hand, is more attractive. It enables you to "sail today and pay tomorrow". But it has its risks, too. Will you always be able to meet your liabilities? The third way, the purchase of an optimally sized yacht in a partly completed condition, makes immediate sailing possible, albeit with certain limitations. The job of completing the yacht may be divided over a number of years. This pre-calculated growth-possibility may also be called planned future.

Designing a yacht with a planned future makes great demands on the skill and creativity of the designer, all the more so because it is meant to prevent unnecessarily high costs. But if anywhere there is scope for creative designers, it is in the field of designing yachts with a planned future.

A The legendary SPRAY, a converted fishing-boat in which Joshua Slocum, well past his middle age, sailed alone round the world in 1895–98. Originally a gaff cutter, SPRAY is here shown in the yawl rig which Slocum gave it during his voyage. Loa: 36 ft 9 in (11.2 m).

B ISLANDER, built and sailed by Henry Pidgeon, twice circumnavigated the world, in 1923–25 and 1932–37. Pidgeon was the first man after Slocum to sail alone round the world. The boat type was designed for amateur construction by Thomas Fleming Day and his staff at *Rudder* magazine. Loa: 34 ft (10.4 m).

E Designed by the Frenchman Jean Knocker for Bernhard Moitessier, JOSHUA, a sturdy fourteen-ton steel ketch, has twice rounded Cape Horn. It is the prototype for a series built by Meta BP, Lyon. Loa: 39 ft 6 in (12.07 m).

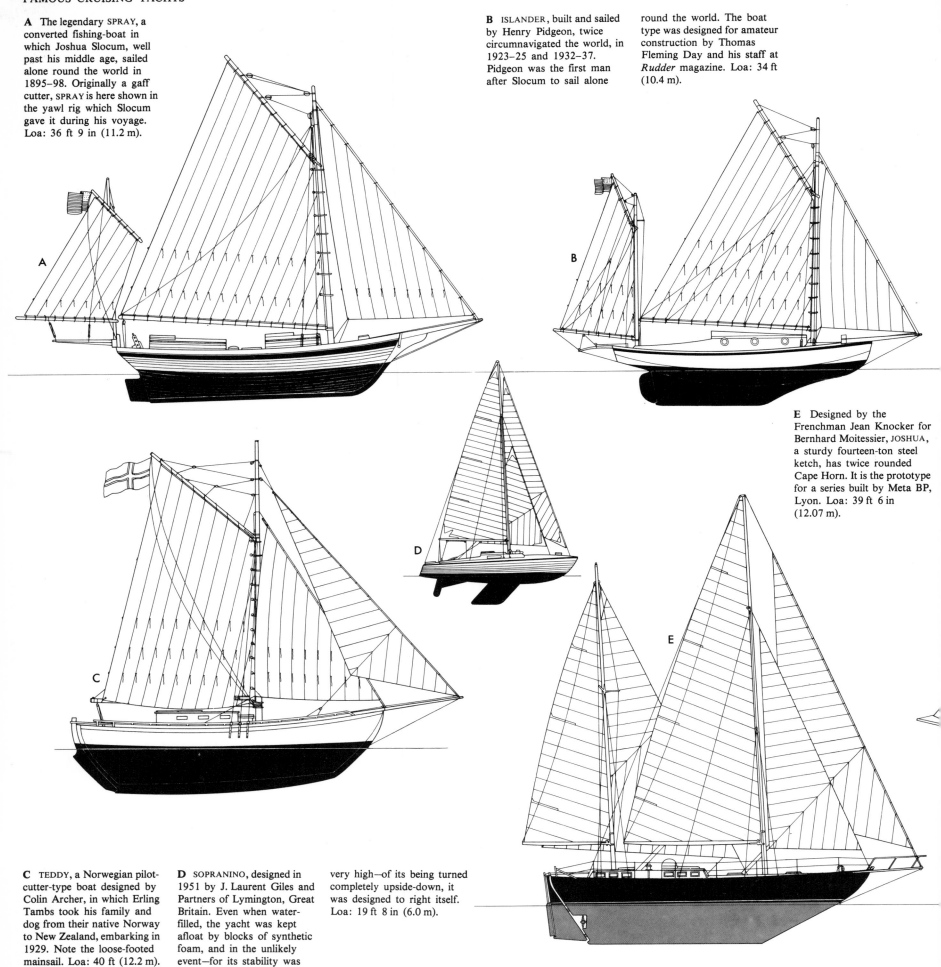

C TEDDY, a Norwegian pilot-cutter-type boat designed by Colin Archer, in which Erling Tambs took his family and dog from their native Norway to New Zealand, embarking in 1929. Note the loose-footed mainsail. Loa: 40 ft (12.2 m).

D SOPRANINO, designed in 1951 by J. Laurent Giles and Partners of Lymington, Great Britain. Even when water-filled, the yacht was kept afloat by blocks of synthetic foam, and in the unlikely event—for its stability was very high—of its being turned completely upside-down, it was designed to right itself. Loa: 19 ft 8 in (6.0 m).

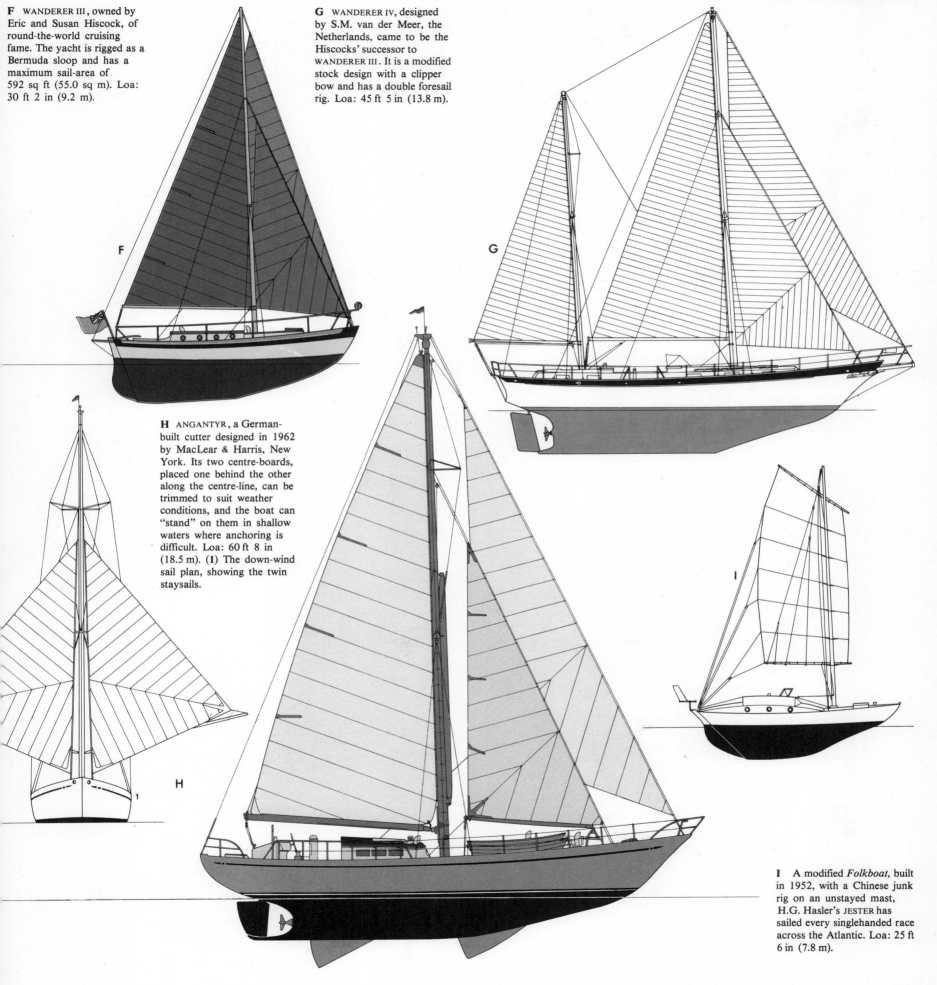

F WANDERER III, owned by Eric and Susan Hiscock, of round-the-world cruising fame. The yacht is rigged as a Bermuda sloop and has a maximum sail-area of 592 sq ft (55.0 sq m). Loa: 30 ft 2 in (9.2 m).

G WANDERER IV, designed by S.M. van der Meer, the Netherlands, came to be the Hiscocks' successor to WANDERER III. It is a modified stock design with a clipper bow and has a double foresail rig. Loa: 45 ft 5 in (13.8 m).

H ANGANTYR, a German-built cutter designed in 1962 by MacLear & Harris, New York. Its two centre-boards, placed one behind the other along the centre-line, can be trimmed to suit weather conditions, and the boat can "stand" on them in shallow waters where anchoring is difficult. Loa: 60 ft 8 in (18.5 m). **(1)** The down-wind sail plan, showing the twin staysails.

I A modified *Folkboat,* built in 1952, with a Chinese junk rig on an unstayed mast, H.G. Hasler's JESTER has sailed every singlehanded race across the Atlantic. Loa: 25 ft 6 in (7.8 m).

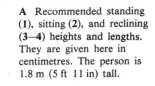
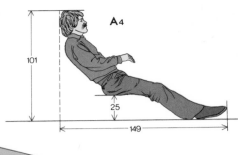

A Recommended standing (**1**), sitting (**2**), and reclining (**3—4**) heights and lengths. They are given here in centimetres. The person is 1.8 m (5 ft 11 in) tall.

Equivalents of the measurements are:
95 cm = 3 ft 1 in;
92 cm = 3 ft; 74 cm = 2 ft 5 in; 150 cm = 4 ft 11 in;
232 cm = 7 ft 7 in.

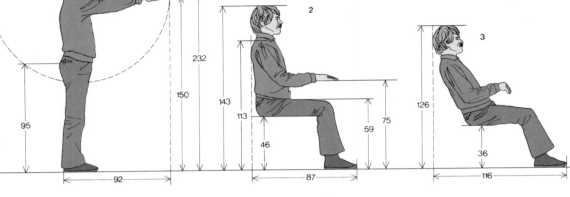

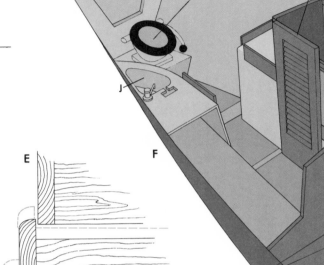

C In the main saloon of this cruising yacht, priority has been given to comfort, ease of movement, and stowage space. There is plenty of sitting space, which can be turned into berths when necessary. There is standing height, both in the saloon and in the doorway to the forward cabin. (*a*) Canned or bottled drinks can be cooled here. (*b*) Milk, fruit, margarine. (*c*) Vegetables. (*d*) Eggs, tomatoes, cheese. (*e*) Bedding. (*f*) Canned goods, drinks. (*g*) Flour, dry goods. (*h*) Salt, sugar, spices. (*i*) Bread.

D If the back rest of the seating is hinged, bedding can be stowed behind it.

E A drawer like this will lock when pushed in. To open, lift and pull out.

F The British-built, van de Stadt-designed *Prospect* cruising yacht is a good example of a well-thought-out layout. (*a*) Cockpit locker. (*b*) Emergency equipment locker. (*c*) Dining table with charts under. (*d*) Main saloon seating and double berth. (*e*) Water tank underneath here. (*f*) Wardrobe with sliding doors. (*g*) Forward berth with locker under. (*h*) WC door. (*i*) WC. (*j*) Wash basin. (*k*) Cabin half-doors. (*l*) Sink. (*m*) Cooker. (*n*) Food store. (*o*) Companion-way steps with drawer under each. (*p*) Gas-bottle locker. (*q*) Life-raft stowage.

G A plate-holder can be made by drilling a piece of chipboard (*a*) in suitable places and inserting wooden pins (*b*) in the holes. The holder can then be varied to suit different plate sizes.

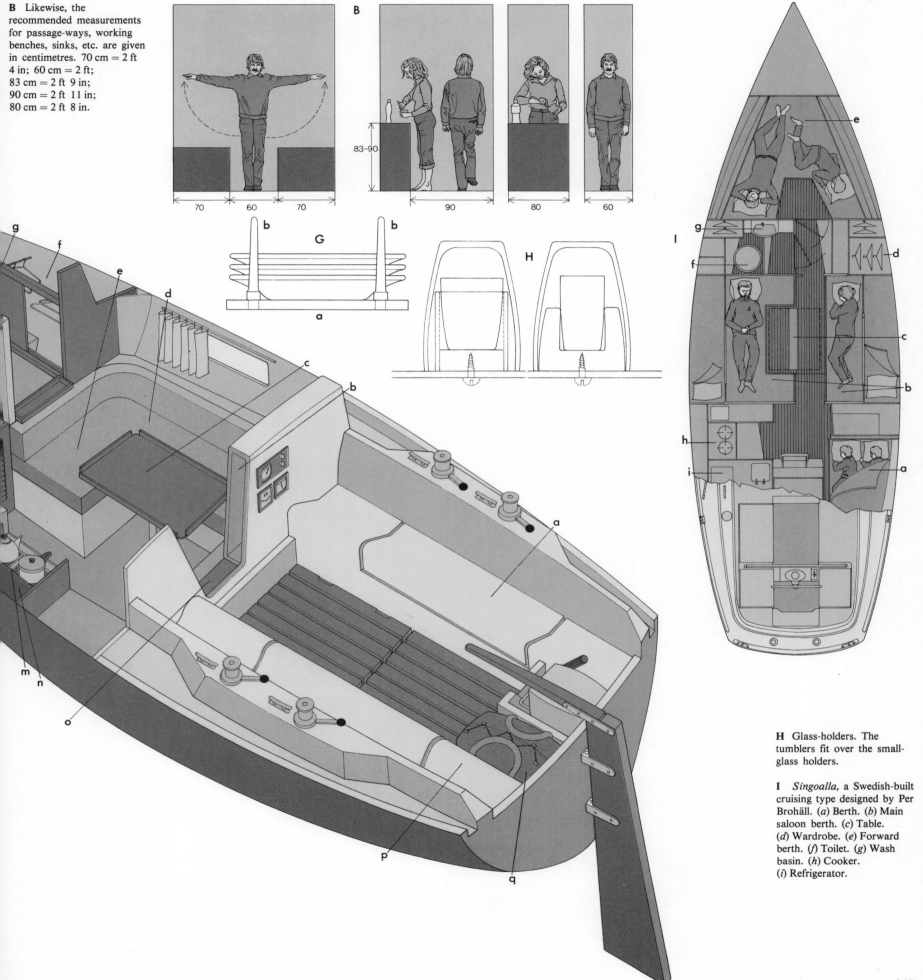

B Likewise, the recommended measurements for passage-ways, working benches, sinks, etc. are given in centimetres. 70 cm = 2 ft 4 in; 60 cm = 2 ft; 83 cm = 2 ft 9 in; 90 cm = 2 ft 11 in; 80 cm = 2 ft 8 in.

H Glass-holders. The tumblers fit over the small-glass holders.

I *Singoalla,* a Swedish-built cruising type designed by Per Brohäll. (*a*) Berth. (*b*) Main saloon berth. (*c*) Table. (*d*) Wardrobe. (*e*) Forward berth. (*f*) Toilet. (*g*) Wash basin. (*h*) Cooker. (*i*) Refrigerator.

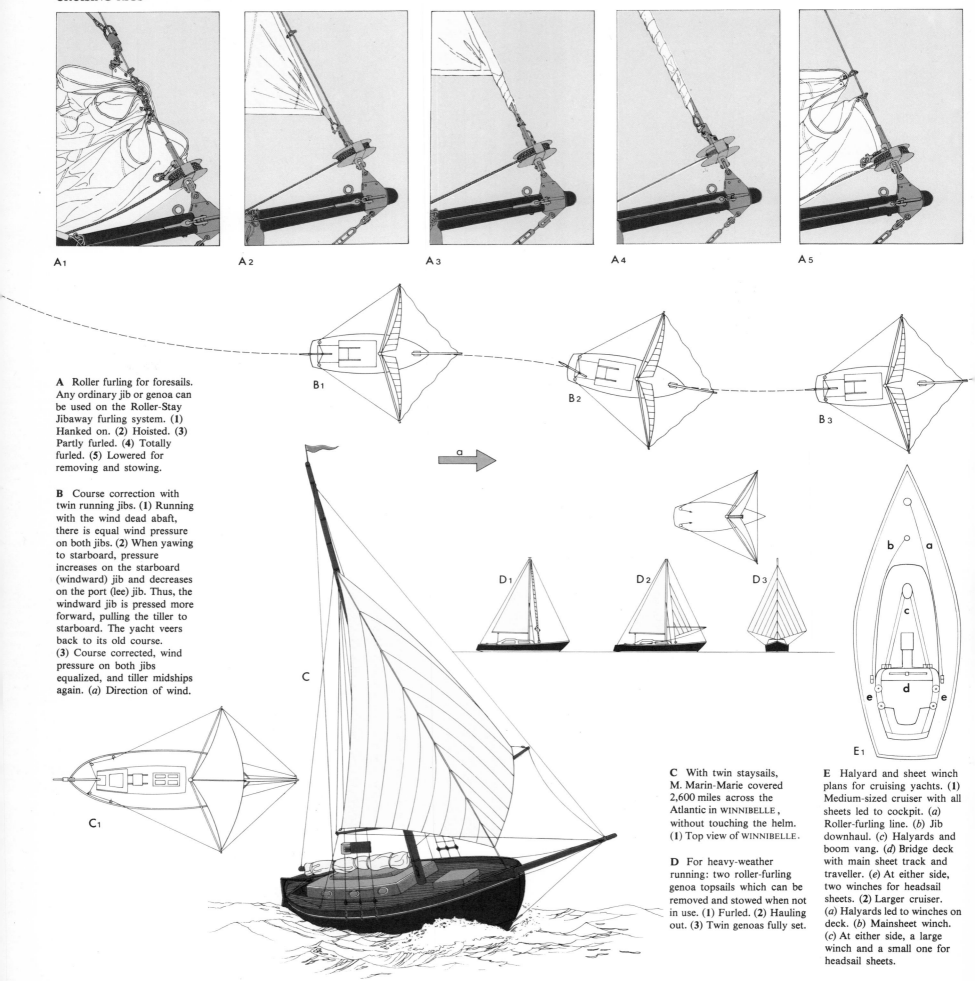

A_1 A_2 A_3 A_4 A_5

B_1 B_2 B_3

A Roller furling for foresails. Any ordinary jib or genoa can be used on the Roller-Stay Jibaway furling system. (**1**) Hanked on. (**2**) Hoisted. (**3**) Partly furled. (**4**) Totally furled. (**5**) Lowered for removing and stowing.

B Course correction with twin running jibs. (**1**) Running with the wind dead abaft, there is equal wind pressure on both jibs. (**2**) When yawing to starboard, pressure increases on the starboard (windward) jib and decreases on the port (lee) jib. Thus, the windward jib is pressed more forward, pulling the tiller to starboard. The yacht veers back to its old course. (**3**) Course corrected, wind pressure on both jibs equalized, and tiller midships again. (*a*) Direction of wind.

C_1

D_1 D_2 D_3

E_1

C With twin staysails, M. Marin-Marie covered 2,600 miles across the Atlantic in WINNIBELLE, without touching the helm. (**1**) Top view of WINNIBELLE.

D For heavy-weather running: two roller-furling genoa topsails which can be removed and stowed when not in use. (**1**) Furled. (**2**) Hauling out. (**3**) Twin genoas fully set.

E Halyard and sheet winch plans for cruising yachts. (**1**) Medium-sized cruiser with all sheets led to cockpit. (*a*) Roller-furling line. (*b*) Jib downhaul. (*c*) Halyards and boom vang. (*d*) Bridge deck with main sheet track and traveller. (*e*) At either side, two winches for headsail sheets. (**2**) Larger cruiser. (*a*) Halyards led to winches on deck. (*b*) Mainsheet winch. (*c*) At either side, a large winch and a small one for headsail sheets.

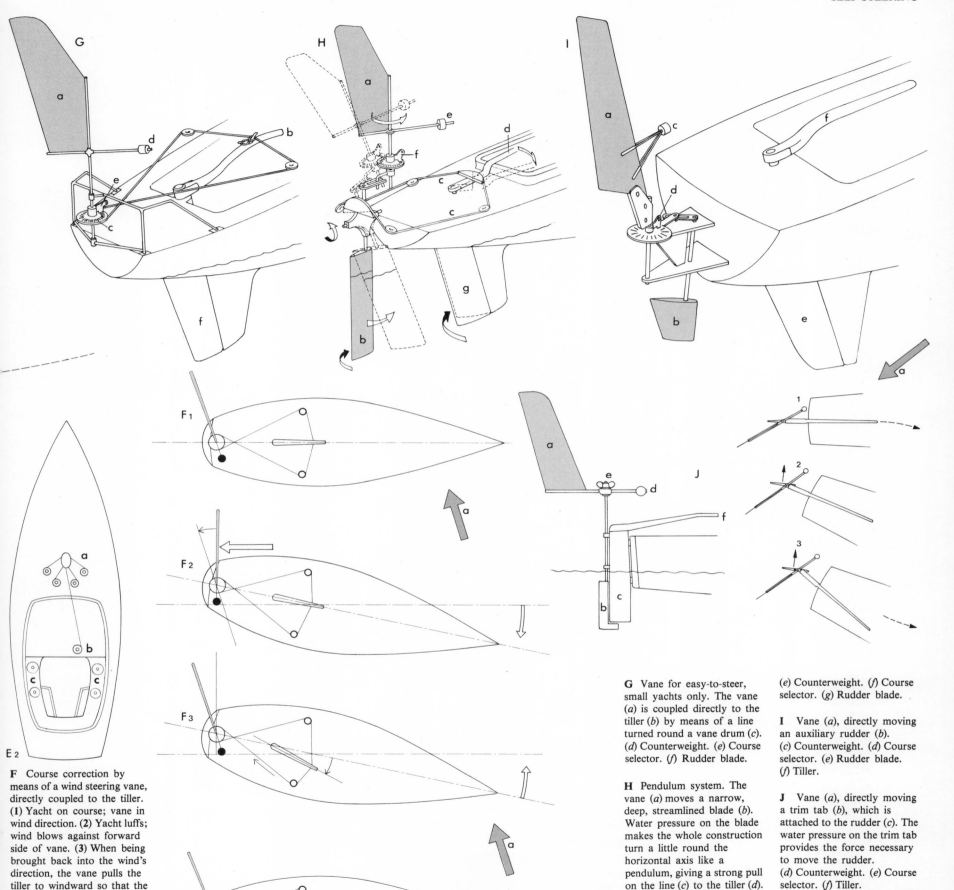

F Course correction by means of a wind steering vane, directly coupled to the tiller. (**1**) Yacht on course; vane in wind direction. (**2**) Yacht luffs; wind blows against forward side of vane. (**3**) When being brought back into the wind's direction, the vane pulls the tiller to windward so that the yacht bears away. (**4**) Course corrected. (*a*) Direction of wind.

G Vane for easy-to-steer, small yachts only. The vane (*a*) is coupled directly to the tiller (*b*) by means of a line turned round a vane drum (*c*). (*d*) Counterweight. (*e*) Course selector. (*f*) Rudder blade.

H Pendulum system. The vane (*a*) moves a narrow, deep, streamlined blade (*b*). Water pressure on the blade makes the whole construction turn a little round the horizontal axis like a pendulum, giving a strong pull on the line (*c*) to the tiller (*d*). When the yacht luffs to starboard, everything starts moving in the direction of the arrows; thus, the tiller is moved to starboard, correcting the course.

(*e*) Counterweight. (*f*) Course selector. (*g*) Rudder blade.

I Vane (*a*), directly moving an auxiliary rudder (*b*). (*c*) Counterweight. (*d*) Course selector. (*e*) Rudder blade. (*f*) Tiller.

J Vane (*a*), directly moving a trim tab (*b*), which is attached to the rudder (*c*). The water pressure on the trim tab provides the force necessary to move the rudder. (*d*) Counterweight. (*e*) Course selector. (*f*) Tiller. (**1**) Deviation from the boat's course. (*a*) Direction of wind. (**2**) Water pressure on the trim tab develops enough force to move the rudder. (**3**) Course correction.

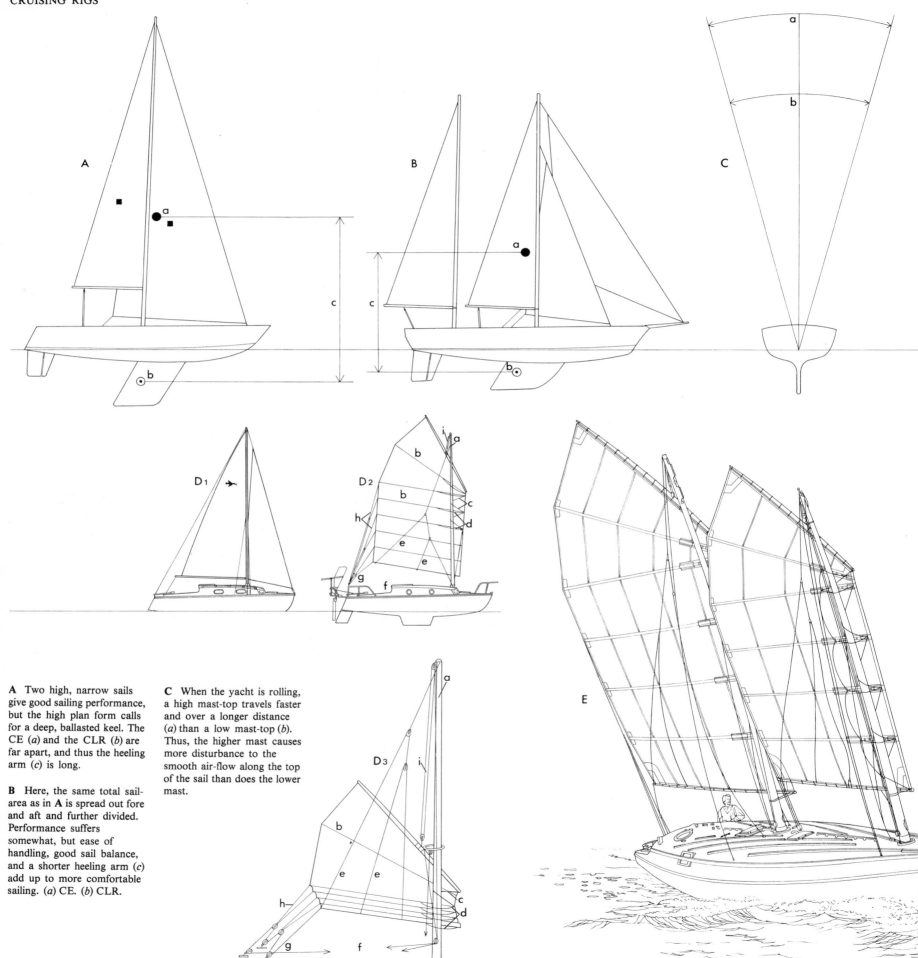

A Two high, narrow sails give good sailing performance, but the high plan form calls for a deep, ballasted keel. The CE (*a*) and the CLR (*b*) are far apart, and thus the heeling arm (*c*) is long.

B Here, the same total sail-area as in **A** is spread out fore and aft and further divided. Performance suffers somewhat, but ease of handling, good sail balance, and a shorter heeling arm (*c*) add up to more comfortable sailing. (*a*) CE. (*b*) CLR.

C When the yacht is rolling, a high mast-top travels faster and over a longer distance (*a*) than a low mast-top (*b*). Thus, the higher mast causes more disturbance to the smooth air-flow along the top of the sail than does the lower mast.

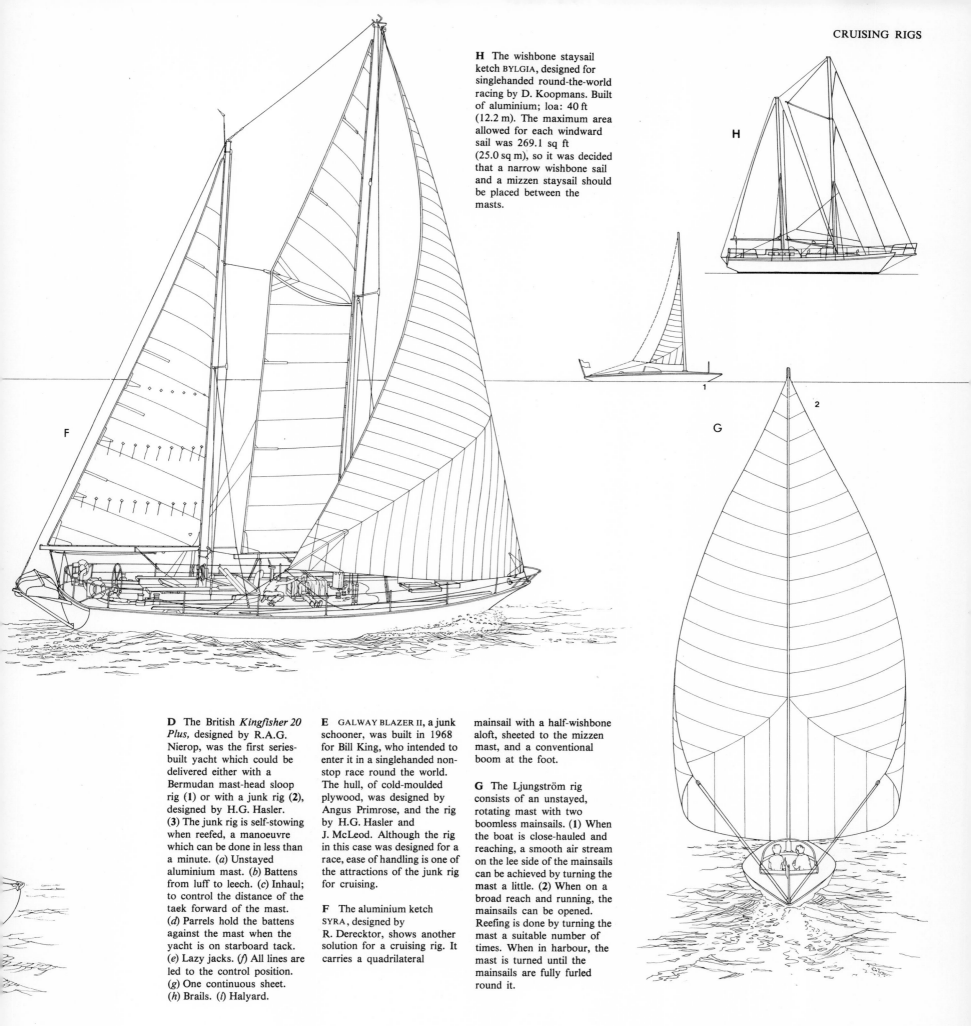

H The wishbone staysail ketch BYLGIA, designed for singlehanded round-the-world racing by D. Koopmans. Built of aluminium; loa: 40 ft (12.2 m). The maximum area allowed for each windward sail was 269.1 sq ft (25.0 sq m), so it was decided that a narrow wishbone sail and a mizzen staysail should be placed between the masts.

D The British *Kingfisher 20 Plus,* designed by R.A.G. Nierop, was the first series-built yacht which could be delivered either with a Bermudan mast-head sloop rig (**1**) or with a junk rig (**2**), designed by H.G. Hasler. (**3**) The junk rig is self-stowing when reefed, a manoeuvre which can be done in less than a minute. (*a*) Unstayed aluminium mast. (*b*) Battens from luff to leech. (*c*) Inhaul; to control the distance of the tack forward of the mast. (*d*) Parrels hold the battens against the mast when the yacht is on starboard tack. (*e*) Lazy jacks. (*f*) All lines are led to the control position. (*g*) One continuous sheet. (*h*) Brails. (*i*) Halyard.

E GALWAY BLAZER II, a junk schooner, was built in 1968 for Bill King, who intended to enter it in a singlehanded non-stop race round the world. The hull, of cold-moulded plywood, was designed by Angus Primrose, and the rig by H.G. Hasler and J. McLeod. Although the rig in this case was designed for a race, ease of handling is one of the attractions of the junk rig for cruising.

F The aluminium ketch SYRA, designed by R. Derecktor, shows another solution for a cruising rig. It carries a quadrilateral mainsail with a half-wishbone aloft, sheeted to the mizzen mast, and a conventional boom at the foot.

G The Ljungström rig consists of an unstayed, rotating mast with two boomless mainsails. (**1**) When the boat is close-hauled and reaching, a smooth air stream on the lee side of the mainsails can be achieved by turning the mast a little. (**2**) When on a broad reach and running, the mainsails can be opened. Reefing is done by turning the mast a suitable number of times. When in harbour, the mast is turned until the mainsails are fully furled round it.

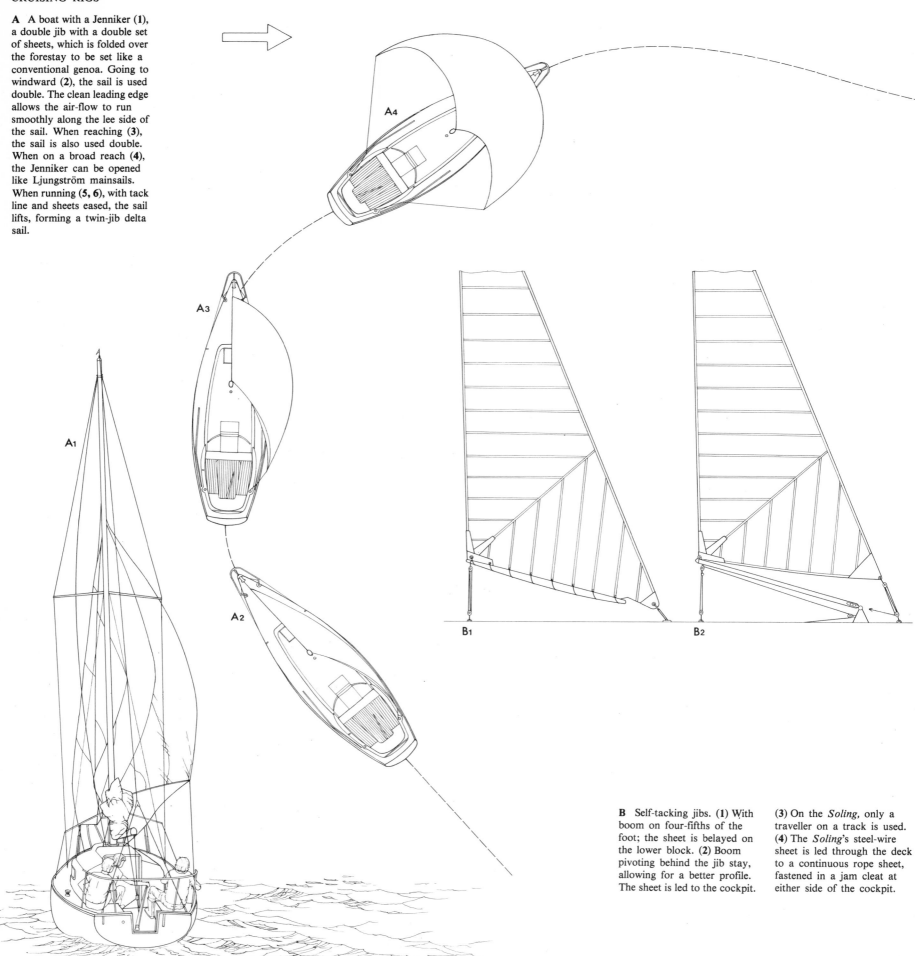

CRUISING RIGS

A A boat with a Jenniker (**1**), a double jib with a double set of sheets, which is folded over the forestay to be set like a conventional genoa. Going to windward (**2**), the sail is used double. The clean leading edge allows the air-flow to run smoothly along the lee side of the sail. When reaching (**3**), the sail is also used double. When on a broad reach (**4**), the Jenniker can be opened like Ljungström mainsails. When running (**5, 6**), with tack line and sheets eased, the sail lifts, forming a twin-jib delta sail.

B Self-tacking jibs. (**1**) With boom on four-fifths of the foot; the sheet is belayed on the lower block. (**2**) Boom pivoting behind the jib stay, allowing for a better profile. The sheet is led to the cockpit. (**3**) On the *Soling*, only a traveller on a track is used. (**4**) The *Soling*'s steel-wire sheet is led through the deck to a continuous rope sheet, fastened in a jam cleat at either side of the cockpit.

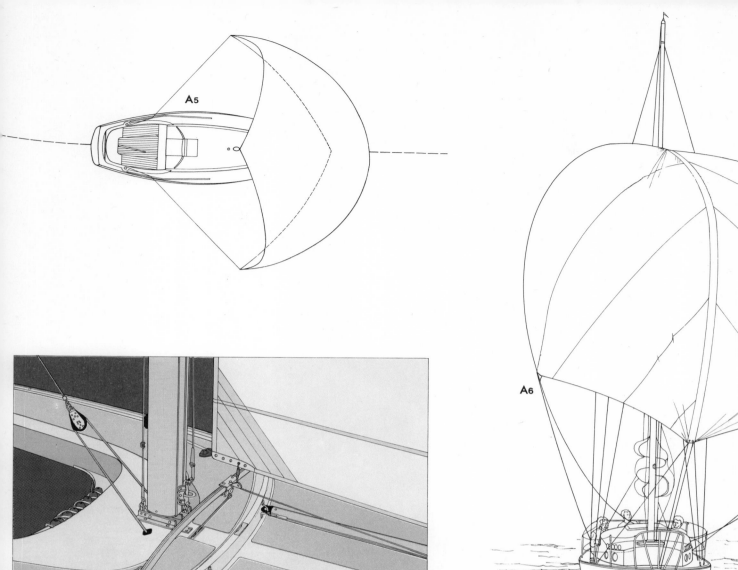

A5

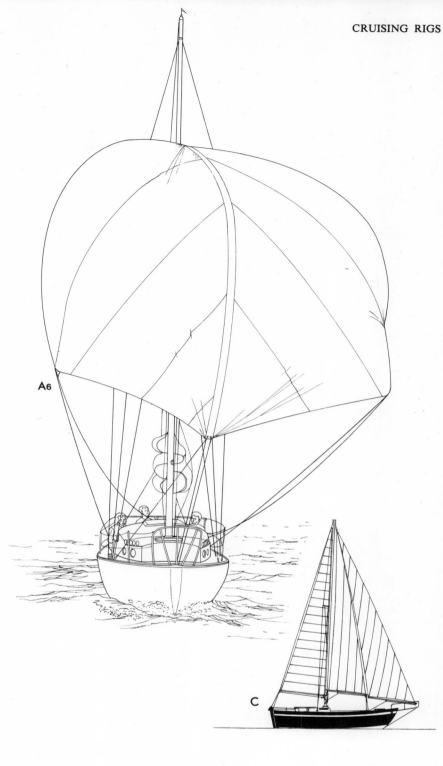

A6

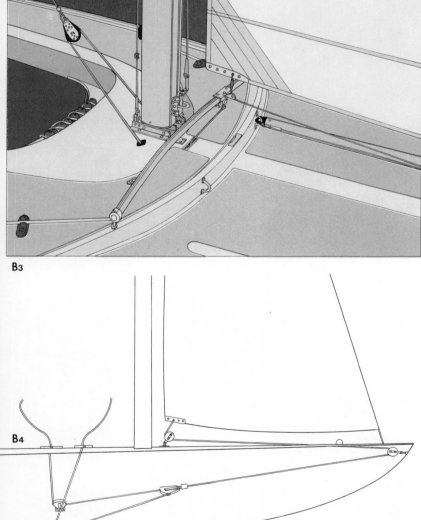

B3

B4

C

C *Brasser 25*, a cruising yacht designed by Robbert Das. The D.A.S. rig has two self-tacking foresails for easy singlehanded sailing.

Cruising has, often, its best moments in the peace and quiet of the early morning. While waiting for the sun to appear, so that the first sighting of the day can be made, the navigator uses the sextant's mirror as a shaving mirror.

Some typical cruising crews and how they may be organized into watches (**A–C**). The colour scheme shows the capacity of each member: *Red:* sailing, steering, and seamanship; *Blue:* can navigate; *Yellow:* can cook; *Brown:* maintenance ability.

A The crew consists of father (*a*), a keen yachtsman; mother (*b*), who can help in sailing and can navigate a little; (*c*) and (*d*), children, who can steer in good conditions. Only one watch (*e*) can be formed, so each night must be spent at anchor. A trip of eighteen hours is possible, but twelve-hour trips are preferred. This crew, sailing on the blue passage line in **D** would take eleven days to make a passage from *a* to *b*, but four extra days should be allowed for bad weather.

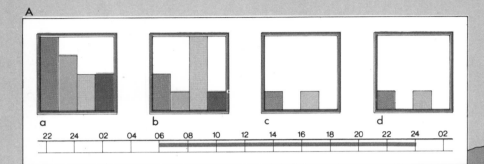

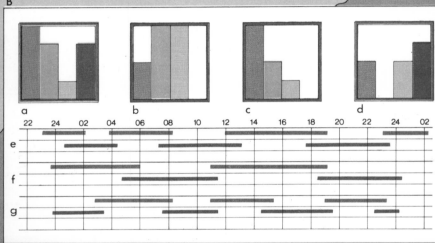

B In another family, father (*a*) is experienced, mother (*b*) can navigate and cook, child (*c*) can sail well and can navigate reasonably, and child (*d*) is a keen dinghy sailor and very handy. A two-watch system is best: *a* + *d* and *b* + *c*. One night can be spent at sea, but the next night must be spent at anchor so that the crew can sleep properly. The two watches can be arranged as shown: (*e*) with overlaps, so that the crew can eat together, or so that the new watch can have plenty of time to be brought up to date on the prevailing conditions; (*f*) long watches; (*g*) short watches. This crew would take the red passage line in **D**, taking eight days to get from *a* to *b*, but three extra days should be allowed for bad weather.

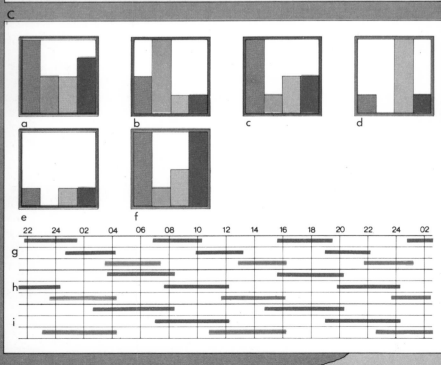

C A six-man crew: skipper (*a*), navigator (*b*), mate (*c*), cook (*d*), young child or passenger (*e*), crewman (*f*). Everybody's capacity is shown in the diagram. The watches can be arranged thus: (*g*) three hours each; (*h*) at the same time daily; (*i*) overlapping. A three-watch system is possible: *a* + *e*, *c* + *b*, and *f* + *d*. This crew would take the brown passage line in **D**, taking six days to get from *a* to *b*, but should allow two extra days for bad weather.

D Passage planning. The blue, red, and brown passage lines have already been discussed. The green passage line would only be taken by a sufficiently large and experienced crew, and the trip would take five days from *a* to *b*, but another day should be allowed for bad weather.

E An example of tactical navigation in an area where the wind is mostly between SW and NE. The green course line leaves with a W wind which is expected to veer slowly through NW to NE. If the boat goes as far as possible in the mean wind direction, then most of the trip can be covered on reaching or broad reaching courses. The red course line shows an alternative, if long distances, close-hauled in unsheltered waters, are not fancied.

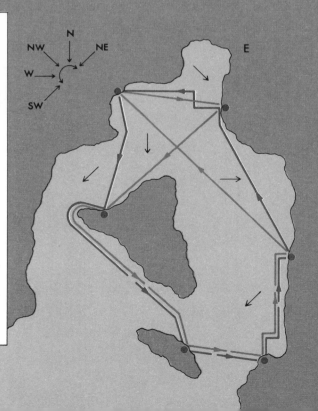

POWERBOAT RACING

John Teale

In many ways, powerboat racing is more akin to car racing than to competition under sail. It is noisy, exciting, fast, and dangerous, and the successful exponent needs to have a "feel" for engines and mechanical equipment just as much as for wind, waves, and currents. Like car racing, too, it has become partly dominated by "works", or factory-sponsored, entries, in which money and specially prepared engines and boats, available only to the chosen few, virtually ensure success. However, such entries are concentrated on a few classes where spectator interest is at its greatest, and this leaves a clear field in many other events for the amateur. He will find well-organized club racing in most countries, with opportunities to attend and race in national meetings in which the "big boys" are also mixing it in their specialized events amid the full glare of sponsored publicity.

The organization of powerboat racing varies from country to country. Racing is in the hands of the competitors, who organize it in a way that suits them and the conditions prevailing in their individual countries. In Europe, for instance, circuit racing (that is, races held inland on lakes, rivers, canals, and so forth) has more support than offshore racing and outboard racing is more popular than inboard. In the United States, it is the other way round, with the greatest publicity going to the big and famous races held at sea and to unlimited hydroplane events inland. In that country, too, circuit racing is supplemented by specialized events like drag-racing, which is practically unheard-of in Europe, though it does take place in Australia. South Africa has, for the most part, a remarkably inhospitable coastline, but there are many dams inland, so that racing there is almost exclusively round the buoys in the sheltered waters. Australia and New Zealand, like the United States, have races for big inboards, but such boats hardly exist as a class in Europe, probably because car engines are generally smaller there, with the consequence that inboard-powered boats tend to be smaller also.

Powerboat-racing world-wide is governed by the UIM *(Union Internationale Motonautique)* with its head-quarters in Brussels, Belgium. This organization makes the rules for racing, decides on classes, and generally arranges the way the sport should be run. In Europe, its decisions are accepted; in the rest of the world, its influence is increasing but by no means dominant. The Australian Power Boat Association, the New Zealand Power Boat Association, and the South African Power Boat Association control the sport in their respective countries, though offshore racing in that part of the world tends to be regionally organized in New Zealand. In the United States, the American Power Boat Association holds sway. All these organizations can and do make their own rules.

Unlike car racing, there are marked differences in configurations between boats designed for the different types of racing. Even for racing inshore on circuits, varying hull forms have evolved for the individual classes. Although the reader may have no intention of joining in the sport, a review of the most common types ought to make watching racing more interesting. Why are certain races dominated by catamarans? And why are these shapes not universally popular? What are tunnel-hulls and pickleforks, those mysterious names used to describe particular boat-types in race programmes?)

At the smaller and cheaper end of the racing scale, we have powerboats intended only for events that take place on sheltered waters. In Europe, these events are called circuit races, while elsewhere, they are known as inshore races and are held on rivers, dams, and lakes, not on the open sea.

Boats may be driven by inboard or outboard engines, and both types are divided into sport and racing classes. Generally speaking, the actual shape of the hull is unrestricted, but a sports boat must conform with certain minimum dimensions related to engine power. In addition, the engine must be a standard production type, with only slight modifications allowed. Sports-boat classes propelled by inboards start with the letter S, and range from the smallest class, S1, which allows engines of up to 1,000 cc (61 cu in), to S6, which allows engines of up to 6,000 cc (366 cu in), to the largest class, S00, where the volume of the engine is from 7,000 cc (427 cu in) upwards. Corresponding outboard sports boats again commence with the letter S, but follow this with another letter. Thus, the smallest class is SJ, where cylinder capacity is up to 175 cc (10.7 cu in). Next comes SA, from 175 to 250 cc (10.7 to 15.3 cu in), and then the alphabet is followed, with gaps, up to SN, 1,500 to 2,000 cc (91.5 to 122 cu in), and SZ, 2,000 cc (122 cu in) to infinity. Generally, these sports boats are privately entered, because the engines have to be standard, and there is no scope for manufacturers' specials.

Inboard racing classes start with the letter R and range from R1 to R6 and R00, with the same engine-capacity limits as in the sports classes. Outboard racing classes start with 0 and also have the same engine-capacity limits as their sports counterparts. OJ is the smallest class; then the scale goes from OA up to ON and OZ. The most popular sizes are in classes OE and ON, and this is where sponsorship comes in.

In racing boats, there are no restrictions or limiting dimensions on hull sizes or shapes, though engines on racing inboards have to be fairly standard, with only certain alterations allowed. Racing outboards are quite unrestricted, apart from capacity, and tremendous secrecy shrouds the building of each new model. Only selected works-mechanics are allowed to handle the new engines, whose general configuration—whether they are four- or six-cylinder, in-line or V—are not revealed. Certainly, the latest models in these classes are extremely potent pieces of two-stroke machinery. Those in the ON class, from 1,500 to 2,000 cc (91.5 to 122 cu in) develop well over 250 horsepower, and drive the boats at a maximum of 120 mph (193 km/h) or so. No mere enthusiast is allowed to buy such engines and, consequently, he cannot hope to match the speed of the factory-entered craft. Even in the OE class (700 to 850 cc or 42.7 to 51.9 cu in), speeds around 100 mph (160 km/h) are reached.

In Europe, outboards dominate the scene, and the principal international events in which they race are those leading to what is known as the European Endurance

Championships. In 1975, there were six venues for both the ON and OE classes—the only two which compete. The former raced at Lecco, Italy; Bristol and Windermere in England; Belgrade, Yugoslavia; and Rotterdam and Amsterdam in Holland. The OE class substituted Rouen, France, for Windermere, otherwise it used the same circuits on the same dates. Drivers counted their best four results, and scoring was done on what is called the "400 points reducing 25 per cent" system. This means that the winner gets 400 points; the second man home, 300 points; third, 225; fourth, 169; and so on, all the way down to 1 point for twentieth place.

In these races, enthusiasts running their own boats can and do enter, but they rarely find a place among the winners. Entries come from teams sponsored by, say, a tobacco or alcoholic-beverage company which may, or may not, have the very latest engines from the manufacturers. If they cannot get hold of these, they have to rely on standard models and hope that the hotted-up competition engines of their principal rivals will simply collapse under the strain. This does sometimes happen, and an unfancied winner then emerges. However, the likely leader at the end of the day, especially in the ON class, will most probably come from one of the works teams.

Courses for these circuit races are usually quite short. A mile or a mile-and-a-half (1.9 or 2.8 km) is the common length. The races are usually of three hours' duration and are run in two heats of ninety minutes each, though some events are non-stop for three hours, and then there are refuelling facilities. The water can get very rough, especially when the race is run in a river or in docks, where the wash from the competing craft is reflected back off the banks or walls, and the water gradually becomes more and more confused as the race goes on. At the speeds these craft reach, great experience and skill are needed to prevent them becoming airborne—this applies particularly to the twin-hull vessels—and to bring them swiftly and safely through a corner.

Nowadays, all big racing outboards can be tilted hydraulically from the cockpit. That is, the angle of the drive leg can be altered, thus changing the angle the propeller makes with the water. During a race, the controlling lever for this tilt mechanism is constantly in use to keep the boat's bow down as it suddenly tries to lift in a puff of wind, or when it is thrown up by a wave. Coming out of corners, the bow will probably need to be lifted, with the engine tilted out, in order to gain maximum acceleration and speed. This also would be the correct attitude for running with waves. However, driving into waves usually requires the bow to be depressed. It is this feel for the boat, this anticipation of its actions just before they happen, and this understanding of machinery that mark out the really good driver from those who are simply waterborne cowboys. It is not enough just to open the throttles and to leave them that way.

In Australia, to confuse the issue, what would be called sports boats in Europe are termed family boats, and European racing boats are known as sports boats. In principle, however, the differences between the two classes remain the same. The family boat is more a production runabout with a standard engine, while the sports boat has a hull free from most restrictions, though the engine must still be a standard production model, except for class X and

Super Sports, in which many engine modifications are allowed. A new class is the 25-horsepower class, in which the hull design is free, but the engine has to be a standard 25-horsepower production model. The idea is to provide good and exciting racing at low cost without inhibiting hull design, and these little boats can do 45 mph (c. 72 km/h) or more. UIM classes are being slowly accepted in Australia, and some meetings cater for them exclusively.

Inboard racing also has its following in Australia. There, imported American K-class craft compete with the more traditional Australian clinker inboards—"hollow logs", as they are termed. In race conditions, with confused water, and speed in turns vital, the local design seems to be superior but, in events such as drag racing, where pure speed is all that matters, the flat-bottomed American boats generally take the honours. Yarrawonga, on the Murray River, is the venue for perhaps the best inboard racing, while outboard meetings are held all over the place, with popular events on the Wyangula Dam in New South Wales, at Goolwa in South Australia, at Brisbane, and at Sydney.

In New Zealand, naturally enough, the racing scene is similar to that in Australia. Twin-hull outboards have come to dominate circuit racing, though there is still a healthy class of big inboard racers. Principal events are held at Karapiro and at Bottle Top Bay.

It is surprising that in the United States, whose outboard engines dominate the racing scene and which has some top-class drivers, circuit racing is not as popular as in the rest of the world. Though there is a public following for the Gold Cup hydroplanes, powered by ex-aircraft engines of 27 litres (1,647 cu in) or more and capable of speeds around 200 mph (322 km/h), crowd support for straightforward racing round the buoys is generally rather poor. As a consequence, the best drivers tend to join engine manufacturers' teams and do much of their racing in Europe.

However, the United States has some excellent venues, such as those at Miami Beach, the Parker Dam, and St. Louis. The Parker Dam 9-hour race is nowadays won at staggering averages of over 100 mph (161 km/h). This gives an indication of the speeds these 2,000 cc (122 cu in) boats can achieve on a course unrestricted by tight bends and short straights. And when considering these speeds, remember that water weighs over eight hundred times as much as air and is about thirteen times more viscous. It obviously takes much more effort to push a boat through the water than an aeroplane through the air, or even a car along the road. That is why designers of very fast circuit racers work hard to have as much of the boat airborne as possible, despite the difficulties in handling and the potential dangers that this creates. That is also the reason why nearly all successful entrants are of ply construction. Without very expensive techniques, GRP cannot better the strength-to-weight ratio of plywood.

Specialized events, such as drag racing, are popular in the United States. Boats are timed, individually or in pairs, through a short course, which is usually about a quarter of a mile (0.5 km) in length. It is here that the traditional American racing inboard, with a nearly flat bottom and a powerful motor installed near the stern, comes into its own. Its powerful acceleration and weight combine to make it a formidable straight-run competitor, though it is

not usually the equal of an outboard-engined boat of the same capacity on a circuit race.

In all fast boats, the main objective of the designer is to reduce the wetted surface. At the same time, the boat must be capable of travelling fast in rough water without falling to pieces or giving the rider such an uncomfortable ride that he is forced to slow down. Furthermore, the boat must be capable of running in a reasonably straight line, without constant work by the man at the wheel, and it must also be capable of turning fast and safely. There are, as will be seen, a lot of factors to be taken into consideration and, over the many years of circuit racing history, hull shapes have constantly evolved and changed. Some ideas that appeared promising on the drawing-board have never quite worked out in practice, and others, which were given up as useless, have returned, often thinly disguised and under another name.

The deep-V hulls would still dominate the circuit racing world—as they do in the offshore classes—if it were not for the fact that catamarans were rediscovered. There were many very fast catamarans before 1914, often driven by airscrews, but they had been virtually forgotten. Occasionally, some of these twin-hulled boats would appear in offshore races, but they were generally rather heavy, and their performances were poor. In addition, they tended to fall to pieces in rough water, due to the enormous strains it put on them. But then, a breed of catamarans was developed for the less structurally demanding circuit racing. These catamarans relied for their greater efficiency on the steadiness and stability given by two widely-spaced hulls and on the air lift provided by a slight modification of the old sea-sled principle. The tunnel between the hulls was arranged to finish above the water-line at the stern, so that the "lift" was mainly of the ground-effect type, and there was no problem with the air bleeding back underwater and ruining propeller performance. Once again, higher speeds were attained and, with one further modification, that is as far as we have got in circuit-racing craft. The modification is to have a V-shaped tunnel to induce the boat to run straighter and to improve its handling in rough water. This has, in fact, taken the catamaran even further back to the sea sled. Catamarans may be called tunnel-hulls, if the tunnel continues all the way forward, or pickleforks, if the tunnel commences some way back from the bows. The idea of the picklefork is that there is less "lift" at the front, and this lessens the risk that the boat may be thrown up and then over backwards by sudden gusts of wind. The picklefork also gives a more comfortable ride in rough water. Since it is the front end of the boat that tends to slam into waves, this slamming can now take place without the top of the tunnel hitting the water, thus bringing the boat to a jarring halt; a very dangerous occurrence, which often results in the boat breaking up.

Offshore racing boats have developed along more or less the same lines as inshore racers, though their greater size, and the fact that they have to operate in what can be very rough water, has brought about some modifications.

Among the offshore classes approved by the UIM, the biggest is Class 1, with a maximum permitted length of 45 ft (13.72 m), and with a maximum petrol engine capacity of 16,400 cc (1,000 cu in) and with double that capacity for diesel engines. Gas turbines are also permitted, but they run in a subdivision of Class 1, known as the experimental class. Speeds of over 80 mph (c. 128 km/h) can be reached by the latest in this class of offshore racers.

Sheer weight can assist a boat to make a good, fast passage in rough water and thus, in bad-weather races, diesel-engined entrants have just occasionally led the field home. These days, however, it is the petrol-driven, twin-engined outdrive craft that are normally the winners. Each engine on these racers develops around 600 horsepower, and the total of 1,200 horsepower can hardly be reached by diesels, or even by gas turbines, with their present rating under the rules. The almost universal success of the outdrive unit has been rather unexpected, and it has come about despite the fact that the lower half of the drive unit impedes a clean flow of water to the propeller, and that to turn the drive from vertical (down the unit) to horizontal (at the propeller) requires a gearbox which must absorb a fair amount of power.

The drawbacks of the conventional inboard set-up, with a straight drive from the engine, are two-fold on racing craft. Firstly, the inclined propeller shaft in the water, the bracket needed to hold it, and the rudder (and remember that there may be two sets of each) are all sources of unwanted wetted surface, and their area is hardly reduced whatever the speed of the boat. The outdrive unit, though, has only the skeg in front of the propeller and, of course, the propeller itself submerged at speed. Steering is done by turning the unit, thus doing away with the need for a rudder. Further, the conventional inboard shaft, bracket, and propeller are always driving at an angle which may not be desirable in the first place, and which, anyway, cannot be changed. The outdrive unit can be tilted, and this allows the drive always to be at its most efficient angle in the various wind and wave conditions.

Another alternative to the outdrive is the surface propeller. As has been mentioned in the first chapter, this is not a new idea, and the surface propeller was actually used in the early sea sled to reduce the interference from water bubbling back under the transom. The idea has been recently revived, and Renato Levi, the renowned racing-boat designer, has been one of its leading proponents. This form of drive has many advantages. As the boat, at speed, lifts in the water, the shaft and bracket run dry, and only the lower half of the propeller is submerged. Provided that the propeller has been designed for this job, its efficiency will be just as high as that of a more conventional type. Another gain for the surface propeller is that, as the boat leaps about in the water, with the bows leaping first and highest, the propeller, trailing well behind the transom, will probably remain in the water for much longer than propellers of the other types. Because of this, the surface propeller provides power for more of the time, thus causing less strain on the machinery, which might otherwise alternatively race and slow down as the propeller comes in and out of the water. Also, the drive on a surface propeller is horizontal, which is what is wanted. A disadvantage is, perhaps, that it cannot be easily altered, as can that of an outdrive.

It is worthwhile mentioning, while on the subject of leaping about in rough water, that a very important member of an offshore racer's crew is what is known as the "throttle man". His job is solely to handle the engine throttle, anticipating the leaps, shutting down the throttle as the boat rockets skywards, and then opening it again in time for the return journey and the maintenance of another burst of speed. An experienced throttle man can tell when an engine needs nursing and, also, if it is safe to keep it flat out for a period. No crew runs its engines harder than is absolutely necessary, and there is no question of opening the throttles to their fullest extent at the beginning of a race, and leaving them like that until the finish. These racing engines are temperamental, highly-tuned, and very expensive. They receive a tremendous hammering during races, and they need looking after.

Generally, an offshore race has a rolling start. That is, the entrants gather behind a boat which moves off towards the start line at a gradually increasing speed to allow for the fact that many of the extreme racing machines are difficult to handle when travelling slowly. When the line is reached, a flag on the start boat is dropped and a flare fired. The boat, which is by now travelling quite fast, normally then turns away from the following fleet and leaves the course. This run up to the line can be uncomfortable, for there are a great number of boats travelling rather more slowly than suits them and creating enormous washes. The start often takes place close to the shore, so that spectators have something to watch, and thus the manoeuvring area is strictly limited. It generally pays to be right in the front line at this time (so missing the wake of the other craft), or well clear at the back, were the water is calmer and where control of the boat is easier.

Races differ, some making more demands on navigational skills than others, but in every case, the navigator plays a vital part. He will have plotted courses to be steered, distances between marks and estimated arrival times at each (for they could be as much as 30 miles —48 km—apart), and probably noted bearings on prominent objects on shore which can be used to give a running check on the boat's position. At every mark and turning point, there will be a committee boat, which notes the race numbers of competitors as they pass. Thus, navigation has to be first class, because time spent looking for a mark can easily lead to the loss of a race and, since race numbers have to be read, competitors must pass close to the committee boats.

The craft become so spread out that there is no way of telling how rivals are doing, and many races have been lost through over-confidence. Engines may be eased in the mistaken belief that the main opposition has been left behind or has dropped out, only for someone quite unexpected to overtake, unseen. This applies particularly when visibility is poor, and in rough-water races, where some boats may take a course sheltered by a headland. The result of this is often that a greater distance has to be covered, but calmer waters will allow higher speeds, and back markers may forge ahead, even though they have not been seen at all by competitors pounding their way through big seas on a direct route to the next marker or turning point.

There are really no race tactics worth mentioning. In any given race, something like half the entrants will drop out through mechanical failure or hull damage, and so the first requirement is to finish. This implies careful pre-race preparation and skilful handling of the throttles during the event. Really accurate navigation is an important factor and, generally, it is desirable to run over the course a few times before the actual race, so as to be able to recognize features on shore that will help pinpoint the boat's position. Fuel consumption at different engine revolutions and, if possible, in different sea states, should be known. Add to all the preparations a large slice of luck, and you will be in with a fighting chance. As has been mentioned, the motors are husbanded as much as possible, and it is probable that throttles will only be opened to their maximum if a rival boat is positively identified ahead, reasonably close to the finish.

Inshore, or circuit, racing is a much more direct confrontation between boats. Here it is innate skill, constant practice to achieve maximum speed through the bends, and optimum trim to suit the water conditions on the straights that pay dividends. Such road-racing techniques as slipstreaming—tucking yourself behind another competitor to get a "pull" along—are not often applicable. Courses are generally short, and turns so frequent that it would be impractical to sit directly behind an opponent. His wash, particularly on the bends, would cause more trouble than the small advantage gained in running in the quiet air behind him would be worth.

The real boat enthusiast will probably be rather disappointed if he looks at the starters in any of the offshore races for the biggest and most powerful classes today. He will find them dominated by boats from a handful of builders and, as far as hull form is concerned, all the boats will be much of a muchness. The craft will be long and narrow, with deep-V hulls, and will have been produced with half an eye to the commercial, non-racing market. It is a sad fact that it has become so expensive to enter this class of racing, with any chance of success, that the "one-off" specials, which used to add so much interest to the racing fleets and which allowed designers the chance to experiment and learn more about the best shapes for very high speeds offshore, are now very rarely built. Boat costs can be reduced if a series of vessels can be turned out in GRP from a single mould, with a few of the series going to racing men and the bulk being sold to people who simply want a boat with a good performance offshore.

Class I under the UIM rules is roughly Class V or VI under the American Power Boat Association gradings, but it is in Classes 2 and 3 (UIM), which roughly correspond to Classes II and III under the United States' system, that most development in new hull forms is taking place. Here, because engine sizes are smaller and costs consequently reduced, people can afford to experiment on hull shapes, and we see quite a number of catamarans, particularly in European waters, plus the occasional three-pointer (as used in hydroplane racing) and stepped hull.

Class 2 boats have a maximum engine capacity of 8,200 cc (50 cu in) for petrol engines and twice that capacity (16,400 cc or 1,000 cu in) if diesels are installed. Class II, under the American Power Boat Association rules, allows an engine capacity of between 4,920 and 6,560 cc (300–400 cu in), while Class III covers 6,560–9,840 cc (400–600 cu in). All rather confusing! The minimum length allowed under UIM regulations is 20 ft (6.1 m) but, normally, boats are rather longer than that. Because the engine-size rule means that outboards can be used without sacrificing too much capacity, they are often the power units. Four 2,000 cc (122 cu in) outboards—the biggest made at the moment—will produce over 600 horsepower and come within the capacity limit, though they will be using petrol at something like 60 gallons (72 US gallons or 273 1) per hour at full speed.

An outboard has precisely the same advantages and disadvantages as an outdrive unit though, since all racing engines are two-stroke, fuel consumption will be greater than on a four-stroke engine used in conjunction with an outdrive. This might be compensated for slightly by the outboard's comparatively low weight.

The smallest boats to race offshore under UIM regulations are those of Class 3, which are popular in Europe (particularly Britain) and in Australia but have no particular following in the United States. These small craft generally race on a shorter and, possibly, more sheltered circuit than the fleets from Classes 1 and 2. Class 3 is subdivided into different engine capacities, ranging from 3K, with engines from 490–900 cc (29.9–54.9 cu in), up to 3N, with engines from 2,000–4,000 cc (122–244 cu in), with the corresponding minimum hull lengths ranging from 14 ft (4.25 m) to 17 ft (5.18 m). Most Class 3 boats are outboard-powered, and many are production-line craft for both racing and pleasure, not specials or "one-offs".

As on the circuit races, catamarans, or twin-hulled craft under one name or another, have made their mark in Class 3 and, to a slightly less extent, in Class 2. In calm water conditions, the catamaran generally wins offshore, for it has several design advantages; but should the weather become bad, the twin-hull craft often have to slow down more than their monohull rivals. The trouble is that there are very great strains placed on the connections between the deck spanning the two hulls and the hulls themselves and, further, should the waves get steep and the underside of that spanning deck start hitting the water, it is liable to crack and split, and eventually the boat itself may break up. Clearly, it would be possible to build a twin-hull boat strong enough to meet any of the likely strains of racing offshore, and this has been done, but the resulting vessel tended to be so heavy that it was uncompetitive except in very bad weather.

All offshore racing is plagued by this dilemma. Should the boats be produced to take bad weather in their stride, with the design features this involves and the probable additional weight of structure; should they be light-weather fliers; or should they be all-round compromise types?

The last-named would not be expected to shine particularly in any extreme water conditions but should always be in the running and ready to take over if the specialized craft came to grief. And that is what happens. The middle-of-the-roaders usually have the best all-round results in a season.

The fact is that, in any race, there are more middle-of-the-roaders than radical types, for if the boat is one of a series intended for pleasure boating as well as for racing, the design must be moderate and not intended purely for use in one particular kind of weather.

It is unhappily true that hull design has made little progress over the past few years, and that speed increases have come about through improvements made by engine manufacturers in squeezing a few extra horsepower, and a little more reliability, from a given capacity of motor.

In the United States, offshore racing is more popular than inshore racing. Though the UIM counts three American races in its world championship programme, this is not a series that arouses much enthusiasm among local drivers, who prefer to concentrate on the American Championships. This has ten heats, very occasionally eleven, which are held on both coasts, as far south as Florida and California and as far north as the Great Lakes and the seaboard near Atlantic City. The principal race is probably the one staged by the New York Offshore Powerboat Racing Association, but all rate equal championship points, which are awarded on the UIM 400-point-reducing-25-per-cent system. To add to the fun, there are a couple of famous events staged by the Bahamian Power Boat Association, the Miami-Nassau and the Bahamas 500. Travelling the vast distances between venues is an expensive business but, despite this, offshore racing is flourishing in America.

This is not really the case in Europe, where Class 3 continues to make ground. In the bigger classes, however, few new boats appear. There are, nevertheless, a series of events staged for Classes 1 and 2 in Europe with, usually, two French races, one in the Mediterranean and one at Deauville; two Italian, one at Naples and the other the famous Viareggio-Bastia; and two British, the Needles Trophy at Poole and the Cowes-Torquay-Cowes, the best-known of all the European events. There are many other less publicized but still well-attended events, par-

ticularly for the smaller classes. For instance, thirteen or fourteen races are staged for Class 3 in Britain, counting towards the national championship and often taking place at the same time as those for the big Class 1 and 2 boats. At the lower end of the engine capacity scale, Class 3 racing is not expensive and competition is not too fierce. Generally, the most popular division is the one permitting engines between 1,312 and 2,050 cc (80 and 125 cu in), but a newcomer could well start one section down using an engine of 902–1,312 cc (55–80 cu in).

Australia holds some ten offshore events per year, and racing is in conformity with the UIM regulations. As in Europe, Class 3 boats predominate, but there is some keen Class 1 racing, particularly among imported American boats. The principal event is called the Cowes-Torquay (held in Melbourne), while the most popular is probably the Sydney-Newcastle and return.

In New Zealand, everything is complicated by the fact that there is no controlling body for offshore racing, and that different organizations in the north and south islands may have different criteria for classing and handicapping boats. Boats as small as 12 ft (3.6 m) compete offshore and, generally, anyone with a soundly-built and properly-equipped hull should be able to find a suitable class to compete in.

Powerboat racing is an exciting sport to watch and to partake in. At times, it can be dangerous for the participator. In offshore racing in the big classes, people have broken ankles as their boats slammed into waves. (Standing up in the cockpit is the general rule, as no more efficient shock-absorbers than a pair of knees have yet been invented.) Many people have retired from the racing scene with bad backs, and a few have been killed when their boats have capsized or been rolled over by competitors. For the man or woman who combines a knowledge of engines with a liking for the sea, powerboat racing offers an opportunity to take part in a growing sport at quite a modest expenditure. There are racing clubs in all parts of the world, and any yachting magazine would be able to put a reader in touch with the national authority, which would then be able to suggest a suitable club. Club members will be helpful, and a visit to watch a few races might then inspire a more active participation.

A A modern racing-boat configuration, designed for home construction. The 28-ft (8.5 m) step-drive was designed by Renato Levi and is powered by a Perkins T6 354 marine diesel engine. (**1**) Profile view. (**2**) Deck plan.

B A big offshore racing-boat with about 1,200 horsepower installed in twin engines. It is capable of, perhaps, 80 knots in calm water. The same hull, fitted with smaller engines, is used for a range of production boats. The class is designed by Don Aronow, Florida, who is also a most successful racing-boat driver. (**1**) Profile view. (**2**) Deck plan.

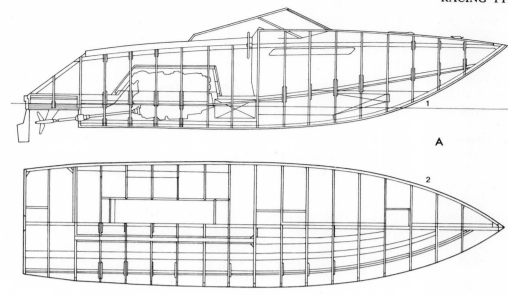

C SURFURY, also designed by Renato Levi, is one of the best known of the big racing craft. It won its first major offshore race in 1967 and would probably still be winning if it could be re-engined to take advantage of the developments in marine engineering and propeller design that have taken place since then. Loa: 36 ft (11.0 m). SURFURY is powered by two Daytona 1,050 horsepower engines fitted in a tandem arrangement. (**1**) Lines plan.

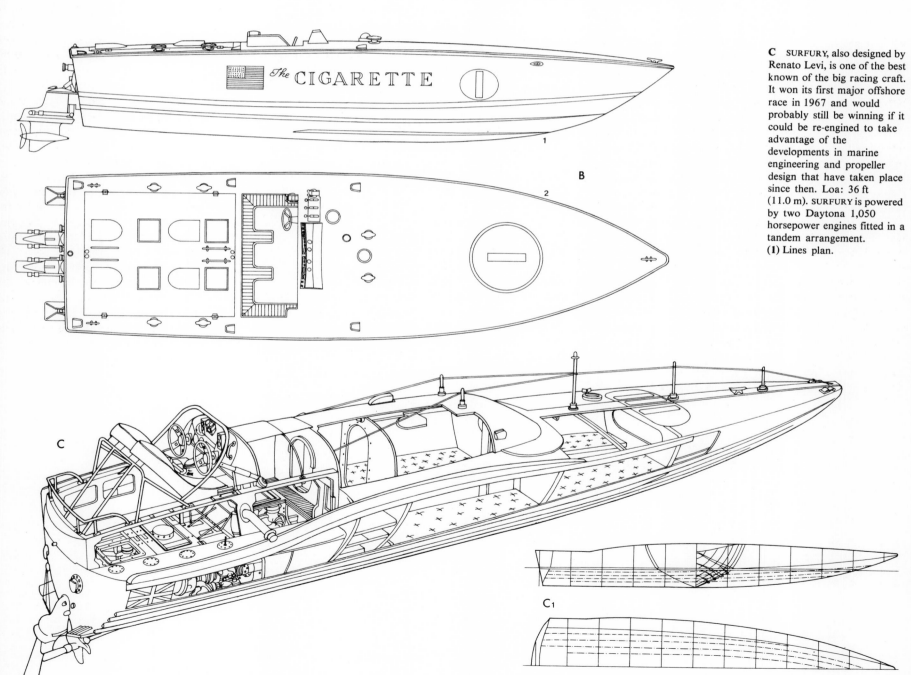

A

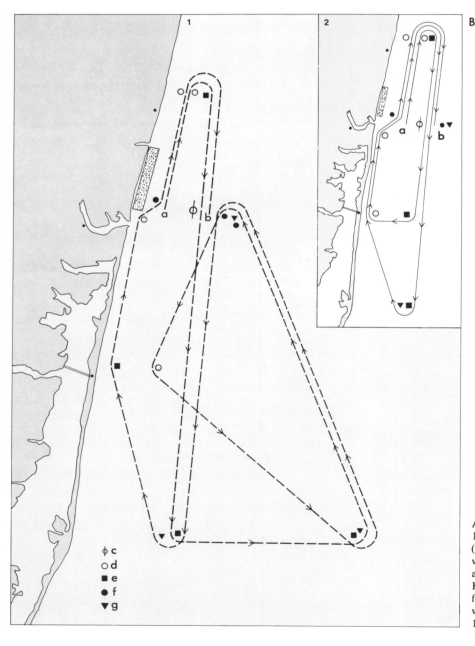

c
d
e
f
g

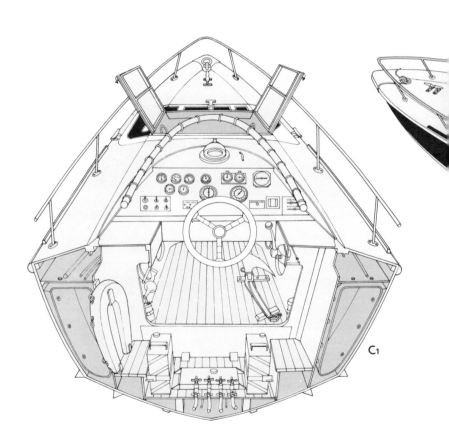

C₁

A UNO-EMBASSY 717, a Class 1 offshore racer, 40 ft (12.2 m) long. Built of GRP, it was designed by Don Shead and is equipped with two Kiekhaefer USA 625 Plus V8 fuel-injected petrol engines, which have a total output of 1,200 horsepower.

B Courses for powerboat racing differ greatly. Usually, they are dictated by the geography of the area in which they are held. We show here the courses over which the Benihama Grand Prix is held, at Point Pleasant, New Jersey. The open-class course (1) is 200 miles long, while the production-class course (2) is 119 miles. (*a*) Start. (*b*) Finish. (*c*) Course centre marker buoy. (*d*) Check-point boat. (*e*) Committee boat. (*f*) Sea buoy. (*g*) Race buoy.

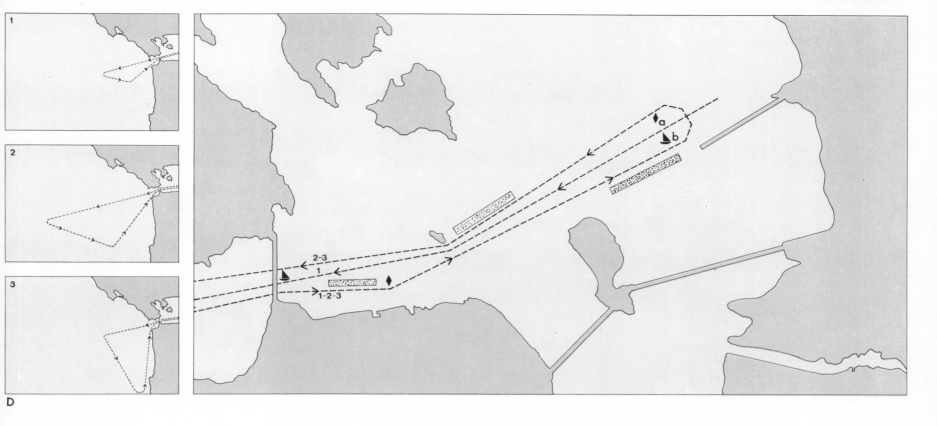

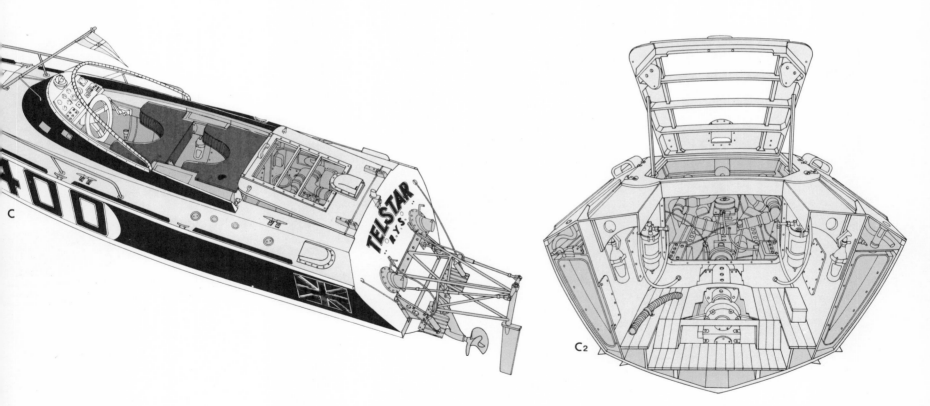

C An unusual craft, which won the Cowes—Torquay—Cowes race in 1968 against much bigger and more powerful boats, is the 25-ft (7.6 m) TELSTAR. Built of wood, it was designed by Don Shead for the famous British racing driver, Tommy Sopwith. The idea of extending the propeller shaft and fixing the rudder well behind the transom was to try to ensure that they stayed in the water for as long as possible, even when the vessel was leaping about in rough water. (**1**) Section of front half, drawn from the driver's position. (**2**) Aft section, with the engine hatch up, drawn from the co-driver's position.

D The course of the San Francisco Power Boat Race is specially laid out so that spectators will be able to get a good view of the race during the boat's several passes close to the shore. Each of the laps (**1–3**) goes under the Golden Gate Bridge. (*a*) Start. (*b*) Finish.

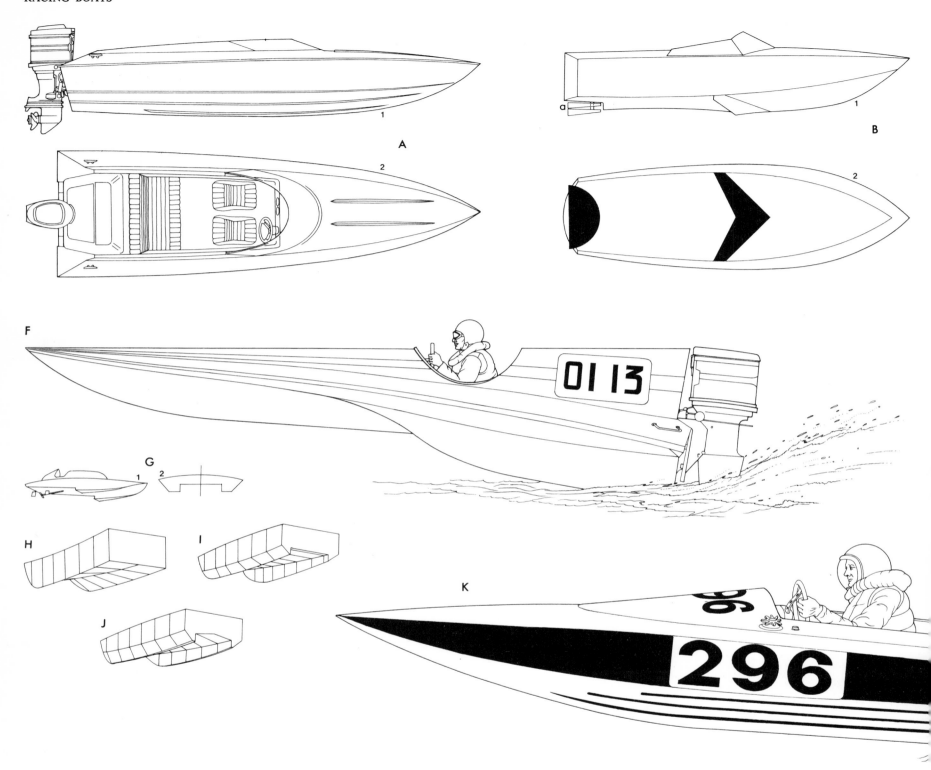

A This is a typical Class 3 offshore racer. It is capable of over 60 knots with its 140 horsepower outboard engine. (**1**) Profile view. (**2**) Deck plan.

B A modern form of the stepped hull, developed in the United States and called the *Dynoplane,* has a planing surface which can be pushed down into the water at the stern. When this is done at planing speeds, the boat will run on the forward step and the aft planing surface, leaving the length of the bottom between the two running dry. This reduces wetted surface and thus the power requirements for a given speed. All stepped boats work basically on this principle. (**1**) Profile view shows the aft planing surface (*a*) in its up and down positions. (**2**) Plan view of the hull shows the wetted surfaces (shaded) at speed.

C Though circuit racers are increasingly of the twin-hull form, in the early days they were of a more conventional shape. This boat, the *Levi 16,* was one of the most successful of them. Indeed, in certain restricted classes it is still competitive, and with its rugged, timber construction, it is a dependable vessel.

D Just a matter of definition differentiates between these two catamarans. **1** would probably be called a tunnel-hull, while **2** would be called a "picklefork", though the only difference is the length of deck over the two hulls.

E Virtually every racing boat is fitted with spray rails. These contribute to the strength of the hull and, presenting a flat surface to the water (unlike the hull, which usually has a steep-V shape), add a certain amount of lift. However, their main function is to reduce the effective beam of the boat at speed, thereby lessening the area of the bottom in contact with the water. As a boat speeds up, it rises in the water, and the spray rails deflect

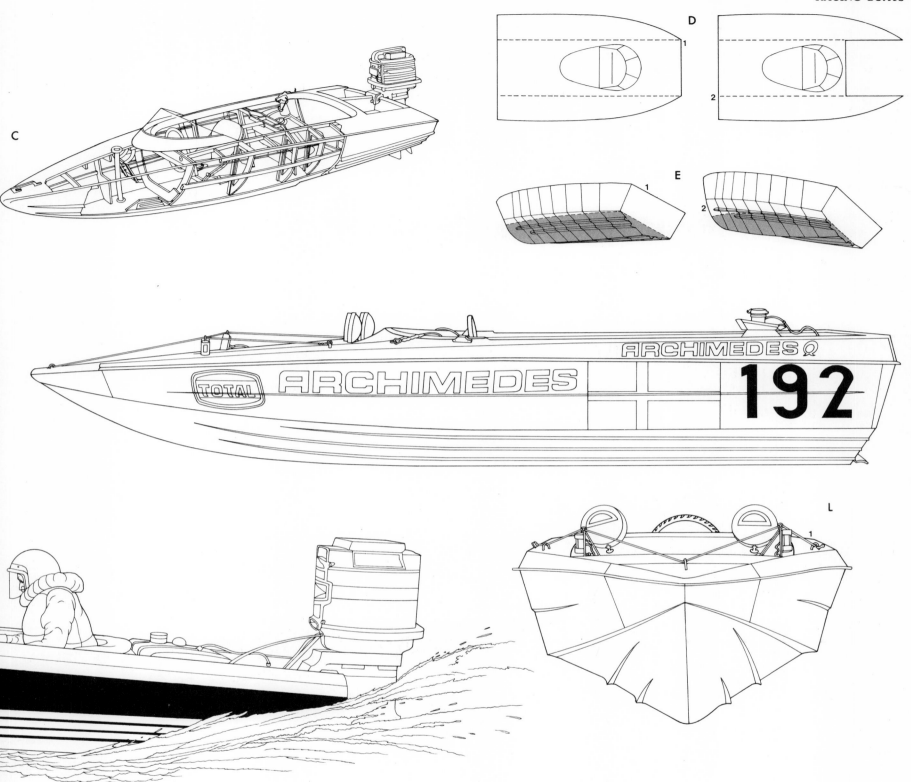

C

D

E

L

water away from the bottom above them. (1) Wetted surface at rest. (2) Wetted surface at speed (defined by the upper spray rail).

F Class *OI* Molinari catamaran for circuit racing. This one is powered by a MerCruiser 1000.

G One type of stepped catamaran hull is the three-pointer, generally used in hydroplane racing. At speed, the boat runs on the widely spaced sponsons forward and on the propeller aft. The rest of the bottom runs dry.

H An early racing form was the inverted-V bottom, or sea

sled, developed in the United States by Albert Hickman. As the boat speeds forward, air is driven down between the hulls, tending to lift them and thus make for less boat in the water.

I A modern tunnel-hull uses a modified sea-sled shape. Air driving down

between the hulls can escape at the stern but still produces lift. Circuit-racing catamarans commonly run, when at full throttle, with the hulls just touching the water.

J Another modification of the tunnel-hull is to have a V-shaped tunnel, a return to the sea-sled principle, though

the air can escape past the stern, not being trapped between the hulls, as was the case with the original sea sleds.

K The French *Cormorant ON* outboard racing class is very popular throughout Europe.

L A sports boat of the *SD* class, powered by an outboard engine of maximum 700 cc (42.7 cu in).

265

POWERBOAT RACING

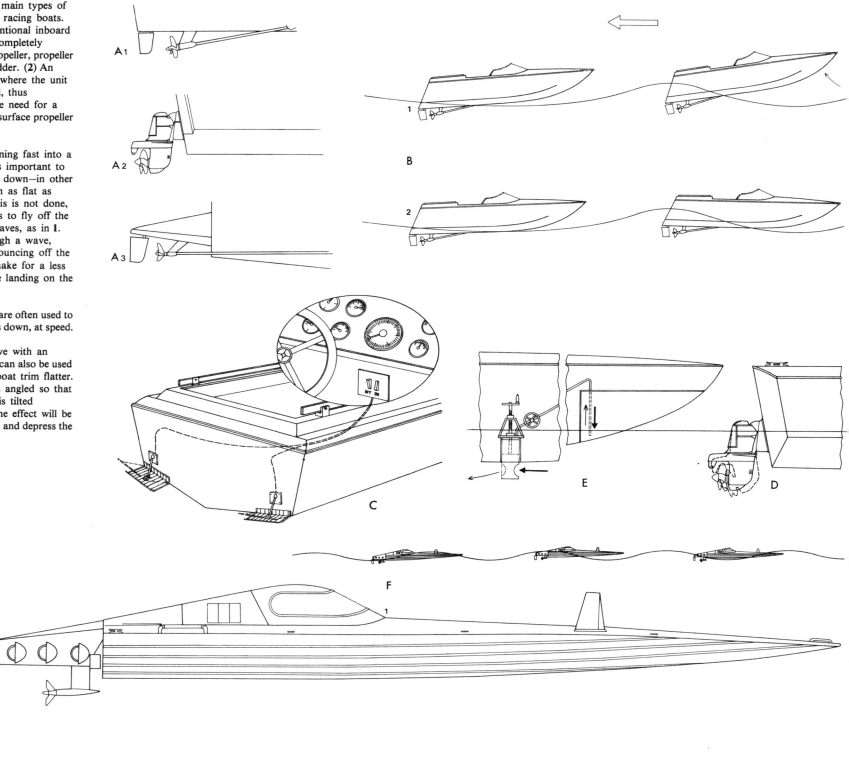

A The three main types of final drive on racing boats. (1) The conventional inboard engine with completely submerged propeller, propeller shaft, and rudder. (2) An outdrive unit where the unit can be turned, thus eliminating the need for a rudder. (3) A surface propeller arrangement.

B When running fast into a head sea, it is important to keep the bow down—in other words, to trim as flat as possible. If this is not done, the boat tends to fly off the tops of the waves, as in **1**. Driving through a wave, rather than bouncing off the top (**2**) will make for a less uncomfortable landing on the far side.

C Trim tabs are often used to force the bows down, at speed.

D An outdrive with an adjustable tilt can also be used to make the boat trim flatter. If the drive is angled so that the propeller is tilted downwards, the effect will be to lift the stern and depress the bow.

E A third method of achieving flat trim is to fit a bow ballast tank which can be flooded with water, when desired. The water can be pumped out, when running down wind.

F Renato Levi, the famous designer, proposes that racing boats could be designed to drive right through waves to give a more comfortable ride at high speeds in rough water. This could be achieved by designing a craft, as in **1**, with a narrow hull forward, which would have little buoyancy and lift.

G In some parts of the world inflatable racing is a popular sport, and high speeds are often achieved.

GLOSSARY

The order of the languages in this illustrated glossary is English, French, and German. Each language is separated by a semi-colon. Alternatives within each language are separated by a comma.

Abandon (to); *abandonner; aufgeben.* A race is abandoned when the race committee declares it void at any time after the starting signal.

Aft; *à l'arrière; achter, hinter.*

Afterpeak; *coqueron arrière; Achterpiek, Hinterpiek.* The space between the stern and the aftermost watertight bulkhead.

Ahead; *en avant; voraus.* See figure 1.

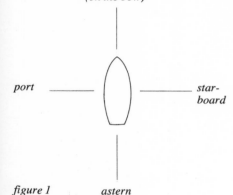

figure 1

Amidships; *au milieu du navire; mittschiffs.*

Anchor; *ancre; Anker.* See page 138, illustration C, and page 198, illustrations C, D, and E.

Anchor (to); *mouiller (l'ancre); ankern.*

Anchor Buoy; *bouée d'ancre; Ankerboje.*

Anchor Light; *feu de mouillage; Ankerlicht.* The white light which all vessels at anchor at night are obliged to hoist. Also, riding light.

Answering pendant; *l'aperçu; Antwortwimpel (des Internationalen Signalbuches), Gegensignal.*

Anti-fouling paint; *peinture antivégétable; Unterwassergiftfarbe.*

Apparent Wind; *vent apparent; scheinbarer Wind.* The wind felt aboard a boat under way. It is dependent upon the speed and relative direction of the boat and the speed of the actual wind. See page 110, illustration D.

Astern; *de l'arrière; achteraus.* See figure 1.

Auxiliary (engine); *auxiliaire; Hilfsmotor.*

Back (to); *contrebrasser; backsetzen.* To force a sail out against the wind so that it fills on the "wrong" side, thus making the bow of the boat bear away from the wind or sail backwards.

Back (to); *adonner; zurückdrehen, krimpen.* The wind is said to back when it shifts in an anti-clockwise direction.

Backstay; *galhauban; Backstag, Pardun (e).* See figure 41.

Bail (to); *écoper; ausösen, ausschöpfen.*

Ballast; *lest; Ballast.* A weight, usually consisting of iron, lead, sand, or water, placed in the bilges to improve the boat's stability and/or to increase the boat's draught so that the propeller and rudder can work properly.

Batten; *latte; Latte, Segellatte.* A wooden or plastic slat, inserted in a batten pocket in the leech of a sail to keep it from curving too much. See figure 2.

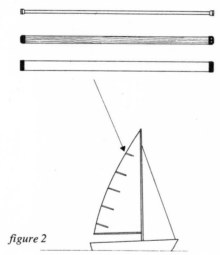

figure 2

Batten pocket; *étui de latte, gaine de latte; Lattentasche.*

Beacon; *balise; Bake.*

Beam (width); *bau; Bootsbreite.* See page 231, illustration A.

Beam; *barrot; Balken.*

Beam reaching; *courir vent de travers; mit raum-seitlichem Wind segeln.* See page 125, illustration 3.

Bear away (to); *laisser arriver, abattre; abfallen, abhalten.* To turn a sailing-boat further off the wind.

Bearing; *relèvement; Peilung, Richtung.* The point of the compass at which an object is seen. A bearing expressed in relation to the yacht's head is a relative bearing. See page 163, illustrations H and I.

Bearing compass; *compas de relèvement; Peilkompass.* A compass with a pelorus (q.v.). The bearing compass is used to define the angle between the line to an object and the meridian through that place.

Beat (to); *louvoyer; kreuzen, aufkreuzen.* To sail to windward by alternate tacks. See page 125, illustration 5.

Becket; *chambrière; Schlinge, (Block-) Auge.* A metal eye, fitted to a block, to take the end of a rope in a tackle.

Before the wind (to sail); *(courir) vent arrière; vor dem Wind (segeln).*

Belly (of a sail); *fond, sein (d'une voile); Bauch (eines Segels).* The area of a sail that bulges out when filled with wind.

Belay (to); *amarrer; belegen.* To make a rope fast by turns round a bollard or suchlike.

Bend (to); *enverguer; anschlagen.* To fasten a sail to its spar or stay, ready for hoisting.

Bend (to); *enverguer; anschlagen.* To fasten by means of a bend, or knot.

Bilge; *bouchain; Bilge, Kielraum.* That part of the inside of the hull where bilge water collects. Also, that part of the outer hull between the keel and the chine.

Bilge pump; *pompe de cale; Lenzpumpe, Bilgepumpe.* See figure 3.

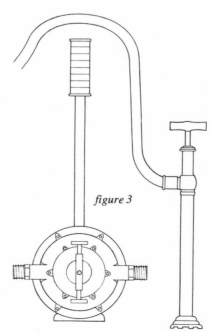

figure 3

Bilge-water; *eau de cale; Bilgewasser, Kielraumwasser.*

Bill of entry; *déclaration en douane; Zolleinführschein.*

Blanket (to); *masquer; déventer; (vom Wind) abdecken.* To sail so that your sails take the wind away from another boat's sails. See page 223, illustration 1.

Block; *poulie; Block (für Tauwerk).*

Board (to); *aborder; ein Boot entern.*

Boat-hook; *gaffe d'embarcation; Bootshaken.* See figure 4.

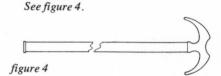

figure 4

Bolt-rope; *ralingue; Liektau, Segelliek.* A rope, sewn to the edges of sails to increase their strength and to allow the sail's foot or luff to be threaded into the groove in the boom or mast. Also, luff rope. See figure 5.

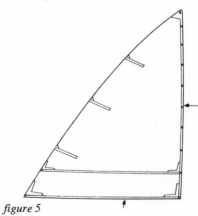

figure 5

Boom; *bôme; Baum, Spiere.* A wooden or metal spar, used to extend the foot of a sail, e.g., main boom, jib boom, jib stick, etc. See figure 41.

Boom out (to); *voile en ciseau; ausbaumen.* To fasten a spar in the clew of a foresail and at the mast, so that the foresail can be fully exploited when running.

Boom vang. See **Kicking-strap.**

Bo'sun's chair; *chaise de gabier; Bootsmannsstuhl.* A harness or short piece of wood, fastened to a bridle, in which a man can be hoisted aloft to carry out repairs or adjustments to the mast rigging.

Bottle-screw; *ridoir; Wantenspanner*. A specially constructed screw fitting for adjusting the tension of shrouds or stays. Also, turnbuckle, rigging screw. See page 58, illustration 10.

Bow; *proue, avant; Bug*. The bow stretches from the stem (q.v.) aft about the length of the vessel's beam.

Bow (on the); *en avant; voraus, über den Bug*.
See figure 1.

Bowline hitch; *nœud de chaise; Palstek*. See page 144, illustration M.

Braided rope; *corde tressée; geflochtenes Tauwerk*.

Breaker; *coup de mer, paquet de mer; Brecher, Sturzsee*. A wave, breaking into foam on a shore or reef.

Bridle; *patte d'oie, pied d'araignée; Hahnepot, Zügel*. A length of rope or wire, fastened at both ends to a boat's hull or to an object to be lifted. The lifting or hauling power is applied to the middle of the bridle.

Breeze; *brise; Brise*.

Broad reach; *largue; mit raumachterlichem Wind segeln*. See page 125, illustration 2.

Broken water; *clapotis; gebrochenes Wasser*. Short, high waves, occurring in what is otherwise a calm sea.

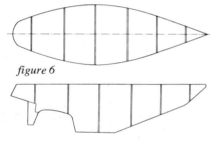

figure 6

Bulkhead; *cloison; Schott, Spundwand*. Partition placed vertically in a boat, athwartships or parallel to or along the centre-line, to separate different sections of the boat and to strengthen the structure. *See figure 6.*

Bunk; *couchette; (feste) Koje*. Sleeping-berth on a boat.

Buoy; *bouée, amarque; Boje, Tonne*. An anchored, floating object, of iron, wood, or plastic, intended to mark navigation channels, sunken dangers, racing marks, or to mark the position of an anchor or mooring line after release.

Buoyage; *balisage; Betonnung*. A system of buoys and perches, marking shallows in the open sea or in a fairway.

Buoyancy; *flottabilité; Auftrieb (skraft)*. The resultant of the upwards-working forces exerted on a floating body by the water in which it floats.

Burgee; *guidon; Stander, Clubstander*. A triangular, sometimes swallow-tailed, flag used to denote rank, and as a club distinguishing mark.

Cabin; *cabine, chambre; Kajüte, Kammer*.

Cable; *câble; Stahldrahttrosse, Ankertrosse*. A chain or heavy rope. Almost synonymous with chain and mainly used in connection with anchoring and mooring.

Calm; *calme, bonace; Windstille, Flaute*. When there is no wind and the surface of the water is smooth.

Calm (adj.); *calme; windstill, flau*.

Cancel (to); *annuler, résilier; annullieren, für ungültig erklären*. A race committee cancels a race when it rules that the race will not be sailed thereafter.

Cancel a signal; *annuler un signal; ein Signal annullieren oder wiederrufen*.

Canvas; *toile (à voiles); Segeltuch*.

Capsize (to); *chavirer; kentern*.

Carvel; *bordé à franc-bord, bordé lisse; Karweel, Kraweel*. A method of boat-building in wood. The edges of the planking lie flush with each other.
See figure 7.

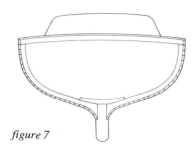

figure 7

Catamaran; *catamaran; Doppelrumpfboot*.

Centre of gravity (CG); centre de gravité; Schwerpunkt, Gewichtsschwerpunkt.

Centre-board; *dérive centrale; Senkschwert, Mittelschwert*. A wooden board or metal plate housed in a case, or trunk, in the middle of the boat along the centre-line. It can be raised and lowered. Its purpose is to prevent excessive leeway. See page 112, illustration C.

Chain plate; *cadène, chaîne; Pütting, Rüsteisen*. A metal plate, bolted to a boat's hull, in which the lower ends of a shroud or backstay can be fastened.
See figure 8.

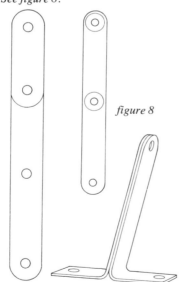

figure 8

Chart; *carte marine; Seekarte*.

Chine; *lisse d'angle; Kimmknick, Kimmleiste*. The joining line between the bilge and the topsides of a hull.

Clam cleat. See **Jam cleat**.

Cleat; *taquet; Klampe*. A fitting used in belaying lines.
See figure 9 and figure 41.

Clew; *point d'écoute; Schothorn*. The corner of the sail where the leech and the foot meet.
See figure 40.

Clinker; *à clins; Klinker*. A method of boat-building. The planks overlap at the edges.
See figure 10.

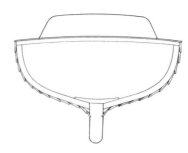

figure 10

Close-hauled; *au plus près, sous l'allure du plus près; dicht, hoch am Wind*. See page 125, illustration 5.

Cloth; *laize; Segeltuch, Tuch*. A term used to denote the material from which a sail is sewn.

Clove hitch; *deux demi-clefs renversées; Webeleinenstek*. See page 144, illustration F.

Coach roof; *rouf; Kajütaufbau, Kajütdach*. The part of the cabin built above the deck to increase head room in the cabin.

Coaming; *hiloire, surbau; Süll, Setzbord*. Strengthening side pieces around openings in the deck, e.g., hatches, cockpit, etc., to prevent water from pouring in.

Cockpit; *cockpit; Plicht*. A sunken space in the afterdeck of a sailing-boat. Originally intended for the helmsman, but now usually large enough to seat helmsman and crew.

Code flag; *flamme du code; Signalbuchwimpel, Signalbuchflagge*. One of the signal flags of the international code of signals. There are twenty-six letter-flags, ten numeral pennants, and one code-and-answering pennant. Also used in a racing context, where it has special meanings according to the IYRU racing rules.

Companionway; *couloir; Niedergang*.

Compass; *compas, boussole; Kompass*.

Compass error; *erreur du compas; Kompass-Fehlweisung*. The angle between the direction indicated by the compass needle and that of the magnetic meridian. Compass error is caused by deviation and variation.

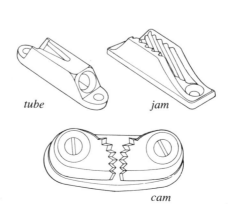

tube   *jam*

cam

figure 9

Clinker ... (covered above)

Corrected time; *temps corrigé; berechnete Zeit*. The actual time taken by a boat to complete a race, adjusted according to the handicapping system employed. It is the corrected time which counts in the final placings.

Course; *route; Kurs, Weg*. A course is laid out and limited by those marks which a participant in a race must round or pass on the prescribed side from the start to the finish.

Course signal; *signal de parcours; Kurssignal*. Signal displayed by the racing committee to indicate which course is to be sailed, i.e., which marks must be rounded or passed.

Cover (to); See **Blanket (to)**.

Covering board; *plat-bord; Schandeck (el)*. The most outer part of the deck. On a wooden boat, the outer plank.

Cradle; *ber, berceau; Slippwagen, Verladebock*. A framework, used to support a hull when it is laid up.

Crank; *jaloux, instable, volage; rank*.

Crew; *équipage; Besatzung, Vorschotmann*.

Cringle; *patte, anneau; Legel*. A grommet (q.v.) or eye of rope in the edge, clew, or tack of a sail, with a metal or nylon ring inside it.

Cross-tree; *barre de flèche; Saling*. A spreader fitted athwartships to the mast to increase the angle between the mast and the masthead shrouds, where they join. *See figure 34.*

Cruiser; *yacht de croisière; Kreuzer, gedecktes Boot mit Wohnraum*.

Current; *courant; Strom, Strömung*.

Dead reckoning; *navigation à l'estime; Koppelung, Besteckrechnung*. A method of estimating position by applying to the previously determined position the recorded log run and the courses run.

Deck; *pont; Deck, Abdeckung*.

Designer; *dessinateur, constructeur; Konstrukteur, Entwerfer*.

figure 11

Dinghy; *dériveur; Schwertboot, Beiboot*. A small, centre-board sailing-boat. Also, a small boat used as a tender (q.v.) for a larger vessel.
See figure 11.

Disqualification; *disqualification; Disqualifikation, Ausschluss*.

Displacement; *déplacement; Wasserverdrängung*. The weight of water displaced by a vessel afloat. It is always equal to the weight of the boat and its contents, and is expressed in tons of 2,240 lb (1,016 kg).

Distress signal; *signal de détresse; Seenotzeichen (SOS), Notsignal*.

Dividers; *pointes sèches; Kartenzirkel, Stechzirkel*.

Double sheet bend; *nœud d'écoute double; doppelter Schotstek.* See page 144, illustration G.

Down-haul; *hale-bas; Niederholer.* A line used to keep the spinnaker boom in the desired position. Also, a line used for hauling down a sail or flag.

Drag; *grappin; Draggen.* A small anchor.

drag (to); *draguer le fond; schleppen, nachschleifen.* To draw the anchor along the bottom.

Draught; *tirant d'eau; Tiefgang.* The maximum depth of water which a boat requires in order to float freely.

Drawstring. See **Leech line.**

Drift; *dérive; Stromversetzung, Abtrift.* See page 112, illustration B. Also, leeway.

Drogue; *ancre flottante ou de cape; Seeanker, Treibanker.* A sea anchor; a canvas cone or funnel-shaped bag, which is trailed from the stern in heavy weather to keep the bow of the boat heading into the waves. See page 198, illustration E.

Echo sounder; *échosondeur, sondeur ultrasonore; Echolot, Schall-Lot.* See page 59, illustration H.

Elapsed time; *temps écoulé; (tatsächlich) gesegelte Zeit.* The time which passes from the moment a boat crosses the starting line to the moment it crosses the finishing line.

End; *but, terme, fin; Ende, Tauende.*

Exhaust pipe; *tuyau d'échappement; Auspuffrohr, Abgasrohr.*

Eye; *œil, œillet; Auge, Öse, Öhr.* A loop, formed in the end or any part of a rope, which goes over a spar or suchlike. An eye can be spliced, seized, or made by knotting. Also, a metal loop or ring.

Eye of the wind; *lit du vent; Auge des Windes.* That point from which the wind is blowing towards the observer.

Eye-bolt; *piton, cheville à œillet; Augbolzen.* A bolt with an eye in its upper end.
See figure 12.

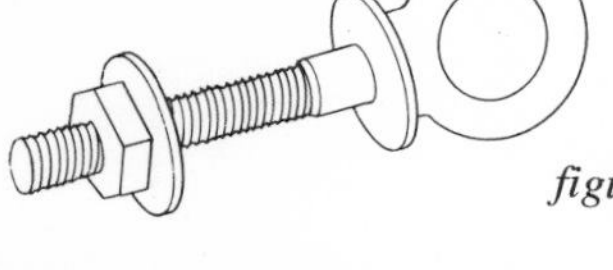

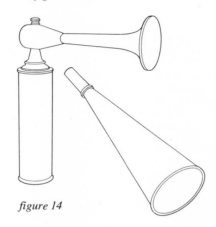

figure 12

Eyelet hole; *œillet, œils-de-pie; Gättchen, Gatt, Segelöse.*

Eye-splice; *épissure à œil; Augspleiss.* See page 144, illustration P.

Fairlead; *conduit, rateau; Leitöse, Leitklampe.* A fitting, usually of metal, which is so shaped that a rope can run through it. Fairleads are often open, so that the rope can be placed in them without having to be "threaded" through them. They are used especially for mooring ropes and suchlike.
See figure 41.

Fall away. See **Bear away.**

Fathom; *brasse; Faden.*

Fender; *défense; Fender, Scheuerleiste.* A device, usually of plastic, which is used to protect the sides of the boat from hitting or chafing against a dock, mooring pole, or suchlike.
See figure 13.

Fibre-glass-reinforced plastic (FRP). See **Glass-fibre reinforced plastic.**

Figure-of-eight knot; *nœud en forme de huit; Achtknoten.* See page 144, illustration C.

Fin keel; *fin keel, bulb; Flossenkiel.*

Finish (to); *couper la ligne d'arrivée; durch das Ziel gehen.* A boat finishes when any part of its hull, or crew or equipment in normal position, crosses the finishing line from the direction of the last mark.

Fit out (to); *armer; instandsetzen.*

Fitting; *accastillage; Beschlag.*

Flagstaff; *gaule d'enseigne; Flaggenstock.*

Floor; *varangue; Bodenwrange.* Athwartships structural member in a boat.

Floor boards; *plancher; Bodenbretter.* In pleasure boats, the floor boards are often raised wooden slats in the cockpit sole.

Fog-horn; *trompette de brume; Nebelhorn, Nebelsignalhorn.*
See figure 14.

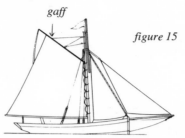

figure 14

Foot; *fond, bordure; Fuss (liek), Underliek.* The lower edge of a sail. It is the foot of a mainsail which is fastened to the boom.
See figure 40.

Fore; *avant; vorder.*

Fore deck; *pont avant; Vorderdeck, Vordeck, Backdeck.*

Fore halyard; *drisse de misaine; Vorsegelfall.*

Forepeak; *coqueron avant; Vorpiek.* Originally, the forepeak was the space between the collision bulkhead and the stem. Nowadays, the term is used to describe the stowage space or the forward cabin in a pleasure boat.

Foresail; *misaine, voile de trinquet; Vorsegel, Fock (segel).*

Foresail sheet; *écoute de misaine; Vorsegelschot, Vorschot.*

Forestay; *étai de mât misaine; Vorstag.* See figure 41.

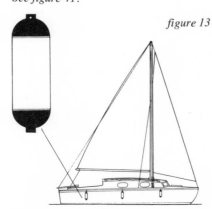

figure 13

Frame; *membrure, couple; Spant, Querspant.*

Free wind; *vent largue; raumer Wind.*

Freeboard; *franc-bord; Freibord.* The vertical distance from the surface of the water to the dividing line between the freeboard deck and the side of the boat, measured amidships.

Full and by; *près plein; voll und bei.*

Furl a sail (to); *ferler une voile, serrer une voile; ein Segel beschlagen.* To roll a sail up or to fold it on a yard or boom, and to secure it.

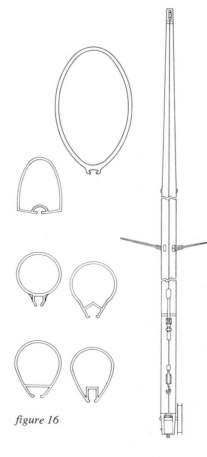

gaff

figure 15

Gaff; *corne; Gaffel.*
See figure 15.

Galley; *cuisine; Kombüse.*

Genoa jib; *foc de près, foc de Genes; Genua, Genua-Fock.* A large foresail which overlaps the mainsail.
See figure 40.

Glass-fibre reinforced plastic (GRP); *résin stratifié, plastique; glasfaserverstärkter Kunststoff (GFK).* Also, fibre-glass-reinforced plastic (FRP).

Grapnel see **Drag.**

Grommet; *bague, erseau; Tauring, Taustropp.* A brass eye in a sail. It is fitted to take the wear of a line. Also, grummet.

Groove; *gorge, rainure; Hohlkehle, Keep.* A channel which runs along the aft side of a mast to take the sail's bolt-rope.
See figure 16.

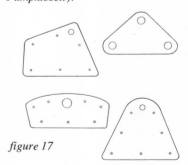

figure 16

Ground Tackle; *ancres et cables-chaînes, appareil de mouillage; Ankergeschirr, Grundgeschirr.*

Guard-rail; *tringle de garde-corps; Geländerstange, Handlauf.* Also, lifeline.

Gunwale; *gunwale; Schandeck, Dollbord.* The bulwark along the upper side of a boat, or the side of a boat which has no bulwark. Also, rail.
See figure 41.

Gust of wind; *coup de vent, rafale; Bö, Stosswind, Windstoss.*

Guy; *retenue, bras; Gei, Backstag.* The control line which runs aft from the outboard end (the tack) of a spinnaker pole. It is used to trim the fore-and-aft position of the pole. Also, a line which is used to support booms, gaffles, davits, etc.

Gybe (to); *coiffer; halsen.* Also, jibe. See pages 134–135.

Hail (to); *héler; anrufen, anpreien.*

Half-hitch; *demi-clef; halber Schlag.* If the end of a rope is passed round its standing part and then through the bight, a half-hitch is formed.

Halyard; *drisse; Fall, Heissleine.* The rope or wire used to raise or lower a sail.
See figure 41.

Handy billy; *pompe à balancier; kleine Deckspumpe.* A hand deck-pump. In Australia, a handy billy is a double-purchase tackle with a hook at the end of each of the blocks.

Harbour authorities; *autorité de port; Hafenbehörden.*

Harden up (to); *embraquer, haler, souquer; anholen.* To bring the boat closer to the wind by using the rudder and hauling in on the sheets.

Hatch; *panneau, écoutille; Luk (e).* An opening in a boat's deck which permits access to the below-deck area.

Hatch-cover; *panneau d'écoutille; Lukendeckel.* A cover or shutter for a hatch which, when closed in heavy weather, prevents the entry of water into the below-deck area. It can be made from wood, metal, or GRP.
See figure 41.

Head; *point de drisse; Kopf (ende).* The top corner of a triangular sail. Also, the lavatory (*toilette, W.C.; Toilette, Pumpklosett*).

figure 17

Headboard; *planche de tête; Kopfbrett, Kopfplatte.* A triangular or semi-circular plate of wood, plastic, or metal, which is sewn into the head of a sail. The halyard is attached to the headboard.
See figure 17.

Heading; *cap; Richtung, Kurs.* The direction in which a boat is actually pointing at any given time.

Head-sail; *voile de l'avant; Vorsegel.* Any sail which may be set forward of the foremast.

Head wind; *vent droit debout; Gegenwind.* The wind which blows from directly in front of the bow.

Heave to (to); *mettre à la cape, tenir la cape, capeyer; beidrehen.* To set the sails so that the boat lies almost still. The term "to heave to" is also often applied to the act of laying a vessel to.

Heaving line; *attrape, passeresse, lance-amarres; Wurfleine.* See page 203, illustrations F and G.

Heel; *bande, gîte; Krängung.* The lateral inclination of a boat due to the pressure of the wind or waves, or to a greater weight on one side.

Heel over (to); *incliner, donner de la bande; krängen.*

Helm; *gouvernail, barre; Ruder (pinne).* The steering apparatus of a boat, including the rudder, tiller or wheel, etc.

Helmsman; *timonier, homme de barre; Bootssteurer, Rudergänger.*

Hoist (to); *relever, hisser, enlever; aufholen, hissen.* See pages 126–127.

Horse; *barre d'écoute; Leitwagen.* An athwartships metal track upon which a sail's traveller (q.v.) slides. Also, hawse or track.
See figure 18.

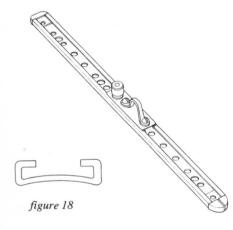

figure 18

Hounds; *épaulette; Backen.* Where the shrouds are fastened to the mast.
See figure 34.

Hove-to; *mis en panne, mis à la cape; beigedreht.* See **Heave to.**

Hull; *coque; Bootsrumpf, Körper.*

Inflatable boat; *canot pneumatique; aufblasbares Boot, Luftboot, Schlauchboot.*

International Regulations for the Prevention of Collisions at Sea; *Règlement pour prévenir les abordages en mer; Règles de route; Internationale Vereinbarung zur Verhütung von Zusammenstössen auf See, Seestrassenordnung.*

IO drive See **Stern Drive.**

Jam cleat; *taquet coinceur, coinceur d'écoute; Schotklemme, Klemmklampe.* A cleat so formed that the line, when pulled, is jammed fast in it. Also, clam cleat.

Jetty; *jetée, extacade, môle; Landungsbrücke, Pier, Kai.*

Jib; *foc; Fock.* A usually triangular foresail, which does not overlap the mainsail.
See figure 40.

Jib furling gear; *envergue de foc à rouleau; Rollfockbeschlag, Rollfockeinrichtung.* See page 59, illustration 10.

Jib stay; *draille de foc; Fockstag.*

Jibe. See **Gybe**

Jumper stay; *faux étai; Jumpstag.* The stays that run over spreaders which are angled forward to give fore-and-aft support to the mast.
See figure 34.

Keelson; *carlingue; Kielschwein, Binnenkiel.*

Ketch; *ketch; Ketsch.*

Kicking-strap; *hale-bas de bôme; Baumniederhalter, Sicherungsstropp.* Also, boom vang. See page 59, illustration 11.

Knot; *nœud; Knoten.* The speed of one nautical mile per hour.

Knot; *nœud; Stek.*

Lace (to); *lacer, transfiler, anreihen, schnüren.* To fasten a sail to a mast or stay by passing a line through eyelets in the sail and then round the mast or stay.
See figure 19.

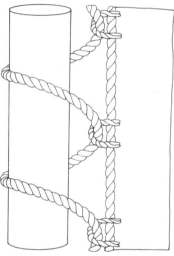

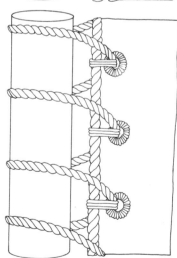

figure 19

Land-breeze; *brise de terre; Landbrise.* See page 187, illustration B.

Larboard. See **Port.**

Latitude; *latitude; geographische Breite.* See page 163, illustration B.

Launch (to); *lancer; zu Wasser bringen, vom Stapel lassen.*

Lay up (to); *désarmer; auflegen, abrüsten.*

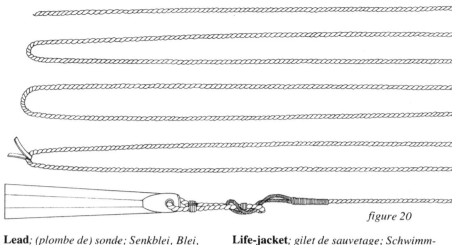

figure 20

Lead; *(plombe de) sonde; Senkblei, Blei, Lot.* A device used when measuring the depth of water by hand. The echo sounder has now superseded the lead.
See figure 20.

Leading marks; *amers de direction; Richtbake (n), Leitmarken.* The name given to two easily discernible objects on a chart which, if kept in line, will keep a boat in safe water. The line made by these marks is called a transit line or a range. See page 168, illustration B.

Leak; *voie d'eau, fuite, coulage; Leck, Undichtigkeit.*

Leech; *chute d'une voile; Liek, Segelliek, Leekante des Segels.* The after edge of a sail. Also, leach.
See figure 40.

Leech line; *cargue bouline; Regulierleine (im Segelliek).* A line attached to the leech of a sail to control leech tension. Also, drawstring.

Lee helm; *mou; leegierig.* A sailing-boat has lee helm when it has a tendency to bear off the wind, when the helm must be kept to leeward to maintain the boat on its course.

Lee shore; *terre sous le vent; Leeküste, Legerwall.* The shore upon which the wind is blowing.

Leeside; *coté sous le vent; Leeseite, Windschatten.* The side opposite to that from which the wind is blowing.

Leeward; *sous le vent; leevärts.*

Leeway; *dérive; Leeweg, Abtrift, Windversetzung.* See page 112, illustrations A and B. Also, drift.

Leg; *bordée; Schenkel, Bein, Schlag.* That part of a race course marked off by two successive markers.

Length over all (loa); *longueur hors tout; Länge über alles, äusserste Länge.*
See figure 21.

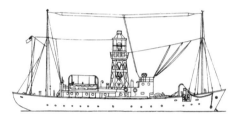

figure 22

Life-jacket; *gilet de sauvetage; Schwimmveste, Rettungsgürtel.*

Lifeline; *filière de salut; Manntau, Greifleine, Sicherheitsleine.* Also, guard-rail.

Life-raft; *radeau de sauvetage; Rettungsfloss, Rettungsinsel.*

Light; *feu; Licht, Lichtschein.*

Lighthouse; *phare; Leuchtturm.*

Lightship; *bateau-feu; Feuerschiff.*
See figure 22.

Line; *Ligne; Linie, Leine, Strich, Strahl.*

Log; *loch; Logge, Log, Klotz.* An instrument used to determine the speed of a boat. See page 26, illustration B, and page 56, illustrations E and F.

Log book; *journal de route; Logbuch.* See page 169, illustrations I and J.

Longitude; *longitude; geographische Länge.* See page 163, illustration C.

Loop; *boucle; Schlinge, Schlaufe, Öse.*

Lower a sail (to); *amener une voile, baisser une voile; ein Segel bergen.*

Lubber line; *ligne de foi; Steuerstrich, Kursstrich.* A mark on the forward inner side of the compass bowl, so placed that a line through it and the centre of the compass card will be parallel to the keel in a fore-and-aft direction.

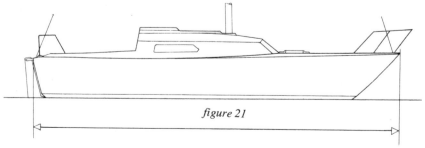

figure 21

Lifebuoy; *bouée; Rettungsring, Rettungsboje.*

Lifebelt; *ceinture de sauvetage; Rettungsgürtel.*

Luff; *guindant, envergure; Luv, Luvseite, Luvliek, Vorliek.* The leading edge of a sail.
See figure 40.

Luff (to); *loffer; luven.* (1) To bring the boat up nearer the wind. (2) In racing, to point high on an opponent to weather. As, in most cases, he must give right of way to you, he is forced to point higher.

Luff rope; *ralingue d'envergure; Luvliektau.* See **Bolt-rope**.

Main halyard; *drisse de grand voile; Grossfall.* See figure 41.

Mainmast; *grand mât; Grossmast.*

Mainsail; *grand-voile avant; Grossegel.* See figure 40.

Mainsheet; *écoute de grande voile; Grosschot.* See figure 41.

Maintenance; *préservation, entretien; Instandhaltung, Wartung, Unterhaltung.*

Make fast (to); *amarrer; festmachen, belegen.*

Make leeway (to); *dériver; Leeweg machen, Abtrift haben.* See page 112, illustration B.

Make sail (to). See **Hoist (to)**.

Mark in the course; *marque de parcours; Bahnmarke, Wendemarke.* A marker on a race course which indicates a point which competing boats must round or pass.

Marline-spike; *épissoir; Marlspieker.* An iron pin, pointed at one end, which is used by sailors to open knots, and to separate strands of a rope when splicing. Also, marlinspike.

Mast; *mât; Mast.*

Masthead; *ton de mât, tête de mât; Masttopp, Mastspitze.*

Masthead rig; *gréement de tête de mât; Hochtakelung, Bermudatakelung.* When the foresail goes up to the masthead. See page 35, illustration A.

Mast step; *carlingue de mât, emplanture; Mastspur.* The fitting on the keelson or deck upon which the mast is placed.

Mast track; *rail de mât; Mastgleitschiene, Mastschiene.* The track on the mast in which the traveller slides.

Measurement certificate; *certificat de jauge; Messbrief.*

Mizzen; *artimon; Besan, Besansegel.*

Mizzen staysail; *foc d'artimon; Besanstagsegel.*

Moor (to); *s'affourcher; genoper; festmachen, vertäuen, verankern.*

Mooring buoy; *bouée d'ammarrage; Festmachetonne, Vertäuboje.*

Multihull; *multicoque; Mehrrumpfboot.*

Nautical mile; *mille marin; Seemeile.* See page 163, illustration E.

Oar; *aviron; Bootsriemen.*

Oar blade; *pelle d'aviron, palette de rame; Riemenblatt.*

Oarlock; *dame de nage; Dolle, Riemengabel.* Also, rowlock.

Offshore; *au large; landentfernt, von der Küste weg, weit auf See.*

Offshore race; *course au large; Regatta auf See.*

Offshore yacht; *yacht de course au large; Seekreuzer, seefähige Yacht.*

One-design; *monotype; Einheits- (Boot, Klasse).*

Outboard engine; *moteur hors-bord; Aussenbordmotor.*

Outhaul; *hale-dehors, étarqueur; Ausholer.* A line used to draw out the clew of a mainsail so that the foot of the mainsail can, if required, be stretched tightly along the boom.

Overhang; *élancement; Überhang, Ausladung.* Those parts of the hull which extend beyond the water-line's foremost and aftermost points. See figure 23.

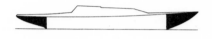

figure 23

Overlap; *engagement; Überlappung, Überdeckung.* See pages 212–213.

Overtake; *rattraper; aufkommen, überholen.*

Parallel ruler; *règles parallèles; Parallellineal.* An instrument used for laying down and transferring courses on a nautical chart. It consists of two rulers, hinged together by cross-pieces of equal length, so that the rulers are always parallel.

Patent log; *loch enregistreur, sillomètre; Patentlog, Schlepplog.* See **Log**.

Pelorus; *taximètre; Peilscheibe.* A navigational instrument which is used to take bearings. It consists of a disc, whose edge is graduated in degrees, which has a pointer that rotates from the centre of the disc. To take a bearing on an object, the 0°-line of the disc is pointed along the lubber line (q.v.), while the pointer is aimed at the object. The angle between the 0°-line and the pointer is the bearing required. See figure 24.

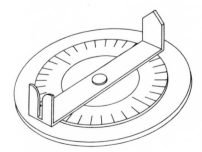

figure 24

Pennant; *flamme; Wimpel, Anhang.* A narrow, tapering flag used for signalling. Also, pendant.

Pilot; *pilote; Lotse.*

Piston hank; *mousqueton à piston; Stagreiter (mit Kolbenbetätigung).* A spring-loaded hank which is used to hold a sail to a stay. Also, snap hook. See figure 25.

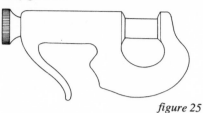

figure 25

Pitch; *tanguage; Stampfbewegung.* Rhytmical, fore-and-aft movements of a boat in a seaway.

Plane (to); *planer; gleiten.* A boat planes when it has broken the surface tension of the water and skims along the top rather than ploughs through the water.

Port; *bâbord; Backbord.* The left-hand side of a boat when seen from astern. See figure 1.

Position line; *droite de relèvement; Standlinie.* See page 166, illustration B.

Postpone; *retarder; verschieben.* A postponed race is one which, not being started at the scheduled time, can be sailed at any time the race committee may decide.

Preparatory signal; *signal d'avertissement; Vorbereitungssignal.* The second signal used in starting a race, made five minutes (unless otherwise stated in the sailing instructions) before the starting signal (q.v.). According to the rules, the preparatory signal may consist of the International Code flag "P" broken out, a distinctive signal displayed, or a blue shape displayed.

Principal race officer (PRO); *président du comité de course; Wettfahrtleiter.*

Propeller; *hélice; Schraube.*

Propeller bracket. See **Strut**.

Propeller pitch; *pas; Pech, Propellersteigung.* See page 116, illustrations B, C, and D.

Propeller shaft; *arbre d'hélice, Schraubenwelle.*

Proper course; *route normale; richtiger Kurs.* Any course which a yacht might sail after the starting signal, in the absence of the other yacht or yachts affected, to finish as quickly as possible.

Protest flag; *pavillon de protestation; Protestflagge.* This is a flag (International Code flag "B" is always acceptable, irrespective of any other provisions in the sailing instructions) hoisted by a boat to indicate that it intends to protest against another boat at the end of the race.

Protractor; *rapporteur; Winkeltransporteur, Winkelmesser.* A transparent, plastic, semicircular instrument, usually graduated in 180°; it can also be triangular in shape. A protractor is used to find a course or bearing between two points on a chart, and when shaping a course on the chart.

Provisions; *provisions; Proviant.*

Pulpit; *balcon avant; Bugkorb, Kanzel.* A security railing of tubing, usually of stainless steel, which runs round the stem of the boat. The security railing running round the stern is known as a pushpit. See figure 41.

Purchase; *caliorne; Takel, Gien.* A system of blocks and ropes, used to increase the power being applied. See figure 26.

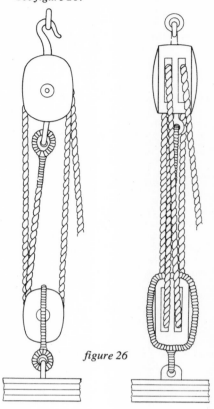

figure 26

Put about (to); *virer au vent; über Stag gehen.* To lay a boat on the opposite tack. Also, to tack.

Quarter; *hanche; hinteres Querschiff, Achterschiff.* The aftermost corner of a boat. There are two quarters: port and starboard.

Quarter berth; *couchette de quart; seitliche Achterschiffskoje, Hundekoje.* A berth in the port or starboard quarter, or at the aft end of the main saloon, with its foot projecting under the aft side-deck. See page 247, illustration 1 (a).

Race; *régate; Rennen.*

Race course; *parcours de régate; Bahn.*

Racing committee; *comité de course; Wettfahrtleitung.*

Radar reflector; *réflecteur radar; Radar-Reflektor.* See page 56, illustration C.

Radio beacon; *radiophare; Funkfeuer, Funkbake.*

Radio Direction Finder RDF); *récepteur gonométrique; Funkpeiler, Bordfunkpeiler.*

Rail; *lisse de plat-bord; Laufschiene, Reling.* See **Gunwale**.

Range. See **Transit line**.

Recall; *signal de rappel; Rückruf.* A signal to those who have started a race that they have not started according to the rules.

Reef (to); *prendre un ris; reffen.* To reduce a sail's working area by taking it in, either by folding it at its foot or by rolling it.

Reef; *ris; Reff.*

Reef cringle; *patte de ris; Refflagel.*

Reef knot; *nœud plat; Reffknoten, Slippknoten.*

Reef pendant; *bosse de ris, itaque de ris; Schmeerreep.*

Reef lacing; *hanet de ris; Reffleine.*

Reef point; *garcette*; *Reffbändsel*. Short pieces of rope sewn at one end along each side of a sail in lines approximately parallel to the foot. Points are used to secure the folded part of a sail by tying their loose ends together in reef-knots under the foot of the sail.
See figure 27.

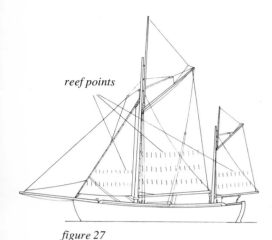

reef points

figure 27

Reeve (to); *passer*; *scheren, durchholen*. To pass the end of a line throught a block or pulley.

Relative wind. See **Apparent wind.**

Retire (to); *abandonner*; *aufgeben*.

Ride at anchor (to); *être à l'ancre*; *ausreiten, abreiten*. To lie at anchor.

Rig; *gréement*; *Takelung, Takelage, Rigg*. The type of sail arrangement a vessel has. See page 35.

Rigging; *gréement*; *Takelwerk, (laufendes und stehendes) Gut*. All the ropes, lines, chains, and cables which support or control masts, spars, and sails in a boat.

Rigging screw. See **Bottle-screw.**

Roller reefing gear; *bôme à rouleau*; *Rollreff, Patentreff*. See page 136, illustration A.

Rope; *cordage, filin*; *Tau, Ende, Leine*.

Round a mark (to); *contourner une marque*; *eine Bahnmarke runden*.

Row (to); *nager*; *rudern*.

Rowlock; *dame de nage*; *Riemendolle, Dolle*. Also, oarlock.

Rubber boat; *canot pneumatique*; *Gummiboot, Schlauchboot*.

Rudder; *gouvernail*; *Ruder, Steuerruder*. *See figure 41.*

Rudder blade; *safran*; *Ruderblatt*.

Rudder stock; *mèche inférieure*; *Ruderschaft*.

Rule; *règlement*; *Regel, Vorschrift, Richtlinie*.

Running; *vent arrière*; *vor dem Wind*. See page 125, illustration 1.

Running rigging; *gréement courant*; *laufendes Gut*. All the lines which are used to control the sails, spars, etc.

Safe leeward position; *position favorable sous le vent*; *sichere Leestellung*.

Safety harness; *harnais de sécurité*; *Sicherheitsgurt, Sicherheitsgeschirr*. See page 196, illustrations B and C, and page 197, illustration K.

Sail; *voile*; *Segel*.

Sail (to); *aller à voiles*; *segeln, unter Segeln gehen*.

Sail-area; *surface de voilure*; *Segelfläche*.

Sailing instructions; *instructions de course*; *Segelanweisung, Wettfahrtplan*.

Samson post; *bitte d'ammarrage*; *Einzelpoller*. In pleasure boats, a samson post is a stout bitt, usually mounted on the keelson and coming up through the deck just forward of the mast, to which the anchor cable or mooring lines are made fast.

Scarf; *écart*; *Laschung, Zuschärfung*. To join two pieces of timber by bevelling and overlapping the edges, so that one continuous piece of timber is formed. *See figure 28.*

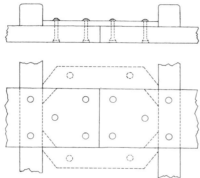

figure 28

Scull; *rame*; *kurzer Bootsriemen*.

Scupper; *dalot*; *Speigatt*. An opening in a hull or deck which allows water to drain off.

Sea anchor. See **Drogue.**

Sea-breeze; *brise de mer*; *Seewind, Seebrise*. See page 187, illustration A.

Sea-cock; *prise d'eau à la mer*; *Seehahn; Seeventil*. A shut-off valve at a through-hull fitting to control the intake or discharge of water through pipes.

Seam; *couture*; *Naht, Saum*. The crevice between planks.

Seam; *couture*; *Segelnaht*. Where two pieces of sail-cloth are sewn together.

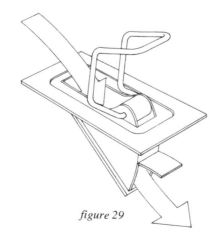

figure 29

Self-bailer; *auto-videur*; *Selbstlenzer*. A valve in the bottom or transom of a boat which, when the boat reaches a certain speed, opens and allows shipped water to drain away. *See figure 29.*

Set a sail (to); *établir, faire voile*; *ein Segel setzen*.

Shackle; *maillon de chaîne*; *Schäkel, Kettenlänge*. A U-shaped metal fitting with a pin across the throat. For example, it is used to attach halyards to sails. *See figure 30.*

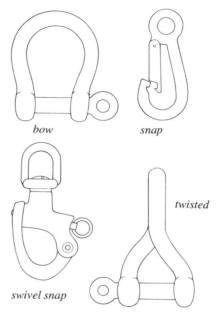

bow   *snap*

swivel snap   *twisted*

figure 30

Shackle (to); *étalinguer*; *einschäkeln*.

Shaft; *ligne d'arbres*; *Welle, Schaft, Griff*.

Shake out a reef (to); *réduire la voile*; *ein Segel ausschütten*.

Sheer; *tonture*; *Sprung, Decksprung*. The fore-and-aft curve formed by a boat's deck at the side. It is measured from the freeboard height to the top edge of the topsides and is usually positive (concave), though it can be negative (convex).

Sheet; *écoute*; *Schot (eines Segels)*. The rope or wire, attached to the clew or clews of a sail, by which the trim of the sail is controlled. Usually, the sheet is named according to the sail to which it is attached, e.g., mainsheet, jib sheet, etc. *See figure 41.*

Sheet bend; *nœud d'écoute simple*; *einfacher Schotenstek, Schotstek*. The sheet bend is used to join, for instance, two ropes of different sizes. *See figure 31.*

figure 31

Sheet lead (er); *filoire d'écoute*; *Leitöse, Schotführung*.

Sheet track; *rail d'écoute*; *Schotschiene*. See **Horse.**

Sheet traveller; *rocambeau d'écoute*; *Schotschlitten, Traveller*. See **Traveller.**

Short sea; *mer courte*; *kurze See*. A seaway with short, high, irregular waves.

Shorten course (to); *réduire le parcours*; *Kurs ankürzen*.

Shroud; *hauban*; *Want, Wanttau*. A wire, running from each side of a yacht to the hounds (q.v.), which supports the mast. *See figure 34 and figure 41.*

Side light; *feu de côté*; *Seitenlaterne*. The navigation lights which a boat over 19ft 8 in (6.0 m) under way at night is obliged to carry. The port light is red, and the starboard light is green. See page 204.

Signal flare; *fusée de signalisation*; *Leuchtkugel, Sternsignal*.

Singlehanded; *en solitaire*; *Einmann*.

Skeg; *talon de quille*; *Kielhacke, Ruderhacke, Leitflosse*. See page 113, illustrations L and M.

Skin friction; *résistance de frottement*; *Oberflächenreibung, Aussenhautreibung*. The friction of the water on the immersed part of a boat's hull and appendages when the boat is under way.

Slide; *coulisseau*; *Rutscher*. A hank fitted along the foot or luff of a sail to be fitted to a boom- or mast-track.

Slip-knot; *nœud coulant*; *Schlippknoten, Laufknoten*. See page 144, illustration H.

Sloop; *sloop*; *Slup*. See page 35, illustration A.

Snap hook. See **Piston hank.**

Snatch-block; *poulie coupé*; *Klappblock, Fussblock*. A block which is open or can be opened so that the bight of a rope can be passed through it, without having to reeve the line. *See figure 32.*

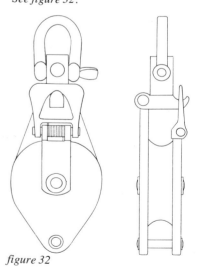

figure 32

Sound (to); *sonder*; *loten*. To measure the depth of water by means of a lead line, echo sounder, or suchlike.

Spar; *espar*; *Spiere, Rundholz*. Any wood or metal pole used as a mast, boom, gaff, bowsprit, etc.

Speed; *vitesse*; *Geschwindigkeit, Fahrt*.

Spinnaker; *spinnaker*; *Spinnaker*. A large, baggy, triangular sail set flying on the side opposite the mainsail with the help of a spinnaker boom.

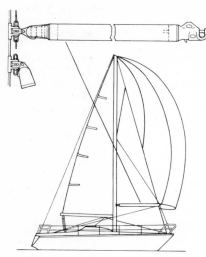

figure 33

Spinnaker boom; *tangon de spinnaker; Spinnakerbaum.* Also, spinnaker pole. See figure 33.

Spitfire jib; *Tourmentin; Sturmfock, Sturmklüver.* A small, heavy storm sail. Also, storm jib. See figure 40.

Splice (to); *épisser; spleissen, einspleissen, zusammenspleissen.* To join two ropes together by interweaving their strands. See page 144, illustration Q.

Splice; *épissure; Spleiss.*

Split pin; *goupille fendue; Splint.*

Spreader. See **Cross-tree.**

Spring-line; *amarre de poste, garde montante; Springleine, Spring.* A shore mooring line which is either led from the stem diagonally aft to a bollard opposite the stern, or from the stern diagonally to a bollard opposite the stem.

Stable; *stable, solide; stabil, fest.*

Stanchion; *épontille chandelier; Stütze, Relingsstütze, Deckstütze.* An upright support, usually of stainless steel, which is through-bolted to the deck along the sides, and through which the lifelines are passed. See figure 41.

Standing rigging; *gréement dormant; stehendes Gut.* Shrouds and stays used to support the mast. They are not movable, though their tension usually can be adjusted. See figure 34.

Starboard; *tribord; Steuerbord.* The right-hand side of the boat when seen from astern. See figure 1.

Starting line; *ligne de départ; Startlinie.*

Starting signal; *signal de départ; Startsignal.* According to IYRU rules, there are three starting signals given at the start of a yacht race: the first is the warning signal (q.v.), the second the preparatory signal (q.v.), and the third the signal for crossing the starting line, which is made by lowering both warning and preparatory signals or by displaying a red shape.

Stay; *étai, draille; Stag.* Wire struts used to support the mast and running fore-and-aft.

Steer; *gouverner; steuern.*

Stem; *étrave; Vorsteven.* The upright bow post where the two sides of the boat meet.

Stern; *arrière, poupe; Heck.* The aftermost part of the boat.

Stern drive; *moteur fixe à embase relevable; Z-antrieb, Segelbootsantrieb, Aussenantrieb mit Einbaumotor.* See page 29, illustration M.

Stiffness; *stable; steif, segelsteif.* The power of a vessel to resist heeling.

Storm jib. See **Spitfire jib.**

Strike the bell; *piquer; die Glocke schlagen.*

Stroke; *nage; Schlag, Streich.*

Strut; *support d'arbre; Wellenblock, Wellenträger.* A fitting for supporting the propeller shaft. Also, propeller bracket.

Suit of sails; *jeu de voiles; Satz (Segel), Garnitur (Segel).*

Swedish jib. See **Genoa jib.**

Swell; *houle (longue); Dünung, Schwell, tote See.* A seaway which remains after a storm has passed, or which has been caused in some other area. Its undulations are long, and have a regular, rounded profile.

Tack (of sail); *point d'amure; Hals.* The corner where the luff and the foot of a sail meet. See figure 40.

Tack; *bordée; Schlag.* A boat's heading with regard to its sails; for instance, a boat on a starboard tack has its mainsail to port (the wind is coming in from the starboard), and vice versa.

Tack (to); *virer de bord vent devant, louvoyer; über Stag gehen, auf den anderen Bug gehen, wenden.* To zigzag into the wind. Also, to change from one tack to the other.

On a tack; *sur un bord; auf einem Bug.*

Tackle; *palan; Talje, Takel.* See **Purchase.**

Take a bearing (to); *prendre un relèvement; eine Peilung nehmen.*

Take in a sail (to). See **Lower a sail (to).**

Tender; *prame, annexe; Beiboot, Tender.* A small boat used by a larger yacht when at anchor some distance off, for ferrying people, supplies, etc., to and from the shore.

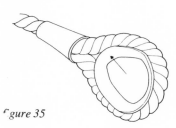

figure 35

Thimble; *cosse; Kausch (e), Hülse.* A fitting, round or heart-shaped, with outwards-curving edges, round whose outer groove an eye may be spliced. See figure 35.

Tide; *marée; Gezeit, Gezeitenbewegung, Tide.* The regular oscillations of the ocean. They are caused by the combined effects of the sun and moon. See pages 164–165.

Tiller; *barre de gouvernail; Ruderpinne, Pinne.* The steering handle which is attached to the rudder. See figure 41.

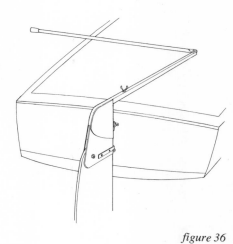

Tiller extension; *allonge de barre; Pinnenausleger, Pinnenverlänger.* See figure 36.

figure 36

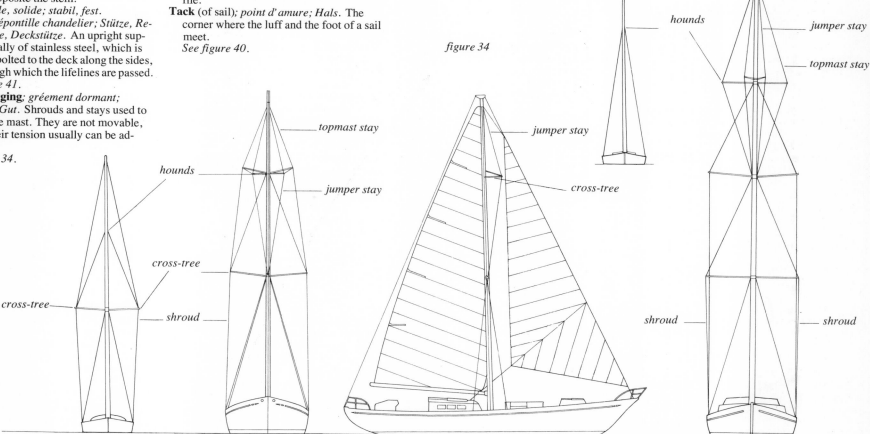

figure 34

Toe strap; *sangle*; *Ausreitgurt, Fussgurt.* Straps along the sole of a small racing-boat which allow the helmsman and crew to hike out on the side of the boat. *See figure 38.*

Trapeze; *trapèze*; *(fliegendes) Trapez.* The wire from the hounds from which the helmsman or crewman in sailing dinghies can hang outside the hull, with his feet planted on the gunwale, in order to counteract the heeling forces of the wind. *See figure 38.*

Traveller; *rocambeau*; *Grosschotschlitten, Laufwagen für Grosschotblock.* The slide which travels along a horse (q.v.), thus allowing the sheets attached to the traveller a certain freedom of play, e.g., the mainsheet traveller, which controls the athwartships swing of the boom. *See figure 39.*

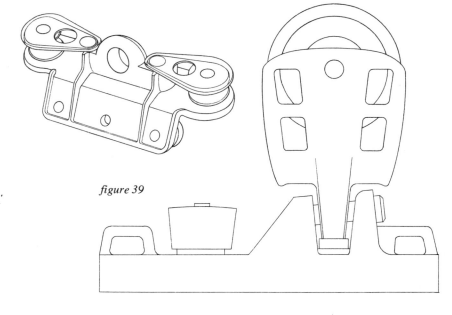

figure 39

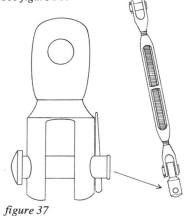

figure 37

Toggle; *cabillot*; *Knebel.* See figure 37.

Topmast stay; *grandétai, étai de flèche*; *Toppstag.* See figure 34.

Topping lift; *balancine*; *Dirk, Toppnant.* A line for raising or lowering a spar; mainly used in connection with a spinnaker pole.

Trailer; *remorque*; *Anhänger-PKW.*

Transit line; *passe, alignment*; *Transit, Deckpeilung, Durchgang.* The line formed when two distant objects are kept in view, one behind the other, thus forming a safe course past a danger or in a fairway. Also, range. See **Leading marks.**

In transit; *aligné*; *in Linie, in Deckpeilung.*

Transom; *tableau arrière*; *Spiegel, Heckspiegel.* See figure 41.

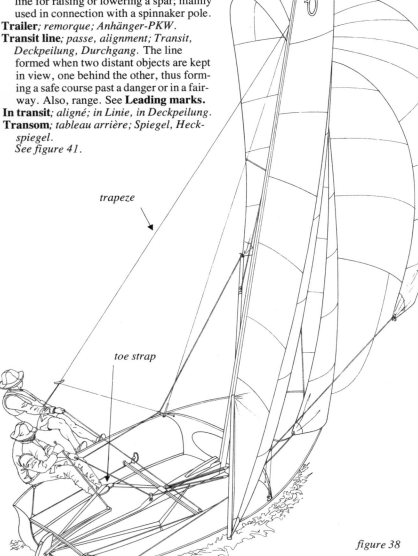

trapeze

toe strap

figure 38

Triangular course; *route triangulaire*; *Dreieckskurs.*

Trim a sail (to); *brasser une voile, orientér une voile*; *ein Segel trimmen.* To adjust the setting of the sail so that it performs at its best in the prevailing wind.

Trim flap; *flap de reglage d'assiette*; *Trimflosse.* One of two flaps, in the transom of a powerboat, which can be lowered to depress the bows. See page 154, illustration G.

Trim tab; *volet de bord de suite*; *Trimmklappe.* A small, extra rudder on the aft edge of the fin keel of a sailing-boat.

True course; *route vraie*; *rechtweisender Kurs, wahrer Kurs, Kartenkurs.* The angle between the boat's centre-line and the true N-S line, when the boat is under way.

True wind; *vent vrai*; *wahrer Wind, atmosphärischer Wind.* The direction of the wind as observed from a stationary boat or from land.

Trysail; *voile de cape*; *Sturmsegel, Treisegel.* A triangular sail which is set loose-footed instead of a mainsail in heavy weather.

Tube cleat. See **Cleat.**

Tune (to); *mettre au point*; *abstimmen, regattaklar machen, trimmen.* To adjust all the fittings on a boat, especially the standing and running rigging, so that the best performance can be achieved.

Turnbuckle. See **Bottle-screw.**

Vane; *girouette*; *Verklicker, Windfahne.*

Vang. See **Kicking-strap.**

Variation; *variation*; *Missweisung.* See page 168, illustration A.

Veer (to); *adonner*; *rechtsdrehen.* The wind veers when it moves in a clockwise direction.

Warning signal; *signal d'attention*; *Vorbereitungssignal, Zeitschuss.* The first of the three signals given by the race committee in starting a race. It consists of breaking out the class flag, displaying a distinctive signal, or displaying a white shape.

Watch; *quart (veille)*; *Wache.* The division of time aboard ship.

Watch; *bordée*; *Wache.* The part of the crew which is working at any one time.

Water-line; *ligne de flottaison*; *Wasserlinie.*

Weather forecast; *bulletin météorologique*; *Wetterbericht.*

Weather helm; *barre au vent*; *Luvruder.* A boat has weather helm when it has a tendency to head up to the wind, when the helm must be kept to weather to maintain the boat on its course.

Weather shore; *terre au vent*; *Luvküste.*

Weather side; *bord du vent, côté du vent*; *Luvseite.* The side of the boat onto which the wind blows.

Weigh anchor (to); *appareiller*; *Anker lichten, Ankerauf gehen.*

Wetted surface; *surface mouillée*; *benetzte Oberfläche.* The submerged part of the hull and its appendages (rudder, bilge keels, propeller shafts, etc.).

Wheel; *roue*; *Rad, Steuerrad.*

Whipping; *surliure*; *Takling.* A whipping is used to prevent a rope-end from fagging. It consists of twine, wound round the rope-end. See page 144, illustrations J and K.

Whisker pole; *tangon de vent arrière*; e.g., *Spinnakerbaum, Fockbaum.* A spar used for booming out (q.v.), the foresail.

Winch; *treuil*; *Winde, Winsch.* See figure 41.

On the wind; *au près*; *am Wind, beim Winde.*

Wind on the quarter; *vent de la hanche, largue*; *Backstagsbrise.*

Windlass; *guindeau (treuil vertical)*; *Ankerwinde (mit horizontaler Welle).*

Wind-screen; *pare-brise*; *Windschutzscheibe.*

Windward; *au vent*; *luvwärts, windwärts.* The direction from which the wind is coming.

Windward shore. See **Weather shore.**

Wire; *fil, cable d'acier*; *Draht, Stahldrahttauwerk.*

Yacht; *yacht*; *Yacht.*

Yacht racing rules; *règles de course*; *Wettsegelbestimmungen.*

Yawl; *yawl*; *Yawl.* See page 35, illustration I.

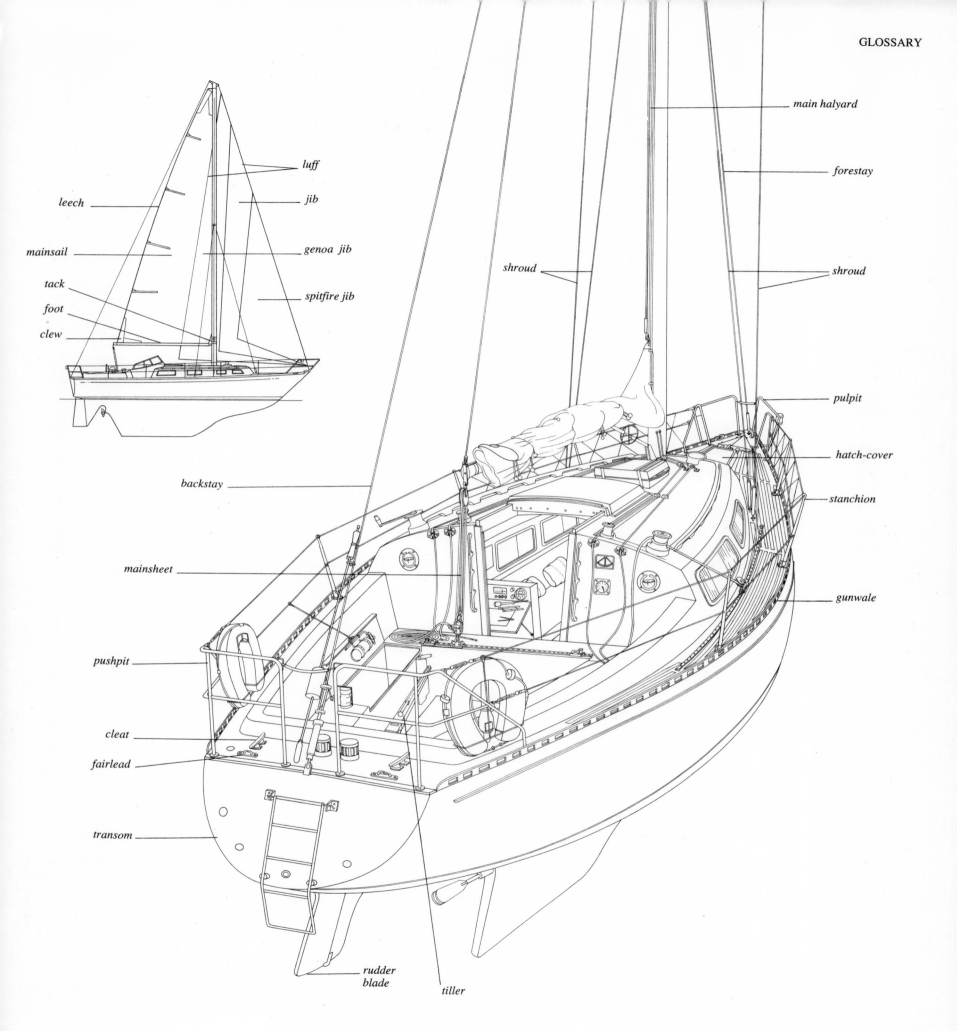

luff

leech

jib

mainsail

genoa jib

tack

spitfire jib

foot

clew

main halyard

forestay

shroud

shroud

pulpit

hatch-cover

backstay

stanchion

mainsheet

gunwale

pushpit

cleat

fairlead

transom

rudder
blade

tiller

INDEX